Kicking Butt and Kissing Saw Dust

Triumphs, Tragedies, and Lessons in the Life of an International Hotelier

DR. PETER W. TISCHMANN

Interior Design by The Book Bureau

Printed in the United States of America.

ISBN: 978-1-960548-36-8 (paperback)
978-1-960548-37-5 (hardback)
978-1-960548-38-2 (ebook)

The Book Bureau

Contents

Dedication

To my wife Denyse, whose love and support
was instrumental to be successful in my life.

To our children Carine and Peter
who are our joy, pride, and everything.

To my many friends and colleagues whose friendship,
and encouragement during difficult moments
was of great help.

And to the hope that our children, grandchildren
and good souls may live in a peaceful world,
where nature is met with respect
and everybody is treated fairly.

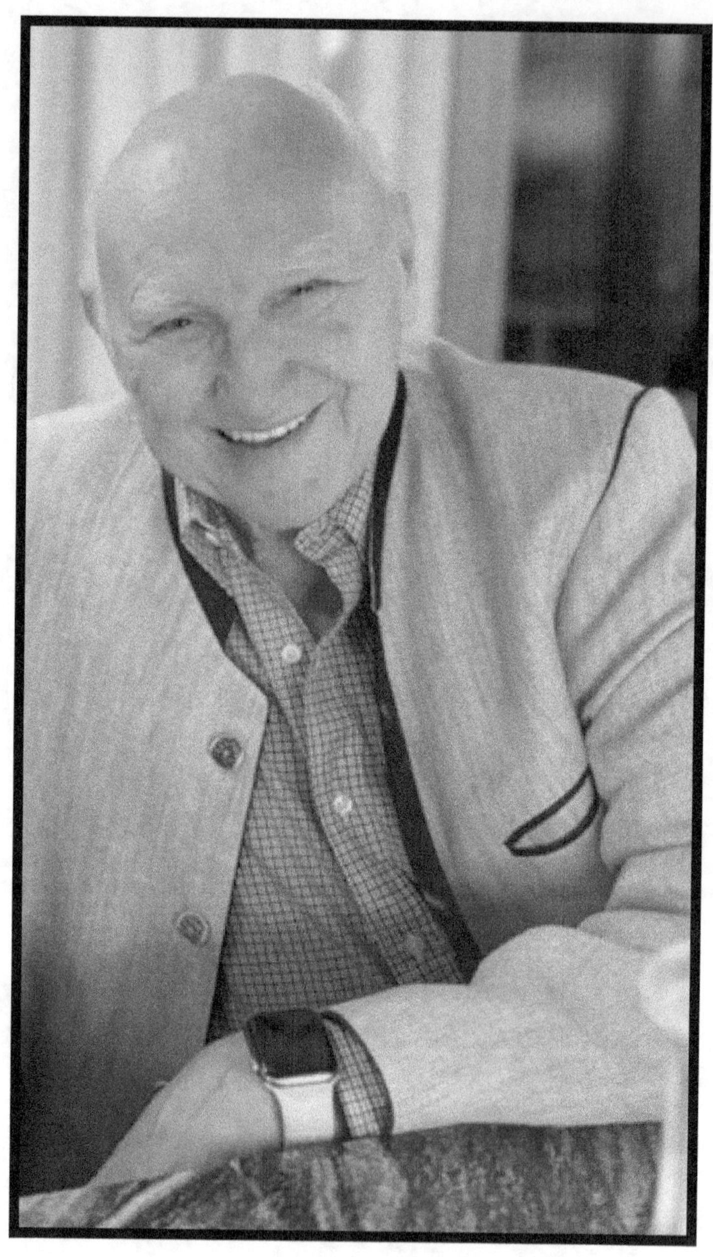

About The Author

Dr. Peter W. Tischmann a native of Hannover, Germany has over 40 years of senior management experience in the luxury hotel industry

Born into the turbulences of World War II in 1939, Dr. Tischmann enjoyed a trouble free childhood during his very young years, until his family was bombed out in 1943 from his native town Hannover and evacuated to a tiny village in the Northern part of Germany.

In the late fifties, the family returned to Hannover, where he completed his schooling and began an apprenticeship as chef.

After completing his apprenticeship with distinction, he worked in different leading luxury hotels in Germany, Switzerland, Monte Carlo and France, before health problems forced him into a career change.

True to his intent to complete every phase of his life, he completed his culinary career earning his diploma as "Master of kitchens" before starting at the Intercontinental Hotel in Hannover at the bottom again, washing dishes and polishing silverware.

His strong will to advance took him to the hotels Front Office department, exposed to guest contact, before joining Steigenberger Hotels in Frankfurt/Main in a corporate management capacity.

A deciding step in his career was his appointment as Assistant to the Divisional Director Food & Beverage of the Sheraton Corporation in Brussels, Belgium followed by his promotion to Vice President Divisional Director Food & Beverage for Europe, Africa and the Middle East less than one year later. Known for his visionary leadership and uncompromising commitment to quality and service, the President of Sheraton ordered Mr. Tischmann to the United States to take over management of the St. Regis Hotel and later entrusted him with the renovation and reopening of this Grand Old Dame of New York hotels.

Exceeding all expectations, the St. Regis was awarded the Mobil Guide Five Star Diamond Award, was voted amongst the ten best hotels worldwide, and "Lespinasse" the hotels signature restaurant had earned three stars by the New York Times for its quality culinary excellence.

Called by Kempinski Hotels, Germany's oldest five-star luxury hotel company, Mr. Tischmann returned to Europe to take the management of the Ciragan Palace Hotel in Istanbul, Turkey repeating his New York City success and positioning the Ciragan Palace Hotel in direct competition to the St. Regis amongst the world's leading hotels.

Committed to the development of young hoteliers Mr. Tischmann was lecturing at famous hotel schools and universities, such as the New York University, the University of Nevada and Las Vegas, the Cornell University – School of Hotel Administration, the Reims Management School and the Berlin School of Economics.

In 2000, Mr. Tischmann completed his European Executive MBA as Summa Cum Laude, followed in 2004 by his PhD – Doctor of Philosophy and Management as "Summa Cum Laude at the Madison University in the USA. He published his first management book, "The Challenges of Change", describing the impact of change on the attitude and human behavior in the environment of repositioning a service product.

Already awarded with the prestigious Leader's Award for Excellence from Leader's Magazine, in 2019 the American Academy of Hospitality Science recognized Mr. Tischmann exceptional career with the "Six Stars Lifetime Achievement Award, which he shares with Donald Trump, President of the United States of America, only other recent recipient of this award.

The life story of Dr. Peter W. Tischmann, working in many different cultural environments, meeting the movers and the shakers of this world, and being a close witness to the history of this world, is indeed fascinating.

Sharing with us the ups and downs during his career, to be finally be confronted with part of his family history unknown to him until the very end, is an unbelievable story, not just entertaining but equally instructive and full of lessons to learn.

His lifetime achievement award reads: "An exemplary career reaching the status level as one of the finest renowned hoteliers who as ever reigned in the luxury hospitality industry worldwide," and finishing with the words "Thank you for setting the highest standards for quality and service and paving the way for all future hoteliers to follow."

Happy reading.

Some of my first Firsts

MY FIRST PARTY IN 1942

MY FIRST TIME ON ICE IN 1962

MY FIRST CAR IN 1961

MY FIRST EARNED MONEY IN 1954

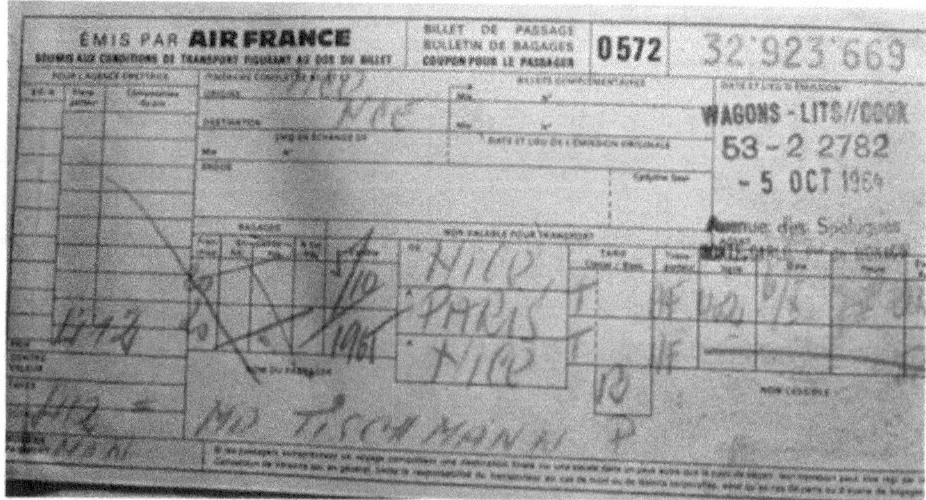

ÉMIS PAR AIR FRANCE
SOUMIS AUX CONDITIONS DE TRANSPORT FIGURANT AU DOS DU BILLET
BILLET DE PASSAGE
BULLETIN DE BAGAGES
COUPON POUR LE PASSAGER
0572
32 923 669

WAGONS - LITS//COOK
53 - 2 2782
- 5 OCT 1964
Avenue des Spelugues

NICE
PARIS
NICE

MY FIRST FLIGHT IN 1964

Proloque

I am not a public figure, not a politician, and not a star of any kind. I am not someone whose memoir people would stand in line to buy because they've read about me in gossip columns and are burning with curiosity. No, I'm not a famous person, but . . .

Who is Peter W. Tischmann anyway?

This question, I was convinced, would keep everyone away from the modestly sized table on which my autobiography might be stacked, if I was lucky enough to publish one.

Despite the urging of friends who know about my unusually dramatic life story, and despite my own desire to share my experiences with my children and grandchildren, I always dismissed the notion of writing anything.

Instead, I contented myself by entertaining family and friends with various colorful episodes from my life.

Until a few former colleagues got pushy, and my daughter began to pressure me too.

"You have to write," they nudged me. "Never mind trying to publish a bestseller. Just tell your story anyway!"

As time passed and I still ignored them, our daughter Carine inquired how far along I was with my writing.

"Papa, why don't you just start writing about anything you experienced? Never mind the beginning, the end, or the middle. Just start writing something and see how it goes."

Her husband, Martin, chimed in: "Start somewhere, and the rest will come all by itself."

So I finally did. I started writing down a few stories, beginning with what I remember from my turbulent childhood.

Eventually, the rest of the story tumbled out. Not quite as easily as "all by itself," but tumble out it did.

As for the question "Who is Peter W. Tischmann?", the short answer—one that might make people walk past the book before they even open it—is that I am a hotelier. But "hotelier" can be a misleading term, and the motives and private lives of people in my field are often shrouded in mystery.

The most flattering description I have received of my work is that I was a culinary ambassador, as the real Belgian ambassador to Egypt used to describe me, if only because of my seemingly opulent lifestyle spent traveling around the world, meeting presidents and prime ministers and celebrities, and experiencing my share of public successes and humiliations.

From my point of view, I was attempting to introduce the art of hospitality in every hotel I led. I witnessed world-changing events with a close-up view, through the most thrilling and terrifying times of the past few decades. I entertained the wealthy and famous, the very brilliant and the very bizarre. I worked hard to fit into every culture in which I lived, often with humorous results.

Despite all the bruises along the way, the path my life has taken is one that I would choose again, with all its joys, catastrophes, victories, and humbling life lessons. Well, most of them.

A Bizarre Twist

01

Competing with the President

"We asked President Trump if it's okay to give this same award to someone else too. To be honest, he said no. He wanted it to be his very own."

My old friend Joe Cinque is enjoying the spotlight, as he speaks to a crowd in a private room at a clubby Upper East Side restaurant in Manhattan. Joe is throwing me a party this evening in honor of a Lifetime Achievement Award that the American Academy of Hospitality Sciences has bestowed on me for my consistent commitment to hospitality, quality, and service throughout my career—and bestowed on the President of the United States of America too, apparently, for his various luxury hotels and resorts.

As I look around the room, I see old friends and former colleagues from my days as managing director of the St. Regis, some of whom I have not seen since my humiliating exit from the hotel more than two decades ago.

I am not an American, although some of my relatives have East Coast roots. So I prefer not to comment on American politics. I have to admit, that amongst my many letters from personalities, is a Thank You letter from George Bush, whom we presented with an original doorknob from 1904 to be used as paper weight.

Another personality, Donald Trump, then the owner of the Plaza Hotel in New York, was very helpful to get an unpaid internship for our son at his hotel. I was very grateful to him at that time, not knowing, that he would become President of the United States a few years later.

So what am I doing sharing a personal achievement award with the President of the United States of America, the sitting president of the United States of America? I will leave that question for Joe to answer. What I do know is that Joe Cinque is a fan of the Trump oeuvre, and he also happens to be a fan of my achievements in the hotel industry. I am mainly grateful for this excuse to enjoy an evening out with old friends.

Cinque's colleague at the Academy, Karen Lynn Dixon, takes the microphone and announces: "Peter Tischmann is an institution. He set the foundation for what luxury would become in New York City."

"There's no one greater. Peter is a legend," Cinque says as he turns to me. I feel my face turning red and my eyes glancing down at the floor. It has been quite a while since I have received an honor of this kind.

Cinque asks some of my old colleagues if they would like to say a few words about me.

John Stavros, who was the head maître d' at the St. Regis, takes the microphone and talks about the success that so many of the hotel's alumni have achieved in the hospitality industry: "The St. Regis mentality under your leadership was a great incubator. That incubator has never existed ever again. The greatest hotel team ever created was under your leadership."

But enough with the adulation. It was time to poke fun at me. Stavros tells a story of when he stumbled into me late one night, standing on a ladder with a hammer in hand, pounding boards to the wall of the hotel's Lespinasse restaurant to get the decor ready for the opening gala the next day. "I said, 'Mr. Tischmann, what are you doing? ' Working, Peter says. 'But it's 1:30 in the morning!'"

My friend Joe Prezioso grabs the microphone and clears his throat. He is a man of great charisma and a loud voice, and he loves an excuse to address a crowd. He worked for me when he was in charge of banqueting operations at the St. Regis, and he was by my side during some of the absurd incidents that can happen when you are trying to keep a luxury hotel and restaurant afloat—sometimes literally afloat.

"This cold night reminds me of a very cold morning in January of 1992," Prezioso's voice booms out as he grabs the microphone. He proceeds to describe the time when the St. Regis building's main water pipe burst at four o'clock in the morning, sending enormous sheets of ice onto Fifth Avenue, blocking traffic, and flooding the hotel's high-end, ultra-exclusive Bijan boutique, located in an adjacent townhouse. The two of us scrambled to try to salvage the famous fashion designer's $50,000-a-piece alligator suitcases, which were now floating in the three-foot-high water that covered the entire floor of the boutique.

"I said to Peter, 'Boss, what are we gonna do?'" Prezioso says, gesturing for emphasis, recalling those ice sheets blocking traffic, and those very expensive, very wet suitcases. "Peter says, 'Go get some pots of coffee, and get croissants.'"

The room explodes in laughter.

"I said, 'Boss, I don't really think anyone wants coffee or croissants at this juncture.'"

More laughter.

"So, that was Peter Tischmann."

What can I say? I liked to make sure people were comfortable and taken care of, even in the middle of a disaster. My mind flashed to a similar situation many years later when I was managing the Ciragan Palace Hotel in Istanbul and a massive earthquake caused hundreds of guests to try to flee the building.

My friend Jude Rozenveld-Woodstock decides now is a good time to play a prank on me. Jude and her husband, Jan, both worked at the St. Regis back in those days, and I have kept up my friendship with the two of them over the years. Jude sneaks up behind my bald head and flips her long, wavy red hair over my forehead. Now I too have a giant mass of red hair.

My wife, Denyse, and my former secretary Maria Peralta see my bald head draped in red hair and begin to laugh and snap pictures, just as when Jude played the same joke on me in a group photo at our staff reunion twenty-five years ago. Denyse brings out the photo that she saved from that party, and we compare then and now. Yes, we have a few more wrinkles in our crowd, a little more gray, but the photos look remarkably alike. Same joke, a quarter century later. Still funny.

Is there anything better in life than loyal friends? You get fired, and you get publicly shamed, and no one will go near you. But these friends will believe in you until the end. You sue the hotel company that fired you, and you become embroiled in a nasty court case, and your friends stand with you all the way. You win the lawsuit, and they are still with you—but they would have believed in you even if you had lost.

I can say this much about the St. Regis team: We endured a frightening roller coaster ride together, during one of the most historic eras of New York City's social life. And at least we can still joke around.

There was a time when no one was laughing. But that's another story.

2018 - LIFETIME ACHIEVEMENT AWARD FOR PRESIDENT DONALD TRUMP

2019 - LIFETIME ACHIEVEMENT AWARD FOR DR. PETER W. TISCHMANN

Born Into a World at War

02

December 26, 1939, was a miserable day. Rain and snow battered the windows from morning to night, replacing the Christmas joy of the day before with a wet, wintry chill. It was a day to stay home, eat gingerbread cookies, and find solace in the smell of beeswax candles on the Christmas tree—real, freshly cut, and still fragrant even after the holiday itself had vanished.

My mother, nine months pregnant, was waiting at home to join her parents for a traditional day-after-Christmas dinner. Her little hospital suitcase was packed and ready to go, just in case.

Although her doctor had advised her that the first child is usually born late and reassured her that nothing would likely happen for another week, my mother was prepared. One never knew.

The rule about first babies arriving late was apparently made without my consent because I decided December 26 would be a wonderful day to enter this world. And so I did. I was born at nine o'clock in the evening, weighing 3 kilograms, 200 grams, and measuring 52 centimeters in length—a screaming, wiggling, belated Christmas gift.

What I didn't realize then is that a birthday on Christmas would have many disadvantages where birthday gifts were concerned, but I was blissfully ignorant at the time.

Entering the world on December 26 was not my only questionable decision as a newborn. That year, 1939, was the beginning of World War II. On August 23 of that year, Germany and the Soviet Union had signed a non-aggression pact, with a secret protocol defining German and Soviet spheres of influence. The pact would ensure that Germany could launch invasions without facing Soviet intervention and risking a two-front war, as had happened in World War I.

Everything changed a week later. Germany, after staging several false border incidents as a pretext, invaded Poland on September 1, 1939. Two days later, France and the United Kingdom declared war on Germany, following their agreement with Poland to assist the country in case of aggression. The Second World War had officially begun.

Meanwhile, daily life in Germany hummed along, as if nothing out of the ordinary was happening. In Berlin's packed cabarets, fashionable crowds did the Charleston, and guests at society parties dined and danced until dawn. The fighting was far away, German troops were advancing and winning in the East and West, so why worry? At least that was how many civilians experienced the war in those early days.

I had my own excuse. I was still an infant, oblivious to the war—and unaware that anything strange was happening with my family.

My father and his close relatives are missing from the pictures of my childhood, but the earliest explanation I remember is that he was at the Eastern front, like many other young German men.

As I grew older and asked more questions, the story changed. My mother told me that my father was missing in action, vanished somewhere in the ever-expanding war. I had no reason to question her story at the time, since many of the other children I was playing with had absent fathers too.

It was not out of character for my mother to say as little as possible about my missing father. When my sisters and I were children, I don't remember her saying much to us, about anything. She was not the type to sit down on the floor and play with us or to take us in her arms and console us. Nor was she especially severe. I do not remember her ever punishing us excessively. For my entire childhood, my mother seemed merely distracted, too busy to bother with us much, except when it came to the necessities.

I guess Mutti was just doing what she thought she was supposed to do as a parent. I know she was working extremely hard to run her household as a single mother in very difficult times. This perhaps drained any energy she might have had to be lighthearted with us or display her affection.

The few memories I have of my mother being playful with us revolve around the classic Christmas Eve ritual that my family liked to perform, like many others in Germany. A grown-up would pretend to check on Santa Claus behind a locked door in the house to see if he was done arranging the presents. My mother dutifully did this, contributing her part to upholding the Christmas tradition, and perhaps she felt her spirits lift a bit during the holiday season.

I strain to find any other images of my mother in my memory as a warm, loving presence, and it strikes me now as strange and a bit sad that I cannot. But at the time, I didn't know any different.

Despite my missing father and my emotionally distant mother, despite the war raging ever closer, the first years of my life were happy, judging by the old pictures I've seen. The few remaining family photos that have survived the war show me in a variety of joyous or peaceful moments: on a weekend excursion to the nearby Harz Mountain , playing in my grandparents' garden under a magnolia tree in full blossom, and again, napping or smiling in my old-fashioned baby carriage.

My own actual memories begin shortly after, but I do retain vivid stories from my early childhood, told to me by my mother and grandparents years later. Some are not quite as cheerful as those photos. I know that during a sleepover weekend at my grandparents' home when I was a toddler, I swallowed a large amount of my grandmother's sleeping pills. Concerned about my unusually long afternoon nap, she went to check on me, found the tube of pills on the floor, and rushed me to the emergency room.

I must have mistaken the sleeping pills for bonbons. How many did I swallow? Nobody actually knew but enough to put me into a long, deep sleep. Luckily, I lost consciousness before I could finish the tube, and my doctors pumped my stomach empty in time. It was a terrifying day for my family. But I emerged unscathed and carried on with my relatively carefree childhood.

The war was still far away, and in Hannover, the familiar routines of life continued. Anyone we knew who worried about the situation did so quietly. After all, the British Royal Family were descendants of the Hannover House, and Queen Luise of Prussia was directly related to the King of England. Hannover should be safe and sound. Or so everyone thought or wanted to believe. Until the unthinkable happened.

Face-to-Face with the War

When I look back now on the events of October 1943, certain details are etched in my memory as vividly as if they'd happened just moments ago. Other scenes from those days, when I was three years old and soon to turn four, are a patchwork of details I remember clearly and ones I learned about later from my grandparents, teachers, and others who lived through that time. As for my mother, I don't recall her ever talking about those days in later years. It was as if a certain era had been erased from our past because it was better not to remember it.

The morning of October 8, 1943, when my life was about to change forever, I knew nothing of politics, of Hitler's murderous regime, of the Axis and Allied powers, or of the war raging in the rest of Germany. In my family, no one talked about what was happening in our country, at least not when the children were awake. I had no inkling of the events that were about to blow up my world and my life as I knew it.

That day, I was visiting my grandparents at their home a few blocks away from my mother's house, when the sirens started blaring, warning of a likely aerial attack. I can still almost hear the sounds of those shrieking, piercing alarms signaling us to take shelter.

As always, we were supposed to go to a nearby bunker, to be crammed in with hundreds of other people in small rooms behind meter-thick walls. The cramped little rooms, the big white painted numbers, and the long benches in that bunker remain as detailed in my memory as a photograph. We had sought shelter there time after time, running to it after each of the siren warnings that later turned out to be false alarms.

The bunker looked like a nondescript building from the outside, except it had no windows. The entrance was narrow, and inside, you walked through a series of rooms on each level of the building. The spaces were like compact apartments, and people would crowd inside, perching along the benches that lined the walls.

When the sirens sounded, I rushed with my grandparents down the stairs of their house. My mother and my sister Bärbel, three years younger than me, were not with us that day, I don't recall why.

For reasons I was never told, my grandparents and I never made it to the bunker. Instead, we ran across the Marienstrasse into a cemetery, adjacent to the Gartenkirche church, opposite the residence of my grandparents.

My grandparents likely thought nothing serious was going on at first and waited for the alert to get canceled, as had happened many times before, instead of evacuating the house right away. By the time they realized this siren was real, there must have been no time to get to the bunker.

The cemetery was a two-hundred-year-old historic landmark called the Gartenkirche Friedhof, and due to a lack of available spaces, it hadn't seen a funeral for many years. The cemetery is the resting place of many celebrities and personalities from Hannover, including Charlotte Buff, who inspired the Lotte character in Goethe's *Sorrows of Young Werther* . Its famous Open Grave—the damaged eighteenth -century tomb of a Hannover city official's wife, its contents accidentally exposed to passersby—became a tourist attraction and popular horror-story setting in the nineteenth century.

Enormous marble tombstones covered the graves at the Gartenkirche Friedhof, lending the cemetery the appearance of a small mausoleum. By the time we arrived at the cemetery, running for shelter behind the huge stones, the sounds of the sirens had stopped. Apart from a few people still running in the street, the city was suddenly quiet, filled with an eerie silence that suggested the terror might have passed. Or the deadly calm was just a prelude to something far more sinister.

It seemed reasonable to hope that the sirens were just another false alarm after all.

History says the British bombers had passed over Hannover that day to give the city a deceptive sense of security, only to make a U-turn to unload their deadly cargo.

After those moments of quiet, we heard the planes return, buzzing louder and louder as they approached. When the first detonations sounded, we realized this was no false warning. I crouched with my grandparents behind a tombstone, and we crumpled our bodies to the ground, hoping the graveyard monument would protect us from what was about to happen.

The first wave of planes crossed overhead, darkening the sky, the humming noise of propellers and engines generating an unbearable din.

Suddenly, a powerful wind, almost like a thunderstorm, swept through the cemetery, followed by an immense *bang* . We watched as the facades of houses across the street detached from the buildings, tumbling to the street in a cloud of dust.

That day turned out to be the start of a massive two-day attack on Hannover by the Allied powers, using bombs designed to create a tremendous amount of air pressure and cause widespread destruction. Nearly five hundred bombers conducted eighty-eight air raids on Hannover, dropping more than 1.5 million bombs and transforming the city into a vast landscape of debris and fire. By the end of the following day, Hannover was over 90 percent destroyed.

Those first moments of the attack gave us a glimmer of the utter devastation underway. The initial attacks instantly turned the residences across from the cemetery into life-sized dollhouses with no front walls, their rooms open to the street, furniture suspended and strewn everywhere. Kitchen stoves dangled in the air on almost every floor, hanging on their gas pipes, waiting to fall at any second.

As detailed as my memories of those moments remain to this day, I struggle to recall the reactions of my grandparents as they witnessed their house getting bombed. In mere seconds, all their belongings disappeared into a cloud of rubble wafting down to the street.

Nearly seven thousand people lost their lives in the attack. We were fortunate to survive, I don't know how. But like almost everyone who lived through those two days in Hannover, we were rendered homeless in an instant.

Evacuated from My War-Torn Hometown

My family's entire life changed in that moment. With nowhere else to go, my grandparents were evacuated to a single room in Hameln, a small town at the Weser River about forty kilometers west of Hannover. My mother, my sister Bärbel, and I were sent to a single room in the attic of a farmhouse in Maasen, a tiny agricultural village about sixty kilometers north of Hannover.

Records show that we moved to Maasen on December 17, 1943. I still have the bombing pass that the military government gave my mother, allowing us to travel to our newly assigned quarters after the destruction of our home. As for where we lived in the two months between the October bombing and our December evacuation to Maasen, I have no recollection of this, and none of our surviving relatives seem to either.

I will never forget the way the horizon looked as we left Hannover for Maasen. The burning remains of our city turned the sky a deep, fiery red. The scene never receded from view as we exited the city's borders, and it followed us all the way to Maasen.

The farm we moved into had no running water and no indoor toilet facilities. We knew no one in the village, and we had brought no belongings. We had each other and absolutely nothing else. But we were alive.

It was now up to my mother to figure out how to feed her family, alone and with no job, no possessions, and no family nearby.

Maasen had only three businesses: a blacksmith fabricating horseshoes and other iron pieces, a Kolonialwarengeschäft (similar to a drugstore), and a small gasoline station with a repair shop attached, frequented by farmers who would bring in their broken agricultural equipment. The rest of the village was made up of a handful of farms surrounded by pastures and arable land. The villagers lived on what they planted and harvested, and nearly everyone had cows. Every evening after milking the herd, farmers would place the containers of milk by the roadside to be picked up by trucks from the local dairy.

It was a typical, self-contained North German village, where everybody knew everybody and everything about everybody. A village with no secrets, no strangers. Suddenly, an unknown family from a big city had dropped out of the blue sky, right into their midst.

Our arrival was a surprise, devoid of any warning or context. None of the villagers seemed to have any idea what we had just gone through and why we had found ourselves stranded in Maasen. The war in Germany was as distant and unknown to them as it had been to me on that early October day in Hannover. Those villagers had no concept of what it meant to be bombed out and to have lost everything in an instant. Their little world was still in order and would likely remain so for a long time to come.

As Hannover suffered new waves of bombing day after day, the bright red horizon of the burning city seemed to inspire no curiosity among Maasen's villagers about what was happening not so far away. The rising smoke from Hannover, a city now destroyed and in flames, was visible as far as Maasen and beyond, and on certain days, it even scented the air of our new village with a rotten stench.

On the other hand, the government had just confiscated any available rooms in homes all over the country to accommodate bombing victims without compensating the owners in any way. What wonderful conditions for a warm welcome. And what a place to send a single mother with two small children and no relatives or job prospects in sight.

In later years, our mother never mentioned how she managed to navigate her way through this difficult time, but I learned later that she had sold some of her remaining jewelry to supplement the meager government payouts that could not cover our family's most basic needs. From the day we arrived, she did an impressive job of shielding us from her daily worries as she tried to raise us and keep us fed, clothed, and housed.

After some time, we began to notice small improvements. Our neighbor, the blacksmith, had two daughters with whom we became close friends. Annegret, the younger sister, spent a lot of time with my sister Bärbel, and Hannelore, who wore two big braids in her hair, appeared to develop an interest in me even though she was older. I think she nurtured a secret crush on the boy who had just dropped out of nowhere, enlivening her family's predictable routines with a sense of wonder and intrigue.

As for me, I found a new hobby of sorts. I spent hours with the blacksmith in his workshop, watching him fit U-shaped iron pieces on horses' hooves. Every day, local farmers would arrive with their horses and ill-fitting horseshoes, and he would adapt the pieces to each animal before nailing them back on to the hooves. He was a man in his forties at the time and always wore a big leather apron. I was fascinated to see how he formed the red-hot iron as his hammer hit the anvil with a singing sound that could be heard from far away.

Weeks after we arrived in Maasen, my mother decided to travel back to Hannover to see if she could recover anything from our apartment. I accompanied her on that trip, leaving my little sister behind with the blacksmith's family.

When we finally reached what was supposed to be the Grosse Wall Straße, we were welcomed by a startling sight that I had not even begun to imagine. Surrounding us were mountains and mountains of stones. Our house's once-proud facade had toppled, reduced to a handful of scattered pieces. There was nothing left of what had been our lives only weeks ago. All that remained was silence, emptiness, an uninterrupted view to the horizon.

Hannover was almost completely flattened, all the way to the ground. Amid the destruction and rubble, only a few houses somehow remained standing. Heavily damaged but still standing. In most areas we saw, it was impossible to find even two stones on top of one another.

Looking through a small basement window, we noticed that the ground inside was flooded. A few boxes floated here and there in the water, remains of items we had once stored in the cellars. In the rubble, I remember seeing a large light bulb drifting around, unbroken. I don't know why I recall that light bulb so clearly, the way it was bobbing along in the wet basement. Everything else around the bulb was dust and debris.

My mother did not say a word. She gazed around for a while, stunned. And then I heard a few muffled sobs. I looked over and noticed that she had started to cry. I had never seen that before, my mother weeping, and I knew it was difficult for her to cry in front of me. But there it was, our family's home, now just a pile of rocks and dirt. Nothing remained from our former life, none of the custom-designed furniture, none of the valuable china or glassware, none of the elegant dresses and clothing, nothing by which to remember the happy days in the Grosse Wall Straße.

After a last glimpse at the remains, we returned to Maasen. It was time to begin an entirely new chapter. We knew now, if we didn't quite grasp it before, that our life in Hannover was over.

Visiting My Grandparents

The shocking sight in Hannover that left my mother in tears did not open any emotional floodgate when we returned to Maasen. Her inner life remained a mystery. I knew nearly as little about my mother as I did about the war or about anything else that was happening to our family. By now accustomed to our awkward but manageable life in Maasen, we engaged as minimally as possible with the outside world and kept our own German version of the stiff upper lip.

But the war found ways to break through the barrier.

In early 1944, we went to visit my maternal grandparents, Opa and Oma, the only grandparents I ever knew. This was a major voyage since scheduled train transportation did not yet exist between Maasen and Hameln, where Opa and Oma were living as war refugees. We had to take a bus from Maasen to Sulingen, change to another bus to Hannover, then take a train to Hameln. This made the eighty-kilometer trip almost a full day's journey.

As we traveled through the countryside, our train stopped abruptly halfway between Hannover and my grandparents' place in Hameln. The conductor ordered us to leave the train and take shelter in the bushes to the right and left of the tracks while the train continued a few hundred yards without us. Only at this moment did we notice a few Allied planes buzzing in the sky overhead.

We stayed in hiding for what seemed like an eternity, cowering in fear from the sounds of the planes. Were they about to bomb us all to pieces? Where was our train going? But after not much longer than a few minutes, the noises stopped. The planes were gone. We were allowed to creep out of the bushes and walk toward the train to resume our journey.

We later learned that the conductor had forced us to leave out of fear that the planes would attack the train and had moved it ahead to protect us from any possible aerial attack on the train. It struck me that he had risked his own life by staying onboard until the planes disappeared and until it was safe to call us back from the bushes to board the train again.

Those few minutes were terrifying, but my excitement about seeing Opa and Oma rebounded moments after. The anticipation of seeing them overshadowed any difficulties along the way.

I felt a closeness with my grandparents that I had never felt with my mother. Oma was a wonderful grandmother to me—caring, affectionate, and devoted to my enjoyment and education. Most of all, she was attentive, if perhaps too attentive. I loved how she paid attention to my every move, even when her observations made me feel awkward. She noticed every detail in my behavior, every etiquette failure, and was compelled to correct me, again and again: "Where is your left hand, Junge?" She affectionately called me by the German term for little boy. "The spoon goes to the mouth and not the mouth to the spoon!"

Even Opa was not spared Oma's keen eye. My grandparents had a wonderful and happy marriage, but there was something about Opa's eating style that drove her crazy. As a relic of his upbringing in the United States, he would take the fork in his left hand and the knife in his right hand and start to cut the meat, then as soon as he had cut a few pieces he would put the knife down and move the fork to his right hand to eat. My grandmother would get frustrated about this again and again, but in all their years of marriage, she never did manage to change it.

She even corrected my mother when she did not sit the way Oma believed a lady should, with legs leaning together side by side instead of crossed at the knees the way Mutti liked to sit.

My face would always redden with embarrassment when she pointed out one of my faux pas, but today I am grateful for Oma's nagging. It has made me conscious of table etiquette in all kinds of settings—mostly my own manners but others' too—although I imagine how annoying this would be to my dining companions if they only knew.

The odd but pleasing twosome of Opa and Oma always made visits to their house a joy before, during, and after the war. Opa was generous and full of warmth, the most gentle and playful person I ever knew even in his old age. I remember how we would stand on the shores of the river Weser and show me how to flip stones across the water and how he would draw creative designs on paper for me.

Later I would learn more about my grandparents' ups and downs in life, some of which foreshadowed my own, but of course, I was blissfully unaware at the time.

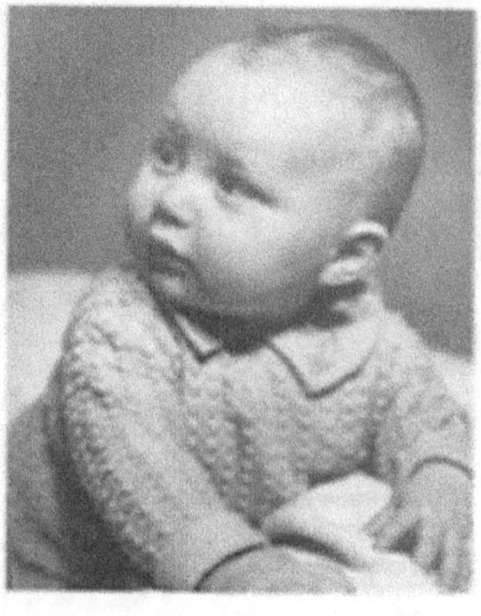

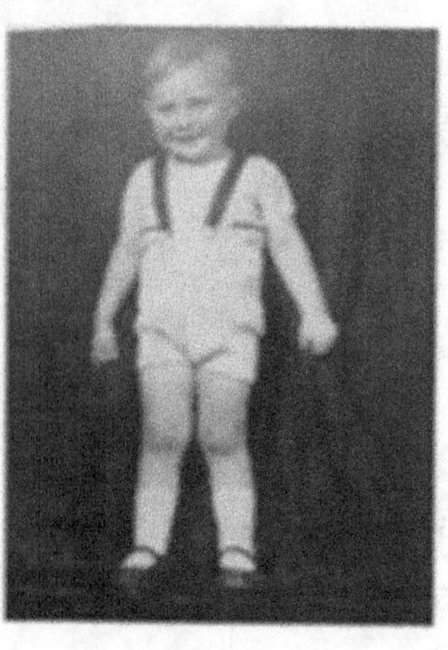

1940 WITH GRANDMOTHER

1940 ONE YEAR OLD

1943 STILL IN HANNOVER

MY PARENTS DURING BETTER DAYS IN 1936

The Early Years

03

My American Grandfather

Opa was born an American—in Hoboken, New Jersey, just across the Hudson River from the midtown Manhattan area where I spent some of the most eventful years of my hotel career. Opa's father, my great-grandfather Julius Ewald Hähnel, had been born in Germany in 1843. The rakishly good-looking young Julius, who favored well-fitting velvet sport jackets and long bangs that brushed away from his forehead, studied lithography and immigrated to the US, where he began to build his reputation as an outstanding lithographer.

Working by day at a prestigious New York City lithography firm, Julius lived with his family in Hoboken, a fast-growing waterfront city and a hub for German and other European immigrants who came to work in its shipping industry. Hoboken spawned its most famous native son, Frank Sinatra, a few decades later, and in 1954 the city starred as the setting of the Marlon Brando classic *On the Waterfront*. During the thirteen years of Prohibition that began in 1920, Hoboken was one of the easiest places near New York City to find bootlegged liquor, a major revenue source for the Mafia that operated in the area.

Julius's son William, my Opa, stayed in Hoboken from his birth in 1872 through his high school graduation with high honors. Opa had always been a good student. A certificate from his elementary school applauded "his punctual attendance with correct deportment and diligent attention to his studies"—although I am sure Opa would agree that the most noteworthy detail of that certificate is the handwritten note next to the official signature, stating that the headmaster who signed it had died shortly after, during the opening of the Brooklyn Bridge.

The note does not say how the headmaster died, but six days after the bridge opened in May 1883, a dozen people were crushed to death in a stampede caused by a panic that ensued when a woman tripped and fell. The process of building the bridge had been riddled with tragedies from the beginning. Ambitious architectural plans coupled with the rumored corruption of construction contracts in Tammany Hall-era New York had caused an estimated three dozen casualties before the bridge even opened.

Just as Opa was beginning his adolescence in New Jersey, near the bustling social scene in Hoboken's lush waterside parks and just across the river from the new skyscrapers going up in Manhattan, his American life came to an abrupt end. A serious kidney problem forced his father, Julius, to return to Germany in 1886 to undergo treatment and to relocate the family with him.

For Opa, this meant a severe dose of culture shock. For Julius, this was not just bad medical news. It brought intense anxiety about his career and his future after the surgery. Julius took a gamble and bought the established printing factory Fürstenau & Co. in Dresden—sight unseen—and planned to profit from running the shop after his surgery. He paid 12,000 Reichsmark for it, about $3,000 in those days.

A crashing disappointment awaited Julius when he visited the printing shop for the first time, already in possession of the ownership documents.

The shop turned out to be a wreck, with outdated machinery that was in no shape to make the kinds of products on which Julius had built his reputation in the United States. He would need to make another major investment or forget about his plans to run a successful print shop in Germany.

Others in Julius's position might have cut their losses and moved on. Not my great-grandfather. He stuck to his plan and modernized the plant, purchasing new equipment and transforming the company within a short time into one of the most successful in Dresden and beyond.

Julius's return to Germany made him an eyewitness to historic events in the industrial revolution. When the first-ever flight by a lighter-than-air vessel made history in July 1900, in an airship owned by Germany's Count von Zeppelin, Julius and his wife, my great-grandmother Ottilie Hahnel, were in Germany to see it. They dressed up in their finest clothes and went to the Rennbahn, the local horseracing track, to join a festive gathering of locals and stare up at the sky. Only three years later and shortly before Julius passed away, the Orville Brothers would launch the era of modern aviation with their heavier-than-air biplane flight in Kitty Hawk, North Carolina.

Meanwhile, Opa, a.k.a. William Hahnel, graduated with honors from the acclaimed Handelsakademie in Dresden, an institution comparable to today's modern business schools. In 1892, he sailed back to America on board *La Normandie*, one of the fastest ships in the North Atlantic in the late nineteenth century, to start work at the Colonial Insurance Company in New York City. Back near his beloved American hometown at last.

But not for long. Once again, Opa found himself bounced back to Dresden. His company had decided to grow internationally and appointed him to lead its expansion in Germany.

Opa was determined to find a way to return to New York yet again. He thought he had the perfect plan as soon as he met Selma Henriette Redlich, a distinguished singer at Dresden's famous Semper Opera House. The talented musician also happened to be a striking beauty, her hair piled high in the fashionable updo of the day, her elegant stature flattered by tailored floor-length dresses with flowing lace sleeves. Opa was in love, and it did not take long for him to propose marriage. But along with the proposal came a request: that she would agree to move back with him to the United States once his Dresden assignment was done.

Selma's answer must have come as a total shock. My grandmother, a highly educated woman with a successful career in Dresden, the cultural epicenter of Germany at the time, wanted no part of William's cockamamie New York plans. Selma announced, "Willi, there is no way I will go with you to the United States, a country without any culture and a lack of education. If you are really serious, you are welcome to stay here!" And that is what he did.

Farewell, New York City dreams. Opa had to resign himself to a future as an American in Germany, in possession of a lifelong nostalgia for his fleeting East Coast days. The couple married in 1907, and more than a dozen years later, Opa eventually applied for and received German citizenship.

I suspect it was Opa's career that eventually brought him to Hannover, where he opened another regional office and was named regional director, a position he occupied until his retirement. He and my grandmother lived in Hannover during momentous times, which saw a high-profile general and politician living in Hannover, Paul von Hindenburg, rise to prominence and win the presidential election in 1925. Hindenburg would later be forced against his own beliefs to appoint his adversary, the rising Nazi Party agitator Adolf Hitler—whose party had won the majority of seats in the German parliament—as Chancellor of the Third Reich.

My grandparents had two children: Wilma, my mother, who loved to dance and eventually opened her own dance academy, and William Jr., her younger brother, who became an aeronautical engineer.

My uncle William Jr. inherited his mother Selma's musical talent. He was a gifted piano player and could play any piece of music after hearing it only one time. His favorite music was jazz, which was not welcome in Hitler's Germany, but he pursued his hobby anyway during his short life.

At age twenty-five, a long bout with pneumothorax, a collapsed lung illness, confined William Jr. to a medical clinic for six months. He returned to his normal life soon afterward , meeting and becoming engaged to an American woman named Ruth Stoll. In the collection of photos from their brief marriage, Ruth and William Jr. are relaxing outdoors at their country home near Hannover, lounging on the grass, looking very much in love.

William Jr. died just six years later, at the age of thirty, after a sudden and severe onset of tuberculosis. I can only imagine what it must have been like for Ruth to write the telegram that sits in my family's archives, informing my mother that her brother had passed away. Ruth remained in close touch with her in-laws until the end of their lives, writing a loving letter to my grandfather Opa on the occasion of his eightieth birthday.

Our son Peter has inherited William Jr.'s ear for music, and as a child, he too was able to figure out how to play a piece on the piano after listening to it only once. Unfortunately, we have not insisted that Peter nurture this fantastic talent, and I still regret that to this day.

My mother's own musical career blossomed in the meantime. She joined a dancing club and performed in competitions in Germany and throughout Europe. She eventually married her dancing partner Fritz Tischmann, who worked in the textile industry and whose American-born father, Benno, owned a shop in Hannover. At the time of the wedding, my uncle William Jr. wrote a warm letter to my mother congratulating her and Fritz on their marriage. My grandparents apparently disapproved of the wedding, perhaps because Fritz was twelve years older than my mother. In group photos from the event, they are noticeably absent, as they chose not to attend.

My parents married in 1934, five years before I was born, so they had time to enjoy life as a couple without children to worry about. A handsome and stylishly dressed pair, the two continued to participate in classical and modern dance competitions and to take automobile expeditions around Germany together.

Like my grandparents, my parents drove cars generally reserved for the high society. My father owned a Horch convertible, compatible with the top-of-the-line Audi, BMW, or Mercedes models of today, and he and my mother would ride in it around Hannover and outside town. Pictures from before the war show my parents and my grandparents living a very comfortable life, in spacious, luxuriously decorated apartments with custom-designed furniture.

After the bombs fell on Hannover during the war, my by-then single mother and my newly dispossessed grandparents faced new realities in Maasen and Hameln that stood in stark contrast to the comforts they had known. In a letter to me from a hospital near Hameln where she was getting treated for severe arthritis, my grandmother told me that Opa would pay long visits to her in the clinic so he could escape their freezing room in Hameln. It would get so cold in their one-room flat that a glass of water Opa was drinking would freeze and crack.

My grandfather passed the time in Hameln by writing me letters too. He would commend me on my improving penmanship and tell me about poems he would like me to memorize and about his hopes that Bärbel and I can enjoy sledding outdoors as soon as it snows in Maasen.

Life in our freezing one-room flats was indeed different from our daily realities before the war. But we had survived, compared to the thousands of people around us who vanished in the bombings of German cities and the millions who were dying in concentration camps, the existence of which we learned about after the camps had been liberated by the Allies.

That is to say, Opa and Oma had survived, and my mother and her children. My father had left my pregnant mother before I was born. Perhaps he was still alive, or perhaps he had died in the war. All I have from my father, besides the few photos taken with my mother before I was born, is a telegram he sent to my mother from Belgium in 1939, congratulating her on my birth. He vanished before he ever met me.

The question of why the telegram was posted in Belgium, while he had supposedly been fighting with the army on the Eastern front, never occurred to me.

Any details of his life, or of my parents' lives together—beyond the few photos that I found after my mother passed away—sat in a collection of locked boxes and later locked cabinets, whose contents I was never allowed to see. The true story remained a mystery that would last for decades.

Daily Life in the Countryside

Daily life in the countryside in Maasen shielded us from the visual effects of the war, of the bombings in the big cities, the torture and deaths of Germans in the concentration camps, and the impoverished lives of survivors. In the early months after the war ended in the spring of 1945, we only saw its traces when we ventured to the outskirts of Maasen and spotted the British tanks and soldiers that now occupied the region.

The soldiers became good friends with the village boys. They gave us biscuits and chocolate and sometimes allowed us to sit on top of their tanks as they drove along the village roads, a view that brought us much closer to the apples hanging from the trees that lined the streets at that time. We loved those rides on top of the tanks.

Those British soldiers provided the only local reminders of the violence all over the country. Except for one incident I will never forget.

I was playing in the fields around Maasen one day when I found an army pistol. This was likely one of the many objects that the local military personnel had shed in a hurry, together with their uniforms and anything else that could mark them as German soldiers, so they could evade identification and capture. I proudly brought the gun inside to show my mother. She suddenly blanched, grabbed it out of my hand, and walked it outside to dump into the Plumpsklo, which is what we called the typical outdoor toilet facility found on farms in the countryside.

"Never ever touch anything of this kind! Do you hear me? Never!" Mutti said, visibly shaken in a way I had rarely seen. Her reaction has stayed etched in my mind, and my disgust for weapons has remained until today. Even now, over fifty years later, when I visit the annual Oktoberfest in Munich, I refuse to take a rifle into my hands and hit targets to win stuffed animals and paper roses. I still flinch when I see firearms.

By the time I had found that pistol, the war was mainly an abstraction to me, but its impact was all too concrete for my mother. She was wearying of the daily fight to get water and food on the table and to keep us alive and healthy in our cold little room in Maasen.

My mother tried to move us back to Hannover multiple times after the war ended, but the military government seemed determined to thwart all of her attempts. She intended to take on her old job as a social dance instructor, but the civil advice office forced her to prove in advance that she had already secured housing and a job. This was impossible, as she had not. Also, as a condition of our departure, the government required the owners of the Maasen farm to agree that they would accept new refugees after we left.

Obstacles kept springing up everywhere. Apparently not satisfied with the challenges it had already thrown her way, the government insisted that my mother provide three certificates of her job qualifications from former employers. But where to find them when Hannover was in rubble and ashes?

Mutti also had to fill out a ten-page English language questionnaire from the public safety board, inquiring about every detail of her past: "For which political party did you vote in 1932? Why?" My mother had been twenty years old that year, with no interest in politics, but that meant nothing to them.

Opa helped Mutti complete the questionnaire, after which she immediately received a new one, requiring proof that she was not associated with the NSDAP, a.k.a. the Nazi Party.

In 1947, she finally received the N rating, which meant "No Concern." But our family's move back to Hannover still did not materialize. Various obstacles kept standing in our way. So we finally resigned ourselves to staying in Maasen—with no idea what the future had in store for us.

My Friend the Farmer

Despite our poverty and our demoralizing existence, my mother always managed to gather enough food to put a daily meal on the table. I do not remember any day when we didn't have at least something to eat.

Most of our meals revolved around turnips picked from the field, normally used as animal food. Meat appeared on our table at most once a week, on Sundays. We called this a "Sonntagsbraten" and considered it a very special treat.

In season, we collected the leaves of the stinging nettle, the young ones that did not burn our mouths, and Mutti prepared them as if they were spinach. On Sundays, we occasionally tasted the luxury of a dessert, usually a vanilla or chocolate pudding. My sister and I couldn't wait to grab a spoon and clean out the leftovers in the pot.

The meager twenty-seven Reichsmark that my mother received monthly as support from the state always ran out quickly, leaving us with little or no money for groceries for the rest of the month. For urgent needs, my mother sent me to the local general store, whose owners were kind enough to let her delay payment until she had collected enough money or food stamps again. But some days, when my mother had overdrawn her line of credit, they sent me home empty-handed.

In those desperate times, when my mother had long since sold the few pieces of jewelry she had saved during the bombardment, she was forced to ask her parents for help. Opa assisted us with twenty or fifty Marks from the small pension he received.

Our farmer neighbor Heinrich and his wife also took pity on us and often gave me a little food to take home: freshly baked bread, fruits, and vegetables in season. Their donations were a welcome change from our menu of turnips or foraged greens, dry bread, and soup made from stray barley grains picked from the fields after they were mown.

I enjoyed spending time on Heinrich's farm and feeding the animals and especially playing with his German shepherd. Heinrich once asked me if I would like to keep the dog. I ran home in a hurry to ask my mother. She nodded absently, "ja, ja" (yes, yes), an answer she routinely gave just to say something. But her distracted reply that day was enough for me. I ran back to tell Heinrich the joyful news.

An hour later, when I arrived home with the huge dog, my mother was in shock. What was I doing bringing a dog home? Sadly, I had to take the animal back to Heinrich.

Did my mother learn anything from this incident? No, I do not think so, because the words "ja, ja" continued to be her favorite answer to almost every question I asked. What I learned that day, even if I had already suspected it, was that "ja ja" didn't actually mean anything, other than that she had heard my voice—even without listening to anything I said.

The now-familiar rhythms of our village continued in this way for the first two years after the war, but the summer of 1946 brought big changes. The British army was building a camp in Maasen for the Allies' German prisoners of war, or POWs as they were called, and I watched as workers put up high barbed wire fencing and light posts everywhere. Little did I realize then that this camp would mark the beginning of a major transformation in my family's life.

Starting Primary School

My own routine was about to change too, in ways both exciting and scary. In that autumn of 1946, I started primary school. The students crowded into a single classroom packed with every local school-aged child from the first through the eighth grades, and the teachers faced a grueling six-day schedule of instructing us for six hours a day. First graders sat in the first row, second graders in the second row, and so on—up through the eighth graders, who sat in the back since they presumably needed less supervision.

Enormous numbers of German teachers had died in the war or been taken captive, so by the mid-1940s, the country had a shortage of educators. I am still in awe of what our few teachers in that one-room school were able to do in order to secure a future for us.

Our teachers' heroic attempts to teach us in that noisy, distracting environment gave many of us the opportunity to continue on to middle school and even to gymnasium, the German equivalent of high school, where we could take the baccalaureate and perhaps go on to university.

Germany's system of education at the time was highly regimented, designed to ensure that every trade and profession received enough educated students to fill its empty positions. As students, we knew we had to work hard to advance to higher levels of education and earn gainful employment and to not embarrass our families or ourselves. In that system, there were no second chances and no allowances for late bloomers.

Students who stopped after the eight years of elementary school generally learned a craft such as baker, butcher, plumber, bricklayer, locksmith, or the like, and were able to provide a comfortable living for their families. The German saying "Handwerk hat goldenen Boden," which means "Craft has a golden bottom," remains true, especially nowadays when finding a genuine craftsperson of any kind is almost impossible. Meanwhile, the students who passed an aptitude test in elementary school were allowed to continue to middle school.

The paths available to Germany's youth forked more permanently after that: Students who went to Realschule could look to a future as an official state employee or as a practitioner of a technical field such as engineering or architecture. Those who made it to gymnasium generally followed through to university and eventually became doctors, lawyers, or professionals in industries demanding an advanced academic degree.

But most of those opportunities were reserved for boys. After primary school, most girls typically continued for three additional years at the Haushaltsschule, to be trained in cooking, knitting, sewing, and other skills related to managing a future household.

There were exceptions, however. Some of the girls who excelled in class went to trade school to obtain jobs as secretaries or in the administrative workforce of large companies. A few girls attended the gymnasium, and later university, and had the chance to pursue successful professional careers.

It was still a world very much dictated by men, and young girls were forced to learn this early in life.

Even for a woman as tough and determined as my mother, daily life in postwar Germany was full of humbling reminders of this reality and full of hard brick walls to keep slamming up against.

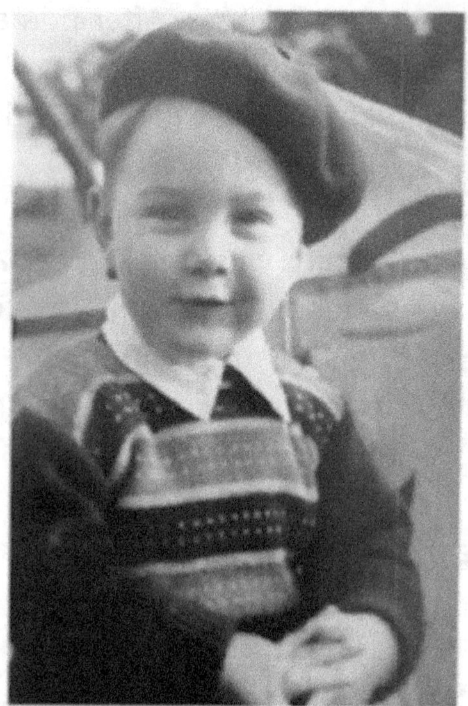

PETER THREE YEARS OLD

LEARNING HOW TO EAT WITH FORK & KNIFE

MY FIRST SCHOOL DAY

WITH MY MOTHER AND TWO SISTERS BARBEL & JENNY

What to Do With My Life 04

Another Man in the Family

The Declaration of Liberated Europe, signed at the Yalta Conference in 1945 by Winston Churchill, Franklin D. Roosevelt, and Joseph Stalin, required the hundreds of thousands of captured German soldiers to provide forced labor to the Allies. In Maasen, we witnessed this development up close, as Britain quickly filled up its local prisoners' camp with German captives.

To avoid any of the human rights guarantees for prisoners of war that were required by the Geneva Convention of 1929, the Allies renamed the captives Disarmed Enemy Forces instead of POWs. Historical records show that many thousands of prisoners who survived the war did not survive captivity and died a few months later from starvation or freezing cold temperatures or from illnesses that went untreated.

In our village, we watched the German prisoners look out from behind the barbed wire fence, staring into an uncertain future. Villagers stopped by the camp from time to time to give them a bit of food if they could afford it. My mother gave the soldiers donations from the little we had or knitted warm socks, gloves, or wool scarves for them to help them through the cold winter.

Many times, people simply went to the camp to talk to the imprisoned soldiers through the fence, to take messages or letters to send to their families, or merely to encourage them to hold on and offer the brief morale boost of human contact with the outside world.

It must have been during one of these visits that my mother met Herbert Dieckmann, a young German soldier who had served in the elite Waffen SS unit, not because he supported the Nazis, but simply because of his physical stature. With his blue eyes and strapping height, he fit the physical ideal that the SS looked for when drafting members.

My sister Bärbel and I had no idea that my mother had made a friend in the POW camp, until one day in the late 1940s when a newly released prisoner named Herbert moved in with us out of the blue.

I guess I was too young and naive to understand why we suddenly had a man living in our house.

This situation caused a scandal, at least for both families. I learned from conversations I overheard at the time, and letters I found later, that my grandparents and Herbert's mother were hard at work trying to end the relationship.

Herbert's mother wrote letters to my mother to beg her to let Herbert go and stop being a bad influence on him. Her letters to her son were even angrier, chastising him about his absurd decision to move in with an older woman, one with two children no less.

My mother and Herbert ignored them and soon got married anyway. This was the second time my grandparents had disapproved of my mother's decision to marry someone with whom she had a substantial difference in age. My father had been twelve years older than my mother, and now Herbert was at least a dozen years younger than she was.

Having this new person around certainly made our living space feel even smaller, but apart from that, Herbert did not make a strong impression on me at first, one way or the other. He was merely another distracted and somewhat remote adult in our midst. I do not recall that he ever tried to get to know Bärbel or me very well, or to play with us or take us on walks anywhere. I think in his mind, he must have been doing his best to fit in, perhaps more by being unobtrusive than by taking an active part in our lives.

Then one day in September of 1950, my half-sister Jenny Brigitte, a screaming newborn baby, dropped into our lives. I was eleven years old, and perhaps because my school provided a sufficient distraction, or my preadolescent mind was otherwise engaged, my mother's pregnancy had not registered as a major development in our lives until Jenny was born.

In any event, the puzzle of my mother's sudden marriage was finally solved, but the mysteries of my family only grew.

Escaping the One-Room Schoolhouse

Life at home was getting even more crowded, and for now, the most urgent question on my mind was whether I would get accepted into the middle school in Sulingen. I had applied and was eagerly awaiting the answer. When the response finally arrived, it was not good news. The classes were full, so my application was put on hold until April of the following year.

This meant my days at school would remain as claustrophobic as my home life. I would stay in that one-room primary school in Maasen for the fifth grade, and perhaps even longer.

Happily, I earned my release the following year. I received an acceptance to the school in Sulingen, with the condition that I had to repeat the fifth grade there. This was a disappointment, but there was nothing to be done. No way would I or my mother give up the chance to advance my education.

Jenny was almost one year old by now, and in addition to my homework, I was helping take care of her. I changed my baby sister's diapers, fed her, and took her for walks in the fresh air.

Since the school in Sulingen was five miles from our Maasen home, the only way to get there when the school year began was by riding a bicycle, regardless of wind, rain, or snow. We had no public transportation nearby.

From time to time, as a service to my school friends, I allowed them to ride along on my bicycle, balancing themselves on the frame in front of my seat. Until one day, a policeman stopped me and penalized me with a ticket of one DM, to be paid within one week. My mother managed to pay the ticket on time, but one DM was a lot of money when we had to count every single penny to make ends meet every month.

Soon enough, my mother and Herbert realized that my long-distance routine was making all our lives even more difficult, so they started to look for affordable housing in Sulingen. The opportunity came when Herbert landed a job as a freelance journalist at a regional newspaper. Our slightly more flexible finances meant we could finally move.

Our new home was a tiny flat in a small house owned by the Logemann family at the Nienburger Strasse. The Logemanns lived on the ground floor and gave us the first floor above them. But other than bringing us closer to my school, the new flat offered no noticeable upgrade in the comfort department.

My family still had to crowd together into one room, and visiting the toilet meant going downstairs and around the house to the farmer-style toilet in the attached stable. Bathing day was once a week, on Saturday. My mother would fill a metal bathtub with warm water, and we would take turns. For the rest of the week, a bowl with hot water had to suffice. We did what is called *katzenwäsche*, washing like cats with as little water as possible.

The new middle school presented challenges I was not yet used to, not just in its academics but in its social environment too. I was terrified of the teachers and principal and of the extremely strict, disciplinarian code of conduct. Whenever we didn't behave properly, we were ordered to stand outside the classroom until the teacher called us back into class. A scary fate since our class happened to be just opposite the principal's office. One time, when I was kicked out of class for misbehavior, I decided to hide in the map room next door to avoid running into the principal. It became clear very soon that this was not a smart move, as my teacher came looking for me outside the classroom door and did not find me in the expected place. Needless to say, the rest of the day did not go well for me at all.

My faster commute to school did make life easier, but since our house was on the outskirts of town, my walk there was long. It took me past the sawmill on the other side of the street, with its mountains of wood piled up along the road. A large, aggressive German shepherd guarded the sawmill. The dog would strain at its long leash, running from one side of the property to the other to make sure nobody dared to come close, and demanding respect. On my walks to school, I stayed as far away from that dog as possible.

As it turned out, our stay at the Logemanns' did not last long. A violent incident in that spring of 1954 forced us to look for other accommodations shortly after we moved in.

Conflicts Escalate

If Herbert had any impact on my life, it was the advice he gave me when I received my official papers to muster for the German army. "Peter," he advised me, "if they give you a choice, never ever go into the Panzer division." Panzer is the German word for tanks. "Tanks are an iron coffin, with no chance to get out if you should get hit." He must have known because he served in a Panzer division, although his capture possibly saved him his life.

Sure enough, during the muster, they gave me the choice: Panzer or telecommunication. Remembering Herbert's strong advice, I had no problem choosing telecommunication, although I had no idea what this would involve.

When I arrived home with my *Wehrpass* military ID, Herbert threw his hands in the air. "Telecommunication? That's worth less than serving in a tank. You'll be the first one at the front to roll the cables out and the last one at the front to roll them back again."

As it turned out, thanks to a special law passed in the government which would free only sons from the military service, I never had to serve either in a tank or in telecommunication.

Although it proved irrelevant, Herbert's military advice was one of the only positive influences he had on my life. His next involvement was less fortunate.

One day, I found my sister Bärbel crying in front of the house when I arrived home from school. The owner's daughter, a few years older than Bärbel, had beaten her. As a big brother, I felt it was my duty to protect my sister. I went looking for the girl, found her, and beat her in return. I had no clue about the domino effect I was about to unleash.

About one hour later, her father came home. Hearing that I had beaten his daughter, he proceeded to hit me over and over again.

Herbert arrived in the middle of this, and seeing our landlord beat me mercilessly and without having any idea why, he started punching him. The situation quickly spun out of control.

Since the girl's father was our landlord, we received our eviction papers immediately. Our family needed a new home right away.

We found an available place closer to the center of town, at Kohlehandel Stagge, a coal merchant who offered us a converted office on the ground floor. This was once again a single room with a toilet housed in a separate building and with even fewer comforts than our previous two arrangements. But we were left with no choice.

Money remained a constant battle. As a freelance journalist, Herbert only earned a check when his articles got published. No article, no publication, no money. Three children needing food and clothing created a lot of stress for him and only compounded the pressures my mother faced daily.

Every day, the two of them argued more than the day before, and it was not long before their arguments became louder and angrier. Overhearing them as I tried to sleep would scare me. I knew the situation had turned more volatile when I noticed that my mother had taken the glass top off the coffee table and hidden it behind the cupboard.

Soon I began to see the outcome of these fights when I woke up in the morning. At times, Herbert beat up my mother badly, leaving her with multiple bruises on her body and face.

Once when I saw Herbert beating my mother, I took a kitchen knife and threatened him, but Herbert was too strong for me and took the knife out of my hand. I am thankful today for what he did because I think I would have been able to kill him.

It came as no surprise when Mutti and Herbert announced they were divorcing, two years after they married. To add to the abuse, it turned out that Herbert was also having frequent extramarital affairs. The official divorce happened in October of 1952, and Herbert agreed to be named as the sole guilty party. One year and another legal battle later, my mother received full custody of my half-sister Jenny Brigitte, who was almost three years old by then. I later found a note in her papers, written by her doctor at the time and confirming that she had been beaten and badly injured by Herbert. That piece of paper must have greatly assisted in winning her custody case.

We were thrust back into a life of stringing together an existence any way we could, mostly through social support and my grandparents' donations. A bit of money came to us through lawsuits my mother repeatedly filed against Herbert, who was neglecting his responsibility to financially support his daughter Jenny and his ex-wife.

Since we were living below poverty level, the state finally granted me DM 25 in monthly support, plus qualifying expenses like schoolbooks, which my mother had to request every single time. This is one of the requests she saved among her papers:

1	Hilf Dir selbst Wörterbuch	DM 1.75
1	Mathematik Arbeitsbuch	DM 2.80
1	Lebendige Muttersprache	DM 2.20

1	Singende, Klingende Welt	DM 1.50
6	Schulhefte	DM 1.50
1	Bogen	DM 0.30
		DM 12.45

To add to the humiliation, my teachers needed to approve and sign any book request before it went on to the local authorities and all the way up to the Ministry of the Interior.

The annual school fees posed another problem. The state would subsidize the tuition of DM 126 only for the top students. Unfortunately, I never reached this level, even though my mother paid for tutoring. I was not a bad student, but no matter how hard I studied, I never excelled. Time was not an excuse since I certainly had plenty of time to study. This was well before the days when televisions, computers, or electronic games took over households, so I had no such distractions to steal my attention. Despite my efforts, I remained an average student, neither at the top nor at the bottom.

This did not bode well for my future. I was anxious about my prospects and frustrated that all my studying didn't propel me closer to the top of my class. But I was about to receive a surprise piece of news.

Grandfather Is the Best

In the early 1950s, soon after my mother's divorce from Herbert, the government contacted us to announce that I was the sole inheritor of two houses in Hannover formerly owned by my father and his sister Lucy.

Since my father had gone missing and was by then declared dead—at least this is what I was told—and my aunt Lucy had passed away after moving to the United States, I was the only known heir. My sister Bärbel had not been listed as an inheritor, but I did not notice this strange omission at the time.

This mystery and other puzzles related to my family did not get resolved until one day three decades later, when I finally found the time to sort through the many documents and pictures my mother had left behind after her death. Buried amid those papers, I found the histories of the past that my mother had kept secret from us all this time.

For now, the sudden ownership of two apartment buildings in Hannover finally gave my family a means of moving back to the city we'd been bombed out of years before.

As an added incentive, my grandparents had already moved back to Hannover. The company where Opa had worked for many years had reopened its regional office in the city and reserved a small apartment on the fourth floor for the use of my grandfather and Oma. The current executives had decided to generously reward the company's long-retired regional manager, who had been instrumental in establishing the firm in Germany and leading it through the difficult war times. They also reinstituted all of Opa's benefits, allowing him and my grandmother to enjoy a comfortable retirement.

Only much later did I realize how much respect my grandfather must have earned in order for his company to voluntarily finance his retirement in this way. The employees of Opa's old company greeted him with the greatest deference when they met him in the staircase. He must have been a legend.

Lessons like this are badly needed in today's profit-hungry business environment, where the commitment of an individual to an employer earns little or no merit or recognition.

In 1957, my mother, my two sisters, and I finally moved back to Hannover, into an apartment in one of my newly inherited homes in the Yorckstrasse 13. Compared to where we were living before, the apartment was huge, and the little furniture we had got lost in the many large rooms.

The chance to spend more time than ever with Opa and Oma brought me a great deal of comfort. While we still lived in Maasen, I had grown closer to Opa from the summers I'd spent with my grandparents after they returned to Hannover. Opa surprised me with his seemingly never-ending array of talents. From ice-skating on the frozen lake in front of city hall to step dancing to the sounds of big band music, he knew it all. He would take his walking stick in one hand and his hat in the other and step dance in the middle of the living room. Fred Astaire had some real competition in my grandfather.

Opa loved piano music too, and his favorite was the British-American musician Charlie Kunz. Maybe this was because Kunz reminded Opa of his late son William Jr., who had played the same compositions in his youth.

Around town, my grandparents still made as striking a couple as ever, and seeing them walk hand in hand when they went out was a pleasure. It was surely an adjustment for them to end up in a small two-room flat after living in a stately apartment before the war and enjoying the luxurious lifestyle of Hannover high society. Then again, a two-room apartment was far better than the conditions in Hameln. I never heard a single word of complaint about their present situation in Hannover.

My grandparents still helped us financially. Since we continued to have limited social income from the state, we depended on the support from Opa and Oma to help us survive month after month.

Pocket money was too much of a luxury for my mother to afford, so I had to look around to earn some money of my own, as little as it might be. I found a job at a private club where members went to play a game called *kegeln*. This was similar to bowling but more difficult, since kegel balls were smaller and harder to control. The pins did not reset automatically, so the club hired a few boys to reset them. As a kegel boy, I would typically earn 5.00 DM for a three-hour shift, usually in the evenings from 7:00 to 10:00 p.m.

I used this money to buy tickets to jazz performances at the Niedersachsenhalle, a local hall that brought in well-known entertainers. My favorite style was New Orleans jazz, and for those shows, I was able to buy a seat on the floor for 8.00 DM. Louis "Satchmo" Armstrong playing his trumpet, George Lewis mastering his clarinet, or Chris Barber and his jazz band playing the trombone—I saw them all. The only jazz hero of mine that I missed was Benny Goodman, whom I could not see because I had to work the late shift and couldn't find anyone to switch with me.

Little did I know in 1959 that almost sixty years later, I would listen to Chris Barber and his trombone again, this time in München in the Prinzregententheater. At around eighty years old, he was still playing, not as forcefully as before but still impressively. And I had no idea that years later I would get to see jazz in New Orleans itself, sitting on the floor at the tiny, legendary Preservation Hall.

The move to Hannover also meant I needed to change schools yet again, to complete the tenth grade. Luckily, I was accepted at a new institution called the Freiherr von Stein Schule, named after a nineteenth-century Prussian statesman. Since my new school had to share space with a gymnasium, as functioning school buildings and teachers were rare during these postwar times, our classes took place Monday to Wednesday in the afternoons and Thursday to Saturday in the mornings. Yes, six days a week and plenty of homework.

Among the many advantages of being back in Hannover was that my new school was only a short fifteen-minute walk from home, past the

Bahlsen cookie factory. Smelling the sweet taste of cookies baking in the morning was a true pleasure, but not as exciting as returning after school with an empty stomach and fantasizing about devouring the entire contents of the factory.

My newly opened school had a lot to prove. Ours would be its first graduating tenth-grade class, so the faculty was focused on establishing the school as one of the leading academic institutions in Hannover. Of the thirty-four students who started tenth grade that year, only eighteen made it through the final exams. That I was one of the final group is due in large part to the training I received at my school in Sulingen and particularly to the efforts of my teacher Mrs. Thiede, who pushed us hard to reach the high standards she had set for us.

Many years later, as a vice president and divisional director with Sheraton Hotels, I decided to pay a visit to Mrs. Thiede and to Mrs. Klose, my former English teacher. They both looked surprised when I described my international career, and after a few moments of silence, Mrs. Thiede said, "Peter, I'm extremely happy to hear this, because honestly, I never thought that you would advance very much in your life."

I could hear a note of pride in her voice, and I'm sure that the success story of one of her past students became a story she told at every possible opportunity.

Polizei-Gruppenposten Sulingen
Polizei-Revier Sulingen
Az. (Behörde – Dienststelle) Sulingen (Ort)

Reihe **C** Nr. A 73514 *

Gebührenpflichtige Verwarnung

An Herrn Peter Tischmann, geb. am 24.12.39
Frau/Fräulein
wohnhaft in .... Straße Nr. 57

Sie haben am 18. 5. 54 in ....

....

....

Sie werden wegen dieser Übertretung hiermit unter Festsetzung einer Gebühr von 1 DM verwarnt.

Sie werden gebeten, die Gebühr von 1 DM **innerhalb einer Woche** unter Vorzeigung dieser Verwarnung bei dem Polizei-

Polizei-Gruppenposten Sulingen
Polizei-Revier Sulingen
(Bezeichnung der Dienststelle)

einzuzahlen oder unter Angabe der Nummer an die genannte Stelle zu übersenden.

Sollte die Zahlung nicht erfolgen, so kann Antrag auf gerichtliche Strafverfügung gestellt werden.

Um zu vermeiden, daß im Wiederholungsfalle eine Anzeige dem Amtsrichter mit dem Antrage auf gerichtliche Strafverfügung zugeleitet werden muß, bitten wir Sie in Ihrem eigenen Interesse, die zur Aufrechterhaltung der öffentlichen Sicherheit und Ordnung erlassenen Vorschriften künftig zu beachten.

(Dienstsiegel)

....
(Unterschrift, Name, Dienststellung des Beamten)

Pol. N. 143 C (DIN A 6)

1954 MY FIRST TRAFFIC TICKET

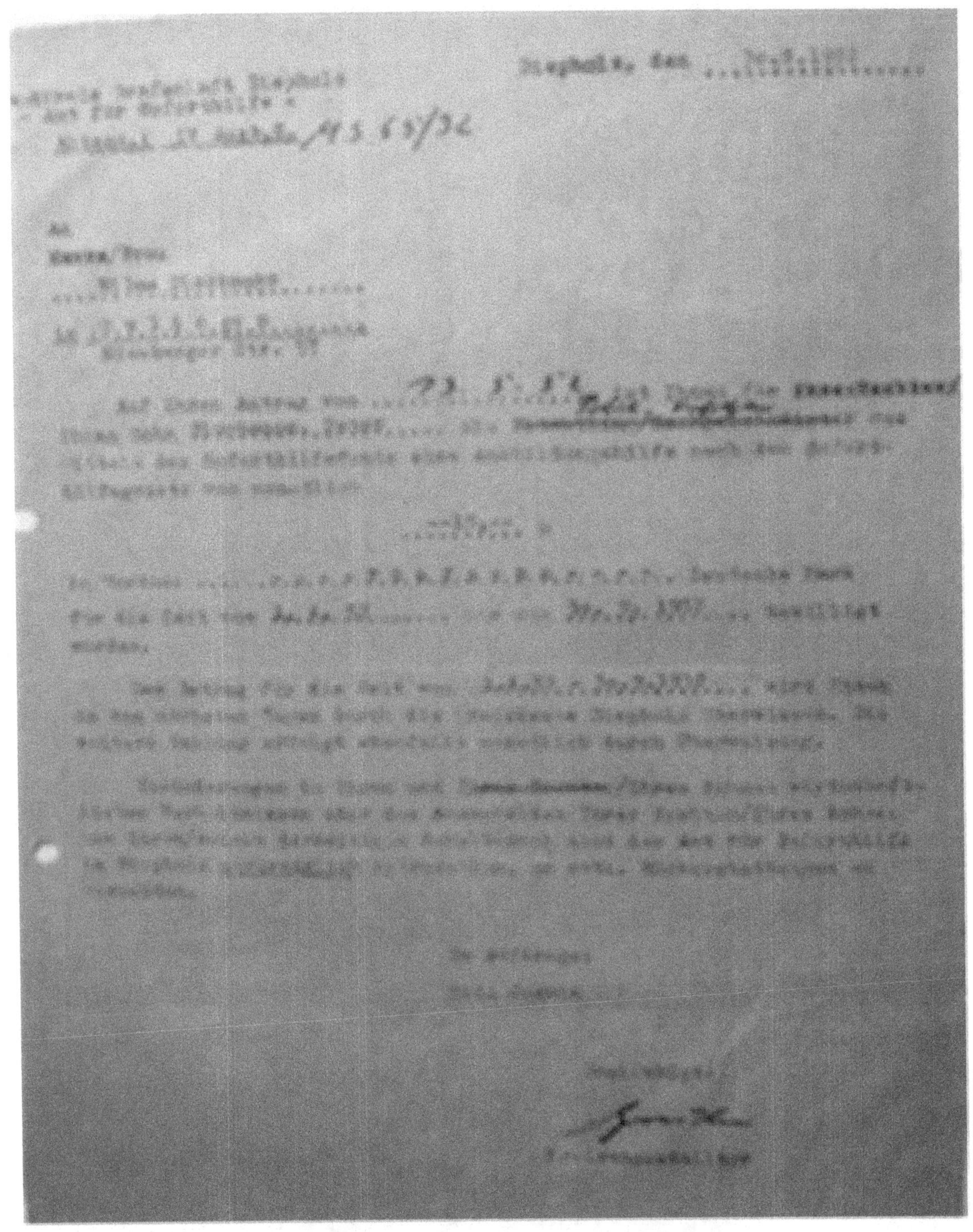

MY MOTHER BEGGING FOR FINANCE SUPPORT

OPA 82 YEARS OLD WALKING AND STEP DANCING

PICTURE TAKEN AT SCHOOL

Starting at the Bottom 05

Krickelkrakel

It's irresistible to guess who we might be now if we had faced different circumstances in life. What kind of person might I have turned into if I had grown up with a father around the house? Would I have made different decisions in my life? Enjoyed other hobbies? Pursued a career I cannot even imagine now?

Questions like these are impossible to answer, of course. But my father's absence had at least one impact I can pinpoint with certainty. It turned Opa into the central male role model in my life.

I craved my grandfather's approval even more than either of us realized at the time. I cherished Opa's attention and felt noticed in his presence in a way I never quite felt with my mother or other authority figures.

It was not until much later that I understood how Opa's letters and his walks along the river Weser with me were more than just expressions of love and playfulness. Opa was doing his best to provide me with the intellectual and creative stimulation that were difficult to come by in times of war and deprivation, adding a necessary balance to the rigors of school.

In every way Opa could, he tried to turn me into a well-rounded young person and give me the confidence to succeed in life.

As an adolescent, I had started to experiment with drawing and painting, and when I showed some of my pieces to Opa, he took a strong interest in my work. I suppose he saw, in my naive efforts, a glimmer of an artistic streak shared by other members of our family, from my great-grandfather Julius Ewald's lithography talents to my grandmother Selma's opera career, to my mother's dancing skills, and my uncle William Jr.'s musical ear.

Opa himself was a skilled artist, although he never pursued his talent professionally. His pencil drawings exhibited a mastery of the form that could have perhaps taken him far had he chosen this path instead of a more traditional business career.

The more Opa saw of my drawings, the more he sensed the potential for a successful career in a creative industry that could not only make me happy but also make profitable use of my skills. He urged me to pursue graphic design. I had just finished school and had no other ideas for what to do with myself. Opa's belief in my talent made me think that maybe he was right.

When Opa offered to use his connections in the Hannover business community to arrange an interview for me at Graphic Oswald, the city's leading graphic design firm and print house, all I could say was yes.

Full of hope, if not confidence, and carrying a knapsack packed with my paintings and drawings, I went off to my appointment with the chief designer and managing director of Oswald. His secretary showed me into his office, where I found him sitting poised in his desk chair, frowning over a stack of papers. I felt a sudden urge to disappear under the carpet.

This man had an impressive title and a lot of important work to do. Why would he waste his time with me? But he looked up and greeted me with a warm welcome. When he began to tell me what he expected of future members of the design team, I had the reassuring sense that he was already treating my candidacy seriously, thanks to the recommendation Opa had put in on my behalf. Then he took my paintings and drawings from my hands and began to page through them one by one, without saying a word.

I tried to read his face for a sign of what he would say, when he broke into a big smile and turned around to look me in the eyes. A shiver of excitement rippled through me. "Junger Mann," which means young man, "what you are showing me here is what I would consider Krickelkrakel."

Krickelkrakel?

"This is far from graphic design. You seem to have some talent in the use of colors, but I suggest you forget graphic design and look for a career in a different discipline."

I could feel my cheeks turning red. I shifted in my chair. He then proceeded to show me a series of designs and drawings that exhibited the professional caliber he was looking for. I immediately saw his point. If I would have shown him the book with my grandfather's pencil drawings, he would no doubt have accepted me on the spot.

Could my grandfather have been so wrong? I assume Opa saw in me a talent worth developing, but a paid job at a professional design firm was apparently not the place to do this—at least, not at a prestigious company like Oswald.

So now what?

I was not yet ready to give up on pursuing a creative career and using my eye for colors and forms, so I came up with a plan: I would become a decorator and create the kinds of eye-catching window displays seen in the top department stores of Hannover. Conjuring colorful three-dimensional worlds would give me much more of a thrill than graphic design anyway.

My hunch seemed correct when I received an invitation for an interview just a few days after I applied for an apprentice decorator position at Magis, the city's most upscale department store.

The meeting with the human resources director at Magis got off to a pleasant start, and he seemed to take a liking to me, enough that I felt confident telling him how my job search was going so far. I mentioned my unsuccessful interview at Oswald, assuming he would shake his head in sympathy. I suddenly felt the tone of the interview shift. "On second thought," he said, "a job as a decorator would not make such a good career choice." Every store has only one chief decorator, and the rest are just helpers with limited opportunities to move up. Why don't I take a job as a commercial apprentice instead?

Commercial apprentice? What was that? Unfortunately, I didn't have enough self-assurance to insist on remaining a candidate for the decorator apprenticeship instead. I still liked the idea of aiming for a chief decorator job down the road, despite this man's discouraging words. But now that he knew I'd been rejected from a creative position at Oswald, I felt cornered and finally accepted the job of a commercial apprentice.

On the morning of Tuesday, April 1, 1958, I reported to the men's clothing department at Magis to start my new job as a commercial apprentice. I wore my best suit, tie, and polished shoes, spick-and-span from top to bottom.

All around me, busy salesmen ran around the floor, selecting clothing items to show customers then tossing the unwanted garments here and there. The job looked stressful but far from boring. I could learn to do this, I thought, and maybe even enjoy it. But I immediately learned that mine was not a sales job. My main responsibility was to pick up the clothes that the salesmen discarded on the floor and put them back on their respective hangers, arranging them by size in the various displays.

This is how you do it, the department head gestured at me, spreading his fingers. He placed one finger between each of the hangers and shook them vigorously until they hung at a perfect distance from each other—but only for a few moments, since they would soon get messed up again.

That first morning, I rushed back and forth across the sales floor, picking up the suits and hanging, arranging, and shaking them, hanging, arranging, and shaking. The boss stopped me once and explained that I also needed to comb the carpet fringes every few minutes to keep them looking smooth.

Magis was the city's most prestigious store, so of course the clothes and hangers and carpet had to look perfect. I understood this, and I fulfilled my duties diligently.

By day two, I decided this job was not going to lead me anywhere, no matter how perfectly I spread my fingers, shook the hangers, and combed the carpet. The boss seemed to enjoy exerting his power over the young apprentices, keeping us breathless and miserable as we cleaned up after salesmen who could not be bothered to hang even one single item on a rack.

I was only twenty years old, but I had worked hard to obtain a middle school degree. I wanted to make at least a minimal amount of progress toward a goal I could get excited about.

After three days of hanger-shaking and fringe-combing, I told my mother I didn't want to go back. She understood and didn't even attempt to talk me out of it. To my surprise, it was the director of human resources who tried to convince me not to resign. A commercial apprenticeship was the best career path for me, he insisted, offering to transfer me to the carpet department: "The people working there are very friendly and supportive to new team members."

Hearing the word "carpet," all I could visualize were days upon days of combing fringes, fringes, and more fringes.

Too embarrassed to say no immediately, I agreed to think about it for a day. At home that afternoon, I asked my mother to telephone the HR guy and decline on my behalf.

A grown man, asking my mother to call an employer to turn down a job. I was not proud of this. But I knew how persuasive this human resources director could be and how badly he needed to fill vacant positions.

After my mother's telephone call, I never set foot inside Magis again—not then and not even once since—even though the store still has the best window displays and merchandise in Hannover.

Now here I was, ready to embark on a career but already failing at it and feeling increasingly lost. I had no idea what to do with myself.

I was ripe for the unexpected meeting that was about to change my life.

A Career as a Chef? Why Not

I ended up in the hospitality business by pure accident. A few days after my inauspicious week at Magis, I grabbed a few jazz records and went to visit my old school friend Lothar Lühring for our weekly musical exchange. He told me he'd just started a chef apprenticeship at the five-star Hotel Luisenhof in Hannover. Lothar sounded excited about this new job, in no small part because there was plenty of delicious free food to eat around the kitchen.

But Lothar also had a genuine passion for cooking, and he sparked a new idea in my mind. A job as a chef? Why not? After all, I liked to cook too, at least when I was helping my mother in the kitchen.

A chef apprenticeship certainly sounded less miserable than smoothing out carpet fringes day after day.

As it turned out, Lothar and I were not the only young people with the bright idea of apprenticing in a kitchen. Every position received a flood of applicants, and employers enjoyed the luxury of choice in those days. Blissfully ignorant of this fact, I sent my application around Hannover.

No luck. Nothing but dead silence for weeks. Lothar's reference was of no use either, as his hotel had no more openings available. But one morning, I was surprised to receive a call from Hirte Betriebe, a major restaurant operator in Hannover.

Barely one minute into my interview at headquarters, the human resources director informed me that before I could start training in the kitchen, I would have to invest one year in the service department.

Waiting tables? No thanks, I politely informed him. At my age, I could not afford to lose a year working as a waiter. I knew that with the unfortunate Magis episode behind me, I didn't want to keep wasting my time. I was already almost nineteen .

Early the next morning, our house telephone rang again. The HR director had found me a position as an apprentice in the kitchen at one of the company's restaurants, the Brauer Gilde Haus. My heart jumped. Turning down a waiter job when I had no other prospects in sight had been a risk, but it seemed to be paying off.

Unlike other dining destinations in the Hirte Betriebe empire, the Brauer Gilde Haus operated as a standalone restaurant. The others, including The Gondel fine dining temple and the Opera Konditorei pastry cafe, occupied the same building, known as the Georgs Palast, and shared one central kitchen. The whole operation was overseen by the well-known executive chef Hans Grünich, a legend in Hannover and a chef everyone in the industry respected.

At the Brauer Gilde Haus, I would be working in a separate kitchen, under a different boss who ultimately reported to Grünich. The smaller setting sounded like a place where I could learn and grow as a young cook. I accepted a three-year apprenticeship contract, and an immediate start date of Saturday, April 26, 1958, at seven o'clock in the morning.

Culinary career, here I come.

That evening, I told my mother that I had a brand-new job, and I needed six cook's trousers, six cook's jackets, six hats, and six neckerchiefs, along with a specific number of chef's knives.

My mother looked at me carefully. There was no "ja ja" this time. She repeated, very slowly: "One trouser, one jacket, one hat, one neckerchief, and one knife."

"No," I said, "you must have misunderstood: six trousers, six jackets, six hats, six neckerchiefs, and at least three knives."

She shook her head. "Let's start with one of each and see how it goes." Considering how my Magis adventure had turned out, I really couldn't blame her. But this time, I was determined to persevere, no matter how menial or demeaning the job.

I had no idea what kind of punishment I had just signed up for.

On the morning I arrived for my first day of work, at seven o'clock sharp, the Brauer Gilde Haus kitchen was a hive of activity, fragrant with the scents of freshly baked bread and regional German specialties. In the dining room, with its red domed ceilings and carved wood detailing on the walls, the tables were draped in white tablecloths, awaiting the well-heeled diners who would stream in a few hours later. I was ready and eager to start my new job. All around me, chefs ran back and forth, busy and active, exuding a sense of purpose and urgency.

The head chef greeted me and escorted me to the locker room in the basement so I could change into my work uniform. As we walked downstairs, he casually turned to me and said, "By the way, seven o'clock means you are fully dressed in a clean uniform and ready to begin work at exactly seven o'clock."

Oh. So I was late on my first day, despite having arrived at the appointed time. From now on, I'd need to clock in at least half an hour before seven so I could have time to change into my chef's uniform. I just got my first lesson in discipline and order in a kitchen.

I frantically put on my cook's trousers, the jacket with twelve black buttons, the tall starched chef's hat, and the high chef's shoes which needed to fit tightly. I tied on my apron, my torchon dishcloth, and my perfectly folded scarf. In less than two minutes, moving at Olympic speed, I was dressed head to toe.

"Let's make a good cook out of you," the chef announced when I found him again in the kitchen. "Have you ever cleaned a chicken?"

"Yes, at home!" I replied. I had helped my mother do it several times, since she hated cleaning the insides of chickens.

The next thing I knew, I was standing in front of boxes and boxes of chickens. Never had I seen so many dead chickens in one place. "Show me how you do it," the chef said.

The moment I placed my knife on the first chicken, I felt a big kick on my butt, as if a horse had hit me.

The chef was standing behind me, both hands on his hips, looking angry. "Do you know why I kicked you?" No. I really had no idea. "I kicked you *not* because you do not know how to prepare a chicken but because you told me you know how. And you know nothing. Nothing!"

Stunned, I focused my full attention on him as he showed me how to clean a chicken, step by step, and prepared it for roasting. Then he turned on his heels and left, but not before pointing to a stack of five boxes, packed with fifteen chickens each. A full morning of work for a novice like me.

After my earlier lesson in discipline and punctuality, I had just learned my first crucial cooking lesson: Never assume you know how to do something, when in fact you know nothing.

I would've been better off telling him I'd never cleaned a chicken before because the way a home cook prepares a chicken is very different from how professional chefs do it. For instance, chefs have a special way of cutting the skin of the neck, by flipping it over the chicken to keep it from drying out. I could tell that working with this guy was not going to be easy.

The chef had certainly earned my respect, or at least my fear.

The chicken cleaning project behind me, I now found myself staring at thousands of potatoes, stacked up like a stone wall. The Germans sure do like to eat potatoes. My job was to first peel the potatoes then toss them into giant round containers that each held around fifty pounds, to get them ready to steam for the lunch service.

Thankfully, I knew how to peel a potato. But even the seemingly easy task before me turned out to be trickier than I had thought since it meant dealing with enormous pieces of equipment I'd never seen before. The steam kettle was big enough that two chefs could hide in it, and the stationary sauté pan was huge enough to fit fifty steaks.

Since I had no idea when the potatoes were cooked enough to remove from the giant steam kettle, I needed to peek. As soon as I lifted the lid, a massive cloud of hot steam escaped into the room, flattening my tall, heavily starched chef's hat. The hat now lay on my head like a pancake. Every chef who walked by me burst out laughing. Just what I needed on my first day.

Those heavy linen hats are now a thing of the past, replaced by lightweight paper hats that chefs change daily. The advantage: no washing, no starching, no pleating, and no ironing. Not to mention, no hat headaches, and no unfortunate comedy routines.

Despite the first few hiccups, the initial days of my apprenticeship went by smoothly. I peeled more potatoes than I'd ever seen in my life, and I occasionally prepared chickens. I kept a respectful distance from the chef and did my best to ensure that nothing went wrong. I did what I was told to do at all times and bravely asked if I didn't understand the assignment. The kitchen lingo, a key to survival in the kitchen, became second nature to me: The stove was the piano, and the pots and pans were called casseroles and sauteuses.

After handling potatoes and chickens all day, every apprentice had to clean the kitchen from top to bottom at the end of service each day.

Our job was to scrub each piece of equipment from the top down and wash the floor. The kitchen had to be spotless, as the chef was keen on maintaining the highest standards of hygiene.

When the chef ordered us to clean the piano, that meant he wanted the kitchen stove to shine inside and outside, top to bottom, just like a Bechstein piano.

One day, while I stood elbow-deep in soap bubbles and sponges, a waiter showed up at the service counter demanding a goulash soup for a guest who had walked in one minute before closing. I looked around for a chef who could take care of this order, only to find that I was all by myself in the kitchen.

"One goulash soup!" the waiter repeated, glaring at me impatiently.

I'd never made the soup before, but I had eaten it, and I knew it was thick and brown. I spotted two bain-maries at the steam table, found the one filled with thick brown soup, filled a preheated bowl, and gave it to the waiter.

Moments later, I heard a yell. "Who is the idiot who served the goulash soup?"

Something must have gone terribly wrong. I rushed to the food service counter and found the chef waiting for his victim. I admitted that I'd handled the soup order since no one else was around. What was the problem?

Suddenly, I felt a foot land firmly on my backside. That familiar butt kick, once again. I had chosen the wrong bain-marie. I grabbed a countertop to avoid falling on my face from the impact. The chef must have been a soccer player in his younger years .

He was a brute, but at least this much was true: Once he had punished one of the apprentices for some ghastly error, the mistake became history, and he did not hold it against us any longer. But woe was anyone who made the same mistake twice.

No doubt about it, the Brauer Gilde Haus was a tough environment for an apprenticeship. Those of us who got through it learned a lot, far more than the average apprentice, and we earned a sense of pride. Yes, the kicks in the butt continued as the months went by, but I started to see them as part of my learning process.

Physical and verbal abuse were common in kitchens at that time, a practice that would be unthinkable today. Even the vocabulary of the profession has shifted since my day. Once known as a "stift," somebody to push around, an apprentice today goes by the more respectable "Auszubildender ," a person to train and mentor.

At least there was one assignment that I looked forward to. Every week, each apprentice had to create a personal report describing what he had learned, so the chefs could make sure the training program was going as planned. For me, the reports were also an excuse to satisfy an artistic itch that I still felt after my rejection from the world of graphic design.

I not only wrote my reports, but I illustrated them too. To show how I had learned to filet a dover sole, I supported every step in the report with a design: from the fresh fish all the way down to the final preparation and service.

The reports got signed first by the individual chefs at each of the Hirte restaurants, then by the executive chef of the Georgs Palast, Hans Grünich. His official title was director of kitchens, overseeing the entire food operation of the Hirte organization.

Grünich was a man of impressive stature, standing at over six feet tall and weighing at least 250 pounds. He looked exactly the way people would expect an executive chef to look, and he demanded the highest respect. Neither I nor my fellow Brauer Gilde Haus apprentices ever dealt with him directly, and we regarded him with equal parts awe and fear.

One afternoon after service had ended and I'd started the cleaning routine, I heard the telephone in the kitchen ring. Everyone else had left, so I picked up the receiver.

"Brauer Gilde Haus kitchen, Peter Tischmann speaking."

A booming voice answered: "Tischmann? Tischmann?"

My heart pounded in my chest. I could feel the blood thumping in my eardrums.

"Are you the apprentice with the report book?"

"Yes," I answered, fearful of the powerful, anonymous voice. I had a guess who the caller might be but did not dare assume.

"Tomorrow morning at eight o'clock, in my kitchen!" the voice bellowed before hanging up.

My mind flashed to the illustrations in my latest report book. I had gotten carried away. Here I was, trying to do a good job at work, establish momentum, and express a little bit of creativity. This was clearly not the place for it. Too many drawings, not enough seriousness.

The most promising career opportunity I'd had so far was about to get smashed to pieces.

The Georgs Palast Is Calling

The hair was still standing up on my arms as I went to see my boss to tell him about the telephone call.

"That must have been Chef Grünich," he said, looking at me gravely.

I nodded and stared at the floor. I'd suspected the same thing.

He paused for a moment, then said, "Sh—" My eyes widened. "He is always taking my best people."

This was the very first time I'd heard from my boss or anyone else that I was doing a good job. No one had ever uttered a compliment, and I had come to expect that I would never hear any commentary on my work unless I had screwed up.

"Get your things ready and be there tomorrow morning," he said, a resigned expression on his face. "You can learn a lot more over there." He shook my hand and added, "I was very pleased to have you. Good luck!"

Just like that, the kicks-in-the-butt phase of my apprenticeship was over. I regretted leaving the Brauer Gilde Haus, a harsh environment that I'd grown accustomed to and a difficult boss I'd learned to appreciate.

But there was no time to get sentimental. I was due at the empire of Hans Grünich first thing the next morning.

This time, I arrived one hour early, at 7:00 a.m. sharp. Entering the kitchen of the Georgs Palast felt like stepping into a giant submarine. The dim underground space had visible piping all over its ceiling, and not a single ray of daylight shone in. I could immediately tell that I'd be doing a lot of cleaning in here, as the entire floor was covered in sawdust.

Seeing a kitchen floor covered in sawdust looks strange at first, but I learned there's a reason for it. Sawdust absorbs any fat and dirt that might fall on the floor and keeps it from getting slippery. After service every day, the sawdust would get swept away and replaced by a fresh layer.

Despite its claustrophobic appearance, the kitchen also looked orderly and disciplined and was divided into various areas of responsibility, known as stations. This system differed starkly from what I'd seen in the Brauer Gilde Haus kitchen, where the cooking staff formed one big brigade and shared all the work.

I surveyed the scene. A large stove dominated the space, with the saucier station and the rotisseur roasting station on one side, and a vegetable station called an entremetier on the other. An extension to the main stove held the soup station, known as the potager, and the fish station, the poissonier. The butcher shop, the walk-in refrigerators, and the cold kitchen, called the garde manger, took up the rest of the central area, while the bakery shop and patisserie occupied a separate space off the main kitchen.

My eyes immediately darted over to a podium hovering over the entire area. This intriguing feature, I learned, was Mr. Grünich's office. From there, he could supervise everything happening in the kitchen and ensure that absolutely nothing escaped his vigilant eyes.

Grünich's perch also overlooked the two heated service counters serving the Georgs Palast dining rooms: three restaurants to one side and the gourmet flagship Gondel to the other side. What appeared at first like a messy sawdust-filled space turned out to be a meticulously organized kitchen, with one station feeding into the other and ensuring a perfect flow of preparation all the way up to the point of service.

My stomach jumped as I saw Mr. Grünich himself enter the kitchen at 7:30 a.m.

I had not expected a ceremonious greeting from him, nor did I get one. After a brief, impersonal hello, Grünich took me to my assigned station, the saucier, and introduced me to the chef in charge there. The saucier station is the heart and soul of the hot kitchen, but I could immediately sense that Chef Ender did not embody "heart and soul" in his approach to the world.

If I thought the Brauer Gilde Haus environment was rough, I had no idea what Mr. Ender was capable of. As I later learned, if you survive Mr. Ender and the saucier station, you will survive anywhere.

As the most junior member of the kitchen brigade, my first task was simply to keep the saucier station clean. Within minutes of meeting Mr. Ender, I started jumping up and down between the cooks, running to clean up after them whenever they dropped something, whisking away dirty pots and pans and replacing them with clean ones, and rushing to resupply clean spoons and ladles for the chefs. In short, my job was to do everything I could to make sure the show could go on, and what a show it was.

The culinary circus of the Georgs Palast had just hired its newest acrobat: me.

Just like any circus, the Georgs Palast had its star performances, and I soon discovered that most of these involved Mr. Grünich. He had traveled the world, and although prone to wild exaggeration, he had more fascinating stories to tell than most of us who were bound to the same kitchen, day in and day out. The man also had a penchant for the dramatic gesture, which he never hesitated to display at every possible occasion.

For any guest wishing to visit the kitchen, walking down the stairs from the restaurant and seeing fifty-plus chefs hard at work in their white uniforms and hats was indeed a sight to behold. It's no wonder the restaurant manager often brought VIPs down to show them the well-oiled operation.

Hans Grünich was at his best during those theatrical moments. Standing up on his podium, he would turn to the service counter and start to announce fake orders in Spanish to impress the visitor. "Uno chateaubriand, cinque escalope, treize New York cut steak," and on and on.

The kitchen brigade knew the game and went along with it, repeating every order out loud—"Yes, chef, uno chateaubriand, yes, chef, treize New York cut steak"—and rushing around in a flurry of activity. The only person who had no idea what was going on was me.

Since part of my job was to supply the saucier and rotisserie stations with all the meat items in an order, I started running back and forth, picking up the meats one by one from the ice box in the butcher shop. Chateaubriand, New York cut steaks, escalopes, entrecotes, tenderloin steaks, and all the rest soon piled up on the preparation table behind the chefs. I wondered why none of the chefs actually made any moves to prepare the meat. Then Grünich stopped announcing orders.

I glanced behind me at the podium. The VIP guest had left the kitchen. The show was over.

A large hand appeared in front of my face, and the next thing I knew, Mr. Ender was pinching my breast nipples, his two fingers twisting slowly. To avoid yelling in pain, I muffled my voice on my sleeve and turned away, only to get pushed to the ground. Flat on my belly in the sawdust, I heard a stream of curse words in my ear. "Stupid idiot!" was the gentlest. Mr. Ender commanded me to put all the meat back into the cooler box immediately. How could I be dumb enough to think the orders were actually real?

In my roughly nineteen years of life, I had never before been treated this way. Mr. Ender's management style was adding a brand-new chapter to my kitchen experience. I should complain, I thought to myself, but to whom?

This was 1958, and earning an apprenticeship at the Georgs Palast was like winning the jackpot. I was determined that I would survive. But more punishment was about to come my way.

An Eight-Hour Workday: Wishful Thinking

Like any other saucier at a high-end restaurant, Mr. Ender expected to find his sauce station clean and ready for him every morning when he arrived. Preparing the station was my job: I needed to line up the pots and pans, position the spoons and ladles by size, and get the sauce pots ready to go on the stovetop.

None of this would have been a problem if the Georgs Palast had enough equipment in its kitchen. But there was a constant shortage, and I had to compete with other apprentices arriving to set up their own bosses' stations. To make matters worse, the pot washer did not get in until 7:00 a.m., so every morning, the apprentices had almost no time to scramble and grab all the clean pieces we needed to set up our assigned stations.

I learned the hard way that if I failed to find enough spotless equipment for my station in time for Mr. Ender's arrival, my mouth would taste the sawdust again.

The only way to get my job done was to come in at 6:00 a.m. and start washing all the pieces required for my boss's station. The pot washer couldn't believe his luck when he started arriving every morning to find a big part of his job already done. Well, at least someone in the kitchen was glad to see me.

Much to my relief, my responsibilities soon shifted. I was allowed to assist the chefs at the piano—how the stove was called lovingly by the chefs— and carry the food plates from the stove to the service counter. The restaurant did three hundred lunch covers a day, so this meant running back and forth constantly to make sure the food got to the customers while still hot.

The food was served on silver plates divided into sections: one for the vegetables, one for the potatoes, one for the meat and sauce. The entremetier station on the other side of the stove would serve up the vegetables and potatoes, then the chef would push the platter over the hot stove to the saucier to serve the meat and sauce. Once the plates were filled, I had to run quickly with one in each hand to the service counter to pass them along to the waiters.

This entire production was timed to the smallest detail and depended on every member of the brigade to execute the job perfectly. Hans Grünich watched over the entire process, checking the presentation on each plate before it went out.

In this high-pressure situation, I learned how to do the job rapidly and efficiently. I had no choice. Soon I could tell that things were starting to go well for me.

Then one day, as I ran around assembling and shuttling plates of pork roast, potato dumplings, and vegetables, something unfortunate happened. As I carefully held the two plates in each of my hands and prepared to sprint to deliver the food, my torchon hook got caught on the gas knob. Unaware, I ran a few more steps, until the hook jerked me to a stop. Suddenly, a potato dumpling went flying ten yards through the air, catapulted by centrifugal force toward the service counter.

The dumpling arrived at the counter before I did. I sheepishly turned around to see if Mr. Grünich had noticed and breathed a sigh of relief when I found him looking in the other direction.

But someone else had seen my dumpling fly. Mr. Ender stared directly at my face and walked over to me without losing a moment. The sawdust that day tasted even worse than it had every other time. Just as I was starting to gain momentum in my job, here I was again, getting punished by my boss.

I can say this much about Mr. Ender: He taught me how to manage a saucier station efficiently, but the most important thing I learned from him was how not to treat people. Those sawdust memories have followed me throughout my entire career.

Luckily, Mr. Ender was the only physically abusive chef I encountered in that kitchen. As for the other bosses at the Georgs Palast, I would soon experience the strange lessons they inflicted on us naive young chefs.

A Day in the Life of a Chef's Apprentice

An old German proverb says, "Lehrjahre sind keine Herrenjahre," meaning the years of training are not years to enjoy.

So far, this saying had certainly come true. Today a chef like Mr. Ender would go to jail, or at the very least lose his license to train apprentices. But I survived his tyranny, true to the promise I'd made to myself. So I celebrated when I received my new assignment at the rotisseur, the meat-roasting station. I didn't know quite what to expect, but at least I would finally report to someone else.

Part of my new job involved preparing the roast beef for the cold kitchen, where it would get served as cold cuts or presented on the buffet. Making roast beef is an art, as I quickly learned. The meat must remain pink all the way through, without even a glimmer of gray on the rim. This meant roasting it with the perfect timing, at the perfect temperature. The raw roast beef had to rest on a layer of bones in the pan to get shielded from direct contact with the heat and avoid that dreaded gray border.

Once the beef went into the oven, I had to turn it every five minutes and continuously pour the jus from the bottom of the pan over the meat to ensure an even roasting process. The head chef at the station checked obsessively to make sure the beef wasn't getting overcooked.

Eventually, I earned his trust. On the first day when he let me take over the roasting process, I wanted to make sure I did everything exactly right. "Chef, how do I know when the roast beef is perfectly cooked?" I asked, thinking this a reasonable question from an eager apprentice.

The chef answered immediately, "When it feels like the breast of a young girl, then it's perfect."

I must have looked at him with gaping eyes and the strangest expression on my face because he turned to me, with his two arms crossed in front of him, and said, "Are you telling me that you've never touched the breast of a young girl?"

My face turned red like a tomato as he smiled, spun around, and walked away.

I still didn't know when a roast beef was done. Without the experience the chef had alluded to, I would need to keep paying close attention to the roasting process and pray I didn't overcook the meat.

During my rotation at the rotisseur, I watched the roast beef diligently every day and developed enough confidence to get the timing exactly right every time. After four months, it was time for my next station: the poissonier and potager.

Compared to the saucier station, every other placement in the Georgs Palast kitchen felt like a vacation, especially the fish and soup apprenticeship. From what I'd observed so far, the station chef, Mr. Erhardt, seemed like a true gentleman. He treated his people well and made sure they got involved in every aspect of cooking. Working for him turned out to be a real pleasure.

Mr. Erhardt had his own way of dealing with Hans Grünich. Every day before the service, I had to prepare a tray with samples of every soup we'd made and bring them to Mr. Grünich. As he ceremoniously sampled each one, he made a critical comment: a little bit more salt here, a little more cream there, too much pepper here, too thick, not thick enough. I don't remember a single time when we had a perfect soup. Or perhaps Mr. Grünich was just keeping us on our toes.

An excellent soup cook, Mr. Erhardt knew that his soups were perfect, but he went along with the daily show. When we went back to our station, he completely ignored Mr. Grünich's comments and left the soups exactly as they were.

Thanks to Mr. Erhardt, I picked up tips on how to handle a boss with a taste for showmanship. I also learned how to handle a live trout.

My first disastrous attempts with the fish provided no end of amusement for the chef. At the fish station, we received lots of orders for the German specialty known as *Forelle blau*, a poached trout served with new potatoes and melted butter. My job was to catch a fresh trout from the basin, kill it, clean it, and prepare it for cooking.

Catching the trout with a net was the easy part, but taking it out to kill it was a real test of agility. The skin is extremely slippery, and I had the hardest time trying to hold it without letting it slide out of my hands. Time and again my trout would end up on the floor, jumping up and down, before I finally managed to grab it and kill it, clean it, and drop it into the boiling water.

But as soon as I'd put the trout into the hot water, it would leap out of the pot and on to the ground. Even though the trout was dead by now, its muscles would contract like a rubber band, then automatically release and send the fish flying out of the pot.

Mr. Erhardt eventually stopped laughing for long enough to let me in on the tip that I'd need to break the trout's backbone to avoid the muscle contraction. Oh, so that was the secret! Another important lesson under my belt, but no more flying trout scenes for Mr. Erhardt to enjoy.

The trout act wasn't the only comedy performance I unwittingly put on, to the chefs' delight.

In contrast to his enormous size and his serious, imposing presence, Mr. Grünich had a sense of humor and liked to entertain his staff with pranks. One morning, as he walked by me in the kitchen, he called out, "Hi, Peter, catch," and I looked up to see a thirty-pound leg of veal flying in my direction.

I caught it, tumbled backward against the refrigerator wall, and started slowly sliding down under the weight of the leg of veal until I was sitting on the floor with thirty pounds of meat on my lap.

Mr. Grünich shook his head and said, "What? You cannot even catch a leg of veal? When I was your age, I could lift the entire animal over my head, with a cook sitting on top of it playing the guitar!"

I was still sitting on the floor when he walked away, a big grin on his face. The other cooks, seeing me on the floor cradling a giant mass of raw veal, doubled over with laughter.

Some cooks managed to play tricks on Mr. Grünich. One frequent prankster was the entremetier, responsible for the preparation of all vegetable garnishes. It was known around the kitchen that he liked to drink. One day, as Mr. Grünich stood watching, the entremetier prepared a choucroute, grabbing a bottle of white wine and visibly pouring it into the pot until the last drop. Mr. Grünich turned away, satisfied that enough wine had gone into the choucroute. A moment later, the chef entremetier, who had secretly stashed a cup in the pot to catch the wine, fished it out, and drank it all.

More and more, I enjoyed the kitchen environment and never regretted my decision, despite the embarrassing moments, the unrelenting work, and the rough times. Not all department chefs were like Mr. Ender. As a matter of fact, most of them were friendly and supportive to the apprentices, as long as we worked hard and did our job. Even Mr. Grünich's humiliating jokes seemed a friendly gesture in their own strange way.

But I did have to face one more difficult trial before I finished my three-year apprenticeship. My final rotation was at the cold kitchen station, the garde manger. Unlike the other all-male cooking stations, the cold section was staffed mainly by women cooks, known as the mamselles. The only man was Mr. Klapproth, the head chef at the station.

The mamselles, like most long-term kitchen employees at the Georgs Palast, took distinct pleasure in making the new apprentice's job miserable. They were not abusive like Mr. Ender; instead, they inflicted their higher rank on the apprentices by making us do the same task over and over again: cleaning a refrigerator that had just been cleaned or washing the salads for the tenth time because they claimed to find a grain of sand.

The mamselles were always right, and I was the apprentice, so the salad needed to be washed again even if I could swear there was not one single grain of sand in there.

Still, I learned much more at the cold station than how to scrub and wash. Mr. Klapproth was an outstanding garde manger and at his best when we had to prepare and decorate cold buffets with showpieces such as a whole salmon, a chicken, and an entire roast beef. If a cold buffet from the Georgs Palast was the best one in town, it was thanks to Mr. Klapproth and his team of mamselles.

In the beginning, I only got assigned the most basic daily tasks: cutting tomatoes, marinating the cucumber salad, preparing potatoes for a potato salad, boiling and peeling eggs for garnishes, and mixing the salad that accompanied most of the menu items. But even that simple routine presented lots of room for error.

It so happened that on one of my trips from the garde manger section to the service counter in the front of the kitchen, as both of my arms were fully loaded with salad plates, I dropped one. I stood watching in horror as the plate flipped in the air and fell to the floor right behind Mr. Grünich. Working rapidly, I unloaded the other salad plates on a nearby table and bent down to pick up the fallen one, but Mr. Grünich was not letting me get away with this. As he turned around to keep an eye on one of the sections in the kitchen, he stepped on the plate with his 250-pound weight and shoe size of 45, crushing the glass with an explosive sound.

I was still kneeling on the floor when I heard him say, "For the plates you have broken, I could take a four-week vacation!" The laughter of the cooks all around me rang in my ears for hours. Let it be known that I had never broken a plate until this moment.

Luckily, the shattered plate was soon forgotten, and things took a more promising turn. A few weeks into my training at the garde manger station, we received a large order for a cold buffet, requiring several shifts of overnight work so as not to interfere with the daytime routine. Mr. Klapproth asked if I could work every night that week to assist him with the order. I said yes without hesitation.

Here was my golden opportunity to pick up skills that went beyond the duties of my training. In the strangely quiet kitchen, I learned how to prepare and decorate a great variety of cold foods under his direction. I didn't quite realize this as I hunched over my workstation night after night, but that first cold buffet order laid the groundwork for my future culinary career.

When the first buffet I worked on turned out to be a success, Mr. Klapproth began to involve me in all aspects of the preparation, even though I was only an apprentice. He also asked me to help with every buffet order we received from then on.

Even Mr. Grünich seemed to notice our excellent work and registered us at the International Culinary Olympics, an international competition, which took place every four years in Frankfurt am Main. As the contest did not allow apprentices, Mr. Grünich bypassed the regulations and signed me up as a chef de partie. I was honored by this newfound trust and wanted to live up to the confidence the chef had placed in me. I pushed myself harder than ever before and achieved a gold medal for my presentations.

Flashing back to all the rough days of my apprenticeship, the physical abuse, and the clumsy errors, I felt proud when I passed my final exams with honors a few months later. Mr. Grünich, Mr. Klapproth, Mr. Erhardt, and even Mr. Ender were the first ones to congratulate me on the successful conclusion of three years of culinary training.

The butt kicks and sawdust kissing behind me now, all that remained were positive memories of learning new skills, meeting new people, and preparing for my career. I had no idea about the unimaginable troubles headed my way.

BECOMING A GRAFIC DESIGNER? HANS GRÜNICH MY APPRENTICE CHEF

NEW YEARS EVE 1958 AT THE GEORGS PALAST IN HANNOVER

A Culinary Career Is Born 06

The Cold Kitchen

Surviving a Hans Grünich apprenticeship opened all kinds of doors for chefs looking for their next job. Restaurants in Hannover eagerly hired Grünich alumni and compensated them well. But I decided to set my sights on a kitchen position at a five-star hotel since I'd learned that those jobs, while lower-paying, led to better opportunities. I began sending out applications, more confidently this time than before.

Weeks later, I hadn't heard back from a single one of the hotels.

So much for my newfound self-assurance. Fortunately, Mr. Grünich wanted to keep me on a little longer, so I stayed at the Georgs Palast for another few months. I used the extra time to keep searching for work at upscale hotels in and around Germany, but I kept hearing only rejection and silence.

I couldn't let myself give up yet. I knew that getting a job at a local restaurant would mean a higher paycheck now. But a reference from a top hotel—even in a poorly paid position—seemed like a smart gamble.

Years afterward, when I was home visiting my mother and sisters, I found many of my former peers still working at the same local restaurant job they had accepted after their apprenticeship. Their salary had not increased much over the years, and they had no real chance to move up or make a career change.

After months of sending my applications to hotels and still reporting to the Georgs Palast kitchen day after day, I finally got an offer. I would start as a commis cook in the cold section at the Frankfurter Hof, a famous hotel in Frankfurt am Main. Best of all, the job included housing, saving me the headache of finding accommodations in an unknown city.

My start date of May 16, 1961, left me just enough time to give notice to the Georgs Palast, say thank you to Hans Grünich, and leave family and friends behind to take my first job away from home.

The train ride to Frankfurt took several hours—this was well before the days of high-speed ICE trains—and from the station, I lugged my suitcase on the twenty-minute walk to the hotel. I stopped to wipe the sweat from my forehead and take a deep breath before entering the grand lobby of the Hotel Frankfurter Hof, flanked by columns surrounding a landscaped inner court.

The receptionist's warm hello changed to a stern look as soon as I asked for the human resources office. If his initial greeting was any sign, the hotel certainly seemed to value its customers. But what about its employees? I would find out soon enough.

After what seemed like hours of signing the mountains of employment forms required by German bureaucracy, an HR staff member showed me to my accommodations, a short twenty-minute walk across the Main River from the hotel. I would be sharing a room with three other employees on a floor that had one bathroom for all to use. I was grateful for the free housing, but the price would be a frantic morning rush to shower and get to work on time.

Things instantly looked up when I entered the kitchen. Mr. Josef Dobler, the hotel's Austrian executive chef and my new boss, gave off the opposite impression from Hans Grünich. It wasn't just his physical appearance. Yes, Mr. Dobler was skinny, lacking the dominant stature of my previous employer. But he seemed kind too, and he welcomed me in with a polite tone I wasn't used to hearing on my first day.

Instead of a podium, Mr. Dobler had his own office with windows on all four sides. This allowed him to watch and control what happened in every corner of the kitchen, but without the imperious showmanship of Mr. Grünich.

The kitchen looked luxurious compared to the one at the Georgs Palast. It had tiled walls and floors, plenty of light, and not a single speck of sawdust in sight. The cooking stations stood in a line, separated by two working tables and facing a long service counter.

My initial impression of Mr. Dobler proved correct. He treated his employees with gentlemanly respect, and I saw cooks at all levels fearlessly approach him with their questions.

Perhaps the slower volume of a hotel kitchen made it easier to be friendly. The Frankfurter Hof kitchen did a fraction of the covers of a busy standalone restaurant like the Georgs Palast. Or maybe Mr. Dobler had a different management philosophy than most chefs I'd met so far. In any case, our staff kept busy enough and never had any shortage of work. Each day saw a steady stream of guests, many of them from overseas, adding a worldly flair to the menu and a welcome new dimension to my routine.

The hotel's VIP guests gave me a crash course in international relations. At this point, I had never traveled outside Germany, so my encounters with the cosmopolitan guests made a big impression on me. I will never forget the king of Saudi Arabia's room service order. He stayed at the hotel for one week and, judging by the quantity of food he ordered for an evening, one would have thought he was throwing a party in his suite. But it turned out the order was only for his immediate family.

As I stood carefully decorating the large silver platters, the Maître d' came running into the kitchen: "Stop! Don't waste your time. Just put all the food on the platter." Apparently, the entire royal family preferred to sit on the floor, around a huge brass platter piled with all the food at once, and eat with their hands.

Needless to say, I knew little to nothing about the Saudi Arabian king's culture at the time. It never crossed my mind that one day years from now, I would be invited to sit on the floor with a sheikh and eat with my fingers as we shared a lavish feast.

My experience in the cold station at the Georgs Palast served me well at the Frankfurter Hof. Mr. Dobler soon entrusted me with special assignments like taking charge of the hors d'oeuvres for the French restaurant and doing the tableside cooking in the dining room. I was exposed to restaurant guests for the first time in my career, as well as to the hotel's owner, Mr. Egon Steigenberger, who frequently ate his lunch in the dining room.

The job passed by in a blur. After a year, it was time to send out applications again, in keeping with the hotel industry tradition of moving around and gaining as much experience as possible.

To my surprise, it did not take long to hear back this time. The Brenner's Park Hotel in Baden-Baden offered me a position almost immediately.

The Brenner's, as it is called in hospitality industry circles, is still among the premier hotels in Germany. Built in 1872, in the lush spa town of

Baden-Baden at the edge of the Black Forest, the hotel has hosted countless celebrities and politicians over the decades. Literary figures like Dostoyevsky, Flaubert, and Turgenev lived at the Brenner's while working on novels.

During the annual event at the famous Rennwoche, in nearby Iffezheim, members of German and European high society convene at the hotel. The events are Germany's answer to the Ascot and the Kentucky Derby, and the Brenner's rooms get booked years in advance.

A main draw for me was that the Brenner's at the time employed Heinz Klinger, who was one of Europe's best garde mangers and the author of *Die kalte Küche*, a book describing the art of the cold kitchen in detailed text and pictures. Mr. Klinger was indeed a culinary artist, and every platter he created looked like a painting, almost too beautiful to eat.

Unfortunately, I did not land a position with Mr. Klinger, but instead started as a chef in the sauce section of the warm kitchen.

My new boss, the chef de partie, was British and had been working at the Brenner's for many years. He had his own distinct way of doing things. "Nur was wenig ist, ist gut" or "only a little is good" was his motto. When serving sauces to accompany a dish, he ordered us to fill the sauce dish only halfway so the waiters would need to keep coming back to ask for more. That was his way of fooling the executive chef, Mr. Lemke, into thinking our sauces were in high demand.

We all had our quirks, but our kitchen brigade worked well together and liked to socialize, going out after long days at work to relax over drinks at the Jockey Club. We'd often stay out until the early morning and reporting to work a few hours later never seemed to present any problem. Who needs sleep? We were young.

On a rare day off, a group of us returned to the hotel after a soccer game when we accidentally witnessed European history in the making.

Approaching the Brenner's, we noticed it was cordoned off by police and security.

As we later learned, France's president Charles De Gaulle and Germany's chancellor Konrad Adenauer were meeting at the hotel to discuss the blueprint for a new friendship between the two adversarial powers. The meeting took place in secret, with no publicity whatsoever.

Did I witness the birth of Europe? Official negotiations started a few months later, leading to the signing of the historic Franco-German Friendship Treaty at Paris's Elysée Palace in January 1963. Despite efforts on both sides to scrap the treaty, the entente between France and Germany survived, reinforced by the idea that without it, Europe as an entity will have no chance of survival.

That 1962 meeting at the Brenner's turned out to be one of the dozens of covert meetings between the two leaders that led up to the Elysée Treaty.

It was the first time it hit me that when you're working at a famous hotel, heads of state might be secretly sharing the same roof, and a momentous event can unfold inches away from you at any moment. It wouldn't be the last time I stumbled into history.

Switzerland Is Calling

It was late August in Baden-Baden, and fancy hats of all shapes and colors descended on the town. The end-of-summer horse race at Iffezheim was underway, and as usual, society women wore their most flamboyant hats to the horse track, a short drive from Baden-Baden and known as the German Ascot. Strolling through the Brenner's lobby at the right moment, you'd think you had accidentally walked into the world's most elegant parade. In the Brenner's kitchen, we prepared banquets for one gala after another.

My year had passed by in a flash, and although I had enjoyed this job, I knew I needed to keep on moving. Once again, my applications turned up nothing for weeks. I should have been used to the slow pace of responses by now, but the job-hunting process always brought out my impatient side.

When I'd decided to give up and stay put at the Brenner's, I received two intriguing responses.

One letter came from the Adelphi Hotel in Singapore, offering me a position as assistant to the executive chef, also known as a sous chef de cuisine. Meanwhile, Badrutt's Palace Hotel in the Swiss resort town of St. Moritz offered the low-ranking position of night cook, or chef de garde. I struggled with the decision for an entire week and finally chose Badrutt's.

The job in St. Moritz would mean less money and a lower status, but I gambled that the reference would make the temporary sacrifice worth it. I also had to admit to myself that I wasn't ready to supervise a hundred Chinese chefs at a luxury Singapore hotel, especially when I didn't even speak the language.

The Singapore contract didn't help matters: a clause in fine print promised that my body would be shipped back to my country of origin if something happened to me.

Switzerland, here I come.

The society crowd at the Brenner's had been quite a spectacle, but nothing could top the scene at the Badrutt's Palace Hotel in St. Moritz.

Perched high in the Graubünden mountain at the shore of a small blue lake, frozen in the winter and draped in a blanket of the whitest snow, the Badrutt's has been a playground for celebrities and royalty ever since it opened in 1896. Alfred Hitchcock stayed at the hotel on his honeymoon, and Audrey Hepburn and Marlene Dietrich famously vacationed there.

The town of St. Moritz itself had been just a sleepy little nook in Switzerland until members of the Badrutt family put it on the map. They'd bought a pension and other properties in the area in the late nineteenth century, built a toboggan run and curling rink, and taken a chance on attracting tourism to the quiet snowbound landscape. Everything changed when the Badrutts bet a group of British summer tourists that if they returned to St. Moritz in the winter, they would fall in love with the alpine sports and landscape or get their vacation expenses reimbursed.

The rest is history. Word of St. Moritz's winter splendor quickly spread, and within a few years, the family's ambitious hotel in the Swiss Alps started attracting moneyed European travelers. The Badrutt gamble turned the town into the birthplace of winter sports, and a cluster of five-star hotels soon sprung up to compete. Two winter Olympics took place in St. Moritz, in 1928 and again in 1948—the first Olympics after World War II—and camera crews from Hollywood later arrived, shooting glamorous ski scenes for movies like the James Bond film *The Spy Who Loved Me*.

A highlight of the winter activities was the illustrious St. Moritz horse race on the frozen lake, an event that drew participants from all over Europe. Hundreds of visitors would line the track and watch the horses gallop across the powdered snow. One celebrity in particular couldn't wait for the horses to be gone so he could take over the racetrack. This was Gunther Sachs, Europe's number-one playboy and briefly the husband of Brigitte Bardot. As soon as the horses were gone, Sachs and his friends would take over the lake and organize a spectacular automobile race involving Ferraris, Lamborghinis, Bugattis, Aston Martins, and all the coveted luxury cars, which would then speed and slide and fly all over the track in pursuit of an enormous trophy.

When I started working at the hotel, much of Europe's elite was already calling the Palace their home away from home, among them the world-famous conductor Herbert Von Karajan, the opera singer Maria Callas, the Greek shipping tycoon Aristotle Onassis, and many more members of the who's who of Europe. They spent the winter at the Palace and showed up for the monthly galas at the hotel's famous Embassy Room.

As a garde cook, I had no time to gawk at celebrities. I worked the overnight shift, while other chefs slept or went out, and it was my job to ensure twenty-four-hour kitchen service to the guests enjoying life in the Kings' Club, a members-only private area at the hotel.

Part of the job was to clean the piano and get it ready for the evening dinner service. And what a piano it was. At twelve meters in length and more than two meters in width, the oven stood at the center of the kitchen and provided enough space for twenty culinary artists to create the best food in St. Moritz.

Badrutt's executive chef Eugene Defrance was a legend at the hotel and had known the current owner Andreas Badrutt as a young boy. Despite his advanced age of eighty-two, Mr. Defrance was still going strong, having survived a series of assistants who'd hoped to replace him one day but given up.

Like Hans Grünich, Mr. Defrance had quite a flair for showmanship, along with some questionable habits.

One day, we received a delivery of live ducks to cook for a gala dinner that weekend. I and the other cooks had to kill and prepare all the ducks for roasting, and after handling dozens of ducks, we thought we'd finished them all. Next thing we knew, Mr. Defrance came sauntering through the kitchen, walking a duck on a leash with a red ribbon tied around its neck.

The chef looked tremendously amused by his own prank, until the duck went flying on to the desk in his office and soiled all his papers. Moments later, the duck followed her peers directly to the butcher block.

When Mr. Defrance wasn't playing jokes, he was developing a strong interest in the knives and special utensils used by the cooks who worked for him. On his way past the various workstations, he would pick up a knife here and a fork here, and the tools would then disappear forever into one of the drawers in his office. Rumor had it that he sold the utensils at a flea market in France at the end of the season, although nobody actually saw him do so.

The vanishing knives and forks were simply a fact of life at Badrutt's, but who had the courage to tell Mr. Defrance to return a missing utensil? Nobody!

Getting any sleep at all was another challenge for us overnight cooks. Our sleeping quarters sat opposite the hotel's carpentry shop, and the wood-cutting machines switched on promptly at 7:00 a.m.—as soon as our night shift ended.

After several days in a row of long nightly shifts followed by sleepless breaks, I complained to the chef. He sounded angry that I didn't inform him earlier and immediately arranged new accommodations for me, far away from the carpentry shop, at the pavilion next to the hotel's ice-skating rink. The pavilion had a few rooms, all unoccupied, and I became the sole person to live in it. It was a strange arrangement, but I wasn't about to complain.

Occasionally I used my rest time for other pursuits. One sunny morning, I tried to learn skiing from one of my superiors in the kitchen, Erhard

Gall, an Austrian I'd met at the Brenner's. Rather than rush back to his room to sleep after the night shift, Erhard liked to hit the slopes for a few hours. He invited me to join him that day, and I reluctantly agreed, unwilling to admit to him that I was terrified. The area of northern Germany I'd grown up in was flat as a pancake, so I'd never skied before in my life.

Naturally, I owned no ski equipment, so Erhard took me to the hotel's ski shop to get fitted for our adventure. The only beginner's pair of skis available that morning was the old-fashioned kind that you'd now only find in a museum or as a quaint decoration at a ski lodge. Security bindings were just entering the market and did not exist on the skis that the shop clerks handed me that morning. To fit the skis on the boots, one had to tie a spiral wire from behind the shoe heel and then bend down to attach it to the front of the ski.

The store's customers, all sporting the latest top-of-the-line equipment, were tremendously amused to watch me do this. I only wish that had been the most embarrassing moment of my day.

Soon after, I found myself perched at the Piz Nair mountaintop, looking down at the postcard view of St. Moritz below, all the way down a steep slope. Erhard took me aside for a few minutes to show me the basics of handling my skis and poles and told me he'd check back soon. Off he went, zooming down the slope.

I stood there alone, looking down, frightened to death by the steep mountain that stretched down below me. I was ready to give up and take the teleferic back down that instant. But I gathered up my courage and decided I should at least give skiing a try now that I had gone through all this trouble.

How hard could skiing be, really? I saw children around me flying down the mountain on their skis, not a care in the world. I took a deep breath, planted my poles in the snow, attempted to push off, and immediately collapsed into a heap. Dusting the snow off my pants, I hoisted myself back up and tried another time, only to fall back down again and again and again.

Half an hour later, I still stood in exactly the same spot. Erhard reappeared, and with a pitying look, he gave me another brief lesson before swerving off again.

Two hours later, and a few more useless visits by Erhard, I had only advanced a few meters. Freezing from my constant falls in the snow, I gave up and walked down the mountain to the Chanterelle train station, my legs sinking deep in the soft powder with every step. I rode back to the hotel and barely had enough time to return my skis, change clothes, and run to the kitchen, arriving breathless just a few seconds before the start of my 3:00 p.m. shift.

The celebrities and ski champions could keep the slopes, as far as I was concerned. This glamorous feature of St. Moritz life was not for me.

Instead, I took up filmmaking with what little free time I had. I decided to buy a Bolex-Paillard movie camera with my hard-earned money to take films of St. Moritz and the surrounding mountains. The only challenge was that the camera needed to be rewound like an old-fashioned clock, and it allowed for only one minute of recording. The roll of 8 mm film needed to be switched around halfway, then mailed to a print shop for developing. Digital cameras were still decades away.

I still own the Bolex-Paillard, and after more than fifty years, it continues to work perfectly. Unfortunately, no one sells the film anymore, so the camera is now just a collector's item and a cherished souvenir of my time at the Palace Hotel.

All in all, my year at Badrutt's was a positive experience. The night shifts took a toll, but I had added valuable skills to my repertoire in that kitchen. For one thing, I learned how to cook at altitude. Boiling potatoes at two thousand meters, for example, takes longer than boiling them at sea level, so getting ready for service at a mountaintop restaurant is an entirely different proposition.

By March, the end of the busy winter season, it was time for me to start applying to other jobs. My contract at Badrutt's was ending, but this time, it didn't take long to find a job at another top hotel. I'd be moving to the Beau Rivage Palace in the Swiss city of Lausanne, about six hours away by train, and working as a commis entremetier, a vegetable cook position that would put me one step away from becoming a department head responsible for an entire station.

In even better news, Eugene Defrance, the chef at Badrutt's, offered to bring me back the next winter after my season in Lausanne and promote me to a department head position. I would come back as a chef hors d'oeuvrier, in charge of the preparation of all cold starters, cold platters, and buffet presentations. The promotion would also mean an upgrade to a double bedroom with its own private bathroom in the staff housing adjacent to the hotel. Goodbye, ice-skating pavilion.

Things were looking up. I now had the Frankfurter Hof, the Brenner's Park Hotel, the Palace Hotel in St. Moritz, and soon the Beau Rivage Palace Hotel in Lausanne on my resume. I had built an impressive catalog of leading hotels and made strong contacts along the way, and I was starting to move up. My decision to focus on references instead of money was paying off, even if not yet in financial terms. Still, I was doing fine on my modest salary, saving a little bit, and enjoying the ride.

In the three weeks of vacation before I started the job in Lausanne, I went home to Hannover and used some of my savings to buy a new car, a DKW F12, to replace the old BMW Isetta 600 I'd bought earlier with earnings from my Brenner's job. My new car wasn't ready yet, but the dealer conveniently offered to drive it to Lausanne for me when it arrived. He also agreed to bring my mother and sister Jenny along with him so they could visit me there.

A few months later, when my mother and sister showed up in Lausanne to drop off my car, the surprising way my boss treated them made me realize my life had taken a new turn.

From White Snow to Green Grass

My days as a beginner were officially behind me by the time, I entered the Beau Rivage kitchen. But I still had a lot to learn—and fast. Most urgently, on my very first day, I needed to learn what an artichoke was. I had never in my life seen one before. This was 1965, and artichokes had not yet made their debut in the conservative kitchens of Germany, nor had they ever appeared in the Badrutt's cold kitchen during my shifts since artichokes were not in season during the wintertime.

My first meeting with an artichoke was no casual encounter. After welcoming me into the kitchen, the chef deposited cases of artichokes in front of me and asked me to clean and prepare them immediately for the dinner service. This had to be a joke. On day one of a new job, when I wanted to hit the ground running, I had to face down a vegetable I'd never seen before. How could I admit I had no idea what this thing was, let alone what to do with it?

But my mind flashed back to my first day at the Brauer Gilde Haus and the raw chicken and the butt kick from Mr. Ender. No, thank you. This time I would tell the truth.

Things went better than expected a few moments later, when I gathered up my courage and confessed. I must not have been the first young cook to be baffled by this spiky vegetable because the chef seemed neither surprised nor upset. He patiently demonstrated how to cut the artichoke leaves and trim the bottom, then cover the leaves with a slice of lemon on both sides and get them ready for cooking. I watched him intently, learned quickly, and managed to get the five boxes done in time for service.

If only I had known years before what a relief it is to admit total ignorance.

The Beau Rivage Palace opened in 1861, an imposing structure on a majestic spot overlooking Lake Geneva and offering a taste of old Europe. But the kitchen provided a surprisingly welcoming environment for young hardworking chefs, despite the grandeur of the Palace and of its general manager, Mr. Schnyder.

A typical old-school manager, Mr. Schnyder never spoke with the lowly employees. I only saw him from a distance when we were setting up buffets or when he came to the kitchen. He would go straight to the executive chef, Mr. Bertolini, and discuss with him whatever he had to discuss, then disappear as fast as he came.

As a matter of principle, Mr. Schnyder never greeted anyone first. But he did expect everyone to greet him, on his way in and on his way out, with utmost respect for his status as general manager.

It was not just Mr. Schnyder's own employees who paid deference to him. He was Switzerland's most respected hotelier, and—in spite of his chilly demeanor—he was the beating heart of the hotel. Little did I know at that time that he had a son who, many years later, would work for me as assistant food and beverage director in an entirely different setting.

Regardless of his deficiencies in the personality department, Schnyder oversaw an incredibly smooth, well-run operation at the Beau Rivage. The kitchen was very modern and well-organized, guaranteeing efficient service to the hotel guests. This was best illustrated by the escalators that went up from the kitchen to the main restaurant, to ensure that the hot food would get to the dining room as quickly as possible. On their way back, the waiters had to take the stairs, enough stairs to keep them fit.

The Beau Rivage took pride in preparing everything fresh daily, from the food in the kitchen to the flowers displayed throughout the hotel and on every table in the restaurant, arranged by the hotel's own florist department.

It was no surprise that the Beau Rivage, like Badrutt's, attracted a constant parade of distinguished international guests. Elizabeth Taylor stayed there often, and William Holden, the famous American actor who starred in *Sunset Boulevard*, had his own yacht anchored in the harbor in front of the hotel. Holden entertained frequently on his boat and often took his guests on a tour across the lake to Evian le Bain and its well-known casino.

I had settled into the rhythms of the hotel and my new job by the time my car finally arrived, a few months later, with my family in tow. It was satisfying to open the car doors and welcome my mother and sister Jenny to the elegant Beau Rivage.

Considering my family's poverty during the war, and the modest middle-class life that my mother now provided for herself and my sisters in Hannover, the trip to Lausanne was a special treat, a rare moment of leisure and luxury. Mr. Bertolini had an empty room available in his apartment and graciously offered to make it available to my family, for which I felt truly grateful.

Mutti and Jenny had a chance to experience the Beau Rivage as guests, and this meant more to me than my boss probably knew.

I even got permission to take a few days off to show my mother and sister around Lausanne and the beautiful Lac Leman, le Mont Blanc in France, Montreux, and the nearby mountains. We took a boat trip on the lake, shared a cheese fondue at the famed Café du Vieil Ouchy, played mini golf, strolled along the flowering promenade at the lake in Geneva, and drove around the Berner Oberland mountains, with their spectacular landscape of towering snow-tipped peaks, pine forests, waterfalls, and bright blue lakes.

My mother seemed relaxed in a way I had rarely if ever seen before and was enjoying her first real vacation in many years. I was glad I could give her something back for everything she had done for us during the difficult war times and after. Having my little sister Jenny with us was a joy. Her natural, friendly character made her enjoyment seem genuine. She was the only immediate family member I felt close to.

Mr. Bertolini's generous gesture did more than cast a warm glow over their entire visit. It also made me feel that he noticed and appreciated my efforts to excel in my job. This gave me the sense, real or not, that I had graduated from my days as a young minion and was now a respected colleague.

The rest of the season soon evaporated, and before I knew it, it was time to say goodbye to the many new friends I made in Lausanne. I would meet some of them again a few years later. The hotel world is small indeed, and contacts from previous jobs always find a way of resurfacing.

Today it's easier to stay in touch with friends and past colleagues, but a job in the hospitality industry at the time was its own kind of Facebook, long before the days of social media or email.

Taking stock of my brief but busy season in Lausanne, I had one major disappointment: I didn't learn any French. I'd accepted the job in large part so I could pick up the language, since Lausanne is the capital of the Canton Vaud, an area of Switzerland where French is the native tongue. The Beau Rivage seemed like a logical place to combine a first-class hotel reference with French proficiency.

Unfortunately, the reverse happened. Mr. Bertolini was a Swiss Italian, and the majority of the kitchen brigade during my time spoke Swiss German or German—and, just like me, they wanted to learn French. But the few locals who actually spoke French outsmarted all of us, since they all managed to learn German from us while we got nowhere with our French.

I did pick up a handful of useful phrases in any case. "Rien ne va plus" means the game is closed, a casino term for when everyone is watching the ball jump from one number to another, praying for a big win.

"Rien ne va plus" also means a tragic end for many who lost their last dime and had to cut short their vacation. For some reason this phrase lodged in my brain and turned out to have a special meaning years later.

A Second Season at the Palace

How much caviar can one person eat in a week? Guests at Badrutt's Palace seemed intent on finding out. Palace guests consumed a gigantic amount of caviar, as I learned during my second season at the hotel after I arrived from Lausanne.

The weekly average at the hotel was a whopping fifteen cans of caviar, each filled with two kilograms of Beluga, making Badrutt's an extremely important customer for the supplier from Geneva.

The coveted eggs of the Beluga sturgeon come mainly from the salt waters of the Black Sea and the Caspian Sea, the biggest inland body of water, bordered by Iran, Russia, and a few other countries. Its eggs range in color from nearly black to golden, and the quality depends on size (the bigger, the better), texture (the eggs should pop in the mouth), and color (light brown to nearly gold is best). High quality Beluga tends to have a buttery, nutty, often creamy taste, and all kinds of subtle flavor nuances. Iranian Imperial golden Beluga caviar is the top of the line, but at the time, it was almost exclusively reserved for guests of the shah of Iran. Many years later, during one of my business trips to Iran, I had the privilege of tasting this exquisite product.

At least one reason for the Palace's high Beluga intake was its own chef. On the caviar supplier's Friday visits to Badrutt's, he always brought more cans than the hotel actually needed, in order to allow the chef to do a tasting of every single can and pick the ones he thought were best. And tasting he did.

As the chef approached the stack of twenty cans of Beluga that the supplier had brought in, he would complain that last week's quality was terrible and he sure hoped this time it would be better, much better. Then the show would begin.

Rather than use the mother of pearl spoon designed for tasting caviar, the chef would dig into every can with his two fingers, and after tasting, he would mumble to himself, "C'est bon" or "Ce n'est pas bon."

At the end, he would accept fifteen out of the twenty cans, and everyone was happy: the supplier because he had weathered the tasting and sold fifteen cans of his best product and the chef because he had a sumptuous early dinner of almost half a pound of Beluga caviar. I was happy too because the show was finally over and I could continue with my work.

During this second season at Badrutt's, I was responsible for the preparation of cold food items, from appetizers to any other special menu offerings. It was the type of job I enjoyed the most, one that allowed me to display all the knowledge and experience I had learned along the way.

In the beginning, the chef would visit my department several times daily to see if I was living up to his expectations. I guess I was because his visits became less and less frequent as the season went on.

The Palace's kitchen felt like a familiar home to me by now, and I was surrounded by good friends. My old buddy and would-be ski instructor Erhard Gall was working this season as chef garde manger, responsible for the preparation and production of all basic food items (meats, poultry, fish) in the main kitchen. This was one of the key positions because without his timely preparations, the rest of the brigade could not function. He seemed to excel at this job, far more than he did as a ski instructor.

In my second season at the Palace, I was determined to learn how to ski properly at last. But not with Erhard this time. When I was finally ready to try again, I asked for help from another friend of mine in the kitchen, Jean-François Neuenschwander, a French chef from the Alsace. He promised not to abandon me on top of the hill, which sounded like a promising start. The hotel's ski rental staff also agreed to give me modern equipment instead of the creaky museum pieces they inflicted on me last time.

Jean-François took a more patient approach than Erhard. He explained to me step by step how to ski, coaching me as I practiced, and he didn't start me off at the sky-high top of the mountain for my first run. After a bit of trial and error, I started to get the hang of the basics. Most important of all, Jean-François always made sure I got back to work on time.

By the end of the season, I was able to follow him everywhere, even to the highest peaks of the Piz Nair and Piz Corvas. At last, skiing became a real pleasure, and I felt comfortable on the slopes of St. Moritz. Skiing downhill, the gorgeous mountains all around me, was a magical, freeing experience, and I could finally see why people loved this sport.

Soon we started gearing up for the highlight of the winter season in St. Moritz, the Embassy Ball at Badrutt's, when celebrities and society members would descend on the hotel with their entourages to see the spectacular shows.

In that 1963–1964 season, the hotel staged a circus, complete with live bears and the most talented acrobats from the circus world. That night, our kitchen brigade served a five-course menu to four hundred guests. The frenzy of producing such a mind-boggling amount of food is a blur to me now, but in my photo album, I still have the picture of our kitchen brigade posing with live bears. I'm glad the bears were well-fed before that photo shoot.

The circus spectacle was a fitting symbol of life at Badrutt's, and just looking at that photo brings back many memories of that remarkable era. That season, I also witnessed the opera star Maria Callas, a Badrutt's regular, getting helicoptered to the top of the St. Moritz slopes so she could ski down. At that exact moment, I happened to be standing at the top of the mountain with the kitchen brigade, providing catering service on one of the trolleys. I grabbed my Bolex-Paillard camera and took a short film of Callas's helicopter as it landed on the mountain and she made her grand exit.

Another celebrity with a penchant for helicopters got everyone's attention at the Palace that season. The dashing Gunther Sachs, the photographer and party boy who married Brigitte Bardot that year—supposedly by courting her with bouquets of roses dropped from his helicopter on to her French Riviera home—was living in the tower suite at Badrutt's and acting very much like a pampered superstar. One of his more outlandish requests was that his suite get redesigned to his tastes.

Mr. Badrutt refused Sachs's demands. The tower building was landmarked and would stay exactly as is, and that was that.

But one year later, I read in the newspaper about a fire that led to a total destruction and rebuilding of the Badrutt's tower. Soon after, Mr. Sachs moved into an entirely redesigned tower suite. I'm not suggesting there was any connection between his design request and the fire. But Sachs was definitely a force of nature in those days. He later committed suicide, in 2011, but in his youth, he reigned over St. Moritz. My brief glimpses of him with his entourage added to the fascinating scene during my stints at the Palace.

A few short weeks later, it was time to pack up all the pots and pans in the kitchen for storage until the following season and to start pondering what my next move would be. In my case, it turned out to be a job in an even more opulent setting.

Moving to a Tax Paradise

One-third of the residents of Monaco are millionaires, and the tiny nation state has the highest per capita ratio of billionaires in the world. Perched along the French Riviera, Monaco is currently ruled by Prince Albert II, son of the late monarch Prince Rainier and the American actress Grace Kelly.

Since taxes do not exist in Monaco, the principality is a tax haven for the fabulously wealthy of the world. Up and down its Mediterranean coastline are glistening beaches, just a short drive away from luxurious hotels, acclaimed restaurants, designer boutiques, and star-studded entertainment venues that cater to the glitterati.

On the day in the spring of 1964 when I drove off in my DKW F12 to start a new job in Monaco's capital, Monte Carlo, I didn't know much about the place, but I was curious to see it. Little did I imagine back then that one day, Monaco's princess Caroline Grimaldi, the oldest daughter of Prince Rainier and Grace Kelly, would become known as the princess of Hannover. In 1999, she would marry Ernst August, the prince of Hannover—my Hannover—and the would-be heir to the nineteenth-century Kingdom of Hannover. But in those days, she was still a child.

I had spent the week before the Monaco trip visiting my mother and sisters at our own family home in Hannover. The city has been restored to its former elegance and charm since the war, but it's a far different place than the one Ernst August's ancestors would have known when the House of Hannover and the United Kingdom's King George III jointly ruled the territory.

At this point in my career, I was still aiming only for jobs at the very best hotels, and Monte Carlo's Metropole Hotel and Hotel de Paris ranked at the top of my list. I was hoping for an offer from the Hotel de Paris, owned by the Societe des Bains de Mer, which had Monaco's then-ruler Prince Rainier as its main shareholder. But they rejected my application, so I was relieved when I landed a job at the Metropole.

Crossing the Alps and Italy, I skimmed the coastline of the Riviera in Menton, home of the famous annual lemon festival, and continued a few miles along the Cote d'Azur, savoring the sight of the sparkling blue Mediterranean and the palm tree–lined coast.

Soon I arrived at the outskirts of Monte Carlo. The city immediately makes its intentions clear: from the rows of neatly arranged multimillion dollar yachts at the marina to the late-model sports cars careening through the hilly streets, this is a place where the wealthy come to play.

The whole city was lush and bursting with flowers on the day I pulled into town. After living surrounded by snow for months, arriving in Monte Carlo and seeing flowering parks and green lawns everywhere was simply spectacular. How could grass be so green? I had to stop and touch it to find out if it was real, and real it was!

I drove around, admiring the red-roofed houses on the rocky beachside cliffs, the manicured center of town with its Beaux Arts–style Monte Carlo Casino and Opera, and the fashionable crowd in designer sunglasses on the Cafe de Paris terrace. Minutes later, I steered my car into the cobblestoned driveway of the Hotel Metropole.

The Metropole's chef de cuisine, Mr. Antoine Berrino, one of the few real Monegasques living in Monaco, welcomed me and escorted me to my accommodations. I deposited my suitcase in my spacious single room in what's called "sous terrain," a level half-below and half-above the ground, with a large window overlooking the street.

It wasn't just Monte Carlo itself that looked and felt different from anywhere I had worked before. My position as a department head, a chef entremetier, was a big step up.

The role meant I was in charge of all soups, vegetables, and garnishes, so I would need to learn how to prepare dishes I'd never made before—and once again, I'd need to learn quickly. The soups, I soon discovered, were less of a priority, since the French clientele that frequents Monaco is not as keen on soups as the Germans are. The Metropole's guests preferred elegant starters like a soufflé de fromage. Sure enough, I had no idea how to make one.

By this point, I knew how to handle a job in a busy hotel kitchen that produced large quantities of luxury items for a demanding clientele. But now I found myself at the epicenter of the gilded universe, and I still didn't know my way around a soufflé. Soufflés were never among my duties in the cold kitchen or vegetable stations I'd worked in before, but all of a sudden, they became my daily reality.

Just as I had conquered artichokes and raw chickens, I had to tame this creature in order to survive. This time, I'd have to admit ignorance again, as I had done with the artichokes, to avoid humiliation later. I confessed to Vincent, the chef saucier, a tall and friendly man with a giant beard. He instantly took me under his wing and was kind enough to show me how to not just prepare a soufflé but how to do it in the huge quantities required in my new job.

A soufflé is a ticking time bomb, ready to implode at the slightest wrong move. I approached my first attempt with caution. As Vincent showed me, rule number one is getting the timing exactly right, which means preparing different orders in different ovens so you can keep absolute control over the process. If you take the soufflé out too early, it collapses, and if you're too late the top hardens. Rule number two is to never open the oven while the soufflé is still cooking because the infusion of cool air would shock it and make it crash down.

I had four ovens at my disposal to make sure I could produce a parade of perfect soufflés for the lunch service. I nervously looked into the glass window of the oven door every five minutes, as Vincent instructed me, until I could see my very first soufflé rise out of its form, nice and brown. I couldn't believe my eyes when I saw it. Vincent had coached me well. I watched and waited anxiously as I made the next batch, and the next one, and I somehow managed not to destroy a single soufflé.

Soon enough, I was producing thirty, forty, or even fifty soufflés for the lunch or dinner service without even blinking.

Working in the Metropole kitchen was a non-stop whirlwind, but our brigade found ways to amuse ourselves during those high-pressure days. I remember one afternoon when Vincent threw off his clothes and jumped into the plonge. This was a basin we kept filled with warm water and lemon for washing copper pots. I suppose that hot, lemon-scented plonge water must have looked tempting to Vincent on that particular day. He splashed right in and bathed himself, paying no mind to us as we laughed hysterically.

During the major events of Monaco's social season, our team kicked into even higher gear, displaying the masterful organization of Mr. Berrino's kitchen. I was producing more soufflés than ever and more of everything, even soups. I and each member of our kitchen staff showed up each day ready to work hard and fast and to perform at our highest level.

Monaco is best-known for its Formula One Grand Prix automobile race, one of the most challenging and prestigious in the world. The track crisscrosses the tight, narrow streets of Monte Carlo, with all of their tunnels and changing elevations, making it a true test for drivers.

Although the organizers try to make the race as safe as possible, two harrowing incidents happened before and after the year I worked there. In 1955, the Italian racer Alberto Ascari came speeding out of the tunnel and, reportedly distracted for a moment, drove his car straight into the harbor. In 1965, Paul Hawkins spun out and went crashing right into the harbor too. Fortunately, both drivers escaped unharmed, which could not be said about their cars.

The two other major social events in Monte Carlo are the Red Cross Gala and the Circus Festival, and just like the Formula One, they sell out every hotel in town. Winning Monte Carlo's coveted Golden Clown, which honors the top talents in the international circus world, is like winning the Oscar in Los Angeles. Prince Rainier used to oversee all three social events, and he would personally hand out the Golden Clown statuette to the circus champion.

Once the around-the-clock workdays for those events were finally over, the rest of the season slowed down a bit. I was able to take a few days off from time to time to make little road trips to nearby Nice, Cannes, St. Tropez, and other locations along the Mediterranean. Since I had my own car, I had no problem finding friends and colleagues to ride along with me. Until I met Helga Klampferer.

Helga was an Austrian who lived in Venezuela and attended hotel school in Vienna, and that summer, she was doing a training at a hotel in Villefranche, a tiny fishing village about half an hour west of Monte Carlo. I have no recollection how we met, but we became very good friends. On our days off, we would visit restaurants in the area and explore the beauty of the French Mediterranean coastline all the way to St. Tropez.

Although we spent many summer days together, our relationship never went beyond just friendship, much to my chagrin at the time. I was glad to spend hours in her company and too reluctant to express any feelings that might not be reciprocated. After three months, Helga returned to her hotel school in Vienna and later to Caracas, Venezuela. We kept in touch and wrote to each other for a brief time, and years later, she married the future heir of the Pschorr Brewery in Munich, becoming Helga Klampferer de Pschorr.

During a trip to Latin America in 1980, Denyse and I went to see Helga and her husband in Caracas. It must have felt strange for Denyse to go meet an old girlfriend of mine, but that summer on the Mediterranean was ancient history by now, and we had a pleasant visit.

My year in Monte Carlo also allowed me to visit Italy often, or at least to get well-acquainted with its gas stations. That year, the Italian government offered discounted gas vouchers to Germans to facilitate them to tour Italy. The vouchers were only sold in Germany, and only valid at gas stations in Italy, and my mother got into the habit of buying them and mailing them to me in Monte Carlo. Gas in Monaco and in France was very expensive at the time.

The gas station attendants of Ventemille, the first Italian town across the border from Monaco, got to know my face very well. Sadly, I didn't darken the doorstep of any other Italian destination in those days, with the exception of the one time I attended a soccer game in Turino. What a shame.

But the year had been wonderful for the most part, and I had lots of new skills and adventures to show for it. I felt no urgent desire to leave the Metropole or Monte Carlo, land of perfect weather and easy access to so many beautiful destinations. The chef de cuisine, Antoine Berrino, had repeatedly expressed that he would love to keep me, and we had become friends. But although I had nothing but fond feelings and gratitude, I needed to attend to a more ambitious goal: a job in Paris.

So far, I had enjoyed jumping from one culinary experience to another, but the idea of applying for a restaurant position had not yet crossed my mind. I was still intent on getting references from top hotels. The likes of Paul Bocuse, Jean and Pierre Troisgros, Georges Blanc, and Fernand Point were still unknown to me, and I had no idea that most of those famous French restaurant chefs would cross my path later and even become good friends.

In the meantime, I had started sending applications to five-star hotels in Paris, from the George V to the Ritz, the Crillon, and a few others. But I received nothing but rejections, one after the other. It seemed I would have to remain in Monte Carlo for another season after all.

One day, I noticed the following advertisement in the *France-Soir*, a leading French newspaper:

Maison of great reputation in Paris, serving an international clientele, is looking for a young chef de partie, specialized in the preparation and presentation of prestigious, quality cold buffets.

The advertisement did not mention the name of this famous maison, only a numbered code to use on the application. Convinced that this could only be one of the top hotels in Paris, I decided to respond, attaching my references and some pictures of my recent work.

Weeks later, I had almost forgotten about my application when I found a letter in my mailbox inviting me to come to Paris for an interview at Fauchon, all expenses and air travel paid. The letter only added to the puzzle. I still didn't know what this strange maison was all about. But I was certainly intrigued.

Who Is Fauchon?

On the morning of my mysterious interview in Paris, I woke up anxious. I had no idea what I was getting myself into. On top of that, at age twenty-five, I had never boarded an airplane before.

In those days, Air France flew a plane called the Caravelle for short distances. To fly to Paris, I had to drive to Nice, the closest airport to Monte Carlo. I was tense during the car ride and throughout the process of boarding and liftoff, but my fear of flying vanished once the plane reached altitude. Not only was the flight extremely short, but it was also perfectly smooth. The Caravelle was a well-designed plane, able to glide over a hundred miles in case of engine failure and land safely at the closest airstrip.

Unfortunately, as with many of its outstanding engineering products, France never managed to commercialize the Caravelle, allowing Boeing and Douglas DC to take over the lucrative air travel market.

My nervousness about the interview still weighed heavily on me as I exited the airplane, but at least I was traveling light. The journey to Paris was only a day trip, so I had no luggage with the exception of a small briefcase with my CV, references, and plenty of pictures of my work. From Orly, which was still the main airport in Paris, the taxi ride to the Place de la Madeleine took about half an hour and cost thirty-five francs.

One thing has not changed since that day in 1964: Parisian taxi drivers don't like to have anyone riding next to them, and they always fill their front seat with paperwork, lunch boxes, or canine companions, like the noisy lapdog my driver brought along.

Despite the barking dog, the ride had a hypnotic effect on me. Approaching the city center, I saw the Eiffel Tower, Notre Dame Cathedral, and Place de la Concorde through the car window, just as if I were flipping through giant postcards of Paris. When we arrived at the unmistakable La Madeleine church, its giant Corinthian columns framing the Greek temple structure, I realized we had reached our stop. My destination was around the corner at 26 Place de La Madeleine.

I had uncovered a few basic facts about my interview location before I left Monte Carlo. When I learned it was at a place called Fauchon, my first thought was: Was there a hotel with this name that I had missed in my research?

It turned out that Mr. Berrino had heard of Fauchon. He told me it was neither a hotel nor a restaurant but a deluxe delicatessen. Apparently, it had been around for decades, so why had I never heard about it? Perhaps it was because I didn't really know Paris. But at least Mr. Berrino did, and despite the fact that a delicatessen job did not fit into my current career goals, he encouraged me to go on the interview.

Stepping out of the taxi in front of Fauchon, I stood at the window, and was immediately spellbound by what I saw. There were beautiful arrangements of fruits I had never seen before. Cherries individually wrapped in cotton. Pastries and petits fours that looked like pieces of art. Tableaux full of temptations. The stunning displays gave me an instant sense of what Fauchon was all about. This was indeed more than just an ordinary delicatessen.

Mr. Roche, the managing director who had invited me to the interview, met me and took me on a tour. He seemed friendly from the start and made an effort to make me comfortable. I relaxed instantly. The chemistry already felt right.

Fauchon opened in 1886, and its reputation in Paris attracted crowds of customers who stood in a queue to buy just one slice of Parma ham, Mr. Roche explained to me. Madame de Gaulle, the French president's wife, Yvonne, had a habit of coming in early every Monday morning to do her weekly shopping. But Mr. Roche admitted that Fauchon had to do better in the decoration of its cold platters.

French chefs excel in the warm kitchen, but the attention to detail required in cold food presentations was not their forte, he acknowledged. The store needed a specialist in this field to raise the quality of its catering services. I did not respond immediately, although I was starting to sense this job was tailor-made for me.

Things took a turn for the worse when the chef de cuisine, Mr. Sutter, showed me around the kitchen.

Housed in a space just above the shop, the kitchen made my heart sink as soon as I walked in. It looked terribly cramped and seemed to be just a large converted apartment. I later learned it was exactly that.

There was one corner for the butcher, one room with miscellaneous kitchen equipment and a deck oven, one walk-in refrigerator, and a few working tables distributed throughout the remaining space. The whole effect suggested a disorganized, unprofessional system, nothing like the kitchens I was used to.

How in the world could Fauchon's chefs produce the quality of food I had seen in the windows?

Aha, the store had a separate pastry shop with its own kitchen in the other building, Mr. Sutter explained. Supervised by a pastry chef who was a "Meilleur ouvrier de France," it supposedly had a reputation as one of the best in France, ranking just under the legendary Gaston Lenotre. From the look of Fauchon's pastries, petits fours, chocolates, and refined showpieces, it did seem plausible that one of the best pastry chefs of France was working there. No wonder Mr. Roche wanted to bring the cold food offerings up to the same level.

My meetings with Mr. Roche and Mr. Sutter ended on a positive if non-committal note. They had more candidates to see, and I didn't know if this was the right place for me, having seen the disappointing kitchen upstairs.

Back at the Metropole, the season was winding down, and I was still wondering what to do next. I had almost forgotten about Fauchon when I received a thick envelope in the mail. Inside was a letter from Mr. Roche asking me to come work for him as chef decorateur and garde manger.

What should I do? Refusing meant staying in Monte Carlo, which would make Mr. Berrino happy and give me the chance to try again for a hotel job in Paris the next year. But it would also mean treading water for the next twelve months. Saying yes would mean settling for a position in a claustrophobic kitchen that seemed like a step backward. But it also meant an opportunity to polish my garde manger skills and get to know

Paris. Much to my surprise, Mr. Berrino encouraged me to accept the offer.

I hoped working at Fauchon would at least open new doors for me, eventually to one of the top hotels in Paris. Adding Fauchon to my list of references would come at a price though. Mr. Roche's offer of six hundred francs a month, including accommodations, was about the same as I was making in Monte Carlo, but Paris had a higher cost of living.

Disappointed that Mr. Berrino wasn't trying hard to keep me, I consoled myself with the thought that maybe he had a better clue than I did about the next logical step in my career. I had no idea then what impact saying yes to Fauchon would have on my professional future, and most of all on my private life.

Paris, Here I Come

Mr. Roche wanted me to start at Fauchon on a Friday in mid-November, namely Friday the thirteenth. This sounded like a bad idea to me, and luckily, he didn't mind when I offered to start a week earlier, on Friday the sixth of November 1964.

Just like Fauchon's kitchen, my own living accommodations turned out to be small and more than a little modest, as I discovered on my first day. My room was on the last floor under the roof, and the only window to the outside world was a tiny opening called a "was ist das." In German, this means "what's that," and the French use the same German phrase to describe the funny hole in the ceiling found in many old rooms around Paris. Besides that, the room had one metal bed, one small table, and one chair—but no closet and no heat—and required me to make some serious improvements.

A few weeks later, the room had become more livable. I had covered the naked walls with some wallpaper, added a few posters from Paris, and completed the missing furniture. Even the floor was now covered with some leftover carpet, adding some warmth to my home away from home. To come back into my room after work now felt much more comfortable, although I still didn't have any heating.

On the plus side, living in the same building where I worked meant I wouldn't need public transportation, and I could show up in the morning already dressed. Also, my new residence was at 26 Place de la Madeleine, Paris 8eme. How many people could claim such a prestigious address, right in the heart of Paris?

Little would anyone know that this fancy Place de la Madeleine home had no heat or hot water and no real bathroom except for a shared toilet and a sink inside a janitor's closet in the hallway.

Despite the tight quarters in the kitchen and in my room, the work at Fauchon immediately suited me. Besides Mr. Sutter, Michel the butcher, and one other cook, there was nobody else in the kitchen. It was a casual environment, and we all got along well.

On my first night, Mr. Sutter invited me to dinner with his family, a gesture I greatly appreciated. The evening was especially pleasant since his wife, of Danish origin, spoke German and made me feel instantly at home—and since he had two good-looking blond daughters who worked in the fashion industry and still lived with their parents.

It took a few days to get used to the fact that all the cooks in the Fauchon kitchen smoked. A Gauloises cigarette dangled from every lip—every lip except mine since I was not a smoker and had always worked in kitchens where smoking was explicitly forbidden. The constant smell of cigarette smoke wafting through the kitchen put me off at first, but soon enough, it was part of the general ambience.

Since Mr. Sutter seemed in no hurry to tamper with the predictable menu in the Fauchon shop and snack bar, we produced the same items every single day, mainly sandwiches, rice pudding, chocolate mousse, and mini quiches of all kinds. There was definitely room to add creative new items, but he felt that the menu suited the clientele and we did not need to mess with it.

Mr. Sutter's lack of ambition about this part of the menu suited me well too because it gave me the free time I needed to concentrate on the aspect of my job that I was expressly hired for and felt most excited about: improving the quality and variety of cold buffet items in the delicatessen area.

On my first days, I assisted Mr. Sutter with his daily work, to learn more about the Fauchon routine and find out what he expected from me. "Son," he said, "you do what you have to do to make the showcase look nice and attractive." He always called me *son*, maybe because he had two daughters. I later learned that he called everybody *son*.

This newfound autonomy was a thrill. I started to develop a weekly program of show plates, a different one every day. Poached Norwegian salmon, roasted poulet de Bresse, Barbarie duck, rack of baby veal, and many others. I presented each item on an elegant silver platter, accompanied with special garnishes, and richly decorated to catch the eyes of passersby. I also prepared an array of finger foods like medallions of lobster and arranged them to resemble miniature pastries.

The irony that I was assembling these delicate, luxurious creations for the Fauchon displays, while living upstairs in a bare-bones room with no heat or toilet, strikes me as humorous now—although at the time, my lifestyle seemed more pathetic than funny. At least I wasn't alone in my sad living arrangements. Other employees were in the same boat, and our shared situation certainly encouraged us to get along well.

I had become friendly with the two Algerian storeroom helpers with whom I shared the janitorial closet that passed for a bathroom. The three of us had to wait our turns to use the sink and toilet, but somehow, we always found a way to get ready in time for work in the morning. Doing laundry meant washing our underwear and socks in that same little sink, using bleach to get them clean since there was no hot water. For more substantial laundry, we went to a nearby laundromat, which we didn't mind so much since it was warm in there, and it gave us the chance to meet people.

When our rooms got really cold in the winter, the Algerians taught me that the best way to warm up is to pour a bit of rubbing alcohol into a copper pot and light it on fire. The flares heat up a room quickly, as long as you don't burn the entire building down. I got into the habit of lighting alcohol in a vessel in my room every night before going to bed, then jumping under the covers as the flames died down.

My Algerian neighbors showed me another way to get warm quickly, at least on the inside. One night they invited me to their room to try their special homemade chicken and pepper soup. The soup was delicious, a bit spicy but not as much as the many peppers floating in the bouillon would make you believe. When I took a big bite of a floating chili pepper—confident the hot broth had surely mellowed the spiciness—a wave of heat suddenly took over my body from top to bottom, giving me the feeling that flames were shooting out of my mouth and ears. My entire body burned from the inside.

My friends, accustomed to the level of heat in the soup, laughed at me as I gasped. "Hey, it's great, isn't it?" they yelled. "It also kills all the microbes!"

Our shared toilet was just a hole in the middle of the floor, with an elevated step on the right and the left to place each foot. I never quite understood why this so-called Turkish toilet existed in the Fauchon building, especially as the last Turks had left Europe more than two hundred years ago and both the French and the Turks had had plenty of time to develop a more suitable facility.

But I soon discovered that even new, modern cafes and restaurants in Paris still offered the same type of toilet.

Using one was quite a procedure, at least for me, as I found it easier to remove the trousers and underpants first, but then had no space or hooks to put them on. I will spare readers any further details about this adventure other than to admit it was a real challenge.

Back in the kitchen, my colleagues and I devised a system for taking our daily showers in what passed for a bathroom. Our work shifts ended at six o'clock every evening, after which we had to take turns in what I called the Turkish shower, because the famous toilet facility also served as a shower. Whoever took the first one had to disinfect the place with plenty of Eau de Javel bleach and rinse with lots of hot water before stepping in to shower. French hygiene at its very best!

In the meantime, my work was getting noticed. The customer response to Fauchon's window displays was overwhelming, and on some days, we sold out the items less than an hour after we had placed them in the showcase. This meant working at an extra-fast pace every day to make sure that the showcase remained richly decorated at all times and never looked empty.

My favorite customers were the ones who reserved the show plate in the morning but requested delivery in the evening. That way, the showcase stayed full for the whole day, which gave me the necessary time to breathe and to prepare the items for the following day.

In early December of 1964, the newspaper *Le Figaro* published an article about Fauchon and its young German culinary artist who was bringing an entirely new dimension to the delicatessen department. After that, everything changed dramatically.

From the moment *Le Figaro* hit the newsstands, our telephone never stopped ringing. Demands for our catering services multiplied exponentially. All of a sudden, this was no longer a one-person job, so Mr. Sutter was forced to restructure responsibilities in the kitchen. From now on, the other cooks had to do all the needed preparation, allowing me time to concentrate on the decorative parts only.

Mr. Roche's vision of making Fauchon a major player in Paris, setting trends and catering to the high society, had just become a reality. I felt very proud to be part of this success.

Even Madame de Gaulle started ordering some of my special hors d'oeuvres, adding them to her purchases on her frequent weekly visits. She had a habit of arriving in her black Citroen limousine two hours before the store opened to the public. Walking through the store with two or three employees, she would pick out a couple of slices of ham over here, some pâté over there, and sometimes the hors d'oeuvres I had created. I only saw her in person once when I was bringing items down for the charcuterie display and noticed her browsing through my section.

Slowly but surely, I was on my way to becoming a culinary superstar at Fauchon. Employees from other departments frequently stopped by to see what I was doing, including Andrée, the woman who was responsible for the fruit display, and even Nicole, the telephone operator. Mr. Sutter insisted that since these particular employees had never set foot in the kitchen before, they surely had more interest in me than in my cooking.

If this was in fact true, it was too late. Fate had other plans for me, as I was about to find out.

AT THE PALACE HOTEL IN ST. MORITZ

COOKING IN THE RESTAURANT - FRANKFURTER HOF

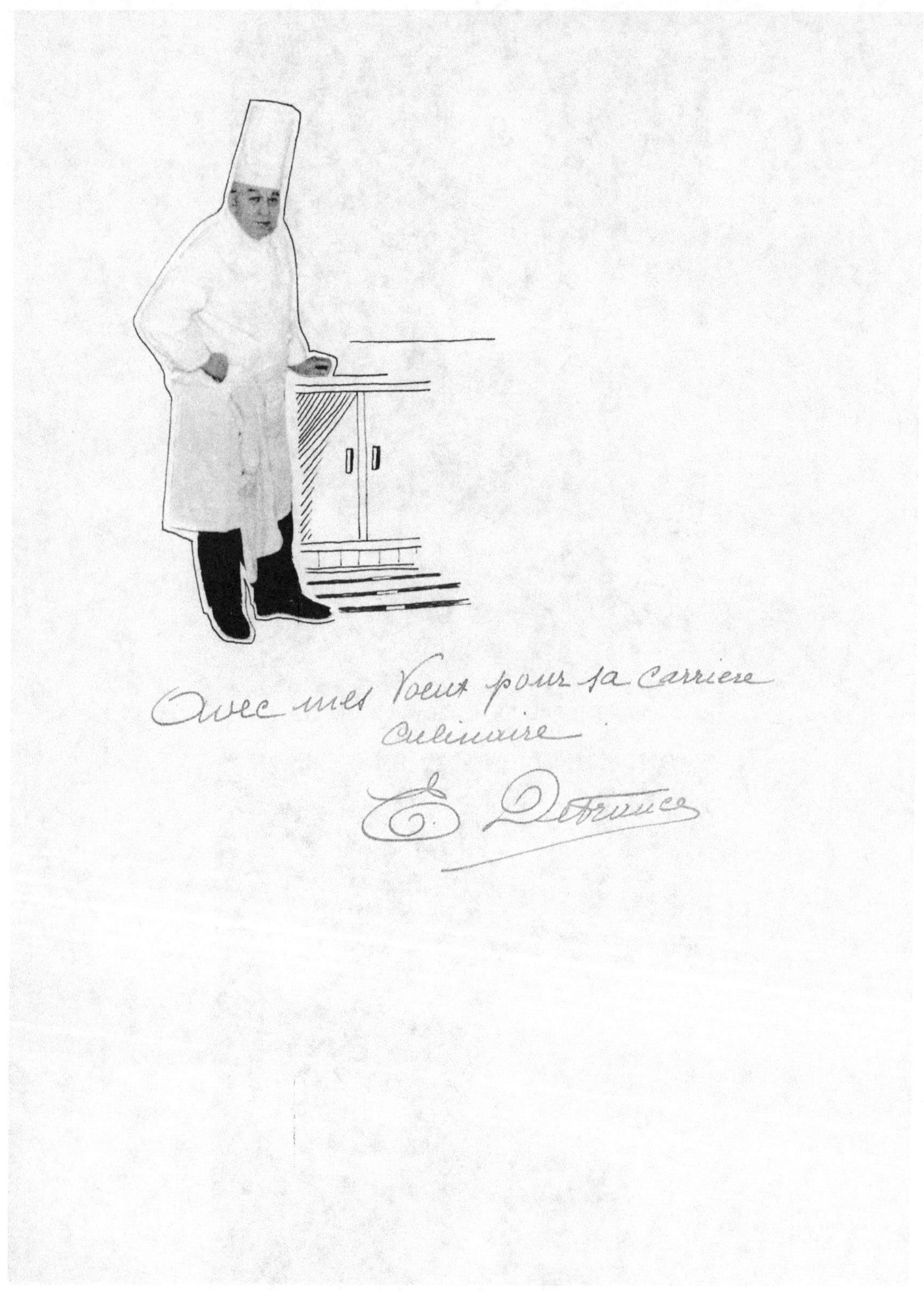

EUGENE DEFRANCE AT THE PALACE HOTEL

J'ai été on ne peut plus satisfait des services de Peter qui joint à de rares qualités professionnelles une grande honnêteté.

C'était un excellent collègue mais aussi un ami

Sutter
Chef de Cuisine
Fauchon

CHEF SUTTER AT FAUCHON IN PARIS

Meeting Mademoiselle Malouf 07

Cafe Madeleine, My Second Home

In Paris, the seasons pass quickly, and soon the cold winter months gave way to spring. In my free time, I strolled along the shores of the Seine, browsing through the hundreds of book stands. I liked to chat with the bouquinistes, asking those well-read booksellers to point me to interesting finds or help me search for rare cookbooks.

The "marché aux puces" (flea market) at the Porte de Clignancourt saw a lot of me too on my days off. Compared to other flea markets selling all kinds of rubbish, this one is a tremendous source of antiques and other unique discoveries. I loved trying to bargain with the sellers or eavesdropping on other customers as they attempted to negotiate.

The city slows down in the summer months, as the high society Parisian customers leave town to travel or spend time at their homes on the Cote d'Azur. Madame de Gaulle's visits became less frequent too in the summer.

With more available personal time, I took on a side job on some evenings, working as a chef de claque at the Olympia, the famous Parisian music hall, where stars like Edith Piaf, Gilbert Becaud, and Charles Aznavour performed in those days.

Journalists showed up for the first night of every star's engagement, so the Olympia made an extra effort to get positive press on those nights. The chefs de claque would be positioned strategically throughout the audience and would clap their hands at key moments to get the entire audience to break into applause and make the show look like a hit. I earned about fifty francs a night for my clapping services. Every little bit helped.

In August, *la morte-saison* in France, the entire country comes to a standstill. Even the Alliance Française school where I'd been taking French classes shuts down for the month.

By September, I felt restless and eager to resume normal life. I looked forward to my routine of working during the day, taking French classes in the evening, and studying with hot chocolate at the Café Madeleine—a place that had the added bonus of a modern European bathroom facility, sans Turkish toilet. My studies had progressed from grammar and writing to literature and conversational French. Just in time, too, for an encounter that took place on a late September afternoon.

I was returning from school on the twentieth of September 1965 and taking a seat at my usual place at the Café Madeleine to do my daily homework, when I noticed an attractive young woman drinking a cup of tea at a table nearby. She looked fashionable, her chocolate brown hair styled in a casual ponytail with bangs. But something was wrong. She glanced around nervously, her face clearly agitated. When one of my waiter friends approached her, she started to argue with him, gesticulating with both hands.

Watching her for a moment, I realized she was not a happy customer. My concern turned to amusement.

The young lady saw me observing her and continued gesticulating with both hands as she complained to me in French, "It's been fifteen minutes since I ordered a sandwich, and I'm still waiting, and my tea is getting cold in the meantime!"

I let out a small laugh, and she went on, even more agitated now: "This is not funny, this is unacceptable." Now her irritation was aimed not just at the waiter, but at me too. Oops, not what I had intended.

Order was restored in the universe a minute or two later when the waiter brought her the sandwich and she sat back to eat her dinner. We made eye contact again, and I asked if it would be okay if I moved closer to where she sat. All the empty tables between us made it difficult to have any conversation. Luckily, she agreed, and I took a seat at the table next to hers.

She looked even prettier up close, her beautiful smile showing off teeth like a string of pearls and her eyes sparkling green. Her French sounded perfect to me, but since she seemed to have nowhere in particular to go, despite her rush about the sandwich, I guessed she was a tourist. I turned out to be right.

"So where are you from?" I asked.

"Where do you think?"

"Latin America?" Her features reminded me of a few Latin American students in my French classes.

"No. Guess again," she insisted.

"Italy? Spain?"

"No," she said with a smile and forced me to guess a few more times before she said, "Beirut, Lebanon."

I knew of Beirut, but I drew a blank when she mentioned Lebanon. "Do you know of Syria?" she asked. "And Israel?" Yes, of course I had heard of both countries even though I had never visited the region.

"Lebanon is right in between those two, along the Mediterranean coast," she informed me, adding, "We have snow-covered mountains on one side and the blue Mediterranean Sea on the other."

This place sounded like paradise, but my blank expression must not have been too convincing. She went on to tell me that in the winter, the Lebanese can ski in the morning and go water-skiing and swimming in the afternoon.

"Wonderful," I replied. "But when do you work?"

I learned that she works for Bank of America in Beirut, from 8:00 a.m. until 2:00 p.m. five days a week.

Tough job, I thought, smiling. Everyone I knew in France and Germany put in much longer hours, sometimes six days a week.

"We work very hard," she continued.

"I'm sure you do," I replied, still thinking: six hours a day, five days a week? What a great job!

"And where do *you* come from?" she asked. "Alsace?"

Alsace! How flattering that she thought my French was good enough to pass for native. Her guess made sense. The Alsatians speak French with a German accent, since the French region of Alsace borders Germany and has changed hands between the countries multiple times before going back to France after World War II. This young woman seemed well-educated and well-traveled.

"Good guess," I told her, "but no. Guess again."

She started listing one European country after the other. After half a dozen, I gave in.

"Germany?" she asked, surprised. Was she disappointed? "No, not really, but I did think you were from France!"

It was my turn to ask a question: "What brings you to Paris?"

She told me her family had sent her on a mission—actually, three missions. One, to travel to England to help her brother settle into his university and to sew a name label into every one of his clothes. Two, to deliver a package to a family friend while she was in Paris. And three, to buy fabric for the dress she would wear to her sister's wedding, from an upscale textile shop in Paris called Bouchara.

The waiter gave us a signal. The cafe was about to close. We had talked for almost two hours, and I'd told her all about my work and learned more about her job and family. But we had been so busy chatting, we hadn't even introduced ourselves. I finally learned her name. Denyse with a Y.

Going back home to my stuffy room felt like a grim prospect on this lovely evening. I took a chance and asked Denyse if she might like to stroll along the Champs-Élysées, glittering in the dusk as the sun went down. The City of Lights was at its best this time of day, and I felt as if Denyse and I could talk for hours.

As I dropped her off later at her hotel on the rue Tronchet, not far from the Madeleine, I asked if we could meet again.

Denyse's answer came like a kick in the stomach.

She had so much to do, so many errands in Paris, and she couldn't make any plans right now. She would have to let me know.

Let me know? This was 1965. We didn't have cell phones. Nor did I have the nerve to ask for her number at the hotel, especially after she seemed intent on brushing me off at the end of our wonderful afternoon and evening. As we parted, I could muster only a crisp "Goodnight, have a nice stay in Paris."

Work the next day felt like drudgery. The memory of the engaging woman with the sparkling eyes would cheer me for a second, but then I would remember how she had turned down my offer to meet again. Still, why had I not persisted in trying to arrange another date?

Back in my room, I opened the "was ist das" to calm myself with an evening breeze, when I realized that I had forgotten to move my car from its prime parking spot in front of Fauchon. The car had sat there all weekend, but on weekdays, those spots are reserved for customers only. As it was already late, I decided to talk to the doorman the next morning, hoping that he would allow me to leave the car for the rest of the day, which he did as business was slow that week.

My normal parking spot was at the underground Invalides parking, on the other side of the Seine. To make the five-minute drive there, I usually turned left around the Madeleine church, then took Rue Royale, home of the famous Maxims restaurant, and crossed past the splendid fountains of the Place de la Concorde, driving past the Egyptian obelisk to arrive at the Invalides parking.

The next evening, acting on a last-minute impulse as I drove my car to the Invalides, I took a right instead of a left from Fauchon and drove into the Rue Tronchet. Stopping at a traffic light and waiting for pedestrians to cross, I thought I saw her. Was I hallucinating?

No, sure enough, that was Denyse. She walked briskly. Maybe she actually was very busy as she had insisted the day before. Where could she be going? I debated whether I should drive away and forget about my intrusive attempt at a chance meeting or veer my car closer to catch her attention.

"Bonsoir, I see you are very busy," I said to her when she looked up and saw me in the car, edging close to where she stood. I regretted that I hadn't come up with a wittier opening line. I was relieved when she didn't send me off right away. She said she was on her way to deliver that package she had mentioned, a box of tea for a young Lebanese medical student from his mother, a family friend in Beirut.

Denyse let me drive her to this mysterious young man, who was living in a university compound at the Rive Gauche, an area full of students and artists. We drove past lively local bars and restaurants, an inviting scene on this moonlit night. My French school was nearby, but I had not yet explored the Rive Gauche much. To my relief, it took only minutes for her to drop off the package with Jean Saleh, a man I would happen to meet again years later when I was managing a hotel in New York City. Then Denyse was back, standing in front of me.

My stomach clenched as I gathered the nerve to ask if she had the rest of the evening free. This time she didn't dismiss me so quickly. I proposed a visit to Montmartre, home of art galleries and painters, and of course the hilltop Sacré Coeur Cathedral, with its views across all of Paris.

We shared a pizza for dinner. Pizza in Paris? I have no recollection of why we made that choice, especially since there are so many bistros in Montmartre offering reliable French cuisine and a truer Parisian experience.

All I know is after that, Denyse's schedule magically freed up. During the day, I worked and she did her shopping, and we passed every evening together exploring the city. We saw the musical *Valse de Vienne* at the Chatelet Theatre, spent an evening at the celebrated Folies Bergeres, and even visited the Moulin Rouge to see the famous French cancan. Somehow, we squeezed in time for stops at the Chateau de Chantilly, about a one-hour drive from the city, and the Marché aux puces too.

A week later, Denyse's shopping vacation came to an end. This seemed impossible, but I had to accept the reality that she had to return to Beirut. Our week together was over, just like that.

She gave me a quick goodbye kiss at the airport and handed me a five-inch record as she picked up her bags and headed to her gate. There's a secret message on it, she whispered, warning me to listen to it only after she had landed in Beirut five hours later.

Making the Postal Service Rich

Keeping my promise to Denyse was easy. I could not listen to the record right away even if I tried. I didn't own a record player and had to find someone who did before I could hear the message, which she told me she had recorded at one of the galleries on the Champs-Élysées. After days of asking around, my suspense growing, I finally found a record player I could use.

Mein lieber Peter,

En ce mercredi, le 29 septembre 1965 je quitte Paris pour mon pays. Oh, des complications maintenant, et en quittant Paris car les vacances sont termines maintenant je quitte un ami, un copain, a qui je dois tout le Bonheur de ces huit jours. Je voudrais tant te remercier pour tout ce que tu as fait pour moi en rendant ces huit jours a Paris plus agreables et les vacances les plus ideals. Je voudrais te rappeler chaque detail, chaque soirée et surtout la dernière soirée.

C'est bien grâce à toi, à ta gentillesse et a tout ce que tu as depensé pour moi que j'ai passé peut etre huit jours les plus heureux de ma vie. J'aurai bien voulu que tu sois avec moi. J'espere le jour viendra ou le hazard nous rencontrera dans un pays hors de la France.

Au revoir cheri et bon courage pour la vie. Je te quitte pour Beyrouth.

Translation

My dear Peter,

At this very moment, on September 29, 1965, I am leaving Paris for my country. This is complicated now, and by leaving Paris because my vacation ended, I am leaving a good friend and buddy to whom I owe all the happiness of the past eight days. I would love to thank you so much for everything you did for me to make this vacation the best I could wish for. I would like to remind you of every detail, every evening, but especially the last one.

It is due to you, your kindness, and all the efforts you made for me that I had perhaps the eight happiest days of my life. I would love so much that you are with me. I hope the day will come when chance lets us meet again in a country other than France .

Bye, my dear, and all the best for your life. I am leaving you for Beirut.

The message sounded sweet and heartfelt, but the last two sentences were not promising at all. "All the best for your life"? Still, we'd vowed to write to each other. So maybe there was hope.

But would we actually write? Distance can change everything. People's lives get busy, and writing to someone far away can feel less and less urgent, especially after the first letter or two.

At least we would always have Paris and one memorable week in September of 1965.

The first letter from Beirut arrived a few days after Denyse left. Reading it, I felt as if we were sitting in a cafe again, talking over tea and sandwiches. An intense longing for that very first meeting washed over me. She caught me up on her life since Paris, telling me she'd had to field many curious questions about her vacation from family and colleagues. She described the upcoming wedding of her sister Mouna and sketched the custom dress sewn from the fabric Denyse had bought in Paris.

In that era, letters could either travel by regular mail, which took weeks, or by airmail, which arrived in a few days. Since heavier weight meant more stamps, letter writers used ultra-light envelopes and thin paper for airmail. The pages were practically transparent, and handwriting shone right through them.

Every week I started receiving letters by airmail, pages and pages filled on one side only with Denyse's news from Beirut. I responded immediately, with the help of a French dictionary and grammar exercise books. I tried to make my letters perfect and often rewrote every single page after discovering little mistakes. I didn't want to send letters full of crossed-out errors.

Soon I realized that even if I tried my very best not to make a mistake, it still happened, as Mademoiselle Denyse made me aware in the gentlest possible way in her response. She clearly saw it as her duty to help me improve my French. Merci, Madame le Professeur.

Unlike my own letters, Denyse's were full of corrections. She crossed out and rewrote words as if it didn't matter. Maybe it didn't to her, but I would have felt it too risky to send a marked-up letter like that. I was trying hard to impress her.

I later learned that she wrote most of her letters at work. She considered it a priority to get the response done in the little time available to her and valued this more than perfection.

By the end of the year, I had received almost twenty letters from Denyse and sent her just as many.

We had no other way to keep in touch. Making long distance calls on the telephone would have cost too much money and raised suspicions. People like Mark Zuckerberg weren't even born yet, and Facebook, texting, or email would've been totally incomprehensible in those days.

Another development that would've been hard to imagine back then is that newspapers would begin to vanish as the years went by. In those days, cafés were still filled with people hunched over newspapers, their hands flipping and folding big broadsheets covered in newsprint. I liked to relax and take my time reading the paper on Sunday afternoons on the terrace of the Café de la Paix, next to the opera house. Sitting in the front row, I could watch people of all nationalities walk by, a show in itself and always amusing.

Opposite the terrace was a kiosk selling international newspapers, owned by a man who liked to know all his customers by their names, or at least nicknames. He knew where I worked and called me Mr. Fauchon when I picked up my German Sunday paper. "Nice vitrine you did this week, Mr. Fauchon," he would sometimes say. I never knew whether he had actually walked by our vitrines and noticed the displays, but I appreciated the personal touch.

One particular Sunday, I picked up my newspaper and took my place on the terrace of the café to read the news from old Germany. Scrolling through the newspaper, I saw an advertisement that made me blink my eyes and stare. I couldn't bring myself to turn the page.

Visiting the Paris of the Orient

In 1965, Beirut attracted tourists from around the world who came to see this little city along the Mediterranean and enjoy its glamorous beaches, tireless nightlife, and treasure trove of ancient ruins nearby. The civil war that would tear Lebanon to shreds was still a decade away. The 1960s were a golden era of cosmopolitan culture and leisurely living for many Lebanese and for travelers who converged on this shining city.

As I sat at Café de la Paix reading the German paper, my eyes came across a promotion for airfares to the Paris of the Orient, Beirut's nickname in that era.

A thousand thoughts rushed through my mind. Should I or should I not take advantage of this opportunity? After all, Denyse and I had only gotten to know each other over a few days in Paris and in the letters we had exchanged since then. Did we know each other well enough for me to parachute into her life on short notice?

I decided to ask Denyse in my next letter. As her birthday was on December 5, I thought she might like the idea of having me fly in during that week. Her answer came about two weeks later.

Reading between the lines, I quickly realized that my idea of visiting mademoiselle had a lot of buts attached.

> *Yes, Lebanon is a wonderful country, but this time of year, the weather is not very pleasant.*
>
> *Yes, I would love to see you, but I have to work and I do not know how much time I can spare.*

After rereading her letter several times and finding no clear answer one way or the other, I felt even more confused than before. Doubts flooded my mind. Maybe the idea of a visit so soon was just crazy.

Her next letter dated October 29, 1965, perplexed me even more. Yes, she would be very pleased to see me again, and she would do her best to make time available. "La decision est a toi" was her last statement, so now the ball was in my corner again. Typical, as I learned later. Never wanting to make a decision.

On November 27, I flew Air France's Caravelle from Orly to Frankfurt to connect with Middle East Airlines, Lebanon's national carrier. The airline was then flying the elegant Comet on this route, a plane with two engines incorporated into the wings rather than attached underneath.

The Comet was the British answer to Boeing, but unfortunately, the model had problems with its engines and wing structure, and after some fatal accidents, it was discontinued. The plane was still in service for my trip though, and luckily it worked well enough to bring me safely to Beirut.

If my flight was smooth and calm, the Beirut airport experience was another story. I exited the airplane into complete and total sensory overload, as porters and taxi drivers crowded every passenger, arguing over who would get to carry his luggage or drive him to his destination. Here I stood in the middle of it all, fending off the screaming and shouting to my right and left, having no idea where to go.

Out of the blue, a representative of the German travel agency miraculously appeared and escorted me away to a minibus. Off we went to the Cedarland Hotel in the busy Hamra district of Beirut.

On the street, chaos reigned again. Drivers jockeyed to pass each other on the narrow, traffic-choked roads. In Beirut, I immediately realized, traffic lights and stop signs are merely decorative. No one paid the least bit of attention to them. My driver leaned on his horn for nearly the entire trip, joining his fellow drivers on the road in the ear-splitting symphony.

Someone I met in Beirut later told me that the Lebanese always makes sure the horn is loud enough before deciding whether to buy a car. I never found out whether this was true, but I wouldn't be surprised.

The driver pulled in front of my hotel, just steps from the American University of Beirut's seaside campus and from hectic Hamra Street. This was the city's most fashionable district at the time, its sidewalks lined with trendy cafés, restaurants, and boutiques, and filled with pedestrians at all hours. The rich "fils à papa" drove their expensive luxury cars up and down the avenue and tried to get attention by tooting their horns, the ultimate Beirut soundtrack. Walking into my room, exhaustion instantly hit me, and somehow, I slept soundly through all the noise.

Even after its late nights, Beirut wakes up early, and so did I. I couldn't wait to explore the city, and after a quick breakfast on the terrace, I took a ten-minute walk down to the Corniche, the seaside boulevard, a curved promenade lined with palm trees. Early risers jogged and walked up and down the Corniche, taking advantage of the fresh air from the Mediterranean and the spectacular view of the sea. Waves slowly rolled into the rocky beach as a few anglers stood on the rocks protruding from the shore, throwing in their fishing lines and hoping for a good catch.

I decided to watch the anglers for a while and sat down on a rock, enjoying the blue waves as they moved in and gently withdrew again into the sea. Too bad I didn't have my bathing suit with me because the sea looked crystal clear, its temperature pleasant even in December. Water pollution was still unheard of in those days.

"Miss Malouf called and will call back later." The hotel receptionist gave me the message a few hours later, when I came back to the hotel for a bite to eat. Denyse had called at 9:45 a.m. I hadn't expected to hear from her so soon given her busy work schedule and her confusing reaction to my Beirut vacation idea.

That missed telephone call turned out to be a fitting start to a visit during which I spent more time alone every day than with Miss Malouf.

Denyse kept me busy, sending me to every imaginable destination in Lebanon and turning me into a tourist par excellence. My itinerary spared no site, from Beirut's iconic Grotte aux Pigeons rock structures to the enormous stalactite and stalagmite caves in Jeita, to the legendary Cedar trees, and to the ancient Roman temples of Baalbek. I saw the archeological ruins at Byblos, Sidon, and Tyr, dating back to Alexander the Great and to the ancient Egyptian and Roman civilizations. I even took an overnight trip to Syria to view the famous Crac des Chevaliers castle built by the Crusaders and the historic cities of Homs and Palmyra.

No doubt about it, spending time with Denyse interested me more than any historical site. But I did receive a crash course in the ancient civilizations of the Middle East and gained a better understanding of the culturally rich place she called home.

Fortunately, Denyse managed to clear some time for me after work on most days, and we visited her favorite local restaurants and other destinations on and off the tourist path. One evening, she took me to the famous Casino du Liban to see a spectacular horse show straight out of Las Vegas, then we enjoyed a delicious ice cream at a favorite local hangout called Ajami. In one of the most epic events of that week, we met her friends one night for dinner at Al Bahri, a popular seaside restaurant in Beirut.

Lebanon's cuisine is famous for good reason. Though many of its best-known dishes found their way into the region during the four hundred years of rule by the Ottoman Empire, the Lebanese gave the recipes a special twist and infused them with local produce and spices. Dining at Al Bahri felt like a front-row seat to the wonders of Lebanese cooking. One of Denyse's friends, Rafic Chehab, sat next to me at dinner and explained each one of the more than fifty different mezze dishes the waiters kept bringing out, from smoky eggplant baba ghanoush to spicy sausages known as mekanek, to a sumac-spiced bread salad called fattoush, and lemony tabbouleh, and creamy labneh, and hummus decorated in swirls of olive oil and paprika, and on and on.

Working in upscale kitchens around Europe had certainly exposed me to splendid food, but I had never experienced flavors quite like these. Culinary fireworks kept going off in my mouth, and I did not miss out on tasting a single one of the mezze dishes. When the waiters finally stopped bringing out plates and started to clear the table, I let out a big *oufff.* I felt full beyond belief and couldn't even look at food anymore.

A few of Denyse's friends lit their big Churchill cigars and continued their animated conversation, part in Arabic and part in French. How nice that I could follow what they were saying, more or less, and join in the socializing. Ah, the Lebanese lifestyle at its best.

Next thing I knew, our tabletop started filling up again. What's this? Apparently, we had only eaten appetizers so far, and now it was time for the main course. Out came a parade of platters piled high with grilled chicken kebabs, skewered shrimp, a beef and lamb specialty called kafta, the Lebanese lamb dish kibbe topped with yogurt sauce, and more.

Overwhelmed by the hospitality, I had to taste at least a few dishes. Denyse's friends chimed in with "You have to try this. Did you taste that? This one is an old recipe from my grandmother."

Even after all this, the dinner still didn't end. Giant platters of fruit soon arrived, along with the sweets known as baklawa. How could anybody eat so much so late in the evening?

Perhaps it was the weight of all that food in my body that caused one of my shoelaces to snap when I stepped on it as I walked to Denyse's home the next day. Luckily, in Beirut shoe polishers lurk on every corner, ready to shine your boots or sell you any and every shoe accessory, including laces. But as with anything else for sale in the Middle East, paying usually involves a negotiation. Arguing about a price wins respect from the seller, not to mention a better deal.

In my few days in Beirut, I had already learned that no price is final, so I started negotiating with the shoe polisher. I got him to reduce the asking price for the shoelace from one Lebanese pound all the way down to twenty centimes. What a deal. The times I had spent negotiating at the flea market in Paris had paid off. If only Denyse had seen me bargain with this guy.

Walking into Denyse's home shortly after, I proudly mentioned my shoelace story to her family. Everyone in the room burst out laughing. Apparently, the going rate for a pair of shoelaces was five centimes, not more and not less. Charging more than five centimes for shoelaces was highway robbery. Despite having fallen victim, I was still happy with the results of my bargaining, although I had made the shoe polisher a little richer than usual. I suppose the Marché aux Puces hadn't quite prepared me for Beirut.

Denyse's family treated me politely, but I couldn't figure out how they felt about me. At least I didn't sense a particularly strong opposition to my presence. I was never asked, "What are your intentions for our daughter," not even by her father, with whom I had a brief conversation in English since he was British-educated. He didn't make me feel unwelcome. I could say that much about the visit. The rest was a mystery.

Days later, Denyse gave me a preview of her own negotiating tactics when we visited Beirut's Basta antiques market. Basta is a web of small, dusty shops crammed with all kinds of furniture and knickknacks, some of them valuable and others worthless. Denyse advised me never to accompany her into a shop. Instead, I should always go in first while she waited outside, and if I saw something I liked, I should slip out and tell her privately. Then she'd walk in and close the deal.

When an antique petroleum lamp caught my eye in one of the shops and reminded me of a piece I'd admired in her family's living room, I sent Denyse in to bargain. She started negotiating with the shopkeeper, and when they arrived at a decent price, she said, "Before I make a decision, I have to check with my fiancé." The seller then saw me walk in, did a double take, and said, "This guy? He was just in here!"

If I'd tried to buy the lamp alone, the shopkeeper would've started at a much higher price, no doubt. I still looked like a novice, and I had a lot to learn before I could bargain like a Beiruti.

In any event, I wasn't serious about buying a lamp on this trip and hauling it back with me to Paris. And there was no time to keep practicing my bargaining skills just for fun. My vacation was already ending. The next day, I had to fly back to Paris on the Comet.

Back Home for Christmas

My week in Beirut created another dilemma for me. Since I had planned the trip at the last minute in the busy month of December, I had left myself no time to arrange my holiday travel. I would have a few days off from Fauchon for Christmas, enough to visit my mother and sisters in Hannover. But I couldn't leave work until December 24, a terrible day to travel to Germany.

How would I get home for the holiday? In Germany, it's not only Christmas Day that brings public life to a standstill. The holiday starts a full day before, when planes and trains start operating on a reduced schedule or no schedule at all. After many phone calls with airline agents, I finally found a flight from Paris to Frankfurt on December 24, but no connecting flights to Hannover were available so late on that day and no trains either.

The only solution was to book a rental car in Frankfurt. When I arrived at the Avis desk on Christmas Eve, I had the dubious honor of being the lone customer, and I could tell the agent had been waiting impatiently for me so she could go home.

It was 8:00 p.m. sharp when I started my 250-mile trip from Frankfurt to Hannover. Christmas Eve on a German highway at that hour felt like a scene from a horror movie. I saw almost no other cars on the Autobahn for long stretches of time, and even most of the petrol stations along the highway had shuttered. Anyone with a mechanical problem or an empty gas tank would face a long, lonely night or worse.

The bells of the Dreifaltigkeitskirche church near our home rang 1:00 a.m. sharp as I pulled into our street, eagerly awaited by my mother and sisters, who stood at the window watching for me.

The smell of Christmas cookies and fresh beeswax candles welcomed me home, along with a beautifully decorated Christmas tree. My family has always treated the tree trimming ritual as an art, hanging handblown glass balls painted in shimmering gold, and stringing lametta on the branches.

As I learned much later, this level of attention to the smallest detail on the tree came from my father, who would spend hours making sure that the gold balls all hung at the same distance, and that the lametta, cut from real aluminum in those days, lined every branch, each tinsel strand the same length as the rest. A picture-perfect Christmas tree: a living legacy from the father I had never met.

We sat down to our traditional Christmas Eve dinner well after midnight that evening, just moments after I walked in. The night-before-Christmas dinner in France is called *reveillon*, and it's typically a lavish culinary feast with wine and champagne, but in Germany, at least in our family, we usually served frankfurters and potato salad for dinner. This was because after an evening spent exchanging gifts and snacking on Christmas cookies and other holiday treats, nobody would feel like having a big meal, an event saved for the following day.

My mother enjoyed slightly better financial circumstances in those days than in the war years, so on Christmas Day, after catching up and helping Mutti in the kitchen, our little family feasted on a holiday dinner of apple-stuffed roasted duck with all the trimmings. It reminded me of our larger holiday gatherings with Opa and Oma in years past, when we used to have Christmas goose, also known as *Weihnachtsgans*, with red cabbage and potato dumplings.

In Germany, the celebration continues through the second day of Christmas, December 26, a time to pay visits to friends and extended family. That day also happens to be the anniversary of that stormy night in 1939 when I made my debut in the world.

My birthday timing always felt unlucky to me as a small child since it meant only one set of presents to cover both Christmas and my special day. But even long after presents no longer mattered, the twenty-sixth always brought more stress than it did birthday festivities. I usually had to work late or travel, and this year was no exception. I had to hurry back to Paris on the twenty-sixth to handle the New Year's Eve rush at Fauchon that kicks off on that day.

In Paris, "le reveillon du jour de l'an," a.k.a. New Year's Eve, involves enormous amounts of food and liquor—even more than Christmas Eve or just about any other French holiday.

Fauchon at that point was the supplier of choice for well-heeled Parisians' New Year's Eve celebrations, which meant that our tiny staff had to produce hundreds of cold buffet platters and orders of foie gras, canard a l'orange, and other elegant party foods. I remember putting together endless orders of coulibiac of salmon, a popular New Year's dish of filet of salmon rolled in chopped mushrooms and pastry dough, then baked and topped with melted butter.

Our biggest order of the night came from Fauchon's own president and CEO, Mr. Boury. He had a New Year's Eve tradition of inviting celebrities, politicians, and the crème de la crème of Paris society to celebrate with him and watch fireworks from his penthouse overlooking the Place de la Concorde.

The pressure to produce perfect platters of food for our boss and his guests was immense, but somehow, I didn't lose sleep over it. I knew we could do it. We had a highly competent, hardworking staff, and

Mr. Boury seemed to trust us. Still, I preferred to take care of the final setup myself, to make sure the buffet and decorations exceeded his expectations.

Creating and delivering all that food to Mr. Boury and to Fauchon's other clients by 10:00 p.m. on New Year's Eve was a monumental task, but we pulled it off. By the time we returned to the shop at nearly midnight, we felt too tired to make any plans or join the celebrations around the city.

I heard fireworks pop off all around as I took a deep breath after the long evening, relieved to have survived this hectic December. Before retiring to my room to collapse into my bed, I toasted a year of exciting new work experiences, a budding romance, and good health.

Drifting off, I wondered, what adventures will the new year bring?

MY FORD TAUNUS 17M

MEETING MADEMOISELLE DENYSE

WRITING LETTERS IN MY ROOM AT 26,
PLACE DE LA MADELEINE

1965 FIRST VISIT TO BEIRUT,
FLYING THE UNFAMOUS COMET JET

Search for a New Direction 08

Getting Sick in Paris

My French would never fool a native speaker, but I counted it as a major victory that Denyse mistook me for an Alsatian. I felt even more motivated to resume my language school routine after the holidays. The new year started much like the old one had ended: I worked at Fauchon during the day, took classes at the Alliance Française in the evenings, then did my homework over hot chocolate at the Café Madeleine.

Until one day, Mr. Sutter told me that my eyes looked as yellow as a canary bird, and I had better see a doctor.

True, I had been feeling more exhausted than usual over the past few days. The holiday stress didn't seem like a convincing reason anymore, already several weeks into the new year. All day long at work, the smells of food disturbed me, and my appetite had vanished. But I hadn't yet noticed my yellow eyes as I squinted into my tiny mirror to shave.

The doctor took one glance at me and announced: "Mon Dieu, vous avez une sacrée jaunisse." My God, you have quite a case of jaundice.

He diagnosed hepatitis and added, "Mais ce n'est pas grave, vous restez bien au chaud pour quelques temps, suivre un regime alimentaire, et cela ira tout seul." But it's not so serious. You just have to stay warm, follow a strict diet, and you'll be fine in no time.

How wrong he was.

Since I had spoken to no one else about my condition, my doctor's advice sounded reasonable to me. But I had no way of following his prescription. My room in the Fauchon building was more frigid than ever in mid-winter, and lighting alcohol in the copper pot wouldn't make it nearly warm enough to relieve my symptoms. I was too busy at work to shop for and cook ingredients that were healthier than the rich creations I was producing at Fauchon. Without fixing my lifestyle, as the doctor had advised, I wasn't going to get better. The only possibility left was to fly home to Germany for two or three weeks to heal properly.

Mr. Sutter understood and sent me off on my health break. The next day, a canary bird called Peter flew home to Hannover. Since I had warned my mother about my appearance, she wasn't too choked up to see me looking practically radioactive with my yellow skin and yellow eyeballs.

Doctors still made house calls in those days, and when our family physician walked into my room and saw me, he looked much more concerned than my doctor in Paris. Suspecting that I did not have a simple hepatitis, he moved me to the Sophienklinik, a small private hospital not far from my mother's apartment.

I was still planning to fly back to Paris in a few weeks at most. I had no idea that this hospital would become my home base for a long time.

The hospital's chief of internal medicine took over my case and started by asking me how much alcohol or beer I had been drinking before.

"None," I answered. "I don't drink alcohol, and I don't like beer."

"Too bad for you," he answered with a smile, "and as of now there will officially be no alcohol, no beer, no wine, no nothing!"

Before I could ask why, he told me the bad news: I had an infectious hepatitis, which meant I would need to stay in the hospital for an indefinite time.

The doctor, a specialist in liver infections, took my case very seriously and began to evaluate it weekly with input from other liver specialists in Germany. I became a case study in how to treat a difficult case of hepatitis. I received one infusion after another and strict orders not to leave my bed, not even to use the bathroom. Ironically, I did not feel sick at all by then and had no physical pain, but the staff wouldn't let me move even one inch.

Trapped in the hospital, restless and bored, I fought hard to keep my spirits up. The letters from Denyse, a lovely treat in the weeks past, became a lifesaving medicine now. We wrote to each other frequently, a habit we had resumed immediately after my Beirut visit. The letters brought us closer than before, albeit at a distance. Denyse too had gone through a rough winter and had recently lost her father. I felt grateful to have met him while he was still alive. I let myself believe that he did not disapprove of me, and if he did, at least it wasn't in my presence. I do think that had we gotten to know each other better, I could have eventually won him over.

My test results began to improve after a few weeks, but there was no immediate relief in sight. The doctors decided to perform a liver punctuation to analyze my infection in more detail, a procedure extensive enough to need general anesthesia. But as soon as the nurses gave me an anesthetic called Evipan, my body revolted. A nurse later told me that it took five people more than half an hour to restrain me and tie me down on the table, where I lay flailing and blocking the entire operating theatre until I finally calmed down.

At least I gave the hospital staff enough to gossip about for months.

The doctor eventually did the liver punctuation, using a local anesthetic instead. Whatever he and his colleagues learned by looking closely at my infection, they decided the hospital was not going to speed up my healing process. I was free to go, six months after the day I checked in. I went home with a detailed diet to follow and a list of things to avoid. High on that list: strenuous kitchen work.

I reread that list several times, not believing my eyes. If I couldn't do any more strenuous work in the kitchen, how could I continue my career as a cook? Did any non-strenuous kitchen jobs even exist? I guess it was time to find out. But first, I had to spend three more months in Hannover, a mandatory rest period prescribed by my doctor.

When I flew back to Paris a few months later, it was only to say my goodbyes. The Fauchon kitchen was too physically taxing as a workplace for me to rejoin it anytime soon, my doctor insisted. I said farewell to the Grand Boulevards, the Place de la Concorde, the Champs-Élysées, and the rest of the city I had grown to love, and I collected the personal belongings that had gathered dust for almost a year. The last thing to do was to go into the garage to pick up my car, so dusty I couldn't even recognize its color anymore, and drive five hundred miles to Hannover.

How did I catch hepatitis? Perhaps by eating seafood and oysters in one of the restaurants in Paris or sharing the Turkish shower at Fauchon or using the unsanitary toilets elsewhere around the city. I could have contracted the infection anywhere. France is a big country, and hygiene is not always at its best. I'll never know, and I never made any attempt to find out because it would not have changed anything. The year lost to hepatitis was a part of my destiny, and I had to accept it.

Back in Hannover, as I tried to regroup, the doctor checked up on me regularly and tried to steer my lifestyle in a healthier direction. First, he warned me against driving cars, which could damage my liver with their insufficient suspension and shocks. He approved only of the Citroen DS, the most advanced car on the road at the time, with adjustable air suspension that made the car feel like it was floating on a cushion of air. A wonderful piece of French engineering.

Four weeks later, I said goodbye to the Ford Taurus 17M and purchased a secondhand Citroen DS 19 with front-wheel drive, air suspension, and a feature that turned the headlights on every time the car went around a curve. Today, more than a half-century later, many of these features are common, but in 1967 they were revolutionary.

My doctor's second piece of advice hit me harder. He told me to avoid kitchen work altogether. The heat, physical labor, and irregular hours would put my liver at risk. I had hoped to find a culinary job that qualified as non-strenuous enough to satisfy my doctor, but he warned me to forget about that and look for a different line of work.

While changing my car had been easy enough, leaving the kitchen would mean a radical reorientation of my career. It would mean saying farewell to a work environment I loved and goodbye to all or most of the skills I had learned so far.

A terrifying question I thought I had answered years ago came roaring back: What should I do with my life?

Touring Germany with Denyse

The summer of 1967 was the Summer of Love. In San Francisco, New York, London, and elsewhere around North America and Europe, young men and women grew their hair long, protested war and social injustice, convened at outdoor music festivals, and launched a cultural movement that remains influential to this day.

In Hannover that year, I was experiencing my own summer of love. No longer ill or confined to bed, I tried to postpone my job anxiety for a few more weeks and soak up the soothing summer air. In the meantime, my long-distance romance with Denyse kept blossoming, and we were writing more frequently than ever.

I had one idea for how to keep busy while I figured out what to do with my life: plan Denyse's first trip to Germany. She would finally get to meet my mother and my sisters, a smaller crowd than her own large family in Beirut, and I could show her around my country. We'd head to Berlin first and then up to the beautiful North Sea area of Heligoland, to the fashionable summer resort of Travemunde on the Baltic Sea, and to picturesque points around the country to see cherry blossoms, do some wine-tasting, visit a famous casino, and experience the best of what Germany has to offer.

Happily, Denyse said yes to the idea. After weeks of planning the adventure down to the last detail, I drove to Frankfurt to pick her up from the airport.

I spotted Denyse instantly. She looked like a knockout in her colorful short dress and her green Tyrolean hat, with a long white feather that moved up and down with every step as she approached. We gave each other a long but cordial hug before we climbed into my car for the three-hour ride.

Denyse had no idea how far Frankfurt was from Hannover, and I could tell this was a much longer ride from the airport than she'd expected. But time passed quickly as we talked and laughed the whole way. My mother and sisters waited for us at the window of our second-floor apartment, curious to catch a glimpse of my girlfriend.

From the moment we walked in, I could sense Denyse's discomfort. Mutti was never one to put people at ease right away, and apparently, she had no intention of doing so with my girlfriend either. Even with her own children, my mother often came off as distant or chilly, just as much now as during our childhood. Denyse never said anything to me at the time about her feelings when she first met my mother, but I knew she was squirming, and I couldn't blame her. The tension never lifted during our two or three days in Hannover. Years later, Denyse admitted that she had hated the entire time she had to spend around my mother.

Mutti tried at times to go through the motions of hospitality, welcoming Denyse to the table for dinner, where my guest had her first surprising encounter with German food. My mother dressed salads with a lemon and sugar mixture, typical in the northern part of Germany. But for someone used to a tart, lemony olive oil dressing, Lebanese-style, the sweetness can come as a shock. Denyse handled it graciously, as she did each of the meals we had with my family.

My sisters made an effort to engage Denyse in friendly chitchat, especially my youngest sister, Jenny, always generous and warm. But my mother's icy demeanor made it impossible to relax, so Denyse and I took every opportunity to escape, spending more time touring the city than we did around my house.

We finally packed our bags and decided to go to Berlin a few days earlier than planned.

As driving to West Berlin would have required us to cross Russian-controlled East Germany, taking a car there was not really an option. We decided to fly instead.

Planning a trip to Berlin was far from easy in those days. After the war, even Germany's former capital, Berlin, was split up into four sections—Russian, American, French, and English—which eventually became two sections: the East, controlled by Russia, and the West, controlled by the Allies.

In 1948, in response to the creation of the new Deutsche Mark as the West German currency, Russia had imposed a blockade that prevented food and supplies from going to West Berlin, only agreeing to lift it if the Western powers retracted the currency. To prevent the West Berlin population from starving, the United States, England, and France organized an airlift that successfully dodged the land and sea blockade and delivered goods into the West. The declaration of East Berlin as the capital of the DDR, the Deutsche Demokratische Republik, in 1949 further enhanced the divisions and restricted travel within Berlin.

Germans living in the East were no longer allowed to visit the West, and people living in the West could only go receive permission to go to the Eastern sector under certain circumstances and with great difficulty. It's no wonder that many people in the East started fleeing to the West to gain their freedom, leaving everything they owned behind them, sometimes even their families.

To limit the exodus and the loss of its elite citizens, the DDR, with Russian permission, started building the Berlin wall in 1961. The wall stopped most citizens from escaping to the West, and it effectively turned Berlin into two cities.

The tour I had booked for us included a visit to the East, and Denyse and I both couldn't wait to see the area typically closed to outsiders. Unfortunately, after a day spent exploring the scenic highlights of the West, including a visit to the Konzerthaus Berlin orchestra hall and a few hours of shopping along upscale Kurfürstendamm Avenue, we ran into trouble.

At Checkpoint Charlie, a crossing station at the Berlin Wall where we were supposed to catch a bus to East Berlin for the remaining part of our tour, the guide announced: "Visitors with a German passport, bus number 1," and after a short pause, "All visitors with a foreign passport, bus number 2." Denyse and I looked at each other.

"Does this mean I have to go alone on the bus?" Denyse asked me, fear in her eyes.

Absolutely not. The bus was going to the other side of the Iron Curtain, and neither of us knew what to expect, especially for a foreigner traveling solo. Let's forget visiting East Berlin!

Years later, after reunification, we finally did visit the East. We discovered that this part of the city had many more of its historic buildings restored than the West did. As a hub for artists, musicians, cutting edge galleries, and cuisines from around the world, the East seemed to have much more to offer than the West.

Our East Berlin plans dashed, we left the city and traveled up north, taking a boat ride through the trading port of Hamburg, visiting the seaside town of Cuxhaven at the mouth of the Elbe River, and stopping in Heligoland, a secluded North Sea island of towering sandstone cliffs, forty miles off the coast of Germany.

The ex-British colony of Heligoland has been part of Germany since 1890, when England's Queen Victoria traded it for Zanzibar, an island she coveted off the coast of Africa. The trade gave Germany an island whose deep, ice-cold waters are ideal for breeding lobsters. Heligoland lobsters are even more delicious than the famous ones of Maine, and Denyse and I enjoyed a wonderful seafood dinner there.

In the Baltic Sea resort of Travemunde, I thought Denyse would jump at the chance to swim. Germans love the area for its relatively warm water, twenty degrees Celsius in the summer, several degrees higher than the North Sea. But the Baltic is not quite the balmy Mediterranean, and Denyse had no interest in wading into what for her was freezing cold water.

As we relaxed by the shore in Travemunde, warm on our beach towels, I reached for my carefully planned travel itinerary to see what came next in our plans. I had winged it so far, since I'd remembered all the places I intended to take us between Hannover and the Baltic resort. But as I searched my pockets and my bags, I couldn't find the itinerary anywhere.

What had I done with it? And where would we go next? All my obsessively detailed planning, weeks and weeks of brainstorming and research, gone to waste. Well, we would have to salvage our trip somehow and just follow our whims.

What a grand time we had. We visited the magnificent Gothic cathedral in Köln and went up the Rhine River to St. Goar, a village embedded among Riesling vineyards. After stopping in the winemaking town of Rüdesheim, which we found too touristy for our taste, we rode a cable car over the vineyards to the top to the Niederwalddenkmal. This monument was built in 1870 to commemorate the unification of multiple principalities and duchies into one Germany, and it was impressive to gaze down onto the entire Rhine Valley. In Heidelberg, an old university city along the Mosel River, we toured a famous castle that also holds the biggest wine barrel in the world.

No tour of Germany is complete without a visit to the legendary Black Forest, home of Baden-Baden and of the Brenner's Park Hotel, my old stomping grounds. The town holds plenty of charm for travelers, and I'd scarcely had time to enjoy it when I worked there. The scenery in the area is stunning, its forested mountains dotted with cottages straight out of a children's storybook, which makes sense since the Brothers Grimm fairy tales were supposedly set in the area. While Baden-Baden's renowned spa inspires visitors to do something positive for their health, its elegant casino invites them to lose all their money gambling. There's something for everyone.

Baden-Baden's casino has a spectacular interior that ranks it, along with Monte Carlo's, among the most refined gaming venues in the world. In 1967, when Denyse and I stopped there on our Germany tour, slot machines had not yet made their entrée into Europe. The casino, with its intimate and luxurious rooms, still attracted a certain level of society.

Guests dressed up for the occasion, the men in tuxedos or dark suits and the women in floor-length evening gowns and sparkling jewels. An evening in the casino generally started with dinner in the restaurant, followed by a visit to the gambling rooms to spend a few hours playing and mostly losing.

Denyse was eager to join in the games. She had experience gambling, she told me, because she'd visited the Casino du Liban a few times. The destination just outside Beirut was among the hottest venues in the Middle East at the time, drawing crowds for spectacles like the horse show we'd seen together.

Baden-Baden's casino is different, I told her. Its gaming rooms are quite serious. Why don't we just walk around and take in the scene? Denyse felt a surge of confidence and was convinced she couldn't lose. I wished her luck. We set our gaming budget at 50 DM each, and off she went. As for myself, I decided to just stand there watching the action at the tables. Observing competitors' faces is an experience in itself.

The next thing I knew, Denyse was standing next to me, whispering, "How much do you still have?"

It took me a few seconds to understand what her question really meant. Her 50 DM was already gone. Her certain victory? Not so certain, apparently. I gave her my money with a silent smile before she disappeared again.

We enjoyed our evening tremendously, and of course the casino always wins! I would discover this truth again many years later when I lived for a while in the city of sin, also known as Las Vegas.

Eating freshly picked cherries in the southern area of Lake Konstanz, also called Bodensee, helped soothe our minor losses. The region borders Austria on one side and Switzerland on the other, and its mild climate even in winter makes it one of the most fertile fruit-growing areas in the country, hence its nickname, the Früchtekammer of Germany.

The end of our trip brought another shock, though a more pleasant one than the loss of our itinerary or the disappointment at Checkpoint Charlie. After spending a day across the Austrian border in St. Johann and Innsbruck, we finished our tour of the south before heading back toward northern Germany and the city of Stuttgart.

In Stuttgart, two unscheduled things occurred. Denyse decided to go to a hairdresser and walked out an hour later having cut her beautiful long hair. She now sported a very short haircut. The style looked sexy and chic on her and accented her features in a lovely way. And later that day, we found ourselves at a jewelry shop, buying a pair of engagement rings.

Denyse might have expected something like this to happen on this trip, but to me, this decision came as a total surprise.

While I do remember discussing a potential engagement someday, I also remember feeling still too young and inexperienced to make any big decisions. Not to mention that I had no idea what I was going to do about my career. I felt smitten with Denyse and had been since the day we met. We had managed to spend more than a week traveling around Germany without getting on each other's nerves. Spending time together came easily and naturally to us. The more I got to know Denyse, the more excited I felt to learn more about her and share time together.

But buying rings? Already? What conversation that day had led us to march directly into the jewelry store? My memory of this part of the afternoon is a blur. Perhaps the hair salon and the ring shop were on the same street.

I wonder if Denyse decided to use her famous casino skills to take a gamble on me that day, steering me into the ring store as she walked out of the salon with her bold new cut. If so, I hope she felt better about the eventual outcome of her Stuttgart gamble than she did about her Baden-Baden casino results.

We were both naive, barely adults, and our spontaneous decision to get engaged felt bewildering. But no question about it, we were in love. The ring-buying, crazy as it was, seemed like a properly grand finale to our fantastic adventure around Germany.

If only my career prospects felt fantastic too. I tried to ignore my creeping anxiety as I prepared to say goodbye to Denyse.

Back On My Feet

My doctor called as soon as I returned to Hannover. I now had his official permission to return to work. Excellent news, except I didn't have a job, nor did I have a career.

I could no longer delay the inevitable. I needed a plan, a new direction for my life. I racked my brain day after day, trying to discover another career passion lurking in the recesses of my mind, a new ambition I could nurture with the proper training and a little patience. Whatever path I chose, I would be starting over at my age, two years shy of thirty.

But the more I contemplated new paths for myself, the more I realized I still had only one idea: hotels.

I knew hotels. I had a basic understanding of how they functioned. Working in a hotel would allow me to leverage the experience I'd gained so far into other opportunities beyond the kitchen. With any luck, I could grow faster in a hotel position than I could if I started over in an entirely new industry.

My list of references already included a few of the best hotels in this part of Europe, so the hospitality industry seemed like a reasonable place to start on my new path. But I needed to gather up my courage to send out job applications all over again, this time with very little momentum behind me. I had been away from work for so long.

Another problem: Hannover was a fairly small town, with a population of only around 300,000. Despite its historical significance and its elegant avenues, the city had mostly provincial hotels, which could never offer the experience and references of a more renowned property. There was just one exception, the InterContinental.

Who knows, I thought, the city's one respected brand-name hotel might offer career opportunities I didn't even know about yet. So I got to work crafting an application and sent it off to human resources, bracing myself to get completely ignored.

My list of past employers must have caught someone's attention because I received an immediate invitation to come in for an interview. Dressed in my best suit and holding a copy of my references and pictures of my work, I went to meet Mr. Rudi Münster , the resident manager of the hotel.

Mr. Münster sounded impressed with my job experiences. But then he sat quietly for a few moments, looking pensive, and announced that hiring me would be very risky for him. Kitchen staff around the world used notoriously rough language, and he assumed I did too, considering the work I'd been doing so far. Kitchen language does not fit in with the tone he aimed to set at the InterContinental, he informed me gravely, looking me squarely in the eyes. "In a high-pressure job," he went on, "you might think there is no time for sweet words, but profane language will not be tolerated."

The way I talked to him during my interview should have set him at ease, but he needed a promise that I would speak with the utmost politeness and professionalism at all times. When I told him what he wanted to hear, he made me an unexpected offer on the spot. Would I like to start immediately as assistant to the chief concierge?

I knew next to nothing about this job. Except that concierges supposedly make lots of money, more than even the highest-ranking employees in a hotel. Well, surely I could learn how to do this job. I thanked him for the offer and accepted without hesitation.

It did not take long to discover that the rumors were true, even for assistant concierges. The concierge desk staff got tips for everything we did for a customer. Everything. If a guest had to post a letter and the stamp cost 1.20 DM, he typically gave us 1.50. At the time, concierges took care of many tasks that the desk doesn't do anymore. We handled phone calls, shipped packages, booked car rentals, and did every imaginable errand, beyond the restaurant and theater reservations that concierges are known for. But we handled those too and profited handsomely.

Anytime we went to restaurants, our dinner bill disappeared as soon as the management found out we were concierges at the InterContinental. For guests' theater tickets, we always booked with venues that we knew would give us a bonus.

Since it was common practice for customers to tip a concierge who helped them, we never held out our hand. If they tipped, they tipped, and if they didn't, they didn't. But usually, they did. We also had other ways of collecting.

One lesson I learned right away is that concierges are known to look out for their own financial interests—despite the cost to the guest and the disadvantage to the hotel—or at least they were in that era. A concierge can make a bundle of money, not only through honest tips but also by taking advantage of customers. We used to increase our revenue by doing things that were not very nice to do with customers, for example telling them that shipping a package to the US was more expensive than it actually was.

We also developed mutually beneficial relationships with local businesses. If a guest wanted to rent a car, he came to us so we could handle the rental for him. The hotel had arranged an agreement with Avis, so every car rental had to be booked through that agency. The management assumed that the hotel would receive commissions for every guest rental. But our concierge desk figured out that if we booked the cars through Avis in another city outside Hannover, we could circumvent the agreement while still appearing to honor it, and the commissions would go straight into our pockets.

Eventually, the executives wised up and created a more detailed contract with the car rental company so that every transaction would have to go through them. But if the head honchos thought they could outsmart the concierges, forget about it. The concierge desk always found a way to take a cut.

After six months in this job, I hadn't even touched my salary yet. I had no idea what my boss at the concierge desk made, but the saying that the chief concierge makes more than the general manager seemed resoundingly true.

While I enjoyed interacting directly with customers all day for the first time in my career, and I certainly enjoyed the money, I also learned how not to run a concierge desk and how not to cheat a customer. Beyond these insights, the job also gave me the chance to build my network.

My French language skills and my limited school English benefited me, especially during the annual Hannover Fair, the biggest industrial fair in the world at the time.

Making connections and learning how to navigate the shrewd ways of the concierge desk would come in handy many years later—although I did not yet know how.

A New Beginning

One of the most important rules in the hospitality business, or any business, is to be nice to everyone you work with. He or she could be your boss someday. I already knew this, but I didn't realize quite how true it was until I met Wilfried Schrader, the new food and beverage director at the InterContinental.

Wilfried, a year older than I, had apprenticed at the Georgs Palast in Hannover at the same time I did, and now his career was taking off. But to improve his department's performance, he urgently needed to hire a chief steward, responsible for keeping the back of the house immaculate and for cleaning and overseeing the inventory of china, glass, and silver. The job is an important link between the restaurant service and the kitchen, and Wilfried felt that my background would be beneficial for this position. He offered me an internal transfer from the concierge desk to his department.

Since I had just completed six months at the concierge desk, the timing sounded perfect to Wilfried. I don't know if he had any idea what kind of money I would be giving up to make the switch, but a job in the food and beverage department didn't seem like a bad idea to me as a long-term plan. As a short-term plan, though, I was in no hurry to leave the tips behind.

The present chief steward, Michael Maas, was about to leave, so Wilfried needed someone right away. But as I learned through the grapevine, no one wanted the chief steward job. And as I experienced myself much later, this position is one of the most difficult to fill in any food and beverage department. Wilfried had struggled to fill the position once Michael resigned. Not only did the job involve constantly cleaning and shining the china, glass, and silver and keeping control of the inventory, but the chief steward had to take orders from every cook in the kitchen. And every waiter felt entitled to boss him around.

"Steward, I need teaspoons. Steward, why are the plates not refilled? Steward, can you send somebody to clean the mess here? Steward, the ice-cube machine is not working!" And so on.

Wilfried knew this, so to talk me into saying yes, he promised that this position would make an excellent starting point for an eventual leadership role in food and beverage. "If you haven't worked as a steward, you don't qualify to work as an F&B director," he told me, "because you don't know what's happening at the back of the house."

A food and beverage director, huh? I was flattered to hear Wilfried mention this. I could picture myself in that role—if not quite yet, then not too long from now. Wilfried's argument did the trick. Within a few days, I had exchanged my dark concierge suit and golden crossed keys for a white coat, bid a silent farewell to the tips, and started my job in the steward department.

I will never forget my meeting with Michael Maas for the handover of steward duties. He stood in front of me, calmly explaining to me the importance of hygiene and cleanliness in the kitchen, then he suddenly grabbed a full bucket and flung the water into a corner behind the dishwasher. He fetched a broom, scrubbed the already clean floor, and said, "You see, this is the way it needs to be done. Good luck!" And off he went.

The cleaning staff kept the floor sparkling at all times, so Michael's gesture seemed a waste. What did he intend to show me? That spotlessly clean is never clean enough? Or was he just teaching me how to mop? I never asked. What I took away from his performance is that the floor needed to stay so immaculate, you could eat dinner off it at any time.

I later learned that Michael had resigned from the chief steward position to take a job as a back of the house manager at the Kempinski Hotel in Berlin, which turned out to be nothing but a glorified title for the same position he just left. But on the way up the career ladder, titles matter. Michael later became the COO of the Kempinski Hotel Corporation.

Little did I know at this moment that Michael would later reappear in my life and help me at the lowest point of my career. It would be the second time in my life that the saying "Be nice to everybody because you never know" proved true.

On my first day as the head steward, I discovered exactly how little respect the position garnered from the hotel's employees. Sure, it was crucial to the operations of the food and beverage department, but it was seen as a custodial position. Which it essentially was.

Here I was in 1968, about to turn twenty-nine and coming off nine years of working in some of the best kitchens in Europe—and all I did now, all day long, was clean and scrub. I washed pots and pans, cleaned the china and glassware, and even polished all the silverware myself.

But I reflected on the success story of Conrad Hilton, who started as a dishwasher and made it all the way to the top of his field, founding and running one of the biggest hotel corporations worldwide. I decided to brush off the other employees' scorn, silent but noticeable.

Against all odds, I enjoyed this job very much, and more so every day. I found it satisfying to guarantee perfectly clean and polished equipment to the kitchen and restaurants and to find new and better ways to accomplish my responsibilities.

I decided to do everything I could to change the image of the chief steward. After all, every job is what you make of it. If you want to make it a dishwashing job, well then, it's a dishwashing job. If you're willing to think a few steps ahead of the role you currently occupy, you can see your job responsibilities in a new way and strategize about your next career moves.

The chief steward job can provide much more than just a link between kitchen and service. It's the heart of a successful operation, and if this heart is not beating properly, the whole food and beverage department can collapse. Yes, my job did involve washing lots of dishes and polishing utensils. But it also meant managing inventories and ensuring that all the departments had what they needed exactly when they needed it in order to run smoothly and efficiently.

The job also meant knowing how to handle the daily teaspoon crisis. For whatever reason, teaspoons in professional kitchens are always vanishing. Customers either take them as souvenirs, or waiters accidentally throw them out with the garbage when they're scraping food into the trash. When that happens, I've noticed that waiters will rarely if ever go into the garbage and dig out a teaspoon. They simply don't care. So I instructed our steward staff to hunt for teaspoons in the bins after the waiters finish scraping. It's shocking how many I and my staff found that way, twenty or thirty teaspoons a day that would have been lost otherwise.

Every task on the chief steward's list had more to it than meets the eye. Running the dishwasher, for instance, meant not only cleaning dishes, but also knowing how to stack the conveyor belt to its maximum capacity to limit the consumption of detergent and water.

My past culinary experience came in handy too, helping me develop a mutually respectful relationship with the executive chef and the kitchen brigade. This rapport helped us all do our jobs more smoothly. We understood each other, and I got the feeling they appreciated never having to explain anything to me. I instantly sensed what they needed and when.

Before I took over the department, the cooks almost never cleaned up after themselves. And if they burned or spilled something, they assumed one of the stewards would come along to clean it. Because of my background in high-end kitchens around Europe, I managed to convince the cooks of the importance of working clean to keep the InterContinental's standards competitive. Bit by bit, they started taking care of their own stations. The steward staff did still have to clean up after cooks as needed, but this system turned out to be more efficient for everyone.

I also improved on the rampant loss of equipment through better inventory management of china, glass, and silverware. By taking a close look at every aspect of the department and making it more efficient, I was able to reduce expenses by 40 percent.

The numbers made Wilfried Schrader look good, but building an effective, unified team brought me even more satisfaction. Training and developing every member of my staff, most of whom had minimal education or work experience, felt like the most important part of my job.

People who sought jobs as stewards often had no other chance of employment. My team included many women from Yugoslavia, hardworking immigrants who had left their country during the rule of Tito, whose government, unlike most Communist nations at the time, allowed citizens to travel and work throughout Western Europe. We also had guest workers from other countries in Europe or elsewhere who could speak no German but who wanted to work hard to start a new life far away from home. Some of the staff had physical or mental disabilities.

Uniting this diverse mix of people into a functioning, productive team was an enormous challenge, one I enjoyed and found invaluable to my own learning process. I had to identify myself with each member of the staff, regardless of any differences we had between us, and make everyone feel like a crucial part of the team.

One important lesson I learned is that a sense of ownership makes all employees, myself as much as anyone, feel committed to their work in a profound and personal way. I tried to instill in all my team members the value of their own individual contribution to our overall effort and encourage them to take pride in their work. Without my having to remind them, my staff started staying past the end of their shifts until their job was completely done and until they'd left their area perfectly clean. Our steward department soon posted the lowest absentee rate in the entire hotel.

Looking back at my time as a chief steward, I not only liked the job, but it was perhaps the most gratifying time of my career. The results of working hard and making good decisions showed up instantly and measurably. The impact of building a strong team was reflected in our department's performance as well as in the job satisfaction of each member of our team. I learned every day that if you respect your staff and make them feel successful in their work, they will pay you and the organization back many times over.

After all, as a manager, you can only be as effective as your staff allows you to be. For myself and for any aspiring leader, this is not just an important lesson. It's also a dire warning.

BY BY FORD TAUNUS, WELCOME CIROEN TOURING GERMANY

DRIVER & CAR A PERFECT FIT CRUISING ALONG THE RHINE RIVER

STOPOVER IN HANNOVER

RETURN AFTER A LONG TRIP

Looking Forward **09**

A Culinary Career Is Ending

A young chef aspiring to culinary stardom would do well to earn a master chef diploma. If you work hard and successfully complete the degree, you can eventually land a leadership role in a prestigious kitchen.

In my case, the entire process happened in reverse.

I had already risen to a coveted chef de partie role at top hotels in Europe, and I'd reached a level of stardom at Fauchon. But then my cooking career abruptly ended, never to return. And it was at this point that I decided to enroll in a master chef degree program.

Why? On the face of it, this decision doesn't make much sense.

But I had my reasons. The first one was pride, I have to admit. It was difficult for me to face the fact that my years of dedication to a culinary career, and all the suffering and learning I had experienced along the way, all the successes I had built up, could suddenly evaporate. Just like that and with nothing to show for it.

The more I debated my next move, the more I realized I could not just give up my love for cooking without bringing my kitchen career to a respectable end. If I could seal this era of my life with an advanced degree from a culinary institution, I could bid farewell to it and embark on the next chapter with dignity.

In the spring of 1968, I came across an advertisement for the master chef diploma at the Dortmund Hotel School. Dortmund was respected for its advanced curriculum in hospitality, and in recent years, it had managed to position itself as the leading hotel school in Germany, ahead of other traditional programs such as Heidelberg's. A diploma from a school like Dortmund would be a feather in my cap. As a bonus, I could complete the program without disrupting my life too much.

My boss, Wilfried Schrader, agreed to let me go for four weeks if I earned a spot, mainly because this would take care of the overdue vacation days and accumulated time off that he owed me.

But first, I needed to get accepted into the program. The application required proof of a completed apprenticeship and a minimum of five years of professional experience. I hoped the high honors I'd earned as an apprentice and my outstanding references from leading hotels would give me a strong chance of getting in.

Fortunately, a thick envelope soon arrived in the mail, and I began making arrangements for my month in Dortmund, about a two-hour train ride from Hannover.

Ironically, as a master chef in training, I'd be spending very little time in the kitchen. The school had accepted its students based on the fact that we already knew how to cook, so to earn the master diploma we'd need to prove that we could do much more. Our program focused primarily on accounting, human resources, and general management, and as a result, most of us had to study endless hours every week. I was no exception.

All this study soon sparked a light bulb in my mind. This diploma was not just about crowning my culinary career before burying it in an early grave. It was also about setting up a basic foundation for a future career. I could not yet foresee what shape my new life would take, but it would almost certainly involve the skills I was learning at school. As chief steward at the InterContinental, I was already in charge of running a department, but this program would lay a firmer groundwork for a management position.

Still, every student had to submit to a cooking test before the session ended. This was, after all, a master chef program, as easy as it might have been to forget that while sitting under a mound of management and accounting books. After passing the various theoretical tests, it was time to enter the kitchen for the first time. Our final assignment: preparing the menu for a gala dinner.

This was the moment of truth. The examination board knew we'd each had extensive training in the kitchen, but now was the time to prove it. Despite all my years in professional kitchens, I felt nervous.

My part of the exam involved making a clear bouillon of beef, known as a consommé, a project that would pose no problem for me under normal circumstances. But normal circumstances do not include creating a perfect specimen under a harsh spotlight, while inspectors observe you closely, waiting for a reason to criticize any move you make.

The traditional first step in making a consommé is to prepare a mixture of ground lean beef, egg whites, fresh vegetables, and ice cubes. You then mix this with the cold beef stock and stir it on low heat until the bouillon turns clear. Depending on the heat applied, the process can take a long time and doesn't allow you to leave the pot for longer than a few moments since the bouillon needs to be stirred continuously and should never reach a boil. This is the classic, old-fashioned method, one that apprentices learn and trade schools have taught for generations.

But everyone knows that chefs benefit from time spent cooking abroad, precisely so they can learn different ways of doing things. Alternate approaches often work better than the classic methods that chefs learn back home.

That's why for my examination, I decided to apply the technique I had learned from Mr. Bertolini, the executive chef at the Metropole Hotel. I had used his method successfully many times in Monte Carlo, and I preferred it to the traditional way. Anyway, I figured it doesn't really matter what technique I use. What counts is the end result.

Mr. Bertolini's way of making a consommé uses the same ingredients and preparation as the classic version, except that you add hot instead of cold beef stock to the pot. After introducing the hot stock, you stir the mixture only once, very lightly, and then leave it alone at low heat. No waiting by the stove, no constant stirring. The cloudier the mixture looks at the beginning, the clearer the consommé will turn out at the end, Mr. Bertolini used to say, and his method worked perfectly every single time I'd used it since.

Remembering those Metropole days filled me with confidence as my exam time approached, although I still felt slightly nervous simply because I was about to take a test. I started by preparing the beef mixture and adding the hot stock. Then I stirred everything together, stepped away, and waited for the clarification to take its course.

It didn't take long before the first exam supervisor showed up at my station and asked me in a brusque voice what I was doing. I explained that I'd learned a better way to make a consommé during my travels abroad, and this was why the contents of my pot might look a bit different from the others.

The supervisor shook his head disapprovingly and walked away. I assumed he was asking himself how I would dare change a proven tradition, a French tradition no less.

"The cloudier it is at the beginning, the clearer it will be at the end." I summoned Mr. Bertolini's voice into my head. I needed the reassurance. Glancing inside my pot, I could see that things looked cloudy indeed. Very cloudy.

Within minutes, every single supervisor in the kitchen had visited my station, walked around my pot, and left with a tight-lipped smile on his face. Seeing them all standing together, whispering and pointing, made my heart sink. My consommé was still stubbornly cloudy. I watched my chances of earning a diploma vanish with every passing moment.

Forcing myself not to stare at the pot continuously, I waited another few seconds then went over to take another look. The consommé still looked cloudy. Should it still be this cloudy by now? I started to seriously doubt Mr. Bertolini's wisdom. Perhaps his method worked most of the time. But it wasn't working now. I had no idea what to do.

The supervisors kept circling around my pot like vultures around their prey, clearly enjoying their chance to prove a rebellious young upstart wrong. A cold shiver ran through my body. I could barely breathe.

Now the mixture in my pot started to bubble. I was still keeping my distance to avoid having to see the disaster again, but I edged over to the pot to cast a quick glance. I had started to prepare what I would say to the supervisors, and to my boss Wilfried, when I failed the exam and went home without a diploma.

The first thing I noticed was a cluster of beef and egg whites forming like a raft at the top. I took a closer look and saw the floating raft surrounded by a golden broth, clear as a sunny summer morning. I couldn't believe it. The clarification had worked.

Wow. Thank you, Mr. Bertolini.

This time I walked away quietly, trying to suppress a smile. I didn't want to look too confident just yet. I couldn't wait for the supervisors to approach my pot again, which they did soon after. It had been their main source of entertainment all morning.

Watching from a distance, I saw them looking at the pot, then looking at each other. Their gestures of surprise explained everything. I couldn't resist walking by, and in a respectful tone, I asked if they had any questions. I heard a muffled "no" and some mumbles, as they walked off, still shaking their heads in disbelief.

When the exam results came out, I saw my name listed as one of two students who graduated with honors, a very clear, consommé-clear triumph! I wouldn't be surprised if the story of my consommé is still circulating in the corridors of the Dortmund Hotel School.

Upon my return to the InterContinental in Hannover, I received a hearty congratulations from Harald Hackbarth, the executive chef. A chef without a master diploma, welcoming back a chief steward just crowned master of the kitchen. Things couldn't get much stranger than that. I wondered whether this new state of affairs would create tensions between us and make my job as a chief steward even more difficult.

My Second Visit to Beirut

It's rare that you come back to a job after a leave of absence then get to turn around and take a vacation. But as it happened, I'd chosen a lucky time to return to the InterContinental.

Not long after I had resumed my routine in the steward department, it was time to prepare for the Hannover Fair, the world's biggest industrial event. The hotel management encouraged employees to take any remaining accumulated days off now, before the fair began, since more days would certainly accrue during the hectic event. I was only too happy to comply.

I knew exactly where I wanted to go on my short vacation. It had been a while since my first visit to Beirut in 1965, and many important life events had happened since then. Not only had Denyse's father passed away, but her sister Mouna had given birth to a baby girl. And, of course, Denyse and I had gotten engaged in secret. We needed to tell the family our news.

My letter to Denyse suggesting a Beirut visit received a far more enthusiastic response this time, so off I flew for a few days in April.

Mouna's husband, Alain, picked me up at the airport, and even though we hadn't spent much time together during my last trip, he had no trouble recognizing the solo traveler with the blond hair and the dazed expression wandering through the arrivals hall. The flight was only a few hours, but I arrived in Beirut exhausted after a few long days at work and very much in need of some Mediterranean sunshine.

Denyse had made a reservation for me at the Hotel Alexandre, a modern and well-appointed if somewhat generic-looking property conveniently located near her family's home. Alain dropped me off with a promise to call and come pick me up after I'd settled in.

An hour later, my telephone had yet to ring. I wondered if something had gone wrong. I tried to distract myself by looking out the window to see what I could glimpse of the affluent Achrafieh neighborhood outside, just a few minutes from Denyse's home.

After what felt like an eternity, the telephone buzzed. Alain was on the line. Apparently, he had been trying to call for some time and asking to speak to Mr. Fishermann. The operator kept insisting there was no such person at the hotel.

"I dropped him off myself at the hotel!" Alain insisted. "He must be there!"

"No, sir, the receptionist answered, "we do not have a guest with the name of Fishermann."

After a series of nervous calls and questions from Alain, the operator asked him, "What nationality is this guest of yours?"

"He is German," Alain answered impatiently.

After putting him on hold, the receptionist came back and said, "We have one German guest who just checked in, but his name is not Fischermann, but Tischmann. Peter Tischmann."

"Yes, that's him!" Alain answered. Tischmann, Fishermann. For him it was all the same.

Soon I was in the car with Alain, en route to meet Denyse and Mouna at a café near Raouche, the famous pigeon rock formation off the seaside Corniche boulevard.

As we all sat enjoying the fresh air from the Mediterranean, Mouna turned to me and said, "Congratulations, On."

It took me a split second to understand what had just happened. Who is On?

Oh, it's me.

Denyse had been using the French impersonal pronoun "on" to refer to the time she spent with me. When Denyse talked to her family about her vacation, it was always "On" instead of "Peter and I." Mouna was fully aware who On was, and what I'd thought was our hush-hush news had not been a secret at all, at least not from Mouna.

Well, at least one member of her family knew the purpose of my trip: to officially ask Denyse's mother for permission to marry her daughter.

"Don't worry, I will prepare the ground," Mouna said as we sat at the café. I felt relieved to hear this. At least I would walk into the meeting with Denyse's mother knowing that she was ready to hear an interesting request from me. She'd probably guess what that was before I even opened my mouth, and with any luck, I wouldn't need to get so nervous about it.

With Easter approaching, we felt the timing was just right. Denyse invited me to her home to meet with her mother and officially ask for her daughter's hand. I arrived at the apartment with flowers for the family and was led directly to the Chaise Maurice, a mid-century modern chair popular in certain Lebanese living rooms of the era.

The problem with this type of chair, with its slatted wooden sides and its back made out of rolled leather cylinders, is that it's a little too big and far too deep. As you sit, the chair sinks lower than you might expect, plunging your bottom down into the upholstery and sticking your feet up in the air.

Needless to say, it's not the most comfortable way to sit as you're facing an already uncomfortable situation. I looked up to find three women sitting opposite me—Denyse, Mouna, and their mother—awaiting what I had to say.

So what did I say? I discussed every imaginable subject. Everything other than the topic at hand. We talked about Lebanon, the sunshine, the weather, the food, the traffic, the history. And meanwhile I sat there, glaring at Mouna, wondering what "Je vais preparer le terrain" actually meant.

Absolutely no ground had been prepared, as far as I could tell. But Mouna looked at me and didn't react. I shot her another sharply inquisitive glance. I had no idea when to bring up the subject out of the blue. Was their mother ready to hear something like this?

As I sat there, sweating in the chair, Mouna turned to her mother and said, "Mama, Peter wants to ask you something."

Was this preparing the ground? Not in my book. But it would have to do. All three women sat looking at me, eyes wide, ears open, waiting for what might happen next. I felt as if a bucket of ice-cold water had just been emptied over my head. I wanted to disappear.

A few moments later, I managed to sputter out my question, heart pounding. The reaction was not at all what I had expected.

Everyone immediately started crying, as I sat there confused, wondering if I had done something wrong.

I sat awkwardly for what felt like an eternity, until Denyse's mother finally began to speak. "Peter, I hope you know what you are doing," she said to me, still sobbing, "because Denyse doesn't know how to cook. She doesn't even know how to cook an egg. As a matter of fact, she has never been in a kitchen!"

"Don't worry," I replied. "I can show her." The issue was of no importance to me whatsoever. I was just relieved that Denyse's mother had no stronger objections to our union.

It later turned out that Denyse actually loved to cook and bake, and she created the most spectacular dinners when we hosted guests at our home.

Mouna's "ground preparing" services were no longer needed the following weekend, when we packed into a car to drive to Hasroun, a mountain village where Denyse's aunt and godmother Odette had a summer house. It was Easter weekend, a convenient opportunity to inform the gathered family that we were engaged. As it turned out, the news had already reached the village before us, and we exited the car straight into a flurry of hugs and kisses.

Odette insisted that for the occasion, we must all go immediately to the local church and pray. So we put on our best outfits and rushed to the church, only to find the doors closed.

Was this a message for me from up above? As I would find out a year later, Lebanese churches and I don't get along very well.

The Culinary Olympics

Back home in Hannover, I had to prepare for another nerve-racking challenge.

Every four years, chefs from all over the world met in Frankfurt am Main to show off their talents in the Culinary Olympics. I had competed once before, during my days working at the Georgs Palast, but back then, it was Mr. Klapproth who was in charge of our culinary team, not me.

This time I wasn't supposed to be in charge either, as Mr. Hackbarth was the executive chef. But when the InterContinental Hotel management decided to send a team and appointed him, he turned to me for help since I'd participated before. Next thing I knew, the entire competition rested squarely on my shoulders. He was delighted to let me relieve him of the responsibility and develop the program, select the team, and finalize all the logistics myself.

I would've been well within my rights to refuse. My job as chief steward kept me busy, arguably too busy to take on a competition like this.

But in truth, I wanted to do it. The Culinary Olympics would give me a rare chance to return to my roots and to pay a brief visit to the parallel career path I'd been forced to abandon.

Mr. Hackbarth helped me in handpicking the most talented members of his kitchen staff, and I worked with them day and night for weeks to prepare. We created sample plates showcasing decorative arrangements of salmon, roast beef, and assorted cold buffet dishes. Seeing what we were up to, nearly the entire brigade wanted to participate, but there was only space for the few members we selected. The others stood on the sidelines with dignity, cheering us on as we worked long shifts to get ready.

Because my specialty was the cold kitchen, the InterContinental signed up to compete only in the event involving decorated show plates. We had no additional challenges to face and no race against the clock beyond creating our plates and getting them to the exhibition hall in Frankfurt on time. I felt at ease with this plan. I could prepare for it without neglecting my own chief steward duties for too long.

The catch was that we had to transport our show plates already assembled because, in Frankfurt, we'd only have time to add some finishing touches before displaying our work for the judges. As it turned out, our biggest challenge wasn't the pressure of creating the actual show plates. It was getting them to the competition in one piece, without disturbing the carefully arranged decorations.

Frankfurt is two hundred miles south of Hannover. What if we hit a bump in the road?

After researching every possible mode of transport, we decided to rent a refrigerated truck big enough to fit all the plates side by side. We covered the entire bottom of the truck with old mattresses from the hotel to cushion any shocks.

We left the hotel at midnight the night before so we could drive slowly and arrive by our 9:00 a.m. deadline for displaying the plates and still have time to do any necessary repairs. The rest of our team drove in a separate car so they could get to Frankfurt ahead of us and prepare our assigned display table.

After six hours of crawling along the Autobahn at thirty miles per hour, watching every car pass us by, we finally arrived at the exhibition grounds. We nervously opened the back of the truck, unwrapped the plates, and gently removed them from their soft bed on top of the mattresses. To our great relief, every showpiece arrived in perfect condition, no repairs needed. Absolutely none!

The hall was abuzz as competitors arranged their booths and judges walked around the hall, evaluating each of the international teams that arrived from all over the world. For our category, we had to present a show plate serving eight people in each of three subjects—for example, one plate featuring salmon, one starring lobster, and one displaying rack of veal—as well as an hors d'oeuvres plate for ten people.

As the judges approached our display table, ready to rate us on criteria such as originality and presentation, my heart beat faster. I could tell our entire team was nervous. We had worked many long nights to prepare our plates, and we faced stiff competition here in Frankfurt. Earlier, I had taken a quick walk through the hall and seen the many beautiful show plates the other teams had created, displays of outstanding creativity and presentation that were certainly equal to if not better than what we had prepared.

Mr. Hackbarth had placed his trust in me, knowing that our performance here would reflect on the quality of his team. The last thing I wanted to do was to let him down.

Try as I might, I could not guess what the judges thought as they looked over our show plates. Each of the judges kept a perfect poker face the entire time, as they stood there for what seemed an eternity, peering at our plates and taking notes. We would not learn the results until later in the day.

Hours later, our patience paid off, as did every minute of the hard work we'd put into the competition. The Culinary Olympics turned out to be a tremendous success for our hotel and team. We returned to Hannover with eight gold medals and six silver ones. The news made it all the way to the InterContinental head office in New York City, and the president of the company sent every team member a personal letter of congratulations.

I felt grateful to Mr. Hackbarth for the chance to oversee the Olympic team. But unbeknownst to me, the awards had put me in an optimal position for a turn of good fortune that was headed my way.

Joining Steigenberger Hotels

Looking back at the hotels I've worked in during my life, some are places I would be glad to return to, and others are not. The Frankfurter Hof is in the first category. Opened in 1876, the graceful cream-colored stone building, with its arched entryway and lush courtyard, its elegant but understated interior, is a place that rings with happy memories of my early hotel days, those challenging but still relatively smooth years of my career.

The chance to revisit the Frankfurter Hof came up in the fall of 1968, soon after I had completed two years at the InterContinental in Hannover. By then, I was more than ready to move on. The chief steward job had taught me valuable lessons in management and back-of-the-house inventory control, and the Olympic medals had reinstated my confidence in the culinary training I'd let lapse since my illness.

I immediately sent in my application as soon as I saw a job listing by the Steigenberger Hotel Corporation, owner of the Frankfurter Hof, for a food and beverage specialist in the company's production and planning department. I wasn't sure what exactly this would involve, but I knew the company also owned other historic hotels throughout Germany and around Frankfurt and had one under construction at the Frankfurt am Main airport.

From what I could tell, the job sounded like an excellent opportunity to strengthen my training in management and food and beverage operations without having to take on any hands-on kitchen duties.

I have no idea how many other people applied. The job, on closer inspection, was going to involve mountains of bureaucratic paperwork, tasks that might scare away applicants with a culinary background. It was probably a hard position to fill. What I do know is that as soon as I applied, I received a call to come in for an interview. The strong reference from my earlier work at the Frankfurter Hof probably didn't hurt either.

This role was certainly not for everyone, as the interview confirmed. The company had an unusual way of doing business. While each restaurant had its own manager, the menu planning and administrative duties were all centralized, to avoid waste and non-productive time.

Whoever did this job would need to manage and improve the elaborate system for organizing the bulk orders and preparations for all of the company's restaurants. Based in the company's main office at the Frankfurter Hof, the position would involve lots of work in the field to test and implement new procedures. It was certainly a departure from the work I had done so far, but the role called for someone with the unique mix of experiences I had managed to gather. I was intrigued.

I had a hunch that helping to develop and streamline the company's system would give me fresh insights on management and expose me to corporate responsibility at a higher level than before. As long as I could stomach the endless amounts of paperwork and learn my way around the company's electronic data-tracking system, this job could be of great advantage for my future career path. I made a strong case for myself in the interview and landed an offer, to which I said yes immediately.

This time my job didn't come with free housing. As part of the management team now, I was on my own as far as finding a place to live near the Frankfurter Hof. I gave my notice at the InterContinental in the early weeks of 1969 and began plotting my move to Frankfurt.

Newspapers were full of housing listings at the time, and one could choose where to live without competing with hundreds of other applicants who had to battle like sharks over every apartment for rent. Within a week, I had rented a furnished room in Frankfurt's centrally located Westend, a business district near my new job and a short walk away from the Alte Oper opera house. Parking was plentiful around there too, and I could safely leave my car on the street day or night.

Adjusting to my new job was another story. I had to learn to use a new system called EDV, an electronic data processing method that assisted the company with its centralized planning, at least when it was working properly. Considered high-tech at the time, the system would seem archaic by modern standards. I had to gather information cards from restaurant managers at each hotel, filled with data relating to their own menus and food inventory, then feed each card into a reader, and print it out on a large fifteen-inch by twenty-inch sheet.

All the managers hated this system. It forced them to do reams of paperwork to benefit the main office, but they couldn't see any immediate value for their own day-to-day work. And right they were. The reports we generated at headquarters arrived much too late to help the managers make any meaningful decisions to impact their operations in the short term. The whole system seemed hopelessly abstract, but I had to convince the managers to have faith.

The truth was that even for the corporate team in the main office, the only immediate advantage was that we could consolidate the results from all the hotels and restaurants onto one sheet, rather than on individual papers. We still had a very limited ability to make decisions in the short term. But the data collection proved to be a wonderful tool for establishing statistics.

Eventually, all that data-gathering paid off, allowing us to make a major move which would benefit all the freestanding restaurants as well as the hotels' food and beverage operations equally. The company made a revolutionary decision to open a central butcher shop that could supply the hotels and restaurants with prepacked portions of meat for their menus, transforming the way every kitchen planned its production.

As we had hoped, the central butcher shop soon turned into the heart of our system. It allowed for perfect inventory and production control, saved managers countless headaches, and helped the company generate significantly higher profits. Later, in my future corporate leadership role at Sheraton, I would look back on the Steigenberger company's data innovations as a key part of my executive training.

Thanks to the increased efficiency and continuous growth, the Steigenberger corporate office decided to hire one additional person to assist us in overseeing the butcher shop and dealing with the additional administrative workload.

On the Monday morning when we had just switched on the new system, a funny-looking gentleman in checkered trousers, two-tone shoes, a white belt, and a Native American-style bolo tie walked into our office and introduced himself in a loud, cheerful voice.

"Hi, everybody, I'm Rudi Rodenbach from Chicago. Pleased to be here!"

Everyone looked up, surprised to see this man come in dressed like he just walked off a golf course.

As unmistakably American as he seemed, Rudi was actually a German through and through, born near the Black Forest and now returning to his country of origin after many years in the United States.

Rudi's initial presentation took us aback, but he turned out to be a real force in the office, a charismatic guy who quickly won over the whole team. He also became an important person in my own life.

RECEIVING THE KÜCHENMEISTER DIPLOMA

THE DAY OF OUR OFFICIAL ENGAGEMENT IN HASROUN

Wedding Bells 10

A Big Decision

Now that I had a career and a future again, I felt more comfortable discussing a wedding date with Denyse. We knew we would get married from the moment her mother approved our engagement, but I needed a job with prospects to give me the confidence to go ahead.

We chose August 3, 1969, as our wedding day, giving ourselves a few months to get everything ready for the big event. Fortunately for me, Denyse's family would be handling all the planning. All I had to do was find elegant invitation cards, order white Paphiopedilum orchids for Denyse's wedding bouquet, and get myself to the church in Beirut on the right day at the right time.

In Lebanon, a country with strong family ties, a daughter's wedding is a huge event. The whole family springs into action. Alice, Denyse's maternal aunt and the youngest of nine children, was the self-appointed leader of the pack among Denyse's relatives. Everyone called her the General because she couldn't resist any opportunity to take command. Since Alice never married, she had plenty of time to involve herself in anything and everything. Sometimes too much so. Denyse found herself waging multiple tug-of-war struggles with Alice so as not to lose complete control over her own wedding.

As August 3 approached, the family got busy planning every last detail. Denyse supervised the arrangements for the cocktail reception at the Beau Rivage Hotel. Her aunt Alice fussed over the decorations, having managed to retain full control of the flowers and trimmings at the Soeurs de Charité church, our wedding site, where Denyse had attended her last years of school. Many of the nuns there still remembered her.

Meanwhile, I was getting more and more nervous by the minute. I started doubting our decision to get married in the first place, because how could I offer Denyse the lifestyle she was used to? I would be taking her away from her family, her friends, her job, and most important of all, an environment she loved. The closer I got to my travel date to Beirut, the more I worried.

Ironically, I consoled myself with the thought that Denyse and I had already crossed the point of no return and could not back out now. I knew I didn't want to lose her, but I felt too crippled with anxiety to think straight.

My mother would probably have preferred it if I did back out. Her chilly reaction to Denyse during our visit to Hannover had never warmed, as far as I could tell from my infrequent correspondence with my mother. Although I had spared my fiancée another trip to see Mutti again after our engagement, I sensed things would not have gone any better the second time. My mother offered nothing more than the faintest congratulations when I told her about our engagement.

Since I wasn't terribly close with my sister Bärbel, I had no idea how she was reacting. But at least Jenny gave me her sincere warm wishes when I called with the news. I was deeply grateful for this.

Despite my mother's attitude, I had asked her several times to join me in Beirut for the wedding and to bring my sisters along, but she never answered.

Was my mother worried about how she would feel, seeing her only son begin a new life with another woman? Was she uncomfortable about traveling to a foreign country? Was she nervous about the cost of airfare? Or was it another reason I don't want to think about, perhaps having to do with Denyse's cultural background?

Mutti repeatedly changed the subject every time I pleaded with her to come to the wedding, so after a while, we didn't speak of it anymore. I was her main source of financial support at the time, and if she had something unkind to say, I suppose she felt it unwise to say so. Which is just as well.

Bärbel was in her twenties by now, but she generally went along with my mother's decisions, so she made no move to attend my wedding either. Unfortunately, Jenny was still a teenager and had never yet traveled alone. I wish I'd gone to Hannover and brought her with me to Beirut.

My flight arrived the day before the wedding, and once again, Denyse's brother-in-law, Alain, picked me up from the Beirut airport to drive me to my hotel. This time I would be staying at the Beau Rivage near downtown. Its name, common to hotels of the era, means beautiful shore. But this hotel was not situated on a lake, as was the hotel by the same name where I'd worked in Lausanne, but on a prime spot overlooking the Mediterranean. At the time, Beirut's Beau Rivage was one of the most desirable hotels in town, and Denyse had chosen it as the location for our wedding reception.

Before Alain left, promising to pick me up the next morning, I handed him the box with the white orchids and asked him to deliver them to

Denyse immediately. The flowers had traveled a long way, from Thailand to Holland and from Holland to Germany to report for duty in Lebanon.

As Alain drove off in his blue Volkswagen Beetle, I felt overcome with loneliness. Here I sat, alone in a hotel in Beirut again. This time, my family's absence made me feel even sadder. I had nothing to do but wait for things to happen, events now beyond my control.

Where Did the Church Go?

The morning of our wedding, I woke up much too early. Alain had planned a big adventure for me to keep me occupied as the family made final preparations for the ceremony. With Denyse's youngest brother, Adel, in tow, he picked me up and off we drove to the Automobile et Touring Club du Liban in Kaslik, a coastal town about fifteen minutes north of Beirut.

A social hub for the rich and famous of Beirut, the Automobile Club had its own private marina filled with boats of all sizes. When we arrived, I noticed that there were far more yachts in the harbor than cars in the parking lot. Sure enough, our morning was going to involve a boat, not an automobile. Alain's friend Marcel Khoury had his own boat docked in the marina, and he was waiting to take us on a sailing trip in the bay for a few hours of sunshine and waterskiing.

By 2:00 p.m., when Alain dropped me back at the hotel, I was red like a boiled lobster. The wedding was three hours away, and Denyse's uncle Michel Samen would be picking me up for the drive to the church. Michel would also act as my witness for the wedding since I had no one else with me.

Denyse later admitted how embarrassed she'd been that none of my family or friends had come to our wedding. She hadn't made a big issue of this at the time, but I could tell that it wasn't sitting well with her.

A couple of months before the wedding, as she was printing the invitations, she had asked me, "Who is coming from your side?"

"Nobody," I'd answered.

This was unheard of in Lebanon, where marriage ceremonies typically draw family and friends from all over. In Lebanon, there's no such thing as a small wedding.

As Denyse had made a special point to visit my family in Germany two years ago, she couldn't help feeling slighted. And what about my friends? Didn't I have any?

Oddly enough, it hadn't really occurred to me to invite any friends. My jobs had kept me moving around too much to make close friends, the kind I would invite to a wedding abroad, and I had lost contact with most of my old school pals. But none of this bothered me as much as it did Denyse. She remained silent about her misgivings at the time, but she eventually told me that all her friends and family had been shocked.

I was relieved to have Michel as my witness. His charm and easygoing personality made the awkward situation seem okay. Out of all of Denyse's family members, Michel and his wife, Edith, were the ones I appreciated the most. I'd connected with Michel from the moment we met on my first visit to Beirut. Denyse was especially fond of him too, so selecting him as my witness seemed a natural choice. I later learned that he too had been baffled that I had no one else.

Since Michel would be arriving in three hours, I had plenty of time to relax and get ready. I could shower, soothe my sunburn, and even wander downstairs to have a look at the preparations for the cocktail reception and make sure everything was in order.

The church was only a few minutes away, so Michel would be waiting for me at a quarter to six, giving us plenty of time to arrive punctually for the six o'clock wedding. Sure enough, I found Michel waiting for me in front of the hotel, smiling warmly as I walked out in the dark blue tuxedo I had bought in Paris, not realizing that it would become my wedding outfit one day.

We wound through the narrow streets of downtown Beirut and crossed over into the hilly Achrafieh neighborhood on our way to the church. I tried to relax by gazing out the window at the old townhouses, with their graceful arched windows and balconies lined with pots of flowering plants. One especially beautiful house caught my eye, but I didn't get a good look at it since we soon pulled off around the corner and into another street. A few minutes later, I looked out the window again and saw what looked like the same house.

Could it be? Yes, I was sure this was the same house. I looked at my watch and realized we had been driving almost for twenty minutes, and now it was after six o'clock.

I glanced up to the driver's seat and saw Michel's lips moving. He was talking to himself. All of a sudden, he pulled the car onto the sidewalk, put it into reverse, and drove backward down the street. I recognized this Beirut maneuver, called "en arriere," used when a driver decides to back out of a street against traffic.

"Is everything okay?" I called out to Michel.

"Yes, yes," he murmured, "don't worry. We're almost there."

Seconds later, Michel stopped the car and disappeared into a grocery store. *Something is not right here*, I thought to myself. Michel returned shortly after and said, in his best upbeat voice, "We'll be there in a few minutes!" Another "few" Lebanese minutes, I thought, increasingly anxious. Now it was 6:15. We were officially late to the wedding.

I detected a rare look of panic on Michel's face. But he had reason to worry. As I later learned, Michel couldn't find the church. After asking for directions in the grocery store, he had called Aunt Alice to let her know we were slightly delayed, sending her into a tailspin.

What Michel didn't tell the panic-stricken Alice is that he'd driven to the old Soeurs de Charité church, which he'd known from years past, assuming it was the wedding site. Michel had no idea the old church had been demolished and that there was a new church and nun's school with the same name in the Sioufi area, close to Denyse's family's home but at least ten minutes from where we now were. He had been circling around and around looking for a building that had long since vanished.

When he finally called Alice again to ask where exactly the church was, chaos broke out in the entire family. Denyse was just about to leave for the church to meet her future husband. But not only was her future husband not at the church yet, no one else had arrived to welcome the guests. That was supposed to be Michel's and my job.

Alice grabbed Denyse's aunt Odette and rushed to the church to tell the guests not to worry. Meanwhile, Denyse's chauffeur drove around in circles for a few blocks to delay her arrival at the church until Michel and I got there.

Finally, our car pulled up in front of the church. The two aunts had been pacing outside on the sidewalk and ran up to Michel, shouting angrily. He immediately went into his typical Michel mode. Calm, cool, completely in control.

"Relax, why are you so excited? We're here!" Michel said, directing me out of the car and up to the sidewalk. Something tells me he would have kept his composure even if we'd missed the wedding altogether. Every family needs someone like Michel.

Once the crisis had passed, everything proceeded as planned. The guests had already taken their seats, and up in front next to the altar, I waited with Michel and the priest for the music to start and Denyse to arrive. And here she came, entering the church on the arm of her brother Adel, who took her deceased father's place to escort her down the aisle. Denyse looked more stunning than ever. I could not take my eyes away from this woman who was soon to be Mrs. Tischmann.

The Greek Catholic ceremony unfolded very differently from any wedding I'd ever been to in Germany. The tradition in the Orthodox denomination of Christianity is to repeat every important aspect of the ceremony three times. Denyse and I, wearing golden crowns connected to each other with a ribbon, walked slowly around the altar three times, while the priest prayed and spoke to us in Arabic.

Obviously, I had a general idea of what we were aiming to do in the church that day, but I didn't understand a single word of what the priest said. This turned into my favorite story about the wedding, one I told over and over again.

> *When the priest finally addressed me in English, all he asked was, "Do you like the weather in Lebanon?" Easy question. I said, "I do."*
>
> *The next thing I knew, we were officially married.*

Denyse never enjoyed this story as much as I did. To this day, it remains one of my favorites. Who ever heard of getting married without understanding a word of the ceremony? But I had no complaints. Sure, I was alone in Beirut, and I'd almost missed my own wedding. But near-disasters aside, this had turned out to be the most magical day of my life.

After leaving the church, Denyse and I rode in a white limousine to the Beau Rivage, to find an impeccably decorated buffet with a huge wedding cake in the center. Denyse had done a superb job of planning the cocktail reception for our nearly two hundred guests. I could not have done it better, and I was delighted by what the hotel created for us.

Did I have the chance to actually eat or drink anything during the reception? Of course not. Denyse and I walked around for hours, greeting everyone and accepting congratulations. Never before did I shake so many hands and learn so many names at once, all of them people from various parts of Denyse's life.

Rafic Chehab, an old friend of hers who had dined with us on my last visit, approached Denyse and asked, "What would you have done if Peter hadn't shown up?" He patted me on the back. Little did he know how close Michel and I had come to being no-shows at the wedding.

When Denyse and I finally retired to our room upstairs as a newly married couple, we discovered dozens of plates filled with all types of foods and sweets from the buffet. As we learned the next morning, Denyse's young cousins Makram and Habib had filled one plate after the other at the buffet and brought them to our room. Who had directed them to do this? We never found out.

As for our first night together, I will keep the details to myself. I'll only mention that when I tried to undo Denyse's hairstyle, I ended up with more than fifty hair pins in my hand—and that we only had a few short hours of privacy before we had to get up and start a marathon of office visits to have our marriage legalized and all the official documents translated.

The hotel reception desk woke us up at seven o'clock in the morning. "Seven a.m. sharp, please," I told the operator when I requested the wake-up call. We had an urgent matter to attend to, and arriving on "Lebanese time" was not even an option.

Moving to Germany

All the anxiety leading up to the wedding day was finally behind us. We were now Mr. and Mrs. Tischmann. I couldn't wait to begin my new life as Denyse's husband. But I couldn't enjoy it quite yet.

We had an important job to do first: prove our wedding was legitimate. This meant wrestling with Lebanese-style bureaucracy, a notoriously maddening system of endless paperwork and arcane procedures the country had inherited from its days as a French protectorate.

Our 7:00 a.m. wake-up call was a cruel necessity. Since government offices in Lebanon were only open in the morning and scattered in different parts of town, we had to run around from one to the other to get our official marriage documents in order. Our papers from the church needed to be approved by the local authorities that morning, then passed on to a certified German translator in the afternoon before going to the German Embassy for registration the next morning.

We had to race against the clock, since we couldn't leave the country without our documents. In the hours between our various office visits, Denyse's friends and family stopped by our hotel to say goodbye, and many of them tried to invite us to dinner before we left. At times, it was as if we were saying bye-bye to the same people over and over again.

Miraculously, we got all the papers together in time for our flight. Now we had to face our second challenge as a married couple: moving to Germany and starting a new home together. We would be living on the outskirts of Frankfurt in Neu-Isenburg, in an apartment I found for us over the summer in the town's Gravenbruch neighborhood. At the time, this was a hub for young couples and families, its new apartment buildings surrounded by a forest and conveniently located near the airport, a shopping district, and a drive-in cinema. The apartment I'd been living in before seemed too small for a married couple, although the new one was hardly spacious.

A crowd of Denyse's friends and family gathered at the Beirut airport to see us off, the two of us plus eight full suitcases stuffed mostly with Denyse's personal belongings and our wedding gifts.

Thanks to friends at MEA, Middle East Airlines, checking in eight suitcases weighing three times more than the allowance did not present a problem. Our suitcases soon disappeared one after the other on to the conveyor belt, each labeled with the destination Frankfurt am Main.

"Peter, I hope you realize you're taking a rose away from us," Denyse's godmother Odette said to me as we bid our final goodbyes and walked off into the airport terminal. Of course, I realized it because otherwise I would not have been here to begin with.

My friend Rudi Rodenbach greeted us a few hours later in the arrivals lounge at Frankfurt, beaming his big hearty smile. His presence seemed a relief to Denyse. Not only was he immediately warm and disarmingly funny, but he could also speak with her in English, no German required.

"Welcome home!" I said to Denyse as we pulled in front of Schönbornring 16, our new address. How strange for her to arrive in a new country, and an entirely new environment, and be told it's home, just like that.

Luckily, we had an urgent assignment that would keep us busy and prevent us from wallowing in anxiety about our new lives. We had to furnish our apartment. Schönbornring 16 was a modern ten-story building, and our eighth-floor apartment had an unrestricted view over the forest and the new condo towers around us. Now we just had to make the inside feel like a place we wanted to live in.

Walking into an empty space is a disorienting way to begin an already overwhelming new chapter of life. But at least the bedroom and kitchen were livable, since I'd already furnished them with Denyse's choices based on photos I'd sent her over the summer. As much as I wanted to take Denyse sightseeing, we decided to spend our first week visiting furniture stores. We bought a Chippendale-style dining room set and an old German-style cabinet for the living room, as well as some decorative pieces to bring the apartment to life.

The problem was we wouldn't receive our furniture for another three months. Taking items home right away was not the custom at the time, long before the days of IKEA and well-stocked furniture markets.

Could we live for three months in this desert of an apartment? The idea seemed bleak, especially as only four hours away, a set of beautifully restored Louis XV chairs sat waiting for us in Hannover, chairs with an interesting background.

Those chairs had made a surprise appearance in my life one day many years ago, when I was walking home from school. Along the route, my attention had been diverted by an enormous pile of broken furniture piled on the walkway in front of our house. As I glanced at the pile, I noticed one chair that wasn't totally destroyed, and I visualized how beautiful these chairs must have looked in their prime. *Why not restore them?* I wondered. I went through the many broken pieces to find the parts that made up a second chair, and another one, and one more. After putting all the pieces in our cellar, I informed my mother.

"Are you out of your mind?" she asked. "The garbage other people throw away, you collect from the street?"

It took me weeks to remove the torn upholstery and the hundreds of nails, and as I did, it became obvious that some decorative elements were missing. Years later, those chairs turned into a project for our Turkish carpenter at the hotel, who luckily agreed to work on them and had no problem fixing the broken parts. The result was four beautifully restored cherrywood frames, waiting to be upholstered. Even my mother was speechless when she saw them for the first time.

The summer leading up to our wedding, pictures of the frames along with upholstery samples went back and forth between Hannover and Beirut. Soon the Louis XV-style chairs were finished and upholstered in an old rose mohair fabric and looked as if they'd arrived fresh from the best antique shop in town.

Making them part of our living environment meant that we would have to visit my mother in Hannover to pick up the chairs along with a few other items that awaited us. Denyse bravely consented to the trip, swallowing her discomfort about my mother's absence from our wedding. We rented a van and drove to my hometown.

My mother's greeting was not exactly brimming with joy, but that was never her forte. At least she seemed resigned to our marriage and willing to be civil with my wife. As difficult a time as I always had trying to decipher my mother's emotions, this time I decided not to bother. I also wanted to spare Denyse the drama of any direct confrontation about my mother's iciness and absence from the most important day of our lives. To be fair, Mutti treated us hospitably all weekend, to the best of her ability, and cooked every meal, even presenting us with a fifty-kilogram bag of potatoes to take home.

A giant bag of potatoes proved too daunting a sight for Denyse, who liked potatoes well enough but not nearly as much as Germans do. We took a few potatoes out of the bag to be polite and returned the rest to my mother's cellar before we left, with the excuse that we have no basement or anywhere else to store them. But happily, Denyse did like the pieces of furniture that awaited us in Hannover and agreed to take them with us.

Back in our new home, our space instantly started to look more habitable. We now had draperies on the windows, and the restored antique furniture from Hannover looked lovely next to the two wooden cocktail tables we'd ordered from a Turkish carpenter at the Frankfurter Hof. By the end of autumn, all the furniture we ordered had arrived, and Denyse had tastefully turned our apartment into a cozy and comfortable space, complete with a charming Oriental corner decorated with textiles and cushions from Lebanon.

The furniture project behind us at last, how would Denyse now occupy her time? She was still a newcomer in Germany, and she didn't speak the language, have a job, or know anyone one except me.

It dawned on me that I was now the main anchor of Denyse's life in Germany. Would this be enough for her? How could it? She was used to a much more social, active, and stimulating lifestyle than either Frankfurt or I could offer her right away.

One ray of light was that my work at the airport was only twenty minutes away by car, and in my corporate job, I had the advantage of regular working hours and most weekends off, very rare in the hotel business. But since we could only afford one car, on weekdays, Denyse was stuck at home. She could use public transportation to go downtown, but she didn't yet feel comfortable doing so without understanding any German.

Our tight budget also meant we didn't even have a TV to provide local news and entertainment and help her improve her German. Even though Denyse didn't complain, not to me anyway, I sensed she was starting to regret her move to Frankfurt.

But our calendar soon started filling up with visits from family and friends, and those plans helped us anchor our days and weeks. My sister Jenny arrived first, expressing her sadness at having missed our wedding. We had fun showing Jenny around Frankfurt, and on the weekdays while I worked, she and Denyse spent the days together exploring the city.

It brought me joy to see my sister and wife get along so well, and I could tell Jenny appreciated Denyse's Lebanese-style hospitality. Denyse had placed silver bowls filled with chocolate, pralines, and other goodies around our apartment, as the Lebanese often do to make guests feel welcome. During Jenny's visit, those containers didn't stay full for long. My sister had a sweet tooth, and Denyse and I were both amused to see her appreciate what our apartment's candy bowls had to offer.

Even my mother paid us a visit, a blessedly short one, and fortunately she arrived without potatoes. Mutti was one of the first to sign our guest list, posted in the entrance of our apartment, and during her few days with us, she complimented our taste in furniture. Things were looking up.

One of our favorite visitors was Denyse's cousin Fadi, who was on his way to the US to complete his engineering studies. He joked about the stifling heat in our apartment, which seemed perfectly comfortable to us. Fadi couldn't handle it and decided to roll out his sleeping bag on the balcony to catch the breeze, despite our constant efforts to convince him to switch to the more comfortable guest bed. He slept under the stars of Gravenbruch and the noise of the nearby highway and seemed to enjoy his outdoor camping adventure. His down-to-earth spirit and humor uplifted us during his entire stay.

Between visitors, we worked hard to whip our finances into shape. Denyse took over our accounting and immediately showed her talent for managing our small budget. She created a series of envelopes designated for the various expenses we had to master: general charges, electricity, gasoline, insurance, food, and beverage. The last envelope was for vacation, and at the end of each month, we filled it with the money not spent on the other categories.

Denyse's accounting system turned out to be brilliant and likely saved us many headaches. Her years of banking experience definitely were an asset for us as we tried to navigate our new lives as a responsible married couple.

In June, her mother came to visit us, obviously curious to see how her daughter was doing so far away from home. Everyone called her Meme, meaning grandmother, and I got along well with her, counting her more as my own relative instead of a typical mother-in-law. I was happy to have Meme around, and she kept us company and helped us warm up our home. From day one, she took over the kitchen and gave Denyse pointers on how to cook the Lebanese homestyle food that I'd grown to love, which made her an even more welcome guest.

DENYSE CUTTING THE WEDDING CAKE AT THE RECEPTION

LEAVING THE CHURCH – MICHEL MY WITNESS BEHIND ME

Our Daily Life 11

A Financial Emergency in Hannover

The summer of 1970 was an especially pleasant one in Frankfurt, filled with day after day of bright sunshine and soft, warm air. The weather, reminiscent of Beirut summers, helped Denyse feel even more at home and made her visiting mother more comfortable too. The three of us took advantage of the beautiful days to take weekend excursions to the outskirts of the city, driving around the lush Taunus mountains and their geothermal springs north of Frankfurt and visiting the Rhine River valley and the Black Forest.

In other good news, I had been promoted to assistant to the general manager at the newly opened Steigenberger Airport Hotel. This change put me back into a hotel environment instead of a corporate office, a move I was happy about. Even more than that, the promotion meant I'd be working directly with the top management team at the company.

A new direction for my career was slowly coming into focus, a path I couldn't visualize in all those months when I lay sick in a hospital bed or even in my first few jobs after the illness.

My time as a concierge, my experience as a chief steward, and my year of wrangling data in the corporate office at Steigenberger had added up to something after all. As an assistant to a general manager, I could see a new path open up: I'd aim to become a general manager in a smaller hotel like the one I was now working in, or a resident manager, the number two position, at a bigger hotel. My path had never seemed so straightforward before, but the promotion gave me a new sense of purpose.

Unfortunately, my new title also meant an end to my predictable work hours and guaranteed weekends off. My workdays became much longer, a new situation Denyse didn't like much. She later reminded me that once, when she asked what time I'd be coming home, I snapped, "I don't know. I'm not working in a post office from nine to five stamping letters all day!"

I'm not proud of my reaction. I suppose I was under stress to perform at work and to be a good husband to Denyse, and now my two top priorities were clashing. At a hotel, the management team's workdays are dictated by customer needs and by the unforeseen circumstances that spring up constantly. For Denyse, who was used to working at Bank of America in Beirut from 8:00 a.m. to 2:00 p.m. five days a week, my six-day work week and long hours came as an unwelcome surprise.

Little did we know that a bigger storm was headed our way.

That year, my mother plunged into financial turmoil and lost control of the two Hannover houses that I owned and had entrusted her to manage. I was shocked when the bank called to tell me that the houses were insolvent and not even in a position to honor the interest payments anymore. The homes had accumulated massive debt, and the bank wanted its money. On top of that, major repairs were overdue. Not only had my mother lost control of the finances, but she had also overspent considerably above her established limit.

Denyse and I were still living on a limited budget, a little more comfortably since my promotion but still in no way free from financial anxiety. We were not in a position to absorb the debts and stabilize our situation without urgent help.

There was no choice. I made an emergency trip to Hannover for meetings with the bank, the tax office, and the companies awaiting payment for repairs on both properties. With the help of the bank, we established an austerity plan and put one house up for sale. The decision pained me, but it was the only way we could cover the outstanding interest payment and invoices and reduce our mortgage so we could afford to keep the remaining house.

The day I had to inform my mother that she no longer had any signature rights or spending privileges for the property, and that she'd now have to live on a restricted monthly budget of 200 DM, is a day I wish I could forget. She was a wreck when I told her, and seeing her this way hurt me tremendously. But I had no other option.

Within four weeks, the situation had stabilized, until we got another piece of bad news. The roof of the remaining house was in dire need of replacement, at an estimated cost of 250,000 DM. How would we get a loan for such a large amount? To our great relief, the bank was impressed by how quickly we'd turned the finances around and agreed to extend the loan. But I would need to secure it with an additional life insurance plan. It was a heavy toll to pay because the premium had to come out of my own pocket since the house could in no way support the additional expenses.

After the tough conversation with my mother, I had to have one with Denyse too, as the bank was demanding to have Denyse countersign the debt of 250,000 DM. At first, she refused to sign, terrified to take on such an enormous financial risk, but she soon realized that, without her signature, the situation was bound to get worse. Today, after many difficult years, the house is finally standing on its own financially. I have Denyse to thank for believing in me.

The house fiasco kept us busy for a few months, but once the situation got resolved, our routine went back to normal. I worked long hours, and Denyse felt isolated at home. Weeks later, she decided she did not want to live this way and decided to look for a job. Her application to Pan American Airways as a ground hostess earned her an offer within days, and I must say that Denyse looked very sharp in her blue uniform. I knew that Pan Am could not have found a smarter, more all-around capable employee.

Happily, I was able to arrange my work schedule so I could take Denyse to work every morning and even pick her up at the end of her shift, although many times I had to return to work in the evening. This was a small price to pay as long as we couldn't afford the luxury of a second car.

Denyse's spirit brightened now that she was carving out her own life in Frankfurt, finding satisfaction in her work, meeting other people, and learning German. One of the friends Denyse met during her work at the airport was Fifi El Karimi, a young Egyptian woman who worked in the same position for PIA, the Pakistan National carrier. Fifi and her husband, Mostafa, became very good friends, and we began having dinner together on a regular basis.

Then one day, less than three months after she had started, Denyse's employment with Pan Am came to an abrupt end.

She woke up feeling nauseous one morning, then the next morning, and the one after that. Denyse saw her doctor and, sure enough, learned she was pregnant. The news surprised us since a baby wasn't in our official plans yet, but we felt overjoyed. Denyse's relatives in Beirut would finally have the news they were waiting for too. Still, it was too soon to share this development with the world, but since Denyse's extreme nausea made it impossible to continue working, she had to tell her supervisors.

A few weeks later, still over the moon with excitement and eager to tell everyone we knew about Denyse's pregnancy, we received bad news. The doctor diagnosed some complications that put the baby in danger. The pregnancy may be too risky to continue, he warned us.

So soon after the thrilling development, we had to confront the sheer terror that things were not going the way we'd hoped.

A Medical Emergency at Home

Almost three months into her pregnancy, Denyse had developed a cyst on her uterus, which endangered the baby and risked an early end to the pregnancy. We consulted a surgeon named Prof. Dr. Walter Schieferstein, who told us Denyse needed surgery immediately, but he couldn't guarantee if the baby would survive.

Denyse underwent the procedure bravely, terrified for the baby's life. I still remember sitting in the waiting room, my heart pounding and palms drenched in sweat. After a short while that felt like an eternity, the surgeon emerged. The surgery had gone well. The baby had survived, and Denyse's cyst was gone. From then on, the pregnancy continued quite normally, but Dr. Schieferstein told Denyse she would need a C-section when the time came.

He jokingly informed us that as of now the child would have two fathers, him and I.

We decided to take an overdue vacation while we still could, and six months into the pregnancy, I requested a week off. Our early months in

Frankfurt had been filled with big changes and stressful episodes, and we needed a relaxing getaway.

How about England? Denyse's brother Adel and his wife, Sandra, had moved into a home in Sharnford, England, about ninety miles northwest of London, so we could visit them after a few days of sightseeing in the big city. I decided I could also use the visit to peek in at some famous London hotels to see what I could learn.

It is considered bad form for hoteliers to show up at other hotels without identifying themselves as colleagues, as my general manager, Walter Mankel, told me when I informed him of my London plans. He graciously printed some business cards for me before the trip. My first business cards ever.

Denyse and I had a wonderful time visiting the famous London sights we had only seen in pictures: the Tower Bridge, the Crown Jewels, the changing of the guards at Buckingham Palace, and the famous flea market on Portobello Road. This time I decided not to try my hand at bargaining and instead simply browsed, watching the city's street life go by. We took pictures of ourselves in front of a classic red London telephone booth and watched double-decker buses and the distinctive black cabs of the era, the pleasingly curvy Austin FX4s, roll by on the street.

We got to know those cabs well on that trip since we had decided not to drive. Getting used to driving on the left side of the street in London was a real challenge, especially when it came to intersections and turns. It required constant vigilance to not to end up on the wrong side of the street. So we were more than happy to take cabs wherever we wanted to go and leave the driving to the experts. After all these years, the British still haven't learned how to drive on the right side of the street.

The hotel I wanted to see most was the legendary Savoy. As Denyse went window-shopping in the busy pedestrian streets around Covent

Garden, I found my way to the hotel, a stately white stone building blending Art Deco and Edwardian architecture.

Entering the Savoy's grand lobby and approaching the front desk, the first thing I noticed was that all the employees wore tailcoats. I handed my business card to the receptionist. After a chilly greeting and a once-over glance at my appearance, head to toe, he finally agreed to show me the hotel and a few rooms, but not without giving me the sense that he was doing me a tremendous favor.

Whether or not my perception is fair, I've often detected a whiff of superiority among the British. Perhaps this is a cliché, but it's frequently proven true in my experience, and my visit to the Savoy on my first trip to London did nothing to dissuade me.

As the receptionist showed me around, I noted that the lobby, restaurants, banquet rooms, and other guest areas looked ornate and palatial and dramatically different from the simple but functional layout of the Steigenberger Hotel in Frankfurt. Maybe it was at the Savoy that I first began paying attention to the details that can create an atmosphere of luxury in a hotel: the gilded and marbled surfaces, the elegant molding along the walls and ceilings, the perfectly arranged flowers, the formal staff uniforms, and all the small, subtle touches that make a big difference.

But my impression changed the moment I was shown into one of the guest rooms. My tour guide unlocked a door and led me into an extremely tiny room overlooking an inner courtyard. A cluster of A/C equipment was visible from the window, along with an adjacent chimney blowing white clouds into the air. I smelled chemicals and realized the scent was coming from the laundry. Turning to the receptionist, I asked if they actually rent this room to paying guests. I couldn't quite imagine how they would.

He looked at me as if he didn't understand my question. In a belittling tone, he answered, "Of course we do. After all, you are at the Savoy!" My point exactly. How could a guest who was paying for the opportunity to stay at the Savoy accept a room like this?

It was time to leave. The next stop: Claridge's. I met Denyse again so she could join me on my visit to this famous hotel on Park Lane in Mayfair, a few minutes away by cab, mainly to experience its English teatime service. Claridge's was known for its tea ritual, and as soon as we entered the lobby of the nineteenth-century red stone Art Deco building, I asked where we could find the tea room.

A gentleman in a black tailcoat asked, "Are you a resident of the hotel, sir?"

I proudly flipped my business card, answering: "No, we are not."

Without even taking notice of my card, he continued, "Sorry, we only serve tea to residents."

Could this be true? Did we not pass his test to allow us entry into Claridge's? Shocked by his answer and sensing that we had just been kicked out of the hotel, we left and continued to the Dorchester Hotel, a little further down on Park Lane.

Another of the iconic London hotels, the Dorchester was known for its large banquet rooms, which made it one of the few traditional hotels able to host substantial events. Approaching the hotel, we noticed that the modern-style curved concrete structure looked plainer on the outside than the other luxury hotels we'd visited that day, but its lushly landscaped entrance seemed inviting. I had no idea what kind of experience awaited us on the inside.

At the Dorchester, five o'clock tea is served daily in the lobby lounge, and as we entered the hotel, we heard soft music playing. A tall, white-haired maître d' stood at the entrance, and much to our surprise, he escorted us, without any questions asked, directly to a lovely table overlooking the entire lounge.

The waiters wore white jackets and long white aprons, and they moved swiftly and silently through the room to the sounds of piano music wafting in the air. Everything seemed perfectly choreographed to create a soothing, elegant atmosphere. This was how I'd imagined English teatime.

Denyse and I ordered tea and a small fruit tartlet, and a waiter soon arrived with a fancy silver tea set. He began to brew our tea, using leaves instead of a bag, pouring the hot water over them as we watched. He told us to wait a few minutes before we start drinking the tea, to let the leaves brew longer and develop their full aroma. I was impressed.

A few minutes later, a waiter passed by and offered us finger sandwiches filled with smoked salmon, eggs and cucumber, shrimp, and many other delicacies. We politely declined, afraid that the price would climb out of our range.

Soon another waiter came to our table with a tray of traditional English scones, homemade marmalade, and Devonshire cream. Again, we said no thank you, but the routine continued. Canapés, English cake, more fruit tartlets, and finger sandwiches once again. Waiters would politely offer, and we would politely turn them down.

Having enjoyed our freshly brewed tea and our fruit tartlet, not to mention this grand parade of delicacies that passed by, it was time to ask for the bill. Much to our surprise, our waiter handed us an invoice requesting 18.00 pounds each for the tea and the fruit tartlet. I made eye contact with the waiter a moment later when I spotted him across the room. He came directly to our table.

"Is this bill correct?" I asked. Surely they had made an error, easy to correct and easily forgiven, considering how kind the service had been.

"Of course, this is the price for the English tea menu, which included all the offerings you so politely denied," the waiter replied, lowering his voice to a near-whisper.

Denyse and I looked at each other. For a moment, we considered asking the waiter to start the service all over again. But no. Lesson learned. Leaving a few minutes later, one experience richer, I promised myself that this would never happen to us again. At least, not this particular embarrassment.

Perhaps a visit to Harrod's would lift our mood. We went directly to the famous department store and straight to its legendary food hall, and within seconds, we had forgotten about our Dorchester disappointment. The hall was a wonderland of beautifully arranged food products, from cakes to hors d'oeuvres to delicatessen displays and much more. As a former chef, I was dazed by all the exquisitely prepared foods, many of them items I had never seen before.

In the tea area, we tasted an intriguing brew called Earl Grey, and entranced by its Bergamot oil perfume and golden color, we decided to buy some to bring to Adel and Sandra the next day.

Our time in London had come to an end, and we made the two-hour drive the next morning to spend a few days with Denyse's brother and sister-in-law in the small residential village of Sharnford.

To welcome us, Adel and Sandra hosted a tea party and invited their friends and neighbors. Denyse offered to prepare the tea, using the leaves we had just brought from Harrods. When Denyse entered the room with the pot of tea and started to serve it, the round of friends looked incredulously into their cups. One of the women asked Sandra, "What tea is this, sweetie?"

Compared to Typhoo, a brand of black tea common in England and as dark as coffee, the golden Earl Grey indeed looked different, and it certainly smelled unlike any other.

"This is Earl Grey tea," Denyse answered, surprised by the question. She thought the English must surely know about this tea we'd just discovered.

After looking into her cup with some skepticism, the woman said, "Earl Grey tea, never heard about," before she finally tasted the tea, as everyone else observed her carefully.

"Oh!" she gasped. "This is delicious, and one can even drink it even without milk!"

Even though Earl Grey was distributed by Twinings, Britain's renowned tea brand, no one in the room had ever tried it before. We later learned it was simply too expensive for the average British person.

We felt grateful for the little tea party Adel and Sandra had thrown for us, a chance to experience this appealing tradition without waiters or topcoats. All in all, our trip had been exactly the vacation we both needed. True, we felt like foreigners in England, uninitiated in the lifestyle, but little did we know that one day not long from now, we'd be back.

The next time, we'd be making our home in London, but our lives would look very different than they did now.

Our Family Is Now Three

The doctor may have been joking when we said our baby would have two fathers, but when the time came for Denyse to give birth, he proved his point. He performed a C-section that delivered our beautiful daughter and left both mother and baby in excellent health. The surgery and recovery were certainly tough on Denyse, but she handled them bravely, and luckily, her mother had arrived to support us.

Deciding on a name was another story. We'd agreed that Denyse would pick the name if it was a boy, and I would choose if we had a girl. Or so I thought.

To tease Denyse and her mother, I insisted that only a German name would be acceptable if we had a girl. I proposed Kunigunde, Sieglinde, Henriette, Klothilde, and a few more, leaving the two women in disbelief. Denyse nearly flipped out, and Meme looked at me aghast, with an "Are you serious?" look on her face.

It quickly became clear that only a French name would do. I went through the list of French names of former colleagues and friends, suggesting a few I happened to like. Genevievre was instantly rejected because my mother would not be able to pronounce it. Good point. Françoise was too widely used at the time, and Nicole was unacceptable because Denyse knew a friend from school with the same name, whom she never liked.

I kept trying, but all my proposed names got rejected by the time we went to the hospital for the scheduled C-section.

An idea suddenly came to me, just as Denyse started to get drowsy from the anesthetics in preparation for the surgery.

"What about Carine?" I whispered.

"Yes," Denyse answered immediately. Finally, a yes! "Carine is a nice name, but with a C at the beginning and E at the end." And then she slipped into sleep.

Less than fifteen minutes later, a girl was born, and Carine was her name. I later realized that we didn't need her name to be so special because our daughter was very special. I could not have imagined any other name. Carine with a C at the beginning and an E at the end was just right.

Carine was born on June 18, 1971, at forty-nine centimeters and three kilograms, with dark eyes like cherries. She arrived perfectly healthy, despite the early problems during Denyse's pregnancy. Thank you to Prof. Dr. Schieferstein, her self-declared second father.

Our entire world looked different a week later when Denyse and Carine arrived home from the hospital. The baby was now the center of our lives, dictating all the activities of our days and nights. Well, almost.

My mother had strongly advised us that we needed to begin the baby's education from the very beginning, at least when it came to her habits and routines. It's important not to react to every little cry, she told us. When the baby has had her meal, burped, and been changed into clean diapers, she had no real reason to cry other than to demand general attention.

The way we reacted to Carine's crying now would set the tone for years to come, my mother insisted. It would determine whether our baby would be trained to expect someone to run to her every time she cried—or whether she'd learn to soothe herself when she had no reason to cry and to fall asleep effortlessly at naptime and bedtime. This would supposedly help Denyse when she was at home with the baby every day.

Mutti talked us into trying this method, but Denyse's mother was skeptical. She probably decided I was a cruel German for going along with this, but she grudgingly agreed.

During dinner one evening, Carine had been fed, burped, changed, and placed in her bed to sleep when she started crying. Denyse's mother immediately jumped up from her chair and ran, but halfway to Carine's room, I stopped to ask her where she was going. She turned around on her heels, saying she needs to go to the bathroom. Nice try. The bathroom was in the opposite direction, as I pointed out. When Meme came back to the table, she didn't look like a happy grandma. But a few minutes later, Carine stopped crying and fell into a deep sleep.

No doubt Denyse's mother still suffered in silence every time the baby cried. But as far as we were concerned, our approach would not only help Denyse get her own schedule on track, it would also turn baby Carine into an excellent sleeper, a skill that would benefit her too.

The ability to soothe herself would soon benefit Carine in ways we didn't yet foresee.

How to Start a Diesel Car

Denyse and I had a lot to learn as we figured out how to be good parents to a newborn baby, but we soon realized we needed to welcome another newcomer to our family: this time a car.

Our dear old Citroen DS19 had rusted all over, and even the mechanic at the service station refused to lift it for an oil change, afraid it might break into two pieces. Relying on a tip from our good friend Rudi, we bought a petrol-blue Mercedes 200D. The 14.500 DM price tag completely eliminated our savings and stretched our budget to the limit, and on top of that, we had to wait four months for delivery. But it seemed worthwhile. This would be our first new car together as husband and wife, and Rudi's word was gold.

To my surprise, as soon as I put the rusty Citroen up for sale, a month before our new car arrived, it only took two days to sell it. A family wanted to buy the Citroen immediately for a vacation to Spain, which would leave us with no car for a month. Fortunately, my sister Jenny had asked me a few days earlier if I could buy her a car, and I had found her a burgundy red NSU TT in excellent condition with very little mileage. She agreed to let me drive it for the month.

Our new car finally arrived in late September of 1971, when Carine was already three months old. Buying a car still felt like a special event at the time, and the dealership made every effort to make this a memorable moment, welcoming Denyse with a bouquet of flowers.

The Mercedes arrived fully loaded, which today means a catalogue of options that could double the basic price of a car. But in 1971, the options were limited to just four: a sunroof, leather seats, a Becker Radio, and an electric window opener. I'd ordered everything except the electric windows, having learned they could be unsafe, and I was excited as I accepted the keys from the sales representative.

Climbing into our brand-new car, I sat there for a moment, realizing I had no idea what to do next. As I'd never driven a diesel car in my life, I cleared my throat and asked the salesman, with no small amount of embarrassment, "Can you please show me how to start the car?"

The guy looked at me, not believing what he had just heard. "You've never driven a diesel? Why did you buy one?"

Saying "Rudi told me to" didn't seem like a satisfactory answer. I sat there for a moment, trying to decide what to do now.

Before Carine was born, we'd heard plenty of advice—good and bad—about how to take care of a baby. But no one had told me what to do when a new car arrives and you don't have a clue what to do with it.

Starting a diesel engine in 1971 was quite different than it is today, requiring a handful of steps to actually get the engine running. I wasn't willing to keep sitting there as the salesman watched me fumble with the key, so I finally got up the nerve to repeat my request. He obliged, offering a few brief instructions.

"Insert the key, then pull the starter button, and keep pulling on it until you see a red light, like the one on the cigarette lighter, begin to glow. Then pull the button further out, and keep pulling it until the engine starts working," he told me, walking off to assist someone else.

The diesel engine didn't start with a soft hum, as in other cars, but gave off a very loud *tack-tack-tack* sound. The entire car shook for a few seconds, until the engine noise became smoother, though still quite loud. I needed to get used to this routine. Soon I realized that the warmer the engine got, the smoother the sound, and before long, the habit was second nature.

Denyse and I truly enjoyed driving the car. It was spacious and comfortable, and seeing its sparkling petrol-blue frame was always a pleasure.

Carine was starting to lift her head and crawl on her own by now, at just under four months old. By Christmastime, she took a strong interest in the lights on the tree and loved to pull the decorations off the branches and knock my electric train off its rails.

By spring, we had kept Carine to ourselves for long enough, and it was time to plan a trip to Beirut to meet the family. We decided Denyse would fly there with Carine first, and I would join them in Beirut for Easter, then we'd return to Frankfurt together.

Flying at that time was still a luxury and not yet as commercialized as it is now. Airfares were high, and the standard cost of a Lufthansa flight from Frankfurt to Beirut in economy was in excess of 6,000 DM. We had to find something less expensive, so we booked with LOT, the Polish national carrier, at less than 4,000 DM per ticket.

The cheaper fare meant we would give up the convenience of a direct flight. A stopover and change of plane in Warsaw with a baby was obviously not the most comfortable way to travel, but it was all we could afford if we wanted to buy gifts for the family and have any spending money left for Beirut.

If I had known what I learned soon after, I would not have booked the flight through Warsaw.

Denyse's stomach was bothering her as we planned the trip, and days later, we realized this wasn't just anxiety about seeing her family. Something else was happening.

A test revealed the news. Denyse was pregnant again. We'd be visiting Beirut with one baby in our arms and another on the way.

I was a little nervous as I took the two ladies in my life to the airport for their flight to Beirut. But I knew that as soon as they stepped off the plane, Denyse would have plenty of help. She could rest while her sister Mouna and the rest of the family took care of Carine.

The days alone in Frankfurt gave me time to plan a surprise. Carine deserved her own room now that she was nearly one, so I decided to transform a corner of the living room into a kids' room designed just for her. She could enjoy it alone until the baby was old enough to move out of the crib in the master bedroom. I painted giant pictures of Mickey and Minnie Mouse, Dagobert Duck, and Goofy on the wall, and I enlisted our friend Alfons Merz to help me make physical changes to the apartment, closing the opening to the living room and creating a door from the hallway.

My short time in Beirut during Easter was, as usual, dominated by eating and drinking with a parade of family members. I ate endless amounts of maamoul, the traditional Easter semolina cookie stuffed with date and pistachio fillings and lightly flavored with rosewater.

Our apartment makeover generated a huge reaction when we arrived back home in Frankfurt. Denyse had no idea I'd decided to do this project, and our daughter was excited to have her own room, complete with the Disney family on her wall.

Carine had her own surprise for us on her first birthday, June 18, 1972. That morning, she walked for the first time. Standing next to Denyse on the playground near our apartment, she started to take a few steps all by herself, walking with open arms toward me. What a day to remember.

Seeing my daughter walk, I felt chills as I realized how quickly the year had flown by. And now we had another baby on the way. I wanted time to slow down so I could watch Carine grow up, moment by moment, and enjoy every second with our new baby. But I had a hunch, even as I stood there on the playground, that life would soon throw some obstacles in my path.

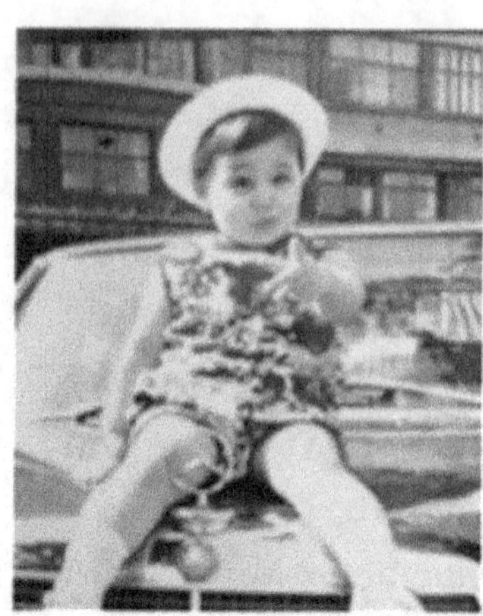

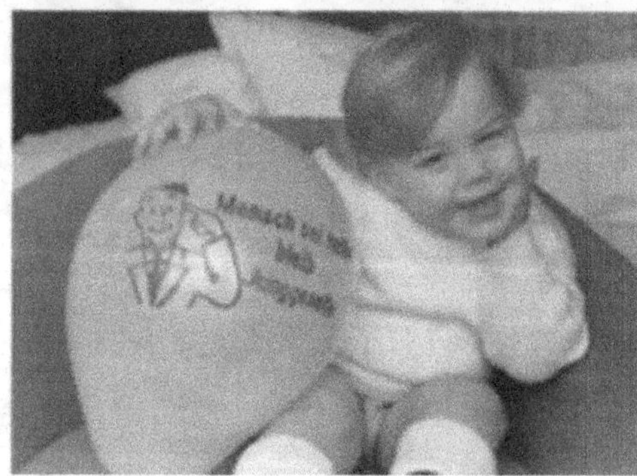

PICTURES OF OUR FAMILY LIFE THROUGHOUT VARIOUS YEARS

Stepping Into the Big World 12

Joining the Sheraton Corporation

That summer, I felt the need to make a major change in my life. Frankfurt had been good to us, and I was enjoying my job at the Steigenberger, but I sensed my career would stagnate if I stayed there much longer.

Shaking myself out of the inertia of a job that had grown a little too comfortable and familiar, I started sending letters of inquiry to the major international hotel companies to find out about any openings that could push my career to the next step.

Faster than I expected, I received a letter in response. The Cairo Sheraton made me an instant offer to take the position of food and beverage director at the hotel.

The problem was I would need to begin immediately. This was impossible as the Steigenberger company only allowed management employees to resign to the end of every quarter of the year. Plus, I had to give six weeks' notice before the end of what would be my last quarter. Obviously, this put managers in a bind. The Cairo Sheraton could not accept this timeframe, and although I was disappointed to miss this excellent opportunity, I had to stay on the right side of my present employer.

Before I started wondering if I'd ever receive an offer from a company willing to accept the Steigenberger's impossibly strict resignation rules, I found another letter from Sheraton in my mailbox. This time it was an invitation from the headquarters in Brussels to meet Sheraton's regional director of food and beverage, Roland Kürsteiner, in their new hotel in Munich to discuss potential career opportunities.

Roland and I hit it off in our meeting, and he asked me if I would be interested in joining him as his assistant director in Brussels. What a question! Of course I was interested. But this was not a job offer because he had more interviews to do. Should I become his candidate of choice, he continued, I'd need to visit Brussels for a follow-up interview with the company president.

He hinted that his decision-making process could take a while, so I realized I'd better not hold my breath. Soon enough, I'd almost forgotten about Roland Kürsteiner, I received a letter from Sheraton inviting me to come to Brussels to meet John Kapioltas, president of Sheraton's management corporation.

I would've flown directly to Brussels that same afternoon if I could. But it was only a few days before I arrived in front of the large French doors of Sheraton's headquarters, located at the Westbury Hotel in the city center.

The first person I expected to meet me in the reception area was Roland, but the desk clerk told me that he was traveling and not in Brussels that day. Instead, a stylishly dressed woman with red hair walked into the lounge and headed directly toward me.

"You must be Peter. I'm Dorothy, Roland's secretary. Follow me. Mr. Kapioltas is waiting for you."

We walked into an enormous office with a huge desk and two visitor chairs on one side of the room and a seating arrangement of sofas and club chairs on the other. Dorothy introduced me to the president.

"Mr. Kapioltas this is Peter Tischmann, Roland's candidate, for you to meet."

"Good morning, Mr. President," I said as I approached his desk, greeting him in polite German tradition.

Smiling as he got up from his desk, Mr. Kapioltas reached out his hand to shake mine and said, "Call me John. How are you, Peter?"

"Very well, Mr. President," I answered, unable to get my mouth to form the word "John." Calling a president by his first name seemed to violate the respect for superiors that I was raised to show.

As we talked, I couldn't stop myself from calling him president. Every time I tried to say "John," I felt as if I had a hot potato in my throat. Initially, he seemed amused by my formality, Kapioltas was tall and gray-haired and wore a perfectly tailored suit that made him look every inch the poised executive.

We didn't get a chance to talk for long before a gentleman walked into the office and informed Mr. Kapioltas that a candidate for the food and beverage manager position was waiting in the reception area. Since Roland was out of the office, who should do the interview?

This man turned out to be the director of human resources, Mr. David Butterworth, and the next thing I knew, John Kapioltas was silently looking me up and down. He turned to Mr. Butterworth and replied, "Peter can do the interview."

Cold shivers ran up and down my spine. I had no choice but to comply. I tried to act confident as I followed Mr. Butterworth into an empty office where the candidate sat waiting to be interviewed. Here I was, not even part of the company, interviewing somebody for a job with Sheraton hotels.

Could this be a setup to find out if I was qualified enough for the job in question? Dorothy later told me that the interview was for real, and as I was the only one around with any F&B background, I had to fill in for Roland who had suddenly decided to go on a trip and forgot all about the interview.

To calm myself, I imagined I was interviewing somebody for the Steigenberger Airport Hotel. There was no way I could admit to this person that I wasn't even part of the organization he was applying for and that I was basically in the same boat he was. I don't think he guessed what was happening during our so-called interview, and twenty minutes later, I returned to Mr. Butterworth with detailed feedback about the candidate.

To my surprise, I never saw John Kapioltas again during my short visit. Instead, Mr. Butterworth asked me some basic interview questions and told me that I would hear from the company in the near future. I politely reminded him that my company requires six weeks' notice and only allows resignations once per quarter, in case Sheraton might be interested in making me an offer. Dorothy, the secretary who greeted me initially, took over from there, giving me an overview of the office in Brussels and how this position fit into the picture. Then she showed me out the door, telling me not to worry.

Walking out, I felt bewildered. I'd never experienced anything like this before, from the surprisingly casual office atmosphere to the president's insistence that I use his first name, to the impromptu interview I had to give another candidate.

I also had the distinct sense that it was Dorothy who was running the food and beverage office and not Roland, as he was apparently traveling most of the time.

Back in Frankfurt, I continued to report for work at the Steigenberger Airport Hotel, taking any free minute to enjoy my family and plan weekend trips in our new car. From Sheraton, I didn't hear a single word, and meanwhile, my August 15 deadline to give notice this quarter was approaching fast. What could I do? Would it be too pushy to contact Sheraton again to remind them of this?

As I grew more worried that I would miss a second opportunity to advance in my career, I finally received a piece of mail from Belgium. It was an offer to join Sheraton as the assistant to the regional director of food and beverage, based in Brussels at a monthly salary of $ 1,000 plus foreign service benefits. This was far better than I had imagined. The pay was about three times as much as I was earning now. Denyse and I discussed it after work that day, but it was clear to both of us that there was no way I could turn this down.

In retrospect, perhaps everything that happened in my career, good and bad, began in earnest on that day. But I had no way of knowing this then.

And Now We Are Four in the Family

Excitement about my new job quickly gave way to an even bigger event in our lives, the birth of our son. The autumn of 1972 was proving to be a time of new beginnings, as well as a season of scary events.

Baby Peter entered the world on September 6, 1972, at nine o'clock in the morning, measuring fifty centimeters and 3.15 kilograms. Just like his big sister, Peter arrived by way of a C-section, as Dr. Schieferstein had predicted as soon as he'd learned that Denyse was pregnant again. The birth went smoothly, and we felt extremely fortunate to have two beautiful, healthy children, a girl and a boy, to keep each other company and fill our lives with joy.

This time, choosing a name for the baby was going to be easy. At least, Denyse thought so because it was her turn to pick a name, and as far as she was concerned, the matter required no discussion whatsoever. The baby's name would be Peter, after me, and his middle name would be William, after my grandfather.

I tried to object, listing one argument after the other, from the potential complications of registering for credit cards to the difficulty in sorting out other official paperwork, to all kinds of other confusion that could creep in later. But Denyse did not want to have this debate with me. Our son's name was Peter William, and that was that.

A few years later, when the whole family attempted to fly to Spain for our summer vacation, my objections proved correct. The four of us arrived at the London Heathrow Airport to check in for our flight to Valencia, only to discover that the airline only had three reservations for us. The ticketing agent had assumed the second Peter W. Tischmann reservation was a duplicate and had canceled it, and now the flight was full, so we had no chance of rebooking it. Our family of four ended up flying in a three-person row. Impossible to imagine nowadays, but Iberia made it happen.

Baby Peter only had a few weeks to experience life in Frankfurt, as we'd planned our move to Brussels for the beginning of October. But just as we had begun our rushed preparations for the move, a major health emergency struck. Carine had developed a high fever and a bad cough, and little white spots appeared inside her mouth. We rushed her to the doctor, who diagnosed a case of chickenpox. He urged us to separate the two children immediately to keep baby Peter from contracting the disease, which is especially dangerous and often fatal for infants and small children.

But how do we separate the kids? We couldn't think of anyone in Frankfurt who could take responsibility for one of our children on such short notice. There was no way to keep them far enough apart in our small apartment, especially with packing boxes stacked up everywhere.

We had no choice but to call my mother. Denyse and I both cringed at this solution, but there was no other way. I let Mutti decide which child she would take, and she felt a baby would be easier for her to handle than an active toddler.

As I frantically got ready for the emergency trip to Hannover with Peter, the packers arrived and miraculously got all our belongings out within a few hours. Denyse flew with Carine to Brussels to begin our move into the new apartment, and Peter and I set off to my mother's house.

Pulling over to feed the baby and change his diapers made our drive not exactly a speedy one, and he was no doubt as relieved as I was when we pulled in front of my mother's house in Hannover five hours later. We arrived to find her ready, with the baby's room already prepared. Peter was fortunately too little to understand what was happening, so I was able to leave in a hurry after a quick kiss on my son's cheek and a big thank-you to my mother. Off to Brussels I went, making the drive in five hours, this time with no breaks.

The new apartment that ITT Sheraton found for us on Avenue de L'Orée felt like a sanctuary after these hectic few days. I was pleased with the location, only a few steps away from ITT's private club and the leafy Bois de la Cambre, a popular park that became the Brussels equivalent of Paris's Bois de Boulogne when it was created in 1861, and that stretches all the way to the city center.

Denyse and Carine appeared from behind a giant pile of boxes to greet me. Luckily, we had the entire weekend to unpack and start arranging our new space before I had to start my new job on Monday at Sheraton's EAME division, overseeing the company's Europe, Africa, and Middle East hotels.

Denyse and I decided we would at least get the kitchen fully functional by the time I started work, then worry about the other rooms later. Carine hovered around us, making a game out of messing up any neat pile we'd created. At least our daughter was starting to get used to her new home.

Early the next day, while moving empty cartons to the balcony, I heard an ear-splitting scream. It was Carine's voice from directly behind me, a sound I can still hear today almost as clearly as I did that morning.

Spinning around, I saw Carine crumpled to the floor, her shrieks getting louder. I dove down to see what was wrong and to comfort her, having no idea what had just happened. She was clutching her hand, and as I looked closely at it, I realized her thumb looked broken. The aluminum door had closed on it as she followed me out to the balcony. Her screaming kept getting louder. I needed to get her some medical attention immediately. Only our second day in Brussels, and already we had an emergency. Not to mention that Carine had not yet completely recovered from the chickenpox and our baby son was far away.

Our concierge recommended that we take Carine to Edith Cavell Hospital on the other side of the park, in the affluent Uccle suburb. As Carine continued to cry and Denyse grew increasingly nervous, we rushed into our car, maneuvered it out of the garage and made our way to the hospital. How we found it so quickly, I have no idea. GPS and navigation systems did not yet exist, but we must have received excellent directions from Mme. Bruylant, and soon we were carrying Carine and running to the emergency room reception.

Denyse and I didn't stop pacing around the waiting room until we saw a nurse emerge with Carine. They were both smiling, and Carine had a big white cast on her thumb. It's broken, the nurse told us calmly, but it shouldn't take long to heal. I couldn't quite share my daughter's smile, but I was relieved that she was so well taken care of and would be back to normal soon.

As Carine's chickenpox symptoms finally started to vanish too, we got clearance to retrieve our son Peter from his grandmother and unite him with his family in Brussels.

As Denyse was busy arranging our apartment and my new job took my full attention, we convinced my mother to take the train with the baby from Hannover to Brussels, where we had arranged in the meantime for Peter to be baptized. When after seven hours of train ride we finally picked up both from the central station, a complicated episode had come to an end, and we were glad to see the family reunited. Mutti seemed no worse for wear either. Whatever her deficiencies in the mother-in-law department, at least we could rely on her in an emergency.

With our multiple health crises out of the way, it was time to tackle the next phase of our eventful move to Brussels: I was about to experience a very strange introduction to my new job.

First Day in My New Office

My new role at Sheraton involved a level of responsibility I'd never had before, and although excited, I was also nervous. I reported to work on Monday at 9:00 a.m. sharp, but not before taking a deep breath as I walked into the lobby of Sheraton's office on the fifth floor at the Westbury Hotel, equipped with my brand-new briefcase and crisply pressed suit.

My polished appearance may have made a positive impression on strangers in the elevator, but it went unnoticed by the top executives. That's because absolutely no one was there to greet me on my first day. No one except Dorothy Crom, the food and beverage secretary whom I had met during my interview several months before.

As this was a Monday morning, most of the executives were on the road again visiting Sheraton hotels or taking other important business trips. Mr. Kapioltas was in Boston at the corporate head office, and my boss Roland Kürsteiner was on his way to Copenhagen.

Needless to say, I had expected a different sort of welcome on my first day. Why didn't they ask me to begin on Tuesday instead, which would have given me one more day to help Denyse unpack? But at least Dorothy gave me a sincere greeting and led me to my new office. I quickly learned she was the eminence grise in the Brussels headquarters. If you get on Dorothy's good side, you're bound to fare much better.

"I've prepared some pencils, a notebook, and a few bits and pieces you may need. Please let me know if you need anything else," Dorothy said, before disappearing.

My office was quite large, furnished with an enormous desk about twice the size of the desk of my former boss Mr. Mankel, the general manager of the Steigenberger Airport Hotel. It had a leather executive chair, two visitors' chairs, a sideboard, and two framed photos of Sheraton Hotels on the wall, and its windows overlooked the city center.

Installed in my plush chair, my hands gliding back and forth over the desktop to convince myself this was all real, I heard the door open. In walked Dorothy.

"Let me introduce you to some of your colleagues in the office," she said, gesturing to the doorway and waiting for me to get up from behind my desk.

The first office we walked into belonged to Mr. Butterworth, director of human resources. "Peter," Dorothy said, "you already know Mr. Butterworth." I flashed back to the day I interviewed a food and beverage manager candidate before I was even hired at the company.

"Welcome to the team," Mr. Butterworth said, "and don't hesitate to contact me if I can be of any assistance. Good luck." He then waved bye-bye with his left hand, while his right hand picked up the ringing telephone, and out I went before I could even say a single word.

Hans Worms was our director of development, responsible for arranging hotel management contracts. Hans was German and thought he was the most important executive in the office. He didn't wait a second to shower me with grandiose words and gestures to prove his point.

The last executive we visited that morning was Richard Chamberlain, chief comptroller for our division and a man of British nationality. Richard had a good sense of humor and didn't miss an opportunity to apply it.

He was also a numbers man through and through, and due to his direct reporting to ITT, he was always struggling to find a proper balance between operational needs and ITT regulations. I left his office clutching two large accounting manuals filled with policies and procedures under my arm. "Happy reading," he said, and out I went.

My new colleagues, at least the ones who were in the office that day, gave me a very friendly welcome, but still I could sense that they were all too busy to have time for me.

Back in my office, Dorothy entered a minute later holding a familiar stack of slim, rectangular papers in her hands. It was a set of airline tickets, and as she handed them to me, she said, "Here. Roland wants you to travel to London tomorrow and check on the opening preparations for the new Sheraton Heathrow Hotel."

Travel on the second day of my new job?

"I've made a reservation for you at the Skyline Hotel," she continued, "and Mike McFayden, the opening general manager, knows that you are coming."

So apparently the timing was non-negotiable. But I had one small question: What exactly was I supposed to check on?

"Are there any documents or anything I should read to prepare?" I asked Dorothy.

"Not that I know of," she answered quickly, "but let me see what I can find in Roland's office."

She came back a few minutes later, shaking her head and handing me copies of several faxes that Roland had sent to Mike McFayden. "Have a look at these. They might give you some ideas."

The faxes had a few brief, scattered notes on them. I looked up at Dorothy to see if she had another pile in her hands, but this was it. Here I was, at one of the world's leading hotel companies, on a mission to supervise the opening of a new hotel in London's Heathrow Airport, but all I had to go on were a few scant notes. No operational concept, no guidelines to check against, no specifications for what Sheraton expected from its new hotels. So far, all Sheraton had provided by way of orientation was a beautiful office, a few pencils, a notebook, and a ticket to fly to London the following day.

There was no point in staying in the office any longer that day since no one was there anyway. I had to break the travel news to my wife and open more boxes before I left.

Denyse's face clouded when I told her I was leaving the next morning. She'd need to take care of the kids alone while trying to unpack the apartment and navigate a new city. At least in Brussels, she could speak the language. And Madame Bruylant had generously offered to help anytime we needed her.

Meanwhile, I tried to focus my attention on my London mission. Since the Sheraton Heathrow Hotel was close to the airport, it took virtually no time to arrive there after I landed. The hotel was Sheraton's first opening in Europe after many years, intended as the company's major entrée into the British market.

Walking in, I tracked down Mike McFayden, the hotel's tall, skinny general manager, originally from Scotland. Off we went on a tour of the site. Even though the building was still under construction and not yet ready to open, I could already tell things were not shaping up well.

I doubt Sheraton intended to build a prison, but the structure looked more like a penitentiary than a hotel. The two-story, prefabricated building had extremely low ceilings, and its tiny windows were designed to remain shut. I saw no architectural features of any kind, and no open spaces anywhere. The public areas, including the restaurants and bars, sat clustered in the inner part of the structure and had no access to daylight or any outdoor areas.

Why would anyone in his right mind choose the Sheraton over its main competitor, the Skyline Hotel, down the road? The Skyline, where I was staying, had open courtyards, restaurants overlooking inside gardens, and high ceilings that allowed guests to breathe.

It didn't require a Harvard degree to realize that there was a difference of day and night between these two hotels. The only advantage the Sheraton could offer was closer proximity to the airport. Was this how Sheraton wanted to be known in Europe? Would this quality and style of hotel make the company stand out in a competitive region? I felt a pang of regret that I had left the Steigenberger Airport Hotel. At least it was well-planned and properly run, a hotel to be proud of.

As we strolled through the half-finished building, Mike showed me the grill room, the coffee shop, and the hotel bar before walking me to the back of the house to see the kitchen and other food and beverage areas. This was all a far cry from what I was used to and what the hotel needed in order to succeed in the European market.

My impression grew worse over the three days I spent gathering information and learning about the opening preparations. I returned to Brussels extremely disillusioned by what I had found. Or, rather, what I had not found. Most disappointing of all, nothing could be done now. The hotel's architectural plans were what they were, and only cosmetic changes were possible at this point.

Back at home, Denyse had worked hard to empty the remaining boxes and put everything in its place, and the apartment looked wonderful. What a breath of fresh air, especially after the grim London trip. My return felt like a true homecoming.

Unfortunately, none of us yet realized that this homecoming would turn into one of many. My new job, it became increasingly clear, would require constant travel and long, frequent absences from home.

Meanwhile, I looked forward to my meeting with Roland Kürsteiner to report on what I'd seen at the Heathrow hotel. He was back in Brussels when I returned, and I'd prepared a detailed report, listing the status of the opening preparations and outlining everything that still needed to be done.

Sitting face-to-face with my boss in his office the next morning, I waited eagerly to start our conversation about the hotel and to impress him with the high standards I would be bringing to my job. Twenty minutes later, I still sat there in silence as Roland filled out his own Scandinavian trip report, took telephone calls, made telephone calls, and prepared his forthcoming trip to Iran. I wondered why he seemed in no hurry whatsoever to hear about the London opening.

Roland must have read my mind because he finally stopped and asked me, "So, Peter, how was Heathrow? Tell me!"

This was my chance at last. I started to share my detailed observations about the London hotel, but before I got two sentences into my description, he interrupted me.

"You're right," he said, "the hotel is a sh——house. But there is nothing we can do. All the planning was done in Boston, and those guys have no idea what Europe needs."

But wait a minute, I thought to myself. Wasn't Roland in charge of making sure Sheraton hotels in Europe got what they needed?

As Roland continued writing his own Scandinavia report and taking telephone calls, I asked him where I could find any information about the opening plans for the Heathrow hotel.

"It's in the filing," he said, his gesture signaling that our conversation was over. I needed to get out of his way and let him do his job, whatever it was exactly.

I hunted down the file and discovered it had virtually nothing in it, nothing that Dorothy hadn't already given me in that useless pile of faxes. At this point, I was starting to feel less and less shocked by this stunning failure to manage a hotel opening. But I decided I wouldn't let myself get discouraged or complacent. Instead, I would use this as my opportunity to take things into my own hands. It was up to me to try to create an organized system that would make Sheraton's many upcoming openings in the region more successful.

During Roland's frequent travels, it was up to me to handle the daily correspondence. Every morning, Dorothy put a pile of letters and memos on my desk for me to read at my convenience and dictate the answers.

Although my command of English was enough to get me through the day, and useful for business meetings and travels, having to handle business correspondence in English was a brand-new challenge.

Thankfully, I had Denyse, who after many years with Bank of America was much more fluent in the English language and could write letters with no problem. I started bringing the correspondence home, and she would help me draft answers to each letter. The next morning, I would call Dorothy into my office and start slowly dictating my prepared answers, one after the other.

Dorothy went along with my game for a few days—never underestimate a secretary's diplomatic skills—until one day she said, "Mr. Tischmann, why don't you give me the prepared papers and let me start typing?"

From that day on, I only informed Dorothy how I wanted to reply to each letter, and she did the rest, indirectly helping me improve my English with each passing day.

A seasoned company executive would've laughed to hear me say this. But I was new and ready for the challenge and blissfully naive.

My First Sheraton Hotel Opening

In the early 1970s, the international hotel world looked much different than it does now. At the time, three main commercial chains dominated the scene: Sheraton, Hilton, and InterContinental. Luxury chains like the Ritz-Carlton, Four Seasons, and Regent Hotels existed too, but on a smaller scale.

To experience the highest levels of luxury, you had to go to a privately owned hotel like the Badrutt's and the Brenner's or icons like the George V or Ritz in Paris. At the time, most of those grand old palaces had not yet been sold to hotel chains.

Sheraton's two major competitors in that era were owned by airlines—Hilton by TWA and the InterContinental by Pan Am—so both companies focused their hotels in cities where their planes landed.

Without an airline as its owner, Sheraton had to figure out its own way of carving up the world profitably. To be more effective, the executives at the Boston headquarters decided that the solution was to divide up the company's operations into regions and to run some hotels as franchises and others as management properties. In the United States, Sheraton would focus on the franchise model, which meant individual hotel owners operate their own properties and pay a branding fee to Sheraton. This did not always work out so well, and Sheraton's reputation was already deteriorating as a result of poorly operated franchises over which it had very little control.

Elsewhere around the world, including in my region overseeing Europe, the Middle East, and Africa, Sheraton mostly followed a management model, taking over the full control of the operation of a hotel and sharing revenues and profits with its owner. Sheraton also committed to opening a certain number of new hotels around the world in those years. But in many cases, the Boston office insisted on doing all the planning for the openings, then bringing in the regional office to take over afterward.

Needless to say, this was a complicated process. One could even say it was a recipe for disaster.

When I joined Sheraton in 1972, its Europe-Middle East-Africa division was still young, with only seven managed properties in its portfolio. But we had a number of new hotels in the pipeline. John Kapioltas had recently been promoted to president of this new EAME division and brought in Roland Kürsteiner, previously food and beverage cost controller at the Boston Sheraton, to oversee all the hotels and new openings in the region.

John's rationale for hiring Roland was that he had European nationality, since he was Swiss-born and could speak several languages. But neither quality could make up for the fact that the man, as I would soon discover, had little to none of the vision required to lead the area into a successful future.

Finally, John did manage to convince the executives in Boston to let the Brussels office handle the architecture, interior design, planning, and coordinating of new hotels in our region. The Boston office had almost no understanding of the needs of European hotels and even less of a grip on what the regional competitors, let alone the luxury hotels, had to offer. In theory, our Brussels office would be better equipped to handle the important decisions. Unfortunately, this move happened too late for the Sheraton Heathrow to benefit.

I did the best I could to save the hotel under the circumstances. I traveled to London on a regular basis to check up on the preparations. I took a microscope to every aspect of the Heathrow hotel's food and beverage operations, including every item on the menu and in the cocktail lounge, and every detail of the customer service. One afternoon, I tried to convince the bartender to learn how to pour a decent drink.

"One-sixth of a gill is a standard in England," the bartender insisted to me, as he demonstrated how he poured a spirit into a glass over ice.

One-sixth of a gill might have been the standard measure for a serving of liquor in Britain, but Sheraton's worldwide standard was four centiliters. Pouring just one-sixth of a gill over ice cubes meant the drink would hardly even show at all, except to make the glass look like it had not been washed before serving.

"Let's give our customers a drink that looks like a drink, instead of like a dirty glass," I urged him.

The bartender gave me a puzzled look. The British did things a certain way, and habits were hard to break. But I refused to give up, as I kept making my rounds and trying to instill an appreciation of quality in the food and beverage operation of this drab hotel. We had to find a way to make the hotel stand out somehow, despite poor design, a claustrophobic interior, and a more appealing offering nearby at the Skyline.

No matter what changes and improvements I tried to make, I could not inspire Roland to show any interest in the Sheraton Heathrow. He continued to find reasons to send himself to his preferred hotels in Copenhagen, in Stockholm, and again and again to Tehran. Only later did I learn that he had established a prosperous carpet business in Iran and was bringing back rugs in his luggage to sell after every trip.

Did I buy a carpet from him? Of course I did. Not one, but two.

Still, my delight over the new carpets I brought home to Denyse did not change the fact that I received very little guidance or help from

Roland, who showed less and less interest in his position. I saw it as my responsibility to cover for his lack of oversight, as his constant absences left me alone to supervise the preparations for the Heathrow opening. I soon realized that nothing would happen unless I made it happen.

It was obvious that the company's clumsy approach was going to spell trouble, again and again. I knew how many contracts had been signed and how many hotels were partially or fully under construction, and I knew all those openings would come my way soon enough. The company planned to open an average of five hotels a year over ten years. This meant that every two or three months, I'd be overseeing a new opening.

No question about it, a steam engine would soon run me over if I didn't make a huge change. And I needed to do it quickly.

Getting the Office Organized

As I suspected, the Sheraton headquarters in Boston had not hidden from me its manual of standards and policies for opening new hotels. There was no such manual at all. At least, I couldn't find one and neither could my secretary, Dorothy Crom, after multiple phone calls to Boston.

If the company seemed lax about quality control, it did keep track of how its hotels spent money. We found plenty of guidelines for accounting, cost control, and corporate procedures. This was because the accounting departments of the Sheraton hotels did not report to the general managers but directly to ITT, the parent company. The company's corporate comptroller also had to answer to ITT, following then-CEO Harold Geneen's philosophy of mistrust, and his appetite for systems of command-and-control.

Time was running out for me to figure out how to improve the quality of the food and beverage offering in our regional hotels in the absence of any standards set at the top. The new hotels in the pipeline were coming at us fast, and it was our regional office's responsibility to make them a success.

I realized my job description had grown far beyond the role I was hired to perform.

If there was no organizational structure for the food and beverage department, I had to create one.

If there were no policies or procedures in place, I had to write them.

If there were no standards of quality and service to aim for, I had to develop them.

If there were no food and beverage guidelines to follow for hotel openings, I needed to establish them.

When I finally found Roland in the office, back from yet another series of trips to Scandinavia and Iran, I told him what I had in mind. He agreed without asking any questions and said we should have had these policies and procedures in place a long time ago. I think he forgot that I had only been working there less than two months. But I was pleased that I now had his greenlight to go ahead with my plans. I was determined to save our region from another badly planned opening.

Luckily, Dorothy typed incredibly fast, even faster than some people could think. As soon as the set of empty white binders she ordered arrived in our office, I began to develop and write concepts, guidelines, and policies for Dorothy to type up. I did this for days on end, in between my frequent trips to London to supervise the Heathrow opening.

Dorothy typed every day until her fingers hurt, and soon the first set of manuals filled up. Within weeks, we had created a series of policies and procedures that took up every inch of the filing cabinet.

Of course, I didn't just want to create manuals for their own sake then watch them gather dust in the cabinet. I made sure every page was packed with meaningful information that would guide staff through every phase of planning each hotel. This started with important guidelines for the architect and interior designer, and standards for the restaurants and bars, and pre-opening policies and procedures that would maintain those standards once the hotel opened. My goal was to create a complete set of instructions for ensuring a structured, well-organized regional food and beverage office.

Roland was traveling during most of this process, and as soon as he returned, I proudly showed him the collection of manuals we had developed. I stood there as he paged through them, preparing myself for any questions he might ask. But he said nothing. He only turned to take a quick glance at the shelves lined with all the manuals, and said, "Looks good, very nice," before walking out to his office.

Was this all? No questions, no discussions, not even the slightest sign of interest in what we had produced? Food and beverage was, after all, his department.

Perhaps Roland knew something I didn't. Wondering why he seemed so detached, and worried that it was because I had basically restructured his department on my own, I asked Dorothy if she knew what was going on. She confided that Roland had lost interest in his food and beverage regional manager job and had been lobbying John Kapioltas for a promotion to a general manager position at one of the hotels that would soon open.

Dorothy had the inside information, as always. She told me John had dashed Roland's hopes by hinting that his lack of operational experience would keep him from getting a GM position anytime soon. He suggested that Roland try for a resident manager first and see how that went. Aha, so this was the reason for Roland's constant travels. He'd been networking with GMs all over the region, trying to promote himself for the next available resident manager role.

Even if no one cared but me, I couldn't conceal my pride in our new set of policies and procedures. Of course, these still had to be tested as we planned and opened new hotels. We'd need the full cooperation of the general manager and the food and beverage staff at each hotel to implement the new system and give us their feedback so we could incorporate their suggestions. But at least we had an actual structure in place for what appeared to be the first time.

Days later, our office got some news. Roland was moving to the Sheraton Copenhagen as resident manager after a staff shake-up there. For the time being, that meant his responsibilities would now land on my shoulders, and those included much more travel than I'd anticipated.

As for my goal of implementing a new structure for the office, I had no intention of slowing down. As long as no one at the top stopped me, I would continue my plans to apply the new procedures at our upcoming hotels. I would also begin to put them into effect at all the existing regional hotels too.

I realized this could mean stepping on people's toes and creating resentment. But if Sheraton wanted to set high standards for itself and compete in this region, we had no choice. I needed to brace myself to do battle when necessary. Because there was no question about it, battles were headed my way.

FIRST DAY IN MY NEW OFFICE WITH
SHERATON MANAGEMENT CORPORATION IN BRUSSELS

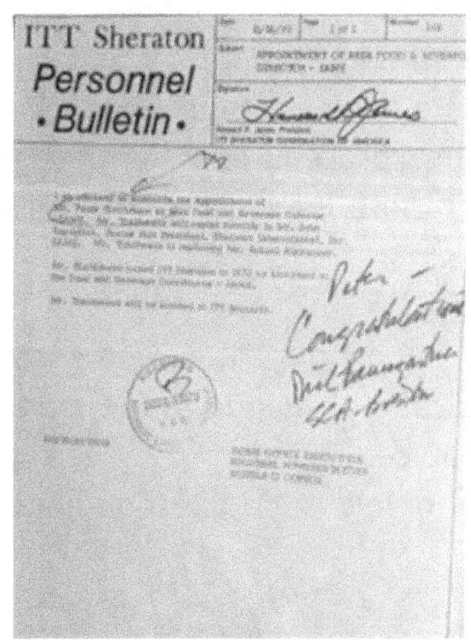

ITT Sheraton
Personnel
• Bulletin •

Peter –
Congratulations

ANNOUNCEMENT OF MY
PROMOTION

AWARDING EXCELLENCE IN
PERFORMING

Exploring Different Cultures 13

On the Move Again

"The devil is in the smallest detail."

A poster in John's office displayed the old saying in large type, and I saw it every day when I walked by or met with him.

Anyone who works in hotels can attest to the absolute truth of this proverb. But I asked myself whether this company had taken its message to heart.

As the acting head of the food and beverage division, I saw it as my job now to pay attention to each and every one of those small details. Immediately after Roland's departure, I started a routine of heavy travel, visiting every hotel in our area to introduce our new food and beverage philosophy, and distribute the new operational manuals to each general manager and food and beverage director.

The only hotel I excluded from my early travels was the Copenhagen Sheraton. I wanted to avoid any confrontation with Roland, the new resident manager, who was involved in straightening out the hotel's many problems in the food and beverage department. It wasn't that I was scared of Roland, but considering our history, it seemed like a smarter strategy to install the new F&B standards successfully in all the other hotels first. That way, the results of the new system could work in my favor in case I encountered any headwinds from Roland when I finally visited Copenhagen.

Besides visiting our own hotels, I made a point of visiting the main competitors in every city I traveled to so I could find out what was keeping Sheraton from ranking as number one there. If Sheraton truly wanted to become the leading international hotel company in our area, we would need to offer an outstanding food and beverage experience in every hotel.

Denyse and the kids had a difficult time adjusting to my constant travel, and I too regretted spending so much time away from my family. But I felt energized by the challenges of my newly expanded job, and I had no plans to slow down my increasingly hectic schedule.

Fortunately, traveling at that time was still a pleasure. Terrorism had not yet turned airports into fortresses, and with the absence of heavy security, there was no waiting in endless lines.

But traveling to new places always brought surprises, and my first trip to Cairo certainly had some in store for me.

As soon as I got off the plane in Cairo, a Sheraton Airport representative named Ali met me at the top of the gangway and escorted me to a Mercedes waiting at the bottom of the stairs.

"Mr. Tischmann, welcome to Cairo. Could I please have your passport, ticket, and luggage sticker?"

Handing over my only piece of identity? And my airplane ticket too? This sounded like a bad idea, but when Ali noticed my hesitation, he reassured me that I would get everything back at the hotel.

Moments later, our Mercedes crossed the airfield, passed through a VIP gate without even stopping, and merged into the heavy Cairo traffic.

The hour-long trip from the airport to the hotel gave me time to start adjusting to my new surroundings. I admired the wide streets lined with flowering trees, bright red as if they were on fire, and I watched as bicycles loaded with multiple passengers rode by. Around us on the streets, we passed pushcarts packed with piles of cotton or stacks of colorful fruits and donkey carts driven by men in long white gowns. Crowded public buses drove by, their passengers spilling out the doors, hanging on by gripping the sides of open windows, and staying on in whatever way they could.

Just as we started to cross the Nile River on one of the city's many bridges, I glimpsed the Sheraton Hotel, a towering building of almost twenty floors, crowned by the familiar sign on top. Turning right into a street along the western shore of the Nile, we arrived to a most spectacular welcome.

The second I stepped out of the car, Klaus Gurny, the F&B manager, welcomed me and escorted me past a line of hotel employees who stood, clapping their hands, in a line all the way into the lobby. What a show! I wondered what they did when John Kapioltas visited.

Klaus took me directly to my room, an enormous suite with a huge private bar, on which rested a fruit and pastry display large enough to satisfy a small reception. Klaus welcomed me once again and asked me to call him when I felt settled in and ready to take a tour of the hotel.

"Absolutely," I said, thanking Klaus for his help but telling him I needed to get my luggage first. It arrived minutes later, along with my passport and airline ticket. But Klaus would still have to wait.

The theatrical greeting by Klaus's food and beverage department did not convince me to change my usual routine, which was to always meet with the general manager first when I visited a hotel. After all, the GM was ultimately responsible for the hotel and had the final decision-making authority. He would be able to give me more perspective on the hotel and fill me on any problems in the food and beverage department.

Turning the department upside down was not my goal. I wanted to assist the hotel with ideas and advice to make the whole operation more successful. So my first business trip to each hotel was mainly a learning exercise to allow me to understand everything I could about that particular hotel and its management, staff, culture, and customs. I also needed to get a sense of the daily challenges to overcome so the hotel could maintain a leading position in the local market.

But no matter what changes I suggested, they could only happen through the general manager, not the food and beverage manager who reported to him.

Peter Birchall, the general manager, was in his office when I came by. He had been with the Cairo hotel for a few years, and as he guided me to a comfortable seat, he asked if he could offer me a Turkish coffee. I accepted with pleasure and gave him a big box of Godiva pralines, a Brussels specialty, for his wife.

His eyes perked up even more when I passed him a copy of our new operational manual and explained the new structure and guidelines. As he listened intently, he broke into what looked like a convincing smile.

"Peter, this looks great, and it's about time that we have common guidelines for all hotels. You have my support!"

What a relief. Having the Cairo Sheraton on my side was an important step in my efforts to introduce our concept throughout the region, and Peter had been at this enormous, busy hotel for enough years to understand the impact of these new standards. What was good for Cairo would certainly be good enough for the other hotels.

Klaus had waited patiently long enough, and it was time to let him give me a tour of the restaurants and bars he proudly oversaw. Despite the competition of other Cairo hotels such as the Hilton and the InterContinental, the Sheraton was a center of social activities in the city, and its restaurants, bars, and nightclubs filled up every night. This was the place to be, and you could sense the energy just by walking through the spaces.

We entered the grill room during a change of shift, and the waiters instantly lined up in an impeccably straight row, giving Klaus another opportunity to put on one of his shows. Like a general, he walked down the line of waiters and checked for polished shoes, clean fingernails, and spotless uniforms. I doubted that this was done with every change of shift, twice a day. But the routine looked so seamless, I was convinced it was done regularly to maintain high standards of hygiene, sanitation, and quality.

Making sure Klaus understood I was not here to conduct an inspection, I asked him to show me around all the other food and beverage outlets in the hotel and to walk me through each kitchen and storeroom.

During that first Cairo trip, Klaus even took me to fruit, vegetable, meat, and fish markets so I could get a feel for the availability and quality of food in the area and see where the hotel purchased its products. I'll never forget my first visit to the meat and poultry market.

Egyptian markets sold chicken so fresh, it was practically still walking, or should I say flying.

The chicken preparation was divided into three areas, with hundreds of cases of live chickens piled up in the front, followed by a line of butcher blocks where workers cut the chickens' heads off, then a place where people plucked the feathers and cleaned the chickens to prepare them for sale.

Butchered in the morning and ready to sell a few short hours later, the product could not be more fresh.

As we walked past the poultry stands that day, I noticed a headless chicken flying midair. Suddenly, it changed direction, so that rather than landing in the hands of the person responsible for plucking the feathers, it was now charging directly at me. I ducked out of the way in the nick of time, thinking that a hard hat would have been a good idea for the market visit.

Ketchup, French mustard, and even sugar were especially hard to find in Cairo, as I learned on my market tour with Klaus. If the hotel wanted to serve those things, it had no other choice than the black market. Trying to explain this to our corporate office in Boston would be another issue, but they didn't need to know.

It was obvious that the Cairo hotel team had to get creative if they wanted to offer outstanding cuisine and attractive menus. This meant they often went outside the city to find certain coveted products, even traveling to Beirut. In Beirut, they could find just about every imaginable item. After every trip, Klaus returned with his suitcases full of merchandise and would use the magic baksheesh system, a.k.a. bribes to officials, to get his bags through customs without paying exorbitant duties.

Baksheesh made everything possible and ensured that the Cairo Sheraton continued to have all it needed to remain the best hotel in town.

Despite my intensive crash-course in Cairo hotel management, I found time to squeeze in a little entertainment during my busy first trip. With Friday the official day off, the weekend starts on Thursday afternoon, and Klaus had organized a sightseeing and entertainment bonanza for me. First, he booked a driver to take me to the pyramids, an hour's drive away in Giza, an experience I felt fortunate to be able to see in person, after a lifetime of looking at pictures of the magnificent structures in books.

During my visit, I had the chance to go inside one of the pyramids, through a metal door that led to a small staircase carved into big blocks of stone and leading down to the inside of one of the great wonders of the world.

The staircase was hardly large enough to hold two people side by side, so it was a real challenge for visitors to squeeze past each other on the way up and back down. More than one hundred steps later, I arrived in an empty room surrounded by stone walls.

The sticky, humid air inside, mixed with the smell of sweaty tourists, made any long stay almost impossible. For those expecting to find something special inside, the whole descent had to be very disappointing.

Klaus also surprised me by arranging for a guided horse ride around the pyramids and all the way to Sakkara, the step pyramid and ancient cemetery a few miles away. I was lucky that my horse, a purebred Arabian, was small and gentle, since this was the first time I ever rode a horse in my life. Many years later, I took another ride around the pyramids, although unfortunately, that one did not end as comfortably.

For my evening entertainment, Klaus arranged an 11:00 p.m. dinner reservation at the hotel's nightclub. Surprised about the time, I learned that Egyptians eat very late. Peter Birchall joined us at our table, set right in front of the dance floor and loaded with a variety of excellent mezze, prepared by the chef of the Sheraton's Lebanese restaurant. Peter seemed impressed that I sounded so familiar with all the dishes in the mezze. Of course, he didn't yet know that I was married to a Lebanese.

A crowd of waiters around our table ensured the best VIP service. This always happens when the GM dines at your table, and even more so if the guest is someone from the corporate office.

Most of the performances that night involved European shows, but the highlight of the evening was Nagwa Fouat, Cairo's very best belly dancer. The Cairo Sheraton was known for always having the best belly dancer in town and had secured Nagwa Fouat exclusively for the hotel. As much as I enjoyed watching a belly dancer for the first time, however, I did not enjoy it when she tried to pull me on stage. Thankfully, the general manager intervened, just in time to save me from an embarrassing experience.

All in all, the trip was a success, giving me an understanding of the hotel's operations and creating a wonderful base for my next visit, when the priority would be less showmanship and more on business.

In my first-class seat on Sabena Airways, flying back to Brussels, I reflected on how one year ago I had received an offer for the job of food and beverage director at the Cairo Sheraton. But since the timing was off at the time, Klaus had taken the job instead. Obviously, I decided not to tell him about this.

The flight time to Brussels was just enough to write my first trip report. My own policies mandated this, after all. As much as I wanted to lean back and nap after an exhausting trip, I forced myself to grab a pen and get to work, knowing that I would not have the time to write my report in the office, as my next trip was already waiting.

On my Cairo visit, I had received the royal treatment from the moment I walked into the Sheraton. But my first trip to our hotel in Kuwait was a different story. Back then, in 1973, the sheikhdom of Kuwait was increasingly dominant as an oil exporter in the Persian Gulf and had grown from its beginnings as a fishing and trading town in the seventeenth century to become a major center of business in the Middle East. I was eager to see it.

Stepping off the plane in Kuwait City, I found two Kuwaiti gentlemen in white galabias waiting for me. Entrance to the country at the time required a local sponsor who would ensure that your visa was ready at the airport when you arrived. The two men took my passport, speeded me through immigration, and led me to customs control, where agents proceeded to search every inch of my luggage looking for alcohol, which was officially forbidden in Kuwait. On the way to the hotel, our car got stopped again for random searches by special custom agents, whose job was to find anything that may have escaped notice at the airport.

In spite of these controls, the black market in Kuwait boomed, and anyone who wanted to buy spirits could get them. The country had a cosmopolitan population with an enormously wealthy, highly educated elite, and it enjoyed a free press and relatively liberal lifestyle. Women drove their own cars, and most didn't wear headscarves at the time, unlike in nearby Saudi Arabia and Qatar.

During the ride to the hotel, I noticed the modern highways and construction everywhere, evidence of Kuwait's growing economy and state of the art infrastructure.

No line of uniformed staff waited to greet me when I arrived at the Sheraton. Instead, I went directly to my first planned meeting with the general manager, Henry Hunold, who briefed me on the hotel and prepared me for my most important rendezvous. I was about to sit down with Mr. Alshaya, head of the influential Kuwaiti family that owned the hotel which had hired Sheraton to manage its operations.

The old man, as Mr. Alshaya was known to everyone, had the ultimate authority on every decision made about the hotel. His two British-educated nephews were more involved in the day-to-day business, but nothing happened without Mr. Alshaya's approval.

The Alshaya family had made its fortune in the shipping and trade industry back in the late nineteenth century, and the hotel it operated in Kuwait City was the first Sheraton outside North America. The company would go on to become an innovator in the franchising business starting in the 1980s and remains to this day a major force in retail and hospitality in Kuwait.

Still, the old man never forgot where he came from. Every year, he paid tribute to his family's roots as Bedouins and retreated to the desert for a month to live the simpler life of his ancestors, taking his two ultra-modern nephews with him.

These retreats must have given Mr. Alshaya a refreshing break from his life as an extremely busy, smart, and demanding businessman. He understood that his hotel was a significant property for Sheraton, a useful toehold for the hotel corporation in a fast-growing country and highly profitable region. I couldn't help noticing that he knew our management contract by heart, especially the chapter ensuring quarterly visits by support staff.

If any of us did not visit his hotel in due time, Mr. Alshaya immediately picked up the phone to call John Kapioltas. The conversation would go something like this:

"John, I have not seen Pablo this quarter," the old man would announce into John's ear, reporting the absence of Pablo Sanchez, the regional chief engineer. "I think we should renegotiate our fees agreement, since you are not fulfilling your part as promised."

If there was one thing John hated, it was an owner complaining that he didn't get the support he was promised in the contract. I made sure to schedule my quarterly Kuwait visits for the coming year as soon as I heard about this, and I instructed Dorothy to inform Mr. Alshaya well in advance every single time.

As I walked into Mr. Alshaya's office with Henry Hunold, the old man got up from his desk to welcome me with a friendly "Ahlan wa sahlan" (welcome) and introduced me to his two nephews, Khalid and Ahmed. Dressed in a white galabia and local headdress, it was hard to guess Mr. Alshaya's age, but his calm, gentlemanly manner suggested a man of maturity and stature, if not necessarily old age.

Mr. Alshaya offered Arabic coffee for all, which I accepted with pleasure, adding that I would like to have it without sugar if possible. The expression on his face made me wonder if I had made a faux pas. I thought I knew this coffee from my multiple visits to Beirut. What had I said yes to?

After a few minutes, a tall man in a long white galabia entered the room, holding in one hand the dallah, an Arabic coffee pot, and in the other hand, a pile of small thimble-shaped cups. Since I was the guest, he served me the first cup, then continued in a round, serving Mr. Alshaya last.

Our host lifted his cup with another "Ahlan wa sahlan" and invited us to drink. The first sip tasted terrible to me, too bitter and overpowered by cardamom. This was not the coffee I knew from Beirut. I later learned that Arabic coffee as served in the Gulf is more bitter and heavily spiced, much more than the version served in Lebanon, and Gulf locals don't tend to sweeten it like the Lebanese often do.

My palate wasn't used to this flavor, so I was relieved to see the cup served only half full. I finally managed to empty it. I had accepted my host's Arabic hospitality, and now we could move on to the business at hand. Unfortunately, I had miscalculated.

The waiter who had brought the coffee leapt up to fill my cup again immediately. Then he did so a third time, and again a fourth time. How could I make this stop? Simply looking at the refilled cup caused my taste buds to revolt. Not drinking the Arabic coffee would have been impolite, but drinking it over and over again meant I would keep suffering in silence, with no end in sight.

This whole time, Mr. Alshaya had been watching me with some amusement. After my third cup, he said, "Mr. Tischmann, if you do not want to have any more coffee, simply shake the cup when the servant comes, and he will not serve you." Mr. Alshaya had not finished speaking when I was already shaking my cup. Other countries, other customs!

Overcaffeinated and ready to carry on with our meeting at last, I told Mr. Alshaya about my career in hospitality and my plans to support our managed hotels more efficiently than ever. I noticed Mr. Alshaya intently taking in every single thing I said and realized he was probably memorizing every promise, word for word. This was clearly not a man who easily forgets.

It was time for me to stop talking and to let Mr. Alshaya take over. He made it clear that he understood how important this hotel was to Sheraton and to its future expansion in the Middle East. During our entire conversation, his nephews sat silently on the sofa, listening. Respect for their uncle and his position would not have allowed them to interfere in the conversation, but I knew that they too were taking extremely specific mental notes about everything we were saying.

I hoped Mr. Alshaya considered our meeting a success. I had no doubt that he would pick up the phone as soon as I left to call John Kapioltas and report every detail of our chat, giving his feedback on this new Peter W. Tischmann person who promised so much. But would I deliver on those big promises?

At least the company seemed to have faith that I was the right man for the job, as I learned in November 1973, a short while after my trip to Kuwait and about one year after I started with the Sheraton Management Corporation in Brussels. That month, I received an official promotion to area food and beverage director of Europe, Africa, and the Middle East, taking over from Roland Kursteiner.

I was not only determined to deliver on my promises to Mr. Alshaya. I was intent on making sure that every food and beverage department in our division would receive the direction and leadership it needed to position itself as the best in town.

But first things first: It was time to celebrate all the hard work our department had put in.

I decided the promotion was a perfect opportunity to invite the entire office to our home for some "socializing," as they call it in the States.

Ludwig Simson, who happened to be in Brussels helping me to restructure the Brussels Sheraton Hotel's food operation, volunteered to help me throw a little party for the staff. After all, when the director of food and beverage hosts an event at his home, the office certainly expects something special. And special this was.

Denyse had prepared the apartment to welcome a big crowd from the office, and Ludwig Simson helped us arrange an irresistible array of French cheeses, crispy baguettes, and bottles of Nouveau Beaujolais, followed by a hearty French onion soup, which we served at midnight to the guests who were still around—and most of them stuck around well past the stroke of midnight.

Everybody seemed to enjoy the wine and the cheese, with the exception of Michael Duffy, who asked me where he could find some water. An Irishman drinking water at a party? Was he sick? I wondered. I showed him to the refrigerator, and as the evening went on, I watched him head into the kitchen over and over again with an empty glass and return with his glass filled with water. Very strange indeed.

Later in the evening, as the first onion soups had been served and French chansons reverberated through our living room, Michael Duffy suddenly flipped over and fell flat on the floor. Everyone rushed over to help him and figure out what was wrong.

"Should we call a doctor?" someone shouted.

"No, I'm fine," Michael piped up, his voice heavy, his eyes already closing as he started to fall asleep right there.

This was no mysterious health condition. The man was obviously drunk, but on water? The answer would be revealed the next morning, when Denyse and I started to clean up our living room and found our two carafes, one that had been filled with Cognac and the other with Whisky, emptied to the last drop.

Surprises Not Permitted

John Kapioltas, with whom I had developed a friendly relationship by the time I was promoted, was a man who hated surprises.

Our warm interactions—I was finally calling him by his first name—didn't take anything away from the respect I felt for John and his position. If anything, I knew better than perhaps anyone that the casual atmosphere he created around the office could be deceptive.

John was smart enough to assemble the most talented professionals he could find to work for him, knowing that he could only be as good as his team. He trusted everyone to the greatest extent and let us do our jobs, as long as no one created problems for him. One of the worst things you could do to John was to catch him off guard with something he didn't know about in advance.

To avoid any ambushes, John liked to have constant contact with his people. He'd open every conversation with "What's new?" This was his way of encouraging his team or any staff member to reveal any issue or piece of news in the departments he oversaw.

Our company claimed to value communication and trust as the tools for success, and we all knew we were supposed to use them to support a common goal: making our division as successful and as profitable as possible. As long as the system worked, John could concentrate on owner relations and the acquisition of new hotels. And we had plenty of those on the way.

For now, my main mission was to reorganize the food and beverage department and prepare it for the rapid growth ahead. I kept filling up the binders, one after the other, and soon we had created an impressive library of policies and procedures, guidelines, quality standards, and operational concepts for the many future hotel openings to come.

John was fully aware about what we had achieved and became a frequent visitor to my office, opening one cupboard after the other to proudly introduce the many manuals to his guests. Every visit to my office became a ceremony, and I made sure to keep him posted about any new binders we added.

Even though our office had what seemed to be a healthy working climate, non-stop travel schedules left the place feeling quiet or empty more often than not. Rarely did all the executives come into the office on the same day, let alone meet in order to exchange ideas or coordinate projects. But through constant check-ins with his staff, John made sure the right hand knew what the left hand was doing.

Only at the annual Christmas parties did all the regional executives make a point to be in the same room at the same time. These were nights when business took second place behind champagne, smoked salmon, and goose liver canapés. At those parties, John, whom I never saw drinking, made sure all glasses were filled at all times.

At first glance, John just wanted everyone to relax and enjoy the evening together. But maybe he had a more devious goal in mind: to test how his staff behaved when they let their guard down or drank lots of alcohol, since some of our colleagues tended to take advantage of the free flow of liquor. I personally had no problem passing his test, as I didn't drink at all.

It was no surprise that John felt suspicious. As convivial as our own staff seemed, I soon learned that the headquarters in Boston were a hotbed of corporate politics and devious maneuvering. In my own job, I mostly remained shielded from any interaction with Boston, but through the grapevine, I learned that certain executives in the main office were more concerned about advancing their own interests than those of the company.

One Boston executive I started noticing around our office frequently was Roger Senter, Sheraton's corporate director of human resources. Senter could be a messenger of good news or, more often, of not-so-good news. Whenever Senter arrived on one of his firing trips, John Kapioltas would be on a business trip, leaving the bad news to Roger.

But being "away on business" didn't necessarily mean he was traveling, as I eventually discovered. Being away could also mean that John worked from home. Did John remain in permanent contact with Roger Senter to find out how things were going? I'll bet he did.

I would be surprised if John ever fired anybody. From what I could tell, he preferred to be the nice guy all the time and possibly never fired anyone in his entire career. Never did I guess that years later, I would become acquainted with the other side of John, the guy who could vanish without a trace at precisely the moment when I needed him most.

The Portuguese Revolution

Lisbon is a place that hooks you for life from the very first visit, at least this is what happened to me. The hilly city, one of the oldest in Europe, has more than its share of beautiful Gothic and Baroque buildings and charming neighborhoods lined with cafés, restaurants, and galleries. Along the winding streets of the Alfama district, one of the city's oldest, food stands give off the tempting smells of freshly grilled sardines and anchovies wrapped in wine leaves.

At night, the sounds of Portugal's classic Fado music fill the air, as female vocalists in long black dresses sing mournful songs of lost love, sorrow, and death, their voices ringing out from dark, crowded little bars.

Planning a visit to the Sheraton Lisboa was always a pleasure. Set on one of the city's many hills, the tall building has a spectacular view overlooking the Belem Tower at the port and stretching all the way to the Christ the King statue on the southern banks of the Tagus River. The monument embraces Lisbon with its open arms, like the famous Corcovado in Rio de Janeiro.

Visits always meant plenty of shopping too, especially for leather goods like shoes and handbags. Many high-quality European brands had manufacturing plants in Portugal, among them Charles Jourdan, a leading French fashion retailer. No wonder Denyse owned Charles Jourdan shoes and bags in every color and shape in the mid-1970s, until after one of my trips, she told me to stop shopping because her closet couldn't fit one more thing.

The warmth and friendliness of the Portuguese, along with the city's reputation for cleanliness, ranked among the reasons why Lisbon was, and continues to be, one of Europe's most popular travel destinations.

For years, Lisbon's most famous hotel was the Ritz, named after the French hotelier César Ritz, the man behind Paris's iconic Hotel Ritz and the founding father of the hotels that became the Ritz-Carlton company. But like so many historic hotels, the Ritz in Lisbon had fallen into disrepair and was mostly coasting on its reputation.

The Ritz's reign came to an abrupt end as soon as the Sheraton Lisboa opened. The Sheraton's modern, well-appointed rooms and facilities turned it within a short time into not only the preferred hotel in Lisbon, but also a social center for the city and Portuguese society.

The Sheraton's general manager at the time was Hans Oppacher, an old Hilton veteran, who knew his business well and managed to quickly position the hotel as the best in town. He ran a tight ship and was tirelessly detail-oriented, and most of all, he welcomed new ideas that would help keep the hotel ahead of the pack.

On my visit to the hotel in the spring of 1974, I found in Mr. Oppacher an enthusiastic audience for the new food and beverage standards I had established. He told me that he would be more than pleased to introduce our new philosophy into his operation, and I sensed his energy was genuine. Likewise, his team, Food and Beverage Manager Herman Simon and Executive Chef Ludwig Simson, were highly competent department heads who could be relied on to execute the new plans thoroughly.

Everything seemed poised to run smoothly, and I felt confident we were off to a solid start. As it turned out, my trip to Lisbon in April of that year involved more drama than I had anticipated.

First, the Sheraton had a big wedding booked during the weekend of my visit. Herman Simon had designed a spectacular show, involving an oversized pineapple structure that would get rolled into the ballroom minutes before the cake-cutting ceremony. The pineapple would then open up as a band played live music, and a young lady would step out of the giant fruit and offer champagne to the newlywed couple.

This was a wonderful idea and definitely a stunning surprise for the crowd, at least to anyone who had never before attended a wedding at the Sheraton Lisboa. The pineapple was one of Mr. Simon's favorite party flourishes, and he had used it over and over again. It worked to perfection and provided the highlight of the evening.

I felt lucky to be around to witness the pineapple extravaganza. That Saturday night, as soon as the lights dimmed on the elegantly dressed wedding crowd in the reception hall, a spotlight appeared and shone down on the giant pineapple as it rolled into the room. The crowd fell silent, watching the pineapple with fascination. Everyone waited to see what would happen. A minute went by. Two minutes. Still, nothing happened. Soon the whispers started. But everyone kept looking and waiting.

Since I knew what Herman had planned, I started to worry about the young woman inside the pineapple, held prisoner in a fruit statue. The music got louder. Still nothing happened, but at this point, it was clear to everyone that something had gone wrong.

Herman wouldn't be Herman if he couldn't figure out a way to smooth out a tough situation. And so he did, inviting the waiters to join him onstage with their trays of champagne, dancing to the music around the pineapple, and distributing full glasses to the guests. Meanwhile, he led the wedding couple over to the glorious cake, so they could start cutting slices with a long, shiny sword.

With the guests distracted and back in the party spirit, Herman and his staff quietly wheeled the pineapple back behind the stage. There, staff engineers took over and freed the prisoner, who stepped out of the pineapple trembling with fear. Apparently, this major stumble didn't keep Herman from bringing the pineapple back again for the next wedding, and the next one after that.

But the malfunctioning pineapple wasn't the only memorable event I would witness on my trip.

As I stepped out of the elevator into the lobby on the morning of April 24, 1974, prepared for another day of work, I was surrounded by noise and commotion.

A crowd of employees ran back and forth, shouting slogans in Portuguese. I spotted some back-of-the-house staff, for whom the lobby was normally off-limits, gathering there and joining the other employees in their loud chants.

At the reception desk, customers jostled and argued with the one receptionist on duty, who looked obviously confused and unable to handle the nervous guests. Standing tall in the lobby, I saw the rooms division manager, who normally stood behind the reception desk but was now gesturing and yelling, trying to bring some order to the chaos.

What could possibly be happening?

As I looked around to try to make sense of the situation, wishing I could understand Portuguese enough to decode the slogans everyone kept shouting, I noticed a huge tank and other military vehicles parked in the hotel's driveway. A group of soldiers in full gear stood in front of the hotel, blocking the entrance.

Maybe the general manager has the answers, I thought and proceeded directly to his office, only to find a group of employees standing in front of his door, arguing. They had locked Mr. Oppacher in his office, and I couldn't get past them to enter. A confusing situation now felt completely bewildering and scary, unlike anything I had ever experienced before, at least not since my childhood.

A few minutes later, I learned that I had just become a firsthand witness to the start of a revolution which, after almost half a century of Fascist dictatorship, would overthrow Portugal's Estado Novo regime. The peaceful uprising had begun as a military coup but was quickly joined by civilians, including some staff of the Sheraton and many other businesses around Lisbon. The event later earned the nickname the Carnation Revolution, after a local restaurant worker named Celeste Caeiro stuffed flowers into soldiers' rifles and tanks in celebration of the revolt.

The crushing dictatorship was finally on its way out, but a long period of instability and social unrest lay ahead. The Sheraton Lisboa would no doubt have a front seat to whatever happened next.

Meanwhile, my ongoing trips to Portugal always seemed to include a side order of drama. Visits to our new hotel in Madeira were no exception.

A part of Portugal, the Atlantic Ocean island of Madeira was about a two-hour flight from the mainland. Each time I visited our hotel in Lisbon, I began stopping in Madeira too.

My visits there became memorable less for the work involved than for the harrowing experience of landing on the island. The volcanic rock formations that made up the island of Madeira descended in a steep, straight line into the ocean. Madeira had no actual beaches, except for the artificial ones created by property owners and developers, the Sheraton Hotel included.

The airport sat on the higher part of the island, and its runway was known as one of the shortest in Europe. Only TAB, the Portuguese

National Airline, was allowed to fly to Madeira, and its pilots received special training to land on that precarious slice of earth.

Shortly before one of my trips to Madeira, I learned that two accidents had just happened there due to planes overshooting the runway and diving into the very deep, very cold Atlantic.

This didn't inspire much confidence, to say the least, but I gathered up my nerves and steeled myself for my flight. After all, I couldn't exactly avoid my responsibility to visit the hotel without humiliating myself. But that particular flight turned out to be one that has remained seared in my memory. Once my plane landed at the beginning of the runway, it shifted immediately into reverse and started to shake and rattle, then lurched forward, stopping just yards away from the end of the runway.

As the plane began turning around, at the tip end of the runway, with its wing extending into the void at the edge, I could see waves breaking against the rocks below us. My back was shaking along with the plane. When I saw a flight attendant pass by, I asked her, my voice surely trembling, "We're very much at the end of the runway, aren't we?"

"Don't worry, sir," she answered, "today was a very good landing!"

I got the sense this was not the first time she'd been forced to put on a brave face and act as if everything was perfectly normal.

So what would a not-so-good landing feel like? I decided it was best not to ask.

Preparing the Next Hotel Opening

On all my trips so far to hotels around the region, I had not faced any resistance from the hotel's management teams. All the general managers assured me they would support the new Sheraton standards that I wanted to introduce, although I knew I would need to keep tabs on the hotels to make sure they actually implemented the changes. But in the autumn of 1974, I ran into an entirely new challenge.

The time had finally come to open the Frankfurt Sheraton, the first hotel in our division entirely designed and developed by our office in Brussels without interference from Boston. This would also serve as my first chance to oversee every aspect of the food and beverage concept, which would take into account the special requirements of an airport hotel. The location near the Frankfurt Airport would mean a constant stream of guests arriving on unplanned layovers, often showing up in big groups and walking into our door demanding service as soon as possible.

Urgent situations like these felt familiar to me. In my years at the Steigenberger Corporate Office and the Steigenberger Airport Hotel, I had seen them all. My experience gave me the perspective I needed to design a back of the house and kitchen operation that could handle walk-ins in large quantities, with no problem.

I found an enthusiastic partner in Karl Schaefer, the hotel's pre-opening manager, who joined our division from the United States. Karl was not only a seasoned hotel professional, but he also had a terrific sense of humor that made working with him easy and fun. Karl knew what the Frankfurt Sheraton needed, and after my meeting with him to introduce our new manuals and concepts, we both felt confident that the food and beverage plans would be a success.

But Karl got his first clue that I meant business on the day we drove together to visit Bauscher Weiden, the hotel's chinaware supplier. Karl loved to drive, so he took the wheel and sped us to Weiden in less than two hours, going at over 120 miles per hour. We enjoyed many laughs during the ride, despite the fact that I was afraid for our lives. When we stepped out of the car at the factory, I noticed his tires were nearly worn to bits. He simply smiled when I pointed this out to him.

Karl sounded equally jovial when he introduced me to Karl Tropmann, Bauscher's managing director. Maybe it was having the same first name that allowed both men to hit it off from the beginning.

Meetings at Bauscher took place at a small Bavarian pub called Bierstube, on the showroom premises. The company had opened the pub specifically to entertain clients and conduct business, in much the same way golf courses are often used in the United States. Mr. Tropmann was a master of the art of hospitality, overseeing a constant flow of draft beer from the taps to guests' tables, followed by a parade of regional pub foods.

Mr. Tropmann's eyes nearly popped out when I told him I don't drink beer. He looked at me silently for a moment. "Beer, we can serve on the spot, but for anything else we need more time," he said, his brow tightening as he tried to figure out what to do with me. Serving up fresh draft beers, one after the other, was a tried-and-true part of doing business at Bauscher, and now here comes the new Sheraton executive in charge of all the regional restaurants, and he doesn't even drink beer!

This would not be the only surprise in store for Mr. Tropmann that day. As he and Karl sipped their beers, he ordered his staff to bring out a variety of china samples so I could have a look. With no idea what I might like, he started showing me the patterns and decorations popular with Bauscher's other clients, including some of our own hotels. I could only shrug and shake my head. I had no interest in any of these patterns.

Creating an individual identity for all our new food and beverage concepts meant using a unique china design for each one. I felt committed to this mission, and I had no intention to back down. Mr. Tropmann seemed surprised when I told him I would not be ordering any of their standard designs. I didn't want Sheraton guests to see our china in other restaurants and hotels. It was important for our concepts to look special and to stand out in our guests' minds.

Mr. Tropmann realized my plan was non-negotiable. He recovered from the momentary shock and offered his full cooperation in developing unique designs for our various restaurants. To prove his point, he immediately called his designer and production manager to join us. He had no idea yet what other new challenges awaited him, but he was a smart businessman. As Karl and I said our goodbyes to him, I could tell he was surprised but ready to take any necessary steps to create a mutually beneficial business relationship.

Alas, I couldn't say the same thing for everyone else who was accustomed to doing business with Sheraton. For instance, some of our hotels in Europe employed one Mrs. Fitze, based in Zurich, to do the menu design, but I was unhappy with her work and wanted to make a change. I found Mrs. Fitze's designs, although attractive, somewhat too childlike and too similar to those of the Mövenpick chain in Switzerland, which also used her services.

Mrs. Fitze shook her head at me as soon as I brought up my plans for new and unique concepts for our restaurants. Not only did she show very little flexibility in adjusting her designs, but she made it clear that she was not willing to accommodate our ideas for our restaurants and bars. She was an artist, after all, and nobody told Gauguin or Picasso how and what to paint!

Unfortunately for me, it was too late to find someone else in time for the Frankfurt opening. But by the end of our meeting, I made up my mind never to work with her again. As it turned out, this would be easier said than done.

No sooner did I start putting the finishing touches on plans for the Frankfurt opening than another hotel dropped into my lap. A Paris property that was originally developed for a competing hotel company suddenly became available, and Sheraton instantly signed a management agreement, eager for a presence in a European capital like Paris.

This decision may have sounded like a good idea to executives in the corporate office, but getting two major hotels up and running at the same time was not the wisest of plans. Our team came under a tremendous amount of pressure to successfully open both hotels. It didn't help that the Paris hotel, a thirty-level skyscraper near the Montparnasse rail station in the 14th arrondissement, had all kinds of problems from the start.

For one thing, the hotel had no room service area. I was wondering how we would be able to serve breakfast to an estimated three hundred guests every morning, in rooms scattered over thirty floors with long corridors. How could architects, designers, and hospitality professionals forget to account for a room service area? Did none of them ever stay in a hotel before?

But with the construction almost completed, we had no time to make real changes, let alone to introduce our new concepts for the various restaurants and bars. Fortunately, the hotel already had two dining areas in progress, each with a distinct personality: an attractive all-day dining space called La Ruche and a gourmet restaurant called Montparnasse, with prints by the famous Italian artist Modigliani decorating its walls. As Modigliani spent most of his active painting life in Paris working in the Montparnasse area, the name of the restaurant and the copies of his paintings turned out to be a perfect pairing.

We still needed eye-catching menu designs for the restaurants, but my search for someone to replace Mrs. Fitze had turned up no other prospects yet. With no time to spare, I called her again, but this time made it clear that if she refused to take any guidance from our team, this would be our last project together.

Two weeks later, Mrs. Fitze delivered one of the most beautiful menu designs I'd ever seen, certainly an asset in helping us open the hotel with a splash.

The Paris opening was a huge success. One reason why it worked so well, even under difficult circumstances, was that we introduced a marketing and promotion plan for our restaurants for the first time. This included not just creating a stunning menu design, but also adding promotional collateral like a series of miniature show plates. The attractive collectors' items helped define the restaurant's identity and created a steady flow of repeat customers.

We soon decided to make the collector show plates a part of every opening in our region. The little plates made perfect coasters, and customers in Paris, after obtaining the first one, wanted a second, a third, and more. As we only gave the plates away to guests who had ordered a minimum amount of food and drinks, the idea became a huge revenue generator.

Another reason why our Paris and Frankfurt openings went so well is that I'd decided to bring in trained staff from our other hotels to assist. Ludwig Simson, the executive chef at the Sheraton Lisboa, and Christine Weigelt, our coffee shop manager in Brussels, did a fantastic job of preparing the new restaurants for the launch. Christine also helped execute my idea of transforming our traditional coffee shops into an all-day dining concept, a space that looked more like a restaurant than an American-style coffee shop with counter seating.

As a first step to implementing our new restaurant concept, we removed the counter seating and eliminated all the visible coffee machines in favor of a more sophisticated style and appearance for the restaurants, and our guests responded with enthusiasm.

This was the first time Sheraton had brought in experienced staff from other hotels to help open a new property, and each launch was such a triumph that the idea of an opening team was born. We would now bring in a seasoned pre-opening team to assist with every new hotel opening, including Ludwig and Christine as well as another Sheraton talent named Rene Schmidt, who joined us from the United States to help ensure that every new hotel we opened became a success.

We certainly needed all the help we could get. Not only did we have a fast-growing roster of new hotels to launch, but I needed to visit the existing properties all year to make sure the general managers were consistently using the new concepts, as promised.

My schedule soon filled up with back-to-back trips to Europe, the Middle East, and Africa. By then I was used to the frequent travel, but managing my home life with the constant need to hop on flights would prove more difficult than I had imagined.

The Importance of Menu Design

Working in a great many restaurants in my life, and visiting even more as a customer, had taught me that details like menu design make a big difference to guests. The impact may be unconscious, but the way a menu looks can set the tone for the entire dining experience. If a menu is poorly designed, its graphic elements outdated or dull, it can damage a guest's overall impression of a restaurant.

Even though Mrs. Fitze, after some urging, had created a menu design for the Paris Sheraton that stood out and contributed to a successful opening, I knew I could not continue working with her. She was too resistant to change and completely unprepared to accept our new approach to design development.

The job was hard to fill, but I was determined to find someone whose vision aligned with mine. Then one day, Toni Yazbeck, director of development for the Middle East, informed me that if I was ever looking for a graphic designer, his cousin Sami Alouf would like to meet with me.

Another Lebanese, is the first thought I had. But I decided to invite Sami into our apartment to see what he had to offer. This pleased Denyse, as did Sami's assurances that there were indeed plenty of other Lebanese expatriates living in Brussels. Sure enough, a few of them later became very good friends of ours.

But my meeting with Sami was intended as an interview, not a social visit. Upon seeing his work that day, I had to admit to myself that his designs involved too many graphic elements that clashed with my own tastes. I could see no rationale for replacing Mrs. Fitze with Sami.

Accustomed as I was to giving direct and specific feedback to the people I supervised, I had no problem telling Sami that my expectations were quite different than what he had shown me and that the chances of working together were almost nil.

Denyse later chided me for being too harsh on Sami and told me I should have explained in more detail what I was looking for and given him a second chance. I regretted that I had invited him to our apartment because now I was stuck in the middle of two people with a shared Lebanese heritage, and I felt outnumbered.

But considering I'd had trouble in the past trying to find another menu designer worth hiring, I decided to take Denyse's advice and invite Sami back for a second trial, this time in my office instead.

What I learned in our second meeting is that Sami worked closely with his wife, Sophie, who was a designer too. On looking at Sophie's own work, I found her creative approach more in line with the look I hoped to develop. Their respective skills complemented each other perfectly, as I discovered, and it was mainly a question of finding the right balance between the two.

Although we had to get over some creative hurdles at the beginning of the process, it didn't take long for Sami and Sophie to understand what I wanted to achieve and to deliver the most extraordinary designs. They did so just not just for our menus but also for the china, show plates, and all the other collaterals we needed to open our hotels with style and distinction.

Sami's Lebanese background turned out to be a bonus, since our new hotels in the Middle East required menus translated into Arabic. Having Sami and Sophie on our team proved to be a win for all sides.

Finally, the era of Fitze was over, replaced by the era of Alouf, which brought with it a budding friendship.

As Sami wrote to me a few years ago, the relationship we've developed since that fateful meeting in Brussels is the last thing he would have predicted. "Our first contact was neither promising nor congenial," Sami admitted, but "the mistrust in the beginning was transformed over the years into a true collaboration."

In that email to me, in French and dated August 3, 2015, Sami reflected on our projects together, dating back to the mid-1970s and continuing for a few decades. He said he found me to be a demanding client "who knows exactly what he wants and can express his thoughts clearly, precisely, and concisely" and that he and Sophie grew to deeply value our work together "even though it wasn't always easy."

One of the parts that moved me most about Sami's letter was when he wrote, "I never would have wagered a single cent that our professional relationship and our friendship would last more than thirty years. I will always be ready to embark with you on new adventures."

Denyse and I are equally delighted that the Alouf family has become such an important fixture of our lives.

The Blue Leather Coat

When work took me away from Brussels, an ever more frequent reality, I made the best of every trip, squeezing in an hour here or there to explore the city and neighborhood around each new Sheraton opening.

One of the company's biggest challenges in those days was the upcoming Istanbul hotel, a long-delayed project with numerous construction hurdles and bureaucratic snags.

The project was a headache, but at least the location was spectacular. The Turkish city is the only one in the world situated on two continents, Europe and Asia, and its setting along the Bosporus, the strait that splits Istanbul in two, is absolutely breathtaking. Istanbul has witnessed three civilizations, the Roman, the Byzantine, and the Ottoman, and each of them has left its heritage behind. Ottoman palaces rise along the shores of the Bosporus, along with stunning mosques, historic mansions, and architectural sites that give the city a profile unlike any other.

Little did I know at the time that years later, I would be returning to Istanbul to host the rich and famous along with many heads of state at one of these palaces along the strait.

But for now, I had to make frequent trips to check on the Sheraton site, centrally located in Taksim Park. For years, the project had shown little sign of advancing and was far behind its original schedule. Hundreds of crates packed with kitchen equipment and other furnishings had sat idly in the park for years, waiting to be installed in the hotel.

Around the time of my visits, Sheraton installed a new general manager, Amletto Abbatangelo, a man of Italian nationality who finally got things moving, although we still had no opening date on the horizon. I befriended Mr. Abbatangelo, and he gave me his useful tips on shopping for leather in Istanbul, which, like Portugal, had an outstanding reputation as a manufacturing site for luxury goods sold by European designers.

Turkish artisans used the finest quality leather and finishes, and there was nothing they could not do, all with the utmost speed. They not only manufactured their own designs, but they could also produce any model and design advertised in any fashion magazine.

When a blue leather coat by Christian Dior caught my eye, Mr. Abbatangelo referred me to one of the finest leather shops in town. Two days and $400 later, I was the proud owner of the most beautiful coat I could imagine. Denyse very much liked the coat too, and it hung in my closet in Brussels, awaiting the moment when the weather changed and I could finally wear it.

One day as I sat in my Brussels office preparing for an upcoming trip, Dorothy popped in to tell me that John wanted to see me. Knowing his standard question, "What's new?" I grabbed the latest reports and zoomed to his office.

"Come here, I want to show you something," said John the moment I walked in. He went to his closet and took out his latest purchase, a blue leather coat. My new leather coat. "It's the latest design from Christian Dior," he said, with a big smile on his face. "The design and the quality are outstanding, the best, and at $5,000, it's a real bargain. What do you think, do you like it?"

Surprised and speechless, I managed to murmur, "Congratulations, what a great coat and a real bargain," because I knew that's what he wanted to hear. What could I say?

This was not the first time John had shared with me some special items he'd bought, knowing that I appreciated quality and style as much as he did, and understanding that those were the standards I tried to instill within our hotels.

Needless to say, I never wore my coat. How could I? But my sister's husband was very happy when I gave it to him as a gift for his birthday.

As particular as John was about his clothing, he had equally precise tastes when it came to his meals, even the most casual ones. As a chef working for a Sheraton restaurant, the sight of John Kapioltas entering your dining room is one that would make your heart rate spike.

One of the openings we had on our docket that season was the Sheraton Hotel in Brussels, and as soon as it opened, in a location overlooking the Place Rogier, our offices moved from the Westbury Hotel to a building within the hotel complex. It was certainly not a pleasant situation for the Brussels hotel's general manager to have the corporate office next door, but it was convenient for us. It also allowed John, myself, and our executive team to dine and host meetings in the various restaurants of the hotel.

The all-day dining room Le Compte de Flandre had dark wooden panels and Flemish scenes as wall paintings, creating an elegant atmosphere that was a far cry from the Sheraton coffee shops typically imposed on us by the Boston corporate office.

John Kapioltas and Hans Worms began to make frequent appearances at Le Compte.

Despite its elegant appearance, the restaurant offered a simple menu of sandwiches, salads, and the like. One day, John, perhaps nostalgic for his American upbringing, decided to order a hamburger. This would generally pose no real challenge for the kitchen, but the executive chef of Le Compte de Flandre decided to unleash his creativity for the benefit of John Kapioltas and reinvented the traditional hamburger for his distinguished customer. Into the burger he slipped chopped mushrooms, onions, and parsley along with some bacon, then he sent it out to John's table.

In that moment, I was entering the kitchen to check on the order, but unfortunately, I arrived too late.

Within a Few Seconds

Passing by his table, John was bellowing in my ear. "Tischmann, when your chef doesn't know how to prepare a hamburger, have somebody run down to the burger shop around the corner, buy one and serve it to your customer." He jumped out of his chair and disappeared back to his office.

The restaurant's hamburger eventually found another enemy in Hans Worms. Hans was less particular in his eating habits than John, and his main habit was to never taste his food without automatically reaching for the saltshaker to add more salt.

One day, when Hans was in the restaurant again, and knowing of his selling habit, I went into the kitchen to watch his hamburger order get prepared, this time without mushrooms, onions, and parsley, and I decided to add some more salt, much more salt to be precise. Sitting at his table distracted, as usual, by the stack of reports he was reading, Hans reached for the saltshaker, showered more salt on his hamburger, and started to eat. His face froze, as he grasped his glass of beer and emptied it in one gulp.

"What happened, Hans? Too much salt?" I remarked as I casually passed by his table, smiling. I had to make sure he understood that this was not the kitchen's screw-up. Did the hamburger disaster teach him to stop salting his meals without tasting them? No, he never changed his habits.

DURING THE PORTUGUESE REVOLUTION
SOLDIERS POSTING IN FRONT OF THE
LISBON SHERATON HOTEL

CORPORATE FOOD & BEVERAGE DIRECTORS
CONFERENCE IN BOSTON

DURING THE OPENING OF THE DUBAI SHERATON HOTEL WITH SHERATON EXECUTIVES
AND THE OWNER OF THE HOTEL H.E. SHEIKH AL MULLAH

Family Is Important 14

Medical Challenges

The year 1974 started much like any other, but it turned out to be a year our family would never forget. Carine was three years old at this point and enjoying her first year in kindergarten, and Peter Jr., age two, was happy monopolizing his mother's attention, at least until Carine returned home from school.

In Brussels, a land of unpredictable weather, people often say that all four seasons happen on the same day. But this particular year saw plenty of sunshine, inspiring Denyse and the children to take long walks in the Bois de la Cambre.

My travels continued to increase, but I tried hard to spend at least the weekends with my family, with varying amounts of luck. I was missing out on more family time than I wanted to, but I could always look forward to seeing Denyse and my children's faces at the airport as soon as I returned from a trip. After one of my visits to Tehran, I returned with a beautiful Nain carpet in my suitcase. I'd struggled the night before to fold the carpet in such a way that it fit into my Samsonite suitcase, but with no room left for my clothes which I had to stuff into my carry-on.

I had informed Denyse about the carpet and asked her to send the children to meet me in the baggage claim area instead of at the arrival hall since I might get stuck at customs for a while. Greeting arriving travelers at the baggage claim was still an option in those days, when airport security was limited to passport and customs control, and the children often liked to meet me as I collected my luggage.

So here I was on that day, waiting at the conveyor belt for my bags to arrive, when Carine and Peter came running into the baggage claim area, each with a rose in one hand. They jumped into my arms, happy to see their dad again, and climbed on to the luggage as soon as I had stored it on the trolley. With Peter sitting on top of my suitcase and Carine holding my hand, we passed custom control with no questions asked. Who would disturb a homecoming dad and his happy kids?

It was around early summer when Denyse started to experience some major health problems, a long-term effect of the difficult childbirth she had had with our son Peter. She would need another operation, a projection Prof. Dr. Schieferstein had already made after Peter was born.

Not having a gynecologist in Brussels yet, we decided to travel to Germany to have the operation performed by Prof. Dr. Schieferstein, who knew Denyse "inside out" and in whom we had developed great confidence, especially after his intervention before the birth of Carine.

This meant I needed to take vacation time so I could be available to travel with Denyse and the kids. We also decided to book one week in a small resort in the nearby Taunus mountains to give Denyse time to rest after the operation.

Things did not go quite as planned, to say the least. What was supposed to be a family vacation and a recovery period for Denyse turned out to be a complete nightmare. Denyse continued to have a sharp pain in her lower belly, forcing us to see Prof. Dr. Schieferstein at the hospital again.

"Everything is fine," he insisted. "These are the pains of a normal healing process after the operation. Don't worry, your wife is too spoiled," he added, signaling the end of our consultation.

The next day, we decided to cut short our vacation, pack our bags, and return to Brussels. If this was a normal healing process, we might as well be back at home, resting and hoping the pain would disappear with time.

Back home in Brussels, Denyse's pain got worse with every passing day. One day, Mrs. Gaypara, a dear friend of ours, insisted that Denyse go immediately to see her gynecologist at the Centre Hospitalier Universitaire. Although he was not taking new patients, her strong recommendation got us an appointment.

By the time we arrived at the hospital, Denyse, wearing a green dress, could hardly walk. "What's wrong with you?" her doctor asked when he saw Denyse. "You are as green as your dress."

He took her into the examination room immediately, only to emerge a few minutes later, extremely angry, and accusing me of not telling him the truth about Denyse's operation in Germany.

I was stunned by his reaction and told him that I had informed him with complete honesty about everything I knew and every detail I was given by Prof. Dr. Schieferstein. I gave him the telephone contact for Prof. Dr. Schieferstein at the Dreieich Hospital in Germany, and he went to his office to place the call.

A few minutes later, the doctor reappeared from behind his office door, even angrier and more frustrated this time, and went back into Denyse's examination room.

Mrs. Gaypara and I stood waiting outside, hoping he would come out to tell us the findings of his examination, but the door remained closed for quite some time. My fears mounted with every passing minute.

Finally, after what felt like an eternity, the door opened and the doctor reappeared, a grave expression on his face.

"You are very, very lucky that you came to see me as soon as you did because if you would have waited any longer, you might have lost your wife," he said to me. My body began to tremble. I stood there frozen, unable to say a single word.

"By the way," he continued, "I called the professor in Germany and he admitted that during the operation he had damaged the urinary canal but had corrected the situation immediately, so you did tell me everything you have been made aware off."

Now I understood why Denyse was in so much pain and why the gynecologist informed me that she almost did not survive. The so-called repair was obviously unsuccessful and was the reason why, as the gynecologist explained to us, her urine had started dripping slowly into her abdominal cavity, causing a painful inflammation and poisoning her body.

I flashed back to Prof. Schieferstein's comments after the surgery: "Everything is fine. Your wife is simply too spoiled." In fact, nothing was fine, and he had put Denyse's life in danger.

He was lucky that he didn't perform the surgery in the United States because a smart lawyer there would've gotten millions of dollars in compensation for Denyse's pain and suffering as a result of the professor's mistake. But what are millions of dollars compared to a human life?

Denyse never left the hospital that day. She went directly to intensive care, where doctors started carefully draining the urine from her abdominal cavity to prepare her for another operation that would fix the problem, for good this time.

The damage that Prof. Schieferstein had done in mere minutes took months to repair. Denyse ended up remaining in the hospital for almost two months, including the time it took to prepare her for the surgery, and the weeks of recovery afterward.

Thankfully, Denyse's mother arrived immediately from Beirut to help and to stay with us during the entire two months of recovery. My vacation time was over, and I needed to return to work and to my relentless travel schedule. Those weeks when I had to fly away on business, with Denyse still in the hospital, and the children without their mother, proved to be one of the scariest and most challenging periods our family had ever faced.

Rushing Home Without a Passport

It's always spring on the island of Lanzarote, near the northern coast of Africa. One of Spain's Canary Islands, Lanzarote has a wonderfully mild climate and a spectacular volcanic terrain that looks like nowhere else on Earth.

In 1975, Sheraton took over an existing hotel called Las Salinas, designed by the famous Lanzarote architect Cesar Manrique. His work appears all over the island, in structures that complement Lanzarote's one-of-a-kind landscape.

Entering the hotel, you felt as though you'd walked into a subtropical forest, with the sounds of parrots chirping all around and waterfalls tumbling down. The hotel's white walls created a pleasing contrast with the black lava on the outside and made for a dramatic setting in which to appreciate the natural beauty of the island.

But aesthetics aside, the hotel operations were a mess. Once Sheraton signed a contract to take over the management, it was up to me to make major changes. I immediately realized the magnitude of the challenges ahead. No one on the team seemed willing to making any improvements, while the owner himself wanted to change everything. He had been unhappy with the previous management contract and looked to Sheraton to transform the hotel.

Ready for a turbulent visit, I arrived at the hotel on a typically warm and sunny day. The receptionist took my passport so she could complete the local formalities, then informed me that the passport would be returned to me upon my departure.

Leave my passport at the front desk for days? I felt uncomfortable about this, but I couldn't do much about it. Anyway, I would not need my passport during my visit, as I was here to work non-stop, with no plans to leave the premises.

On day two, I received a telephone call from Denyse at the front desk. Denyse never called me, so as soon as the receptionist found me, I knew something must be wrong.

Denyse sounded nervous. Our three-year-old son, Peter, was very sick and needed urgent surgery on his left ear. As I didn't get any further details and Denyse didn't know much else, I was overcome with worry. Another family health crisis, so soon after Denyse's terrifying episode? I decided to return home immediately. But this would not be easy since direct flights to Brussels only left Lanzarote once a week.

After making multiple telephone calls, the general manager's secretary, Carmen, announced: "I did get a flight via Madrid, but your flight from here leaves in two hours. In Madrid, you only have one hour to catch the Iberia flight to Brussels."

I packed my luggage in record time and jumped into a waiting taxi to the airport. Luckily, it was only a short drive, and I arrived just in time to join the passengers boarding at the gate. What a relief. I couldn't believe the plan had worked.

Our on-time arrival in Madrid gave me a full hour to catch my connecting flight. "Your passport please," the agent said to me as soon as I reached the transfer desk.

Passport? Where was my passport? After frantically searching my travel bag again and again, I remembered that I didn't have it with me. It was still at the hotel reception desk in Lanzarote.

I hadn't noticed that my passport was missing until now, since Lanzarote is part of Spain and I was flying to Madrid, so no one at the airport had asked for it. But without my passport now, I was stuck. No leaving Spain! On top of everything, I didn't speak Spanish and couldn't explain my situation to the airline agent, not that this would have helped. Anyway, the next flight from Lanzarote did not arrive in Madrid until tomorrow, so there was no chance of getting my passport sent to me from the hotel today.

Looking around for any help, I saw the Lufthansa desk and ran over to it, explaining my crisis in German. The station manager recommended I go to the German embassy in Madrid and ask for a temporary travel document. If I could manage to do this in four hours, he said, he could get me on a Lufthansa flight to Frankfurt with a connection to Brussels.

First, I had to change my Deutsche Marks into Spanish Pesetas, as I'd had no need for currency at the hotel in Lanzarote, then quickly jump into a taxi. Minutes later, I arrived at the embassy in the center of Madrid. So far, so good.

Except not yet, because I needed two passport pictures in order to get my documents. Who carries passport pictures while travelling? The desk agent suggested I go to the Cortes Ingles department store one block away to get my photos done.

One block turned out to mean a fifteen-minute walk, followed by a rushed attempt to get coins for the photo booth, take the photos, wait for the pictures to come out of the machine, and walk back to the embassy. I felt as if I was running a marathon.

My documents took only a few minutes to prepare at the embassy, and I managed to arrive at the airport in time to get my new tickets issued and board the flight to Frankfurt.

A few hours later, I landed in Brussels and sped home to see what was wrong with Peter.

The surgery was over, Denyse told me. The worst was behind us. Prof. Van Eyck, the Otho-Rhino specialist at the hospital in Brussels, decided to operate on Peter as soon as he saw him that morning. He was concerned about the amount and pressure of pus collecting in Peter's inner ear and worried it could break the bone and flow into his brain. Apparently, the infection had been building for days, but no one had noticed.

Thankful the emergency surgery had gone well, I went to the hospital immediately to see my son who would need to remain there another few days for observation. Soon after, we would discover that Peter had lost part of his hearing as a result of the infection and operation. Ever since, he would always sit in class with his good ear facing the teacher, and he still turns it so he can hear any important conversation.

What a nerve-racking few months this had been for our family. The French proverb "Jamais deux sans trois" or "There's never two without three" ran through my mind. With Carine breaking her thumb in the balcony door, Denyse going through a nightmare hospital experience, and now Peter getting emergency surgery on his ear, I wondered, are we done now? Will the proverb turn out to be true, or was there a fourth disaster in store for us?

A Conflict of Philosophies

The miserably wet December day in Hannover when I was born, in 1939, was nothing compared to the harshness of Boston winters. During a particularly snowy winter week in Boston in 1975, Sheraton was getting ready to host its annual meeting of divisional food and beverage directors. Despite the grim weather forecast, I eagerly anticipated the event. I was eager for the chance to meet my peers from the other divisions and to discuss the many changes I'd introduced in the two years since my promotion to area F&B director.

The Boston Sheraton Hotel management team knew it needed to rise to the occasion and please all the corporate executives in town for the meeting. They reserved suites for us at the very top of the hotel, on the thirtieth floor, with the best views of the city. But little did anyone know how badly this move would backfire. When an especially giant snowstorm hit in the middle of the conference, the hotel lost its power, and each of us had to walk up thirty flights of stairs to our rooms and back down again. We were fortunate not to have been among the many in the city who were injured or killed in the storm, but suffice to say, things did not go exactly as planned.

Spending some time with us in the main kitchen of the hotel were some cops from the nearby police station who were happy to warm their hands on a hot cup of coffee and enjoy a soup for lunch. Certainly, I wouldn't have liked to change places with them and have to be out in the cold and responding to emergency calls all the time.

The constant power outages defied all our efforts to have a productive conference, and we finally gave up. Trapped in the hotel for several days, we spent most of our time in the kitchen, talking about our individual divisions and exchanging experiences and updates on what we were doing back home. In truth, these casual talks in the kitchen might have contributed to a more beneficial exchange of ideas than the conference ever would have.

Meantime, the city's roads and trains all ground to a halt, with only a few streets cleaned and reserved for emergency services. Boston was at a total standstill, and we were continuing to climb thirty flights up as the elevators were still operating only sporadically.

Finally, later that week, the trains started running again, but the big question was how to get to the railway station since the streets were still not open to traffic. When a few of those cops offered to drive us to the railway station, we didn't hesitate for a second to say yes. With the roads still clogged and reserved for official vehicles only, the only way to get to the station was in a car equipped with blaring sirens.

Not wasting a moment, I packed up my bags and piled into the police car along with two other regional directors, and off we sped to the Amtrak station. Suddenly, the walkie-talkie comes on in the car, and I hear the dispatcher asking the cops, "Hey, where are you guys?" The police officer who was driving didn't miss a beat. "We're on our way to take some nurses to the hospital!" he shouted into the speaker.

I laughed quietly, but I was a little embarrassed. Nurses were working around the clock to save lives during this storm. What were we Sheraton executives doing to deserve this ride? Well, we had busy hotels to return to and meetings to attend. Not quite the same level of urgency. But who was I to argue with the chance to finally escape?

Although the Boston conference that year did not quite accomplish its goals, I had one encounter that has stuck in my mind all these years. During a discussion about ways to increase customer loyalty with Sheraton's corporate food and beverage director at the time, our different philosophies became more than visible. From past encounters with him, I knew that he believed profit should always supersede everything else. Quality and attention to detail were words that were not part of his vocabulary, and he didn't seem to consider these for even one second if they didn't produce an immediate profit.

I said to him, "Listen, the most important thing is to have satisfied customers because they will come back. And the more customers come back, the less we have to spend on advertising and so on."

He looked me in the eye and said, "Peter, if you don't have profit on your mind all the time, then you're not working for the right company."

Obviously, our understanding of quality of food, presentation, service, and guest satisfaction were miles apart, and I had no idea, until years later, just how right he would turn out to be.

More Family Problems

That storm in Boston signaled more disasters to come, as I soon found out. By the time the snow melted, other catastrophes loomed in my life and in the world at large.

Our family had already battled a series of scary health crises over the past year, made no easier by my ballooning job responsibilities and increasingly hectic travel schedule. But by the time spring came around, we had a more serious cause for anxiety. Lebanon's long-simmering political tensions erupted into a civil war, endangering our relatives' lives along with the fate of the country and the entire region.

Lebanon was no stranger to sectarian conflict and had already endured a short-lived civil war in the late 1950s, as well as various regional outbreaks in the past. Lebanon's Christian and Muslim denominations had long been vying for political power, though they managed to mostly coexist despite the tensions.

But in April of 1975, all hell broke loose. The Palestine Liberation Organization—a group that had established a foothold in Beirut after the creation of Israel in 1948 and the forced exile of the mostly Muslim Palestinians into neighboring Lebanon—tried to assassinate Lebanon's Christian president, Pierre Gemayel. On the same day, Christian militia members took revenge, attacking a bus full of Palestinian refugees. The event was enough to tip Lebanon into full-scale civil war.

The fighting at first raged mostly in Beirut, forcing schools and businesses to close and normal life to come to an almost complete standstill for days and weeks at a time. But many optimistic Lebanese people we knew kept thinking the conflict would clear up before long and life would return to more or less normal. But from our vantage point in Europe, the mess looked far too complex to resolve anytime soon, especially now that various foreign powers were trying to take advantage of the conflict to advance their own interests in the Middle East.

Denyse's sister, Mouna, and her husband, Alain, wanted to stay in Beirut and wait for the war to end, but this sounded like a bad idea to Denyse and me. We worried about their safety in Lebanon and kept trying to convince them to get out. We hoped they would at least bring their daughter Carol to Brussels so she could continue her schooling until the hostilities in Beirut calmed down. They refused to come to Belgium, but a year later, they finally agreed to leave Lebanon when the Beirut bank where Mouna had been working agreed to transfer her to a branch in Paris.

Alain had a hard time finding a job in Paris within his field of experience in the airline industry, but I was able to get him a temporary position at our Sheraton hotel there, starting as an order taker in the room service department. This was obviously a difficult step down for a man of Alain's education and achievements, but at least it was paid work that helped the family make financial ends meet in Paris for the time being.

Carol later completed her studies at the renowned Paris Pantheon-Assas University and became an accomplished lawyer. Denyse and I still feel proud of the small role we played in our niece's success, if only by endlessly harassing her parents to escape war-torn Beirut.

Ultimately, the pessimists turned out to be right, at least for another brutal fifteen years: The war raged on and on, with only brief cease-fires, until it ended in 1990. Fortunately, no one that Denyse and I knew personally was killed or injured in the war, but more than 150,000 civilians lost their lives by the time the fighting ended.

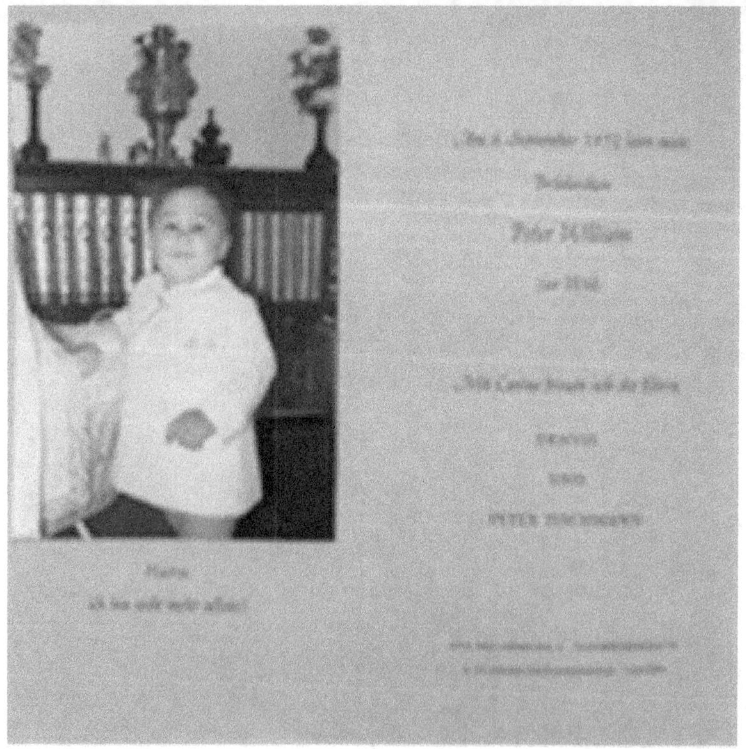

SEPTEMBER 1972 PETER JUNIOR IS JOINING THE FAMILY MAKING CARINE VERY HAPPY

The Sheraton Corporation

HOWARD P. JAMES
CHAIRMAN, PRESIDENT
& CHIEF EXECUTIVE OFFICER

June 3, 1980

Mr. Peter Tischmann
Sheraton Management Corporation
Brussels

Dear Peter:

Please let me add my sincere congratulations, along with your many friends and family, on your being chosen a winner of the Quality Ring Award. I am delighted at this splendid tribute to your ability and achievements, which you so well deserve.

You have my very best wishes for your continued success.

Very sincerely,

Bud

Howard P. James

HPJ/pt

cc - Mr. John Kapioltas

617/367-3600 • SIXTY STATE STREET, BOSTON, MASSACHUSETTS 02109

RECOGNITION FROM BOSTON

BUSINESS TRIP TO WAR TORN BEIRUT

PLAYING TENNIS WITH THE PRESIDENT BUD JAMES

A Vision for Success 15

The Search for Good People

Building a missile to kill a mosquito: that's what companies often do when faced with a challenge. In reality, the solution to a problem is often much simpler and closer at hand, but corporate bureaucracy always finds a way to make things harder than they need to be.

Nothing illustrates this point better than the case of the München Sheraton Hotel. When Karl-Heinz Hatzfeld, the general m anager, needed to hire a new food and beverage manager in the winter of 1975, he immediately started placing calls overseas and even tapped a headhunter to help him find a suitable candidate.

When I got involved in the search, I didn't have to look too far. With Siegmund "Sigi" Steber, the executive chef, already working in the hotel, I knew the right person was at our fingertips. Sigi had an impressive background as an executive chef in restaurants around the world, and he'd been with the hotel since it opened. He had enormous talent, knew the hotel's operations inside out, and was well respected by his peers. What more could we want in our F&B manager?

Well, there was a slight problem. Karl-Heinz Hatzfeld had somehow convinced himself that Sigi was not interested in the job, so he never brought it up. Sigi meanwhile doubted his own ability to succeed at the job and thought that Mr. Hatzfeld would never consider him anyway, so he refused to ask for it. I tried to talk both parties into approaching each other, but no one wanted to go first. Each clung to his own stubborn beliefs.

I realized that if I wanted Sigi in the job, it was up to me to find a diplomatic solution to this bottleneck without stepping on anyone's toes. One morning that week, I found Sigi in his small office in the kitchen, and I walked in with what I thought was a convincing argument that he should ask for the position. I reminded him that I had started in the kitchen too, and I offered him my fullest support as he adjusted to the new role. But he still hesitated.

Sigi admitted that he felt far more at ease in his chef's jacket than in a business suit at the front of the house and was afraid he was not up to the task. But after I pressed him more, he finally agreed to at least give it a try, on one condition: that no new chef would be hired for six months, should Sigi decide to change his mind after the trial period. I agreed to this plan, knowing that Sigi had a well-trained sous-chef who could take over in the meantime, and suspecting that the cost-conscious general manager would only be too happy to save on payroll.

My next stop was Karl-Heinz's office. He welcomed me in and asked for the list of candidates I had come up with to interview for the open position.

"You have the best food and beverage manager right here in the hotel," I responded.

"Who would that be?" he asked me, a surprised look on his face.

"Sigi Steber, your executive chef," I answered. "You cannot find a better person for this job."

Without even stopping for a moment to consider my proposal, Karl-Heinz responded at once, "Sigi will never take the job. He is not interested. Subject closed!"

"Did you talk to him? Why don't you ask him?" I replied. He picked up the telephone and ordered Sigi Steber into his office.

To his surprise, Sigi accepted the job on the spot. We did not hire any new chef for six months, just as Sigi had requested.

But true to our agreement, and to make sure everybody knew Sigi was ready to return to the kitchen at a moment's notice, he hammered a nail into his office wall and hung up his chef's jacket and toque for all to see.

The rest is history. Of course, Sigi never went back to the kitchen and his executive sous-chef, Mr. Ehrenfelder, got appointed executive chef, making two people happy with their promotions. He turned out to be the best food and beverage manager the München Sheraton ever had, and he eventually earned a promotion to general manager.

Why is it that big companies and corporations are always looking abroad to fill an open position rather than looking into their own inventory of potential candidates? Why look far for a solution when one is right in front of our face? I've found this principle to be true time and time again. But as with so many important lessons in life, this one is all too easy to forget.

Success Begins in the Mind

Hotel restaurants, with a few exceptions, are typically not known for serving creative, first-rate cuisine or for their high quality of presentation. As a result of this image problem, hotel guests generally visit outside restaurants, so hotel restaurants tend to lose money. This leads general managers to cut costs in order to save on the bottom line, thus creating a downward spiral that further damages the reputation of their restaurants.

To my mind, hotel restaurants everywhere had the potential to greatly improve their offerings and to draw crowds that would rival their stand-alone competition. I took it as a personal challenge to turn every one of our hotel restaurants in the Europe, Africa, and Middle East region into a destination in its own right. I wanted to create a sense of excitement not just for our newest openings, but for our already established hotel restaurants too—and I wanted to achieve this goal in all parts of the region, including in the more challenging cities of Europe.

So far, my efforts to restructure the food and beverage operations had succeeded in the new hotels, where it was easier to automatically implement the standards and operational concepts I'd developed. Thanks to the hard work of the entire hotel team at each new Sheraton, our openings around the region wasted no time in establishing themselves as the best hotels in town, and their restaurants played a role in that distinction.

No one was happier about all this than John Kapioltas, who took pride in bringing hotel owners who were considering a Sheraton management contract to our F&B office. There, he would open our filing cabinets and introduce our future clients to the many quality and operational manuals of our hotels, promoting what a management contract with Sheraton could do for their property. Meanwhile, our development department made use of Sheraton's string of recent successes to attract a steady stream of contracts.

This was all well and good, but I was not yet quite satisfied with our progress. I wanted our F&B operations to shine in every city, and I wanted the chefs at each of our hotels to produce food that could hold its own among the top fine-dining establishments in their cities.

I felt proud of the new F&B manuals we'd developed, but I knew they could never guarantee success on their own. No matter how many times John Kapioltas walked into my office to show off the volumes to his visitors, those manuals could only go so far in triggering major change. I needed to make sure those manuals became living documents instead of collecting dust on the shelf. Chefs had to learn to embody those philosophies in their daily work, food and beverage managers had to take ownership of our new concepts, and the general managers had to support and encourage the food and beverage departments to achieve these goals.

But how could we radically transform the way our chefs thought about their cooking? In order to motivate every one of our chefs to create exciting, original menus and feel passionate about their work, we needed to light up their ambition from within. Getting our chefs to take pride in their cooking would be a more effective strategy than making them listen to lectures from me about what they must do or handing them a manual off the shelf. Once our chefs realized they had license to take the creative reins, I could offer them guidance and encouragement along the way. But first, we needed to jolt our chefs into seeing their potential in an entirely different way.

It was time to get our chefs out of the kitchen and our food and beverage managers out of their offices and take them all into an entirely different environment for a weekend, a place where we could all discuss the new approach, brainstorm ideas, and get excited about our new direction. It didn't take long to figure out where to host the symposium: France, of course, land of bountiful culinary inspiration.

The Paris Sheraton was kind enough to offer accommodations and meeting facilities for all participants, and I knew that Paris, the city of lights—with its multiple three-star restaurants—was a destination nobody would want to miss.

Realizing that no dramatic changes in our food and beverage operations would happen without the support of the general managers, it was important to include them in this process. But I had been working in the corporate office long enough to know that you cannot just ask general managers to attend a food and beverage workshop, which they would consider below their level, and expect them to show up. For the GMs, I had to come up with something much more special to get their interest.

Every one of our executive chefs and food and beverage managers showed up, and I couldn't be more happy about this audience. Now it was up to me to make it an exciting and productive gathering.

On the day our workshop started, I had a surprise in store. That year, the French chef Paul Bocuse was rapidly becoming a media superstar, with articles about him appearing in nearly every publication in France, Europe, and worldwide. Paul Bocuse today was what Auguste Escoffier had been at the turn of the century, as his cuisine gained fame at the elegant hotels Cesar Ritz opened in Paris, London, and beyond. There was not a single chef around the world who would not know who Paul Bocuse was. But few chefs had met Bocuse in person yet, and certainly none of our hotel chefs had.

When I announced to our chefs and food and beverage managers that a mystery guest would be joining us, everyone in the group looked around and whispered, trying to guess who it might be.

Shortly after my announcement, in walked Paul Bocuse. The chefs recognized him immediately, and the room erupted in loud applause.

I had met chef Bocuse once or twice in the past and had maintained a friendly acquaintance with him, so I was honored that he agreed to speak to my food and beverage team. Bocuse had a remarkably approachable personality, especially for someone with the culinary celebrity that he had by now amassed. But the most refreshing thing about Bocuse, a quality he displayed back then and during his entire career, is that he came across as a man completely unimpressed by stardom, his own or anyone else's.

During his talk at the workshop, Bocuse looked and acted every bit the hardworking chef, sounding like a complete professional as well as a normal human being. He forged an instant connection with the chefs gathered in the room. During his visit, he gave generously of his time to our chefs, talking with them about cooking techniques and philosophies.

Of all the ideas that Bocuse imparted to our chefs that day, and all the skills and wisdom he gave them to take back to their hotel kitchens, one of the most significant was the absolute importance of using fresh ingredients instead of the prepackaged foods typically found in hotel kitchens. He also emphasized how crucial it is to cook a la minute instead of in advance. Our chefs had been mostly in the habit of precooking nearly everything and refrigerating it so it would be ready to heat up when someone ordered the dish—an outdated approach, although still prevalent in hotel restaurants worldwide.

It took someone of stature like Paul Bocuse to convince our chefs and F&B managers that it was time to abandon their old habits. Focusing on freshness would make a huge impact on the flavor and quality of their menus and would take the overall dining experience at our restaurants into a new realm. If I or another executive had tried to emphasize this idea to our chefs, it would have sounded like just another management directive. But Bocuse brought the idea to life with his characteristic humor and charisma.

When the subject turned to "Nouvelle Cuisine," a trend promoted by the Gault Millau restaurant guides—which had recently emerged as new competitors to the Guide Michelin—Bocuse could not resist ridiculing the entire concept. The Nouvelle Cuisine–style involved pureeing vegetables and serving them in small portions as part of a degustation menu. I'll never forget Bocuse's comment as he spoke to our chefs that day.

"Of course," he said, "it's easier to puree vegetables in a mixer than to cook them properly. I don't know," he continued, "are those chefs thinking that France is a nation without teeth?"

The room erupted in laughter, and he went on: "If these chefs could figure out how to prepare scrambled eggs the right way, this would be what I would call 'la Nouvelle Cuisine.'"

This was a devastating comment, even funnier than the first one. But this time the laughter in the room was more muted. Our chefs surely realized that cooking scrambled eggs properly was a challenge in their kitchens too.

Bocuse explained the importance of treating even a deceptively simple dish like scrambled eggs no differently than the most elegant items on the menu and doing it properly every time.

After the meeting with Paul Bocuse, our chefs returned to their hotels on fire, and I felt confident they would be ready to do their part to improve our restaurants.

But as the final say in every hotel is with the general manager, I realized that the next big challenge was to get their support and convince them that reinventing our food and beverage operations would be a benefit not only for the hotel but for them personally as well.

Talking to John Kapioltas, I proposed that we call our general managers for a meeting to get their interest and support and to give them a taste of our new ideas for what the food and beverage operations should be all about.

Realizing that we could not simply call it a meeting, I proposed to name it a Divisional Food and Beverage Symposium, and I made attendance mandatory for all general managers.

John immediately supported my ideas and personally signed the invitation to the general managers, leaving the GMs with no excuse not to attend.

"Tischmann, don't screw it up," John said when I left his office, committed to making the symposium an event nobody would ever forget.

This time, the Paris Sheraton would not be good enough. We decided to hold the first two days of the symposium at the Chateau d'Artigny, a magnificent chateau hotel south of Paris. The location, facilities, and service there certainly helped prepare the ground for my presentation, outlining our new food and beverage approach and the role the GMs would have to play.

The discussions we held throughout the symposium made me feel comfortable that the general managers were at the very least prepared to give our ideas a trial, which was more than I had expected in the beginning. I also knew that the rest of the program would turn their tentative agreement into an attitude of full support.

Next stop was Reims en Champagne, where a tour of the champagne cellars of Laurent Perrier and a spectacular dinner in the cellar awaited us. The best was just good enough to impress our general managers.

By this point, the company's top executives had joined us. John Kapioltas flew in from Brussels and Howard P. (Bud) James, Sheraton's CEO and president, arrived from Boston, in time to accompany us on the tour of the champagne cellars and to enjoy the gala dinner prepared by a three-star chef from Reims.

The presence of the two top executives from Sheraton certainly made a statement. I felt extremely thankful for the strong support their attendance conveyed, as I strove to make the restaurants in my region competitive with the best restaurants in their respective cities.

John had already expressed pride in the improvements we had achieved, and the presence of the company's president and CEO, Howard P. James, just added another level to it.

By this time, the general managers seemed to have undergone a change in attitude too and had begun to better understand the crucial role that an improved food and beverage operation could play in the success of their hotels.

But during the gala dinner that night, one of our general managers nearly gave me a heart attack. Grabbing a sauce spoon from the elegantly set table, he asked in a very loud voice, "What is this for?" There was a moment of stunned silence as the other general managers looked at each other. "Is this a shoe spoon?" the general manager continued.

Everyone laughed. I hoped he was just joking.

On our way to the Bordeaux region, to add another notch to our food and beverage tour, we stopped in Collonges Mont d'Or to have lunch at Paul Bocuse's restaurant. What a show Paul prepared, giving us a taste of his outstanding regional creations, starting with his famous Soupe aux Truffes Valery Giscard d'Estaing, followed by his Poulet de Bresse, and closing with his extraordinary Ile Flottante. I was confident that most of our general managers had never experienced anything like this lunch.

A photo session with Paul Bocuse and a souvenir menu concluded this extraordinary lunch, before Paul took us over to his collection of organs so we could listen to the French national hymn. This was a lunch event no one could forget. Bocuse's death in 2018 at the age of ninety-one was a reminder of how fortunate we all were to have benefited from his tremendous talent and wisdom. I regretted that John Kapioltas and Bud James had to leave us in Reims and could not experience the outstanding display of food and beverage that Bocuse offered us during that lunch.

The weekend ended with a bus ride to the Bordeaux region, to familiarize our general managers with France's most exquisite wines at Chateau Margaux, Chateau Petrus, Chateau d'Yquem, and several other Grand Cru vineyards.

I admit I was chagrined to see a few general managers playing poker on the bus, rather than looking out at the vineyards of France's outstanding Grand Crus. Had they really understood the purpose of this trip? I wondered. Were they soaking in the atmosphere of luxury and refinement? Basking in the finer culinary arts so they could understand what we wanted to impart to our guests?

In all fairness, they likely just needed a break from an exhausting few days. Surely they understood that when they got back to their desks, a big challenge lay ahead of them, bigger than any they had faced until now—and they knew that corporate was watching every move they made.

Menu Changes and Much More

Any chef who planned to return to the normal routine after a few days of wining and dining in France could expect a rude awakening. Back in my office, I set about doing everything possible to ensure that these trips would remain etched in the minds of every chef and every general manager, for as long as they lived, or at least as long as they stayed on our payroll.

The changes started immediately. I asked the chefs to reengineer all their menus, making sure they reflected only fresh, high-quality ingredients and a la minute preparations. Steak, for instance, must always be cooked to order, and the same with risotto. Obviously, some items are an exception: You can't make a roast beef a la minute, which I knew from my days in the cold kitchen. But for the most part, the rule would be: Make it fresh, or forget about it.

The days of relying on previously refrigerated dishes or processed ingredients were now over forever. I knew the chefs needed time to implement these changes. In some hotels, that would mean hiring one more chef to execute the new menus, and in others, it would mean budgeting for fresh products with a higher price tag. Another hotel might have to print a whole new set of menus even if they'd recently printed two hundred copies of the previous version. I braced myself for resistance from general managers who would no doubt need convincing that these expensive measures made sense. But I found that the lessons of our symposium had truly sunk in, between all the poker-playing.

It didn't take long for the food and beverage transformation to show results. After a short time, our restaurants became busier and busier. Most importantly, repeat business from the local community increased substantially, to the extent that most of our hotel restaurants were not losing money anymore. Each hotel restaurant had a distinctive menu reflecting the best and freshest ingredients, expertly prepared, displaying the chefs' own skills and the techniques they'd learned from Paul Bocuse.

We elevated our wine lists too, to appeal to even the most sophisticated wine connoisseurs. Obviously, as a large hotel company, we had limitations. We couldn't put a fifty-year-old Mouton Rothschild on our lists. Acquiring the highest-priced wines wouldn't be profitable for our restaurants, but we created impressive wine lists within our budgets. Instead of encyclopedic volumes of a thousand wines, we offered 100 or 120 excellent choices at attractive price points.

Seeing our restaurants get recognized by the local press in their cities filled me with pride. We were on the way to cementing Sheraton's reputation as not just a hotel company but a food and beverage powerhouse too.

Admittedly, our hotel restaurants in the Middle East were already successful before the France experience, although each of these vastly improved afterward. But it was in Europe that our new approach truly shone. Since European cities typically have more stand-alone restaurants, filling our hotel dining rooms had always been a challenge. So it was a triumph to watch our restaurants in Europe become more popular with guests as well as locals and post profits for the first time. Our restaurants in Stockholm, Copenhagen, and Brussels became exceptionally successful, and in most other European cities, we finally positioned our restaurants within the mainstream of successful local establishments.

I do regret, however, that we did not achieve the same distinction in Paris. No matter what our chefs tried, they had a hard time getting their menus to stand out from among the large number of outstanding Parisian restaurants. Our two restaurants at the Paris Sheraton, the all-day dining room La Ruche and the fine-dining restaurant Montparnasse 25, now served excellent food in attractive settings. But we never quite managed to attract the Parisian clientele, even after Montparnasse 25 won an award for best hotel restaurant in all of Paris.

The challenge surely had something to do with the hotel's location next to the Montparnasse railway station, not a terribly appealing spot for locals. But I suspect too that Parisians tended to think of Sheraton as an American company, so what the hell did we know about food? I would have loved to make our Paris restaurants successful, but habits are difficult to break, especially in Paris.

Still, we never gave up trying. Our chefs continued to reinvent their menus, to see if they might finally discover a winning strategy. After all, "The road to success is always under construction." That's a phrase I read somewhere once, and it helps keep things in perspective. Our chefs and our entire team had to be willing to keep building that road.

Meanwhile, little did my team know it, but I was about to throw another challenge their way.

Golden Moments

It's easy to get lost in the kitchen. Chefs can disappear into their own universe for hours, days, years at a time, and rarely interact with the world outside their kitchen door. Paul Bocuse considered it one of the major achievements of his career that he inspired chefs to get out of their own kitchens, to talk with their guests and peers and engage with what others were doing, in restaurants down the street or across the globe. Bocuse later joked that perhaps his innovation had been too successful, and chefs had developed outsized egos from all the attention they started getting as they gained higher profiles and turned into media stars. But for many chefs, including our Sheraton teams working away in their hot kitchens, it's rare to get the chance to meet peers and mingle with competitors who can infuse new ideas and energy.

As I thought about new ways to expose our chefs to the wider world, I recalled a favorite event from my former life as a chef: the Culinary Olympics. Participating in an event like this requires a huge amount of extra work, not to mention extreme organization and the willingness to sacrifice sleep. But I had a hunch that giving our chefs the chance to compete for a spot at the Olympics would motivate them to do their very best work. The event itself would be a bonus. Not only could chefs win career-boosting awards, but the event is a fantastic opportunity to get out there and see what their talented peers are doing. The pride of having their company fly them to Frankfurt to compete in an international competition was itself worth the effort. And if they earned a medal at the Olympics, what better motivation could they have to keep striving for success?

Frankly, it wasn't just the chefs' own success I had in mind. The Culinary Olympics would give me an excuse to bring together all the key players from the F&B departments in my region and make them feel part of a team, enhancing their morale, and I hoped, generating even more new ideas and energy. The event would also have significant public relations potential. Winners might earn coverage in the international media and, at the very least, would earn attention in the Sheraton EAME newsletter, which went to every one of our hotels and every hotel owner in every region. Success in the Culinary Olympics would make an excellent showpiece for the owners of the hotels our company managed: "Look what a Sheraton contract can do for you."

Watching my team succeed at the Olympics would earn me a little bit of glory too. I knew it would take a monumental amount of work to get everyone ready for the event, but I made a bet that it would pay off.

The Culinary Olympics happen every four years, just like the actual Olympics. They're sponsored by a German culinary association and always takes place over eight days in Frankfurt, in the city's giant 14,000-square meter exhibition fairgrounds. That year, 1976, more than twenty countries representing every continent sent teams to the Olympics to compete against one another, and all the big hotel chains made an appearance.

I couldn't resist the temptation to compete too, to put on a chef's hat and get myself back into the kitchen, cooking side by side with the chefs we selected for the event. Since I'd already participated in the Olympics as a chef earlier in my career, I knew what to expect.

In the years since my last Olympics, I had conveniently forgotten about all the other challenges involved in the contest. Presenting the food on silver platters, for instance. This is a requirement at the Olympics, and one of the event's biggest challenges. It sounds simple, but the arrangement takes a huge amount of skill and finesse because you can never put food directly onto a silver platter. Acidity turns silver black, so you have to create an isolation layer between the platter and the food without losing the shiny silver effect. How? By spreading a thin layer of aspic on the silver, waiting until it hardens, then presenting your food on top.

Every team does this, but some do it much better than others. The challenge has been known to drive chefs crazy. The aspic has to reach a specific temperature and end up without any bubbles or movement, looking as clear and transparent as if there is nothing on the plate at all. Some chefs end up trying and failing and trying again and again, meanwhile losing time and losing their minds. It's a wonder that I never saw a chef simply throw the whole thing out the window.

Unlike my first Olympics with the Georgs Palast and the InterContinental Hotel, both in Hannover, this time my teams were able to use the kitchen of the Sheraton Hotel in Frankfurt. As if trying to share the facilities with the hotel's own kitchen brigade did not present enough of a puzzle, when the National Team of Italy was also assigned to the hotel for their preparations and needed to use the Sheraton kitchen too, things started to get complicated. With the thirty-two additional chefs from Italy running through the kitchens, chaos was inevitable, and the situation soon drove the Frankfurt hotel chefs crazy as they tried to cook for their restaurant guests in the middle of it all.

Fortunately for us, the Italian team only needed our facilities for a few days, and we were relieved when we could finally go back to our well-prepared schedules.

While the logistics of accommodating the various Sheraton teams presented a big enough challenge, equally challenging was the attempt to get our budget approved by John Kapioltas.

Putting the pieces in place so we could attend the Olympics at all took a tremendous amount of effort, and without the help of my two assistants Ludwig and Rene, this would have been a "Mission Impossible." We had to prepare a detailed plan, then get a yes.

When I mentioned to John that I would be participating together with our chefs, he most probably thought, "Now Tischmann has completely lost his mind." But he still bet me six bottles of Vintage Dom Perignon that I would return empty-handed.

Much to my surprise, John approved our plan without any hesitation. Now that my boss had said yes, I was determined to prove to them that this would be a worthwhile undertaking, not only for the benefit of the participating chefs but for our division as a whole.

We did not waste any time, and as soon as we received the go-ahead from John Kapioltas as well as from our media director, Ludwig, Rene, and I started to put our well-developed plan into motion.

I had no doubt that John's approval would come with a few raised eyebrows and comments such as "Oh, Tischmann, here he comes again with another of his wild ideas," and I pictured him shaking his head and looking at Simon Cardew, our director of media and public relations, for support and answer.

We asked all the Sheraton chefs chosen for the Olympics to write down the dishes they planned to create and the ingredients they needed so we could approve everything and get it shipped to Frankfurt in time. With thirty Sheraton hotels participating, organizing the logistics turned into a monumental task, a project that took more than a year to plan and execute.

In the end, after all the stress we put our chefs through, and their tireless work in planning show plates and executing them under extremely difficult conditions, our biggest dreams came true. We won a total of forty-one medals, including thirty gold ones.

I even won a gold medal myself for my participation, and John Kapioltas, who was doubting my culinary talents, lost our bet. I went home with a case of Dom Perignon from him.

Earning so many gold medals and seeing our victory heralded in the international media was a total vindication. News of our success instantly reached the executives in Boston, and even the president of the company showed up for the ceremony. Our PR department promoted our triumphs far and wide, and our sales department used the results to generate more business.

As for me, seeing the look of pride on our chefs' faces made this relentless yearlong project worthwhile. I knew the results of their morale boost and creative exchange would manifest in all kinds of ways in our hotel kitchens.

Our Olympics victory was an outstanding success for Sheraton, and as a result, a special edition of the company's worldwide magazine was sent to all the owners. I was extremely happy with the results and committed to keep building on our gains. But first, another crisis was headed my way.

SPECIAL ISSUE

Sheraton EAME

SHERATON HOTELS EUROPE AFRICA & MIDDLE EAST

OLYMPIC TRIUMPH !

GOLDEN MOMENT AT THE INTERNATIONAL CULINARY OLYMPICS

The Price of Hard Work 16

The ITT Psychological Test Exercise

To survive as a hotel executive, you must not only know how to handle stress. You must also thrive on stress. Otherwise, you will run screaming out of the office on your first day at work. But apparently, there is a limit to how much stress even a seasoned hotel professional can take.

After our year of intense preparations for the Olympics, I knew that things were not likely to return to a saner pace. In the hotel industry, it's rare to have the luxury of time to sit back and savor any successes. There is always another big plan brewing or a crisis afoot or an urgent reason to hop on the next flight out.

Sheraton had ambitious plans for the years ahead, and I now stood face-to-face with the reality that I would be overseeing dozens of upcoming hotel openings, stacked one on top of another. Our EAME division set a goal of growing from six hotels in 1972 to more than fifty by 1982, and the thought of that number, coupled with my unrelenting need to succeed on every front, was keeping me up at night. I was also traveling more than ever and finding almost no time to relax with my family on the weekends.

My compulsive need to excel in everything I took on was perhaps not the healthiest approach to my job, but I was about to find out that I wasn't the only victim of my own perfectionism. That year, ITT decided to give a psychological test to all its employees. This might sound hopelessly outdated now, but in reality, many companies, including most of the Fortune 100, are again using personality assessments and psychological tests to make decisions about hiring or promoting employees. The decision to give everyone at ITT a psychological test came as something of a shock to us at the time, since many of us, myself included, had already been working at the company for years.

I tried to get out of it. "Why do I have to take this test?" I asked John Kapioltas. "Don't you know who I am? I've been working for you for five years."

Ever the company man, John shrugged me off. "Of course I know who you are, but this should always be in your files. Someday I may not be here, and someone else won't know you at all."

The exam was easy enough, a Rorschach-style test that asks you to look at various shapes and talk about what you're seeing. The results were another story.

I either did very well or very poorly on the test, depending on how one looks at it. During the feedback session afterward, my test administrator said, "Of all the hotel people I know, you've scored the best." At first I did not believe him and assumed he said this to everyone. But then he added, "If there's something we should talk about, it's your perfectionism."

"What's wrong with being perfect?" I replied, defensively. This man had just met me. How could he possibly have the insight to critique my character after such a brief test?

"There's nothing wrong with being perfect," he said with a smile. "But your tendency to be perfect could be frustrating for the people who work for you. If you're never happy with 99 percent, they'll feel they can never please you."

Admittedly, he raised a good point. But as a director responsible for exceeding expectations at each one of the hotels under my supervision, I always felt that demanding 110 percent from my staff would be the only way I could get close to a 100 percent effort. Because if I ask for 100 percent, I will get 85, and that's not enough. I know I'm very demanding, but I demand the same of myself too. I thought about arguing the point with the administrator, but I decided to let his words sink in. Maybe I needed to hear this.

Many years later, when I reached out to some of my former employees after a devastating earthquake in my professional life, some admitted that it had in fact been difficult to work for me. Others told me they had been grateful for the pressure I'd put on them, saying they never would have achieved what they did, especially during the historic transformation of the St. Regis Hotel in New York, if I had not always pushed them to excel and asked for 110 percent. I suppose that some looked more kindly on this tendency than others did, but I hoped it helped them all form habits that benefited their careers.

In any event, soon after the ITT test, all the years of pushing myself to the limit finally claimed their first victim: my stomach.

Excruciating pains sent me directly to my doctor, who diagnosed me with gastritis. "You'd better take some time off, as soon as possible," he ordered me. "Going fishing would be an ideal vacation for you."

At first, I thought he was joking. Me going fishing, staring for hours at the rod, waiting for a fish to bite?

"Doctor," I said, "if you want my gastritis to get worse, send me fishing!"

But his point was well-taken. No, there would be no fishing for me, but Denyse and I did decide to take his advice and rent a small house on the Cote d'Azur for a relaxing family break.

The time away did more than cure my stomach. It inspired Denyse and me to start making brief getaways like this one a regular part of our lives, for the sake of our family and our health. Should we buy a little place in Southern France? We asked ourselves over a glass of wine one evening on the terrace. The Mediterranean landscape reminded Denyse of Lebanon. After all, it was the same sea. I had fallen deeply in love with it too.

But our real estate dream proved short-lived. We quickly learned that we could not buy our own house in France because bank regulations didn't allow foreigners to receive credit. Paying in cash was out of the question for us.

Back at work, I confided our disappointment to my colleague George Cavenaille. Soon after, he arrived in my office with an advertisement for houses in Spain that could be purchased with financing. The development company behind the new homes was offering complimentary flight and hotel accommodations for potential homebuyers, regardless of whether we actually bought anything or not. A few weeks later, Denyse and I flew off to Spain, with George in tow.

The development sat 120 miles south of Barcelona and 80 miles north of Valencia, in a charming area called Costa del Alzahar, known as the orange coast. The hillside project rested on a slope leading down to the coastline, offering a spectacular view over the Mediterranean.

Even more spectacular was our discovery that all we needed to do was make a small down payment to get registered as the owners of the land, then we could finance the construction at a very reasonable rate. This sounded too good to be true.

Alas, it was. The company went bankrupt shortly afterward, leaving us with a piece of land in Spain where nothing would happen for years to come. Our Mediterranean dream had blown up yet again.

A year later, we received a surprise call. A real estate agent named Fernando, whom we'd met in Spain, phoned to tell us about a piece of land for sale only steps from the shore. Tempted to say "no thanks," suspecting this was yet another fantasy likely to turn out just like the others, we finally agreed to take a look. Fernando even recommended an architect who could take care of all the formalities if we were interested and a local contractor to build and finance the construction.

We booked a flight to Valencia to see Las Fuentes, a small resort on the coast. The land took our breath away. It looked like the perfect spot for our dream house, with its beautiful pine trees, Mediterranean views, and appealing location just a five-minute walk to the beach, albeit down a steep hillside that made the walk back up quite strenuous. But never mind, we finally seemed one step closer to our vacation home on the Mediterranean Sea.

We should've been prepared for what happened next.

In the summer of 1978, shortly before we were ready to start construction, a wildfire burned down the hills all the way to the sea, scorching our land and all the pine trees and leaving the entire area charred to a crisp. Blackened trunks shot up like skeletons into the blue sky.

But this time, although the land was burned, the pleasant weather, the beaches, and the sea remained intact, encouraging us to finally complete our project a little while later. As for the initial property we had purchased, I received a telephone call many years later from a promoter who offered to buy my land, which I was very happy to sell to him.

The hillside house that we built allowed our family to spend many happy vacations over the years, with relatives and friends visiting us from around the world. Or at least, Denyse and the kids vacationed there often, and I would pop in for a few days at a time. I couldn't manage any more than that because of my work and travel demands, but at least I was now spending more time relaxing with my family and friends on a beautiful coastline. Doctor's orders. After all, who am I to argue?

Purchasing a Vacation Home

When you decide to become a hotelier, you relinquish any fantasy of living a serene existence. Eventful, yes. Peaceful, no. Even a general manager of a hotel in the quietest little village in the middle of nowhere will experience drama and headaches of some form on a regular basis.

Our new hillside vacation home in Spain provided a lovely escape from the pressure and made my doctor happy, but my real calling was in the middle of the action, for good or ill.

And so it was that, in 1977, I found myself visiting Beirut, two years into its increasingly treacherous civil war.

Despite the war, Sheraton had decided to maintain its regional office in Beirut, probably because the regional director, being Lebanese, wanted to continue operating fully staffed as usual.

The office was located halfway between the airport and the city center at the American Life Insurance building, a striking modern structure surrounded by a lush garden and secured by high gates.

Although security at the building seemed to be at an acceptable standard, the location did have one major disadvantage, as it was near

Shatila, one of the Palestinian refugee camps. This had not been a problem in the past, but now that one of the main access roads into the area passed through the camp, I wondered if Sheraton should perhaps reconsider this.

Meanwhile, the company's regional office continued its daily business more or less as usual, and I made my trip to the city just as I did for all the destinations overseen by my regional office.

But it was difficult not to notice that moving around Beirut in those years was a unique experience. In the first moments of my arrival on the tenth of November 1977, the car that picked me up from the airport was stopped on the street by a group of people in civilian clothes holding machine guns over their shoulders and addressing the driver sternly. "Sir, your passport, please," the driver asked me politely.

"Who are these people?" I asked. No uniform, no identification, no nothing.

"Don't say anything," the driver replied to me. "Just give me your passport. Everything is under control."

"Nationality!" the man holding my passport shouted at the driver, his machine gun pointing inside the car.

"Alemani," the driver answered, which means German.

"Tamam," said the man, meaning okay. He handed my passport back to the driver and off we went, entering through the large metal gate of the American Life Insurance building.

I later realized those men were probably Palestinians, guarding their refugee camps and the surrounding areas in a city that was increasingly controlled by militias representing various populations and factions. The Lebanese authorities had lost any grip on this situation.

The Phoenicia Intercontinental Hotel, where I usually stayed, was now in a volatile part of the city, so I changed to the Bristol, a socially well-established hotel near the Hamra shopping district. Throughout the war, the Bristol was not damaged by the fighting in the way other hotels were, including the Phoenicia, which sustained major damages. I later learned that the general manager of the Bristol was paying officers from the Syrian occupying force to protect the hotel.

Denyse's relative Michel, my best man at our wedding, and his wife, Edith, lived near the Bristol, so one evening during my trip, I decided to surprise them with a visit. When Michel opened the door, his mouth dropped open. He stared at me, speechless, his eyes popping, before he composed himself enough to ask, "What are you doing here?" When I explained that I was staying close by at the Bristol, he smiled but still yelled at me: "Are you crazy? Nobody walks outside during the evening. Come in!"

Seeing the two of them was wonderful, and of course, we reminisced about our experience trying to find the church on the wedding day. Michel and Edith have always been two of my favorite members of Denyse's family. They asked whether I'd told Denyse's mother, Yvonne, that I was in Beirut. I planned to visit her the next day, Sunday, as the Sheraton office would be closed.

At this point during the second year of Lebanon's civil war, the fighting had intensified, but most Lebanese people I spoke with remained optimistic that it would end soon. The violence during the day was sporadic, becoming more explosive at night, so people circulated during the day, visiting friends and family and doing their errands.

On that Sunday, I took another walk from the Bristol Hotel to Ashrafieh, the neighborhood where Denyse's mother still lived. When Yvonne opened the door, her facial expression looked as if she'd just seen a ghost. It was a few moments before a smile took over her face.

Yvonne and I took a walk through the neighborhood, amid the rubble of destroyed buildings, and headed to Rue de Damas, the demarcation line between the strongholds of opposing militias. Our walk would strike many people as crazy, but since it was daytime and Yvonne knew the landscape well, I knew I was in good hands.

Walking down the street among the wreckage, I took pictures of collapsed buildings, glimpsing from a distance the people still living inside them in bombed out rooms without any windows, their laundry hanging from broken balconies. Suddenly a group of Syrian soldiers appeared in front of us. "No photos!" one guy grunted at us, stretching out his hand for my camera. I don't know what Yvonne told him in Arabic, but her kind words and my ten-dollar note helped me keep my camera. I promised to put it away.

Welcome to the Middle East, where even during a war, baksheesh seems to do the job.

As it turned out, this was my last trip to Beirut during the war. The fighting intensified month after month, with occasional deceptive ceasefires, but by then, even the most optimistic did lose hope that things would be over soon. Sheraton moved its regional office from Beirut to Cairo, where it would remain for many years to come.

It took another thirteen years and two Israeli invasions before the civil war officially ended, with no winner but plenty of losers. Beirut, the ancient and proud city by the Mediterranean, was reduced to crumbling ruins, its once robust business activities and cultural life coming to a near total standstill.

Those who had the chance to leave the country had mostly done so by then, including Denyse's sister and family. Her mother joined them not long after, allowing Denyse to breathe more easily. When could we return to Beirut as a family? The situation grew more ominous every day, and no one had any answers.

Damascus–Beirut and Return

John Cleese's famous character, Basil Fawlty, had to battle one crisis after another as the general manager of a hotel in England in the BBC series *Fawlty Towers*. But one thing Mr. Fawlty never had to contend with was an actual war, complete with militias and car bombs. Still, perhaps a man like Basil Fawlty would have been useful for Sheraton, if only to provide comic relief as the company expanded its Middle Eastern presence in the volatile, unpredictable 1970s.

It might sound odd that Sheraton decided to open one hotel after another in the region in the seventies. This beautiful but conflict-ridden part of the world had more than its share of flare-ups in that decade. Beyond the civil war in Lebanon, which had started in 1975, various other regional conflicts were brewing or on the horizon. Syria itself had recently allied with Egypt in the 1973 Yom Kippur War and had begun to intervene in the war across the border in Lebanon in 1976. Meanwhile, the Iranian Revolution was soon to erupt in 1979, followed by the Iraq-Iran War of 1980. But expand its regional presence, Sheraton did—a decision credited mostly to a charismatic and highly effective Lebanese-born executive, who drummed up hotel contracts for Sheraton all over the Middle East. So off we went.

Among the first hotels we opened in the region was in Damascus, Syria's capital. The country had been under the rule of the oppressive Hafez al Assad regime as of 1970, but the political situation in Syria was calm for the time being. By the time we prepared to launch our new Sheraton in Damascus in 1978, we had succeeded in generating excitement and anticipation among locals and visitors to the city.

I too felt enthusiasm about the opening, but by the time the project landed on my lap, it was already too late to make any significant changes—a situation that reminded me of the Heathrow hotel opening a few years ago. I immediately noticed a problem with the design, namely a structural feature in the facade that looked like a huge cross. In a majority Muslim country, this appeared to me and to some other observers as a bizarre architectural decision. But I'd learned long ago not to bother pointing out problems when it was too far along in the process to get them resolved. Ultimately, the cross shape did raise some eyebrows but apparently not enough to tear down the construction and start over. Anyway, the debacle was soon forgotten.

Denyse and the kids were eager to join me in Damascus and attend the grand opening, part of a deal I had struck with John Kapioltas. John knew that ITT's corporate policy promised executives at least one weekend at home every second week, but my constant travels had made it impossible for me to see my family on weekends. John suggested that I could bring Denyse and the kids to the hotel openings instead of flying myself home, since it would cost the company the same.

I couldn't resist the chance to show our kids around Damascus, a historic city displaying that unique Middle Eastern blend of ancient ruins from Greek, Roman, Egyptian, and Ottoman civilizations alongside the busy life of a modern metropolis.

The grand opening of the Damascus hotel went smoothly, but my family's drive to Lebanon to visit family afterward put everything into perspective. Even if the opening had not gone smoothly, what drama could compare to the anxiety of getting my family safely through a war zone? I had not anticipated feeling quite this nervous when I planned Denyse and the children's drive to the Lebanese town of Brummana to visit relatives and spend a bit of time in the quiet mountain area, where some of Denyse's family had moved to escape the bombs falling all over Beirut.

The drive from Damascus to Brummana normally takes about two hours. I hired a driver who doubled as a bodyguard, as many people did in those days, to accompany my family across the Syrian border and into Lebanon. The driver knew how to get to Brummana without steering into the major conflict areas along the way, but there was no way to avoid driving through parts of Lebanon controlled by various militias. I had confidence in his abilities, but I was still slightly anxious, and so was Denyse.

Luckily, the driver knew what to do when he had small children traveling in his car. Whenever he approached an area with a heavy militia presence, he yelled to Carine and Peter Jr., "Sleep!" This startled Denyse, but our kids must have obeyed him, because when they all finally arrived, Denyse told me that Carine and Peter did not seem shaken in the least. They had slept, or at least closed their eyes, through most of the trouble spots. When the car finally drove into the courtyard of Denyse's family residence, the surprise could not have been bigger. That they considered me crazy to send my family to Lebanon was another story, but maybe they were not so wrong.

Fortunately, we didn't have to contend with any more battlegrounds, at least not literal ones, at our other Middle East openings in those years. While each new hotel we launched came with its own share of hiccups, as hotel openings almost always do, the problems were typically minor and caused more amusement than stress.

The Dubai opening, for example, had its own quirks. Dubai itself is now an ultra-modern metropolis, a glittering city full of the world's tallest buildings, fanciest malls, and most ambitious construction projects. But back in 1978, it was still a mostly sleepy town.

The new Sheraton we opened there distinguished itself as the first modern hotel in Dubai and the first one to have an escalator. Today, if you go to Dubai and see the Sheraton along the creek, you might say, "My god, what is this little hotel? They should knock it down." It seems shockingly modest compared to the city's other stratospheric hotels and buildings, like the Burj al Arab. But at that time, it looked impressive.

The sheikh of Dubai even came to our opening. This meant, of course, that we had to bend over backward to accommodate any request he might make. Before the sheikh arrived, we learned that he does not want to see any women whatsoever when he walks into the hotel or shake any woman's hand. His request took us aback, but we knew it was in our best interest to comply. We wanted to avoid a situation experienced by the InterContinental Hotel, when the sheikh had walked in for a moment, spun around, and walked back out when a woman employee attempted to present him with a bouquet. As for our opening, we were committed to following the local protocol line by line, especially as one of the sheik's advisors had alerted us to make sure that female staff members would stand nowhere near the entrance and would remain out of sight as soon as the sheik arrived.

This had ridiculous consequences. As our famous escalator went from the ground floor to the atrium where the lobby was located, and where the ceremony was scheduled to take place, we had to ask every woman, including Denyse, to proceed to the balcony of the highest guest floor so they would be far enough away from the lobby when the sheikh arrived. When he walked in, the whole group peered down at him from above, but they managed to do so discreetly.

When the sheikh arrived, he decided to take the escalator rather than using the elevator we had prepared for him, which suddenly redirected our attention from the women to his galabia. What if his long galabia got caught in the moving escalator so that the sheikh found himself standing there, undressed, in full view of everyone gathered in the lobby?

In the end, everything went fine, the sheikh remained clothed, and the opening was a success. Our international fine-dining restaurant Lulua made a big splash at the launch. I was proud of the elegant dining room, the top-notch Middle Eastern cuisine, and the poetic name, which means *pearls* in Arabic and honors Dubai's historical status as the center of pearl fishing.

As the weeks went on, however, one specific problem arose at the hotel, making the general manager a very unpopular figure with the staff and putting into jeopardy his position as the general manager of the hotel.

All staff had been hired exclusively from the Philippines, as this country was known for supplying skilled hospitality workers. After completing a thorough interviewing process in Manila, 350 qualified hotel employees were flown on a 747 plane to Dubai to undergo final pre-opening training before starting to work. Our Filipino employees immediately began to make us proud with their excellent work ethic and their service-minded, friendly demeanor.

But one day, as the GM walked through the guest corridors, he passed by an open door to a guest room. Inside, he glimpsed a bellboy with his hands in a customer's suitcase. The GM immediately yelled at the bellboy, "What the hell are you doing there?" and slapped him on the face. As soon as word spread about the incident, the entire staff went on strike. Since we had only one nationality of employees in the hotel, Filipino, their decision to go on strike in a gesture of solidarity meant that all services in the hotel came to a complete standstill.

Under no circumstances should the GM ever have slapped the bellboy, no matter what he was doing. And as it turned out, the bellboy was in fact just packing the suitcase of the guest who had requested a room change and was doing so with the door open to avoid any question of impropriety. But the GM had hastily and cruelly jumped to conclusions and failed to give the bellboy the benefit of the doubt.

One lesson we learned, besides the obvious lesson which we hopefully already knew—never mistreat an employee—is that hiring an entire staff from the same country is a recipe for trouble. You never know when one staff member might bring up a labor complaint and rally his colleagues to his side. While it's true that a staff without a national bond might still protest in solidarity, it is unlikely that 100 percent of employees would walk off the job at the same time.

At least when it came time to launch our next new Middle Eastern opening, the Sheraton Abu Dhabi, we had already learned our lesson and decided to staff the hotel from multiple Far Eastern countries in order to prevent a similar situation during this opening. But we had more surprises in store.

Expansion, Expansion, and More Expansion

The glamorous shopping centers, impressive museums, and stunning new mosques that draw visitors to Abu Dhabi nowadays did not yet exist back in 1979. The Emirate of Abu Dhabi had joined the newly formed United Arab Emirates only eight years before, and the capital city of Abu Dhabi still had no international airport and no modern hotels except for the Hilton and one or two others. The opening of the spectacular Sheikh Zayed Grand Mosque was still nearly three decades away. People still shopped in the old souk—now gone forever after a 2003 fire—and took a boat ride to Saadiyat for picnics, well before the island became the site of Abu Dhabi's own Louvre and a future branch of the Guggenheim.

But at the time, the former fishing village and pearl-diving site held a great deal of promise as a center for development in the oil-wealthy Emirates region, enough that Queen Elizabeth II decided to pay a visit to Abu Dhabi in February 1979. She arrived by yacht, to pay her respects to a country in which the United Kingdom had vested economic interests, especially in a time when much of the Middle East region was ripped apart by war. The Iranian revolution had erupted only weeks before her visit.

Sheraton, too, saw a huge amount of promise in Abu Dhabi. After all, we could not simply leave the lucrative high-end hotel business to our competitors at Hilton. So in July of 1979, only months after the Queen's visit, we opened our first Sheraton Hotel in Abu Dhabi.

This time we hired an international staff, assembling our team with people from Thailand, Indonesia, the Philippines, and other countries around Asia and elsewhere. We ensured that the general manager received thorough preparation and training in how to manage his staff, show cultural sensitivity, and avoid unnecessarily punitive or antagonistic behavior.

One thing we did not quite anticipate, however, was the level of local excitement around the opening. We had placed a large sign on the front of the hotel site, announcing "120 days to go," changing the sign every day, reducing a day. But at one point when the hotel forgot to change the sign for a few days in a row, we received so many calls asking, "What's the matter? Are you having trouble with the opening?" Apparently, locals had kept close tabs on the progress, perhaps in their eagerness for novelty and for an alternative, at last, to the same old hotel lounges and restaurants around town.

As this was the Gulf, temperatures spiked during the day, reaching levels I had never before experienced and going upwards of forty-five degrees Celsius. Denyse and the kids visited me in Abu Dhabi in the days leading up to the opening. With daytime temperatures so high, making it too hot to even go to the pool, activities such as tennis were scheduled for the late evening times, around 9:00 or 10:00 p.m. to avoid the heat. One night as I walked with Carine along the path to the tennis courts, we heard crunching underfoot. Crickets. Masses of insects were flying up into the air to avoid being smashed by our shoes. Carine jumped up as soon as she saw the bugs and spent the rest of the walk hanging from my neck. That was the last time I could convince Carine to play tennis with us in the evening.

The Sheraton Abu Dhabi opened to great fanfare and wasted no time in establishing itself as a social center for the city. I felt relieved once again that the opening went smoothly, even more so than our previous launches. By this point, we had a solid grounding with our new operational concepts and philosophies as a result of our ongoing training with our chefs and our food and beverage managers. The corporate higher-ups were taking notice. I had strong and vocal support from Bud James in Boston and John Kapioltas in Brussels.

In that era, I also accompanied Sheraton's development director Andre Mas on trips to seek out sites for new Sheratons. One memorable trip I took with him was to the Seychelles, a country made up of 115 lush granite islands in the Indian Ocean. Formerly a French colony and later part of the British Empire, the Seychelles had won independence a few years earlier, in 1976. Not long after this, a coup d'état had replaced the new government with a Socialist regime. Andre and I participated in a government meeting held in a school classroom, with the goal of convincing the ruling party to allow us to open a hotel. The prime minister attended the meeting, along with members of his militia. Our presentation must have impressed that intimidating collection of individuals, since in the end, they approved our hotel plan. By the time the hotel opened years later, I had moved on in my career, but a few unique moments from that visit stand out in my mind.

Among the most memorable was the scene that unfolded when our airplane landed, as members of the local sanitation department boarded the plane, walking from the front to the back to disinfect the cabin and the passengers with spray cans. I had never seen this anywhere else, and I still have not to this day. I can still smell the terrible scent that pervaded the airplane after the spraying, an aroma that trapped us as we sat there and waited for one hour until they finally deplaned us.

I also remember one extraordinary tree on the islands, the coco de mer. The nut that grows on this tree is shaped like a human backside and was once valued at extremely high prices and reserved for royalty. According to one legend, the Seychelles are the biblical site of the Garden of Eden, and the coco de mer's nut is the original forbidden fruit. But since the nut weighs upward of fifteen kilograms, it is difficult to imagine how Eve could have carried it. These nuts, too, I've never seen anywhere else.

My trips around South Asia were also filled with wonderful discoveries and memories, along with their share of hotel challenges. In 1979, I traveled to Karachi, Pakistan, to oversee the construction of our hotel, an old project that had still been planned by our Boston office. The trip happened not long before Pakistanis burned down the US Embassy in the capital, Islamabad, in November of that year, based on suspicions that the Americans were behind the bombing of the Masjid al Haram mosque in Mecca. Those were turbulent times indeed across our EAME region, but we were pressing on with our plans to develop and expand Sheraton's presence wherever we sensed an opportunity.

When my team and I met with the local architect in Karachi, we discovered that Sheraton's technical services in Boston had no clue about lifestyles or customs in this part of the world. For one thing, the Boston office knew nothing about the local cooking traditions. The architect had designed a huge banquet kitchen and an enormous ballroom in a way that might have made sense in most Western countries, but not in Pakistan, as my first visit to Karachi would prove. To prepare the local food for big banquets, I saw how Pakistani cooks were arranging large bricks on the ground, lighting up charcoals placed between the bricks, and putting copper pots into the red-hot charcoal to cook the meals. The chefs then walked in between the charcoal from brick to brick to check on the food in the pots and to move them around to make sure they cooked properly. Meanwhile, unaware of local customs, Sheraton's architect had designed a multimillion-dollar banquet kitchen that made it impossible for chefs to prepare the food in the traditional manner.

The architect had also designed a giant ballroom without taking into account that at Pakistani social functions, women and men rarely celebrate in the same room, so two separate ballrooms are typically required for the same function. As a result, we had to undertake a complete redesign to reflect the local customs. Unfortunately, this was not the last time that Boston executives had signed off on hotel plans in complete ignorance of the local culture.

As for Karachi, we noticed and fixed the problems in time, and from the moment the Karachi Sheraton opened on the city's posh Club Road, it turned into one of Karachi's iconic hotels. The hotel continued to operate as a Sheraton until 2013, when the Kuwait-based owners switched management contracts to Mövenpick. According to rumors at the time, the owners, Arabian Sea Enterprises, increasingly worried that an American-based management company like Sheraton represented a security risk, a fear heightened by a spate of bombings at high-end hotels around Pakistan. The owners, on the other hand, claimed they had switched management for business reasons, not security concerns.

During the era when I visited Karachi often to check on the hotel, I enjoyed shopping in the city and browsing its markets for beautiful Pakistani art. Once, in a carpet store, while the owner flipped rugs over to show them to me, I noticed something wrapped in a newspaper and asked the owner what it was. As he was ignoring my question and kept on flipping the carpets over, I flipped the carpet back to the mysterious package, only to have the owner flip the carpet over again. After flipping the carpets back and forth a few times, he finally unwrapped the object and showed it to me: an unusual-looking Buddha made out of a bluish type of basalt stone. He told me it was from Burma, and initially, he refused to sell it to me. I finally convinced him to sell me the Buddha for US $400.

That evening, at a dinner party in the home of the owner of the Sheraton Karachi, I complimented his carpets and told him the story of how I wanted to buy a carpet and ended up buying a Buddha. He said, "Mr. Tischmann, you know you cannot take these Buddhas out of the country, right?" In fact, I did not know that. He said, "I hope you didn't tell the guy you bought it from any details about where and when you will be traveling?" I said I did. He shook his head and said: "I guarantee you customs will find you and take the Buddha out of your luggage, give you a fine, and share the profit with the man who sold it to you."

Sometimes you get lucky in life. Due to a late meeting, I missed the flight to Istanbul and instead had to fly with MEA via Beirut to Istanbul. A representative from Middle East Airlines picked me up at the hotel and transported my luggage directly to the plane, bypassing customs and antiquity control. In that luggage was the Buddha, which arrived at my final destination of Istanbul with no questions asked.

But the story doesn't end there. The food and beverage director in Brussels was married to a woman from Malaysia, and when I told her about the Burmese Buddha I'd bought in Karachi, she asked me what it looks like and, more specifically, inquired as to the position of its hands. I showed her a picture.

"This is a very special Buddha, a good luck Buddha," she said, frowning at me. "But you should never buy it. You should always receive it as a gift. Because if you buy it, it will bring you bad luck."

At home later that day, I took the Buddha down from the shelf and turned to my wife.

"This is for you," I said to her.

"What do you mean?" asked Denyse. "We've had it for a while now."

"Please accept it as my gift to you," I replied.

Years later, I found myself wondering if my so-called gift to Denyse had backfired. Did my purchase of the blue Buddha unleash the wave of bad luck that came at me like a tsunami not long after?

On the Indian Subcontinent

The name Bollywood earned worldwide fame in the 1970s when India's thriving film industry began to surpass America's, producing more films and more blockbusters than Hollywood. India itself was well on its way to passing the five hundred million population mark at that point, and it was on the rise as a global power after a turbulent era. Partition in 1948 had split Pakistan and India into two separate nations in a brutal struggle, and Gandhi was assassinated that same year. But even as the turbulence continued into the subsequent decades, India expanded its international footprint as a political and nuclear force—it tested its own nuclear weapons in the mid-1970s—as well as a pop-culture powerhouse.

I had the good fortune to visit India multiple times in the seventies, traveling mostly to Bombay, now officially known as Mumbai, and Delhi. Around India, Sheraton had multiple hotels already up and running and new ones in the pipeline.

At the time, the international media had fixated on the issue of overpopulation of the earth, but I had never sensed the problem up close in quite the way I did in India. In Bombay, you could not walk on the sidewalk without seeing a wave of people coming at you. You had to fight your way through the massive crowds at every step, every turn.

Once you grew used to this, you were better prepared to take in the magnificence of Bombay. The city is built on an archipelago of seven islands, and it has a spectacular cultural heritage, from beautiful Buddhist sculptures and ancient engraved caves to architecture that reflects India's centuries under the Mughal Empire as well as the more recent colonial influences of Portugal and the English East India Company. Skyscrapers fight for space amid the historic skyline, creating the sense of a pulsing cosmopolitan metropolis.

In Bombay, you will see tremendous wealth contrasting with a staggering amount of poverty. As I walked through the city, I would see people sleeping on the street in front of buildings, crowding under awnings when it rained. In the morning, in certain parts of town, people who were no longer moving, having passed away during the night, were piled in a giant heap at the back of a passing donkey cart with an unknown destination.

Another local tradition concerning death stood out to me at the time too. The Parsi sect of Zoroastrians, originally from Iran, had a practice of placing dead bodies in a Bombay park at night so the vultures would eat them, a ritual considered to create less pollution than burial or cremation. Although this religious park was closed and off-limits for passersby, one could still see flocks of vultures flying around, sometimes with pieces of corpses in their beak. The tradition has since faded, mostly because the population of vultures has vanished from Bombay, casualties of a now-banned drug that had been used on cattle. However, I read recently that the practice may soon return to the city, once the vulture population bounces back.

I won't make any obvious connections here between hotel companies and vultures. But suffice it to say that negotiations over hotel management contracts often feel like a blood sport.

Sheraton had a management contract with the Oberoi brand in Bombay at the time, and at the same time, we were in talks with ITC, the Indian Tobacco Company, about upcoming hotel projects in Delhi and Agra. But as soon as our partnership with the tobacco company became official, the Sheraton sign suddenly came off the Sheraton Oberoi Hotel, a not-so-subtle punishment.

Corporate warfare aside, our involvement in the Delhi hotel meant that I would get to make frequent trips there, to meet with the architect so I could ensure that our operational concepts and standards were being observed. I was excited about this and awed by the scale and energy of Delhi, a very different place from Bombay but impressive in its own right. But visiting the construction site proved to be a grim experience. I saw how cruelly the locals and immigrant workers were exploited on building sites. I would see pregnant women and women with babies in their arms working long hours, carrying the brick stones on their heads up and down the ramps from the morning until it got dark, when they would sleep in tents close to the hotel. It was misery from A to Z.

Watching the workers labor under these conditions was so infuriating and embarrassing to me, I could not manage to take any pictures of the construction site for fear of humiliating these people and invading their privacy. Years later, as Qatar prepared to host the World Cup in 2020, I read about the workers' conditions at construction sites there and flashed back to those days in Delhi.

But those Delhi workers did a beautiful job building the hotel. Back then, the style for hotels, even new ones, involved plenty of decorative details and golden carved structures. The Sheraton was no exception, the seeming grandeur of the new hotel masking the degradation that took place behind the scenes.

An Invitation to Latin America

"Accentuate the positive. Eliminate the negative." Bing Crosby's classic song gives wise advice indeed.

If only that advice was easier to follow. Still, during those years of rapid expansion at Sheraton, we had a constant stream of positive accomplishments to celebrate, even if the new openings came with their share of challenges, cruelties, and mishaps.

One ongoing victory was the increased profitability of our restaurants across the EAME region. I felt tremendously proud of all the hard work my team had put in to implement our new culinary concepts and honored that the Sheraton executives in Boston and around the world had taken note.

One day in 1980, John Kapioltas called to tell me the president of Sheraton in Latin America wants me to travel to Lima, Peru, to give presentations to the general managers about our food and beverage achievements. He hoped his teams around the area could pick up some valuable lessons from us and boost their own revenues.

As a bonus, Denyse and I were allowed to fly from Paris to Caracas by Concorde. This was the heyday of that fast, futuristic airplane, and only four years after commercial Concorde flights had begun in the mid-seventies. Inside, the plane actually looked tiny and had only two seats on each side, all of them first-class. When Denyse saw the plane in Paris, waiting at the gate for us to board, she got scared and instantly called her sister, Mouna, from the airport. "If anything happens to us," she said, her voice trembling, "please take care of our children."

The flight turned out to be an outstanding experience. We flew from Paris to the Azores to refuel, then continued on to Caracas. The crew provided top-notch service, from the quality of the beverages to the blankets and the cheese platters. We enjoyed a serene flight in the first cabin up front, the one I'd heard was the quietest. It was amazing that we heard no noise whatsoever, since I noticed a sign on the wall in front of us showing the speed of the plane, which reached Mach 1 per hour during our flight.

Three years later, in 2000, the Concorde went out of service after Air France flight 4590 from Paris caught fire during takeoff, crashed, and killed everyone on board.

Investigations later showed that the departing Concorde had picked up a turbine blade lost from the plane that was taking off in front of it, causing damage to the gasoline tank and leading to the fire with the catastrophic ending.

My presentation in Lima was the first time I had the chance to explain our new F&B operating philosophies to a big crowd of Sheraton executives outside our EAME region. In a room full of the company's Latin America GMs and F&B directors, I talked about how we had dramatically improved our restaurant revenues and how I had revised the idea of food and beverage marketing.

Marketing is not done by just putting advertising in the newspaper, I explained to the crowd, but it means taking all kinds of subtle steps to address the six senses and get the attention of your audience.

Marketing to the senses means challenging the eyes, the smell, and the taste buds of your guests before they've even taken the first bite. As an example, imagine a waiter walking through a restaurant with a platter of French-style escargots, trailing behind him the irresistible smell of garlic and fresh herbs and tempting other guests to order the escargots too.

Maybe none of the guests were thinking about ordering escargots, but the waiter's stroll inspired them to ask for the dish.

In food and beverage, successful marketing is anything that creates a desire for your product. It's everything from the welcome greeting a guest receives at the restaurant the moment she arrives, to the last smile and goodbye she gets from a staff member when she leaves. If you drive up in your car and don't find parking right away, you're already annoyed. Or you enter the restaurant and say, "My name is Tischmann, and I have a reservation for four," and the maître d' says, "What is your name please?" This creates a negative feeling that you are not important and results in a bad impression right away.

The Lima event lasted two days, and in that time, I spoke with executives at length about how to improve food quality, polish an image and reputation within the marketplace, and raise revenues. Quality in the kitchen starts with purchasing the right ingredients and focusing on freshness instead of dishing out precooked food. I explained how we had recently made that switch in our own EAME restaurants and seen nearly immediate results.

Ultimately, I believe the meeting paid off because the Latin American division soon became the best division after EAME in the categories of food quality and service. I wouldn't say it was necessarily a direct result of the meeting we had since they were undertaking other improvement initiatives too. But I think the new concepts did help contribute to the positive results. In any case, outcomes like this do not happen overnight. You can give all the explanations and examples you want, but it's up to the GMs to find the value in what you say and implement it if they wish.

As a thank-you, Sheraton offered me a trip to Machu Picchu after the seminar. Denyse and I flew from Lima to Cuzco in the Andes, eager to see the ancient ruins for the first time. When we landed, the flight attendants instructed us to move as little as possible for a while as we adjusted to the altitude. And so we did, relaxing for some time at the hotel, following their instructions, before we boarded a train that lurched mercilessly forward, backward, forward, and backward again on its route up to Machu Picchu, where small minibuses were waiting to take us up the last miles to the ancient ruins. At that time, most of the world had only learned about the fifteenth-century Incan city six decades before, and restoration was still underway in the 1970s. The site had not yet begun to attract enormous crowds. Denyse and I spent a wonderful day walking around and gazing in awe at the ruins.

We briefly visited Caracas in Venezuela, and in a shop there, Denyse found the beloved cherimoya fruit that she had only seen before in Lebanon, where it's prized for its sweet, pulpy white flesh. In Lima we learned that the cherimoya is Peru's national fruit, due in part to its ample presence. We stopped in Brazil too, and in a Rio shop, I bought a huge purple amethyst rock, cut open from both sides. As it didn't fit into our suitcases for our flight back from Rio to Paris via Dakar, I had to carry the giant rock, weighing twenty-two kilos, wrapped up in newspapers and tied with a cord. I carried it along as if it had no weight, so I could take it as hand luggage on to the Concorde, and then I lugged it through the airport in Paris for hours after our connecting flight was canceled. Now the rock sits on a shelf in our Munich home, looking lovely but never budging an inch.

The Secret of Grapefruit Juice

What does grapefruit juice have to do with corporate decision-making? When Sheraton announced in 1980 that our corporate office would soon move from Brussels to Denham, England, the decision took employees by surprise. Denham? Where was that? And why did we have to move? Rumors soon began to spread. My favorite was the one about John Kapioltas and grapefruit juice. In all his years in Belgium, the story went, our president had never managed to learn any French whatsoever, except for "jus de pamplemousse."

So off we headed, to rural England. As it turned out, the move had everything to do with taxes, but it also had a little bit to do with grapefruit juice. Belgium had been giving lots of tax incentives to foreign companies to establish themselves in Belgium, and international employees working in Brussels received a tremendous tax benefit as well. In my case, during the time we lived in Brussels, I paid taxes on my salary only for the number of days I actually worked in the country. So traveling more than 250 days a year left very little tax to pay. But when England started offering similar corporate tax benefits, Sheraton decided to move its head office from Belgium to a country where John Kapioltas could do more in the local language than order his jus de pamplemousse.

Our kids, meanwhile, felt less enthusiastic than John did about the chance to switch cities and languages. As we arrived in London on our flight from Brussels, and the stewardess announced, "Welcome to London Heathrow," our son Peter Jr. turned to me and said, "Oof, now we have to start speaking English." He'd started out life speaking German, and in Brussels, he had become fluent in French, and now there we were, creating more linguistic whiplash. To tell the truth, I was not excited about the move either. I never felt comfortable during my trips to England, and London was not a city I could warm up to, so I was not eager to subject myself or my family to it full-time.

But even though Denyse and I were less than thrilled about Denham, we suspected that the cultural change would do both of our children good, an attitude we wanted to maintain throughout every move. We had a hunch we had more moves coming up in our future.

The new office in Denham was located in an impressive old mansion surrounded by a manicured park and lush lawns. As the staff of the

Sheraton corporate office soon learned, the building's landmark status didn't even allow us to select the interior colors of the walls. But the setting was perfect for conducting business. Potential hotel owners would get picked up in a Rolls Royce from the airport, driven through the British countryside down a long tree-lined alley, and deposited in front of our mansion, where a Sheraton executive would welcome them and escort them to the president's office.

If our prospective owners were not impressed by now, they certainly were after John gave them a tour of our office, opening all the cabinets and introducing them to our manuals of operational standards, quality, and service.

The only thing left for them to do was to sign their name on the management contract.

As Denyse and I drove through the countryside around Denham to look for appropriate housing, we saw picturesque houses lining the roads, set amid lavish, flowering gardens. The British call these homes cottages, and owners are very proud to explain that their house is a hundred-plus years old, sometimes embellishing that detail with stories about the previous inhabitants.

The problem with these cottages was that they actually looked like dollhouses on the inside, with entrances so tiny that our furniture would neither fit through the doorway nor find a place in any of the rooms, not to mention that there was rarely one straight wall to be found.

After visiting almost every available cottage in the area, listening to stories of their history, and being told multiple times how beautiful these homes are, we decided to look for a modern house instead. A place with less history, but with straight walls and doorways which would fit our furniture. We wondered if such places even existed in the area. Comfort and convenience at this point were more important to us than honoring British history.

We finally settled in Marcham, a tiny community close to Abingdon, but near the European school where our children were scheduled to go. As we were making the house as homey as possible and arranging the garden, we tried to get used to life in England.

On Saturdays, I would see our neighbor mowing his lawn adjacent to ours, and as we were both driving our lawn mower up and down the garden, the following conversation would develop:

"Nice weather, isn't it?" our neighbor would say, passing by while mowing his lawn.

"Roarbabraroarboar," the lawn mower would say, at a deafeningly loud volume.

"Ideal weather to mow the lawn, indeed," I would respond.

"Roarbabraroarboar."

"Yes, it certainly is," the neighbor would say as our paths were about to cross again.

"Roarbabraroarboar," the lawn mower would say again, until we met once more at the next round.

The lawn and the weather seemed the only subjects of interest that could draw our neighbors into a conversation, until the lawn was cut and the lawn mower put back into the garden shed.

Despite those failed attempts, we eventually made friends with Penny and Bob from across the street, and our kids did enjoy playing together.

We even visited each other occasionally and had supper together from time to time.

One day, when Penny was visiting, she said, "Denyse, I saw a shopping bag from Harrods in your garbage. I have never been to Harrods. Would you mind taking me with you when you go the next time?"

Denyse was shocked. Were the neighbors actually going through our garbage? Otherwise, how would Penny know about the Harrods shopping bag?

Of course, we never asked. The next time Denyse went to London, she kept her promise and invited Penny, and the two of them explored Harrods together from top to bottom.

Another occasion I'll never forget is our New Year's Eve get-together with the neighbors. As was the tradition, everybody would bring something for the evening, so I brought half a dozen bottles of champagne to pop at midnight. But much to my surprise, by 8:00 p.m., all the champagne was gone and the only thing left were a few bottles of beer which the other neighbors had brought along. Welcoming the new year with beer was something I never experienced until now, but it showed me a side of our neighbors which surprised me.

Throughout our time in that house, Denyse and I tried to make the best of our move to the neighborhood, looking for bright spots even as we hoped this new situation would not last forever. John Kapioltas had to adjust himself too, although I suspect he did not mind the move, all in all. For one thing, his office in Denham was about three times the size of the one he had in Brussels, a huge space with dark gray leather furniture and a Dior-style palette of gray and white, a far more prestigious-looking suite and a perfect fit for a president.

I remember that space quite well, especially because of one incident I'll never forget.

During one of my infrequent trips to the US for meetings with the corporate director of food and beverage, I learned about the Corning Tableware that Sheraton had introduced into the coffeeshops of all their hotels in the States.

The tableware was made not from porcelain, as the kind we used in Europe, but from a special type of glass with an extreme resistance to breakage. No breakage meant fewer replacements, which meant more profits. So needless to say, the Corning Ware quickly distinguished itself in the bottom line-oriented world of Sheraton USA.

The lack of breakage intrigued me too, admittedly. I saw a presentation by the Corning Ware representative, who threw one plate on top of another without breaking any of them, and felt duly impressed. There was only one problem. Corning Ware could not be decorated with a design but was available only in one off-white color. We would have to see about that, I figured.

Thinking there must be a trick to this supposedly break-proof glass, I asked to throw the plates myself. I tossed one plate, then two, three, four, and more plates on top. Nothing happened.

I asked for a handful of samples to present to John Kapioltas. Maybe I could find a way to introduce this tableware in our own regional hotels, I thought. John would surely agree as soon as he witnessed what I had seen.

Back in my office in Denham, I tested the plates by throwing them one on top of the other on to my carpeted office floor, and again, nothing happened.

I called John to tell him I wanted to show him something unusual.

"Come on down," he said. I rushed down the two floors and into his office, carrying a box of plates under my arm.

I started with a short introduction about this strange, nearly unbreakable tableware, then I proceeded to throw the first plate on to the carpet. I threw a second plate on the top of the first one, and then a third plate—when, with a loud bang, the last two plates smashed together and fragmented into a thousand small pieces.

John looked at me, puzzled. What was the point of all this?

I stood there, gazing in disbelief. How could this happen? I had tried this trick several times before. Why was it failing me now? John slowly got out of his executive chair, looked at me, and said, "Tischmann, I give you five minutes to clean up the mess," and he walked out.

It took me more than five minutes to vacuum the entire carpet to remove any evidence of these so-called unbreakable plates. But when John returned, his office looked impeccable.

Needless to say, this was the end of Corning Tableware in Europe.

During our two years in England, our relationship with John became friendlier and warmer, to the extent that John visited us a few times in Marcham to join us for dinner. John did love Lebanese food, and Denyse is an outstanding cook. I believe we were the only people from the office John ever visited, and he didn't mind returning, since he knew that we would not publicize the fact that he was socializing with us, nor take advantage of the friendship and the evenings spent in our home. Both Denyse and I appreciated that John made the effort to drive forty miles from his home in London to spend time with us in Marcham.

As we prepared to move out for my next assignment, Denyse and I began to bid our neighbors goodbye and accepted invitations for last meals together. The night before we left, at a farewell supper of scrambled eggs and toast, our neighbor Penny turned to Denyse and said, "Now that you're leaving, I have to tell you something."

Denyse looked at her, wondering what the woman was about to reveal.

"When you moved here, everyone was asking themselves, what are those foreigners doing here?" the neighbor said to my wife.

Denyse's mouth dropped, but she said nothing. Later at home, she confessed how much this comment had offended her. It took our neighbor two years to mention that everyone had considered us foreigners? That they had not wanted us here when we first arrived? Our kids played together all this time and our families became friends, and we never knew that they had all thought of us as invaders in their little oasis.

Well, perhaps it was fitting that we would soon move to a place where, not so long ago, the British were the invaders—at least until they got decisively kicked out.

Driving Architects Crazy

"Vision without action is a dream. Action without vision is a nightmare."

A friend wrote this in a note to me many years ago, and it has proven wise time and time again. But the saying truly came to life when I flew to Cairo to oversee a new hotel project outside the city.

The soon-to-be Sheraton occupied a sprawling site in Heliopolis, the city of the sun, a desert area between Cairo and the airport. The history of Heliopolis dates back more than five millennia, to a time when it was one of the largest and most vital parts of ancient Egypt. Nowadays, Heliopolis exists mainly as a suburb of Cairo and is home to the Presidential Palace along with several other notable government buildings—as well as lots of sand. But in 1981, when I first visited Egypt—not long before Egyptian prime minister Anwar El-Sadat was assassinated in October of that year for signing the Egypt-Israel peace treaty with Israel's prime minister Menachem Begin—there was not much else in Heliopolis. The future Sheraton Hotel was still in the planning phase.

Originally designed as a Novotel, the project could have been located anywhere in the world and did not take into consideration local dining habits or the operational needs required to create a successful hotel. I immediately sensed that creating a dynamic new hotel with bustling restaurants and a lively social scene there, practically in the middle of nowhere, was going to be no easy task. But Heliopolis was situated close enough to Cairo that I knew the dream had potential if we executed it the right way. But at this moment, as I saw it, the dream looked more like a nightmare.

Over the past few years, I had witnessed my share of poor decision-making, as I oversaw one after another of the fifty hotels Sheraton aimed to open in the next ten years. But the Heliopolis hotel project was already threatening to rival the others as far as shortsighted planning and bad ideas.

When the hotel's Kuwaiti owners switched management contracts to Sheraton in 1981, they made it clear that they would accept any renovations necessary to bring the hotel up to Sheraton's standards and expectations, not realizing the extent of the changes that would have to be done to reflect the ambitious vision we had for this hotel.

My partner in the hotel relaunch would be General Ahmed Zaki, a man of impressive stature, who functioned as the owners' local representative. During his active time in the military, the general had been in charge of training for the Egyptian army. He impressed me from the moment I met him. The man stood six feet tall, with a heavy build and a face dominated by large, dark eyeglasses. I could instantly sense that he was a real character.

The first thing General Zaki did after we met to discuss the project was to propose that we hold a meeting in New York City where the architects were based. Why New York? I wondered. There was no reason for this meeting to happen in the US. The owners could have simply asked for the New York-based architects' team to come to Egypt instead, to present their plans for the renovation on the site of the actual hotel. But they insisted on going to New York instead. I suspected they wanted to use the opportunity to travel abroad at the owner's expense.

So off I flew with General Zaki to New York City. I was eager to see the architects' plans, and we arranged our first meeting to take place on the morning after we arrived. We met in the architects' office, where Mr. Adler, of the firm Adler and Partners, proudly presented us with his team's plans for the redesign.

I looked at the plans carefully for a few moments, and it took me only thirty seconds to realize that they would never work. Not only did the new hotel concept appear completely unimaginative, with no special elements that would give anyone any reason to go all the way out to Heliopolis instead of staying in Cairo, but the plans for the back of the house made no sense. They practically guaranteed that the restaurants and the entire F&B department would never function properly. Those plans totally disregarded the proper flow of merchandise from the back of the house reception area into the food preparation spaces and the restaurants, never mind the movement of trash from all these areas into a refrigerated garbage holding area.

Watching how food moves from place to place in a hotel gives a strong clue about what the back of the house plans should look like. Food gets delivered into the kitchen first, then cooked, then sent into the dining room, and finally it gets dumped in the garbage. All those actions must flow smoothly from area to area, without interrupting service or causing needless delays. The plans I saw would disrupt this flow and create an inefficient, unprofitable operation. These architects, I guessed, had never designed a hotel before. They also seemed to have no idea what the competing local properties looked like or what guests would expect from an ambitious new hotel in the Cairo area, especially located outside the city.

As I looked again at the plans stretched out on the table, I told General Zaki that I would need more time to study the design concept. I would need to make big changes, I warned him.

"Can you do it by tomorrow?" the general asked me.

"I'll try my very best," I promised. I had no choice. We needed to start the changes on a tight schedule, but first I needed to save Sheraton from hemorrhaging money out in the Cairo desert.

I rolled up the plans and prepared to take them with me to the Sheraton Center, the hotel where General Zaki and I were staying for our trip. But first, I asked for stacks of tracing paper and boxes of pencils and erasers.

At the next morning meeting, over breakfast, General Zaki asked me if I had come up with a solution to the problem. With a big smile on my face, I told the general: "If you find us an empty table to roll out the plans, I will present your hotel to you."

"Right here," General Zaki said. "Breakfast can wait."

"General, if we want to make this hotel successful," I continued, "we have to create a new, innovative concept, unique for Cairo, or we have no chance." I paused to give him a moment to absorb the reality that we had a tremendous amount of work ahead of us.

First of all, I explained, we needed to reject the predictable two-restaurant concept, the same concept adopted by every competing hotel in Cairo. Our new hotel should offer something totally unexpected: a spacious central lounge, for instance, decorated with an eye-catching design element—an Egyptian water wheel, perhaps—and surrounded by an array of tempting restaurants offering a variety of cuisines and environments. We could offer an Italian restaurant alongside a German and an Egyptian eatery, a pastry shop, an all-day dining space, and of course a nightclub, a necessary feature of any successful Cairo-area hotel.

Visitors could take their time strolling through the lounge and deciding which restaurant to choose, while people-watching and observing the lively scene around them as they walked. This would create an exciting new experience that no other hotel offered and would help us attract the attention and the clientele Sheraton had promised the owners.

To ensure that the back of the house runs efficiently, each restaurant would have its own display kitchen but would also connect to a main production kitchen, which would also handle room service and banquets.

I looked up from the tracing paper to see if the general was still paying attention.

General Zaki paused. I could see how he was absorbing the ideas and thinking. A moment later, he broke out into a big smile. He rolled up the tracing paper and announced, "Let's have breakfast." It was time to gather the architects again. I could tell the general was eager for this meeting.

An hour later, we walked back into the office where Mr. Adler and his design team sat waiting for us.

"Do you have a large table?" the general asked. Directed to a large surface he could use, he proceeded to roll out the architects' original plan.

"Gentlemen," he started, "if we want to make this hotel successful, we have to create a new, innovative concept, unique for Cairo, or we have no chance. Your design does not fulfill this criteria."

A tense silence filled the room. The general then rolled out the tracing paper on top of the original plans and began to explain the new idea I had discussed with him, appearing to enjoy the rapt attention of the architects as he spoke.

Having now finished, he looked over at Mr. Adler and his team, who stood quietly next to the table. After a few moments, Mr. Adler finally spoke up. "General, do you realize that this is a completely new design and has nothing to do with the concept we presented?"

"I know," the general answered, "but it works!"

And that was that. General Zaki and I soon exited the room, leaving behind us a stunned Mr. Adler. His team had a lot of redesigning ahead of them, on a tight deadline, and the clock was already ticking.

In the meantime, General Zaki and I turned our attention to the smaller details of the F&B operation, such as kitchen equipment. I insisted on ordering specific materials, expensive ones, that would need to get shipped from France.

"Why do we have to spend so much money on the kitchen equipment?" the general asked me.

"Because chefs don't treat the equipment gently," I explained. "You want to buy the best and most heavy-duty equipment your money can buy if you don't want to start having to replace equipment right away. Also, we need the oven doors and their hinges to be of the highest quality," I told him. "Chefs will drop the very heavy pots from the top of the oven on to the open door below, so the doors have to support this heavy weight, which could reach 150 pounds and sometimes more. If a chef can stand on the door and bounce, and the door can support this, we'll be fine." I had worked in kitchens for long enough to witness cooks using, and abusing, all the materials within reach.

Visiting the kitchen equipment factory in France, I demonstrated to the general what I was talking about, as I stood on an open oven door and bounced up and down. The oven door remained solidly in its place.

Stepping down, I noticed the general carefully putting one foot on the open door, bouncing a little bit with it, and then stepping with his full weight on the door. He didn't bounce his 250 pounds' worth of body weight on the door, but when he stepped down from the door, I noticed a smile of satisfaction on his face.

By this point, General Zaki and I had developed a pleasant rapport. I respected his questions and concerns, and he listened to my ideas and most of the time adopted them.

With the redesign finally complete and the new equipment ready to go, the hotel opened about a year later. The launch made an instant splash in the local community and the social scene of Cairo, and the media raved about the creative concept of the newly opened hotel.

From the first week, locals from the surrounding area flocked to see this exciting new destination. The lounge and the restaurants filled up with well-dressed customers arriving to see and be seen and to dine and socialize and spend the evening in the nightclub. The Heliopolis

Sheraton's food and beverage offerings soon ranked among the most envied concepts in Cairo and across the Middle East.

Karl Foerster, the GM at the time, did a wonderful job opening the hotel as well as hiring and training a big staff, a challenging accomplishment for a property in the middle of the desert, twenty miles away from Cairo. I had much respect for what he was able to accomplish. It was now time for me to return to Denham and turn my attention to the next assignment.

While in Heliopolis, I had occasionally heard the Egyptian saying, "Whoever drinks from the water of the Nile once shall return." I should have taken the saying to heart.

Because even though I didn't know it at the time, Egypt was not done with me yet.

RECEPTION OF THE CHAIRMANS AWARD FROM HOWARD P. JAMES, CHAIRMAN, PRESIDENT AND CEO OF SHERATON

Sheraton Management Corporation

W. G. MORIN
PRESIDENT

DENHAM PLACE VILLAGE ROAD DENHAM
UXBRIDGE MIDDLESEX UB9 5BT ENGLAND
TELEPHONE 0895/832388 TELEX 894533

WGM:jw

25th January 1984

Mr. Peter Tischmann,
Heliopolis Sheraton Hotel,
Uruba Street,
Heliopolis,
Cairo,
Egypt.

Dear Peter,

Many congratulations on being recognized by Mr. James and selected to be a recipient of the very prestigious Chairman's Award. Peter, the continuing effort that you contribute to one of our most visible hotels is well recognized by your colleagues. You have proved that you have the ability to translate your creative style in Food and Beverage to hotel operations and the additional selection of being Manager of the Hotel of the Year for the Middle East was well deserved.

The challenge in 1984 continues to be great. The new competition in your market will test all of your creativity at the Heliopolis Sheraton and I feel quite confident that you and your team will succeed.

Again my congratulations on receiving the Chairman's Award.

With kind regards.

Sincerely

W.G. Morin

Incorporated in the USA with limited liability

INTERNATIONAL TELEPHONE AND TELEGRAPH CORPORATION
320 PARK AVENUE
NEW YORK, N.Y. 10022

HAROLD S. GENEEN
CHAIRMAN EMERITUS

June 1, 1981

Mr. Peter Tischmann
V. P. Director Food & Beverage
Sheraton Management Corporation
Denham Place, Village Road
Denham UB9 5BT, England

Dear Mr. Tischmann:

I am happy to inform you that you have been nominated for the Harold S. Geneen Creative Management Award.

Your nomination has been forwarded to the selection committee where it will be given a complete and thorough review. By mid August, the committee will have selected ten to twelve finalists that will be invited to New York for the awards banquet.

Please accept my personal thanks for the contribution you have made to the continued success of ITT.

Very truly yours,

NOMINATION FOR THE HAROLD S. GENEEN CREATIVE MANAGEMENT AWARD

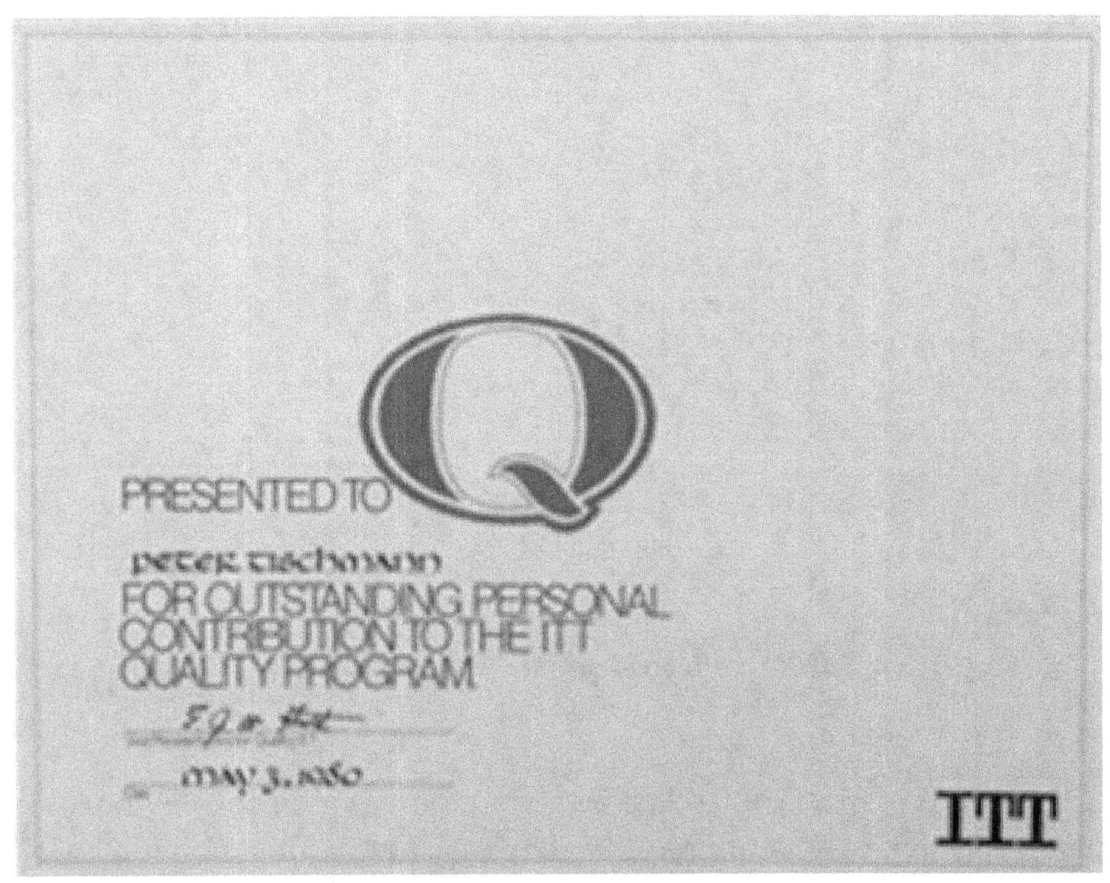

ITT QUALITY AWARD

Transferring Into Operations 17

The City of Sun Is Calling Again

Our departure from England came not a moment too soon. By the time we finally left, we had no regrets about saying goodbye. Denyse, ever the good sport, had made an effort to adjust to the rhythms of the town during our time there, but I knew she did not envision living in England for the long run.

The opportunity that got us out of Marcham was a result of a shift in my career goals, a shift that I had been contemplating for a while but that was finally triggered by something my daughter said.

One night after I had just returned from a trip, Carine rushed up to me and said, "Daddy, you're never here when we have a show in school or a soccer game."

She was right. I rarely had any time to participate in these memorable events in my children's lives. Even though I enjoyed traveling around the world, my constant absence was taking a toll on my family and on myself, even more than I had realized. Kids grow up so fast, and it's too easy to miss out on the important milestones and even the simple everyday moments when you want to be present. I realized it was finally time for a lifestyle adjustment, time to find a position that would allow me to sit still for more than five minutes.

John Kapioltas expressed support for the idea. "Just tell me where you want to go," he said.

My mind immediately flashed to Qatar. I had been heavily involved in the plans for a hotel we were building in the capital, Doha, and I thought, why not throw my hat in the ring for the general manager job there?

But the idea fell apart as soon as Denyse and I flew to Doha to look at schools. The British elementary school in Doha was only able to keep the kids for two years, after which time they had to go off to boarding school in England.

"No way, no boarding school in England for our kids," Denyse said. End of story and end of my plans to transfer to Doha to take over the job as general manager of this striking new hotel.

According to Denyse, I replied, "This is the first and last time I give up a job for the sake of the children." I don't remember saying this. But Denyse has a terrific memory, so I probably did.

Fate was about to take an unexpected turn, but I had no idea at the time. For the first few weeks after I turned down the Doha opportunity, I had worried that another opportunity like it would not come up again anytime soon and brooded about how much longer my family would be forced to live in England while I continued to travel extensively.

Meanwhile, General Zaki was busy interviewing candidates for the GM role that had just opened up at the Heliopolis Sheraton. The opening GM, Karl Foerster, was getting transferred to Brussels, and Sheraton had presented General Zaki with three candidates. He swiftly rejected them all. "This hotel merits better GMs than what you have sent me," he complained to John Kapioltas.

To this, Kapioltas replied, "Wait, I have a GM for you."

"John," General Zaki responded with irritation, "why do you think that you have a GM for me who is better than the three you have sent me, when you were supposed to send me the three top candidates Sheraton has to offer?"

Kapioltas said simply, "I'm sure you will like this one."

"Who is it?" the general asked.

"You know him well," John answered. "Peter Tischmann."

General Zaki was immediately suspicious. "Peter Tischmann? Why do you want one of the best people from your team let go?"

Kapioltas replied, "General, if you want Peter Tischmann, you get Peter Tischmann."

He made the commitment behind my back while I was on a business trip, visiting other parts of our area. As soon as I returned from my trip later that week, John took me aside. "Peter, you said you wanted to go into operations. The opportunity is here. You'll go back to Heliopolis, and you will start work on the first of the month."

I was speechless. "John, that's only three weeks away."

John looked at me with his typical smile and said, "So what? Where is the problem?"

But no question about it, I was delighted to hear this piece of news. When I told Denyse and the kids, they got excited too.

The following month, I reported to General Zaki at the Heliopolis Sheraton. By now it was 1982, and much had happened in Egypt since my last trip. After Anwar El-Sadat's assassination the year before, Egypt had a new president, Hosni Mubarak, a former Air Force commander. Mubarak would go on to stay in power for another thirty years, until he was forced to resign during the Egyptian revolution of 2011, with a legacy of corruption and human rights abuses that left him facing life imprisonment.

The move to Egypt in 1982 sounded like an appealing idea at the time, for myself as well as for my family, and not only because it finally rescued us from a place we never enjoyed living in and a job which kept me away from the family for 250 days a year. Yes, I had risen to the position of corporate VP, but the last time I had actually worked in a hotel was more than ten years ago. This job would refresh my skills and challenge me in ways I craved.

I could see the hands of destiny at work. Since I had taken on such an active role in the redesign of the Heliopolis hotel, taking over as GM now felt like a homecoming. My family would get to live in an apartment at the hotel too, and we could finally spend more time together. This chapter promised a new adventure for us all.

Happily, the food and beverage offerings were humming along smoothly by the time I took over. The hotel overall was doing very well too. This meant that I could spend my time learning how to run the rooms division, the sales and marketing, and all the other departments that I had not yet overseen directly. Beyond that, my main challenge would be to come up with innovative promotions and ideas that would establish our Heliopolis hotel as the place to be in the Cairo area, for the local social set as well as for tourists.

Since I already had a friendly working relationship with General Zaki, I felt confident that he would welcome my ideas, no matter how ambitious. Of course, working for him day after day in a hotel would be different from my interactions with him in my former role as corporate envoy, but I had a hunch that we would continue to get along very well.

The general welcomed Denyse, the kids, and me with a big smile on his face, and I could see how happy he was to have me now permanently installed as a general manager and not just visiting. We toured the hotel frequently together and often walked hand in hand through the hotel garden, a common custom in Egypt among friends and relatives.

I could sense that the general had turned into something of a father figure for me, perhaps the latest manifestation of my subconscious attempt to replace my absent father.

I certainly needed all the trust and encouragement I could get in this new job. In my former role, I was in charge of making ambitious plans for dozens of hotels and selling those ideas to the GMs and F&B directors. Now, in my role as GM, the final decision was mine. I also now held all the responsibility for the profits and losses at the hotel, so I could no longer rely on generating creative ideas and leaving it up to other teams to implement them. My ideas would need to directly benefit the bottom line.

Sheraton was also now expecting me to send them a monthly check for their management and incentive fee. Rather than sending the check to the comptroller as outlined by policies and procedures, instead I mailed the first check to John Kapioltas with a personal note saying, "John, for the last ten years, I have been receiving monthly checks with your signature. Now I am very pleased to send you a check with my signature on it."

I quickly adapted to my new role as general manager and felt very much energized by this new responsibility.

Nonetheless, managing a privately owned hotel comes with its own distinct set of challenges, as I soon learned.

General managers who run privately owned hotels face a unique dilemma: Do you prioritize the owners' interests—which means that you sometimes have to go against your own company—or do you protect the company's interests, even if that means going against the owners' wishes when necessary? Well, I discovered, it means both.

This can get awkward, to say the least. But I soon came up with my own philosophy to help me navigate the choppy waters: What is good for the hotel and good for the owners is ultimately good for the management company as well. I sincerely believed this to be true, and I acted according to that principle when presented with a difficult choice.

But ultimately, no matter what decisions you make, you have to retain the owners' confidence that you're doing everything you can to protect their investment. It's their money, after all. With the exception of the operational capital, Sheraton didn't invest one single dime in the construction of the Heliopolis Sheraton Hotel, leaving the risk of the investment entirely with the owners. So as a GM, you have to earn enough credibility from the owners' side as well as from the corporate side, and both sides have to trust that you're not taking advantage of them.

I eventually got used to this paradox as my daily reality. Now came the fun part.

For New Ideas, the Sky Is the Limit

After a wildly successful launch, the Heliopolis Sheraton continued to build on the momentum, filling up day after day, night after night. But as with every hotel, some parts of the operation do better than others. One of our less successful concepts, for instance, was the Egyptian restaurant. For whatever reason, not enough visitors walking through our dining promenade chose the Egyptian eatery as their destination. I realized we needed to rethink the concept, to keep generating a steady stream of innovative ideas to cement the Heliopolis's status as the most exciting restaurant destination in Cairo, if not in the entire Middle East. I realized what was missing was a restaurant offering fish, served fresh from the sea to the table.

General Zaki had once described to me how fishermen coming back to the beach in Alexandria would take a stick and draw a big circle in the sand, marking a space reserved for them to display the fish they had caught that day. This circle was called a *halaka*, and in the morning, one could see a circle next to another, with fishermen standing next to those *halakas* selling their catch of the day.

When we decided to divide the huge space of the former Egyptian restaurant into two new outlets, this story came to my mind again, and I knew that the idea of creating a fish restaurant was the logical choice. Along with the idea came the perfect name, Al Halaka. The concept was to serve fresh fish from the sea to the table and to express absolute simplicity in the preparation, with a concentration on high quality and flavor.

As the first fresh seafood restaurant in Cairo, Al Halaka turned into an instant hit from the day it opened. To bring in enough fish, our refrigerated truck would drive to the Alexandria beach every day to bring back the freshest selections from one halaka to another. The cars following the driver would see on the back of our truck a sign saying, "Follow me to Al Halaka."

I don't actually know how many followed this invitation, but it was a marketing gimmick everybody talked about.

As for the remaining space available, it seemed only natural that we should create another Egyptian restaurant, also to take advantage of the many beautiful pharaonic replicas we owned.

However, offering an exclusive decorative environment alone was not enough if the food served did not live up to the expectations of our future guests. After some serious thought, the idea of creating a modernized Egyptian cuisine was born.

Rather than serving the kind of homestyle food that the local cuisine was known for, we would take the same fresh, traditional ingredients but serve them with a modern twist where the preparation and presentation were concerned.

The opening of the new King Tut restaurant too was an instant success and became within a short time the benchmark for Egyptian food in Cairo, making General Zaki the undisputed ambassador of modern Egyptian cuisine.

Now that we had added two new restaurants to our culinary repertoire, I turned my attention to the underperforming shopping center and meeting area located in the basement. The location never really took off, not nearly as well as the small souvenir shop selling local handicrafts that we had set up in the lobby. This one did a steady business from day one, enough to keep people from going downstairs. So what to do with the shops and conference rooms in the basements?

I could not blame companies and their executives for ignoring our basement conference spaces. Those dimly lit rooms held little appeal, despite our design efforts. We needed to start from scratch, with an entirely new basement concept.

"What if we built a pub downstairs?" I asked General Zaki. "But it has to be the only place in Cairo serving draft beer!" I added. Plenty of English expatriates lived in the Cairo area, and the British colonial history in Egypt meant that pubs already had a presence in the city—although I felt sure ours would be the best. The general sounded intrigued, even though as a devout Muslim he didn't drink alcohol. He agreed to accompany me to London to visit a company specializing in selling furniture from English pubs that had been closed for one reason or another. The company had bought the entire contents of each pub, offering buyers the chance to recreate the interior of an authentic vintage pub with all its original furnishings and decor.

"What kind of pub are you looking for?" the company owner asked General Zaki. Ha, I thought, that's a funny question for two men who don't drink beer. But we both enjoyed browsing through the furniture and discussing our concept and finally agreed to try a pub-restaurant hybrid.

"Now we just need the right name," General Zaki said. We knew it had to be easy to pronounce but memorable. As we walked through one of the showroom's storage spaces, I noticed a stained-glass window with a white swan in the middle. I said, "I have it! General, take a look at that window. What if we call it The Swan?"

General Zaki glanced over at the window, then looked at me, nodding. Two months later, the pub arrived in Cairo and a team of specialized carpenters from England fitted the paneling, the decoration, and the furniture into the assigned space in the basement. It couldn't have looked more British.

Under the patronage of the British embassy, the opening of the pub was a tremendous success. The British ambassador arrived for the opening in his Rolls Royce, cutting the ribbon together with General Zaki, escorted by two beefeaters, before General Zaki was pumping the first beer, something the clientele had never seen before in Egypt.

An electric, old-fashioned upright piano played famous songs for the crowd to sing along with, and everybody did.

The party was a smashing success, and General Zaki himself didn't stop drafting the beers for our distinguished guests. It was a fantastic night, and it set the tone for many years of lively socializing downstairs in the basement.

Promotions Are the Key to Success

Catapulting a hotel to the center of social life in a competitive city like Cairo involves a very important strategy: mastering the art of the promotion.

At the Heliopolis Sheraton, I kept busy brainstorming one promotion after another. My ideas ranged from the modest to the outrageously ambitious. I got General Zaki and the rest of our staff involved in generating ideas too. We tested the most promising ones, and we never stopped, week after week, holiday after holiday, year after year.

For a Mother's Day promotion, our chefs made three hundred heart-shaped puff pastry cakes filled with strawberry cream and topped with glazed strawberries and placed them on skirted banquet tables all along the sides of restaurants on the main promenade. We put out the cakes at 10:30 a.m. that day, and by 11:30 a.m., they were all gone. For Christmas, we baked three hundred German stollen cakes, and they too sold out within two hours. We felt lucky that everything we touched turned into a success, or maybe it was our detailed planning, which left nothing to chance.

In honor of my first New Year's Eve in Heliopolis, we unveiled a theme called Winter Wonderland, transforming the hotel into a fantasy landscape to celebrate the season. A teaser campaign alerted the public that snow was predicted in Egypt, followed by more advertising recommending that Cairenes get their skis ready. The whole city was curious about what we were planning, and the telephone didn't stop ringing with calls from people wanting to get additional information.

To produce the event and handle all the decorations, I brought in a company from the States, and within a few days, the entire lobby and all the restaurants were transformed into a winter wonderland scene, complete with artificial snow and sculptures of snowmen and reindeers. The dance floor was a silver-colored vinyl that mimicked the mirrored surface of a lake, giving the impression that guests were gliding on water.

Although we spend a lot of money on the decoration, the return on this investment was multifold, but most importantly, we had happy customers who couldn't stop talking about the event. The promotion was so popular, we left the decorations up for one extra week after the event officially ended to make sure everyone who heard about it and came by had a chance to see it and snap photos.

The German expression "austoben" means to go wild. I and my creative staff certainly came up with crazy ideas during my time at the Heliopolis, but we did everything with taste and style. We relished the chance to try out all kinds of new concepts, with the full support of General Zaki and the corporate side. Our team's innovation and tireless work generated immediate results. The Sheraton Heliopolis soon ranked as the most successful hotel in Egypt and the company's top moneymaker in the country. Although the hotel was already making money by the time I took over as GM, the average room rate and restaurant revenues had risen significantly.

Our blockbuster Winter Wonderland event inspired us to outdo ourselves the following year. But what could we plan the next time? I didn't want to settle for repetition or take the easy way out. We started brainstorming in meeting after meeting, until we finally landed on an idea that we all got excited about: For New Year's Eve, we would turn our hotel into the Land of Make Believe, set in a lush summertime landscape, offering a completely opposite experience from the Winter Wonderland. This proved equally successful, as hundreds of people strolled through our colorfully decorated summer panorama every day during our December promotion and toasted the new year around the pool as they socialized with old and new friends.

One day, Samir Zabre, our musical consultant, came to me with the idea of promoting the old but still famous musicians and belly dancers of Egypt's musical heyday of the 1950s and 60s. "Why don't we host an event that brings in world-class Egyptian artists of bygone days, which the younger generation in Cairo never had the chance to experience?" Samir suggested.

"Fantastic," I said. "Let's do it, but what do we call this event?"

After some discussion, we decided to name the event "Layla Al Kabira," which means the big night in Arabic. And a big night we wanted it to be.

What we needed most of all was a marquee performer to make the event a success. But who could we find who would be prepared to come out of retirement? "It has to be a belly dancer," I mentioned to Samir, "because only a known, famous belly dancer will guarantee us a successful event."

"Well," Samir said, "if you're talking about a famous belly dancer, there is only one name coming to my mind, and that is Samia Gamal."

"Perfect," I responded, "let's get her."

"I agree," Samir said, "but there is only one slight problem. She doesn't dance anymore. As a matter of fact, she stopped dancing many years ago, since her husband passed away, and no one has seen her onstage in years."

"One reason more to get her for Layla Al Kabira," I responded. "Let's go and get her."

After asking around, we found out how to reach Samia, and we invited her to the hotel to meet with us about our concept.

"Samia, you have such a famous name," I said to her, "but the younger generation only knows you from old films or stories. Why don't you want to dance anymore?"

"I'm scared," she said, to my surprise. She confided that it had been too long since her last performance. She felt out of practice. I think she was over fifty at this point.

By the end of the meeting, we had convinced Samia to take the stage for our Layla Al Kabira. We couldn't believe our good luck.

Unfortunately, the opening night of Layla Al Kabira turned into a total catastrophe. Despite all our planning and attention to every detail, we had underestimated the reaction of Cairo society to this event, and we didn't think about the local custom that for a reservation for two, more than two people might actually show up. In Egypt, people thought nothing of making a reservation for four, then showing up with eight people.

Not to accept the entire group at the door would be impossible and would expose the hotel to bad press and negative reactions in society. So we decided not to turn down anyone who had a reservation, even if they brought in a group double the size they'd booked. But our flexible approach proved disastrous.

We were overwhelmed by the amount of people showing up, and it became very clear to us that we would not only be running out of space, but we would be short of food as well.

Nonetheless, this night would go down in history. No belly dancers performed anywhere else in the city that night because they all showed up at the Heliopolis to watch Samia Gamal dancing. Hers was a name they all knew, but they had never before experienced her in person.

Samia was already nervous about making her grand comeback, and the size of the crowd only scared her even more. Before she stepped out in front of the audience, I saw her looking terrified backstage. I held her hand as she shook with nerves, appearing crippled by a case of stage fright that I found surprising in a seasoned performer.

But Samia's professionalism triumphed over her nerves. A few moments later, she walked out on to the stage to the sounds of loud cheering from every corner of the pool deck. When she moved across the stage, it was as if her feet didn't touch the ground. She was elegant, graceful, a class act. The crowd was enchanted. There was no question: Samia was still the queen of belly dancing, with no equal anywhere in Egypt.

This all happened on a Monday, a night when Cairo's nightlife is not usually bustling. Earlier, when we had debated which night to host the Layla Al Kabira, colleagues suggested Thursday night: "Everyone goes out on Thursdays." But I reminded them that we already have a booming Thursday business in our restaurants. We could use the help on a slow night like Monday. No one goes out on a Monday, they protested. Exactly, I insisted.

I knew it was a risky move. But not only did we sell out the house on that Monday night launch, we also booked it completely every week after that. After the first night, we enforced a stricter reservation policy and made sure we had enough food for everyone, and we ended up running the event for the entire summer.

The Layla Al Kabira experience taught us a lesson about Cairo nightlife, but the promotion turned out to be easy compared to the even more ambitious events we threw later that year.

How ambitious? The sky was the limit. The only rule was that we wanted each event to be unique. When I heard about the rocket man who had performed at the Olympics in Los Angeles earlier that year, flying into the stadium and impressing the audience by swooping around in the air, I knew we had to bring him to the Heliopolis. But I had no idea of the difficulties that awaited us.

Having the rocket man agree to recreate his show in Egypt was the easy part, but arranging his visit turned out to be more complicated than I'd expected.

Luckily, I had developed a friendly relationship with Abd Al-Halim Abu-Ghazala, the defense minister and commander-in-chief of the Egyptian military, with whom I played tennis twice a week, and twice a week he cheated his way to win. His serves would nearly always land outside the lines of the service box. He would say, "15 to love," as he walked over to the other side of the service line. Then the next ball would land well beyond the service box again, and I would hear him say, "30 to love," and on he went. I let this slide every time. How could I contradict him?

After the game—the fact that I never won should come as no surprise—we would sit in one of the poolside cabanas, enjoying a platter of fresh, prepared fruits and trying to save the world with our discussions of global politics. Abu-Ghazala had witnessed important moments in world history since he joined the government in 1981 and was sitting right next to Anwar Al-Sadat on the night of Sadat's assassination.

With Abu-Ghazala, there was never a dull moment. I enjoyed his company, and his friendship came in handy when it was time to execute my wild ideas, like sending a man flying over the Heliopolis Sheraton to land on the pool deck.

Getting the rocket man and his jetpack to Cairo on an airplane was not a problem. But as I soon discovered, the rocket fuel was another story. Since we couldn't find the same type of gas in Egypt, we had to send it over by ship from the US, and we had to order the kerosene early enough so it would arrive on time. There's nothing that good advance planning can't conquer, I thought to myself.

But as soon as the rocket man arrived at the hotel with his jetpack, the problems began, and our program started taking on new directions. Abu-Ghazala suddenly decided he wanted to host a preview of the show for his Egyptian generals. The rocket man luckily agreed to the request to do two separate shows, one for the VIPs and one for our big public promotion at the hotel. There was just one issue. The rocket fuel was blocked at customs in the Alexandria harbor.

At this point, I was panicking, and I called my buddy Abu-Ghazala for help. We had marketed the promotion far and wide, and everything was ready to go, except the most important part, and now we had a certain failure on our hands.

"Don't worry, I'll take care of it" was all Abu-Ghazala said. I hung up, still feeling anxious. I trusted Abu-Ghazala, but tracking down the rocket fuel at the Alexandria port and getting it to Heliopolis in time sounded like a far-fetched proposition to me.

Four hours later, the rocket fuel magically arrived at the hotel, in time for the first flight.

Two dozen generals stood outside the next day, looking up at the sky, when the rocket man suddenly appeared in the sky from behind the hotel, flew around, and twenty seconds later landed safely next to the pool. It was a magnificent sight. The generals cheered with enthusiasm, and I wondered if they considered doing this in one of their military operations.

The next day, we hosted our grand jetpack show at the hotel, and the large crowd erupted into loud applause at the sight of the man flying over the building. No one had seen a performance like this before. Neither had I, and neither had the majority of people in the world, except on TV during the LA Olympics.

How could we possibly top this?

It would surely be difficult. But we were determined to do it. In a developing country, as the general manager of the most successful hotel, and with access to the connections I had developed, everything was possible.

Tina Turner, Our Son, and a Kiss

The Heliopolis Sheraton would soon celebrate its fifth anniversary. To toast five successful years, we needed to do something absolutely spectacular, even more spectacular than sending a man into the sky strapped to nothing but a jetpack.

What could beat a flying human? A flying saucer, perhaps. Especially if we could trick people into believing it was real.

We began planning the anniversary promotion immediately. After a series of designs, changes, and redesigns, our engineers enthusiastically started to construct an enormous flying saucer. When I saw the result, I was impressed. The huge object of metal and wood looked like a real UFO, with round bullseye windows and lights on the inside. It looked so real, one could expect aliens to come out of the UFO at any moment.

The big challenge now was how to get this UFO flying and hovering over the crowd of invitees at our birthday party?

Again, my friend Abu-Ghazala helped me, picking up the huge model of the UFO via military helicopter from the hotel and flying it to the nearby airbase, then parking it there until our party.

On the night of the event, a large crowd of invitees gathered on the pool deck enjoying the entertainment, food, and beverages we had prepared, when at about 10:00 p.m. we turned off the exterior lights, leaving the hotel in near darkness. Electricity cuts were not rare in Egypt, so the guests stood quietly, waiting for the lights to come back on again. Then out of the dark sky, the UFO with its flashing lights appeared overhead. It was hanging on a long steel wire from the bottom of the unlit helicopter, which the crowd could not see. A strange sound filled the air as the UFO hovered above the guests and a metallic voice started to address the crowd.

"Good evening, we are from outer space. We heard there was a big party going on here. Congratulations, Sheraton Heliopolis, for being the very best hotel."

Even I felt goosebumps.

For anyone who was alive in 1938, the year before I was born, this might have sparked memories of a certain famous radio broadcast. That year, Orson Welles narrated H.G. Wells's *War of the Worlds*, the science fiction novel about Martians invading earth, on the BBC. As he spoke, many listeners thought they were hearing an actual news announcement about an alien invasion.

Our own Egyptian UFO flew around for a while, then disappeared. The crowd continued to stare up at the sky for a little while, waiting to see if it would come back. Even the office of the president of Egypt took notice of the spectacle, calling the military base to ask, "What the heck is going on there with all this noise?"

They said, "Don't worry, Mr. President, everything is under control."

The event made it into every newspaper the next day. General Zaki told me how thrilled he was about all the media attention we were attracting at the hotel.

Week after week, month after month, articles about us continued to appear in the press. Our events continued to generate vast amounts of ink in newspapers, and even more so when we began to host major international celebrities at exclusive events. In particular, I remember the time when we held our own private Tina Turner concert for VIPs and loyal guests of the hotel.

Ms. Turner's visit to our hotel had come about through unusual circumstances. Her agent had called me one day, unexpectedly. I don't know why he chose me, but I guessed it was because we had become the top hotel in Egypt. He told me Tina Turner believes that her ancestors came from Egypt and were once Pharaohs, so she wanted to visit the land of her ancestors. The agent wondered if our hotel could assist her in arranging this, in exchange for a small concert she would give at the hotel.

My immediate answer was yes, of course. Who could say no to such a golden opportunity and to Tina Turner? Within a few days, we had organized Tina Turner's trip to Upper Egypt, managed to hire a private plane, and ensured her team that we would take care of her during her entire trip. The expenses involved were very low compared to what we would have had to spend for a private concert.

When Ms. Turner arrived at the hotel, Denyse and I and our two children welcomed her in our lobby. "Are these your children?" she asked us.

"Yes," Denyse answered, "this is our daughter Carine, and this is our son Peter."

Ms. Turner looked at them with a big smile and said, "What a cute boy you have. Let me give him a kiss!"

Peter, hearing the word *kiss*, turned around and started to sprint away. Tina Turner followed him at high speed, all the way down the corridor toward our apartment. Peter was eleven years old at the time, and I still don't know how he managed to get to the end of the corridor, open our apartment door, and close it in a hurry, but by the time she got there, he was already inside. Many people would have killed for a kiss from Tina Turner, but our son actually ran away from this opportunity. I have no doubt this was a rare experience for her.

Tina Turner held her concert in our members-only nightclub, the Baron, open only to the two hundred or so guests who paid a few thousand dollars annually in membership fees for access to exclusive events. A crowd of about two hundred was the perfect size for an intimate concert, and we filled every seat in the club on the night of Tina Turner's show. What a success it was. Ms. Turner gave an absolutely outstanding concert, wearing a leather dress with fringes and singing with her distinctive energy and charisma. Our guests could not take their eyes off her for the entire show.

No Limits for Creativity

The Tina Turner concert ranks among the most memorable events at the Heliopolis Sheraton, but plenty of other stars showed up too. We invited celebrity chefs to cook in our hotel for restaurant promotions, and I was delighted to host Georges Blanc, Michel Troisgros, and other culinary superstars. On special nights like these, we invited Egyptian officials to attend, among them Abu-Ghazala, Prime Minister Kamal Hassan Ali, and others from the high ranks of government. They all came.

Denyse and I also enjoyed inviting VIP guests and their spouses to our apartment at the hotel. As a perk of my job, my family not only got to live in a private apartment at the Heliopolis, but we also benefited from the privilege of having the apartment decorated to our taste.

During Ramadan, we hosted the Egyptian government elites for an iftar dinner in our apartment, with the vice president, prime minister, chief of the armed forces, commander of the air force, and the governor of Alexandria all sitting at our table. Our Lebanese chef prepared the most delicious food, stretching the iftar until late into the evening. Fortunately, terrorism was not yet a subject of the day because if someone had dropped a bomb on our apartment, they would have taken out nearly the entire government—except for President Mubarak, the only top official who wasn't in the room.

But even as I worked hard to attract attention to the hotel, to please the owners, and to create an aura of glamour around the Heliopolis Sheraton, I also managed to make enemies during my time there. One morning, I woke up to find my name in the newspaper, along with accusations that I had built myself a most luxurious palace, with a bathroom fit for a king and gold-plated fixtures and furnishings. I was frustrated to read this, not yet realizing that this was only the beginning of a hate campaign that would land my name in the paper every weekend. Knowing that the journalist who wrote this worked for a Communist newspaper in Cairo didn't help restore my good mood.

Why had he singled me out for this attack? I wondered. Why was he printing nothing but lies to gain publicity for himself and his newspaper?

Then I learned that not long ago, when the hotel had hosted an Easter Egg Painting promotion for guests and their children, this journalist had felt left out when we invited a group of social columnists to judge the egg-coloring contest. To make things worse, when he had showed up anyway at the hotel, he was refused entrance to the contest and had left the hotel fuming and irritated. I admit we should have handled the situation more intelligently, but from that point on, he did not miss an opportunity to attack the hotel, and myself as the GM, nearly every week in his column.

Noticing how much this frustrated me, General Zaki tried to reassure me. "Don't let it bother you," he said. "Everyone knows who this journalist is. Visualize yourself stacking every edition of his smear paper, one on top of another, and then stepping on top of the pile. All of this writing only makes you taller."

I was impressed by General Zaki's fatherly approach, but still, the situation gave me an upset stomach. After some time, the hate campaign finally stopped. I suppose the journalist eventually had to come up with some new stories to write about.

Meanwhile, I took comfort in the more positive feedback I received. My friend Sami Sabet, the chief of protocol for the Egyptian government, took it upon himself to write a letter to John Kapioltas, saying: "Through Peter's initiative, warmth, and amiable personality, he has succeeded not only in making so many friends in so short a time, but more important still, in making the Heliopolis Sheraton the talk of the town. In my official functions, there is hardly an evening when I am not called upon to attend some diplomatic social event. When the location happens to be the Heliopolis Sheraton, my colleagues and I look forward to the event with added pleasure." This letter remains among my belongings, after all these years.

In my collection, I have also kept certificates of the corporate awards I received in those years, including the ITT Quality Award, the Chairman's Award, and the President's Award, prestigious Sheraton recognitions given to only one executive annually.

I also felt honored when Sheraton's corporate office chose the Heliopolis as the site of the annual general managers meeting for the entire region. Around forty or so GMs would be attending, and I wanted to do something special, with a local flavor, to welcome them to the hotel.

We might as well have some fun, I thought. Since we had two talented artists from Thailand working for us, I commissioned the carving of a giant pyramid out of Styrofoam and placed it in the lobby. We built a tunnel winding all the way through the lobby and ending at the entrance of the nightclub, which had been decorated to appear like the inside of a huge Egyptian tomb. As they entered the pyramid, the GMs had to crawl through the tunnel on their hands and knees, across the sandy floor, with no idea where they were going. When they finally arrived on the other side, they'd look up and find themselves inside the pyramid. Our female waitstaff, wearing ancient Egyptian dresses, greeted the managers as if they were Pharaohs.

The success of the Heliopolis Sheraton in those years owes a tremendous amount to the dedication of our wonderful staff. I appreciated being surrounded by so many hardworking, talented people, some of whom became good friends. Our chauffeur Mohamed, in particular, helped to make Heliopolis feel like home during our years there. He treated our kids as if they were his own and drove Carine and Peter safely to school every day, the Cairo American College, forty-five minutes in the car through the desert. Interacting with people like Mohamed every day helped our family cope with the stress of living in a big hotel, where we rarely had the luxury of privacy or quiet.

Still, I would not trade my years in Heliopolis for anything in the world.

If only I could have predicted what was coming around the corner, maybe I would've decided to stay in Egypt.

Finally, Family Time

Despite all the glamorous events we hosted at the Heliopolis Sheraton, the VIP concerts and celebrity chef dinners and spaceships, seeing my family every day remained one of the greatest perks of the job. Carine had been right all along. In the years when I had always been away on business during my children's events and milestones, I had not even realized how much I was missing. I would see them looking a bit more grown up every time I returned. In the Egypt years, I was lucky to get to watch Carine and Peter Jr. experience life day by day and to stop time just a little bit.

We grew closer as a family in those years. The chance to see my wife and children more also helped me cope during the difficult weeks in 1983 when my mother was dying.

Mutti had undergone surgery for cancer of the intestines several years earlier, and since then, she had gone for checkups every three months to see if the cancer had returned. Her doctor had said that if she showed no sign of cancer for five years, then he would declare the surgery successful in removing it entirely. Every checkup looked fine, and as the five-year mark approached, the doctor said she could start coming in every six months instead.

By the end of five years and six months, my mother was gone.

The cancer had returned with a vengeance, growing rapidly in those months when she didn't see the doctor. Mutti passed away two days after my sister Jenny was able to have her admitted to palliative care. When Jenny called to tell me the news, I cried on the telephone. I had not managed to get to Hannover in time to see my mother before she passed away. Jenny had kept me up-to-date on her condition the entire time, and none of us realized that the end was only days away.

At the funeral, I saw only my mother's cremated remains. She wanted her ashes in the same cemetery where her parents and brother were buried. The cemetery is a special place for our family, and it held just enough space for her ashes, right next to her mother, father, and brother. During the ceremony, I kept my eyes on the urn carrying Mutti's ashes, the only tangible part of her left in this world, soon to go back into the ground. I had a difficult time watching. But I forced myself not to miss a single moment this time.

In the months after the funeral, I threw myself into my work even more than before. Even though Carine and Peter had not seen their grandmother much over the years, we all grieved her absence. Even Denyse expressed regret that Mutti had never had the chance to visit us in Egypt, although I had invited her many times.

I would always say to my mother, "When you feel better, you have to visit us in Egypt, and we will go skiing in the desert."

What was meant as a joke back then is now a reality. These days, sand-skiing in Egypt and other Gulf countries is very popular, but at the time, the idea of skiing of any kind there seemed absurd.

Ever since my attempt to learn skiing in Switzerland finally succeeded, I have relied on the sport for relaxation, exercise, and an effective form of therapy during challenging times. Denyse, Carine, and Peter Jr. are enthusiastic skiers too, and although we were certainly not skiing in Egypt, we took every opportunity to do so on vacation.

When we lived in Brussels, we would go to Munich after Christmas, spend New Year's Eve at the Sheraton there, then continue the following day to the ski town of Saalbach-Hinterglemm in Austria.

The hotel occupancy in Munich was very low at the time, and the general manager would close most of the hotel's restaurants for the holiday season. Arriving in Munich on December 31, we usually ate lunch in Die Mühle, the all-day dining room, where we were usually the only guests.

One year when we arrived and sat waiting for our lunch to arrive, feeling exhausted from the long drive from Brussels, I watched Peter Jr. complain and squirm in his seat, making a scene at the table. I warned him that I would have to discipline him in front of everybody if he didn't behave.

Peter turned his head slowly from one side to the other side, looked at me, and said, "In front of everybody? I don't see anybody."

It was hard to argue with his observation. Fortunately, he still hasn't lost his deadpan sense of humor.

Saalbach-Hinterglemm is a charming Austrian Alps ski resort perched at about eight hundred meters in elevation and offering ski facilities that felt just about right for a family with two small children. We always looked forward to our vacations in a small family-run pension there. But as time passed, we searched for a ski area situated higher up in the mountains, one that was more secure in its snow levels.

Konigsleiten in the Salzburger Land looked like such a place, with its 1,600 meters of elevation and guaranteed snow in the winter. Several of my colleagues in the Brussels office had bought apartments there, and Denyse and I decided to investigate the options. But at first, we found nothing available.

So we waited. Then one day, my colleague's wife Alice Steber telephoned to say she had read about a new building going up in Konigsleiten, with eight apartments for sale. The next week, I made a stopover in Munich on my way to the Middle East, and I drove with Alice to the site. The weather was terrible that day, rainy and foggy. At the address she gave me, we found nothing except gray clouds hanging heavy and dark over Konigsleiten.

Alice pointed at the location, a few steps away from the lift, and said it seemed perfect for us. I felt it would have been even more perfect if I had been able to see anything at all. But the only image I had was on a postcard created by the developer.

Still, on my next trip through Munich, I decided to jump in with both feet. Life is short, and sometimes you have to take a risk and have faith it will work out. I signed a contract to buy an apartment in that building. Luckily, fate rewarded my daredevil move. The apartment became our ski destination for years to come, throughout our stay in Heliopolis and long afterward. The vacation home was a beautiful respite for our family, not just in the winter, but in the spring and summer too, when chanterelles and berries appeared all over the fields, waiting to be picked and enjoyed by our kids and all the guests we invited to share our memories with us.

Exploring the Far East

You steal with your eyes. That's what you do when you run a hotel. Everywhere you travel, you take note of ideas that impress you, ways of living and decorating and offering hospitality in other cities, countries, hotels, shops, and restaurants around the world.

In 1984, our family traveled to Asia, on a trip intended partly as vacation and partly as an idea-gathering mission. We went to Bombay, Delhi, and Agra in India, where the kids enjoyed riding on elephants and watching a musician play the pipe as a snake twisted out of a basket in front of him. I nearly fainted when he tried to put the snake around my neck. We went to the Philippines, Thailand, China, and Hong Kong, which was still a British colony and not part of China at the time.

During the trip, Carine decided to cut her hair very short. It suited her well. When we were about to return from the airport in Canton, now known as Guangzhou, to Hong Kong, I handed over our family's passport to the passport control officer. This was the only document we had, since in Germany an entire family shares a single passport. It had a picture of all four of us on it, and I worried that Carine looked so different with her short hair that the guard would not let us in. But the guard said nothing about this. A moment later, he looked up at me and said he did not know if the passport would be valid in China since they rely on individual passports instead.

He then disappeared for twenty minutes, then came back and said, in perfect German, "Your passport is absolutely valid in China. Have a safe trip, and by the way, you have two very nice boys." Carine must have decided not to cut her hair short anymore after this episode because since that trip she has worn her hair long.

The trip was a success, enjoyable in every way, and a wonderful educational opportunity for us all. We stayed in different types of hotels throughout Asia, providing me with a daily learning experience in various styles of hospitality.

We were impressed when we arrived in Guangzhou and noticed a huge supermarket located inside of our hotel, selling everything from refrigerators to TVs, radios, kitchen appliances, and even cars. Anything imported from the West or made in Hong Kong, you could buy in that supermarket. I later learned that Guangzhou was the primary meeting point for separated Chinese families living in mainland China and Hong Kong, with the rich family members from Hong Kong buying everything their poor family from mainland China could not afford and needed to pay for in hard currency. Most amazing to see was the main road in Guangzhou, where bicycles took up most of the lanes, squeezing the cars into one narrow lane on the side. This situation has changed by now, as the streams of cars squeeze bicycles into the small lane.

I always thought the finest European hotels gave their staff exemplary training, but even the best service I've seen in Europe could hardly measure up to what I found in hotels around Asia. In part, this was because of the number of employees at Asian hotels. Labor costs less in Asia, so hotels could afford to hire more help. When Sheraton was busy opening one hotel after another in the Middle East, we hired mostly employees from Thailand, the Philippines, and Indonesia for far less than we paid staff at our European hotels. In Europe, if we had 0.5 employees for each room, in the Middle East, we had 1.5 per room. Consequently, the service was far superior to what we could afford in Europe, and with the additional staff came increased attention to the smallest detail.

At the Mandarin Oriental in Bangkok, I stood in the lobby absorbing the beautiful decor, when an employee appeared next to me, seemingly out of nowhere, and asked, "Sir, is there anything I can do for you?" I must have looked lost, and he didn't waste any time in coming to my assistance.

I noticed only one receptionist behind the reception desk at the Mandarin, but as soon as a guest walked into the lobby, the receptionist walked out to greet him while another employee instantly appeared to take over his spot. The entire routine looked seamless. If another guest had walked in, I am sure that a third staffer would have appeared to fill the empty desk position. In Europe, none of this would happen, not in my experience. You would walk into the lobby, even at a fine hotel, and see a few employees standing in the reception area talking to each other. When a guest walked in, they would hardly even take notice.

At the Raffles Hotel in Singapore, if you had to return to your room shortly after you left, you would find your room already tidied up. This happened to me on our first day in Singapore. How did anyone already know that I'd left the room? I had not passed a single person in the hallway. I later learned there's a trick to this. At the bottom of a guest room door, a needle is positioned in such a way that it falls as soon as the door is opened again. A staff member passing by will notice the fallen needle, knock politely, and say "Housekeeping. Is there anything we can do for you?" If there's nobody in the room, they will refresh everything for you.

The level of customer service in the East impressed us day after day, beyond anything I had ever seen before. Even a Holiday Inn in Asian cities likely offers a level of service far beyond what you would ever get in a Holiday Inn in the States or Europe.

That trip was a revelation for me. I picked up hundreds of ideas about service that I later implemented in the hotels I oversaw. When I returned to Heliopolis, I immediately knew what we were missing. Our staff already treated guests with warmth and friendliness, but they lacked the level of professionalism and focus that I had seen in the East.

In Egypt, it could happen that after you order a tomato soup, that the waiter would spill it over your freshly dry-cleaned suit as he attempted to serve it to you. He would apologize a million times, with a big "sorry" on his face, and look so upset that you could not remain mad at him. But still, professional service staff should never allow this to happen.

In the Asian hotels we visited, it would simply never come to that. The staff would never spill the tomato soup on you in the first place.

WELCOME BY GEN. AHMED ZAKI

THE STAFF OF THE HOTEL WELCOMES MY FAMILY

FIRST SCHOOL DAY IN CAIRO

شركة الخليج مصر للفنادق والسياحة
ش.م.م. طبقا للقانون ٤٣ لسنة ١٩٧٤ وتعديلاته
GULF-EGYPT FOR HOTELS & TOURISM (S.A.E.)

Our ref : 110/1 — رقم القيد: 147

Your ref: — رقم الملف:

Date : May 18, 1982 — التاريخ:

Mr. Peter W. Tischmann
Vice President
General Manager
Heliopolis Sheraton Hotel
Urouba Street, Heliopolis
Cairo

Dear Mr. Tischmann,

Reference is made to your letter dated April 30th, 1982.

It gives me great pleasure to welcome you as General Manager of Heliopolis Sheraton Hotel.

In welcoming you to your own hotel, I am confident that it will continue to prosper and develop more and more, having faith in your capabilities, thorough experience, devotion and enthusiasm.

My sincerest wishes for continued success to all your endeavours and a pleasant stay to you and your family in Egypt.

Sincerely,

A. Zaki

GEN. AHMED ZAKI
PRESIDENT

Address: Misr Travel Tower
Abbaseya Square, Cairo
P.O.Box: 42 Abbaseya, Cairo, Egypt
Cable : GULF MISR - CAIRO
Tel. : 822465 - 822481
Telex : 93892 GEHTM UN

العنوان : برج مصر للسياحة
ميدان العباسية-القاهرة
ص.ب : ٤٢ العباسية -القاهرة مصر
تلغرافيا : جلفمصر-القاهرة
تليفون : ٨٢٢٤٦٥-٨٢٢٤٨١
س.ت : ١٧٩١٩٠
تلكس : ٩٣٨٩٢

WELCOME TO CAIRO LETTER

MEETING THE PRIME MINISTER KAMAL HASSAN ALI

OMAR SHERIF A FREQUENT GUEST AT THE HOTEL

Boston Is Calling 18

No Time to Pack

Fairy tales don't always have a happy ending. Stories that end tragically often have the most seductive beginnings. Little did I know it when I first received a phone call from Boston, but I was about to enter a fairy tale. As with so many fairy tales, this one involved a castle. And it had princely figures and princesses and other regal characters. The setting was, after all, the St. Regis, known in its prime as the most majestic hotel in New York City and perhaps the world. But that's only part of the story.

On a typically sunny Monday morning in Cairo, in early February 1985, my secretary informed me that I had a phone call from Boston. John Kapioltas wanted to talk to me. John was by now president and chief operating officer of the Sheraton Corporation, having replaced his predecessor Howard P. "Bud" James, who stepped down as president in 1983.

John and I had a close working relationship after so many years together in the Brussels and Denham offices, but he never called me in Heliopolis.

I wondered what I possibly had done wrong for John to telephone me himself.

After the warm hellos, I launched into small talk to delay the awkwardness of what was surely going to be an unpleasant conversation. John interrupted me. "Peter," he said sternly, "I want you to see me in Boston on Wednesday."

"John," I said, "today is Monday and the day is almost gone."

"Have you forgotten how to pack a suitcase fast?" he answered. "And bring Denyse with you. See you on Wednesday morning, end of conversation."

Two days later, I sat in the reception area of Sheraton's Boston HQ, waiting to meet with John. A few minutes later, I heard my name, but when I looked up, I found Tom Hewett, area manager for Sheraton's New York City hotels. No sooner did we shake hands than he began to give me a detailed account about the St. Regis Hotel and its many problems. As I stood there looking confused, Tom went on. "The St. Regis is a magnificent old-world charm hotel," he continued, "but the service and guest experience are not living up to expectations."

Okay, I thought, why is he telling me this? As I stood there contemplating why we were having this conversation, Tom looked at me, seeming puzzled that I didn't already know why I was in Boston that morning.

"John wants you to take over the hotel and make it Sheraton's flagship in New York," Tom explained, as if he were merely stating the obvious.

I paused to let Tom's announcement sink in.

Me, Peter Tischmann, running the St. Regis? This was one of the most legendary hotels in the world, its name still signifying grandeur and exclusivity even though the hotel itself had in recent decades fallen into decline.

I knew something about the history of the St. Regis, but the hotel had not crossed my mind in years. John Jacob Astor IV, one of the richest people in the world at the time and a member of the socially prominent Astor family, built the hotel in 1904. He conceived of it as a destination for prominent international guests, much like his wealthy friends, who were used to living in luxury back home in Europe and who sought the same level of accommodations on their travels.

In the year when it opened, no other hotel in the United States came even close to offering the same level of opulence as Astor achieved with the creation of the St. Regis.

On the day in 1904 when Astor opened the St. Regis, horse-drawn carriages and motor cars pulled up to the door, dropping off high-society guests in front of the hotel's limestone Art Nouveau facade. The area around Fifth Avenue and Fifty-Fifth Street where the hotel sits was known at the time as Millionaire's Row, and the name was apt. For the hotel's guests, Astor created an opulent environment of Louis XV furniture, Waterford crystal chandeliers, intricately carved balustrades, and gilded mailboxes. Every guest room had electricity and its own telephone, the ultimate high-tech status symbols of the time.

I had heard about the exclusive society events that took place on the St. Regis roof in that era. The hotel continued to make history in its first century of existence. A bartender famously invented the Bloody Mary in the St. Regis's King Cole Bar (he called it the Red Snapper) in the 1930s, and as the decades went on, the hotel attracted a steady stream of the wealthy and the famous and the culturally prominent, from presidents and royalty to artists and celebrities such Salvador Dali to Marlene Dietrich, John Lennon, Alfred Hitchcock, and many more.

The St. Regis was now facing difficult times, but I was confident it had potential to return to the magnificence of its early days.

The hotel had, in fact, weathered tough storms from its very beginning, long before ITT Sheraton bought it in 1966. John Jacob Astor had to fend off complaints by socially prominent neighbors including the Vanderbilts and the Rockefellers, who resented the construction of a hotel that might spoil their views. But the St. Regis quickly found its way to the center of the New York social scene from the moment it opened, then eight years later, Astor drowned in the Titanic tragedy of 1912. The hotel continued to flourish after his death, due in part to the charm, intuitive hospitality, and social ease of the extraordinary Rudolf M. Haan, the hotel's first general manager.

Haan's stewardship of the St. Regis, guiding the hotel after Astor's death into its long-held position as one of the world's regal hotels, had turned him into a legend. How could I possibly live up?

As Tom spoke, my mind drifted at times, as I contemplated the legacy of the St. Regis and wondered about my own presence in the room. It took effort to focus on what Tom was saying during our hour-long talk. I felt anxious that I would not be ready for this job. Tom was busy trying to explain to me the importance of the hotel for Sheraton and the great opportunity it would represent for me. Then he realized we were late for our next meeting. "Roger Senter is waiting for you," he said in a hurry, as we got up and walked down a long corridor to the corner office.

Roger Senter was senior vice president and director of human resources, and I knew him from his many trips to our offices in Brussels and later in Denham. Since Roger and I had already met many times before, he welcomed me warmly. He was an expert at disarming people with his friendly, easygoing greeting. And the fact that Tom Hewett had already spilled the beans to me meant I didn't have to worry that Roger had some bad news in store.

He started by telling me how much John Kapioltas trusted me and wanted me to take over the St. Regis, a hotel to which he felt a personal attachment. The St. Regis was ITT's crown jewel, and the GM job would come with many benefits, Roger added, far superior to the ones I had in Europe.

"Why don't you discuss this with Denyse, and we'll meet with her tomorrow morning?" he said, wrapping up the meeting and subtly steering me to the door.

"Yes," I replied, "I will discuss this with her, especially as we have two very young children, who would be affected by this move much more than I."

My hunch that Denyse would feel just as skeptical of this move turned out to be correct. The two of us spent all afternoon walking through the streets of Boston, trying to sort out the pros and cons of what would be one of the biggest decisions we'd ever made for our family. At the top of the cons list: New York in 1985 was not the best place to bring up two young children, especially kids who had been protected and coddled until now. We worried they did not yet have the street smarts to be safe in a city like New York. The crime rate there was high at the time, and we'd heard enough stories about violence and drugs in New York City schools to make our stomachs clench.

The job itself did appeal to me, however, and Denyse too felt excited about the prospect of a career move like this. But our fears about raising our kids in New York kept tilting our decision to "no." Then one of us would bring up another benefit of living in New York or another reason why it would be wrong to turn down a role like this, and we would tilt to "yes" again. Then back to "no." By the end of the day, we were both totally confused, and for the first time in my career, I had no idea what to do.

Avoiding a meeting in the Sheraton office the next day was not an option, unfortunately, so Denyse and I dutifully showed up at 9:00 a.m. sharp at 60 State Street. Roger Senter smiled at us when we entered his office. But this was our second day in Boston, and I had yet to see any sign of John Kapioltas.

Without wasting a moment, Roger started telling Denyse about the many advantages that our move to New York would offer. *Our move to New York?* I thought. He was talking about it as if it were a done deal. Denyse and I did not see it this way. We had come to his office planning to raise our concerns and perhaps buy ourselves more time to decide or attempt to wiggle out of this situation altogether.

"You want the best private schools for your kids in New York? Not a problem. Granted," Senter said.

"But our children have never taken public transportation at all, never mind in a city like New York," Denyse responded.

"You'll have a car and a driver. What's next?" Roger answered.

"Would we be living in the hotel?" I asked.

"Yes, there is an apartment on the eighteenth floor," Roger answered, "and if you don't like it, you choose another one."

I had more questions. "What about medical and dental insurance?"

"Same as in Europe, 100 percent," he replied quickly.

Soon I had run out of questions. Every query that I had hoped he would answer with a no, to give me an opening to turn down the job, he had addressed with an instant yes. I felt I was standing with my back against the wall, with no chance of escape.

"So, what are we going to tell John?" Roger asked, raising his eyebrows.

After a few moments of silence, I made a giving-up gesture with my hands. "Tell John I'll take the job," I said, glancing over at Denyse. I felt my nerves tense up, then slowly give way to a sense of relief as we looked at each other, smiling anxiously, but with a palpable sense of excitement. At least the decision was done. Now would come the truly difficult part. I knew this, but at least Denyse and I could finally take a break from the yes and the no and turn our attention to the next challenge.

"A good decision," Roger said. "By the way, John wants to see you and Denyse for lunch at one o'clock in the executive dining room on the top floor."

I had a hunch that John would have never even shown his face at all during our visit had I refused the job.

The moment we sat down to lunch, Denyse had a question for our host. "John, we are very happy at the Heliopolis Sheraton, and you have more than three hundred general managers to choose from. Why do you have to take Peter?"

John looked at Denyse with a very serious expression on his face before he answered: "Because I have only one Peter Tischmann."

Years later, when my lawyer Steven Eckhaus interviewed him during one of the worst days of my life, John refused to admit that he said those words.

Denyse and I made a brief stopover in New York after Boston and woke up in shock the next morning in our room at the New York Sheraton. We still couldn't quite believe we had made the decision to uproot our family once again, to New York of all places.

On a stroll around the city that would soon become our home, we looked up from the Fifth Avenue sidewalk to see the St. Regis looming over us at the corner of Fifty-Fifth Street. I told Denyse we should make an incognito visit to the lobby to get a first look at the hotel. I wanted to get a sense of what I would be up against. My brief would not be easy, to say the least: bringing European elegance back to a declining hotel and transforming the St. Regis into Sheraton's flagship operation in New York.

No sooner had we entered the big bronze revolving door into the lobby when a heavyset bellman with an outstretched hand walked right toward me and said, "My name is Joe. Welcome to the St. Regis, Mr. and Mrs. Tischmann." Murmuring something like a thank you, we turned around and left the hotel lobby in a rush.

I had barely just accepted the job and the bellman at the St. Regis already knew my name and what I looked like. Amazing how fast news travels.

Back in New York a month later, Denyse and I arranged private school visits with Carine, now fourteen, and Peter, thirteen. We scheduled tours at most of the prestigious ones, but our experience at one of the most famous schools stands out in my mind. As we walked through the hallway, I saw groups of teenage students sprawled out on the floor, stretching their legs into the middle of the corridor and not making an effort to allow us to pass. This forced us to step over their legs and books on the floor. They seemed to have no manners, and the comment from my grandmother when William Hahnel was proposing to her about "how America was uncivilized" crossed my mind again.

We struck that school off our list almost immediately.

Another top-ranked school that we nearly deleted from our list was Trinity, where the director of admissions refused us even the courtesy of an interview, claiming all the classes were full. But a few weeks later, spaces must have miraculously appeared, since a strong letter of recommendation from Günther Brandt, the headmaster of the American College in Cairo, resulted in an interview for Carine, followed by a quick acceptance.

Peter received an acceptance from another top choice on our list: Collegiate, a boys' school known for its discipline and high academic performance.

While the kids felt intrigued by the new adventure on which we were all about to embark, Peter did not generate the same level of excitement about having to wear a uniform, a relic of the past at the schools they had attended in Europe and in Cairo.

Nonetheless, with the major decisions about my job and their schooling out of the way, the impending move to New York became less daunting. We all looked forward to conquering the big city.

But as we would soon learn, nothing in New York is ever easy. The city threw an immediate hurdle in our way.

A German in the Big Apple

As I prepared to hand over the reins of the Heliopolis, and Denyse and I packed up our things to move to the US, the hotel world in New York underwent a major disruption. In early June of 1985, the city found itself in the middle of its biggest hotel strike in a half-century, as thousands of housekeeping staff, bellmen, waiters, cooks, and other employees at hotels all over the city walked off their jobs.

The strike affected every major New York hotel, but most of them continued to operate, with limited amenities: no room service, no restaurants or entertainment, no help carrying suitcases. But the hotels kept accommodating guests who had made reservations.

Employees tried to hinder guests from entering, forming picket lines outside the hotels and protesting. The demonstrators did what they could to deny access to deliveries, sanitation workers, and taxis, and in some cases, the confrontations turned violent. Mayor Ed Koch made a statement denouncing the behavior, threatening labor as well as management with arrests and jail time if either side resorted to violence.

Negotiations went nowhere for weeks. All signs indicated that this would be a long strike, intentionally timed to interrupt a summer tourist season that typically brings around 1.5 million travelers to New York City. Meanwhile, I was supposed to start my new job at the St. Regis that month, with very high expectations of what I might accomplish as general manager.

Luckily, the higher-ups at Sheraton postponed my start date, asking me to wait in Egypt until the strike ended. Almost four weeks later, on June 29, the strike finally reached a resolution. I gathered my suitcases and prepared to cross the Atlantic to start my new responsibilities in New York City. Denyse and the children planned to join me shortly after, to give me time to get settled in my new job.

Arriving at JFK, I saw a long stretch limo and a driver standing outside the baggage claim area, holding a sign with my name on it. Inside, the limo was fitted with a bar, a bottle of champagne, and crystal glasses. Limousines like this only existed in the United States, as far as I knew, where everything looked huge and over-the-top compared to Europe and the Middle East and nearly everywhere else in the world.

As if to offer a soundtrack for my excitement and anxiety as I started this new chapter of my life, the limousine took a sharp turn on to the FDR, sending the glasses, champagne, and ice bucket flying. The sound of shattering crystal rang through the limo. I hoped this was not an omen.

The glass-filled limo soon pulled up in front of the St. Regis, and August Cerradini, the resident manager, welcomed me at the entrance and escorted me to my room. I recognized Joe the bellman as we proceeded to the elevator, and all the way to my accommodations, I felt the eyes of curious employees staring at me.

Work began early the next morning. August had arranged a meeting with all the department heads, so they could introduce themselves and hear what I had in mind for the hotel.

Sensing they were suspicious of this newcomer, who had a reputation for making major changes, I focused on each one of them closely as they spoke. I wanted to send a message that I would be an attentive and accessible boss. Then came my turn to speak.

"I can imagine the thoughts and questions you are asking yourselves: Why is the company bringing somebody from Europe, who doesn't know the city, to improve this hotel, to install a new philosophy, and to try to reinstate the St. Regis again as one of the leading hotels in the city? Are there no Americans who could do the job?"

I looked around, and from their faces, I could tell that I had guessed correctly. I continued.

"You are right, but before I start, I wish to share two things with you. Yes, I do have one disadvantage: I don't know New York. But I do have one big advantage: I don't know New York!"

A few people laughed, and others looked at me blankly. I couldn't tell if they understood what I had meant with my comment. But I figured I would have plenty of time to explain later. I proceeded to tell them a little about myself, my career, and my achievements within the Europe and Middle East region, just enough to let them know who I am without giving the impression that I wanted to show off.

Back in my office, my new secretary, Dorothy Button, waited to get me settled in and show me around. After Dorothy Crom in Brussels, here was Dorothy Button in New York, preparing to brief me about the hotel and the many things I should be aware of. This Dorothy, much like Dorothy in Brussels, had detailed knowledge about the inner workings of the hotel, probably even more than the departing general manager ever knew. But the most important thing was I could tell right away that she was an honest, reliable person, someone I could trust.

I did not have the same impression when I met Ilona Oosthuisen, the director of human resources. Expecting to find a person presenting herself with style and elegance, the person I met was instead dressed in a careless manner, lacking the polish of other department heads I had seen at the St. Regis and other hotels of this caliber.

Even more disconcerting, Ilona quickly revealed herself to be someone who plays politics and stirs up trouble. In our first meeting, she tried to impress me by informing me that I should not worry about the unions because she knows the game they're playing and knows how to handle them. I sensed that she's a person who tries to make herself indispensable by exploiting difficult situations, then swooping in to solve them.

She took her game to the next level a few days later, when she told me she'd heard that some union members were planning to demonstrate that afternoon in the lobby to protest what they saw as unsatisfactory working conditions in the hotel.

"Mr. Tischmann," she said to me gravely, "I would recommend that you leave the hotel for a few hours and let me handle this."

Ilona's tactic might have worked with the former general manager, but it was definitely not going to work with me. I needed to establish immediately that I had no intention of giving up control of this hotel and that her approach would fall on deaf ears.

"We don't know each other very well yet," I said to her, "but please understand once and for all that, first, I will not be leaving the hotel. I'll be standing in the lobby. Second, if I see anybody in the lobby who has no business being there, I'll personally turn the revolving door to throw that person out of the hotel. Third, the only way any of the people I throw out will be allowed back into the hotel will be through your office, to pick up their papers before they are fired."

True to my word, I spent the whole afternoon in the lobby, waiting for something to happen. But with the exception of the front office staff and the bellmen carrying luggage for arriving guests, no one else showed up, let alone any protestors. I believe the director of human resources got the message that this was a new era at the St. Regis.

My hunch that she was a person who could not be trusted turned out to be true, especially as I discovered that she maintained a close relationship with Kevin Richwood, the director of union relations in Boston. Was she working for the hotel or for Kevin, or for both? I decided to keep an eye on everything she was doing. This turned out to be a wise move, even if it could not save me from the trouble that awaited me not long after.

Sheraton's President Visiting Bijan

Denyse nearly had a heart attack when she arrived in New York with the children a few weeks later. The former general manager who had been transferred to Hawaii had moved out of his apartment, and we finally got to glimpse our future home. We were in for a shocking surprise.

The apartment on the eighteenth floor that Roger Senter had told me about was nearly uninhabitable. It looked as if it had been neglected for years. The beds were broken, the blankets filled with holes, the curtains torn up, and the upholstery on the furniture so dirty and covered in stains that we could no longer identify the original color of the fabric.

In the kitchen, we found an even worse situation. The cupboards felt sticky and dirty, with piles of partly broken chinaware stacked on their wobbly shelves. In the refrigerator, we found the remains of meals consumed weeks ago.

What a sight, and at the St. Regis no less. If the general manager's apartment looked like this, why was I surprised about the miserable conditions I found in other parts of the hotel?

I maintained no illusions that the Boston executives had any real understanding of what a luxury hotel was all about, and I suspected they had no idea just how bad things had gotten at the St. Regis. I knew no one in the corporate office would have believed me if I described the horrendous state of the eighteenth-floor apartment, so I decided to take pictures and send them to Roger Senter. Sure enough, he was as shocked as Denyse and I, and he instantly approved my request to make badly needed renovations. For the duration of the work, my family stayed in another apartment in the hotel.

The condition of the eighteenth-floor apartment represented only the tip of the iceberg. Ever since I arrived, I had been taking exhaustive notes on all the ways in which the St. Regis had fallen well below the level of a top hotel, not to mention the competition nearby in the city. We had nowhere near a physical product that lived up to the standards one would expect to find at the St. Regis.

When it came to bringing the St. Regis up to a level where it would meet, and even hope to exceed, the expectations of a luxury hotel, no one at Sheraton had any idea what to do. I understood that this was why John Kapioltas had brought me to the US. I had an enormous job ahead of me, and already, I had started planning all the changes that needed to happen at the hotel.

The St. Regis had always been a very special place. Even now, no other hotel in America offered the luxury and elegance that the St. Regis emanated back when it first opened. But now, only the name remained, a mere hint of the bygone days.

Sad examples of the decline abounded all over the hotel, some sitting there in plain sight and others hidden deep down in the basement. At this point, the St. Regis offered little to nothing to distinguish it from other Sheratons in the city. This was partly due to money-saving efforts by Sheraton and partly the result of a complete lack of vision.

All of the St Regis staff, from the bellman to the receptionists, wore the same exact uniforms as the staff at the Sheraton City Squire and the New York Sheraton Hotel on Sixth Avenue. It was cheaper for Sheraton to purchase uniforms for its four hotels in bulk instead of allowing one hotel to have its own identity. As far as operational concepts too, nothing distinguished the St. Regis from the others. The company treated it just like a regular hotel despite its history and its past reputation for grandeur. The hotel simply got lumped in with the cluster of other New York Sheratons.

By the time I arrived in 1985 to begin my new job, the St. Regis's clientele consisted mainly of business travelers who patronized the hotel primarily because of its convenient location in mid Manhattan. The occasional celebrity booked a room too, but our guest list lacked the society sparkle of years past, to say the least.

Nonetheless, a few exceptions stood out. The fashion icon Pakzard Bijan, known by his first name Bijan, had for the past year been leasing a retail space on the ground floor of the St. Regis. If there was nothing otherwise distinctive about the St. Regis under Sheraton, at least we had Bijan.

Bijan's fashion boutique for men had no rivals anywhere on Fifth Avenue, or in New York City for that matter. The spectacular shop displayed outstanding taste and sophistication from top to bottom. To simply call it a shop would not do justice to the experience Bijan created for his clients.

Although Bijan was a fashion designer, his store displayed no garments whatsoever. The clothing hung in closets, discreetly placed along the walls of the boutique. The only visible items were the accessories, displayed not on traditional shelves but on beautifully handcrafted antique wooden doors from Persia and Afghanistan. From the center of the shop, a round Lucite and brass staircase led upstairs, its spiraling steps hung with a giant Baccarat chandelier, sparkling as if it had a thousand diamonds hidden among its crystals.

Bijan reserved his office, atelier, and showroom upstairs for his important customers from the US, Europe, and worldwide, their pictures displayed in silver frames throughout the boutique. Into his private showroom walked the most exclusive VIP clients: from Carlos the King of Spain to the Aga Khan, to presidents and prime ministers, corporate leaders, and Hollywood stars, international celebrities from every walk of life found their way to his boutique. Bijan dressed most of the living US presidents, from Carter to both Bushes and Clinton.

For his clients, who visited by appointment only, Bijan had set up a handcrafted table, comfortable armchairs, and variety of closed wardrobes, ready to unveil presentations the likes of which no one had ever experienced before. Whatever his clients were looking for, Bijan had the answer, and he proudly opened one wardrobe after the other to display exquisitely tailored blue suits, brown suits, white suits, evening garments. Bijan could satisfy any and every item on his customers' wish lists.

His many wardrobes not only contained suits of all colors and all styles, but also matching shirts, socks, and even shoes. Once you left this room, you could count on ranking among the best dressed elite in America.

In order for clients not to mismatch items in their wardrobe, Bijan and his team made sure every item was numbered and grouped with other matching elements. Once a client had made his choices, Bijan and his team custom-tailored and identified every item. To wear suit #1 , his clients only had to look for shirts and ties and socks and of course shoes marked #1. That way, one was certain to always make the perfect choice and to show up impeccably dressed for any occasion. Bijan kept information about each client's size, weight, preferred colors, and favorite styles, even the color of their eyes, on file in his office. His attention to the smallest detail was absolutely unrivaled.

The experience did not end once the customer left the store. Packages sent to his VIP clients traveled by private plane and arrived hand-delivered by stylishly dressed hostesses, no matter where in the world the customer lived. Yes, all this service came at a high expense for Bijan, but his customers did not just order one suit. They ordered suits by the dozen and changed their wardrobes frequently. Bijan once claimed that some of his clients spent upward of $800,000 in his shop in one day.

Bijan split his time between New York and Beverly Hills, the site of his main boutique on Rodeo Drive. There, many of Hollywood's biggest stars shopped, counting on Bijan to keep them on the best-dressed list. The Beverly Hills boutique had a reputation as the world's most expensive store.

One day, while John Kapioltas visited the St Regis, he asked me if I could arrange a visit to Bijan's boutique, which he had never seen. At first, Bijan was surprised that the president of Sheraton wanted to see him, but then he gladly seized the opportunity to show John around.

John had spent many years in Europe and had refined taste. The boutique impressed him, and he did not hold back his compliments on everything Bijan showed him. Until he saw a set of crocodile luggage, attractively displayed in one of the corners of the boutique.

"How much is this luggage?" John asked.

"$75,000 a piece," Bijan answered proudly, showing John the particular finish and detail of every individual item.

John interrupted him. "Did you say $75,000 a piece? That's too damn expensive to put on a plane."

Bijan waited some time before he answered. "No, Mr. Kapioltas , this is not too expensive because my clients who buy this luggage have their own planes."

This answer rendered John speechless, and he left the boutique shortly after.

All day long, passersby peeked into the window and gawked at the beauty of the shop. Even the window-cleaning ritual made passing pedestrians stop and watch, to see the sheets of glass that protected Bijan's treasures receive an elaborate, theatrical washing worthy of a palace.

Unfortunately, Sheraton never recognized the value that Bijan brought to the hotel. For Sheraton, Bijan was a tenant like any other, and the most important issue was that he paid his rent on time.

But it was a terrible mistake to view Bijan as just another tenant. On a short list of retailers that included the Belgian chocolatier Godiva as well as a high-end jewelry shop at the corner of Fifth Avenue, Bijan was by far the most important tenant at the hotel—not just because of the astronomically high rent that he paid every month, but because of the quality, image, and reputation his shop brought to the hotel.

Unfortunately, tenant relations did not exist as a concept in Sheraton's universe, at least they did not rank as a high priority. So it came as no surprise that Bijan had some reservations when we first met. When I introduced myself as the new general manager of the hotel, Bijan said he was surprised that I had decided to pay him a visit in his shop.

"Who was the old general manager?" he asked me. "I don't think that I ever met him!"

Soon enough, he realized that my attitude about our tenants was quite different from what he had experienced in the past.

My relationship with Bijan improved from week to week, and although I never made it onto his private client list, he did once offer me a new tie, insisting that my tie was not the right one for the suit I was wearing. I hoped he would decide that my suit did not match the tie, but unfortunately, this didn't happen. Still, I felt quite lucky to have my own complimentary tie, chosen by Bijan himself, a gift that would make me the envy of any pedestrian who walked by the shop.

But as amicable as my relations with Bijan had become by this point, on two evenings, our interactions took an unpleasant turn.

On one particularly icy night in New York, his store flooded as a result of frozen pipes exploding and leaking water into the boutique. The entire shop turned it into a tragic aquarium scene, with expensive rugs and handmade furniture submerged in water. I grabbed a few members of my team, including our director of banquet operations, Joe Prezioso, and we worked through the night, calling for emergency plumbers and attempting to calm Bijan down as they addressed the leaks. This was a catastrophic situation for a shop like Bijan's, but luckily, he had a generous insurance policy. Even more luckily, he decided not to abandon the St. Regis, although it would have been perfectly understandable if he had.

Another night, the phone in our family's apartment rang, and I picked up the receiver to hear Bijan screaming into my ear. "What is Sheraton doing to me now? Can you come down to the shop immediately?"

I arrived to find the floor flooded once more and water pouring down the walls, inundating his boutique, and ruining his merchandise all over again.

Without any discussion, and despite the heavy rain, I followed Bijan on to the roof of the townhouse. The water up there had formed a giant pool, the blocked rain gutters having allowed water to back up on the roof and find its way into Bijan's boutique again.

As we cleaned the rain gutters, swept water off the roof, and covered all possible leaks with plastic sheets, working side by side all night long, Bijan's goodwill eventually returned.

It was at this moment that, I believe, our mutual respect turned into a genuine friendship.

The St. Regis managed to keep Bijan as a tenant even after this second disaster, perhaps more as a testament to the allure of that corner of Fifth Avenue and Fifty-Fifth Street rather than as any display of loyalty to the hotel.

The St. Regis, and even more so Sheraton, had yet to do anything to deserve the faith of plum clients like Bijan. I had been working steadily to bring the hotel back from its sad state of decline, but the Bijan incident proved to be nothing compared to the problems that awaited me.

Opportunities to Reduce Costs

Life along Fifth Avenue resembled a theater performance that went on and on. Around the corner and just steps from the St. Regis sat luxury designer boutiques and department stores displaying the latest and most extraordinary fashions, a scene that could rival any upscale shopping district in Monaco or Paris.

Denyse and I enjoyed walking up and down the avenue, especially the few blocks that stretched north from Fiftieth Street, starting around St. Patricks' Cathedral and La Maison Française, the striking Art Deco building with its intricate bronze engravings of figures personifying beauty, elegance, and poetry. We would stroll up to Fifty-Ninth Street, where the avenue touched the southern edge of Central Park near the Plaza Hotel. The real Fifth Avenue was actually much longer, but this particular stretch encompassed much of the glamour and sparkle of Manhattan. Crossing Fifth Avenue at Fifty-Seventh Street, where the intersection opened wide into a panorama of high-end design shops, exclusive restaurants, and soaring office towers, one felt a sense of occasion, a feeling of being at the center of the world.

Window shopping with Denyse on Fifth Avenue became a favorite pastime, a way to relieve the daily stresses involved in bringing the St. Regis back from its compromised condition. We walked along the avenue on weekend afternoons, admiring the windows of Tiffany, Fortunoff, Bergdorf Goodman, and all the famous brands that called Fifth Avenue their home. In the windows, mannequins wore the latest couture by Christian LaCroix, Jean Paul Gaultier, Azzedine Alaia, and all the major fashion icons of the era, and carried the most coveted handbags by Hermes, Judith Leiber, and Chanel.

Walking west on Fifth Avenue to Rockefeller Center, we would find ourselves in front of the NBC building, where Saturday Night Live hosted its weekly comedy show. In late November, a giant Christmas tree lit up Rockefeller Center, as it does to this day, illuminating the plaza and joining the twinkling lights of the boutiques and buildings along Fifth Avenue. During the Christmas season, the department stores would attract long lines of pedestrians who flocked to the windows to see the famous seasonal displays, intricate winter scenes, populated with detailed mechanical puppets that moved around a tiny stage. From the now-defunct Lord and Taylor all the way up to Bergdorf's, we would join the tourists and New Yorkers lining up in front of the magical windows.

We loved to walk out on to the avenue at Easter time too, when it turned into a spectacle of colorful bonnets and crazy costumes, as pedestrians and their pets showed up wearing their most creative getups for the annual holiday parade. The event looked to us more like a costumed street party than like any organized parade we had ever seen anywhere else.

One of the things I liked most about living in New York was the chance to be Mr. Nobody, to stroll the avenue without getting recognized by someone at every corner, as used to happen in Cairo. As the general manager of the best hotel in the Cairo area, I would get stopped wherever I went.

Living in the Big Apple, you are one of millions, and no matter who you are, even a major Hollywood celebrity, you can typically walk around simply being yourself. Seasoned New Yorkers, if not tourists, will generally leave you alone. Even if you strolled down the avenue in a pajama, mingling with the hundreds of New Yorkers and tourists window shopping on Fifth Avenue, people would most likely be too busy and distracted to care.

This situation has its downsides too. One warm evening, as Denyse and I waited for the light to change at the Fifty-Seventh Street intersection, my wife got nearly knocked over by two women who were crossing the street next to us.

"Can't you watch where you walk?" Denyse shouted to the women, who by then had disappeared into the crowd. I noticed Denyse's shoulder bag was open, so I alerted her.

"No, my handbag was closed," she said, but as she reached for the zipper, she realized it was open and the purse inside was gone. Did those women steal it as they bumped past us? We looked around, walking Fifty-Seventh Street and Fifth Avenue in all four directions, but could not spot those women or turn up any other clues. Whoever did the deed was long gone, a professional pickpocket who was surely robbing someone else the very next moment.

Back at the hotel, the doorman said, "Mr. and Mrs. Tischmann, this happens every day all over the city. These people are professionals, and all they want is money. The rest they dispose of as fast as they can throw into the next garbage can." I was worried less about the money than about the legal documents in Denyse's purse, so I sent her ahead to our apartment and returned to the scene of the crime. I must have checked every garbage can on Fifty-Seventh Street between Fifth and Sixth Avenues and between Fifth and Madison, as well as Fifth Avenue all the way to Fifty-Ninth Street, competing with the beggars as they dug through each trash can in search of empty soda cans or other items they could turn into money.

If this would have happened in Cairo, no doubt someone would have noticed. I would have hit the first page of the *Al Ahram* newspaper the next morning.

But this was New York, and here I was, walking with beggars from garbage can to garbage can, digging through empty soft drink cans for Denyse's purse. It should come as no surprise that after some time, the beggars' plastic bags were filling up with discoveries while my own search had failed. I returned to the hotel empty-handed, but all the richer for having learned an important lesson about living in a big city.

In case I had any doubt about this before, a night spent digging through the trash can attracts absolutely no attention in New York City.

If only every humiliating incident could be ignored in the same way.

New York's Barbers Are Truly Special

The sidewalks of Fifth Avenue are too public to truly call home, but those blocks soon began to feel like our family's intimate little neighborhood, our own window on to the spectacles that made New York one of the world's most thrilling cities. For Denyse and I and the kids, the area around Fifth Avenue and Fifty-Fifth was also the place where we tried to meet the simple errands of daily life, not always an easy feat in a neighborhood that caters primarily to shoppers and tourists.

I still remember one time when I tried to get a haircut along the avenue.

Not wanting to use the barbershop in the hotel, I had asked the concierge where to find a good barbershop, and he recommended the one in Rockefeller Center. "Ask for Jim, and tell him I sent you," the concierge called out to me before I walked out the door.

The Rockefeller Center barbershop looked enormous, with at least twenty chairs on one side of the room and a row of customers sitting on the other side, waiting for their turn. On the floor, I saw cut strands of hair clumped in bunches, from black to brown and blonde and red, and all the naturally occurring hair colors in the world, along with some colors that did not exist in nature. I watched as the barbers sharpened their knives the traditional way, on leather stripes.

Asking for Jim, I learned it was his day off, but after I waited for a while, a barber named Frank showed me to his chair.

New York City barbershops are an institution, and the vintage ones that remain around the city provide a nostalgic experience, an old-fashioned environment where clients can gossip and enjoy a break from their daily grind. The most in-demand barbers tended to have a talent for chitchat and would stay up-to-date on the news and gossip their customers enjoyed. They had a reputation for discretion, whether well-deserved or not, and customers often felt they could entrust them with personal news they wanted to keep private. The barbershop was a place to discuss business, get tips on how to play the stock market, talk about last night's Yankees game, or hear opinions on any current event in the headlines, and the one in Rockefeller Center proudly carried on this tradition.

A minute or two into my haircut, Frank asked me about my work and learned I'm the new general manager at the St. Regis. "It's about time that they bring somebody who knows what the hell he is doing," Frank said, and continued, "Unfortunately, the good days of the St. Regis are long gone."

I was interested in hearing his opinion on this. But my first New York haircut took exactly five minutes, after which Frank efficiently escorted me to the cashier before going to get his next customer.

"That will be twenty-five dollars," the cashier said. I thought I hadn't heard him correctly.

"Twenty-five dollars?" I repeated. "That's a lot of money for so little hair to be cut."

"Sir, we don't charge by weight," the cashier answered, stretching out his hand to receive the money. He returned five dollars in change to me, which I handed to Frank with a "Thank you and see you again soon."

That was my first and last visit to the barbershop at the Rockefeller Center. Not long after, I would find myself embroiled more deeply in the world of New York City barbers, but for the time being, I had to continue my search for a decent place to get a haircut, somewhere other than the St. Regis. The barber at our hotel was simply too close for comfort. Considering the tendency of many barbers to excel at gossip, as the general manager I was better off steering clear.

A Weekend at the St. Regis

New York City winters felt far more severe than the winters I had grown up with in Germany. Even when it didn't snow, the icy winds blowing through the tunnel-like Manhattan streets, bordered by tall buildings on both sides, made the temperature seem twice as cold. When the thermostat dropped below freezing, no mere winter coat could keep anyone warm on the frigid streets.

Winter coats could not keep certain St. Regis guests warm inside their rooms either. Bijan's plumbing issues proved only a small part of a much more serious structural problem. The St. Regis was in a slow-motion state of collapse, and on the coldest winter nights, or even on merely rainy nights, guests might find themselves in a leaky or freezing room, with the outside weather blowing directly into their private sanctuaries.

This was no joking matter, of course. But in order to cope with the stress of a hotel that was falling apart, and to comprehend the stunning contrast between the hotel's reputation and its current reality, I documented all the shortcomings in a little booklet.

Together with a series of incident reports and Polaroid shots documenting the leaks and floods, I turned my findings into a fake brochure titled "A Weekend at the St. Regis." The cover photo depicted a happy couple preparing for a romantic stay at our hotel. But instead of images of the couple enjoying a champagne toast in their room or sharing an elegant room service dinner, the brochure showed page after page of leaky ceilings, broken plumbing, and flooded floors. One photo displayed a toilet filled with frozen water and a pen sitting on top of the ice. I had placed my own pen there to see what would happen, and it stuck, so I had to snap a photo. These images were quite funny to look at, and they offered a break from the endless catastrophes. But surely no one at the corporate office would have been amused.

The truth was that nearly every aspect of the St. Regis needed major repairs, significant improvements, or a good renovation. We had problems everywhere, on every floor, and in nearly every space in the hotel.

The famous luxury hotels in New York at that time included the Plaza Athenee, the Pierre, and the Mark. When I took over the St. Regis, the room rate was less than half the others. But we didn't have any business charging higher rates. We could not even come close to what the other hotels offered.

I received angry letters or calls from guests on a regular basis. One day, a customer called me to complain, "How did we dare to rent a room without a toilet?" A room without a toilet? How could that be? I knew the hotel inside out by now, and I had no knowledge of any room that was missing a toilet. I went to the room to investigate.

Opening the door and walking in, I looked around and thought, this man is right. Where is the toilet? How did we not know about this toilet-less room? Then I realized what was happening. When the door to the bathroom opened all the way, it blocked the entrance to the corner where the toilet was, hiding it from view. Walking in without closing the door, you might well believe that the room had no toilet. But there it was, lurking behind the door, tiny and awkwardly placed, yet another feature that needed a complete upgrade.

There's a saying in the hotel business: If someone has a positive experience, they'll never talk about it because that's what they expect. But if they have a negative experience, they'll talk to at least ten or twenty people about it.

The St. Regis was no doubt becoming a victim of bad word-of-mouth, not just in New York but among its former clients around the world. And we deserved it.

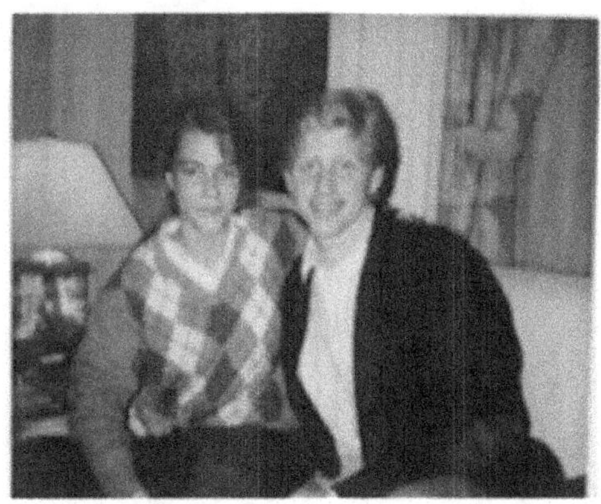

BORIS BECKER RELAXING
AT THE ST. REGIS

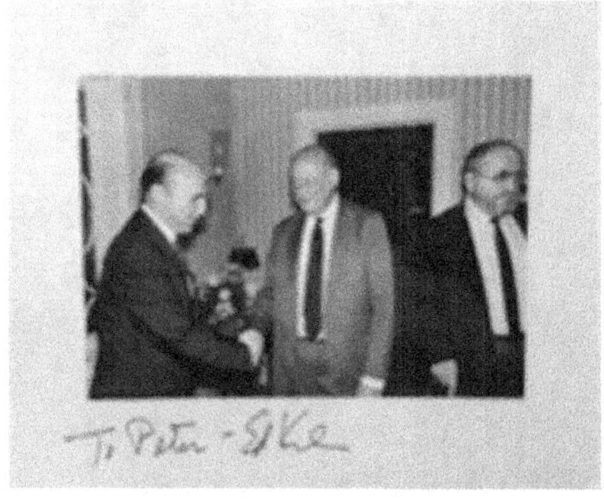

ED KOCH, MAYOR OF
NEW YORK VISITING

THE NOUVEAU BEAUJOLAIS
ARRIVED

PRESIDENT CARTER AND
THE TISCHMANN BOYS

IAN TIRIAC
MANAGER OF BORIS BECKER

PETER JR. INTERVIEWING
PRESIDENT CARTER

Return to Center Stage 19

Settling the Children in New York Schools

The floods and leaks that plagued much of the St. Regis had so far kept a safe distance from our family's apartment on the eighteenth floor. The renovations that we'd made when I started my job had kept disaster at bay, allowing us to enjoy our apartment as a relaxing place to spend time together when I wasn't at work.

In truth, I was always working, but I still had more time to myself than I ever did at the Sheraton Heliopolis. Managing the St. Regis, at least in the early days, was a different proposition than running the Cairo hotel. In Cairo, hotel guests expected the on-demand attention of the general manager, but in New York City they mainly wanted privacy. The rhythms of the day and night also differed in each city. Guests in Cairo generally arrived for dinner after 9:00 p.m. and never left before midnight, while restaurant guests in New York showed up much earlier and were gone by the time guests in Cairo were arriving. This meant I could retire to the apartment early and enjoy dinner or evening time with my family more than I could in years past.

Whatever my hesitations about uprooting my family to New York, and whatever the significant challenges of my current position, I had become convinced this move was the right decision, both professionally and personally. I remembered what Carine had said to me years before, that I had missed many important moments that she and Peter wanted me to experience with them because I was always traveling.

In New York, I found the time to participate more fully in the lives of both children. Despite the hectic pace of my job at the St. Regis, we made time for family vacations too, including a trip to Rio de Janeiro in the year after I started my new position, a trip made all the more memorable because of a birthday party that broke out in the middle of our Pan Am flight to Rio.

Carine and Peter Jr. had comfortably settled into their new schools in New York. Patrick, our driver, dropped them off every morning in our blue Lincoln Town Car in front of their school entrance, as instructed, and picked them up in the afternoon at the same spot, right in front of the door. But our children were no longer children, a point made all the more emphatic one day when Carine told Patrick not to drop her at the school, but to instead leave her on the corner so she could walk the rest of the way on her own.

Obviously, Patrick refused, insisting that he had specific instructions from her parents, and he was not prepared to risk his job. Carine was already a tough negotiator even as a teenager, and she reached a compromise with Patrick, who from then on dropped her a few yards away from the school entrance, so she could walk the last stretch as if she had just arrived from the subway. None of her classmates got dropped off by a chauffeur, we later learned, and she felt embarrassed about arriving in the big blue Lincoln.

Three months into the fall semester, Denyse and I attended a parents' evening at Carine's school. When we bumped into the director of admissions at the entrance, he gave us a distracted hello and welcomed us in, and we realized he did not recognize us. We introduced ourselves as the parents of Carine, and his tone shifted.

"Mr. and Mrs. Tischmann, congratulations to your wonderful daughter. We are so happy to have her at our school," he said, his voice brightening. "Her language knowledge and upbringing in so many diversified cultural environments are a real asset for her class and Trinity."

Was I hearing correctly? Was this the same person who had told us only a few months ago that we shouldn't bother to come to an interview because they had no room for new students?

At first, I felt like reminding him of this gently, with a smile. But I abandoned the thought and instead thanked him for the opportunity for Carine to study at such a great school as Trinity. Carine Tischmann would be in the company of many impressive alumni, from William P. Lauder, chairman of Estee Lauder Companies, to actor Larry Hagman of the popular TV series *Dallas*, to tennis champion John McEnroe—although McEnroe's behavior on the court was not necessarily a good reference for Trinity, truth be told.

Meanwhile, Peter Jr. would soon impress his teachers and classmates at Collegiate in his own way. Assigned to write a report in history class, he chose to examine the impact on the Middle East of President Carter's 1978 Camp David peace treaty between Egyptian president Anwar El-Sadat and Israeli prime minister Menachem Begin. As Peter concluded his presentation to the class, he said, "Why don't we ask the person who was mandatory in this agreement, President Jimmy Carter, how he feels about the agreement today?"

Students began to laugh until Peter turned on a tape recorder and played an interview he had just done with President Carter, who was a guest at the St. Regis while Peter was doing the assignment. Peter was the class hero that day. What could the teacher do but give him an A?

All in all, our family's new adventure together appeared to be going very well. We had dinner together at home most nights, and Denyse and I would go out to the theater often. On nights when we were invited out for dinner, we would order food for the kids from room service. But this was more of a convenience when we needed it, as Denyse was a wonderful cook and we were fortunate to eat homemade meals nearly every weeknight.

Little did I know how valuable this family bonding experience would become for us in the future, when times got much tougher.

Another Union Experience

The reality that enormous changes needed to happen at the St. Regis seemed obvious to me, but not everyone saw it that way. The crippling hotel strike of the previous summer still loomed large. I faced an uphill battle convincing my employees, from the housekeepers to the engineers, that we needed to overhaul the way we did business at the hotel. The attitude I kept encountering was that everything was basically fine, so why change it.

But as I saw more intimately than anyone, having examined every detail of the guest rooms and the service, and handled a steady stream of plumbing calamities like the ones in Bijan's shop, everything was far from fine.

Since I knew that changing the staff's attitudes would be a tremendous challenge, I had decided to let some time pass before beginning my reeducation campaign. Instead, I concentrated on the astronomical expenses that were killing our profits. Sheraton considered this a priority too, so I began to chop any line items that seemed expendable.

The garbage expenses struck me as absurdly high. I instructed our purchasing manager to look into alternative sanitation companies, until one day, the telephone rang in my office.

"Peter Tischmann," I responded.

A voice with a strong Brooklyn accent answered. "Peter Tischmann, you must be the new general manager. I understand that you are looking for an alternative garbage removal company." Before I could answer, the voice continued, "Let me tell you, you have the best garbage removal company in town, and the price is very competitive. So stop looking. Did I make myself clear enough?"

Before I could even answer, this man hung up. End of conversation.

When I called August Cerradini and spoke to him about the call, he laughed. "Mr. Tischmann, welcome to New York. You are now on their list."

"Which list?" I asked.

"Well," August said, "the garbage business is run by a group of people you don't want to get involved with, and if I were you, let's just say you should forget the garbage removal. You won't win."

It took me a half-second before I understood who was on the other side of the line. Ah, so this is how it works in New York. Needless to say, we never changed the garbage company, not even after we started a major renovation of the St. Regis a few years later.

"Nice hotel you've got there. Be a shame if anything happened to it."

The saying always sounded funny when mobsters said it on TV. I wanted to keep it that way.

A Careful Beginning

I needed to tread carefully every day if I wanted to avoid a rebellion by my staff. Determined as I was to improve the St. Regis down to the smallest detail, I knew that doing so would mean asking for much more from my staff. Hospitality employees know they can disrupt an entire hotel, an entire tourism industry, by walking out on strike. That was the last thing I wanted. So I plotted my moves strategically.

One thing I knew is that a higher level of service would mean higher tips. Improving the guest experience would pay dividends for everyone, so I focused on that angle as I tried to inspire every member of every department to adopt a new mindset about customer service. It was not that I wanted staff members to work longer hours; it was that everyone needed to focus more on anticipating guests' needs and making each and every customer feel valued and attended to. We needed to vastly improve the quality of service in our guest rooms, our lobby, our public areas, and our restaurants if we had any hope not only of surviving but also of restoring the magnificence of the old St. Regis.

If I were a guest accustomed to staying in the finest hotels around the world, the St. Regis would make a bad impression from the moment I walked in. I would notice the bland chain-hotel uniforms and the old-fashioned brochures and the menus that seemed dated. Never mind the look of the rooms and common areas, which had been renovated in 1977 but already looked dated, thanks in part to a pink and green springtime color scheme that was not exactly timeless.

We needed to start with elements that we could change immediately, the faster, the better. I was determined to fix every single fixable detail that could impact customers' experiences, from the first impression down to the last greeting they received on the way out.

Of course, that also meant preventing our guests' rooms from flooding in the middle of the night. But I soon discovered that the biggest roadblock to improving the condition of the hotel was the engineering department. The engineers on staff spent more time explaining to me why things couldn't be done instead of presenting solutions and attempting to make changes.

After several months with no major breakthrough in the attitude or behavior of anyone in the engineering department, and with ongoing leaks and structural issues all over the hotel, my patience ran out. I remembered an old saying: "Either people change, or we change people."

I knew that hiring and replacing the head of the department was my only hope if I wanted to bring about the much-needed changes. Over a period of weeks, I had secretly searched for a new chief engineer, and I finally found my ideal hire in a man named Vasos Michael.

Vasos came from Cyprus and had been working at New York's InterContinental Hotel, which had similar problems as the St. Regis. He was also well-connected and respected by the unions for his demanding but fair management style. After a thorough inspection of the hotel, Vasos confirmed my worst fears about the back of the house and the basements. But Vasos seemed undaunted by the problems, as big as they were. In him, I sensed a dedicated team member who would match my own commitment to improving the hotel. I made him an offer and was relieved when he agreed to leave his job and come work at the St. Regis.

As we walked all over the basement together, we found flooding that had remained unaddressed for years and shoddy attempts to patch up leaks. The area was now not only waterlogged but also dangerous. The engineering staff had told me these conditions dated back years, and I wondered if the previous general managers had ever made it into this part of the hotel. Why had this area not been addressed during the last renovation?

"There is nothing down there anyway," was the standard answer that the engineers kept giving me. I didn't believe them.

Equipped with Wellington boots and flashlights, Vasos and I explored every corner, and indeed we found nothing at first other than old and broken furniture. Then we stumbled onto a locked room. When we finally managed to get inside, the first thing I noticed were the remains of a table from the Astor era. This was a real treasure, even as damaged as it was, and soon we found other valuable pieces in there too.

We used our best judgment to determine which of the antiques we found could be repaired, and which ones were now merely firewood. Alas, all those years in the humid basement had taken a tragic toll on some of the most beautiful old pieces. We brought the ones worth salvaging upstairs, cleaned them, and placed them carefully in our general store.

The furniture around the St. Regis at the time included very few of the original pieces that dated back to the 1904 opening. This was a shame, and unsurprisingly, it turned out Sheraton executives had made the decision to do away with the antique furnishings. Apparently, during the most recent renovation, they determined that buying new furniture was cheaper than restoring the old pieces. This was how the hotel ended up with replicas instead of actual antiques—another nail in the coffin of the St. Regis's once-unrivaled splendor.

I discovered another reason why so much of the antique furniture had vanished. General managers, for years, had picked the nicest pieces to furnish their own private apartment at the hotel, and when they received a transfer, the furniture moved with them. No wonder so little furniture remained, in the guest rooms or basement or anywhere else, to reflect the hotel's original charm and individuality.

As the weeks went by, Vasos wasted no time in transforming the back of the house into a more presentable area. Even though guests never saw these parts of the hotel, it was important that we turn them into cleaner, tidier, not to mention safer spaces for the staff. The water soon disappeared, the walls received a new coat of paint, and the employee locker rooms and staff dining room looked refreshed.

Even Lynn Mitchell, our executive housekeeper, started to smile again, as the space she spent time in every day finally got a much-needed makeover.

All those improvements inspired us to hold an upcoming travel industry event in the basement, rather than in the fancy Versailles Room on the first floor overlooking Fifth Avenue. This was an annual event for travel agents and corporate customers, and for the first time, we invited not only the sales department but also all the department heads to present and promote their respective parts of the hotel.

The party generated a buzz in the industry, and travel agencies and other decision makers talked about it for a long time after. I was pleased to see what the change of one department head could achieve, and I added a few more potential candidates to the list.

One department I'd found disappointing so far was sales and marketing. Instead of doing what they were supposed to do—sell, sell, sell—the staff in our sales department seemed to have a different idea about how to do their jobs. I would find them all in the office every morning, chatting with each other about their evening plans, taking time to sip their morning coffee, and waiting for the phone to ring.

Selling through order-taking was not my idea of a sales department. An attitude adjustment was in order if the St. Regis had any chance to increase its visibility and success in the local marketplace.

In hotel lingo, selling is also known as cleaning doorknobs because in order to sell rooms, one had to go out to look for customers, which means knocking at doors and opening them—in other words, to polish the doorknobs.

Since Sheraton had only recently hired Martin O'Brien to head the sales and marketing department, I held out hope that he had not yet been affected by the dolce far niente virus of his sales staff. I quickly discovered that he agreed with me: Only a radical change would give us the expected results. So we dismissed the so-called sales staff at the end of the week and within two weeks had replaced them with an energetic, hungry sales staff.

Finally, we saw a rapid uptick in the sales of our hotel rooms, banquet functions, and even restaurant reservations. The corporate sales department in Boston was not too happy that we had made this radical decision without their involvement, but considering the past poor performance of the sales staff, they wisely refrained from making an issue out of it.

Now, when I walked through the sales office in the morning, I would see only empty desks. The staff was finally out on the road every day, polishing doorknobs and bringing badly needed business into our hotel.

Filmmaking with Woody Allen

Bit by bit, the St. Regis was starting to wake up from its deep slumber. The hotel began to function better in nearly every department. We had fewer leaks, due in part to the improved structural condition of the building. Our rooms looked cleaner, the result of a preventative maintenance program I was trying out where we took five to ten rooms out of service every day so we could do a thorough sprucing-up. We had almost four hundred rooms at that time, so we could accomplish this without hurting our occupancy.

The more enhancements we made, the more guests took notice. We had a steady influx of new guests now, thanks to the efforts of our sales department, and our word-of-mouth reputation grew more positive. I had made some headway in improving the attitudes and customer service skills of our guest-facing staff, but the real change came as they noticed that the higher quality and satisfaction of our guests meant more cash in their pockets. The only way to motivate certain staff members was through money, and finally this was starting to happen.

We even raised our room rates, not yet to the level of our luxury hotel competitors but within striking distance. Our occupancy and revenues were going up steadily too. Everything was clicking along.

Now it was time to tackle the most challenging part of my job and the part I looked forward to the most. It was time to deliver on the promise of the old St. Regis.

I wanted to not only restore the St. Regis to its original magnificence, but I wanted to bring back the spirit of the original hotel when it was a place for festive times and grand events. I introduced a new slogan for the St. Regis: "Back to the good old times."

As luck would have it, we soon had an opportunity to give our new slogan a dose of much-needed exposure. Woody Allen's agent called one day to say the filmmaker had chosen the St. Regis as the site for his next movie, *Radio Days*. Would we be interested in hosting the film shoot?

What a question!

Within days, the film crew had transformed the King Cole dining room into a stylish period restaurant, complete with crystal chandeliers, plush upholstery, and luxurious table settings that reflected the grandeur of those good old times.

Despite the electrical cables that ran all over the floor during the film shoot, and the spotlights that gave the public spaces an almost daylight harshness, and the movie crew dispersed all around the hotel, our guests did not appear disturbed in the least. On the contrary, many told us how excited they felt to experience Woody Allen in action and to witness the creation of his newest movie.

When the film shoot ended, I asked the foreman what they intended to do with all the decorations and settings. "It's garbage," he replied. "We can't use it a second time. Do you want it?"

So that is how the King Cole ended up with a new interior decor scheme, not to mention a formidable marketing tool. Our hotel restaurant was now the home of Woody Allen's movie *Radio Days*, and guests came in just to see it.

That same month, we started our enormously successful Saturday Night Dinner Dance series. The only other restaurant that had dancing at the time was the Rainbow Room. I decided New York City needed at least one other venue for dining and dancing. We brought in a band made up of young musicians wearing tuxedos and red sneakers to play the sounds of Lester Lanin, New York's famous big band jazz musician from the thirties. Now the good old times were finally back at the St. Regis. But we still had a long way to go.

In the Limelight

The St. Regis was becoming the talk of the town once again. But this was no time for rest. We needed to keep getting the word out, to keep fighting for our space in New York City's ever more competitive hotel scene. That meant coming up with constant promotions. I felt as if I were at the Heliopolis all over again, but this time without General Zaki as a sounding board.

When I brainstormed ideas for promotions, I always researched events that the hotel had thrown in the past or that dated back to an earlier heyday in the city. I tried to connect the past with the present. At the Heliopolis, I had come up with the Layla Al Kabira concert by talking to the older generation in Egypt who remembered the way things used to be back in the golden age.

As a general manager, you have to develop your curiosity and absorb everything like a sponge if you want to generate successful promotion ideas. Happily, just about every promotion we tried at the St. Regis brought in enthusiastic crowds, from the Dinner Dance series to the Big Band Night. At one point, we hired a piano player named Bobby Weatherbey, after I had tried and failed to bring in Michael Feinstein, the famous pianist who had a cult following at the Regency. But Bobby turned out to be wonderful and brought in his own eager crowds.

We did steal another concept from the Regency: the power breakfast. At the time, the Regency was the prime power breakfast spot, but we decided to go head-to-head with our competition. We placed an hourglass on every table and told customers that if they didn't receive their bread, jam, croissant, and coffee within five minutes of ordering, breakfast was on us. This was a successful promotion too and improved our breakfast business.

I saw another opportunity to get guests excited when it was time for the release of the Beaujolais Nouveau wine. The St. Regis managed to win a citywide race to serve the coveted French wine first, generating a buzz in the media. The tradition goes back for decades in France, but most New Yorkers had yet to experience it.

On the fifteenth of November every year, the Beaujolais region of France releases a new wine, and restaurants and wine bars race to be the first to serve it, sending staff to bring it back via motorbike, automobile, or airplane—and even by Concorde in the airplane's heyday. On that day in mid-November, banners all over France announce that "Beaujolais Nouveau est arrivé." Around the early 1950s, the craze went global, thanks in large part to George Duboeuf, a prominent Beaujolais negociant with connections all over the world.

George Duboeuf was also a personal friend of Paul Bocuse, and through the chef, I had the pleasure of meeting Mr. Duboeuf in person and visiting his famous winery.

Now that the St. Regis had a European general manager and a French food and beverage director, it was perhaps no surprise that we decided to participate actively in this race to bring the first bottle of Beaujolais Nouveau to New York.

I owe a debt of gratitude to George Duboeuf, who personally carried the first bottle of his Beaujolais Nouveau on a Concorde in less than six hours from Paris to New York, and an even bigger thanks to Joseph Prezioso, our director of banquet operations, who met the Concorde at the airport and waved George's limousine with a police escort through the heavy New York traffic, straight to the doorstep of the St. Regis.

The St. Regis was the first hotel in New York to proudly fly the banner, "The Beaujolais Nouveau has arrived."

As with many other classic rituals, business greed has by now ruined the tradition. Today the wine sits waiting in warehouses worldwide, waiting to get shipped to restaurants. The only remaining restriction is that this cannot be done before November 15. But the mystique and suspense are now relics of the past. At least the St. Regis got to join in the party while it lasted.

A Surprise at the American Consulate

I've heard it said that it's easier to get away with murder in the US than to cheat the Internal Revenue Service, and there's apparently truth to this. The notorious Mafia boss Al Capone was never convicted for his multiple crimes, but what finally got him was tax fraud.

As a foreigner working on an L1 limited work permit and residence, I had to take extra precautions to make sure I did everything correctly on my taxes, so I started to look around for an accountant who could help me with my tax returns.

The guy I hired on a friend's recommendation, Howard Cohen, at first could not believe the paperwork I handed to him. Since I had only been working in the US for a few months by then, I had very little to bring him besides my monthly pay slips. "That's all you have?" Howard asked me, in disbelief. "You don't owe any money to any bank, no interest payments, no credit card debt, no sales taxes?"

"Peter," he continued, shaking his head, "you are in the States now. You have to owe money somewhere, or you are going to make Uncle Sam very happy and pay taxes you should avoid."

I never owed any money to anybody. My credit cards were paid the day I received the statement, and my only relationships with banks were the accounts that received my monthly salary deposits.

Sales taxes? I didn't even know that they were deductible, so I never collected the sales slips. Obviously, I had a lot to learn, and Howard Cohen was a good teacher.

Meanwhile, Denyse and I met many Lebanese people in New York, as the city was full of them. Among these was Dr. Jean Saleh, a famous gastroenterologist, whom Denyse knew through her family connections and with whom we developed a close friendship.

One day, Jean invited us to his weekend home in New Hope, Pennsylvania, about a two-hour drive from the city. Weekend residences outside New York City were de rigueur among those who could afford them and a welcome escape from the hectic pace of urban life.

New Hope, a small town and artists' haven on the Delaware River, is close enough to New York City to make for a popular weekend destination and a coveted site for second homes. Jean's house was a lovely Dutch Colonial within a private estate, surrounded by substantial acreage that gave him the privacy and tranquility he craved.

We began to visit Jean more and more often as our friendship grew. During one of our visits, I happened to overhear people hammering a "For Sale" sign into the ground on the other side of the street from Jean's house.

"Look," I said to Denyse, "the house across the street seems to be for sale. Should we have a look?"

Four weeks later, I followed Howard Cohen's advice and closed on the purchase of the house. Now I owed the bank a lot of money. I hoped Howard was happy.

We chose to work with Bank Audi on the purchase, based on an introduction by friends of ours. The bank was owned by a Lebanese man named Joseph Audi and was one of the major banks in Lebanon.

Joseph Audi, or Joe, eventually became a close friend of ours in New York and advised us on all our banking and investments. The fact that his bank was located just behind the hotel on Fifty-Fourth Street made banking with him even more convenient.

I have to admit, living in a house that the bank owned was not a feeling I was used to, and it took me quite some time before I stopped losing sleep over it.

The home was not just an investment, of course. Having a weekend home in New Hope meant driving to Pennsylvania every weekend and undertaking projects to improve the house, beautify the landscaping, mow the grass, and rake the piles of leaves that landed on our acre-and-a-half property in the fall. But I found that I enjoyed the work. It provided a welcome distraction from my job in New York. Getting my hands dirty in New Hope turned out to be an effective way to clear my mind from all the stress of managing the St. Regis.

Even Carine and Peter Jr. enjoyed the weekends, with the exception of fall. As much as they enjoyed riding the tractor to cut the grass, they disliked having to collect the endless layers of fallen leaves on the ground.

As time passed, we redecorated the house to our taste and fitted it with new carpets, parquet flooring, and wallpaper.

We enjoyed relaxing in our warm and cozy house and invited many friends from New York, who were glad to know somebody who had a weekend escape. We were equally glad to have some friends around us to share our home.

As for Denyse's Lebanese connections, they soon came to our rescue on another occasion, this time a more important one than buying a weekend home.

We had applied for a Green Card, but we ended up waiting a year before we finally got accepted. At that point, the whole family had to go for a final interview at the American Consulate in Frankfurt. As we sat in the waiting hall, Denyse heard the consul summon her up for the interview.

"Mrs. Tischmann," the consul asked my wife, "you are applying for a Green Card? What is your maiden name?"

"Malouf," said Denyse.

"Malouf? Are you from Lebanon?"

"Yes, I was born there."

"Let me tell you a story," the woman said, perking up. "My first assignment abroad for the US was in Sudan, in Khartoum. I arrived in Khartoum all by myself, and there was a doctor whose name was Dr. Nicolas Malouf, who welcomed me and took care of me and introduced me to everybody. He helped me to establish myself."

Denyse said, "Yes, that is my uncle, the brother of my father."

From that moment on, the discussion was only about Sudan and how great her uncle was and what a wonderful family she had. The Green Card was just a formality at that point.

Denyse turned to me with a smile as we walked out, saying, "You see what family you married into?"

The St. Regis Is Back

The lobby of the St. Regis looked and sounded different than it did when I first took over as general manager. It wasn't simply that the staff smiled more often or greeted guests more warmly. I did feel proud of this shift in the customer service attitude, a hard-won battle on my part, but something else had changed. Day after day, week after week, I started overhearing more foreign languages in our reception area than I had before. More business executives and international guests were booking rooms at the St. Regis than in recent years. Elite travelers arrived at a steadier clip.

Slowly but surely, the St. Regis began to stand out among the three other Sheraton hotels in New York, attracting more cosmopolitan, affluent customers and offering a higher level of service.

Yes, we still had a tremendous amount of work to do, but the results were encouraging.

My connections with the leading travel agents in the city and the relationships I had built with international corporations had started to pay off too. It was important to remain visible as a general manager in the modern business environment, and I could already see the rewards of making myself accessible to staff, clients, and industry contacts alike.

True, the St. Regis had not yet rejoined the upper ranks of the Pierre, the Plaza Athenee, and the Mark, but we seemed well on our way.

At this point, it did not come as a big surprise when one day we received the reservation of the young German tennis star Boris Becker. At seventeen years old, he had just won Wimbledon in 1985 and 1986 as the youngest male player ever to triumph at the tournament. He arrived with his trainer Günther Bosch and his manager Ion Tiriac and stayed with us over an extended time. Boris was preparing to compete at the US Open, which several years before had moved to Flushing Meadows in Queens, where it remains to this day.

I invited Boris and his entourage to our apartment for "Kaffee und Kuchen ," and when he showed up, Carine and Peter were starstruck.

Boris could have easily said no to the invitation, but maybe the presence of a German general manager looking after him made the hotel feel like a home away from home for this jet-set young star.

One afternoon, Boris asked me if I knew a place near the hotel where he and his friend, the Serbian tennis player Slobodan "BoBo" Zivojinovic, could hit a few balls, as they didn't feel like driving all the way to Flushing Meadows. I made them a reservation at a facility on Fortieth Street where I sometimes played tennis when time allowed, and I asked if I could watch the practice.

Seeing up-close how Boris and Slobodan hit the ball made me realize how much more powerful professional tennis players were than us normal beings. When BoBo took a break, Boris asked me if I wanted to hit a few balls with him. I accepted hesitantly, suspecting my tennis skills would seem like ping pong to him, and I probably turned out to be correct.

Boris wanted to practice his serves, and as I stood behind the line waiting for the ball, I heard a loud smash. It was the ball, hitting the wall about fifteen feet behind me at a speed above a hundred miles an hour. How could anybody respond to such a serve?

I was happy to give my place back to Slobodan when he returned. Now I understood why Boris's competitors called him Mr. Boom Boom.

That year, Boris Becker faced John McEnroe at the Davis Cup in Hartford, Connecticut, which I was privileged to attend. That tournament earned its place in tennis history when Boris, after six hours and thirty-nine minutes, won a match point with an ace to finish off the last game. At 11:17 p.m., the crowd broke out in jubilation, having just witnessed the most dramatic tennis game ever played.

John McEnroe, devastated about losing this important tournament, put on his usual show, screaming at the linesmen, complaining to the umpire, and insulting everybody else. It didn't help. His young opponent kept his cool, in typical Mr. Boom Boom style.

As John McEnroe still stood at the net, not quite believing what had just happened, Boris ran around the court waving the German flag.

It was a historic moment for the Davis Cup and for Germany, not to mention for a certain German general manager who was delighted to host the winner at his own hotel.

I was very proud of Boris, and I have to admit, I was proud of the St. Regis too. The hotel was not exactly a young, up-and-coming star like Boris Becker, but we were finally starting to reclaim our place in the sun.

OUR WEEKEND RETREAT IN NEW HOPE

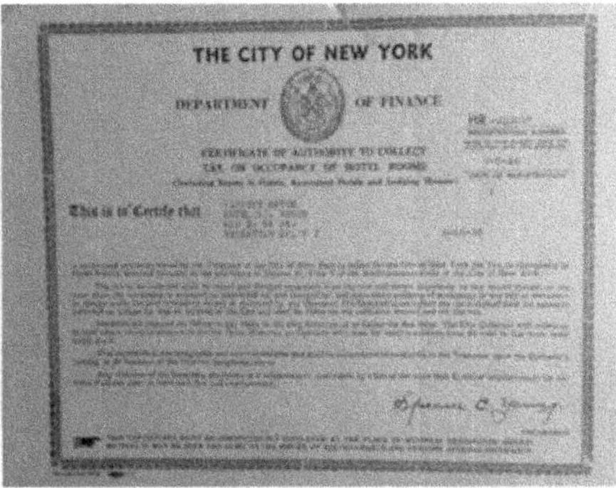

THE CITY OF NEW YORK

DEPARTMENT OF FINANCE

CERTIFICATE OF AUTHORITY TO COLLECT TAX ON OCCUPANCY OF HOTEL ROOMS

This is to Certify that

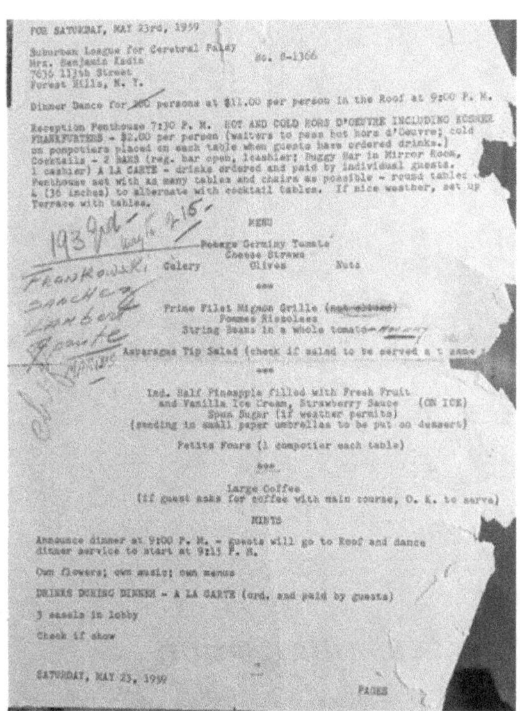

FOR SATURDAY, MAY 23rd, 1959

Suburban League for Cerebral Palsy
Mrs. Benjamin Kadin
7636 113th Street
Forest Hills, N. Y.

No. 8-1366

Dinner Dance for ~~200~~ persons at $11.00 per person in the Roof at 9:00 P. M.

Reception Penthouse 7:30 P. M. HOT AND COLD HORS D'OEUVRE INCLUDING KOSHER FRANKFURTERS - $2.00 per person (waiters to pass hot hors d'Oeuvre; cold on pompotiers placed on each table when guests have ordered drinks.) Cocktails - 2 BARS (reg. bar open, 1cashier; Buggy Bar in Mirror Room, 1 cashier) A LA CARTE - drinks ordered and paid by individual guests. Penthouse set with as many tables and chairs as possible - round tables 4 (36 inches) to alternate with cocktail tables. If nice weather, set up Terrace with tables.

MENU

Potage Germiny Tomate
Cheese Straws
Celery Olives Nuts

Prime Filet Mignon Grille (~~not sliced~~)
Pommes Rissolees
String Beans in a whole tomato

Asparagus Tip Salad (check if salad to be served at same

Ind. Half Pineapple filled with Fresh Fruit
and Vanilla Ice Cream, Strawberry Sauce (ON ICE)
Spun Sugar (if weather permits)
(sending in small paper umbrellas to be put on dessert)

Petits Fours (1 compotier each table)

Large Coffee
(if guest asks for coffee with main course, O. K. to serve)

MINTS

Announce dinner at 9:00 P. M. - guests will go to Roof and dance dinner service to start at 9:15 P. M.

Own flowers; own music; own menus

DRINKS DURING DINNER - A LA CARTE (ord. and paid by guests)

3 easels in lobby

Check if show

SATURDAY, MAY 23, 1959

PAGES

KING EDWARD VIII ABDICATED KING OF THE UK & MRS. WALLIS SIMPSON AT THE ST. REGIS

Salvador Dali at the St. Regis 20

The Celebrities Return

As celebrity guests go, Boris Becker was one of my favorites of that era. This was partly because I was a tennis fan but also because he took the time to visit our apartment and show me a few moves on the court. As the hotel continued to improve, we saw more and more VIPs pass through our doors, as guests staying at the hotel or as diners at the King Cole—or as speakers at the many events we hosted at the St. Regis.

The illustrious New York City mayor Ed Koch made a number of appearances at our hotel. Koch was very PR minded, and I remember that, at one point, he held a press conference at the St Regis. It was around the time when a Japanese buyer purchased Rockefeller Center. Koch got heavily attacked by the press: How could he allow Rockefeller Center, this landmark of New York City, to get sold to the Japanese? Taking the podium at the St. Regis, Koch said this to one member of the media who posed the question: "I don't understand why you're getting so excited. They can't take it to Tokyo." That was typical Koch.

Margaret Thatcher, who was prime minister of the UK at the time, also hosted a private press conference at the hotel. I remember that a question came up about her management style. Her answer still rings clearly in my mind. She said that if you try to please the media and let them tell you what to do, you are not displaying leadership. You are displaying followership. I have held on to those words, particularly in the tough times of my career when I felt I had to forge a path through the wilderness alone.

Former New York governor Hugh Carey visited the hotel regularly, but this was not so much of a surprise since his son worked for me as our director of catering. Other frequent guests included the famous divorce lawyer Raoul Felder, who often had breakfast in the King Cole restaurant, and Donald Trump.

I met Trump once or twice when he came to the hotel for breakfast. We shared a few similar interests at the time. We both took an active role in the Fifth Avenue Association, as he didn't want food carts in front of Trump Tower and I didn't want the carts parked in front of the St. Regis. Trump was a major real estate mogul at the time, and I was the small hotelier on the corner.

Years later, I encountered him again when Peter Jr. did an internship at the Plaza Hotel, which Trump owned. One day during his internship at the Plaza, Peter came to me, telling me that he had been laid off since the hotel was reducing employees to cut losses. I was furious when I learned this news. I could not understand why the hotel was dismissing a student who was obligated to take an internship as part of his training as a hotelier and was receiving very little pay. I decided to use my relationship with Donald Trump to do something about it. The following day, Peter was back at the Plaza, completing his internship. Thank you, Donald Trump, for the fast decision.

The Iranian businessman Charles Dabiri was a regular at our hotel in that period too. He owned a hair replacement business on Rodeo Drive in Beverly Hills, with a VIP client list including the likes of Elton John and many other famous Hollywood stars and starlets. Dabiri had opened an office in the Trump Tower too and was living there, on Fifth Avenue, not far from our hotel. I learned that his business was hair extensions and that the rich and famous were his clientele in New York City too. He would fill your thinning hair for you with new strands, which he would attach to your existing hair with clips. His system of attaching the additional hair obligated his clients to come back periodically to have the hair fixing redone. He never told customers that once their natural hair grew, the clip would eventually detach from the skin and move around, requiring a refitting every four weeks. He charged a fortune for his services and became a very wealthy man.

Although we were now receiving more and more VIPs and celebrities in our hotel, I never used their names to get publicity. I respected their privacy and required the staff to do the same, just as we would for anyone else at the hotel. Still, we constantly received calls from journalists hungry for news. "Who are the important people staying at your hotel right now?" they would ask. The answer was always the same: Every guest is important.

I knew that if we ever became known as a hotel that did not respect the privacy of its celebrity guests, we would never again see a celebrity walk through our doors.

We had worked too hard to rebuild the cachet of the St. Regis to risk ruining everything by leaking a silly item to the gossip pages. My staff seemed to understand this too, even as the media continued to circle around us like sharks.

Putting Lipstick on a Pig

Putting lipstick on a pig. That's a phrase American politicians like to say, and it was a fairly accurate description of what we kept trying to do at the St. Regis as the months and years went by. The St. Regis wasn't exactly a pig, or it was certainly a very expensive and elegant breed of pig, at any rate—but our attempts to make superficial aesthetic improvements to a building that was gradually falling apart were ultimately going to go to waste. We needed a more dramatic solution if we wanted the St. Regis to truly reprise its original role as the most opulent, gracious, and impeccable of hotels for the most elite guests in the world.

The St. Regis had made impressive strides so far, returning to a prominent position among New York City's top hotels, despite the minimal structural repairs we were allowed to make. We had already succeeded in improving the quality and service, raising the average room rate, and generally rehabilitating the image of the hotel. We heard fewer guest complaints and improved our guest satisfaction feedback. But the more improvements I introduced at the St. Regis, the more the corporate office began to realize there was a limit to what we could achieve without fundamentally changing our product.

At long last, the word "renovation" started coming up at corporate meetings. A smart person in the Boston office must have said, "Hey, if we can achieve this level of success with this old, tired hotel, imagine what we would be able to do if we completely renovated it."

It's possible that it was I who dropped the initial hint about renovating the hotel during one of the many conversations with John Kapioltas. Perhaps I said, "Well, if we could spend some money in the hotel and do the necessary renovations, we could do much better."

Wherever the idea originated, the decision needed to be made at ITT on Park Avenue, and if we wanted to get the process going, John had to bring it to Rand Araskog, CEO of ITT. As the ultimate decision was Rand's, my job at that time was to provide John with the necessary ammunition to sell the idea to him.

I believe that, with the exception of John, I was the only person who actually had a love affair with the hotel. I treasured the St. Regis's history and all the original details in the magnificent old building. The hotel was absolutely unique and had a tremendous amount of potential, and it did not deserve to be undervalued as it had been for so long. Since I knew so many of the palaces and luxury hotels in Europe, I would not be surprised if I was the only hotel executive Sheraton had in North America who could visualize what the hotel could become if we were in a position to fix it.

John did such a thorough job of convincing Rand Araskog of the value of the St. Regis that Araskog soon turned the hotel into his own little hobby. But even after the corporation decided to move ahead with the possibility of renovating the hotel, nothing happened overnight. Equitable Life Insurance was a part owner of the hotel at the time, and that company was not interested in investing any more money in the St. Regis. ITT eventually bought them out for something like $85 million. Once Equitable was out of the picture, ITT had a freer hand to make decisions about the future of the St. Regis.

Corporate executives began to debate whether it made sense to close the hotel for a while and gut-renovate it or to make the renovations without closing. The company investigated every other option too, from not doing anything at all to getting rid of the hotel altogether.

The decision to renovate finally prevailed. But new dilemmas sprang up in its place. For example, what should we do about our staff? If you have 350 employees and you keep the hotel open, or close it for a short time, you cannot replace them with fresh new employees. You have to keep the workers on staff and pay them according to the union contract. But it was clear in our minds that we would need to start from scratch if we reopened the hotel. This might sound cruel, but I knew that we could not rise to the level of service we'd need to achieve if we kept the existing employees. The service attitude that had been in place for so long at the hotel could not change dramatically without a change in staff.

True, I had seen incremental improvements in certain employees' attitudes, especially as their tips got higher, but those little changes struck me as tentative. We needed staff members who approached service differently and trainees who were eager to learn—not people who had already developed a jaded idea about working in a hotel.

When ITT finally decided to shut down the hotel to embark on the renovation process, an announcement was made that the closing would be indefinite. The company would not even confirm that the hotel would ever open again. The uncertainty made headlines.

An article in *Crain's New York Business* was headlined, "The mysterious closing of the St. Regis: Why a hotel long on history but short on profits shut down indefinitely."

Was the company's non-committal stance merely a way of getting around union regulations? Skeptics might have adopted that theory, but based on my understanding, the decision to reopen was actually in flux when the hotel closed. Whether the St. Regis would reopen depended, as I understood it, on whether the costs of the renovation ended up matching our estimates. It also depended on what it would cost to remove the asbestos from the building.

All along, I suspect Rand Araskog kept asking himself this question: "Can I justify spending $100 million to renovate this hotel, or will they take me apart at the next board meeting?"

He had good reason to worry. It was unclear whether the St. Regis would ever live up to its potential and whether $100 million was a wise investment to make in a building with as many problems as the St. Regis.

Luckily, Rand had fallen in love with the St. Regis too by this point. Perhaps not as madly as I had, but I sensed that I now had an ally in what would surely turn out to be a bloody battle.

Salvador Dali's Time at the Hotel

Kicking everyone out and gutting the St. Regis building would no doubt come with a price tag beyond the renovation costs that ITT hashed over at corporate board meetings. I worried that the celebrities and other elite guests who had developed an attachment to the St. Regis would find another hotel to call home and never return. As much as I favored the idea of a top to bottom renovation, I did not want to pay this particular price. My mind drifted to the renovation of the 1970s, which had displaced a famous resident of the hotel, the surrealist artist Salvador Dali.

Dali had been a permanent guest in the hotel for many years, and when he was asked to move out because of the renovation, he left with the promise that he would be able to return to the hotel once the work ended. But this never occurred because the main reason to renovate the hotel was to achieve a higher room rate, and guests living permanently in the hotel at a very low rate simply didn't fit the objective, even if their name was Salvador Dali. I don't believe he ever returned to the hotel after that. I understand that a low room rate for a permanent celebrity guest can place too much of a strain on revenues, but a resident like Dali does bring a certain cachet, and it's difficult to put a price on that.

If we ever did open the St. Regis again after finishing this round of renovations, I hoped that we would not only raise our room rates but also retain those clients who act as unofficial ambassadors for the hotel.

Rumor has it that once Salvador Dali moved out of his suite, the St. Regis staff went in to find the bathroom walls decorated with his designs. Even the toilet bowl was adorned with a giant eye. Unfortunately, none of these details survived the renovation, as no one at Sheraton had the foresight to guess how much value the maintenance of a Dali suite would represent as a marketing tool.

A few years later, I too would experience the same lack of vision involving Salvador Dali's memorabilia and the same careless attitude about the original St. Regis's heritage.

When I began my job at the St. Regis, well before we began to talk about an extensive renovation, I learned that a close personal friend of Salvador Dali, named Carlos Alemany, had his office in the townhouse adjacent to the hotel. I also learned that Dali had been a jewelry designer as well as an artist. His friend's business, Alemany & Company, was now executing Dali's jewelry in close cooperation with Salvador Dali himself. Needless to say, the right to exclusively promote the Salvador Dali Jewelry Collection was hugely profitable for Carlos.

The jewelry itself was exquisite and quite unusual, as one might guess about accessories made by this visionary surrealist. Dali intended his jewelry to be worn, not to "rest soullessly in steel vaults," as he wrote in a coffee table book called *Dali: A Study of His Art in Jewels.* "The viewer, then, is the ultimate artist. His sight, heart, mind—fusing with and grasping with greater or lesser understanding the intent of the creator—gives them life," Dali wrote.

As I got to know Carlos, I discovered that not only was he acting as Dali's right-hand man and handling all his business and financial matters, but that he also had access to a collection of memorabilia from Dali's long-term residence at the hotel: everything from restaurant invoices to deliveries from the pharmacy, sketches on hotel menus, personal notes, and even an old copper plate that was scratched and devalued after two hundred prints.

Carlos and I became good friends, and when I mentioned to him the idea I had at the time, to write a book about the St. Regis and its famous guests, he handed me a stack of Dali's memorabilia as a gift and as material for my book project.

Unfortunately, circumstances beyond my control never allowed me to start this project. Then, shortly after the closing of the hotel for the full renovation in 1989, Carlos offered the St. Regis two original Dali paintings for the ridiculously low price of $22,000 each.

What did the Sheraton corporate office say to this staggering offer? They said no. We are in the hotel business and not in the museum business, they replied.

When I suggested the idea of creating a Dali Suite in the new St. Regis after we reopened it, they again said no. Carlos eventually sold the paintings to the Salvador Dali Museum in St. Petersburg, Florida, where they remain on display to this day, and are valued at a price exponentially higher than what it would have cost the hotel to buy them from Carlos.

Why did I not buy one of the paintings for myself? Unbelievably, that idea never crossed my mind.

Closing a Landmark

Forcing a hotel as old and grand as the St. Regis to grind to a halt in four short weeks felt like a surreal act. If Salvador Dali were still living at the hotel, perhaps he could have created a painting to depict this madness.

I had exactly four weeks to dismiss the entire staff and to end all events and activities and plans that the hotel had agreed to undertake beyond that period. Every commitment we had made, from promotions to food festivals to banquets and every other imaginable event, we had to cancel if it was happening more than four weeks away.

As for hotel reservations beyond that date, we had to give a complete list to our sales and marketing department so they could ask guests to change their booking to another Sheraton hotel in New York.

The first person I fired was Ilona, the head of human resources. I had always been suspicious of her motives and tactics, and I never felt I could trust her. One potential problem that I did not take into account when I let her go, however, is her close relationship with Kevin Richwood, the director of union relation in the Boston corporate office. This friendship would later come back and bite me, but for now I had simply overlooked it.

I kept only two people from the current staff. One was Vasos Michael, the chief engineer I had hired about a year before. He was one of the best engineers in New York, and he knew the hotel inside out. He would help me communicate with Sheraton and ITT about the renovation and help us determine whether it would in fact be feasible to reopen the hotel.

The other person I kept, in a manner of speaking, was Joe Prezioso, the director of banquet operations. To Joe, I could only make the promise that if the hotel did reopen, I wanted him to come back to work for me. In the meantime, Joe had no trouble finding a job at the Plaza Hotel to ride out the St. Regis renovation. Of course, I risked losing him forever, but what could I do?

Laying off every other employee at the hotel proved extremely difficult for me. It was the first time in my life I had to do something like this, and it made me feel extremely uncomfortable. We also had many employees who were over fifty-five and who had worked at the hotel for decades. Since the St. Regis over the years had developed a reputation for not having the best staff, it was clear to me that the majority of those people would never get a job again.

Still, we promised everybody the best possible support. We organized a job fair at the hotel, and we invited other hotels to set up tables and send their human resources directors. That way our employees could meet the decision makers in person and present their papers and, with any luck, land a job.

About a week before we physically closed the hotel, I threw a huge farewell party for all the employees. It was one of the least festive parties I have ever thrown. Our employees put on a brave face. Nobody seemed bitter or eager for revenge. It was just a very sad moment for everyone. We were closing one of America's grande dames hotels, and we weren't yet sure if it was going to reopen ever again.

To keep up my own spirits, I decided to put my faith in the eventual reopening of the St. Regis. Because if ITT ultimately decided not to restore it or chose to sell it to someone else with deeper pockets instead, I would be out of a job or they would have to find another hotel somewhere for me. But I had developed a very strong attachment to the St. Regis, even in its badly diminished state, and I wanted to be the one to see it through its renaissance.

Having Vasos around felt like a good luck charm. After everyone on staff packed up their belongings and vacated, the building would surely have felt like a mausoleum had it not been for Vasos's smiling face and friendly personality.

The eyes don't lie, as the saying goes. I can look someone in the eye and know right away if the chemistry is right or not. With Vasos, the chemistry had been right from the beginning. I could tell from the start that he was committed, professional, and trustworthy, the kind of guy who would go through fire for you. But I always hoped it wouldn't have to come to that.

For the first six months after the staff bloodbath, the ghost town formerly known as the St. Regis had only four residents staying in it around the clock: my family. None of us ever quite got used to living in a desolate building. But soon enough, staying on the premises became impossible.

When the company finally decided to gut the hotel and begin the extensive renovations, the real work began. Everything had to go, from the electrical wiring to the plumbing, the insulation, everything. The rotten infrastructure needed a complete overhaul. The outside and inside walls would remain standing, but that was about all, and even some of the inside walls would get knocked out later and rebuilt.

The St. Regis of the current era consisted not only of the original 1904 building, but also an extension that dated to 1927. After John Jacob Astor's death on the Titanic in 1912, his son Vincent Astor had inherited the hotel, eventually selling it in 1927, during the Great Depression, to the industrialist Benjamin Newton Duke. Before he died in 1929, Duke built a new wing on Fifty-Fifth Street and brought the room count to 550, almost double the original number. Duke's daughter Mary Duke Biddle eventually sold the hotel back to Vincent Astor in 1935 for a shockingly low $300,000, and Astor began a new round of renovations. The last time the hotel had been renovated was when Sheraton bought it in 1977.

You could easily notice the difference between the original hotel and the new wing. The room with the bathroom hidden behind the door, the one that had upset our guest so much, was one of Duke's newer rooms, created on an economy budget. I don't know what Sheraton accomplished in the 1977 renovation, but from what I had seen, I was not impressed.

For this major renovation, which we started working on once we closed the hotel in 1988, we aimed to blend the new part of the hotel into the old part, as if the two had always made up one seamless whole. I wanted to make sure we got rid of every trace of those cheap rooms. We had a great deal of work ahead of us, a three-year project that I hoped would end up worth the many millions the company was pouring into it. We needed to do it right this time.

Soon my family had no more water or electricity to live on, and with all the systems shut down, we packed up and moved to an apartment on Fifty-Seventh Street and First Avenue.

During the day, it was just Vasos and me working in the building. My office was now in the old library, which had doubled as an event space. Vasos and I needed to stick around on the premises to keep an eye on the old building while the company planned the renovation. Otherwise, it would have started rotting from the inside out. A building falls apart very fast, especially one as old as the St. Regis.

Shortly after my family moved out, the asbestos removal crew arrived. They ran around every day with their yellow suits and masks and vacuum cleaners to suck all the asbestos out of the building. You would think they had just landed on the moon.

Removing the asbestos alone cost something like fifteen million dollars. For decades, the construction industry had recommended asbestos as a fire retardant, and as long as the material stayed solid, it wasn't dangerous. But when traces got suspended in the air and inhaled, they became a serious health hazard. Under the new construction standards, every inch of asbestos had to go.

The challenge, as I saw it, was convincing my company not to treat the entire heritage of the hotel as if it, too, was as outdated and toxic as asbestos. I was determined to preserve as much as possible, but this likely meant waging a lone battle. I vowed to gather my strength for the fight ahead.

Understanding Luxury

Spending $100 million to renovate the hotel would amount to nothing more than a stupid decision if the company decided to throw all the value of the old St. Regis out the window.

I knew that the hotel's history and heritage were its most important assets. I was certain that the valuable relics of its past would not only help resuscitate the grand old St. Regis, but that they would lift the image of the entire company as well.

In the King Cole Restaurant, for instance, we had a giant 1932 mural by Maxfield Parrish. The mural had once adorned the wall of John Jacob Astor's former Knickerbocker Hotel, which his son Victor had closed during the Depression. Even though we were creating a new restaurant concept, it was important that we salvage the mural, which was by now a part of the St. Regis's identity. I knew we would find a perfect place for it, even though we didn't know exactly where at first.

The lobby formed a major part of our identity too, as it does with nearly any hotel, and even though it would be getting a new layout, I wanted it to recall the old St. Regis as much as possible. The architects drew up plans for a tea lounge just off the hotel entrance, where a bar and meeting room used to be, but they made the ceilings higher. I liked that plan, as it would boost the grandeur and elegance of the ground floor while also seeming to form a natural outgrowth of the original layout.

This was, to me, one of the most important goals of the renovation: to transform the hotel completely, while also making the spaces feel as if they had always looked this way.

The devil, of course, is always in the details. Upstairs along the walls of the guest room corridors, white Carrara marble came up waist-high. I liked that elegant touch and I wanted to preserve it, but the architects said no, it's too old-fashioned. In the lobby, we had an antique gilded mailbox that I adored and a vintage reception counter where cashiers sat in booths protected by brass bars. Outside we had an old doorman booth. In the end, much to my chagrin, many old features disappeared, casualties of the new era. But at least I was able to salvage many of those charming relics, such as the mailbox, the reception counter, the revolving doors, and the doorman's booth, which would distinguish the new St. Regis from the other luxury properties in the city.

The mail chutes on the guest room floors were charming relics too, and fortunately, those stayed. But we closed up the chutes so you could no longer throw a letter in. It was too easy for letters to get stuck inside the chute, never to be seen again. We had one incident when a guest complained that a postcard he sent never arrived, and he thought the concierge had pocketed the money for the postage and thrown out the card. When we started the renovations, we found many letters trapped inside the chute, dating back months and even years.

I knew that the wines in the St. Regis cellar were worth a small fortune, but what would we do with those bottles during the renovation? I wanted to rent wine storage and keep the old bottles there until we reopened the hotel. We would need those wines to give the new wine list some weight. But the answer I received from Boston was: "We are not in the wine business, and we're not going to spend money storing wines outside."

"What do you want me to do with them?" I asked.

"Sell them at book value," said my colleagues in the Boston office.

Since a wine's book value does not increase over the years, I asked if I could buy some of the wines myself. Sure, said the Boston higher-ups. So I bought fifty bottles of wine, including about a dozen of Chateau d'Yquem 1972, for ten or twelve dollars per bottle, and I bought some Mouton Rothschild and Chateau Latour. The remaining wines we sold at book value.

Many years later, when Peter Jr. went to the Cornell Hotel School, acting as an assistant professor, he was organizing a wine tasting in one of his classes. I gave him a bottle of Chateau d'Yquem to taste in class. The professor, because of the special value of the bottle of Chateau d'Yquem, decided to save it for the last day of the semester, as a highlight.

A few days later, Peter Jr. called me, "Dad, do you have any idea how much that wine costs now?" I said no. He sent me a page from a *Wine Spectator* issue, and I learned that the wine was trading at about $1,000. A bottle. Once again, our corporate executives had proven they had no idea what to do with some of the most valuable, unique items that came their way.

The Salvador Dali paintings, the vintage wines, the broken-down antique treasures in the basement. These were only the beginning. If we weren't careful, everything that was unique about the St. Regis, everything that mattered, would soon dissolve into a cloud of dust.

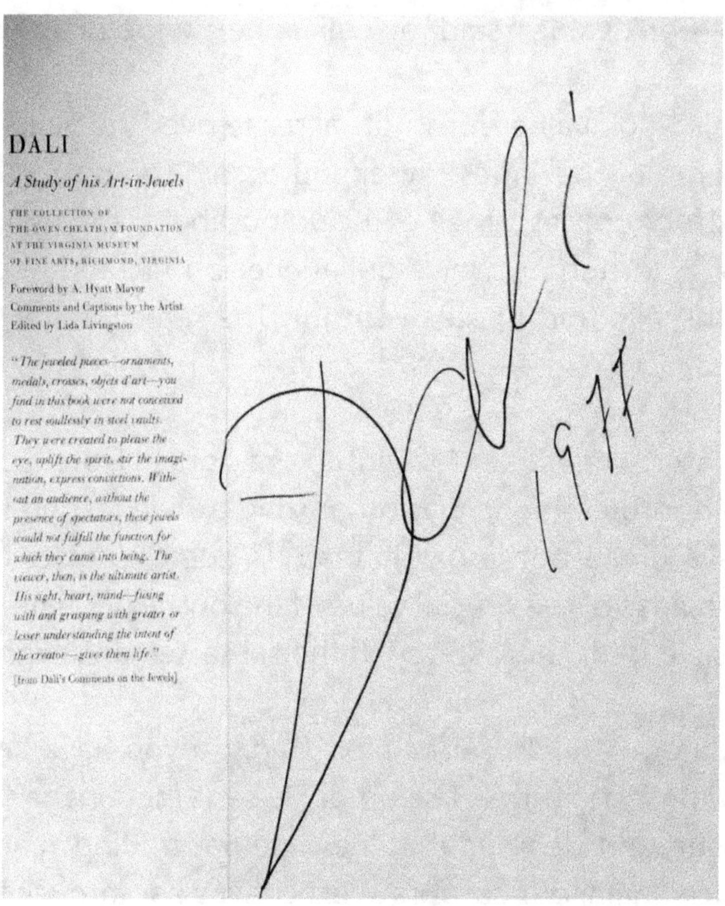

DALI

A Study of his Art-in-Jewels

THE COLLECTION OF
THE OWEN CHEATHAM FOUNDATION
AT THE VIRGINIA MUSEUM
OF FINE ARTS, RICHMOND, VIRGINIA

Foreword by A. Hyatt Mayor
Comments and Captions by the Artist
Edited by Lida Livingston

"The jeweled pieces—ornaments, medals, crosses, objets d'art—you find in this book were not conceived to rest soullessly in steel vaults. They were created to please the eye, uplift the spirit, stir the imagination, express convictions. Without an audience, without the presence of spectators, these jewels would not fulfill the function for which they came into being. The viewer, then, is the ultimate artist. His sight, heart, mind—fusing with and grasping with greater or lesser understanding the intent of the creator—gives them life."

[from Dali's Comments on the Jewels]

Dali 1977

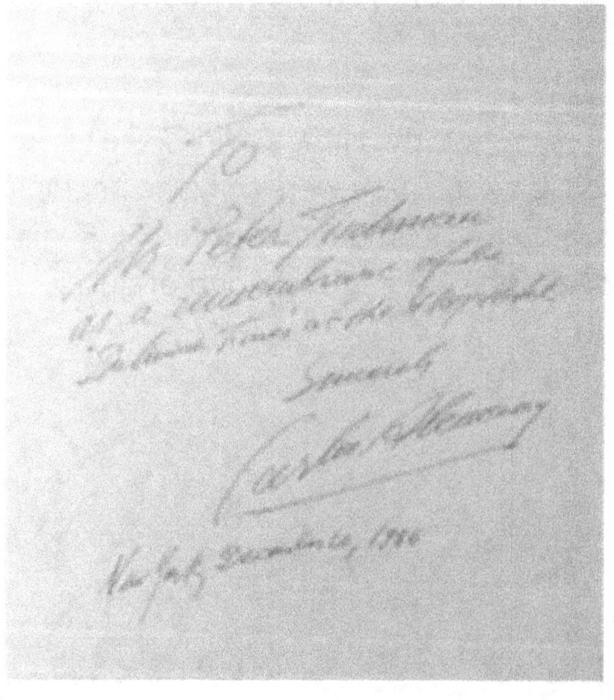

THE HONEYCOMB HEART

There's a little bit of sweetness in the heart of every woman.

DALI

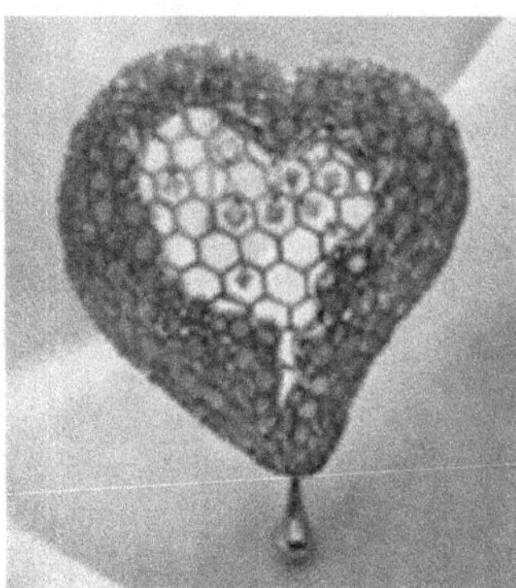

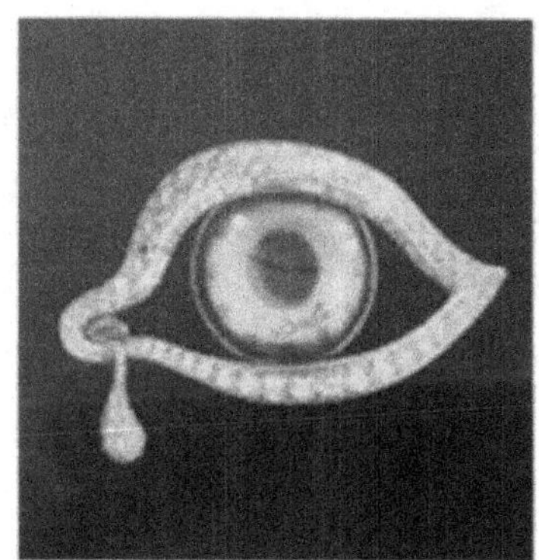

DALI - A STORY OF HIS ART IN JEWELS, AUTOGRAPHED FROM DALI IN 1977 AND RECEIVED AS A PRESENT FROM CARLOS ALEMANY, PERSONAL FRIEND OF SALVADOR DALI AND PROMOTER OF HIS JEWELRY COLLECTION

The Remaking of a Legend

21

A New Beginning

"Garbage in, garbage out."

This is a saying that computer scientists like to use, but the concept applies to nearly everything in life. If your efforts are garbage, don't expect your results to be anything other than garbage.

Sheraton would have done well to adopt this principle across all of its hotels. Unfortunately, I had the chance to witness the concept in all of its glory when I received a new assignment from the company. I was to supervise the reopening of another luxury hotel, the Carlton in Washington, D.C., while the St. Regis remained closed for renovations.

The Carlton had just gone through an extensive renovation of its own, handled by our technical services department in Boston. The hotel was about to have its grand relaunch, and Rand Araskog asked me to go to Washington on the day before the opening party to make sure everything was up to the high standards the company had set for this property.

Was the service staff thoroughly trained? Did the amenities look up to par? Did the guest experience appear poised to live up to Sheraton's promises about the luxurious new Carlton Hotel?

All these questions and more, I knew how to answer, and I knew how to fix any areas that needed improvement. At least, I could have done so if Sheraton had given me the chance to oversee the details before the renovation was complete and the champagne was already on ice. But by now, it was too late. Rand had invited several of his VIP friends, among them Fortune 500 CEOs and other influential figures in Washington, to spend the night at the hotel before the grand reopening gala.

Things had not gone as planned during the pre-opening visits, to say the least. I later learned that Rand had received quite a bit of feedback from the guests he had invited. The issues they discovered ranged from large to small, and every size in between. The water pressure was too weak, the drawers were too small to fit a folded shirt, the closet had no place to hang ties, the bathroom had no space for toiletries. The list went on and on. But I didn't have any inkling about those complaints when I arrived on the morning of the gala.

What I did notice was that Rand appeared quite agitated at the party that evening. He came up to me, looking tense and anything but festive, and asked me to meet with him the next morning. I went to see Rand at 9:00 a.m. the next day, with no clue as to what was upsetting him. But I soon found out.

With every complaint he listed, he grew more agitated. He wasn't blaming me for the problems in the hotel. The restoration had started long before I was put in charge, and I had no knowledge of any details until the day of the reopening gala. But I could tell Rand needed someone on whom to offload his frustration. He had spoken proudly about the renovation with his friends, and now their reactions to the pre-opening visits had humiliated him.

We walked through the hotel together and took note of all the problems we found, not just the issues the guests had complained about, but everything else that caught our eye. To our dismay, we found ourselves walking through doors that were too small, doors that opened on the wrong side, bathrooms that had no telephones, and an endless number of omissions and trouble spots. Not only had this renovation been poorly thought out, but the results came nowhere near the luxury experience Sheraton had promised to deliver.

By this point, ITT Sheraton had already finalized the decision to pour $100 million or more into renovating the St. Regis.

As we came to the end of our tour, Rand turned around and said to me, "Peter, I hope we don't have the same people renovating the St. Regis."

"Rand, I'm very sorry to tell you that we have exactly the same people," I replied. "We have the same architects, the same interior designers, the same decorators, all handled by our technical services office in Boston. The same people that handled the Carlton restoration are in charge of the St. Regis renovations too."

I was concerned about this decision from the minute I learned about it because none of the people involved had ever visited a luxury hotel—forget about designing one. Surely Rand knew that he had already signed off on this plan.

No matter. The next day, the architect was gone, the designers were gone, the decorators were gone, and the people in technical service were taken off the St. Regis project after what had happened at the Carlton.

Boston had to quickly find a new team to handle the St. Regis. Soon we had new architects—the New York City firm Brennan, Beer, Gorman, and Monk—and we had a new interior decorator too, Jinnie Kim.

My role suddenly changed too. Rand put me in charge of overseeing the details of the St. Regis renovation, in consultation with the architect and designer. "Peter," he said, "you make sure that you get everything you need to make the St. Regis the best hotel in New York." I would now be responsible for supervising everything except the construction. This move was a welcome one for me, but it put me in a difficult position vis-à-vis technical services. The office still had the same department head, Henry Fake, and would still play a role in the renovation. I would be responsible for major changes at the St. Regis without having any supervisory role over the department itself. Technical services answered only to Henry and to the corporate office. Not an ideal scenario, to put it mildly.

But I trusted that Rand Araskog and John Kapioltas wanted the St. Regis renovation to succeed, above all, and that they desperately needed to avoid repeating the embarrassment of the Carlton.

"Make sure you get what you need," John repeated to me.

Henry was someone I knew from my years in the EAME regional office. He had never been my favorite person, to put it mildly, and I suspected he must be quite angry now. When key responsibilities get taken away from people, they tend to make it known that they don't like it, through various means at their disposal. I felt sure that during the entire length of the St. Regis renovation process, certain people waited anxiously for a decision that I made to go terribly wrong.

Planning the New St. Regis

What is the difference between a classy gesture and a mere gimmick? What kinds of amenities inspire well-traveled luxury guests to fall in love with your hotel and to remember it above all the others? What details bespeak refinement and individuality, and which ones give away the fact that a chain hotel with tight budgets and no imagination is making all the decisions?

There is simply no way to create a hotel with the ambitions of the St. Regis without understanding the difference between true luxury and empty gestures, between a world-class product and mass-produced mediocrity. Unfortunately, certain people in charge of ensuring the quality of our hotels had no idea what a luxury hotel even looked like.

Obviously, John Kapioltas fully understood what I wanted to achieve with the St. Regis. Rand Araskog understood this too. Their vision for the hotel was almost exactly like mine: to restore the splendor John Jacob Astor had created when he opened the hotel for his worldly, socially prominent friends. But the people working in technical services in Boston only knew Sheraton hotels and business hotels, and they had no idea what I was talking about. It was clear that we spoke entirely different languages.

At one point, Rand asked Henry, the head of the technical services department, "How many luxury hotels have you visited?" Henry shrugged and didn't answer. Not only did he not seem to know what the inside of a luxury hotel looked like, but he appeared to have no understanding of the customers who patronize such hotels.

Looking at the St. Regis, even as it sat hidden behind construction beams, I had a crystal-clear vision of what the hotel could become once again as soon as the scaffolding came down. The St. Regis was a one-of-a-kind, highly prestigious property when John Jacob Astor first opened it, and it remained so for decades afterward. I am told that the St. Regis had the first air conditioners of any hotel in New York and the first mail drop. Details like those, among many other unique amenities, catapulted the St. Regis well above the competition at the time. Guests at the St. Regis knew they were part of a special experience, an experience they could get nowhere else in America.

Times have changed, needless to say, and so has the hotel world. The St. Regis had done a poor job of keeping up with those changes over the years, and when I first arrived, I saw the evidence of this decline everywhere. To reclaim the St. Regis's place at the top, we had to not only renovate every inch. We had to recapture all of the charm of the old St. Regis, while ensuring its appeal to the modern luxury clientele.

How would we set about reinstating the St. Regis as the grande dame of New York City, while modernizing it in subtle ways? I wrestled with this challenge day and night. It was important that we maximize the comfort of our guests, using all the state-of-the-art means at our disposal, but without letting the technology get in the way. While high-tech innovations can improve comfort, service, and the customer experience tremendously, they should remain invisible to the customer whenever possible.

During my decades of working and traveling around Europe, I stayed at the Ritz, the Bristol, and the Plaza Athenee in Paris, the Imperial in Vienna, and dozens of other hotels representing the highest levels of luxury. Anytime I traveled to an old European city with a famous luxury hotel, I would book a room and take extensive photos and notes on everything that impressed me.

At the Ritz in Paris, I admired an amenity called the Ritz Switch. This was a brass switch that a guest needed to turn in order to switch on the lights in the room. It looked like an old wind-up toy, but it had its own aesthetic charm. To summon a member of the service staff, a special button was located on the night table, a simple way to provide comfort and assistance to guests whenever needed. By preserving these old, charming relics, the Ritz had managed to combine the heritage of the past with modern needs.

On my travels in the East on business and with my family, I visited the top palaces, from the Raffles in Singapore to the Mandarin Oriental in Hong Kong and Bangkok. I took note of the physical details that made those hotels stand out, and I analyzed how the quality of service, the amenities, and every aspect of the hotel added up to create a spectacular experience for guests. I was stealing with my eyes, always, everywhere I went.

When it came time to plan the St. Regis renovation, I used all the tidbits I'd gathered over the years as I set out to craft my vision. But I had a difficult time convincing certain Sheraton executives that the details mattered. We had a big argument over bed sheets, for instance. I requested Frette sheets from Italy, made from 100 percent Egyptian cotton. Yes, the sheets were more expensive than standard hotel sheets, and they cost more for upkeep since they needed ironing, special care, and even special washing machines to handle the high-quality cotton linens.

One Sheraton executive asked me, "Why do you need 100 percent cotton sheets? We don't have these in any of our other hotels."

I said, "Yes, but the St. Regis will be serving a different level of guest and achieving a $450 room rate that other Sheraton hotels can only dream about."

What did he think these guests slept in at home? They had 100 percent cotton or even silk sheets in their own bedrooms. I found myself constantly arguing with people who have no idea what luxury means and no concept of what that clientele expects.

I ended up in another argument over the quality of the printed menus at Lespinasse, the St. Regis's new signature restaurant. Designed to be printed on handmade paper, every menu would cost $15, a unique piece of art and a business card for the restaurant.

"How many more covers are you going to serve every day in your restaurant because you have such a fancy menu?" I was asked more than once.

How to answer questions like this? The Sheraton executives who were all the way at the top and still asked questions like that should know better or shut up.

Still, I kept thinking about the advice Rand Araskog and John Kapioltas gave me: "Make sure you get what you need." So I did. Or I kept trying to, anyway, as I felt myself always split between Rand and John on one side and technical services on the other.

Bigger questions loomed too, like the controversy over what we should name the reopened hotel.

The corporate side wanted to name it the Sheraton St. Regis or the St. Regis Sheraton. In one of our meetings, I said, "I think it should be called simply the St. Regis, period."

Rupert Jones, the VP of operations for North America, chastised me in front of everyone at the meeting. "Peter, if you don't like the name Sheraton, maybe you should find another company that can build you your hotel."

Hearing this from an executive higher up on the chain, it can sound pretty threatening. But I knew I was right, and that others in the room who had any concept of luxury would support me on this point.

In a later meeting, Rand Araskog finally spoke up. "Are you sure that you want to call the hotel the St. Regis Sheraton? I think we really should just call it the St. Regis," he said, looking around the table.

Rupert Jones looked at Rand and said, "I agree with you. I think we should call it the St. Regis. After all, that's what we call it internally."

Jones likely had no clue what the right decision was, since as far as I was concerned, he did not understand the luxury hotel market at all. But going along with Rand was in his best interests, so that was that.

Shortsighted corporate politics aside, at least we ended up with the right name. I didn't need to take credit for it. I was simply relieved Rand spoke up and didn't let Jones make a decision we would all regret.

Around the same time, I received an unexpected opportunity to get an inside look at the business operations of a competing luxury hotel in New York City. Donald Trump had bought the Plaza Hotel on Central Park South in 1988 for a $390 million price tag. As Trump stated in a full-page advertisement he bought in the *New York Times*: "I haven't purchased a building, I have purchased a masterpiece—the *Mona Lisa*. For the first time in my life, I have knowingly made a deal that was not economic—for I can never justify the price I paid, no matter how successful the Plaza becomes."

Well, not only could Trump not justify the price, but he also failed to retain ownership of the Plaza as a result of the giant debt he took on to purchase it. Although he had appointed his then-wife Ivana Trump as president of the hotel and the Plaza was doing a robust business, it was not enough to keep the balance sheet in the black. Trump tried to sell some of the suites as condo units, but eventually, he gave up control. His creditors at the banks began to look for a new buyer to take a controlling stake in the hotel.

It was during this time that my phone rang one day, and on the other end of the line was Michael Maas. Over the past few years, he had advanced to become an executive member of the board at Kempinski, and he asked me if I would be willing to do a feasibility study on the Plaza for them.

Apparently, Deutsche Bank was prepared to keep their interest in the hotel, under the condition that a new management company would take over the operation. Kempinski, a leading German luxury hotel company, operating outstanding hotels throughout Europe, therefore became their natural choice to run the Plaza for them.

After a conversation with the GM of the Plaza, a study of competition shopping reports and information about occupancy and average room rates, plus other key data available from the New York Hotel Association, I called Michael Maas a few weeks later.

"Michael," I said, "I don't know the financial situation of Kempinski, but to successfully operate a hotel like the Plaza, it is important to have substantial financial reserves. The Plaza can produce a lot of money for a company, but at the same time can send a company into bankruptcy if they don't have the resources to support the losses in the soft shoulder seasons."

In the end, the top brass at the company decided not to get involved in the Plaza. They probably realized that one or two years of losing money in the hotel would spell the end of their company.

I had no inkling at the time, but years later, Kempinski would enter my life again, under far more dramatic circumstances.

A Chance of a Lifetime

Imagine that you are staying at a hotel with your spouse and planning to attend a gala in the evening. You will be picked up at a quarter to eight, but you've just arrived back at the hotel from a late meeting, and it's already twenty minutes before the hour. You and your spouse are both in the bathroom at the same time, rushing to get ready in just a few minutes before your car arrives. Is the bathroom equipped to handle this situation?

Design elements like these reflect the priorities of a particular hotel. Decisions about how to offer guests the maximum amount of comfort and convenience set luxury hotels apart from standard accommodations.

Once we switched our architecture and design team for the St. Regis renovation, we found ourselves in much better hands than before. The architects at Brennan, Beer, Gorman, and Monk did an excellent job drafting plans for the renovation, as did the new designer we appointed, Jinnie Kim. They had all obviously done their homework and had stayed in the important luxury hotels in Europe and taken pictures, just as I had. They were prepared and knew what they needed to do at the St. Regis. We all agreed that the hotel needed a complete overhaul.

Still, in order to create the guest experience I felt we needed at the St. Regis, I involved myself in overseeing every detail and anticipating every possible situation. Every renovation involves hundreds or even thousands of individual decisions, and the architects and designers and I—not to mention the corporate side—did not always agree about every issue.

Winning over the architects to the idea of taking all the tiny rooms from the 1929 addition and combining them to make one larger room was a battle, but I felt that all the guest rooms needed to recapture the spaciousness they once had in the initial hotel that John Jacob Astor had built.

An additional issue was the number of suites we had in the hotel. I lobbied strongly to create a larger number of suites, which I was convinced would be necessary to drive up the average room rate, but technical services fought me on this. They were not willing to reduce the room count, as this would have increased the overall cost per room, and with the budget already increasing, even Sheraton's executive board was not prepared to give Rand Araskog the bad news. Clearly, they had no interest in listening to my reasoning, and I eventually gave up.

Years later, the hotel ended up creating significantly more suites by combining two rooms into one, to satisfy customers' demand for suites. But simply joining two guest rooms together and calling the new space a suite is not the same thing as designing a proper suite and taking into consideration the need and comfort of a guest who books such an accommodation.

In any event, at least everyone agreed at the time that we needed to address the rest of the hotel, including the 1927 addition, to give it the glamour and feeling of the original 1904 building. This would require an even more dramatic change, a complete gut renovation, to ensure that the 1927 part of the hotel looked like it was part of the original St. Regis.

Fortunately, we had hired an immensely talented team led by the architect Julie Monk, the interior designer David Beer, and the interior decorator Jinnie Kim. They brought ingenuity to the exceedingly difficult job, and they fully understood what I was trying to achieve. Even though our cooperation was not always without conflict, I held them in the highest respect, and still do.

In addition to our weekly project meetings, I got into the habit of stopping by the architects' office a few times during the week to have a look at the plans, measure progress, and make sure that I got what I needed. Many times, I would ask for tracing paper to sketch over the first set of designs, so I could initiate changes and make sure we had a design that would satisfy our guests and our operational needs alike. My mind flashed back to the hours spent with General Zaki and a pad of tracing paper at the Heliopolis.

I inspected every plan for the rooms and suites to ensure the new spaces would fulfill the needs of a clientele accustomed to staying in luxury hotels, not just a business or chain hotel. I kept bringing up details that created more work for the architects and designer. But I stubbornly advocated for my changes.

To take into account every aspect of a guest's interaction with the rooms and common areas, it was important to be able to walk the plan and visualize every step through the eyes of the future customer.

I would look at the room designs and ask questions like these: What happens when guests order room service? Where does the waiter place the gueridon table? Are there enough chairs for both guests to sit comfortably? Or does one person have to sit on the bed and another on the luggage bank? Unacceptable.

How about if a couple arrives with four or five suitcases? Where do they put all their stuff? And are there two opposite full-length mirrors so a female guest can view her outfit from top to bottom and front to back?

When you open a desk drawer, are the writing paper, envelopes, pencils, and paper clips arranged in such a way as to make it easy to use them?

And when housekeeping performs the evening turndown service, where do they store the beautiful bedspread and the decorative cushions so they stay out of the way of the customer and service?

Do the surfaces in the room provide enough space for guests to spread their things? Are the surfaces too small or already cluttered with needless information from the hotel? I always hated to see the available spaces taken over by the hotel's promotional materials, leaving guests hardly any place to store their belongings. We would not have that kind of clutter at the St. Regis.

In my visits to hotels around the world, I often noticed how the bathroom spaces flowed and whether they created a comfortable environment for a guest. Looking at the sketches for the St. Regis renovation, I would spot a problem and say, "This bathroom doesn't work."

"What do you mean it doesn't work?" the architects would ask.

"Because there is no space for a couple to get ready at the same time. We need two vanities, so they can get out of each other's way."

I insisted that we have a shower as well as a tub in every bathroom. I wanted deep, European-style bathtubs, the kind you can lay in and have the water come all the way up to your chin. The basic American tub isn't deep enough. You can barely fit into it, let alone soak in it up to your head.

In every shower, we installed a bench so guests could sit if they wanted to. We put a rain shower at the top and hand showers on the side so guests could bathe in the style they preferred.

The type of mirror in the bathroom mattered too. Imagine you're standing in front of the mirror fixing your makeup, and your husband is taking a shower. The mirror gets all fogged up. It's annoying. We made sure the bathroom mirrors were heated from the back to avoid fog.

In business hotels, you see hair dryers hanging on the wall. We would not have that at the St. Regis. Our dryers would go into a drawer. And I wanted to make sure that our bathrooms didn't appear too sterile and cold in their design. They should look like extensions of the guest room.

Having stayed overnight at hundreds of hotels around the world, I knew how annoying it could be for guests to have to find and switch off every light before falling asleep, then go back to bed and realize they forgot one. When every light has a different type of switch, it's even worse. Why not minimize the number of switches in the room and make sure every lamp has the same kind of switch? Why do hotels like to subject their tired guests to these lighting games?

It was this relentless drive to perfection, attention to the smallest details, and barrage of thousands of questions that drove our architects and designers crazy, to the extent that once when I was passing by, I heard Julie Monk shouting, "Peter Tischmann is coming. Hide the tracing paper!"

Loud air conditioners are another problem I've noticed at hotels, even at luxury properties. In my opinion, one should not be able to hear the hum of the AC or even feel the air but simply enjoy the comfort of a perfect temperature in the room. But this is not a simple problem to solve since AC noise depends on the size and placement of the ducts. The sound comes from the air flowing through the ducts, and the smaller the duct, the more the air has to push through it. Vertical ducts tend to be quieter too. To ensure quiet air-conditioning throughout the hotel, we needed to specify how the duct work is done during the early phase of the renovation, or it would be too late. The architects worked closely with Vasos Michael to make this happen.

Near the end, when all the planning was done, it was time to build a sample room, reproducing even the smallest details as faithfully as possible, so as to translate the plans from paper into a physical, visual product.

When the sample room was ready, it was time for company executives to visit. And that's when a new round of questions and comments began, this time from the corporate office. Perhaps predictably, some didn't like the stripes on the curtain, while others felt the upholstery of the chairs was too bright, and so on. But nobody bothered to try to see the room through the eyes of a guest.

"What do you think, Peter?" Rand asked me.

"I think the room looks very nice and displays the elegance we were looking for," I replied, "but give me three days, because I want to live in the room to find out if it functions as nicely as it looks, and if the room responds to the needs of our guests."

John and Rand nodded their heads in agreement, while the architects and designers were probably afraid that more changes would come their way.

The process was challenging for everyone, but we committed ourselves to addressing the tiniest details and more with one goal in mind: When guests enter a room or a suite, they have to feel as if they are entering a comfortable, luxuriously appointed private home—not just a hotel. Not even the best hotel. The St. Regis must feel like home to our guests, just as John Jacob Astor had intended when he first opened the hotel in 1904.

Furthermore, I knew a second disaster like the one that had happened at the Carlton in D.C. was out of the question for the St. Regis. This was not only for John and Rand's sake but for the sake of not jeopardizing my future with ITT Sheraton.

A New Concept, a New Culture

Perfecting every room and suite at the St. Regis was only half the battle. The common spaces had to feel seamless to guests as they arrived and moved through the hotel. Even the areas that guests never saw had to contribute to the magic, to the sense that everything was flowing smoothly and easily behind the scenes. The smoother the experience, the less guests would even notice how seamless it actually was. This was the ultimate goal.

To give our guests that magical experience, every seemingly tiny part of the whole needed to do its part. That meant we had to ask ourselves questions like this: If we have ten people checking in at the hotel with two pieces of luggage each, what do we do with those twenty pieces of luggage while the guests are going through check-in? At no time did I want to see any luggage sitting in the lobby, creating clutter. So we invented a system in which the luggage would get immediately transported from the street to the lower basement, and from there, it would go up to the individual floors and guest rooms.

As for room service, what could we do to create the most elegant, stress-free experience for our guests? I requested a butler pantry measuring at least twenty-five square meters. Why? Because I wanted the room service rolled over to the guest rooms on mobile gueridon tables, not carried on trays. When guests finished eating, I didn't want to see the used gueridon tables with dirty dishes and service items piled up in the corridor. Guests could push their mobile table out into the hallway if they preferred, rather than calling and waiting to have it removed, but staff would need to roll the table into the butler pantry as quickly as possible to get it out of sight and out of the way. During the breakfast rush hour, we would need a big butler pantry to accommodate all those tables.

The St. Regis's famous banquets would need to project impeccable style and grace, even more than before. The banqueting department had done a spectacular business in recent years under Joe Prezioso's direction, and I saw an even brighter future ahead. Hotel restaurants are typically money-losers, and ours were no exception, but the profits from our banquets carried the entire food and beverage program. Joe was at the Plaza Hotel now, having been recruited by Ivana Trump, but I hoped he would take me up on my offer to return after the renovation. By then, the banquet hall and the event space on the rooftop would look the way I hoped they would, elevating our private parties to the best in New York City. But we had work to do first.

I consulted with Joe on the plans for our renovated rooftop and second floor banquet space, and together, we sketched out a new arrangement for both. The architects' sketches for the rooftop had placed the bathrooms and the coat check in an area that broke up the flow of the entire space, so Joe and I made the necessary adjustments on tracing paper. We needed to get these spaces right. Too much revenue was dependent on the decisions we made. I only wished we could hold even bigger groups at our private events, but we were limited by the space we had. Of course, I knew that however many guests our renovated banquet spaces could legally hold, Joe would find a way to squeeze in another dozen or two. He had a special genius for fitting in more people than officially allowed, but somehow the number of guests always felt just right.

Even when I did not agree with the initial solutions the architects offered for various parts of the hotel, we worked together to come up with an acceptable compromise. Sometimes I would bring out my tracing paper, and other times, we would all sit together to establish the important criteria for the new space, so they could create a suitable answer.

Long after the work was done, Julie told me that she had almost gotten fired for agreeing to give me tracing paper. I think they all grew to resent and even hate me at times as the project went on.

I think Jinnie Kim, the designer, hated me too, at least in the beginning. But eventually, we all agreed that the hotel looked fantastic. Jinnie wrote to me many years later: "You drove us crazy, but we were able to achieve a perfect product in the end."

I regret that I drove everyone crazy, but at least we ended up with a result that made us all proud.

NEWSPAPER

$1.00

CRAIN'S NEW YORK BUSINESS

JULY 4, 1988

VOL. IV, NO. 27

At Deadline

Judge freezes assets of Wedtech execs

A U.S. Bankruptcy Court judge signed orders late last week freezing the assets of four former Wedtech Corp. executives and entering judgments against them totaling $5.1 million. Since they pleaded guilty to bribery and fraud charges early last year, the four have spent money on luxury cars, gambling junkets to Atlantic City and Las Vegas, vacations in Europe and the Caribbean, jewelry and mink coats, according to lawyers for the Wedtech estate.

The four—Fred Neuberger, Anthony Guariglia, Mario Moreno and Lawrence Shorten—were key government witnesses at the racketeering trial of Rep. Mario Biaggi, Wedtech founder John Mariotta, and

(Continued on page 22)

Catch-22: Why Alcott must find new money

By PHYLLIS FURMAN
CRAIN'S NEW YORK BUSINESS

Four years ago, two Federated Department Store executives offered their company what was then a unique concept: a specialty retail chain targeted to career women. When their conservative employer turned them down, the pair found financing elsewhere and created Alcott & Andrews—a specialty chain that defined a whole new niche in retailing.

Now their original backers want out, and once again the pair, Alcott & Andrews Inc. president Michael Jeffries and executive vice president Coleen Brady, are seeking an investor. Only this time the $52 million chain won't be an easy sell.

Hurt by high operating costs, slow sales in some stores and low gross margins, Alcott & Andrews has lost money in three of the past four years. As other, better-financed retailers, including most major department stores, have crowded into its market, Alcott & Andrews has been squeezed in a Catch-22: The retailer needs to keep expanding to reach a critical mass before it can make a profit. But it's running out of money and needs fresh capital.

"The question now is can they afford to operate until they get enough stores?" says Carol Farmer, president of Carol Farmer Associates, a Manhattan-based retail marketing consulting firm.

When Alcott & Andrews debuted, it attracted enormous attention as a startling concept that was quickly and widely imitated.

Despite its current problems, the retailer hopes to lure a buyer that still has faith in that concept and is attracted by the chain's solid reputation with career women 25 to 50 years old who have a minimum household income of $50,000. Already such names as The Limited Inc. and Sears Roebuck & Co. have been mentioned as possible buyers.

"The niche exists and Alcott & Andrews has the best position. The consumer is focusing on work clothes and that should be terrific for the chain," says Ms. Farmer.

But prospective buyers must find a way of valuing a company that isn't likely to

(Continued on Page 22)

INSIDE

Peter Tischmann, general manager of the St. Regis, in the hotel's King Cole Room

The mysterious closing of the St. Regis

Page 11

Spring's capricious for area's stocks

By TIMOTHY MIDDLETON
CRAIN'S NEW YORK BUSINESS

Wall Street has some advice for you if you own a stock that's a mutt: Go away.

"I just can't talk about it," says Barry Brant, the Drexel Burnham Lambert Inc. analyst on Crazy Eddie's case. "That's the beginning and end of the conversation."

"I'm not going to talk to you," says Goldman, Sachs & Co. analyst Rick Shurland, on the subject of On-Line Software Inc., another big second-quarter loser. "I'm not going to do it."

And who could blame them? Who could foresee those companies wouldn't grow at compounded annual rates of 40% forever? Who could imagine their managements weren't infallible?

After all, just because *toute la* Wall Street once touted these outcasts doesn't mean that they are somehow *responsible* for them.

In other words, last quarter it was business as usual at Broad and Wall—takeover stocks went up, bankrupt ones went down (like big loser Zenith Laboratories) and

(Continued on Page 23)

The dogs' days

Second-quarter losers among New York stocks

① Berkey	− 57%
② Zenith Labs	− 50%
③ Crazy Eddie	− 41%
④ On-line Software	− 36%
⑤ Electrosound Group	− 35%
⑥ Emery Air Freight	− 30%
⑦ MacGregor Sporting	− 26%
⑧ University Patents	− 21%
⑨ Integrated Resources	− 21%
⑩ Western Union	− 19%

For a complete listing of how the key 250 firms performed, see Page 19.

War begins in Queens over EDO defense firm

By BILL STERNBERG
CRAIN'S NEW YORK BUSINESS

Queens-based EDO Corp., which has been in the defense business for the last 53 years, now faces the prospect of defending itself in what analysts predict could be a drawn-out takeover battle.

EDO, long considered a target in the consolidating military electronics industry, learned last week that a group of investors has acquired 5.9% of its stock and may seek control of the company.

EDO had no comment on the developments, but analysts and former employees say they expect the company to fight to remain independent. The company's alternatives include restructuring, going private through a leveraged buyout, finding an acceptable merger partner, or simply sitting back and seeing what develops.

"I think it's going to be a long, drawn-out process—a siege rather than a blitzkrieg."

(Continued on Page 20)

THE LOCAL MEDIA IS QUESTIONING IF THE ST. REGIS WILL OPEN IT'S DOORS AGAIN

The Sheraton Corporation

To: Mike Bloomer

From: John W. Russel

Date: August 1, 1989

Subject: The St. Regis

Copy to: Rand Araskog
Bob Collier
Bob Durban
John Kapioltas
P. Tischmann

It was agreed, that the name of the hotel will be "The St. Regis", with a small indication, that this is an ITT Sheraton Hotel.
I believe you have the Type face and special writing of this tag line already. If you have any question, please contact me.

JWR/led

617/367-3600 • SIXTY STATE STREET, BOSTON, MASSACHUSETTS 02109

AFTER A LONG STRUGGLE, THE HOTEL WILL BE NAMED FINALLY "THE ST. REGIS"AGAIN.

CUSTOM DESIGNED TABLEWARE MANUFACTURED SPECIALLY FOR ST. REGIS

Building a New Team 22

The First Hire

In case anyone around me had forgotten that I'd worked as a chef and F&B director for most of my career, they were soon reminded of this fact. I involved myself in every detail regarding our kitchens and dining rooms. I felt I had no choice, although I am sure my colleagues would disagree.

For our Lespinasse restaurant, for example, I felt that the glass entrance door needed a special handle to make a statement, something that would fit in with the style of the room and become a conversation piece. During my frequent travels, I had seen many memorable door handles on restaurant entrances, but none was as fitting as the handles to Paul Bocuse's restaurant in France: a chef statue, molded in bronze with a saucepan in one hand and a chicken in the other.

Having secured Paul Bocuse's approval to copy his door handle, I proposed this idea to the architects and designers as they sketched plans for the restaurant, and they made it happen.

A much bigger challenge, however, was to convince everyone that the Maxfield Parrish mural, the one salvaged from the former King Cole restaurant, would not fit into the atmosphere of the new restaurant. I certainly wanted the mural in the hotel somewhere, but where?

"How about in the new bar?" David Beer suggested. "The bar even could inherit the King Cole name?"

Said and done. This also solved the problem of having to find an attractive name for the bar, one that everybody else would go along with. We already had one, it turned out.

The mural itself, based on the old English nursery rhyme about King Cole the merry old soul, is famous around the world, but the story behind the painting was known mainly to staff and regulars at the hotel. Apparently, John Jacob Astor, who commissioned the mural, wanted his own face to represent King Cole in the painting. Maxfield Parrish resisted, but since Astor was paying for the mural, the artist finally concurred. As a subtle revenge, Parrish's artist friends told him to paint the king passing gas. In the mural, the guards around the king are holding their noses and turning away from the king's smelly cloud.

A painting depicting a royal fart would not fit quite as perfectly into the new fine dining restaurant we had in mind, but it would have an ideal home in the bar, as a colorful decoration and a conversation piece.

Luckily, Jinnie Kim's partner Sam agreed with this idea, and it was eventually approved by the architects and designers.

Many years after the mural was originally painted, as a professional photographer took pictures of the newly renovated St. Regis, he also took a picture of the King Cole mural, and knowing the original story, he made a photo montage incorporating my face as King Cole into the picture just for fun. Obviously, the picture was never used anywhere and is still among my collection of souvenirs from the hotel's opening.

I was happy that we were finding a way to retain the personality of the old King Cole restaurant in our new bar because the old King Cole restaurant was a place filled with memories, for hotel guests, New Yorkers, and for myself too. It was the place where in 1986, not long after I began working at the St. Regis, I met the former Sheraton president Bud James for a lunch that I still think about.

Bud had stepped down from his president role at Sheraton after corporate politics caught up with him, but he and I had stayed in touch, having developed a warm working relationship since the days when he paid visits to our offices in Brussels and Denham. I always appreciated Bud's support for what we had tried to achieve in the food and beverage department. When he called me that day in 1986 to tell me he was in New York City, I invited him to lunch—but to my surprise, he immediately asked me if I was sure that being seen with him would not cause a problem for my own job. Obviously, Bud knew his former company all too well, but he did not realize that I didn't care in the least about how our lunch would be perceived by the corporate office, if they even found out about it.

I cherished the opportunity to sit down with Bud and catch up about the old times in Sheraton, although we avoided talking about the dirty corporate politics. We merely enjoyed each other's company and had a wonderful lunch. I intended for the new restaurant to create an environment for old friends or family members or business associates to feel at home, relaxing over a memorable meal.

Years later, Sam reminded me of a certain meeting with the architecture team, at which one of the firm's partners, David Beer, proposed a layout for the new fine dining restaurant. Apparently, I did not like the plan at all, just as I had disapproved of many other areas in the new design of the hotel. Sam remembers that I spoke up in frustration and said, "Toujours la même merde!"

Well, what can I say? Creating a one-of-a-kind restaurant at the St. Regis was a goal that was close to my heart. I was not ready to sacrifice my vision in the face of an uninspired idea about what a hotel restaurant should look like.

Eventually, the architects came up with a design that looked more like the sophisticated, world-class restaurant I had in mind. But I continued to intervene to make sure every detail would be exquisite. I had a concept for every piece of equipment in our restaurant. I found an old china pattern used during a previous era at the St. Regis. It had a gold outline around its circumference and a gold laurel outline inside. I wanted this pattern back in use, so I hired Bauscher from Germany to replicate it for banqueting china.

Not only in the restaurant, but in our other F&B departments too, I wanted every detail to exude elegance and grace. I ordered Tiffany china for each department, and I made sure every department had its own special pattern, so there could be no stealing between them. I still had crystal-clear memories of my days as a chief steward at the InterContinental, where china and silverware always seemed to go missing. Staff members would accidentally dump it into the trash, or lose it, then they would take pieces from other departments. Not at the new St. Regis.

It was important to me that our banquets too would set a magnificent new standard, even exceeding what we had done before. So I designed serving equipment that would provide a unique elegance and style that no other hotel offered. I created a custom set of Escoffier server ware, along with special caviar settings and the multi-tiered fruit platters.

John Stavros, the St. Regis's maître d' for banquets, likes to tell a story of how one pre-opening night when he was working late, he found me at 1:30 a.m. standing on a stepstool with a hammer, hanging up a structure I had designed for storing the heavy silver tiered trays we used in our tea service. I had designed the special shelving unit to ensure that the trays never suffered a single dent or scratch. To this day, John still likes to point out that I always managed to have a smile on my face, even as I stood on that stepstool in the middle of the night, and even during the worst days that came my way not long after. It's good to hear that I at least managed to appear cheerful at times when I probably should have stayed in bed.

My preoccupation with every object, every element of the hotel extended to each item that would appear on one of our restaurant or banquet tables. I wanted even our glassware to be the absolute best in town, so I ordered exceptionally thin, delicate glasses from Zwiesel. Yes, the glasses are quite expensive and tend to break easily, but the important thing was that they make wine taste better. For the holloware, I asked a German company to create a custom line for the St. Regis, based on a small collection of antique silver pieces I found at the hotel. I ordered Tiffany flatware for every department. The tablecloths and linens for the restaurant, room service and banquets all came from the French company Porthault, the best of the best, 100 percent Egyptian cotton all the way.

The corporate naysayers in technical services spoke up, again and again: Why does our flatware have to come from Tiffany? Why do we need Zwiesel glasses? Why Porthault linens?

I responded the same way every time: Because the St. Regis is not just any hotel. The St. Regis has style, class, and elegance. That's why.

Maybe they were jealous that despite the exquisite, custom-made operational equipment I insisted on, I never exceeded the budget I was responsible for.

It was the same story with the bedroom and bathroom linens. I started to sound like a broken record. I wanted quality, plush terry cloth bathrobes from the US because, in my opinion, that is where the very best terry cotton in the world comes from. For the beds, I ordered linens with elegant designs from the luxury Italian brand Frette. My insistence on Frette linens too did not win me any friends in the technical services office, but so be it.

Still, I had far bigger headaches to contend with than bathrobes and bedsheets. Since the St. Regis was in a landmark building, we could not do anything to change the facade or the windows. The windows were all made of single-glazed glass in a copper frame, but many of them were deformed and wouldn't close anymore. This was the reason we had so much cold air coming in and why we had ice in the toilets and so on. To change the windows and get approval from the landmarks commission took months. In the end, we won their approval because we recreated the same type of window—this time with a state-of-the-art frame and double-glazed glass—that still looked like the old, original window frames.

Every month during the entire renovation process, I met with Rand Araskog , John Kapioltas, and a representative from the accounting department, to keep them all informed of any problems we faced or any updates on the opening date. I also made presentations in front of Pete Thomas, who was the second-in-command at ITT at the time. They all approved of my presentations, since those three people were the rare executives in the corporate office who had any concept of luxury. I always thought it was wise to keep them in the loop, even about details like chinaware. Rand generally did not object or try to make changes. He only became heavily involved in the last three months of the process, by which point he could walk into a restaurant space or a room and see what it was actually going to look like.

This is when all the slow, dusty work of the previous two years started to get more exciting. The architects created a mockup room so we could test the guest experience. I stayed in that room for a couple of days, then I assigned others on the team to do the same and to take detailed notes on what was working and what was not. At that point, it wasn't important if a wall or a surface was pink or red or green. We would leave that to the interior designers. We were just looking into the functionality and practicality of the space: Does this room answer the guest's needs?

So it was extremely important to pay attention to every single aspect of the room and to every tiny detail of the layout and the equipment and the flow and make sure everything worked perfectly. Not just perfectly, but in a way that reflected the absolute highest standards of luxury and refinement.

This was the moment to get the St. Regis renovation right. My chance to get it right. It was a moment of intense pressure, but a kind of pressure that I relished.

The renovation was only one piece of the puzzle. To do my job correctly once the hotel reopened, I needed to have the right people around me. I needed to create a culture where only the best of the best would do. It was now time to start building my team from scratch. It was time to start creating the new St. Regis experience, an experience that would be unrivaled by any other hotel in the world.

Vision and Mission Statements

One morning, as I heard a knock at my door and invited the person to come in, I looked up from my desk to see a giant hat zooming into my office, followed by a blur of long hair.

The woman introduced herself as Maria Peralta, the secretary candidate from the Park Avenue Agency.

Maria made a positive impression from the very beginning. She sounded smart and efficient, and although this would be her first job in hotels, I considered that an asset. I preferred to train my staff on how to work in a five-star hotel, instead of hiring people who had worked for lesser hotels and would then need to unlearn everything in order to do their job properly.

My hunch about Maria turned out to be correct. She became my first hire after Vasos Michael, the chief engineer I had brought onboard before the shutdown. Now we were a team of three. Maria immediately started proving she could take the initiative, and she seemed to never miss a detail. The door between our offices was always kept open, so if I needed something while I was on a phone call, she would overhear it and bring me any documents I required without my having to ask.

Maria had a keen ability to track down any document or piece of information, but I remain stumped about how she did it. I say this because her desk looked like an absolute disaster at all times. As for myself, I can only function in a tidy space, and I did not understand how Maria could do her job amid such apparent chaos. I tried to clean up her desk at one point, forming neat stacks of paperwork—mainly for my own comfort—but I could tell this annoyed her. Still, it was not until the second time I attempted to straighten up her office that she became angry. This was on a day when I walked by her desk and saw what looked like the remains of a tornado. I made neat piles once again and tried to tidy the drawers and shelves too, but this time she stormed out. "If you don't like how I do my job, maybe you should hire someone else," she said. I knew she meant it.

She did have a point. I had overstepped, and I had to accept that not everyone works in the same way as I do. Once after that incident, I was meeting with restaurateur Joseph Baum in his office, and I saw a sign that said, "Those proud of keeping an orderly desk never know the thrill of finding something they had irretrievably lost." I had to admit I'd been missing out on that thrill all my life.

Mess or no mess, Maria's job performance was stellar, and she often stayed late to finish her work even though she was paid a set 9–5 salary. Maria also displayed a quality I hoped to see in every employee I hired, namely the willingness to roll up her sleeves and pitch in anywhere.

Later, after we reopened the St. Regis and found ourselves occasionally short on butlers on a weekend, Maria would put on a tuxedo and learn on the job. She took the opportunity to soak up whatever training she could. This turned into a benefit for me too, since she had her eyes and ears all over the hotel, and she befriended staff members who kept her informed about the goings-on in various departments.

Maria's friendships with staff helped me stay in the loop, although she kept her confidence and didn't share any personal information about anyone. But even idle gossip gave me helpful hints. At least, until a catastrophic situation came up not long afterward, shocking many of us on the staff.

But for the time being, everything moved along smoothly, as our fairy-tale hotel prepared to leap off the pages and spring to life.

The Search for Exclusive Amenities

"We, the associates of the St. Regis, are dedicated to making the St. Regis a symbol of luxury and distinction, recognized worldwide for its high standards of excellence in guest service."

I sat at my desk one day, drafting this mission statement for our new hotel.

"Our aim is to provide unobtrusive personalized service in an atmosphere where each of us takes pride and ownership in giving attention to even the smallest details."

The statement continued for a few more lines, emphasizing the entire staff's tireless commitment to the needs and wishes of every guest at our hotel.

I knew this could easily turn into another piece of corporate blah-blah that new hires would find in their orientation folder and toss in the garbage. But I would not allow that to happen, not at the St. Regis. Once we finished hiring our staff, I would require every rank-and-file employee to carry around the mission statement at all times. Mine would remain in my shirt pocket too, to show to employees as they walked by so they would do the same. This way, none of us would forget what we were doing here, every single day.

Reestablishing the St. Regis as the grande dame of New York City was not going to be easy, to say the least. In the increasingly competitive world of luxury hotels, we needed to do whatever it took to succeed. This meant not only a beautiful, newly renovated building with magnificent spaces. It meant a new approach to service and a new philosophy of how to run a hotel.

My vision of what the new St. Regis would look and feel like was already starting to come to life, as a result of all the hard work of our talented architects and design team. Not to mention all the patience it took to deal with someone like me.

Now it was time to create a culture of world-class service and to build the most luxurious guest experience imaginable. We needed to be the best of the best in absolutely everything if we hoped to create and keep a competitive edge in this most cutthroat of cities. Even then, I knew it would still be a fight.

We certainly had aesthetics on our side. Walking into the lobby, guests would now be greeted by a spectacular, soaring reception area, reminiscent of the old St. Regis—with its hand-painted ceiling mural, marble floors, gilded crown moldings and stunning Waterford crystal chandeliers—but looking sparklingly fresh, and giving way to an elegant tea lounge appointed with Limoges china and Tiffany flatware. Entering the rooms, guests would experience much more spacious surroundings than ever before, some nearly three times the size of the previous rooms, and all with twelve-foot ceilings. In every room, individualized design elements radiated elegance and grace once again, from the Louis XV-style furniture to the marble bathrooms and handwoven carpets. We'd found subtle ways of introducing state-of-the-art technology, making sure to enhance instead of intruding on the guest experience. In each room, for instance, a button on the phone could open and close the draperies or dim and switch off the lights.

One of the challenges of my job that I enjoyed the most was thinking of ways to anticipate guests' wishes and delight them at every turn. As soon as the hotel reopened, we planned to introduce amenities like a daily-changing pastry in guests' rooms every afternoon, left as a sweet invitation to recharge after a business meeting or a shopping trip along Fifth Avenue. Every morning, rooms would receive a delivery of the day's newspapers, in the language of that particular guest, carefully ironed in order not to leave traces of ink on the hands of the guest.

Each time a new guest registered at our hotel, or a guest returned for the first time, I would leave a handwritten letter in his native language welcoming him to our hotel. No, I would not write fifty or sixty letters per day. I would have a system: I would copy the letter in advance on to our elegant stationery, and on the day the guest arrived, I would fill in the greeting and the date with the same fountain pen I had used for the letter, so no one could tell if it was handwritten or printed in advance.

Details like these are what makes the difference between one hotel and another. It's the personal involvement of the general manager, and the attention to the special details. At the St. Regis, I would insist that we give customers more than they expect every single day and that we treat them in a personalized manner that no other hotel would think of doing or even know how to do.

This was not just about cake and newspapers, of course. It was about survival. The hotel industry is war, and we needed our best, most elegant, most graceful ammunition.

Our Secret Weapon: the Butlers

It would be silly for a hotel that treats its guests to a piece of cake in the afternoon to then chase them away with horrible soap. I resolved never to allow Sheraton's embarrassingly bad amenities into our guest rooms at the St. Regis after the renovation. Not under my watch.

Before we closed the St. Regis, guests staying there or in any other Sheraton would receive the same kind of soap. You would wash your hands with it and then have to put on cologne to get rid of the awful smell. Just as I had thrown out the Sheraton staff uniforms, the Sheraton restaurant menus, and all signs of the company's brand image, I intended to start from scratch with the amenities.

By this point, I had developed a friendly relationship with our tenant Bijan, helped in part by the less frequent plumbing disasters in his shop. It occurred to me that I should ask him to supply the new St. Regis with a line of amenities under his own brand. Bijan did everything with style and perfection, and he would surely do the same with soap. I wanted Bijan's name, his flair, his magic touch on our amenities when we reopened.

The minute I asked him, he gave me an immediate answer. No.

"It's not my line of business," Bijan said to me, shaking his head. "I don't even have the time to think about it."

End of discussion.

Even though I held out a slight hope that he would change his mind, as we got closer to the opening I finally gave up and selected Bulgari for our amenities. Many of the finest hotels used Bulgari, and although I liked them, they were not exactly unique. But I was ready to sign the purchasing order, when Bijan walked into my office, a big white leather box under his arm.

"Mr. Tischmann," he said, "here is your amenity line for the St. Regis." He then proceeded to open the white box and begin to place an entire assortment of amenities on my desk. As usual, Bijan did everything with originality and class. Anyone else would have carried the samples in a shoebox. Not Bijan. And the amenity samples? I had never seen anything like these in any hotel anywhere.

Arranged on my desk like pieces of jewelry were two exquisite lines, one for men and one for women: attractively shaped and oversized soap bars, bottles of shampoo and bath gel scented with the finest perfumes, and body lotion with an unusually luxurious texture. As a special touch, his lotion for women even contained a touch of gold dust, which gave a little sparkle to the skin once applied.

No question about it, Bijan won the contract. His line of amenities struck me as the finest ever offered at a hotel. They would help make a stay at the St. Regis very special indeed. There was only one issue: Bijan's amenities would cost us $18 per set. Remembering that the $15 menus I had proposed for our new restaurant led to endless arguments with corporate, I knew I would have some tough convincing ahead of me. Moving an elephant would be easier to do than getting this through the corporate office. But I promised myself I would not give up.

The Challenge of Finding the Absolute Best

"Excellence can be attained if you care more than others think is wise, risk more than others think is safe dream more than others think is practical, and expect more than others think is possible."

I don't know who made this statement first. Perhaps it was the American football player Vince Lombardi, although the quote has been attributed to others too. In any event, I came across it once while passing the time between flights at a newsstand at LaGuardia Airport. Those words have stayed with me ever since, and I don't think any other philosophy more accurately defines the decisions I made for the new St. Regis.

Dreaming more than others think is practical. I did this every single day, as our staff planned the renovation and relaunch of the St. Regis. One of the dreams that excited me most was to introduce a private butler service at the hotel. Taking a page from the exceptional service I had witnessed in my visits to the top hotels in Asia, I decided that every floor at the St. Regis should receive its own butler staff, assigned to look after the guests, and to offer personalized, around-the-clock assistance.

Picture an entire roomful of corporate executives raising their eyebrows at once. This is, essentially, the reaction I received from the Sheraton office when I introduced the idea. But however expensive and impractical Sheraton might have thought it would be to hire and pay three dozen butlers, I knew the concept would be a major difference-maker for the St. Regis, something no other New York City hotel offered.

To offer our guests the best service they had ever experienced, we planned to place on each floor a team of three butlers, who would play the role of mini hoteliers.

After a guest arrived in the lobby, the receptionist would welcome him and immediately inform the butler on duty on this floor, before escorting the guest to the elevator. This would give the butler sufficient time to greet the guest as soon as he stepped out from the elevator. From this moment on, the receptionist's job would be done, and the guest would be in the capable hands of the butler, who would introduce him to his room and complete the check-in process. The butler would then invite the guest to ask for any assistance he might need throughout his stay.

Unlike in a traditional hotel, the mini hotelier at the new St. Regis would be responsible for the entire floor, including the housekeeping staff and room service waiters from the moment they entered the floor. This way, everything that happened on each floor fell under the immediate supervision of the butler. The butler would be ultimately responsible for every aspect of a guest's experience on that floor, even down to the smallest details.

A butler I hired shortly after the opening, Arndt Oesterle, told me years later that he had once spent time cleaning the pantry on this floor and was feeling proud of his attention to detail until I walked in. Apparently checking the pantry, Arndt told me, I had noticed a few spots of water drops in the sink. When I asked him to wipe them off, Arndt told me, he felt sad that he had not done a perfect job. But despite my perhaps excessive attention to details like this, I feel proud to have helped turn Arndt into a consummate professional, who now runs a very successful high-end concierge service for the global elite.

The butlers would also oversee the steamer trunk service, another innovation we introduced for the new St. Regis. On request, repeat customers could leave any of their laundry or accessories (anything from clothes to shoes, toothbrushes, and grooming supplies) behind in the room after they checked out. Our staff would then clean their clothes and fold or hang them in the steamer trunk to get them ready for the guest to arrive next time with just a briefcase and find all his belongings stored in the steamer trunk, carefully placed in the room's wardrobe.

We would offer extra toiletries and necessities free of charge. You forgot your toothpaste. A butler would arrive with a silver tray arranged with a wide variety of toothpastes, and you could pick your choice, on the house.

Needless to say, the butlers could also help with tickets, reservations, mail, and other errands. Guests would only need to go to one person with any request. Simplicity: the ultimate luxury.

No question about it, the St. Regis needed to offer the best guest rooms in New York City, and the absolute best guest experience, in order to charge the highest room rate in the city: exceeding $400 a night. This was ITT's ambition for the hotel, and every detail from the scent of the Bijan shampoos to the cut of the butlers' tuxedos would play a role in earning that rate.

But guest rooms are only one front in the luxury hotel wars. To set the St. Regis apart, we needed to offer the most unforgettable restaurant experience too, and the classiest social spaces, and the most seamless room service, and the most exquisite banquets.

I did not just want a restaurant that our hotel guests would rave about. I wanted one that the *New York Times* would rave about, and to which it would grant its rare four-star rating, or at least three stars. Our restaurant would attract a sophisticated local and international clientele, well beyond merely the hotel guests.

During my dinners and lunches out with Denyse or business associates, I had started taking mental notes on chefs whom I wanted to approach for our signature restaurant. But before I did this, I told Rand Araskog about my plan—that I intended to hire not just one but two excellent chefs. I needed one chef to run most of the hotel's food service and banqueting, and one whose main role would be to establish our fine dining concept as the top restaurant in the city. To my relief, Rand approved that idea, with no arguments from anyone in corporate.

Room service is its own challenge, a tricky game that most hotels lose in one way or another—mainly by bleeding money. But no self-respecting hotel in New York City can afford not to offer room service. If we couldn't make our room service profitable, at least we shouldn't lose too much money on it. I didn't want other departments to have to subsidize the room service.

If we weren't going to make any money on room service, we should find a way to put it to some good use. Why not turn it into a showpiece for the extraordinary quality of customer care at the St. Regis? Offering an outstanding menu was only part of the story. I wanted our service to be the best in town. Again, I turned to some of the most noteworthy practices I picked up from the top hotels in Asia.

As an example of a small detail, but one which would be important enough to leave a long-lasting impression on guests who ordered in-room dining, I instructed servers to never turn their back on a customer as they walked out the door of a guest room. Instead, they should walk out backward, facing the guest the entire way. For me the ultimate in gracious hospitality. Why should a guest have to watch a server leave with his back turned to him all the way to the door? Facing guests is not only polite, but it also gives them a chance to ask any questions about their room service order while the server is still in the room.

Our banquets, too, needed to serve as a gilded business card for the hotel. Before we closed the hotel, our banqueting service was one of the best in town, even though the rest of the hotel had long since stopped performing at a high level. I was confident that our new event spaces were going to look spectacular, and even if they wouldn't be the biggest banquet rooms in New York City, we would offer the finest banquet service. The St. Regis rooftop, which hosted the most exclusive, A-list society galas in town in decades past, would become the most coveted event space in town again after the renovations.

The era of white-glove service would return to the St. Regis. In every department, from the restaurants to room service to the banquets, servers would wear white gloves at all times. The doormen would too. To ensure a polished presentation, gloves would need to get changed every hour or so, if not more often, and staff members would carry plenty of spare pairs around every day.

But not everyone would deserve to wear the signature St. Regis gloves. Among the entire world of hotel professionals, and among the tens of thousands of resumés we received from the moment we began posting job openings, we would select only a few to join our staff. I knew exactly what kind of person I was looking for and exactly what kind I would reject on the spot.

The Best Chef Is Just Good Enough

Companies excel at throwing around lofty slogans without having any idea what they mean. Building a culture of excellence. That sounds like an empty slogan, and most of the time it is. I wanted to breathe life into that concept, to make our staff understand what excellence actually means and what it looks like and how to embody it in their work every single day.

Every member of our team would need to show an absolute dedication to each and every customer. They would strive for nothing more or less than creating the most luxurious hotel in the world, with the most impeccable service, and they would deliver on every detail necessary to make that happen.

So where would we find staff members ready to meet those almost impossibly high standards?

"Peter, you will never find these employees in New York City." I kept hearing this from colleagues in the corporate office and friends in the hospitality industry.

To which I replied, "I only need about three hundred people. And I see no reason why I cannot find three hundred talented staff members in New York."

As it turned out, I found many of our top employees outside the confines of the city. To search from coast to coast, I tapped a woman named Sheila Skolnick to conduct secret headhunting missions on my behalf. Sheila had a business selling amenities for hotels, and at a time when Sheraton was spending about four dollars per guest on amenities, she had a share of this expenditure.

But despite her involvement in Sheraton's low-cost amenities business, Sheila also had an eye for quality and style and traveled constantly to hotels around the US as part of her work.

One day I said, "Sheila, do me a favor. When you travel, if you see any items in a hotel that look different or interesting, buy them or steal them so you can show me. And if you notice an outstanding personality that I should consider hiring for the St. Regis, let me know."

This arrangement worked out wonderfully for a while. Sheila collected bits and pieces and brought them to my attention. Some I thought were interesting, others I rejected, but I did gather ideas through her observations. Her most important contribution, however, is that she found some fantastic people whom I eventually hired.

Tony Fortuna was one of these people. Sheila identified him at one of the top hotels in Beverly Hills, and I hired him to manage the fine dining restaurant we would open in our renovated hotel. Tony knew the New York City restaurant world because he had worked at the Swiss hotel where Jean Georges Vongerichten had been the chef, and to this day, Tony remains a friend and a valuable resource for me.

Through Sheila, I also found a young Lebanese man from L'Ermitage in Beverly Hills, Simon Malouf who spoke several languages and made an ideal choice to run our front office. We needed as many languages on our staff as possible, and I knew I would be assembling a multilingual team once the hiring for the entire hotel got underway.

Later, as we hired more staff, I sent some of them out on competition-shopping missions, just as I had done with Sheila. Tony Fortuna and his assistant went to the top New York City restaurants at the time, from Daniel to Bouley and dozens of others, to see what they were doing right so we could incorporate some of those elements into our operational concepts. I sent the bartenders to famous bars in order to experience firsthand what our competitors were up to and see what kinds of ideas we should steal.

The front office managers and assistants went on undercover visits to other luxury hotels like the Carlyle, the Mark, the Pierre, and the Plaza Athenee, and spent the night there so they could report back to me about their impressions, good and bad.

Six months before we reopened, I started filling the key department head positions. In Singapore, I found the man I hired as director of sales and marketing. His name was Richard (Rick) Fleming, and he had been working at the very successful Sheraton Tower there. Although it was a Sheraton, it did have the type of luxury customers we were looking for. Rick was the typical sales and marketing type, full of himself, but that's what you get when you look for the best in this field. I had a good feeling about hiring him, at least in the beginning. We also hired a personal assistant for Rick, a young woman named Jude Woodstock.

From the moment Jude entered my office, I was impressed with her self-confidence and the way she presented herself. I guess she was not even twenty years old, but she seemed to have everything needed to survive with Rick. Although she had no sales experience, she instinctively understood the St. Regis customer we had in mind. She carried herself with poise, but also seemed like a sensible, hardworking person who would help balance Rick's personality quirks.

And quirks, the man did have. Once, as we were each standing at an intersection, waiting to cross the road, Rick tripped and nearly fell. He looked up, his face red with embarrassment, and said to me, "Can you imagine if I had fallen down?"

"And?" I asked. "What would you have done?"

"I would have stayed on the ground until dark, so no one could see that it was Rick Fleming who had fallen down." This incident stayed in my mind for quite some time afterward, as a clue that could hint at potential trouble.

Much to my delight, Joe Prezioso agreed to come back and work for the St. Regis as the director of banquet operations. He had spent the past two years working for Ivana Trump at the Plaza while our hotel was closed, and I think he was as relieved to return home to the St. Regis as I was to have him back in charge of banquet service, our most profitable department.

Choosing the right person for the head housekeeper position is crucial for a hotel, and for this job, I hired Christel Schmitt. She was very warmhearted but tough when it came to running her department, someone who wouldn't take no as an answer from her staff and always pursued perfection. Hotel housekeepers have to be tough. As with Rick, she seemed like the correct choice at the time.

For one of the most important positions in the hotel, the director of human resources, I hired a graduate of Harvard University who had done academic studies in human resources. But he didn't turn out to meet expectations, to put it mildly. While I value politeness in my colleagues, this man did not have a strong enough personality to handle the demands of this type of job. With him, everything was always "as you wish, if you want."

As he was new to the hotel industry, we brought in Jennifer Hall as associate director of human resources, a hire who came to us from another Sheraton hotel. She passed all the interviews and knew all the Sheraton policies and procedures, so this seemed like a bonus. But the two of them did not have a productive working dynamic, and I don't believe he had the guts to discuss this with me. Nor did he have the guts for the job in general. I needed to look for a replacement.

This was no time to be without a human resources director, but the man had to go. Now I had to find someone else to run the department, and I needed to do it in a hurry. Through internal recommendations from Sheraton executives, the name Anne Power came to my attention. Jennifer Hall had worked with Anne Power before and gave her an excellent reference, so I decided to hire Anne, which turned out to be a big mistake, one that I regret to this day.

Typically, companies search all over the world for key team members, and even pay headhunters good money, while neglecting to look in-house. I was no exception. I should have known better, as I went through this same issue at the time when we promoted Sigi Steber from executive chef to director of food and beverage in Munich. Sometimes the perfect person is right in front of our eyes, and you're somehow too blind to notice him or her.

Such a person was Kathy Ransom Kiernan, whom I had hired as director of training. She did a magnificent job as we brought in and trained staff members for the hotel. When we fired the first HR director, I should have thought of Kathy to fill his job. If I had, I am confident that I would not have had the problems I eventually faced. Not appointing Kathy turned out to be a big mistake, if not my biggest mistake at the St. Regis, one that would come back to haunt me soon after we reopened the hotel.

Building Commitment and Passion

Executive chefs are notoriously difficult characters. Since I worked in kitchens for a large portion of my career, I've witnessed many colorful personality traits of all shapes and sizes. I knew that finding the right chef for the St. Regis would not be easy. But I had some names in mind from my visits to the best restaurants in New York, and I felt optimistic we would find the perfect person for the job.

I had won approval from the corporate office to hire two executive chefs, as I had requested. This might sound extravagant, but I knew that overseeing our signature fine dining restaurant—the one that I hoped would earn a four-star rating from the *New York Times*—would be a full-time job at the very least. The second chef would handle primarily the banqueting and all other food and beverage programs at the hotel, including the King Cole Bar and Lounge, the Astor Court social area off the lobby, and the room service.

I needed to find someone who was not a typical hotel chef to run our fine-dining flagship. Restaurant chefs think differently from hotel chefs, and I wanted our restaurant to stand out in the city's highly competitive culinary arena.

My attempts to distinguish this restaurant from others in the city had so far expressed themselves in details like door handles and tableware, and they had also informed our search for the restaurant name. After extensive brainstorming sessions, one that even involved a linguistics professor from Princeton University, we decided to call the restaurant Lespinasse, after Madame Jeanne Julie Éléonore de Lespinasse, a prominent French woman who hosted a famous salon in eighteenth-century Paris, entertaining members of society and the political elite.

Now it was time to tackle arguably the most important decision: choosing the chef. To turn Lespinasse into a smashing success, we needed a chef like Jean-Georges Vongerichten, a rising star at the time who was working at the Lafayette restaurant at the Swissotel. As he was my "Wunschkandidat ," my first choice, I called him in for an interview.

After presenting to him our thoughts and vision for the restaurant, he said, "Mr. Tischmann, I want to be very honest with you. I am working to have my own restaurant. I should know in the next three or four weeks. If it doesn't work out, I will join you. If it does, I will not."

Shortly after this conversation, Jean-Georges opened his own restaurant, JoJo, which led to his namesake Jean Georges and a string of other critically acclaimed restaurants in the city and worldwide. I was disappointed that I couldn't get him for Lespinasse, but I was very happy for him that he ended up with such a fantastic career. Until today, we are very good friends and often talk about the time he almost joined the St. Regis.

When Jean-Georges fell through, my attention shifted to a chef named Gray Kunz. He was the executive chef at the Peninsula Hotel across the street and responsible for a restaurant called Adrienne. After visiting the restaurant a few times incognito, I could tell that his style of cooking was what I was looking for. Gray was not just a hotel chef but somebody with an amazing instinct for refined cuisine. Based on the meals I had enjoyed at his restaurant, I knew he was an outstanding chef.

After our initial interview, Gray Kunz and I proceeded to talk for nearly six months. Salary, benefits, bonuses: We went on and on. Gray remained stubborn and hard to convince, though I knew he wanted the job. I wanted to hire him too.

Eventually, I called on Phillp Alfus, a headhunter I had hired to assist me with searches. Philip was specialized in finding exquisite culinary staff, and he finally helped me to close the deal with Gray. Philip also helped me find the talented chef Michel Carrer, to lead all our other food and beverage programs.

But to get Gray to sign our contract took another endless round of negotiations. He wanted a larger restaurant staff than we felt we needed, and he had all kinds of demands about the kitchen itself.

I finally said to Gray, "Tell me why you need twelve people instead of ten. What will the additional people do for you?"

He couldn't answer the question on the spot. Another general manager might have caved in to his requests, if he had the budget to do so, but based on my extensive kitchen experience, I knew his request was unreasonable. I had every intention of giving him all the support he needed when it came to producing an extraordinary menu and helping him procure all the materials and products he would need. But when it came to the kitchen and the space and the decision to hire more people, I showed him what his limits were. Because I had worked as a cook for years, there was not one chef who could tell me anything when it came to kitchens, not even Gray Kunz, especially since I knew that Jean-Georges Vongerichten was running his new restaurant with six chefs only and producing a most extraordinary cuisine.

After all the back and forth, we hired Gray at last. This turned out to be absolutely the right decision. Gray was instrumental in establishing Lespinasse as one of the top restaurants in New York City. I told him that I expected us to make at least 120 covers every day in the restaurant, and he achieved this quite soon after we opened. Not long afterward, we received three stars from the *New York Times* food critic Bryan Miller.

Miller reviewed the restaurant two weeks after the opening, which is unusual, as it does not give enough time for the kitchen to work out the initial kinks. If he had waited a few weeks, I feel sure we would have received four stars for the first time around. But Lespinasse was already making waves, and three stars were enough to command attention from the media and food industry elite of New York City.

The headaches turned out to be well worth it, although the negotiations did not stop after Gray came onboard. He kept making demands about the size of the staff, the size of the kitchen, and virtually everything else. Even after I left, the arguments continued. Several years later, in 1996, he got the kitchen of his dreams, designed by himself. The million-dollar kitchen renovation shut down Lespinasse for a summer, but when it reopened, the media collectively dropped its jaw to the ground.

It also earned Gray Kunz a reputation for making astronomically expensive demands for his kitchens but not producing the revenues to pay for them.

Even though our working relationship ended more swiftly and tragically than I could imagine, Gray and I would remain on good terms through the years, and we still occasionally called each other until he sadly passed away in March of 2020.

THE BUTLERS CONCEPT OUR SECRET WEAPON TO MAKE THE ST. REGIS NUMBER ONE AGAIN.

TO CREATE THE BEST RESTAURANT IN TOWN WITH CREATIVE FOOD NEVER SEEN BEFORE THE BEST CHEF IS JUST GOOD ENOUGH

THE RESTAURANT LESPINASSE MERITS NOTHING BUT THE BEST WHEN IT COMES TO QUALITY OF SERVICE.

FINAL MEETING WITH ONE OF THE ARCHITECT TO GIVE THE PROJECT THE LAST TOUCH AND POLISH PRIOR TO THE OPENING

Preparing for the Opening 23

Advertising to the Senses

"Perfection not only consists in doing extraordinary things, but in doing ordinary things extraordinarily well."

This philosophy is at the heart of everything we wanted to accomplish at the St. Regis. While it's true that doing extraordinary things was the "raison d'etre" of the new St. Regis, doing all the seemingly simple, daily, ordinary tasks with seamless perfection was what truly mattered. That is what would ultimately make our hotel stand out from the rest, day after day, week after week, year after year.

This meant hiring people willing to take pride in even the simplest task, a mission more difficult than it sounds.

Meeting this challenge was of the utmost importance when it comes to hiring butlers in particular. With our butler staff, our maîtres d'etage, we had absolutely no room for error. Butlers would have the most personal and frequent interaction with our guests, sometimes in, shall we say, compromising situations.

Each butler would need to have not just the know-how but also the right instincts for how to pamper guests, how to give them the personal attention that would set our hotel apart, and how to remain discreet at all times. Yes, the butler would have to arrange theater tickets and so forth, but that is only a minuscule part of the job. The most important goal was to make each guest feel special, a mission that our entire staff would share too, from myself as the general manager to each and every staff member who comes in contact with the guest. This included every detail from the moment guests arrived until they left the hotel, and even afterward, as it was important to take the time to make follow-up calls.

When the guest arrives on his floor, the butler must not only greet him and show him to his room, but also take care of any errands or questions the guest has on arrival. The butler must act like the consummate host. This is even more time-consuming than it sounds, and the most dedicated staff members would likely find themselves getting up early in the morning or staying late to get all their work done. But my feeling was, if you don't like what you do, you should get a job somewhere else.

We received almost ten thousand resumes for the 350 openings we needed to fill—an unusually high number of applicants, but not surprising. The soon-to-reopen St. Regis was by this point generating a great deal of interest in the hotel industry, and our talent search became a magnet for aspiring hoteliers and anyone who wanted to learn the luxury hospitality business from the ground up.

Obviously, we saw a lot of rubbish among those applications. Our stringent selection process kept the vast majority out, and the human resources department narrowed the initial stack to about one thousand that we considered to be acceptable candidates.

What did we look for? Signs that the candidate was an eager learner and could adapt to new situations successfully. Contrary as it sounds, I didn't want people with extensive experience at other hotels for the simple reason that you not only hire the experience that the person brings along, but you also hire all the bad habits that he has accumulated in past jobs. We wanted to start fresh at the St. Regis, so we needed to make sure the people working with us would be receptive to the spirit of what we wanted to achieve.

What surprised some of my department heads is that I insisted on meeting with every single candidate that we were considering hiring, from the lowest positions up to the senior ones. I asked the key department heads to screen the applicants first, then to decide on a short list of candidates who would meet with me. Toni Fortuna interviewed his candidates for food and beverage, Joe Prezioso met with the top applicants for banqueting, and so on, then they scheduled interviews for the finalists in my office.

To get into my office, applicants had to survive three interviews—first with human resources, then with the director of training, then with the key department head—and finally with the general manager. This can feel scary. I understood this and tried to make everyone feel comfortable despite the high-pressure situation. Instead of sitting behind my desk, I would get up and sit in the visitor chair, next to the candidate and the department head. You can sit like a big boss behind your desk or you can try to create a human interaction with a potential employee. The second approach made more sense to me. Years later, I still hear from former employees who say they were relieved by my efforts to make the interview less formal, at least on the surface.

As much as I may have sounded casual in those conversations, I paid close attention not only to how the candidates answered my questions, but also to the expressions and gestures they made. Some of my questions were basic interview protocol. Others would force the candidate to think about and articulate challenging ideas and not just to say yes or no. "What do you expect the St. Regis to do for you?" I would ask. "What do you think you can bring to the hotel?" But at least 80 percent of the interview was just about watching how the candidate behaves and trying to assess how his personality might fit into our team and impact our guests.

As for more specific skills and attributes, I made those clear in the hiring strategy and training philosophy manual which we put together with the help of Kathy Ransom-Kiernan. Although the manuals I had developed in our divisional office in Brussels and Denham were of great value, the St. Regis hiring manual went far beyond what we had created in the past.

"The common bond between all St. Regis employees, line staff and managers alike, must be an unbending dedication to the service of our guests," I wrote. "Beyond a desire to serve, the St. Regis employee must be a true citizen of the world. Knowledge and excellent command of English and at least one additional language will be necessary for all front of the house employees," along with "good awareness of geography and social customs," especially of the countries from which many of our guests arrive.

An employee's smile mattered too, but not just any smile would do. It was important to have a "warm and natural smile," as I wrote in the manual, along with "maturity which is unrelated to chronological age."

All these traits would matter to our guests, along with a sophistication that expressed itself with subtlety and grace: "Our high-profile customer will demand a type of employee who can relate interpersonally at more advanced levels."

People who lacked these characteristics were immediately obvious to me. In the beginning, when the department heads would bring me their top candidates for various positions, I would reject eight or nine people out of ten candidates presented.

"How can you present me with someone like this?" I would ask, after the candidate had given a particularly thoughtless answer to a question, or appeared immature, or revealed a shiftiness in his eyes, or generally seemed to lack the right attitude for customer service.

"When you bring people to my office," I explained to the department heads concerned, "I assume it is because you have interviewed them thoroughly and feel confident that these are candidates you want to hire, in which case you should defend these people against my objections, unless you are not sure you made the right choice."

Eventually, the quality of candidates I met with began to improve, and it was simply a matter of choosing the very best of the best. Soon I was rejecting only two or three out of every ten.

The butler interviews were among the most challenging. I wanted to see an exceptionally rare blend of attitude, experience, instincts, and personal presentation. Some of those skills and traits are teachable, but others are not. Many of the butlers we ended up hiring came from European hotel schools in Germany or Switzerland or Holland. Those programs required candidates to do an internship and complete one or two years of professional experience first, then to undergo a rigorous training to polish their hospitality skills. Graduates of those schools spoke at least three languages. I also hired butlers from Latin America, from India, and from other regions around the world, and a handful from the US. The people I selected from the US either had parents who worked in the diplomatic services or had lived internationally during their youth, giving them exposure to different cultural environments. It was crucial for our butlers to be able to relate to guests from around the world.

But more than anything, I looked for signs that the butler applicants had natural reflexes when it came to navigating difficult situations. Yes, we would train butlers extensively in the weeks leading up to the opening.

But we can never predict every scenario that might transpire with a guest, and butlers need to know how to handle themselves. They must be nimble enough to remain discreet if confronted with difficult and compromising situations.

We would certainly host celebrities as well as prominent diplomats and governmental figures at the St. Regis, and there would be no telling what these guests might do on occasion, from consorting with individuals who are not their spouses to throwing wild parties in their rooms, to undressing in front of a butler.

What to do in a situation like this? Well, the butler would know. At least, this is what I hoped for. Because one thing was certain: What happened in the St. Regis had to stay in the St. Regis.

A Workplace Called Home

"I met your grandmother on New Year's Eve 1918. There was a big party at the Mellons'. Or was it the St. Regis?"

"'24 Mouton Rothschild isn't something you forget. We were at Claire's summer place. Or was it the St. Regis?"

Our new ad campaign for the soon-to-reopen hotel was a work of genius. We aimed to woo back the coveted St. Regis guests who had since moved on to other hotels like the Pierre or the Carlyle, as well as to flatter a new clientele by assuming that they, too, moved in the most exclusive circles.

But attracting and flattering potential guests would be only half the battle. We needed to flatter our staff too. The people we hired had joined a very special hotel, and we intended to make them cherish their role at every opportunity. I had several ideas for how to accomplish this. First, we would make sure every piece of collateral, including even the employee handbook, reflected the elegance of the St. Regis. We would not simply hand our staff members the typical photocopied, stapled employee information. We hired a quality design firm to create an elegant little book, with an attractive font and New Yorker–style illustrations that added a touch of humor.

Second, we would find ways to remind staff members of the exclusive, handpicked team they had joined, with unexpected gestures such as welcome gifts and birthday presents mailed to their homes.

Everything would reflect the St. Regis's impeccable style, whether it was intended for guests or for employees. In my opinion, if we offered ultimate luxury in all the visible parts of the hotel, we must do so in the less visible back-of-the-house areas too.

Those tacky brochures that littered hotel lobbies everywhere had no place at the St. Regis. The design firm we hired created absolutely smashing pieces of collateral, using creamy paper, translucent overleaf, and beautifully rendered closeup photos for all our hotel and banquet brochures. One of the brochures, for instance, had a softly lit photo of an afternoon tea service, complete with a sterling silver tiered cake tray, perfect petits fours, and a vase of fresh flowers. "Only the finest . . . Limoges China . . . Tiffany & Co. Silver . . . Waterford Chandeliers," said the caption.

Today, many hotels don't bother with brochures anymore, relying on their websites instead. But as we were preparing to reopen the St. Regis in 1991, before the Internet age, brochures still played an important role in promoting the hotel to potential customers and travel agents.

Even though our brochures looked lovely in my opinion, we still refused to litter guest rooms with all that paper. I hate it when you walk into a hotel room and the first thing you have to do is stash away those piles in a drawer. Instead, we placed a folder in each room, so guests could look inside and find the brochure if they wanted to, as well as the room service menu and a directory of services in five languages.

The St. Regis stationery was kept in the drawer of the desk, together with sharpened pencils, paper clips, and everything else that someone traveling on a business trip might look for. Guests could easily find everything. As beautiful as it looked, we still kept it all hidden.

We took a far less discrete approach in our marketing efforts. Our goals were quite aggressive: to steal customers away from all the competing luxury hotels in New York City. Now that we were about to open the most luxurious, grandest hotel of all, we wanted to ensure that our potential guests from around the world knew about it.

Together with Rick Fleming, we began to take trips to Paris, London, and other European capitals to meet with executives and taste makers who had a wide circle of influence among our desired clientele. We entertained and arranged presentations at luxury companies such as Hermes and Cartier and Chopard in Paris, Trussardi in Milan, and a list of competitive luxury brands in other cities. We typically booked individual meetings with decision makers, but occasionally, we would throw a cocktail party to introduce a group of luxury brand representatives to the St. Regis.

We hosted a reception at the famous Automobile Club of France at the Place de la Concorde and entertained individual decision makers in hotels when necessary. Everyone who was anyone in the French society belonged to the Automobile Club, and its address was the place to be. Listing that location on our invitations motivated our target clientele to come to the party.

I think our attractive new collaterals intrigued people as well. We offered white-glove service at the reception, and we showed slides of the new

St. Regis. At that time, we still relied on slide presentations. I stepped on to the podium and explained the philosophy of the new St. Regis and our unique approach to service, then Rick followed with a marketing hard sell. It was a successful evening.

Meanwhile, in the personal meetings with our contacts at luxury brands, it became immediately obvious that none of them had ever seen a Sheraton sales representative before, for the simple reason that their president or CEO would have never stayed at a Sheraton, not even the St. Regis. There were plenty of other luxury hotels in New York City that had not allowed their standards to erode, as the St. Regis had by the time I arrived there in 1985.

"What do we have to do better to get you out of the Pierre or the Plaza Athenee and into the St. Regis?" We asked the same question in every meeting, and we used the answers we heard—about service preferences, amenities, restaurant environments, room service—as an opportunity to promote the new St. Regis and to detail the specific changes and innovations guests could expect. Most importantly, we used the answers to fine tune our operational concept, in areas where we felt we could still improve, and in training sessions to prepare our staff for the moment of truth when they would be facing the first St. Regis guest.

For instance, one of our contacts said, "I hate being asked at reception, 'Sir, did you have anything from the mini bar?'" This question seemed particularly bothersome when guests were already paying a very high room rate in a luxury hotel. As a result of this conversation, we decided to fill our mini bars with a large choice of juices and soft drinks, free of charge, allowing our guests to drink as much as they wanted, with the exception of wine and other alcoholic beverages that needed to be ordered through room service.

Another person complained about the room service at his favorite hotel. "Why do I have to sign a check for room service? Doesn't the hotel trust me?" So we implemented a policy where guests never have to sign a check in the room. They simply order food, we deliver it, and the charge goes on their room bill. That's that.

We convinced many of those potential customers to book a room in our hotel, but we realized that it would be much harder to keep them, especially when they already had loyalties to other hotels. We were aware that most just wanted to try the St. Regis out of curiosity but had little intention of switching permanently. It was up to us to give them a compelling reason to stay with us in the future.

I was convinced that our level of service would impress them and win them over to the St. Regis. But I intended to take extra measures with those guests, such as welcoming them to their floor in person and escorting them all the way up myself until the butler took over.

We knew that we would have only one chance to win them over to the St. Regis and were determined not to miss this chance.

During my trips with Rick, it became increasingly clear that if we want to win over this coveted clientele for the long term, we needed our own individual sales and marketing representative in Europe. We needed someone who understood the needs of that particular customer, someone who knew what luxury was all about and could communicate effectively with our target clients.

Creating this position turned out to be easy. John Kapioltas understood why we needed to hire a person like this. His only condition was that we find the right candidate, not just a sales representative but someone with polish and class who knew how to move in the right circles.

We found this person in Arlette Hagedorn, a tall, elegantly dressed marketing professional who spoke many languages. Arlette had worked for the Leading Hotels of the World marketing organization and for the

Oetker Collection brand of luxury hotels, which includes my alma mater, the Brenner's in Baden-Baden, Germany, and the Bristol Hotel in Paris, making her a natural choice for the position.

I knew immediately that we would hire Arlette as soon as she arrived at the St. Regis to view the renovation and meet our staff. She fit in perfectly with our team. Arlette could have worked from anywhere in Europe, but when she accepted our offer, we decided to base her at the regional sales office in Frankfurt. This way, she could benefit from the backup support of the local staff and infrastructure there.

What a disastrous decision this turned out to be. We unknowingly unleashed a wave of hostility toward Arlette by having her report directly to Rick, the St. Regis's director of sales and marketing, instead of to Sheraton's own regional director of sales. From her very first day, the staff in the Frankfurt office viewed Arlette with suspicion, and they never relented. Thinking back to the situation now, many years later, I remain awed by the challenges Arlette navigated in order to succeed in that toxic environment.

And succeed she did. The results she generated for our hotel left no question as to who was right and who was wrong. Arlette produced far more customers for the St. Regis in Europe than the entire Sheraton system ever did. Her previous contacts along with her tireless networking and personal charm resulted in greater access to the types of customers we wanted, the ones willing to pay a nightly rate of $400 or even $800 and upward for a room.

Still, no matter how much revenue Arlette generated for our company, the damage had already been done. Despite her impressive results, or perhaps because of them, she never received anything but pushback and interference from the Sheraton office.

I had no choice but to change the situation, for Arlette's sake and the St. Regis's sake. I needed to figure out where to put Arlette so the St. Regis could derive the maximum benefit from her skills. But little did I know that I was running out of time to do so.

Only the Best for Our Associates

At any moment, anyone on our staff could abandon us and go work for a competitor. A defector could reveal all our strategies and operating philosophies, from the big picture to the tiny details, and damage us quite severely. I was aware of this risk, so I knew that we needed to constantly win over our own team. We had no choice if we wanted to triumph over other competing hotels. Marketing our hotel to an elite international clientele was one thing, but marketing the St. Regis to its own staff was an equally important job, one I could not neglect.

I knew that if I could create a positive environment for our hotel staff and keep them happy and engaged, then I would have no problem keeping our customers happy too. The logic worked both ways.

Our staff restaurant, I decided, would not be the typical employee commissary, not one of those drab rooms filled with workers slumping over dull cafeteria food, desperate for a break. It would not have cheap chairs, institutional furniture, fading paint on the walls. Ours was going to look and feel like a real restaurant. We would offer appealing choices on our menu and delicious food created by our top-notch food and beverage staff.

I made a promise to myself that I would have lunch in the staff restaurant almost daily. But instead of congregating at the same table as the managers and department heads, I would sit with the line employees, a different group each day. This would give me the chance to interact with my staff on more casual terms. I would encourage them to tell me about their concerns, their proud moments, their frustrations, or to discuss any questions or matters they wanted to bring up.

We decided to call our staff restaurant Chez Nous, and in the corridor leading to Chez Nous, we hung clocks showing the time in each of our employees' native countries. We had forty-four different nationalities on the St. Regis reopening team, so when we launched, we had forty-four clocks ticking along the wall.

Looking back on my lunch hours at Chez Nous, eating there daily turned out to be one of the best decisions I made as a general manager. Chez Nous became the place where our employees gathered not only to eat but also to socialize and form bonds. From day to day, I would eat with the housekeeping staff or the engineers or the butlers and so on. I appreciated hearing what was on their minds that day, anything they wanted to share. The departments often had their own inside jokes, and I would stay long enough to enjoy the camaraderie, then excuse myself when I felt that perhaps the employees should be left to relax on their breaks without the boss listening in.

Apart from the staff restaurant, we made sure our other employee facilities were worthy of the St. Regis. We gave our staff members spacious, clean, comfortable locker rooms, for instance, so they could change into their uniforms and keep their belongings in a secure, well-maintained space.

The hotel would get nowhere without the dedication of our team, day in and day out. I knew that, and so did every department head at the St. Regis. I considered no detail too small or insignificant if it would make our staff members feel valued and keep them loyal to us.

I would need their loyalty soon, even more than I would have ever predicted.

Finding the Right Barber

"Sir, we don't charge by weight."

I remembered those famous words from my visit to the Rockefeller Center barbershop that had charged me an absurdly high price to cut my little remaining hair.

After that visit a few years ago, I never went there again. Nor did I ever visit our hotel's own barbershop for a cut or a shave or anything else. The St. Regis barbershop had always looked unappealing to me, dirty and rundown and infused with an attitude of carelessness. I thought, if this barber cannot run his shop properly now and keep it clean, why should I expect him to do so after we reopen? I was convinced that the old St. Regis barber was not a candidate for our new hotel.

The last thing I wanted was to get offered a free haircut there or to receive any special treatment as the general manager. I did not want to owe anyone any favors.

What I aimed to do, from the moment when we closed the hotel and began the renovations, was to find a new barber. We would redo the entire space and introduce in its place a barbershop that would not only live up to the St. Regis standards but in every aspect would be the best barbershop in town.

For months, I looked around for the ideal barber for the hotel. When the old barber understood that he would not be returning once we reopened, he did not take this lightly. The man had been working at the hotel for twenty or thirty years, and for some reason, he had a dedicated clientele. His customers began writing letters to Rand Araskog, to ITT Sheraton, to the press, to everyone the barber could think of as he launched an impressive promotional campaign to get himself hired back at the hotel. I wish he had worked half as hard on maintaining a decent barbershop as he did on lobbying all of the top executives as soon as he realized his head was on the chopping block. But there was never any question of him coming back.

Eventually, I did find a barber who impressed me, a man by the name of Sal Fordera who had his shop at the Warwick Hotel, not far from the St. Regis. I liked how Sal kept his barbershop perfectly clean. Everyone who worked there wore a uniform. The place stood out from the typical New York City barbershop, at least in its appearance. But I needed to try it for myself.

One afternoon, I went in for a haircut without identifying myself. I noticed that the sheet they put over me during my haircut looked clean and freshly ironed. It was obvious that they had not simply shaken the hair out of a used sheet and placed it over my clothes. The haircut was impeccable, and the price seemed fair, neither comically high nor too low—merely the price you would expect to pay for a basic haircut like mine at a high-quality establishment. I went back a second time and was impressed again.

I knew that the corporate executives would have an opinion on this matter since many of them had known the previous barber for years and even decades.

First, I went to Pete Thomas, the second-in-command at ITT, and told him I had found a better barber for our shop. I asked him if he might like to visit incognito and get a haircut. Pete went to Sal's not once but twice and was just as impressed as I was, both times. Meanwhile, Sal still had no idea the St. Regis executives were eyeing him.

I said, "Pete, I think this is the right guy. How do we sell this to Rand?"

We agreed I should first talk to Sal to make sure he would take the job if offered. After I identified myself, I told Sal about our plan to have a super deluxe barbershop at the new St. Regis. Would he be interested in moving there? To my surprise, he immediately said yes, without any hesitation.

The next step was for Pete to arrange a visit with Rand to get their hair cut together. This visit, also incognito, went seamlessly too. As I predicted, Rand was delighted with the barber and gave us the go-ahead. Sal came onboard right away, just in time to consult on our plans to outfit the barbershop with all the professional equipment it would need to truly stand out. Once we renovated the space, it looked like a showpiece, a movie set version of an iconic barbershop, but an exceptionally clean and well-appointed one. After we reopened the St. Regis, Sal's perfect professionalism along with the loyalty of his longtime clientele helped to quickly distinguish it as the best barbershop in the city.

It would seem absurd that I had to go all the way up to Rand Araskog to get approval to hire a new barber. But I had a hunch that I should proceed with caution, partly because of all the letters we received in defense of the old barber, and because I had started noticing the detailed attention Rand was putting into the hotel. His office nearby, at the ITT office on Park Avenue, allowed him to pay regular visits to the St. Regis, visits that grew only more frequent as we approached the reopening date.

Rand apparently considered no detail too small to get his hands on. He even wanted to help choose the colors of the flowers and assist with the bouquet arrangements for the reopening. Imagine the president of the global conglomerate ITT getting involved in the selection and cutting of flowers. In any other context, this would have seemed ridiculous. And it surely was. But I also saw it as a sign of Rand's growing adoration for the St. Regis, which gave me a sense of satisfaction. This had become

Rand's pet hotel, and he seemed to want to tend to it as a homeowner dotes on a beloved house.

In retrospect, Rand's over-involvement should have flashed as a big red warning sign. But at the time, I was so immersed in pre-opening preparations that I didn't see what was right in front of my eyes.

*For those of you who
missed New York's Golden Age,
we invite you to its re-opening.*

AN ITT SHERATON LUXURY HOTEL

NOW RECEIVING GUESTS • FIFTH AVENUE AT 55TH STREET, NEW YORK, N.Y. 10022 • TEL 212.753.4500, TELEX 148368, FAX 212.541.4736

CREATIVE ADVERTISING TO THE SENSES NEVER SEEN IN THE HOTEL INDUSTRY

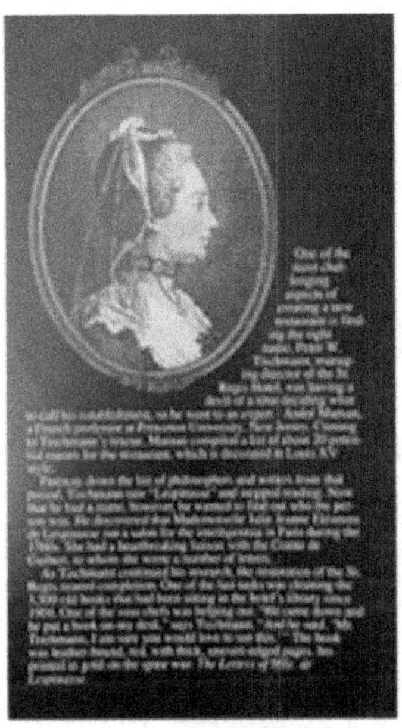

THE CHALLENGE WAS TO FIND A NAME FOR THE RESTAURANT

WE ARE EXTREMELY PROUD TO HAVE SAVED THE HISTORIC MAIL BOX THROUGH THE TIME OF CONSTRUCTION

METHOD

- Use the guest's name, smile and make eye contact.
- Be natural and friendly, but never familiar.
- Anticipate the guest's need.
- Be polite and always positive.
- Treat every guest's wish with utmost urgency.
- Always look your best, spotless uniform and appearance.
- Respect our guests privacy and confidentiality.
- Be obsessed to give service.
- Escort our guests within the hotel, never point where to go.
- Be knowledgeable about our hotel and related services.
- Retrain and educate yourself in all areas of your responsibilities.
- Be part of a team and respect your fellow team members.
- Never say no, but take personal responsibility to satisfy every guests need and question.

THE MISSION STATEMENT FOR EVERY ASSOCIATE TO CARRY ON HIM AT ALL TIMES.

Time Is Sprinting By 24

Family Time

Days, months, even years can disappear in a blur. Living with my family in our newly renovated apartment next door to the St. Regis meant I could spend more hours with them, at least in theory, and attempt to slow down the onward march of time, even for a few moments. Our new home eliminated the commute, removing even the short walk I had to make during the time when we lived in our temporary apartment a few blocks away. This helped tremendously, as the closer we came to reopening the St. Regis, the more my days became completely absorbed in the hotel preparations, morning to night.

As a family, we had to make an extra effort in those days to book hours or days together. Our family time was precious, and I tried to prioritize it even above the demands of my increasingly nonstop workdays. The challenge became even more difficult now that Carine had left home for college at Dartmouth. The New Hampshire campus was close enough that she could come home for visits on occasional weekends, but suddenly, it was just the three of us living in the apartment. Peter Jr., meanwhile, was approaching the end of his high school days. Denyse and I both felt these changes acutely, aware of how seemingly fast and how permanently our reality was shifting.

One day during the height of the pre-opening phase, my family surprised me with a gift: a bright red 560 SL convertible. I had been admiring this car, a beautiful and well-made automobile, forever, and I was delighted by the gift, even though our family rarely had time for long drives anymore. But we still had our home in New Hope, a relaxing haven that we continued to enjoy whenever any of us had a free weekend or whenever I managed to slip away to meet them there for a Saturday or a Sunday, or both if I was lucky. The car became our transportation of choice in New Hope, and it helped cheer my spirits during the exceptionally stressful days before and after the opening.

Denyse and I felt very proud of our children and their accomplishments in school. Sending Peter Jr. to school at Collegiate had turned out to be a good choice for him. The young boy who complained on the plane to London that he had to learn English managed to master the language in no time. The rigorous demands of the school had a positive impact on his previous tendency to be what Denyse calls "un partisan du moindre effort," meaning someone who gets by with minimal effort. He had to work hard to succeed at Collegiate, and I believe the academic environment helped set the stage for his future success.

Soon, before we could even blink, it was time for Peter Jr. to choose a university. He had put together a list of colleges he wanted to visit, with the help of the college advisor at his high school. It was now important to arrange personal visits to these schools, as is customary in the United States. I had my hands full with the St. Regis opening preparations, so Denyse took off with Peter, driving up and down the East coast to visit one college after another, from Cornell in upstate New York, to Lehigh in Pennsylvania, all the way to Duke in North Carolina. Each of these colleges had high standards in the technical, computer, and engineering disciplines, and Denyse and I thought Peter's interest in these fields provided a fruitful direction for him.

But much to our surprise, Peter had other plans.

Acceptances soon began to arrive from a number of his coveted schools. But several weeks passed by without any apparent decision by Peter.

Shortly before the deadline for accepting offers of admission, we had still heard nothing from our son. "Peter," I finally said, "have you decided which college you wish to go to? Because I should know where to mail the first check!"

Peter looked at us, his special mischievous smile creeping across his face, preparing us for the unpredictable.

"I decided to go to Cornell," he said.

Wonderful news. Denyse and I could barely contain our pride. "Congratulations!" I said. "Cornell is an Ivy League college with an excellent engineering department. You could not have made a better choice. Bravo!"

Peter looked at us with that same smile still on his face, and said, "But I'm not going to the engineering department. I'm going to the hotel school."

Denyse and I stood there, speechless. It took some time before I found my voice again. Meanwhile, I heard Denyse muttering to herself, "I thought one hotelier in the family was enough."

But after the initial shock passed, I patted my son on the back. Apparently, all these years of living with a hotelier for a father had not dissuaded him from a lifestyle of traveling constantly, changing cities every few years, working with people who display a variety of personality disorders, and keeping very late and very early hours, never knowing what each day might bring. If this career seemed exciting to Peter, and if this was what he wanted to do with his life out of all the other options he had considered, he could not have made a better choice than Cornell, one of the top hotel schools in the world.

Would hotels turn out to be the right career for my son? It was too early to tell, but I committed myself to supporting him every step of the way and assisting him with any experience or connections he might need. Of course, I realized he might just prefer that I back away entirely.

Since I had never known my own father, I could not know what it felt like, as a son, to have your father offer guidance in your professional life. When it came to my own career, I had done it all myself. Perhaps Peter Tischmann Sr. should simply step away and allow Peter Tischmann Jr. to make his own mistakes and find his own triumphs.

As it happened, I was about to receive my own education in how things work in the hotel industry, at least in my own corner of it. This would be a lesson I would hope Peter Jr. would never have to learn himself.

OTSU—the Opportunity to Screw Up

Five stars. Five diamonds. Two years.

ITT Sheraton hired me to lead the St. Regis so that I could achieve this mandate, a lofty goal for any hotel. The St. Regis needed to earn the highest accolades in the industry within two years after reopening, and preferably less. That meant we had practically zero opportunities to screw up. We needed to impress the most sophisticated guests in the world, exceeding their expectations from the moment we opened until the moment when we earned those distinctions, and then every moment after that.

The guest experience at the St. Regis needed to achieve perfection in every regard or get as close to it as humanly possible. Everything we did during the pre-opening phase was aimed at achieving this goal. For instance, I showed employees in our food and beverage department a chart outlining an ideal guest experience at our restaurant. The chart had a line across the middle, and above it were all the moments our guests would experience if they came to dinner at Lespinasse, from the time they booked their reservation to the time they arrived, entered, ordered, ate their meal, paid the check, and exited. Below the line were all the details we had to get right every step of the way, from valet-parking a guest's car to greeting him/her properly to making sure every ingredient and menu item showcased the highest quality to storing every wine in our cellar at the right temperature—to all the smaller steps in between. We had to excel at every big and small detail involved in creating an experience that would put a smile on guests' faces, whether they were visiting us for business or for pleasure.

"OTSU," I wrote at the bottom of the chart. Admittedly, this was a strange acronym, but it was a hard one to forget. What did it stand for? Opportunity to Screw Up. Every guest's visit provided ample opportunities for us to screw up. We as a staff needed to work hard to avoid each and every one of those opportunities, each and every day.

This did not mean that every decision every staff member in every moment had to be absolutely perfect. Mistakes would happen daily, but the way in which an employee handled an error would make all the difference. I wanted to empower staff members to make decisions on the spot, to feel confident responding to guests' questions, and doing whatever it took to ensure that guests felt comfortable and happy during their stay. This was the utmost goal. Even though we cannot maintain full control of everything that happens, we can control the way we treat our customers.

I explained to our line employees that it was they, not our department heads, who have the most power to impact a guest's experience.

Imagine a pyramid, where the point at the top represents the employee with the highest position, the general manager. Below this person are the key department heads, and below them are all the line employees.

How many times does each employee interact with a guest during a three-day visit? The GM might see a guest maybe five times, and certain department heads might see him six or seven times. But a line employee would likely see a guest twelve, twenty, even thirty, or more times. So who then is the most important person in the hotel?

Now flip the pyramid over, so that the wide base is at the top. The line employees belong at the top of the hierarchy because they have the most opportunities to impact the guest experience. In this way, they are more important than the GM.

This philosophy resulted in a radical way of viewing customer service and employee training. I committed to giving every member of our staff the authority to make decisions on the spot, based on what's best for the customer.

Empowering our line staff would help deliver a better guest experience than requiring employees to ask permission for every little decision. Not only was it a more efficient way of doing things, but I knew it would raise morale too. If a guest asked for extra bathroom amenities, for instance, or wanted to stay a little bit past the checkout time, we didn't want employees to have to say, "Sorry, I don't know. Give me a minute, let me find out." Employees could go ahead and make the decision themselves. Might they make the wrong decision at times? Yes. But I felt confident that none of our line employees would do so in bad faith.

If an employee made an error in handling a guest request, it was important that we remain supportive and respond with constructive criticism. "Congratulations, you made a decision," the supervisor might say. "It was important that you did so. But maybe next time you want to try this instead." We didn't want to discipline employees for making a decision or to scare them away from taking the initiative again next time.

Just as we had placed a clock at Chez Nous showing the time in every staff member's country, we wanted to reinforce our belief in each member of our team, every step of the way. Every small decision about empowering our employees added up to something larger. It was not just that I ate my lunch with line staff in the cafeteria every day. And it was not only that I visited each department every month and spoke individually with everyone on the team. I wanted each staff member to feel listened to, respected, valued, and entrusted with upholding the image and reputation of the St. Regis.

If you want to create a team of 350 employees who stand out above and beyond every other hotel employee in New York City, you have to make them feel invested in the hotel, train them to take pride in their work, and earn their trust every day. The department heads and I worked hard to instill these values from the moment we hired every person, up through the extensive pre-opening training that started in the weeks before we reopened.

Once the doors of the St. Regis flung open and guests began to arrive, I knew we would have no time for inadequate training and no time for bad morale.

During the entire three years of our closing, people kept asking us, on the sidewalk and in the press, if we were ever going to open again.

Now, at long last, ITT made the official announcement. The St. Regis would reopen in September of that year, 1991.

The news made a splash in the media. I knew that from this moment on, the anticipation would be so enormous, the scrutiny so microscopic, we had no choice than to create the most magnificent experience imaginable for all the world to see.

It certainly helped that all the key department heads and nearly all the line employees had been on board for almost three months before we reopened, doing extensive training and soaking up the culture of the new St. Regis.

We still had time to polish our act and add the final pre-opening touches. But before we launched the last phase of training for the entire staff, I had to make sure the department heads were ready to do their jobs under the highly stressful circumstances they would surely face the moment the hotel reopened. I decided to send them on a secret mission to see how they would cope in a brand-new, pressure-cooker environment.

I had all kinds of other surprises in store for the final pre-opening phase. This was shaping up to be an exciting time for the staff, even if they didn't know it yet.

Checking the Smallest Detail

Crowding into a tiny, inflatable boat, navigating rough waters, trying to make it down the river and keep everyone in one piece. What kind of person takes charge in a situation like that? Who manages to get the whole group to their destination, safely and efficiently? You might be surprised. It's not necessarily the person you might think it would be.

One late summer day before the hotel reopened, the department heads and their deputies boarded a bus to travel a few hours north to a secret location. Our director of training, Kathi Ransom, had given everyone only one hint: Dress for the outdoors. Ready for an adventure, we rode along, wondering where we were all headed, until we arrived at the Connecticut River reservoir. Waiting for us there was a collection of zodiac boats, the kind you blow up like a lifeboat.

Kathi instructed everyone to pile into the boats in groups of five or six. The mission: to navigate the boat down the river to the designated stopping point, coping with rapid, slow, or choppy water, and any obstacles that got in the way.

It was time to discover who was a true leader and who wasn't.

The river was not for the weak-minded. The water that day moved very slowly at times, which presented a challenge for a boat like the zodiac. The point of the exercise was to see how the people in each boat would communicate under pressure and to see who takes leadership and manages the whole group in order to get the zodiac boat from A to B.

I watched from the sidelines with Kathi and found it absolutely fascinating to see how the group in each boat fared and how everyone interacted intelligently, or sometimes not, to safely maneuver around the rocks in the river and arrive at the ending point. Some boats never made it because everyone talked at the same time and had conflicting opinions and wanted to give orders. In other boats, one person had the most vocal opinions, made all the decisions, and was accepted by the others as the leader.

One group kept arguing about how to paddle and who should sit where, and at one point, their boat ended up going off to the side and getting stuck. They all got out of the boat and rearranged their seats, and their trip went smoothly after that.

One interesting case study was team number 3, which included Rick Fleming, our director of sales and marketing. As good as Rick was at his job, in this exercise, it emerged that he had a serious problem communicating with his team in challenging situations. In his boat, he refused to accept advice and leadership from anyone else and could not effectively lead the group himself, so his team's boat was the last to arrive.

Kathi took notes as she watched the boats. At the end of the exercise, she debriefed each group on what they had learned, what went well for them, and what did not. By watching the boats and listening to the postmortem discussion afterward, she could tell which people on our team would need more training and assistance. She could also get an idea about which department heads we could count on implicitly in difficult situations.

Because if there was one thing we could count on, it was that tricky scenarios were sure to arise. Every hotel experiences its share of challenging moments, or moments of truth as they're known in the industry. Some more than others, as we would soon find out.

Running Faster Than Time

"To every person, there comes in his lifetime a special moment when he is figuratively tapped on the shoulder and offered the chance to do a very special thing, unique to him and fitted to his talents. What a tragedy if that moment finds him unprepared or unqualified for that work."

My former St. Regis secretary, Dorothy Button, gave me this quote that she found in a newspaper years ago. I still think about it at times. In the weeks before we reopened the St. Regis, I thought about this quote every day. I did feel that I had been tapped to do a very special thing, and I wanted to be prepared and to excel at it.

I felt the same way about the rest of our team too. Even if the chance to work at the St. Regis was not a defining moment in their lives, it was important for them to understand the value of the experience and to transmit that sense of specialness to our guests.

We were all about to take part in a historic moment for a historic hotel, a piece of New York City's heritage. My team and I had chosen each member of the staff for the unique talents, intelligence, and instincts that he or she would bring to the St. Regis. I knew that for many of our line employees and department heads, this was ultimately one of many jobs they would do in their lives. To them, this may not be the chance of a lifetime that it was for me. But no matter what they did next, this moment of their lives would, I hoped, remain in their memories as a special time.

I took every opportunity to emphasize our philosophy of empowerment, and I decided we would call every employee an associate, regardless of rank.

Our new uniforms had to reflect this sense of dignity too. All our uniforms were custom-made from 100 percent cotton, no synthetics. If you wear synthetics and move around all day, you sweat. If you sweat, you smell, and then imagine if you have to get on to an elevator with a guest. Each department received its own style of uniform, crisp and tidy and well-cut. The steward department, in charge of washing dishes, polishing silverware, and general cleaning in the kitchen, wore white uniforms with a crossed knife and fork on the back, and the words "Sanitation and Hygiene Department." White uniforms show stains more easily, so an associate would know when it was time to change. Traditionally, back-of-the-house team members would never meet a customer, but they might run into guests if they had to go up to the banquet floor and bring down some china or silverware. I wanted to make sure each person would look professional and walk around with a sense of pride.

This was their hotel, our hotel, and together we would make it the absolute best it could be.

Now it was time to put the final touches on the training, to make sure the reopening would find us all eminently prepared to greet the world. We needed to wow a city that had seen it all, or so it thought. But New York City had never seen anything like the new St. Regis.

Our preparations kicked into high gear during the last month before the reopening. I created customized trainings for each department and built in fun surprises.

To train the butlers, I flew in Ivor Spencer, the man who trains Queen Elizabeth's own butlers at Buckingham Palace. We were the first hotel in America to hire Ivor. With his own unique flair, Ivor educated our staff on how to properly greet guests, how to unpack their suitcases swiftly and discreetly, and how to prepare their room. He had his own special tricks, such as ironing newspapers to dry out the ink so it wouldn't stain guests' hands. He explained how to take detailed notes about every guest's preferences, from a distaste for diet soda to a specific way of arranging the shampoo and conditioner in the bathroom.

Our butlers needed to be the best in the business. Just as John Jacob Astor had hired maîtres d'etage for every floor of the hotel when he opened it in 1904, I imagined he would expect the same if he were alive today to see the reopening. Our fleet of butlers would surely impress Mr. Astor, in their perfectly tailored black tailcoats. Now, they needed to practice the refined maneuvers that would match their outfits. Ivor taught our butlers how to perform the trickiest movements with grace, not least how to walk across a ballroom with a silver tray balanced on their head.

Whiskey was becoming fashionable in that era, so we taught our butlers how to speak knowledgeably about it to any guest who asked.

We had somebody from Dewars' come over from Scotland to teach butlers to recognize the various types of whiskey and discern the flavor nuances among them. We also taught them how to serve wine and spirits correctly, how to know which bottles need to breathe first, and how to store champagne. Most important of all, we emphasized the importance of never acting ruffled if, for example, a couple of guests in a room decide to enjoy a private moment in front of the butler. Never acting ruffled at all is a trait we hoped to instill in all our staff.

The butlers learned to brush their teeth at least a dozen times per day. Ivor himself set an impeccable standard of personal hygiene. On his multiple visits, he always arrived with his wife and daughter, and judging from the number of towels they requested to their room every day, they must have taken four showers a day each.

It was not just the butlers who needed to present themselves with polish. Back-of-the-house employees needed guidance in how to interact with guests too. It would be a mistake to assume that customers would never see the engineers. If there's a mechanical problem in a guest room and the butler calls for assistance, the engineer would need to walk down the guest corridor before he enters the room. In this way, he has plenty of opportunities to pass by guests, and he needs to know what to do: Never ignore a guest, and never avoid eye contact. Always greet every customer as you walk by: "Welcome to the St. Regis. I hope you enjoy your stay."

For our front-of-house employees, we conducted basic knowledge training. We knew guests would have questions like, "How high is the World Trade Center?" The St. Regis was scheduled to reopen almost exactly ten years to the day before the city tragically lost the buildings on September 11, 2001.

A guest might ask, "What's special about the Statue of Liberty?" or "How many people live in New York City?" or "How long does it take to get from here to Grand Central Station?" If employees memorized the answers to common questions like these, they would avoid having to say "I don't know. I'm sorry. I'll find out for you" all day long. We created quizzes to speed up the learning. After all, we are a hotel based in New York City, and we all live in the area and work in this hotel. Even though it may have never before occurred to us to find out the answers to such questions, now was the time.

First-time visitors might have a hard time finding a specific part of the hotel and may ask for help from the first employee they see. "Never simply show a customer where to go, but escort him instead." We taught the whole staff to represent our service culture in every interaction with a guest.

What are the most respectful ways for employees to treat guests from different cultures or backgrounds? We role-played a variety of scenarios and discussed expectations around customs such as tipping. For instance, tips are not customary in Japan, so don't make a long face if you don't get a tip from your Japanese customer, we explained to our staff. Don't make a long face at all, with any guest, for that matter.

Staff members got to switch roles for a day or two to see what it feels like in each other's shoes. This helped cement a sense of teamwork, making staff members realize no one is better than anyone else. For example, front-of-house staffers spent a day at the back of the house, helping out in the stewarding department. This way everyone could understand that each job is challenging and valuable, and that every person has the responsibility to make guests feel comfortable and to provide them with excellent service.

We hosted a fashion show of the line staff uniforms at one of our weekly all-employee meetings. The bellboys, receptionists, chefs, stewards, and every other department promenaded around the room in its uniforms. At those meetings, we kept staff abreast of our progress in preparing for the opening and answered any questions or concerns. Those gatherings also gave staff members a chance to see and touch the equipment used in each department throughout the hotel. At one meeting, I would bring out the new china so everyone could get a close-up look at the plates and pass them around. "Every piece costs $20," I would announce, "so please be careful!" We did this with the silverware too and every piece of operating equipment we received for the kitchen. Gray Kunz wanted copper pots—nothing else would do, he insisted—so he got copper pots. Copper distributes heat better than other materials, so I could not deny his request. Staff members would pick up a copper pot for the first time: "Wow, it's heavy."

As soon as the linens arrived and we started setting up the rooms, everyone knew the hotel would be ready to reopen in a matter of a few weeks. By now, the whole group started to seem like a family. I sensed a strong bond across the departments, as the staff began to act as if they belonged to one big team.

Now it was time to put all our hard work to the test. It was time for every member of the line staff to stay overnight in a St. Regis hotel room and report to us about their experience.

I asked everyone on the team, from the housekeepers to the bellboys, engineers, stewards, and members of our front-of-the-house staff to check into the hotel with their families and stay the night. Some were eager to do this, a chance to experience life as a guest but for free. I learned that certain staff members felt uncomfortable bringing their families and showcasing their private lives at the hotel, and we did not pressure them to do so.

These practice visits provided helpful feedback from our associates about what staying at the new St. Regis actually feels like, and I also saw them as a chance to get staff members from one department to experience the work of associates in another area. Housekeepers staying a night with their families saw how the way they and their colleagues did their jobs can impact a guest's visit. Engineers staying in a room overnight could view the rooms through a customer's eye. I wanted our whole team to understand how their individual role and everyone else's fit into the bigger picture of what we wanted to achieve. I felt this would create a sense of ownership. This way, if an employee witnessed an issue or a request arising outside his own department, he would pitch in to help instead of saying, "That's not my business."

We adopted the same strategy with our fine dining restaurant, Lespinasse. To find out whether our flagship restaurant was ready for prime time, we needed to test the Lespinasse experience before we could invite outside guests in. Staff members were asked to come in as customers and bring another guest with them for lunch or dinner, then evaluate the experience. For the employees, this was an experience they may never have again, the chance to sit in an elegant restaurant, dine on expensive china, and sample Gray Kunz's exquisite cuisine. Total bill: Zero dollars.

Nobody was left out of this training exercise. Every staff member had a chance to stay in the hotel for a night and eat a meal in the restaurant if they accepted our invitation to do so. Most did both, and everyone learned from those experiences. Kathi Ransom even picked up employees at the staff exit door and drove them around to the front door in her red Chevy Nova. When they emerged from the car, the bellhops and doormen and front-of-house staff would practice greeting them and showing them up to their room.

It was not as if we expected detailed feedback on each aspect of every guest room or the nuances of the Lespinasse menu from each employee who visited our restaurant or stayed overnight. But we found their experience valuable even if it was the very first time they had experienced service at this level. From our interviews with each person afterward, we took any information that would help us improve our offerings.

I hoped the entire staff would feel as if their opinions and comments were welcome, not just in the pre-opening phase but after we opened the hotel too. In fact, we could not survive without that feedback. How often do executives make all the decisions, then after they implement their plans, everyone wonders, "Who was crazy enough to make a decision like this?"

I knew that from the moment we opened the hotel, if anything appeared flawed or out of step, the press would take us apart—especially because of our much-heralded room rates. Any missteps we made by not taking the proper care before opening could hurt us, causing potentially irreparable damage.

INTRODUCTION OF CUSTOM DESIGNED EQUIPMENT TO
THE SERVICE AND CULINARY TEAM

LAST INSTRUCTION TO THE EXTRAORDINARY BUTLER TEAM
ANOTHER FIRST FOR NEW YORK

The St. Regis's Grand Reopening 25

Almost Open

The clock started ticking louder every day. We now had less than a month before our publicly announced reopening date, and it was time for one last reality check, a chance to give our associates the opportunity to practice our vision and mission with customers who were, for all intents and purposes, almost exactly like true hotel guests.

As part of our final opening preparations, we had scheduled a ten-day dry run, inviting selected outside guests to stay at the St. Regis for free and to enjoy everything the hotel had to offer. The luxury of our accommodations, the exquisite flavors of Gray Kunz's cuisine, the special cocktails in our King Cole Bar, and every other service designed to turn the St. Regis once again into the finest hotel in New York City and beyond.

During that ten-day period, a number of ITT and Sheraton executives, as well as some CEOs and presidents of Fortune 500 companies, owners of New York's leading travel agencies, VIPs, and other dignitaries arrived to put us to the test, checking into the hotel and using its amenities as if it were already open. Obviously, we only set aside a limited number of rooms to be booked for this exercise to allow the staff to stay focused on delivering the best possible experience to our pre-opening customers.

Every guest we invited had the chance to stay for up to three nights during the dry-run phase and to take advantage of all the services the hotel had to offer for free, well, almost for free, because the price of getting chosen as part of this privileged group of guests was to give up a bit of valuable time for an exit interview before leaving the hotel.

This did not come as a surprise to any of them because when they accepted our offer to stay at the St. Regis as our guests, they knew we would ask for their comments and feedback. In particular, we wanted to know their impressions of how our service compared to what they find at the other luxury hotels where they typically choose to stay.

The interviews were conducted by all the key department heads, including myself, and we made sure that we collected as much information as possible, which we then consolidated into a final checklist and an action plan to make sure that the smallest details were taken care of.

Conducting a pre-opening test run is certainly not a normal part of a hotel launch, even for a luxury property like the St. Regis, and I was grateful to Rand Araskog and John Kapioltas for approving this exercise. I'm confident that they must have understood the value of doing so, as it would ensure that we would have a picture-perfect opening when there was no longer any time for errors.

Both the invited guests and the hotel employees took real ownership of this exercise and treated it with the seriousness it deserved, and each contributed to its success. But this phase was not free of a certain amount of confusion. Since we had our doors open, with guests coming in and leaving the hotel, some passersby refused to understand why they could not visit the hotel as well. Eventually, we had to turn them away.

After those ten days, we closed the hotel again for two weeks. We took all the feedback we had received and compared it to what we were already doing. We made changes wherever we saw the need. Mostly, it was just fine-tuning, and we were happy that the exit interviews did not reveal any major surprises. We heard things like, "My mini bar hasn't been filled up." Or "The breakfast should be served a little faster." Or "I had to wait too long for the luggage to come into my room."

Happily, most of the feedback was positive. Everybody loved the afternoon amenity in the room, the piece of cake the butler left on the table, with a personal note saying, "When you return, please call the butler and inform him if you would like coffee or tea."

This phase provided invaluable training, especially for the butlers and the staff, allowing them to get used to the rhythms of a guest visit and to practice getting the timing right.

Rand Araskog essentially moved into the hotel at this point. While he did not sleep at the St. Regis, he spent at least three or four days a week at the hotel, examining every detail. He and I would walk through the hotel together, and he would comment about things like the lighting—"Should we dim it here and raise it there?"—and the background music. "Don't you think the music is a little too loud," he would ask. I would explain that the music might seem loud at this moment, but when the room fills up with guests, it won't seem loud at all.

Knowing that Rand and his colleagues at the highest levels were taking such an interest kept the staff on their toes. It certainly kept me on my toes.

I always said to my staff, "If anything goes wrong with the opening, I will be out so fast that I will not even have the time to pack my baggage."

Thank God I didn't have to pack my suitcases. Because we had a fantastic opening. I still think back to that day, moment by moment, the way an unsuspecting character in a horror film might savor every minute of a beautiful day in the park just before a horrible shadow peers out from behind a tree.

Finally Open

On September 10, 1991, momentous events were happening in America and the world. The Soviet Union was in the process of dissolving after the failed August Coup of President Mikhail Gorbachev. In the US, the Senate Judiciary Committee had, on that day, begun its televised confirmation hearings on Clarence Thomas's nomination to the Supreme Court, amid accusations that he had sexually harassed his employee Anita Hill. I watched a few tidbits of this hearing with fascination, not realizing how this event would become a particularly memorable one in my life.

In my own universe, the relaunch of the St. Regis was the biggest event of all on September 10, 1991. After three years of tireless work and anticipation, we had finally reached the moment of truth.

But we could not simply fling open the doors of the St. Regis on the morning of September 10 and tell the world, "We're ready. Come on in."

We had to open in grand style, in a manner as opulent, graceful, and impeccably choreographed as the new St. Regis itself. And we needed the right person to help us do this.

As it happened, the Trump organization had just lost ownership of the Plaza Hotel around this time, so Ivana Trump had left her position at the hotel. Her personal public relations attaché was now available to take on other clients, and we immediately contacted her. What a public relations person she was: Eleanor Lambert, the doyenne of fashion in New York City. The woman who had created New York Fashion Week and the Best Dressed List and the Council of Fashion Designers of America. Eleanor Lambert, the woman had won international attention and a higher profile for America's fashion designers. Her list of close personal contacts included nearly every socialite in New York, every famous designer, every supermodel, and the entire who's who of New York City in the early 1990s.

We had no choice but to hire Eleanor. She was in her late eighties at this point, but she was still visible on the society circuit and as elegant as ever, a woman of stature all the way up to the day she passed away at a hundred years old. I asked Mrs. Lambert if she would be interested in helping the St. Regis with public relations for the opening. "Your job is to get the society people of New York into our Lespinasse restaurant," I said. "Every day, I want you to invite up to ten people of standing into our restaurant."

And this is what she did. She brought everyone who was anyone to our doors, and she really helped put Lespinasse on the map. She brought these people in to have tea in the lounge and luncheon in the restaurant, and sometimes a cocktail at the bar, and almost instantly Lespinasse, the Astor Court, and the King Cole Bar became known as the places to be. Lespinasse for lunch filled up to three-quarters capacity, and for dinner it was packed. You could not find a place to sit in the Astor Court. The biggest compliment I received from our hotel guests was that they could not get a reservation at Lespinasse because it was so in-demand by locals. This was quite a different situation from my days of working on Sheraton's hotel restaurants in Paris, when we could hardly ever get anyone other than tourists into the seats.

Eventually, we decided to reserve a couple of tables every day for hotel guests. After all, we didn't want Lespinasse's popularity to turn into a liability and to create the impression that guests from around the world did not stand a chance of eating in our suddenly famous restaurant.

Lespinasse and the social spaces at the St. Regis were not the only parts of the hotel that launched with a bang. We opened the rooms and suites with tremendous fanfare too.

Rand Araskog and his wife, Jessie, presided over the ribbon-cutting ceremony in the presence of Mayor David Dinkins and many celebrities.

While the golden scissors cut through the ribbon, the famous singer Judy Collins performed one of her most beloved songs. Among the many other guests and local dignitaries was Archbishop Iakovos, head of the Greek Orthodox community, who had joined Martin Luther King Jr.'s march to Selma, Alabama, and had been decorated by President Jimmy Carter with the Presidential Medal of Freedom.

We had red velvet ropes around the whole area. A member of the Landmarks Commission made an appearance, someone with whom we had developed a close relationship after all the battles about how big the windows had to be and what we were allowed or not allowed to do to the building.

Later I discovered that Joe Prezioso had added his own sneaky touch to the ceremony. One of the gas valve covers on the manhole next to the St. Regis door had become worn and rusted over the decades, and Joe had a feeling that the sight of this cover would bother me. So he went down to the engineering department to retrieve black spray paint and masking tape, and he painted the entire cover black before the ribbon-cutting. Joe knew me well. He was right that if I had seen the rusty manhole cover out of the corner of my eye, I would not have been able to take my mind off it even as everything else about the ceremony proceeded perfectly.

When the first guests walked in the door, a nice-looking older couple, we greeted the woman with a bouquet of flowers and her husband with a bottle of champagne. As it turned out, those two were not only our first guests, but they had actually celebrated their wedding at the hotel many years ago. I can still see them standing in front of me. She was a medium-sized gray-haired woman; he was a little bit taller. They were not fancy people. They came from out of town, not New York, and had reserved a room at the St. Regis for their wedding anniversary. I remember the surprised look on their faces when we greeted them. They seemed overwhelmed by the champagne, the flowers, the welcome from the GM. It all seemed too much and almost embarrassing to them.

As a thank-you to all the customers who had booked with us for the very first night, we charged the same rates as the hotel did back in 1904. This amounted to $4 for a room, $6 for a suite. Those room bills definitely came as a surprise to our guests. Who would have expected this, after booking the opening week at the St. Regis and expecting to spend a small fortune?

The first part of the opening phase was an enormous success. My staff did an exceptional job every step of the way. I could not have hoped for a more spectacular beginning to the new era of the St. Regis.

The second part? That was another story, which began the week after we officially reopened the hotel, when ITT scheduled a big opening gala and charity event and sold every table of ten for $20,000. The public relations department of ITT handled all the details for this event, from the date to the invitation list to everything else. Rand Araskog personally invited every guest. The St. Regis public relations department had no involvement in the gala, other than being available should somebody from the ITT publicity team need assistance.

Unfortunately, for whatever reason, most of the CEOs and other prominent guests Rand had invited did not show up. Maybe they were traveling, or they simply booked a table because they couldn't afford not to, to stay on Rand's good side, but when the time came, they asked their secretary to send whoever had the time to go. As a result, regardless of the excuse, Rand did not get the level of guests he wanted in the rooms that night to provide him with the big social splash he was hoping for.

It also happened that on the same day, another major society event was taking place nearby, a major oversight on the part of ITT's public relations department. Even a partially competent PR person would have known to check for any competing events before booking a gala. But ITT's publicist obviously neglected to check the social calendar. The repercussions were an absolute disaster for the St. Regis, for our entire team, and for myself.

The event that killed us was Saks Fifth Avenue's traditional fall fashion show, a society event benefiting five different charities and attracting the rich and famous of New York. These were many of the same people we were looking forward to having at our opening gala, but they chose to attend the Saks Fifth Avenue event instead.

At least we had Brooke Astor in our corner. Mrs. Astor, following the ribbon-cutting ceremony, had attended our official opening cocktail reception, as well as the press conference for our launch. When we walked her around the hotel and showed her the guest rooms and public spaces, she said, "Mr. Tischmann, if John Jacob could see what you have done here, he would be very proud." Mrs. Astor herself had been involved in redecorating the hotel in the late 1950s, shortly before her husband William Vincent Astor, the philanthropist and son of John Jacob Astor, died in 1959. In a letter to me months earlier, during the renovation phase, Mrs. Astor had written, "I kept thinking of Vincent and of how very proud he would be to see the hotel coming back even more beautiful than it was when his father built it."

Mrs. Astor was the eminence grise of New York society at the time, occupying the very highest echelon, so much so that whenever she threw a party, society members who did not receive an invitation left town in order to avoid the shame. It filled me with gratitude and humility to think that her late husband would have been delighted to see the hotel his father created restored to its splendor.

Alas, Mrs. Astor's approval was not quite enough to avoid the humiliation that soon followed.

The day after our gala, the *New York Times* published a full-page article about Saks Fifth Avenue's fall fashion show and all the VIPs in attendance. As for our own opening gala, the *Times* mentioned it two pages later, in a paragraph or two. Rand Araskog's name did not appear anywhere in the article. Needless to say, Rand was not pleased. No one at ITT was pleased, not in the least.

Suddenly, we had a giant debacle on our hands.

My phone rang shortly after the article appeared that morning. It was John Kapioltas, instructing me to get rid of the St. Regis's PR person because she had not done her job in securing prominent media coverage for the gala.

My attempt to explain to John that ITT had chosen to exclusively handle all the public relations for the event, sidelining our director of PR, did not reach his ears, as he kept cutting me short, saying: "Tischmann, did you hear what I just said to you?"

Rand Araskog must have given him an earful that same morning, leaving John with no other choice but to instruct me to fire our totally innocent PR lady.

As for the director of PR from ITT, Juan Capello, he took no responsibility whatsoever, sticking his head into the sand like an ostrich. A typical reaction for a corporate executive. After all, why risk your career if there was an easy scapegoat you could blame instead?

A few days later, several newspapers outside New York City, from Florida to Connecticut and beyond, published lengthy articles about our gala. Rand's name appeared prominently in most of these. But it didn't matter anymore. Only New York mattered. And that was already a lost cause.

Another catastrophe followed a few days afterward.

Since we were without a director of public relations at the hotel, I requested that ITT send somebody to join me for an interview with a *New York Times* journalist who wanted to speak with me about the renovations and the relaunch. Sitting in the Astor Court for the duration of the interview, I answered all his questions politely, careful to avoid any missteps. When the interview finally ended, with the journalist's notebook and pens packed away, and as we were finishing our tea and cake, he asked me this: "Mr. Tischmann, by the way, what do you think about the Peninsula Hotel on the other side of Fifth Avenue?"

Jokingly, I answered, "Which hotel?"

"The Peninsula," he repeated.

"Ah, you mean the hotel on the west side. Well, let me ask you this," I said to him, again in jest, "if you had a choice between booking your hotel on the east side or the west side, which one would you choose?"

The journalist and even the ITT person were laughing at my joking statement and nodding their heads in approval.

I didn't realize this at the time, but it was as if I had just announced the end of life on earth as we know it.

The next day, the journalist's *New York Times* article about the St. Regis reopening appeared with this headline: "St. Regis General Manager Considers Peninsula a West Side Hotel."

I have very little experience with New York media. I thought the headline was meant humorously, in the same spirit as the comment I had made. But I turned out to be wrong about this, very wrong. Moments after I saw the headline, I received a phone call from Rand Araskog, followed swiftly by a phone call from John Kapioltas. John said, "You do *not* joke around with journalists." I wish I would have known better, and I was wondering why ITT's PR person had not been able to stop this headline from appearing. After all, my understanding was that good PR people should not only be able to ensure that articles get into the press, but they should also be able to steer journalists away from a negative slant like the kind reflected in that headline.

The irony of this is that two days later, the electric transformer station below Fifty-Fifth Street outside the hotel exploded, throwing the manhole cover on the street twenty feet into the air and leaving the St. Regis without electricity. I had to call the GM on the other side of the street—at none other than the Peninsula Hotel—asking for help: "I'm sorry but do you have any rooms available for our customers?" Graciously enough, he said yes. Of course, the St. Regis paid the Peninsula for these rooms since our guests had already paid us before the manhole disaster. But I can only imagine how tempted the GM must have been to say, "Sorry, Mr. Tischmann. We cannot do anything for you."

During the Holy Roman Empire in the eleventh century, Pope Gregory VII excommunicated Emperor Henry IV for his attempts to oppose the papal power. But in the year 1077, Henry IV made a pilgrimage to Canossa in Italy to see the Pope and plead for his forgiveness. To do so, he had to kneel in front of the pope's gates for three days and nights, in the snow and rain, before the pope agreed to see him. Since then, the Walk to Canossa has described desperate attempts to seek penance from people you have wronged. Calling the Peninsula's general manager to plead for rooms was my own Walk to Canossa.

I later invited him for lunch at Lespinasse so I could apologize for my statement in the *New York Times*, and I explained in detail how this had happened. He nodded his head with a big smile on his face, possibly knowing that I had already received my share of heat from the organization I worked for. And right he was.

Little did he know that in this moment, I would have traded jobs with him with pleasure. Because from the minute we opened the hotel, with a level of quality and elegance that earned us compliments from none other than Mrs. Brooke Astor, I began to receive calls from my boss John Kapioltas every single morning at 8:00 a.m. I could have set my clock by his phone calls.

"Hi, Peter, what's new?"

"Everything is fine. What can I do for you?" I would answer, holding my breath for the next question.

"What's the occupancy today, and what's the average room rate? Also, who do we have as a VIP in the hotel?"

I was prepared for these daily questions, and I had no doubt that a few minutes later he got a call from Rand, his own boss, asking the same questions.

Our average room rate after the opening was somewhere in the neighborhood of $500—much higher than we had predicted. But our occupancy at 45 percent stood below the 65 percent we had hoped for, raising some concern from John, who requested that I do something about it.

I tried to explain to John that we had succeeded in getting the right guests into the hotel, and they were paying a room rate higher than we had expected, but it would take some time to build the occupancy. John suddenly said, "Just do it. I have a call coming." I was almost sure that Rand Araskog was the one calling him.

For some hoteliers, the occupancy might be more important than the rate, and they are even prepared to sacrifice the rate for a higher occupancy, a strategy I could not agree with. In the case of the St. Regis, we were getting the customers we were looking for, and I was confident that we would be able to build the occupancy over time, while keeping the same quality of customers we were already enjoying so soon after the opening.

Although John might have agreed with me, I'm sure he was pressured by ITT to generate a higher occupancy to ensure a faster rate of return for their investment because he kept asking the same question again and again: "What are you doing to bring the occupancy rate up?"

I would reply that we are doing everything we can think of, but that we have to appeal to the most discerning customers in the world one by one, and this takes more care than merely booking the kinds of tour groups that other Sheraton hotels base their occupancy rates on.

There was no doubt in my mind that if we tried all kinds of tricks and maneuvers to raise the occupancy, we would have lost the high-end guests. They want to be among people like themselves, and so far, the St. Regis was succeeding in marketing ourselves to this exclusive group and exceeding the room rates of every other hotel in New York City.

I agreed with John that we should increase our occupancy, but we had only been open a few months. I saw no need to reduce our rate or discount the rooms, a typical Sheraton approach, as long as the company gave us a realistic amount of time to attract more and more high-paying guests, one at a time, as we were already doing.

Analyzing where our guests were coming from and how the booking was generated, we noticed that Sheraton's sales and marketing department was hardly contributing to our occupancy, confirming what we had known all along: that Sheraton's salespeople had no access to the level of customers we were aiming for.

An analysis of the first three months of operation showed that Sheraton was contributing only 8 percent of our occupancy, while the remaining 37 percent were direct bookings or the results of Arlette Hagedorn's sales efforts.

When I communicated our analysis with the corporate sales and marketing office, I once again did not make myself many friends in Boston.

One guest I would not have personally chosen was someone I knew very well by this point, for better or worse. It was Rand Araskog, who, after his near-daily visits to the hotel during the pre-opening phase, had now decided to make the St. Regis the home base for himself and his wife as they awaited renovations at their Park Avenue apartment.

That's exactly what I needed: My boss's boss breathing down my neck at all times.

I grew used to Rand's presence soon enough, however, and while it no longer bothered me to have him around in between his travels, it did create added pressure on my staff. Rand ordered room service or went to the restaurant as often as he could, and he used all of the hotel's services. This kept everyone on their toes, which I considered a positive thing because it gave our team the kind of boost we needed to maintain the absolute highest levels of quality in every inch of the hotel.

But as it turned out, one well-intentioned customer service error was all it took to set off a tragic domino effect.

No Room for Errors, But They Happen

What do they say about the best-laid plans? In the St. Regis's reception area, we had a brilliant front office manager named Simon Malouf, the smart and multilingual hotel professional whom I had hired from L'Ermitage in Beverly Hills. The staff adored Simon, and he was doing an excellent job. He always found ways to take the extra step for our guests, to go above and beyond, and this is what he did one morning as Rand Araskog prepared to leave the hotel for the airport.

Simon sent not one bellboy but two up to Rand's suite to gather and bring down his luggage as efficiently as possible. As one bellboy came down with the luggage on a trolley, it got loaded into a car. The bellboy nodded to the driver that he was done loading luggage, and the driver took off with Rand in the back seat.

Two seconds later, the second bellboy came down with Rand's briefcase, which the two of them had not wanted to load onto the already packed luggage trolley. Oh no. I saw this and realized the driver had left too soon, and the first bellboy had perhaps not realized that the second bellboy was still on his way with the briefcase. So I called the driver, who had one of those big car phones that certain automobiles had in the early 1990s, before cell phones became popular. I said, "Patrick, where are you?"

Fortunately, he was not far, and I asked him to swing by again to pick up Rand's briefcase. I waited on the sidewalk, and when I opened the car door to give the briefcase to Rand, I saw him sitting there with the stoniest expression I had ever seen on his face.

The car took off, and the next thing I knew, I received a phone call from John Kapioltas. I'm sure that Rand had called him from the car to report the incident.

"Peter, what happened to Rand?" asked John.

I explained how the head receptionist had sent up two bellboys and how the driver had taken off after the first bellboy loaded the car, not realizing there was another bellboy behind him carrying Rand's briefcase.

"Who is in charge of the front office?" John asked.

I said, "It's Simon Malouf. He's great. You know him."

John did not wait even a half-second. "Fire him."

Was this the way we were doing business now, apparently: "Fire the PR director." "Fire the front office manager." Why bother finding out what actually happened in such incidents, when you can simply fire conscientious employees who did nothing wrong? I had no choice but to obey John's orders, unless I wanted my own head on the chopping block too. But I was very concerned that our hard-won staff morale would go down the drain fast.

This was the corporate culture of ITT in those days, at least the part of it that I witnessed. Truly something to be ashamed of as we continued to keep up the facade that all was gracious and genteel on the corner of Fifty-Fifth and Fifth.

On the Road to Success

Despite the disasters of the gala, my poorly timed joke about the Peninsula, and Rand's delayed briefcase, our hotel flowed smoothly from the day we reopened.

Our constantly packed restaurant earned stellar reviews, our King Cole Bar maintained a lively crowd every night, and our Astor Court attracted VIPs every day. Plus, our banqueting department quickly distinguished itself as the best in town, just as I knew it would. Every plate looked like a painting. Guests complimented our service throughout the hotel, and we heard daily about the various ways in which the new St. Regis exceeded expectations and surpassed its peers in its attention to detail.

As everything was going well, I could now focus my attention on the puzzle at hand: how to raise the occupancy rate, while retaining our high average room rate and superior clientele. Yes, we had the right customers, but we didn't have enough of them. Rick Fleming continued his overseas trips to meet with contacts and drive business to the St. Regis, and I started to take some of those trips too, visiting the leading German corporations and meeting with private businessmen along with Arlette. Rick and I both felt confident that we were on track to bring in even more of the guests we had succeeded in attracting.

By external measures of success, we had nothing to complain about. We had established the St. Regis as the number 1 hotel in New York City, according to *Conde Nast Traveler's* well-respected hotel ratings. *Institutional Investor* ranked us number 1 in the US too, and number 14 internationally out of 100, based on their polls of executives who travel frequently and stay at crème de la crème hotels. On that list, we ranked far higher than any other New York City hotel and higher than the Bel Air in Beverly Hills, the prestigious hotel where I had found my restaurant genius Tony Fortuna.

Our hard work and success only motivated me to achieve ever greater heights for the St. Regis. What will we set our sights on next? I would ask myself. I would sit down with my key department heads to brainstorm ambitious goals we could conquer. But then two unexpected newcomers arrived.

MRS. BROOKE ASTOR THE GRAND OLD DAME OF NEW YORK AT THE HOTEL OPENING

778 Park Avenue

May 29, 1991

Dear Mr Tischman,

This is just a little note to thank you for lunch yesterday. I was quite overcome by all that you have done to make the St. Regis such an extraordinarily attractive place. It is not often these days that one sees such wonderful workmanship, and of course, the Library was just its old self, only with a marvelous facelift.

I am enclosing a list of people whom you might write to in England.

With re-newed thanks
for a delightful time
Sincerely
Brooke Astor

LINCOLN W. ALLAN
328 ANDREWS AVENUE
DELRAY BEACH, FLORIDA 33483

October 4, 1991

Mr. Peter Tischmann
General Manager
The St. Regis
Two E. 55th St.
New York NY 10022

Dear Mr. Tischmann:

Forty-four years ago today, my wife and I were married on the roof of your hotel. It was the first occasion for the hotel when both the ceremony and the reception were held in the ballroom. The maitre d' was "Joseph".

Two weeks ago, we were visiting in New York and stopped in at The St. Regis to see all the changes and revitalization of the "grand dame"! Everyone was so very nice to us. A man, named Vincent, greeted us in the lobby and offered to show us the redecorated roof. Unfortunately, we were in a hurry at the time and had to decline.

Later that evening, we visited the King Cole Bar and had a most delicious dinner. Once again, everyone was so friendly and nice. We met John Duffy, the cordial bar tender, and Arthur Backal, director of catering. They both made us feel right at home.

We thought you would enjoy seeing the enclosed hotel bill for October 4, 1947...a room for $15... how about that!

Best wishes for all success in the years to come and thanks for keeping the St. Regis in the same gracious tradition that it has always been famous for.

Cordially,

Lincoln W. Allan

OUR FIRST GUEST AFTER THE REOPENING

RAND ARASKAOG IN FRONT OF THE KING COLE MURAL

The Writing on the Wall 26

Politics Are Finally Catching Up

One day shortly after our reopening, a man by the name of Donald Crossfield was tapped by John Kapioltas to oversee the luxury hotels of Sheraton. At this point, Sheraton only had two luxury properties, the Carlton in Washington D.C. and the St. Regis in New York. We had no luxury division yet. Only those two hotels.

So, I wondered, why did the company suddenly decide to put this Donald Crossfield person in charge of a division that had yet to exist? And why did I now have to report to him instead of to John?

Donald had never before managed a luxury hotel. However, before going to the Boston office, he had racked up quite a colorful resumé.

Donald had spent the previous five years as the GM of the Sheraton San Cristobal in Santiago, Chile, during which he won the Harold S. Geneen Award for Creative Management, the prize named after the ITT chief executive who turned the company into a multinational conglomerate in the 1960s and 1970s. Interestingly, Harold Geneen was, according to reports and books on the era, instrumental in a chain of events in Chile that led to the ousting of the country's newly elected socialist president Salvador Allende in 1972. ITT at the time owned a 70 percent stake in the Chilean Telephone Company (Chiltelco), and it feared the socialists' plan to nationalize telecommunications in the country. Reports on the era show that ITT extensively lobbied US president Richard Nixon and the CIA to bring down Allende. There is also evidence suggesting that the funds paid to Allende's political opponents to destabilize the country and force a coup were channeled by the CIA through ITT's Chilean telephone company. When the ITT headquarters in New York City were bombed later in 1973, many believed this was done as payback for ITT's involvement in the Chilean coup.

By 1979, when Rand Araskog became the chief executive of ITT and needed to reestablish ties with Chilean business and government leaders after the coup, Donald Crossfield helped him in his capacity as a well-connected GM of a prominent hotel in Chile's capital.

Rand, of course, was himself no stranger to dealings with governments and intelligence services. He was a graduate of the West Point military academy, and in the 1950s, he had worked with the United States' National Security Agency to interrogate Soviet defectors.

But Rand had no connections in Chile, which remained a prime market for ITT in the years after the coup. Don Crossfield introduced his new boss Rand Araskog to the top levels of business and government in Chile.

Was Donald Crossfield's appointment as senior vice president of Sheraton's so-called Luxury Collection in 1991 done as a reward for everything he had done for Rand and ITT in Chile?

I could not answer that question. But I could find no other explanation for why this man would possibly get appointed to a job like this. Day after day, week after week, I had to sit down with Donald and explain our policies and our standards and all the countless concepts involved in running a hotel like the St. Regis. Even though he had no luxury hotel experience, I was now in the position of reporting to him. Every day, he would ask me a million questions. And I would basically train him, as if I were training a novice who also happened to be my new boss.

In my gut, I knew something didn't feel right. What the hell was going on here? I kept my mouth shut and continued to do my job, trying to look out of the corners of both eyes at the same time.

The next thing I knew, John asked me to provide an office for Donald Crossfield so he can sit and work in the hotel when he was in New York, once or twice a week. Since Donald was rarely around, I offered him a place where he could sit and make telephone calls. The next day, John called to inform me that Donald was not happy with his office, and that I needed to give him a space on the executive floor.

Obviously, this was another clue that something was amiss.

Donald started walking through the hotel on his visits, talking to employees, poking his head into every department.

At this point, I should have asked John a direct question: "What is happening here?"

But I didn't. I observed everything quietly, even when Donald asked me to give him all the information I had about the hotel, from the operational philosophy of each department to our hiring strategy to our training manuals. Everything.

Something was cooking, but I had no clue what was going on or that much harder times were waiting for me.

I remained quiet too when Boston pushed me to hire a woman by the name of Anne Power to replace the director of human resources. Since I had no other immediate replacement in mind, I went along with it.

In retrospect, I should have pushed for Kathi Ransom-Kiernan, our highly capable director of training. She was the perfect person for the HR director job.

By this point, I was in a strong enough position that I could have promoted my own candidate, but Kathi didn't cross my mind for an instant. I think what stopped me is that Kathi was doing too good a job as director of training, and I didn't want to lose her in that position.

In any event, this would prove to be a tragic error soon after. But for the time being, I continued to work day and night to keep the St. Regis at the top of its game and to scale new heights. But always, I watched my back, now more than ever.

Unbeknownst to me, I was the proverbial frog in the pot, sitting there as the water slowly heats up, not realizing that it's boiling until it's too late.

The Higher You Go, the Deeper You Fall

My secretary in Brussels once said, "Peter, in corporate life, the higher you go, the deeper you fall."

Her comment sounded obvious when I first heard it, but it has stayed in my mind. At the time, my career was on an upswing. I was getting recognized through a string of promotions and awards at Sheraton. The senior vice president and managing director role at the St. Regis was still years away, but I was rising quickly in my career, and felt I would keep doing so year after year, at this company or another one.

When John tapped me to head the St. Regis back in 1985, I immediately set about making it the absolute best hotel it could possibly be. I never stopped thinking about this mission, from the years before we closed the hotel all the way through the renovation. Day and night, I occupied myself with creating a hotel that would stand out above all the others in New York City and reach the shortlist of the top-ranked hotels in the world. I did not occupy myself with worries that I should watch my back. I had taken Dorothy's comment as a mere statement of the obvious—everyone falls at some point, even if that point is only retirement—but I had failed to see it as a warning.

It was only when Donald Crossfield arrived at the St. Regis that my stomach told me something was wrong.

At first, I could not point to anything specific. It was the simple fact of his presence and the realization that a position above mine had been created expressly for Donald, even though he seemed completely unprepared to do the job. Donald appeared to have somebody's unwavering support.

Within days of Donald's arrival, it became clear that he intended to snoop around in every department and eavesdrop on every possible conversation. As if this was not disturbing enough, the situation did get worse when John Kapioltas requested on Donald's behalf that I get the engineers to punch a hole in the wall to connect Donald's new office directly with Maria's cubicle. Suddenly, I had to share Maria, my personal assistant, with Donald Crossfield and his constant administrative demands.

The three years that I and my team spent envisioning and creating the new St. Regis, focusing on every detail big and small, seeking out and hiring the most talented staff, training our new hires to be the best in the business, meticulously planning every step of the pre-opening phase, accommodating Rand's meddling, navigating all of the operational challenges of the reopening, launching a hotel worthy of the highest room rate in town, and catapulting the St. Regis to the rank of number 1 hotel in New York City: What did all this amount to?

All I knew was that three years' worth of intensive work and the unrelenting pressure to get everything right added up to nothing compared to the small, unsettled feeling in my gut that overtook me from the first day Donald Crossfield arrived.

As it turned out, I had every reason to feel unsettled.

Dark Clouds Over My Head 27

Dirty Games Are On Their Way

In March of 1992, three months after Donald's arrival, my family was scheduled to leave before me for a ski trip to Austria. This was a long-awaited break, a chance to spend a full two weeks vacationing together, something we had not yet done in the three and a half years since we left Cairo. Denyse would be flying to Austria a few days before me, along with Carine and Peter Jr.

On March 6, a few days before my family left for Austria, I received a visit in my office from Kevin Richwood, the director of labor relations in Boston.

His office has received some complaints, he said to me, dispensing with the small talk and getting straight to the point.

"What kind of complaints?" I asked. Was this a union matter?

Only a few of our departments were unionized, and our agreement with the union seemed to me to be working well for all sides, at least for the time being. Kevin was the person whose job it was to communicate between the union and management, and he had successfully negotiated a standstill agreement in order to allow us to open the hotel successfully without any union involvement.

As the majority of our employees were not in favor of joining the union, we were hoping to be able to extend the agreement for as long as possible.

Unfortunately, we had made our calculation without the union, who was pressuring Kevin to get into the St. Regis to the point that they were threatening to strike the Sheraton Center and all other Sheraton hotels in the city. So when Kevin showed up in my office that day, it was the union threat which was on my mind.

From what I could sense, morale was high at the hotel, even though everyone on staff had worked long hours around the opening. This was part of our agreement with the union, that the reopening phase would involve longer hours than usual, before the more restricted schedule would take effect. I had not heard any complaints from staff members myself. I was trying to imagine what kinds of complaints would have prompted an unannounced meeting with Kevin. He jumped in to interrupt my chain of thoughts.

Sexual harassment, Kevin said to me. I looked at him, wondering which employee might be harassing coworkers. We had all labored long hours for months together and had developed a collegial working environment. I felt proud of our team spirit and our camaraderie. Who was now putting this in jeopardy?

"Complaints about you, Peter." I heard those sounds come out of Kevin's mouth, but I did not immediately register them as actual words. My mind drifted, attempting to make sense of what he had just said. Then he continued.

Two women have accused me of sexual harassment, Kevin told me. The company would now need to investigate the claims. I would receive an update on the matter soon from John Kapioltas and Jim Smith, the corporate director of human resources in Boston.

I scanned my mind and tried to create a mental picture of our entire staff, wondering which employees could have thought that I was sexually harassing them. My face felt numb. All I could manage to say was, "Who?"

He cannot reveal their names, Kevin said, since the investigation is now underway.

"How come those allegations have reached your level?" I asked Kevin. "Who spoke to you?"

Anne Power, our HR director, had informed him of the allegations some time ago, he told me.

"Why didn't Anne speak to me first?" I asked.

Because she was afraid of me, her general manager, Kevin replied.

"Bullshit," I blurted out. This sounded fishy to me, to say the least. Anne Power was not someone who would have any reason to be afraid of me. She was an outspoken and tough director of HR, and I valued her as a dedicated and productive member of the staff. She was not a colleague with whom I had a jovial working friendship, as I did with Joe Prezioso and others on my team, but she got the job done well and was highly competent.

I also knew that Anne and Kevin had a close friendship and often went out drinking together after work. So I asked Kevin, why had he not told me before that these sexual harassment claims had been made against me?

He told me that he was instructed not to.

Before Kevin left my office, I said, "I would recommend that you investigate and talk to as many people as possible in the hotel so that you have a fair evaluation of those charges."

Kevin asked me which staff members he should speak with. I told him to go out and speak with anyone and everyone at the hotel. "You can start with my assistant, Maria," I said. He left, and I saw that he stopped by Maria's desk for less than two minutes before walking away. I later learned Maria had recommended he talk to Ann Barzola, a banquet manager. Kevin apparently spoke with her very briefly too, and that was that.

As Kevin left my office, I tried to sort out the thousand questions racing through my mind, above all: What was this all about?

A Call from My Friend the President

The next thing I knew, John Kapioltas called to speak with me. At first, I thought he was calling to express sympathy and encouragement, but his voice had a note of resignation as he told me that the whole matter had been taken out of his hands and there was nothing he could do about it. He then hung up, appearing to be in a hurry. More likely he was trying to avoid any of the questions I might ask him.

Strange. This did not sound like the John Kapioltas I knew, my longtime colleague and friend, one of the most powerful executives at the company. Then my mind flashed back to our days together in Brussels, when John always seemed to be absent from the office anytime a personnel issue reared its head or whenever Roger Senter was in town to fire someone. Where was John? No one really knew. He remained invisible, pretending to be traveling so he could avoid the moments he hated most.

This time around was no exception. John was supposed to check into the St. Regis the following day, but he had cancelled his reservation and moved to the Sheraton Centre. I should have known that something was cooking.

For the following three days, I did my job in a daze, sensing a giant storm brewing behind my back but unsure what to do, as I had no information whatsoever and no instructions. Anne Power avoided my calls, even though we needed to communicate in order for both of us to do our jobs. When I finally spoke to her, I said, "Anne, I respect this. I don't want to put you in an uncomfortable position, but we have to go on with business as usual, so let's put this aside for now."

Thinking back, I should have contacted an aggressive, street-smart lawyer right away to take the initiative, to go into an offensive mode, and threaten ITT with a defamation of character lawsuit before they confronted me with a fait accompli. But at this very moment, the idea to do so was far from my mind.

I didn't hear any more about the issue until that Wednesday, the day of the routine board meeting for Sheraton executives. Jim Smith, the corporate director of HR in Boston, had come to New York to sit in on it. Jim called me right before the meeting started to tell me that he wanted to see me in the afternoon, after the board had convened. I later learned that Anne Power had been called in to attend the meeting. As for myself, I typically did not attend board meetings, and I was not called in to this one.

I sat in my office, nervously waiting for Jim's call. I had planned to see Denyse off to the airport that afternoon, and I tried to occupy my mind by helping her with last-minute trip preparations. I informed her of nothing at this point, not wanting to worry her unnecessarily before vacation.

At around 4:00 p.m., I received a call to go up to Jim Smith's suite at the St. Regis. I found him sitting there with one of ITT's lawyers. At this moment, I should have walked out of Jim's suite and tried to find legal assistance immediately instead of sitting there all by myself, but again I was not prepared for this. The element of surprise was definitely on Jim Smith's side.

The investigation is over, Jim told me. The appointed committee had interviewed the two women and found their statements believable.

Over? How could the investigation be over? No one had spoken to me about anything yet. Who were the two women? Could he at least tell me now? I was still in the dark about everything.

One was Anne Power, the HR director, and the other was Jennifer Hall, assistant director of HR, Jim told me. After he said their two names, he sat there looking at me.

Anne Power? Jennifer Hall? Those were the two women making the claims? My mind was racing. How? Why? What did they say?

As Jim read the complaints aloud to me, I must have heard only 10 percent of what he said. I sat in the chair across from him, trying to make sense of what I was hearing.

Apparently, Jennifer had complained that on Valentine's Day I gave out roses to the female staff of the pre-opening office, and I asked her for a kiss.

The Valentine's Day roses? Yes, it was my idea to give roses to all the female employees for the holiday, but my assistant Maria usually handed them out. Last year, I remember that Kathi Ransom gave out the roses. We had also recently started to include the male staff members too, since some of them joked that they were jealous.

As for Jennifer's other claim, I never asked her, or anyone, for a kiss. It would be ridiculous to do so. I did vaguely remember a joking conversation with Jennifer after the roses were passed out one year. I remember her asking something like "Are you my Valentine?" and I may have replied by tapping my cheek in jest. Our work dynamic had always been positive and professional, in my mind, and our entire pre-opening office tended to joke around and maintain a humorous camaraderie. Most of us have remained friends to this day. Jennifer's claim seemed confusing, and I kept running the scenario through my mind.

But there was more. Jim told me that Jennifer said I had once attempted to push her into the office closet. I again tried to understand what she was referring to. In our pre-opening office, the hallway door and the closet door were side by side. Jennifer was claiming that one time, after she accidentally opened the closet instead of the hallway door, I had tried to push her in. But there was no way I could have done this, as I had traditionally remained at my desk when an associate was leaving my office, and the closet was completely full of unpacked boxes and other stuff stored in this closet to keep my office clean and tidy. It was impossible to even open the door without some of the stuff toppling out.

As we were working together closely as a team, jokes were made, some perhaps ill-conceived. But our whole team—perhaps wrongly—made humorous comments in those days when we all worked in the same space for long hours. Why was this coming up now? Especially since Jennifer and I and our entire pre-opening staff had maintained what I thought was a supportive and cheerful working atmosphere for all this time?

I was also surprised and puzzled by Anne Power's claims. She alleged that I would sometimes put my arm around her and that this made her uncomfortable.

While it was true that I frequently put my arm, in a fatherly way, around a colleague or clasped a shoulder as a show of support, I did this with men as well as women on staff.

Again, today I would not do this, and perhaps I never should have. But to me, it was always a gesture of goodwill and certainly not intended as flirtatious or sexual.

I thought of myself as a difficult boss who also made a point to show support to my team and perhaps, at times, to act as a parental figure. Patting people on the shoulder was part of this. Another is that I tended to correct what I thought were poor grooming practices that did not serve employees well and could also hurt our hotel's image. My colleague Jeremy Schuster once got upset because I put my hand on his face and told him he needed to shave. He protested that it was Sunday night and that he always shaves twice on workdays but not on Sunday. He did not complain that I touched his face, but then again, perhaps I should not have done so. Perhaps grabbing his face was too physical, and I had no business doing this.

Today I'm still in friendly contact with Jeremy, who now lives with his wife in Paris, and when the discussion turns to this subject, we both laugh.

Our dress code asked the female staff at the front of the house to wear heels instead of flats to work, since in my opinion heels create a more polished look and project a style more consistent with the St. Regis image. I understand that this is now an outdated point of view, but this is what I had seen in the many luxury hotels I had worked in and visited.

My sense had been that what was good for them should certainly be good for the St. Regis.

My management style was partly a function of what I had learned from my past jobs in Europe and partly my own tendency to communicate in an old-fashioned manner, with gestures that understandably no longer had a place in the environment of a modern American hotel.

Perhaps I was out of touch with reality. But I strongly believe that no one should be harassed, sexually or otherwise. I had labored every day to create an atmosphere of respect and professionalism among the entire staff. I suppose when people are in close working quarters from morning to night for months or years, sensitivities can arise. I experienced this from both sides, but in my mind, the incidents that I witnessed or participated in represented clashing work styles, not harassment or anything other than misunderstanding.

Some time ago, at the Carlton Hotel in Washington, D.C., which I continued to oversee during the time when the St. Regis was closed for renovation, I had put my hand on the elbow of a restaurant hostess who was resting her arm on the podium and turning her back to the restaurant entrance. Since she was leaning over and appearing to nap on the podium during work hours, I found her behavior unprofessional, and I had attempted to correct it. My reaction made her angry, and she brought sexual harassment charges against me. Then she changed her mind and claimed physical assault, then changed the claim back again to sexual harassment. The judge dismissed her case.

Jim brought this incident up again as I sat in his office, listening to him describe Jennifer and Anne's claims.

By this point, the numbness in my mind began to fade, and I could focus again. I was upset now, and felt I was getting bullied by HR and the lawyer. They gave me no chance to ask questions or attempt to understand what was happening to me.

"How come nobody from the committee ever contacted me to ask for my response or my side of the story?" I asked.

Jim said this was not necessary anymore because the statements from the women in question were believable enough.

"We've made the decision to remove you from your role." As Jim spoke these words, I felt I was not hearing him correctly at first. I had the sense that the floor had disappeared under my feet.

He sat there looking at me, silently. I could feel my body tremble. My head was spinning. Everything around me seemed surreal, like a sinister dream that I kept trying to wake up from but could not.

Jim appeared to be done speaking with me. I would have no chance to give my response to all of this, to attempt to reach an understanding and make sense of the situation. The decision to fire me was already made. As I sat there motionless, Jim continued. "By the way, as of now we don't want you to talk to any employee of the hotel." Nothing could surprise me anymore at this point, but I was wondering what they are afraid of if I were to speak with employees.

As they didn't want me to go into my office anymore, Jim said, I should pick up my personal belongings immediately. From this point on, Donald Crossfield will be taking over my GM duties.

In a day full of surprises, this was the only development that did not surprise me.

But I soon found out there was no danger of my making any forbidden revelations. The word was already out. The news had spread like wildfire through the entire hotel.

In a daze, I stuffed the personal materials in my office into a big box, then I went to my apartment. Denyse, Carine, and Peter Jr. were en route to Austria. I had no idea how to tell my family about what had just happened.

I needed to talk to a friend, but everyone at the hotel was off-limits now according to Jim. So I left the building and went to see my acquaintance Philip Alfus. Philip had consulted for me in identifying candidates for the St. Regis chef positions and had helped with other searches. Philip and I had a friendly working relationship, and I felt I could confide in him.

It was a good thing that Philip's office was on Sixth Avenue, far enough from the hotel but still only a short walk away. After I told him the news, I broke into tears. I almost never do this in front of people, and I felt embarrassed. But in that moment, as I began to understand the full reality of what was happening to me, I was relieved not to be alone.

I spent the rest of the day in my family's apartment. In the early evening, I reached Denyse in Austria. She had just arrived in our apartment in Konigsleiten.

"Do you want me to come back?" Denyse asked immediately when I told her what had just happened.

I wanted to say yes, to ask her to please cut the vacation short and come back right away. But I insisted that she stay.

"Don't worry," I said. "I will find a solution to this."

Denyse wasn't convinced she should stay in Austria, but she agreed, for now. During our entire conversation, she did not say, "What did you do?" She did not say, "How could you?" All she said was that she loved me, and she wished I could be in Austria with her right now. "Are you sure you don't want me to come back?" she repeated.

I was overcome with emotion once again. Yes, I wanted Denyse and my family here with me. I needed their support. I needed to talk about what was happening to me and attempt to make sense of the situation and begin to pick up the pieces if I could. But ending their vacation on the day it began seemed to me a cruel thing to do to my family, after a very stressful few years, and especially now on top of the news about my immediate termination.

My head was still spinning. I had promised Denyse that I would find a solution. But what solution? I had no ideas at the moment. My company had already made up its mind. I could not speak to my now-former colleagues, not the ones who had made claims against me, and not any of the other team members either. I sat on a sofa in our living room, wondering if I should simply begin to count the days until my family was back and I had someone to talk to.

My isolation ended quickly. The doorbell rang soon after I hung up with Denyse.

Standing at my doorstep were a few of my colleagues. They had come by to express sorrow about what had just happened. Some seemed sad, some angry. Monika Krebs, the assistant director of housekeeping, told me that the employees in her department wanted to put down their work and protest on Fifty-Fifth Street. I convinced her not to do this. Nonetheless, she had with her a list of all the employees who had so far signed a petition protesting my termination. I saw a pile of stapled pages, dozens of names on each page. I appreciated the effort, but everything seemed futile at this point.

Maria, my assistant, called soon afterward to express her regrets. Even though Jim had asked me not to talk with anyone, my colleagues already knew, and I needed their support and friendship in order to keep my sanity as my life fell to pieces around me. Back in my apartment, the rooms felt quieter than ever, a chilling emptiness all around as I tried in vain to fall asleep.

The next day, I called my former resident manager, August Cerradini, who was now the president of Circle Line cruises. I trusted his advice, and since he no longer worked for Sheraton, I could call him without violating any agreement.

"You need a lawyer," August said to me as soon as I briefed him on the events. "I know somebody."

The next day, I called August's contact, a lawyer named Robert Thompson. "It looks like you have a very good case," Robert told me, "because this situation has not been properly handled." But he said he cannot defend me because he typically represents companies in cases like this. He doesn't take employee cases, but he might have someone else for me.

At least these conversations gave me something to do other than merely sitting and waiting for my family to return from vacation. Staying busy has always been my coping mechanism, and now my suddenly busy agenda of phone calls and visits was coming to my rescue.

I needed every distraction I could think of to keep my mind off the catastrophe that was unfolding in my life. Why had this all happened so suddenly? Why did I have no chance to answer or apologize or explain or create any kind of reconciliation?

Only one person would know the answers to all these questions, John Kapioltas, but he was in hiding, and despite various attempts to get in touch with him, he never called back.

I kept turning these questions over in my mind, as I picked up the phone to make a call that could change my life.

My Family, a Strong Support

Letter from Denyse in French, from Konigsleiten, dated Saturday, March 21, 1992:

> *We will get over these difficulties together, and I'm sure that one day you'll see happier moments . . . I'll be by your side in a few days . . . I know the day will come when these problems created by an unprecedented jealousy will be in your past. A thousand kisses. Denyse.*

Fax from Peter Jr. and Denyse, from Konigsleiten, dated March 15, 1992:

> *We send hugs and kisses and bon courage. Keep the faith. Peter Jr. and Denyse.*

Letter from Carine, from Dartmouth, dated March 17, 1992:

> *I want you to know that no matter what, you are and will always be the family's superhero . . . Things will work out, I know it . . . You'll end up in a place where your hard work and dedication are well-respected . . . If not in the Big Apple, then maybe California or . . . The world is a big and exciting place. Where do you want to go? . . . Daddy, I just want to say, keep your head up. We are all with you!*

Steven Eckhaus, the litigation lawyer whom August Cerradini's friend recommended, had his office in the Helmsley Building on Park Avenue, a historic thirty-four-story tower with a soaring marble and bronze lobby. I would come to know this man quite well over the following months, but our first meeting began with a conversation similar to what happens when you are deciding whether to buy a car and you try to kick its tires first.

Guessing from his name that he was Jewish, I asked him whether he might have any issues representing me, a German. I wanted a lawyer who would believe in my case completely, not someone who might have any reservations about me as a result of what had happened not so long ago in Germany.

I posed this question to him directly. Perhaps I raised it too abruptly, but he did not seem perturbed. He answered me by saying that his grandparents were killed by the Nazi regime in Germany, but that no, he had no problem defending a German client. So here we were, a German executive wrongly fired by his company and a Jewish lawyer whose family members had died in the Holocaust, agreeing to take the case and promising a strong defense. I could tell he was a talented lawyer, and as the weeks went by, we developed a very close relationship. I began to spend so much time in his office that he joked about hiring me as a legal assistant.

Given the financial straits that Denyse and I found ourselves in all of a sudden, maybe I should have asked him where I could pick up an application for this job.

From the moment Steven agreed to take my case, I knew I would be in good hands.

Meanwhile, Denyse and I had not only lost our livelihood, we were also in the process of losing our apartment. ITT informed me that as I was no longer employed by them, I had to evacuate the apartment immediately. Company representatives had already removed some of our personal belongings from our home and placed them outside in the hallway. Again, I needed legal help in fighting this move. Steven suggested I hire a special attorney who knows real estate law, so I took his advice. But despite that lawyer's efforts, Denyse and I ended up having to vacate the apartment in the end. We rented an apartment on Fifty-Seventh Street for a time and later stayed in studios or empty rooms that friends let us borrow, a situation as unsettling as it was humiliating.

My opponents on the ITT side continued to unravel every aspect of my life that they could get their hands on. First, they canceled my medical insurance, then they objected to my application for unemployment-related medical benefits. They also denied me the severance package in my contract. As it appeared, they wanted to demolish me to the point where I would give up, pack my belongings, and leave the country. The faster, the better; the further, the better. But I was not prepared to do them this favor.

Steven had a very big job to do, and we spent hours talking every week as he planned my defense. But even though I could have easily spent all day working with Steven on the case, I needed to find a job. Denyse and I had two Ivy League tuitions to pay, not to mention our rent and living expenses. We had no money coming in, not even New York State unemployment benefits since ITT had tied those up in court too. My wife, who had not worked since her first pregnancy, became the chief financial officer of our family. By finding ways to tighten our belts in every area of our lives, she kept our heads above water for the time being.

We still needed paid employment, however, and Denyse managed to find a job before I did. Fortunately, close friends of ours who own an antiques shop on Madison Avenue offered her a position doing the bookkeeping for their store.

My own attempts to find work went nowhere. The hotel industry is a very small world. I must have written a hundred applications to every major hotel company, but the only responses I received, if I received any at all, were "No, we're sorry." News spreads quickly. My reputation was destroyed based on manufactured facts and lies, but ITT had achieved their objective. Finding a job in America was close to impossible for me now because no hotel company in the world would touch a hot potato like me. I understood their reasons because none of them could afford to take any chances in a highly competitive industry like this.

If only I could have included, along with my job application and resumé, some of the letters my staff wrote to me.

"I feel terribly hurt for you and for your family. We have lost a lot, a great leader. The St. Regis is your dream, our dream, my dream. No one will forget that. I want to thank you again for having given me hope and a dream," wrote Jocelyne D'Amblard, a member of the butler staff.

"Your enthusiasm and your kindness are the reason I joined the St. Regis team. You have given me much inspiration," wrote Holly Walsh, another of the maîtres d'etage.

"When you weren't racing, you often took the time to place your hand on my shoulder and ask in your unforgettable accent, 'How are you doing today, Miss Woodstock?' Those moments were meaningful to me and gave me strength," wrote Jude Woodstock some time later. Jude was the assistant sales and marketing director who worked with Rick Fleming. She later married Jan Rozenveld, one of the most talented butlers on the team.

"The St. Regis will stand as a monument to your memorable tenure and above all, what you achieved in its restoration for all of America to see," the chief telephone operator Kathleen Kennedy wrote.

"You have shown yourself to be a gentleman, a man who listens to all sides and then decides on the best option, a man who is proud of and supportive of those who work beside him," wrote Geoffrey Haberer, "a man who loves his family, speaking highly of his wife and gifted children. I hope and pray you can forgive those who attacked and denigrated your character and abilities."

Meanwhile, the letters Denyse had started writing to me while she was in Austria continued for quite some time afterward. My wife's handwritten notes expressed her love and loyalty and her pain and confusion about this crisis.

"Who are these enemies? Can these people go to sleep every night with their mind in peace? Their bad conscience is going to hurt them all their lives," she wrote in one letter. In another she said, "Life can be very hard sometimes. But thank God we still have hope."

Denyse wrote some of the notes to herself at first and shared them with me only later. One of those caused me enormous pain when I read it.

"I thought I knew Peter," she wrote, during the early phase of the crisis. "I know he doesn't like to share his professional problems with the family, but in a situation like this, I don't understand why he left me in the dark. He doesn't think I can handle problems? I only understood yesterday from Carine that a week ago, he knew that there is an investigation going on against him. He had no idea from whom or where. Why didn't he tell me? He probably didn't want to worry me. So what? Either we share our problems and our happiness together or why am I still with him then? He has no confidence in me. Am I not strong enough to take it?"

But as the weeks went by, most of Denyse's letters expressed a hopeful note despite our struggles, and they kept me going during the days when I was losing strength. "Hope is the only thing to get us through our daily problems. Hope for better days. Maybe this is a sign that there's something better waiting," Denyse wrote.

Carine and Peter Jr. called frequently, week after week, to check on how I was doing. Joe Prezioso, Jude Woodstock, Philip Alfus, Maria Peralta, and many other colleagues and friends called on a regular basis too, offering support and strength.

Meanwhile, the petition Monika Krebs had shown me continued to circulate among staff to protest my firing. "Some of us have known this man ever since he came to the St. Regis in 1985, and we cannot take the charges that were made against him. We are angry at the way this company has treated a loyal employee who has devoted twenty years of his life to the ITT Sheraton company and demand that he receives justice and that he be treated fairly." By the time the petition made its way to the corporate office, more than 150 employees had signed it.

But not everyone took my side.

The Punishment Which Doesn't Fit the Crime

Oprah Winfrey, the famous talk show host, once made the following statement:

> *Lots of people want to ride with you in the limousine,*
> *but what you want is someone who will take the bus*
> *with you when the limousine breaks down.*

One afternoon not long after I was fired, I had a disturbing encounter with my former travel companion Rick Fleming, the director of sales and marketing. As Rick and I walked toward each other on a sidewalk on Madison Avenue, we made brief eye contact. Just as I was about to greet him from afar, he crossed over to the other side of the street. Perhaps he thought I hadn't seen him yet. In any event, it was obvious he wanted to avoid interacting with me, even to risk simply saying hello, because somebody could have seen him talking to me. And just as he would have continued to lay down on the street until it got dark, as he confessed to me that day when I saw him trip years ago, Rick was not prepared to jeopardize his career by getting noticed with his former boss. His instinct was perhaps right, because a few months later, Rick was named resident manager of the hotel.

Rick was not the only former colleague who avoided me, despite our formerly friendly working relationship. Christel Schmitt, the director of housekeeping, sent me a letter of support around the time of my firing, but she too avoided me soon afterward. Her deputy, Monika Krebs, continued to check in with me and express solidarity as I endured ITT Sheraton's campaign to discredit me and deny me all my unemployment benefits. The rest of the housekeeping staff remained on my side too, at least vocally, but Christel perhaps felt she was better off cutting off any contact with me whatsoever, following the example of Rick Fleming.

I later learned that Donald Crossfield too had repeatedly warned the employees not to talk to me if they didn't want to jeopardize their employment with the St. Regis.

Even if only a few of my former staff members dodged me, or seemed unsure what to say, and even if the majority of the team took my side, the fact that some ex-colleagues began to doubt me was enough to demoralize me in the weeks after my life fell apart.

All I could think about, every day and every night, was how or why this was happening to me.

If my management style was too brusque at times, or too physical, for example when I patted associates on the shoulder or grabbed a cheek to tell an employee to shave, and if my joking remarks were inappropriate, then I should have been told to change my habits. I would have apologized to the staff members who were affected. I would have done so, if I had known at the time that they were upset, just as I had apologized to Maria, my secretary, when she became angry with me for tidying up her office. Perhaps my style was out of touch with contemporary norms, and if so, I realized it was my own responsibility to make adjustments.

But I had worked hard to build a supportive team atmosphere, one in which everyone felt equally respected and valued. If I made some people uncomfortable, it should have been the responsibility of the human resources department to give me feedback about this, even anonymously, instead of using the comments as a strategy by which to fire me without giving me any chance to defend myself. Was my behavior so egregious as to deserve this kind of treatment? I was not sexually harassing anyone. I believed this strongly, and I felt my actions had been misunderstood and used as a welcome excuse to remove me from the hotel for reasons I did not know about until now.

The punishment did not fit the crime. Something seemed fishy.

Was there another motive behind this all? I began to wonder. Was my salary perhaps too high for ITT's comfort, in an era when the luxury hotel sector was facing economic challenges? Was the St. Regis's room occupancy too low, at a time when ITT was under pressure to achieve a healthier bottom line, especially after the $100–$200 million the company spent on the renovation?

Should I have been focusing more intently on occupancy and taking more frequent marketing trips with Rick Fleming to secure more business for the hotel, as GMs of competing luxury hotels increasingly started to do? It's true that I preferred to spend all my time running the hotel and perfecting every aspect of it, but would I have been in a better position had I played more of a part in marketing the hotel?

How about Kevin Richwood's role in all this? Did he consider me an obstacle in his attempts to secure contracts more favorable to the unions? When he brought the supposed charges against me to the attention of Jim Smith in the Boston HR office, was it a revenge tactic because I had fired his friend Ilona?

Was it significant that one of the women making the sexual harassment charges was Anne Power, with whom Kevin had a drinking-buddies friendship and, perhaps, similar goals?

Did Jennifer Hall, who seemed to worship her boss Anne and do everything she said, go along with this scheme as a means of remaining loyal to Anne?

Was Kevin's move merely part of a long-brewing plan by ITT to place Donald Crossfield in the plum position?

Not all the theories I came up with were true, perhaps, but I became more certain that there was more to the story than I had been told. Pieces began to fit together. I remembered that John Kapioltas had asked me the previous summer if I might be interested in moving to Santiago in Chile. "Why? Are you trying to get rid of me?" I had asked him jokingly at the time.

"No," he answered, "but I thought you might like to know about other opportunities."

I later learned that in January, two months before the sexual harassment debacle, John had discussed with ITT executives the potential of moving me to a Sheraton in Bangkok.

There was no doubt about it: I should have sought the help of an aggressive lawyer from the minute Kevin Richwood walked into my office to confront me with these unfounded accusations.

Oddly, the media's coverage of my departure made no mention of sexual harassment in the initial weeks after my firing. Somehow, the word had not yet leaked to the press. Instead, columnists advanced a variety of theories and stories about my sudden disappearance from the St. Regis.

An item in a column in *Crain's New York Business* on March 30, 1992, appeared under the headline "Dethroned at the St. Regis" and suggested that ITT Sheraton's decision to fire me was because they were "reportedly miffed at the swank property's less-than-sterling performance."

A column in the *New York Observer* by Deborah Mitchell, on April 4, published the news about me as its lead item, noting that ITT was calling my dismissal "a management action." It quoted Dolores Sanchez, a company spokesperson, saying, "We're not defining that management action as actual dismissal." The column also disputed a rumor floating around at the time that I was whisked away from the St. Regis in a limousine and never came back.

And even Cindy Adams, the *New York Post's* famous gossip columnist, devoted a few words to questioning why I had left the hotel so suddenly. "Que pasa, I don't know," she wrote.

Another article in *Crain's* the week after, this one by the journalist Yolanda Gault, carried the headline "Why Hotel GMs Are Checking Out." The article noted that "General managers at five deluxe properties have left their posts over the past few weeks. These veterans have become casualties of a market whose harshness continues to grate on operating profits and occupancy levels." It added that "though explanations vary with each hotel, the St. Regis, Drake, Helmsley Palace, Regency, and Peninsula New York all replaced general managers last month."

The *Crain's* report mentions myself and the other general managers by name, but it doesn't say anything else about why I was fired. The article also describes a shift in the role that GMs of luxury hotels are expected to do nowadays, including marketing and sales. Hoteliers, the article notes, "are having trouble meeting one of their chief performance criteria, profit per room."

The company's behavior toward me had been so swift and secretive, and its reasons for firing me so lacking in any believable grounds, that I could not keep myself from trying to puzzle out what had motivated the firing beyond what they told me. ITT was certainly no stranger to secret motives and dark behind-the-scenes maneuverings. In fact, ITT had a long history of behavior that would make the Mafia jealous.

Soon after it first launched in the 1920s as a telephone company, ITT expanded into manufacturing and sold planes to Axis forces during World War II. One of its co-founders, a naturalized American citizen from the Virgin Islands, named Sosthenes Behn, reportedly visited Hitler in 1993 and referred to him later as a "gentleman," according to a book titled *The Sovereign State of ITT* by Anthony Sampson.

Over the decades, ITT had grown into a conglomerate, selling everything from Wonder Bread to military radars. Even though it was well-known in certain circles that the company had worked with the CIA to instigate Allende's ouster in Chile in order to keep the government from nationalizing phone services, ITT continued to expand its worldwide influence into the twenty-first century.

Although ITT was in more difficult financial straits by now, and Rand Araskog was under fire for an extravagantly high compensation package that was completely out of step with the company's performance, ITT still had deep pockets. But the hotel world was tough and getting even more competitive, and perhaps attacking me in this way seemed an effective strategy for cutting costs, avoiding paying me an expensive severance package, and replacing me with someone who was more of a corporate game-player.

Whatever the motives, I knew this much: The company to which I had devoted the past two decades of my life was now engaged in destroying everything I had and everything I had built. However, one thing seemed to become clearer every day since ITT published its statement concerning my departure: That the decision about my firing was made on Park Avenue, and all the false, fabricated accusations were simply tools used to follow those orders.

It was time to fight back.

An Emotionally Draining Nightmare

My life as I knew it was over. A hurricane had blown through my world and wrecked everything in its path. But at least one thing gave me some sense of order. I had hired the right lawyer.

Steven Eckhaus knew how to battle companies like ITT. He wasted no time in starting our campaign, filing a claim in labor court in mid-April. Steven disputed ITT's claim that I had been fired for misconduct, which would have disqualified me from collecting my severance package as well as my New York State unemployment benefits.

Our first move succeeded. After several days of hearings in labor court, the New York State Department of Labor's Administrative Law judge Irwin Silberlicht filed a decision stating that my firing was unjust, as was the denial of my unemployment benefits.

"The evidence fails to establish any sexual harassment on the part of the claimant and therefore there is no misconduct in connection with employment on the part of the claimant," the decision stated. "The witnesses' testimony regarding these acts of sexual harassment is suspect and rejected. Claimant's contention that he did not do what he is accused of is accepted . . . I find that the claimant's testimony regarding these events was honest and truthful and I reject the testimony of the Director and Assistant Director of Human Resources."

The judge's decision felt like an enormous victory and a vindication that I had done nothing wrong. I knew that ITT would appeal the decision, but if upheld, it would mean that I could now receive my $364,000 severance package plus interest. I could also receive unemployment benefits from the state and recoup the retroactive benefits payments I had been denied until this point.

This victory came soon after another piece of good news, even though by this point I could hardly enjoy it. A few weeks before, in December 1992, I had received a letter from Mobil announcing that the St. Regis had earned its coveted five-star award. One of the goals of the reopening had been to earn this distinction within less than two years, and now the hotel had done so well in advance of the goal, although several months after I had been fired.

Steven felt that our victory in labor court gave us solid grounds to file a complaint suing for reinstatement of my job at the St. Regis, along with punitive and compensatory damages and attorney fees.

"Although this is an important decision and supports our claims," I wrote in my personal notebook after our labor court success, "we still have a way to go."

Mr. Eckhaus's next move was to file a complaint against ITT in the United States District Court for the Southern District of New York, seeking a judgment that I was entitled to severance. In response, ITT filed a motion for summary judgment, seeking to dismiss the complaint. ITT also appealed to the Appellate Division of the New York State courts, seeking to reverse the decision of the labor court.

In a written decision, United States District Judge Shirley Wohl Kram denied ITT's motion for summary judgment, ruling that the matter should proceed to trial on the question of my entitlement to severance.

At least Judge Kram had denied ITT's efforts to dismiss our case. But I braced myself for the grim experience of sitting in court and watching the ITT lawyers attempt to make their case.

When the trial finally began in September 1996, it was a sordid spectacle for everyone involved. I found myself in federal district court for a twelve-day jury trial, one of the longest week-and-a-half periods of my life. Anne Power and Jennifer Hall each took the stand and made their accusations against me, detailing the claims that Jim Smith had told me about.

Denyse, Carine, and Peter Jr. sat in the courtroom and watched, day after day. I felt humiliated that my family had to hear these accusations and to bear witness as my reputation and career fell apart. But my wife and children offered nothing but love and support and loyalty, through every miserable hour of every day in court.

When Jennifer Hall was called as a witness, she appeared drugged, speaking in a halting way that I had never seen her do before as she elaborated on the charges she had made against me. In addition, she started bringing up some more fabricated details, ones she had never mentioned in her earlier deposition. She was lying from the beginning to the end in a performance that seemed to have been orchestrated and rehearsed with Paul Anthony, ITT's lawyer.

To relieve anxiety, and sometimes just to pass the time, I drew sketches as I sat there in court during those long days. I drew pictures of the witnesses and created cartoons or designs to represent what I thought was happening: Jennifer Hall and Anne Power getting manipulated by ITT's lawyer Paul Anthony, or John Kapioltas not willing to hurt his own career and suddenly not remembering anymore what he had testified in his deposition and contradicting himself as Steven Eckhaus cross-examined him. John looked extremely uncomfortable on the witness stand, and I didn't know if I should feel sorry for him or if I should be happy to see his testimony working in our favor.

At long last, after the testimonies finally ended but before the jury began its deliberations, ITT Sheraton's side tried once again to move for summary judgment on the basis that I had failed to prove that I had been fired and denied severance payments arbitrarily or in bad faith. But the judge denied their motion, and the trial went to the jury.

After an agonizing wait, filled with a growing sense of terror about what the future would hold for me if this case ended badly, the jury finally announced its verdict. They had found in my favor.

I won the case.

Perhaps I should have been relieved, but the whole experience had been such a long and vivid nightmare that it was hard to wake up from all of this.

But the bad dream was far from over, as I would soon find out. Even though the jury determined that I had not sexually harassed anyone and I should receive my severance, ITT asked the court to reconsider whether I was entitled to severance under the Employment Retirement Security Act.

In the end, exactly six months to the day after the jury verdict, United States Magistrate Judge Michael H. Dollinger, who now presided over the case, decided that under ERISA I should not have had a jury trial. He treated the jury's verdict as advisory only and reversed the jury verdict. Suddenly, ITT had won the case. What I thought had been a victorious result turned out, after all the twists and turns, to have a devastating conclusion.

"We find Ms. Hall and Ms. Power to be entirely credible in recounting their dealings with the plaintiff," Judge Dollinger wrote in his opinion. "As for Mr. Tischmann's account of these incidents, his testimony was equivocal as to some of the charges—typified by failure to recall incidents rather than denials—and he denied certain of the more lurid events. To the extent that his testimony conflicted with that of the complainants, I reject his version as not worthy of belief."

At this point, the Appellate Division handed down its decision on ITT's appeal of the Labor Court findings. The Appellate Division dismissed ITT's appeal, holding that the evidence did not support the charge of sexual harassment, and the Labor Court's decision was supported by substantial evidence.

So the Labor Court found in my favor, the Appellate Division found in my favor, Judge Shirley Wohl Kram found in my favor, and a federal jury found in my favor. Only Judge Dollinger, finding me "not worthy of belief," ruled against me.

Not worthy of belief. So that was that. This was the end of the road. There was no point in continuing with more appeals, more misery, more months and years spent on this chapter.

In the final analysis, I got nothing. Not my job back, and not my severance. Only a reputation in tatters. I could not conceal my suspicion that ITT had interfered in the judgment. Six months was certainly enough time to do so, and the final results were enough to severely damage my trust in the United States justice system. Money talks, even in court, or so it appeared to me.

Fortunately, some happier developments were taking place in the meantime, including Carine's graduation cum laude from Dartmouth in June of 1993. A few months before that, in April of that year, Denyse and I had attended a parents' night with Peter Jr. at Cornell, where we saw none other than Donald Crossfield and his wife, who were also parents of a Cornell student. On the program for the evening, the guest biographies listed me as vice president and managing director of the St. Regis Hotel in New York City. Donald's biography simply stated that he works for the St. Regis.

This was a dark irony, but it struck Denyse and me as quite funny, at a time when we needed any excuse for humor. That evening, I noticed Donald was acting even more uneasy than I felt and appeared to go out of his way to avoid any coincidental meeting.

Back home in Manhattan, the grim reality of our new lives continued, without many rays of light except for the achievements of our children, and the strengthened bond Denyse and I felt with each other in the face of the current situation.

At least by now, I had started collecting the state unemployment benefits that were owed to me, along with the back pay that was withheld when ITT tried to prevent me from receiving the payments. The checks amounted to only a few hundred dollars a month, but that was better than the zero I had been receiving since my dismissal.

The only positive outcome is that the experience was finally over, an experience that had emotionally drained me and my family and everyone involved and dragged out the humiliation for years. By the end, I felt completely depleted and even angrier and more perplexed than when this all started. How could two decades of hard work and loyalty to the company, of dedication to my staff and to the hotel, end in this way?

But in life, as I have learned, it does not pay to simply feel wronged about a situation that does not go the way we would like. Wallowing in anger, week after week, month after month, year after year, only threatens to eat away at everything else that remains positive in our lives and prevents the possibility of moving forward into a new chapter. I needed to take a step back and reflect on what had happened.

In my career so far, anytime I faced a challenge, I had always attempted to think about the big picture. I tried to do so now, as overwhelmed as I still felt by the outcome of the case.

I thought about my career and my life and my family and my future. I examined the decisions I had made along the way, and my motivations and actions and behaviors, to see what I could learn from what had transpired in my life so far and how I could improve as a person and as a professional.

This was a time for me to meditate on the events that had shaken up my life. I knew that I may not come up with any answers immediately, but I committed myself to thinking through the past few years of my life, through the dense fog of the court case and the despair that I now felt.

My thoughts kept coming back to this: If the so-called sexual harassment charges had been made sincerely, if someone truly felt uncomfortable and believed I had been creating a hostile work environment, to use the legal term, then it would upset me to know that I had done this. I do not respect or support this kind of behavior in others, and the last thing I would ever want to do is to create any sense that I was defending such actions, not to mention partaking in them.

But it would seem only fair that I or anyone accused should have the benefit of a complete investigation. Instead, I found myself subjected to a kangaroo court atmosphere from the very beginning of the crisis, and I had received a quick and haphazard judgment from my company. ITT Sheraton had made decisions with absolutely no input from me and with only the most minimal input from the hundreds of staff members at the hotel who vouched in my favor.

I have to admit that when the Clarence Thomas case went before the Supreme Court in the late summer of 1991, during the week when we reopened the St. Regis, I initially felt sorry for the man. A colleague had accused him of sexual harassment, and he had no way of proving that he did not do the things of which he was accused. Although he was eventually confirmed to the court, his name became forever associated with these charges.

I realize that these situations are difficult to assess and that they often take place behind closed doors. When sexual harassment occurs, how can the victim prove that it did in fact happen? I know that women often face resistance or ridicule when they bring up charges like these and that they often decide not to bring them forward at all for fear of risking their reputation or their career. The perpetrator often pays no price at all. This is an unjust situation, and I understand that the complicated legal procedures related to sexual harassment are an attempt to remedy this. But what about the accused person? If someone is accused of an act that he or she did not commit, and that no one witnessed, how can this person receive justice in an environment like the one that ITT Sheraton created?

In my own specific case, and for others like me who make an inappropriate joke or give an unwanted shoulder pat without realizing that this violates the law—I was not at the time aware of any policies against such behavior—is there any middle ground? Is there any solution between, on the one hand, asking the recipient to simply ignore the unwanted behavior (which seems unjust) or, on the other hand, completely destroying the life and career of the accused?

I now had plenty of time to reflect on such matters because my career was effectively over. At least, my life as a hotelier appeared to be buried in the dust forever.

But I have always heard it said that when one door closes, another one opens. And, as it happened, my life was about to take a very strange turn.

Questioning Justice

Doing jail time for a crime I never committed. This is what my life felt like in the days, weeks, months, and years of the trial, and for an extended period afterward. The nightmare in which I now found myself threatened to define the rest of my days. After decades of working tirelessly, receiving a steady stream of promotions and accolades, and making my mark in the hotel world, I had suddenly turned into a pariah in my industry, unable to get a job in the US or anywhere else in the universe.

It hardly seemed to matter that I had won the court case or that multiple judges and a jury had found the charges against me baseless. The final judge's last-minute reversal had sealed my fate, handing me a severe punishment that rippled through my entire life. This penance was not limited to the consequences that I now faced from the outside world, in the form of financial losses and a series of seemingly never-ending rejections from every job to which I applied. I was also punishing myself. In my own mind, I wrestled daily and nightly with the question of how I might have brought this crisis upon myself. Had my old-fashioned European style of communication and camaraderie, all the back-patting and the silly joking, kept me from sensing differences in the cultural environment of an American hotel? Had I inadvertently turned into an insensitive boss and set myself up for the events that overturned my life?

While I was struggling with these questions, the tremendous support from almost all my former employees, and the countless letters of encouragement I received, seemed to tell a different story. Regretfully, none of that changed what had already happened to me, or to be precise, none of it was of any importance in the game Sheraton's executives seemed determined to play. As I learned later, it was only two associates out of 350 who were involved in the accusations that led to my downfall.

Perhaps I should have been more aloof in my interactions with these employees or noticed the ways in which my attempts to create a collegial environment seemed at odds with their personalities. But then, they had never uttered a single word or reacted in any way that would have hinted to me that I should change my way of interacting with them. Would that have made any difference, though? Evidently, in the last few months, a sword was already dangling over my head, ready to behead me at a moment's notice. As it appeared, I was doomed regardless of what I did or did not say or do, for business-related reasons to which only a few were privy.

Yes, the financial results could have looked better in those first few months after the reopening, but in a very short time, we had positioned the St. Regis among the best hotels in the world. We were delivering an outstanding guest experience and hosting entrepreneurs and corporate executives from around the world. Our average room rate had reached a level never seen before in the city, and we were confident that the occupancy rate would follow suit, as we were succeeding in expanding our base of highly affluent, discerning, and loyal customers. But although every hotel in the city was watching our performance with envy, maybe for some of our own executives and their shortsighted strategy, our steady growth was not quick enough.

AT THE OPENING WITH PETE THOMAS VICE CHAIRMAN OF ITT CORPORATION

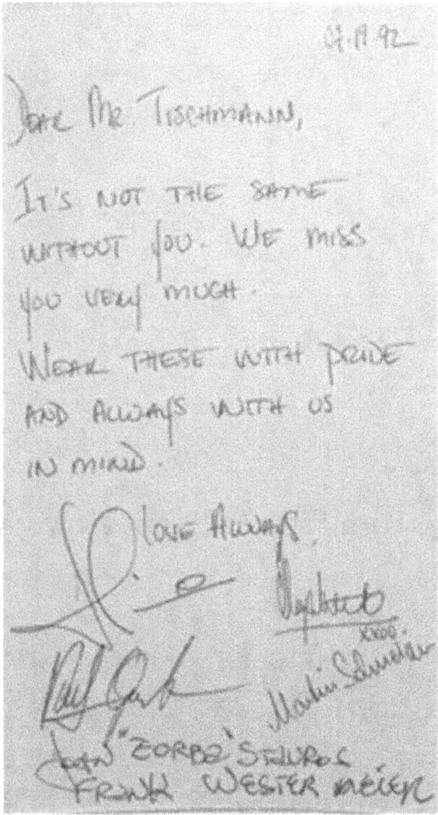

07.11.92

Dear Mr Tischmann,

It's not the same without you. We miss you very much.

Wear these with pride and always with us in mind.

Love Always,

XXOO.

"ZORBA" STAVROS

FRANK WESTERMEIER

LETTERS OF SYMPATHY FROM FORMER ASSOCIATES.

What is happening at the luxury ***St. Regis-Sheraton*** in ***New York City?*** Career hotelier ***Peter Tischmann,*** who was General Manager and orchestrater of the hotel's $150 million redo, has suddenly departed, leaving staff and clients in a anxious wake. Does this signal a Sheraton change of mind and a return to tight-fisted, cost-control management? All of us are waiting to see.

MIXED COMMENTS AND A LOT OF QUESTIONS BY THE LOCAL MEDIA

Back On My Feet 28

From Hotelier to Hair Replacement

My punishment took other forms too, beyond the constant thoughts like these that kept me up at night and beyond the jobs I failed to get. My penance came in the form of a new line of work that I would never have anticipated, in a field that was as far from my plans as it was possible to get: the hair replacement industry.

Yes, hair replacement.

While it's true that I had lost most of my hair several years before, a toupee was the last thing on my mind. I liked myself the way I was, and it had never occurred to me to get a hair replacement for the strands I had naturally lost. In any case, the look was by now a part of my personality. After all, my grandfather had lost his hair by the time he turned thirty. My own hair had lasted many more years before it vanished, and I had long ago made peace with its absence.

But one day, while I was still embroiled in the legal mess, I received a call from the St. Regis informing me that a guest named Charles Dabiri was trying to reach me. He had left his telephone number for me to contact him. Filled with curiosity, I decided to call the man back.

Mr. Dabiri answered immediately, getting directly to the point. He had been impressed with the St. Regis each time he visited the hotel during my tenure there, and he wanted to speak with me about a business opportunity. I was deeply skeptical, but I agreed to schedule a meeting with him. I had no clue who this person was, nor what type of business opportunity he was talking about, but my phone was not exactly ringing off the hook with job offers.

I learned over coffee that Mr. Dabiri was an Iranian-born entrepreneur who owned a hair replacement business on Rodeo Drive in Beverly Hills and on Place Vendome in Paris. Faithful to his philosophy that the most opulent location is just good enough, he had recently opened a new location in Trump Tower.

He listed his celebrity customers, including Elton John, and told me that everyone knew him simply as Dabiri. He explained that he had made his fortune by developing a technique by which he customized hair extensions for clients, attaching the pieces to a customer's original roots with numerous tiny clips. This allowed his clients to shower without disturbing their hair pieces and to never have to worry about the wind blowing their hair away as they cruised in their Bentleys along Rodeo Drive. The process, he told me, worked for men as well as for women, and he was able to charge fees of $50,000 and up for it.

Mr. Dabiri expressed sorrow that I had been fired from the St. Regis and immediately offered me a job helping him organize his business. Surprised at the idea, I paused to think this over. Both the man and his industry were still virtually unknown to me, but managing a business was a skill I could easily transfer from hotels to another arena, even hair replacement. Dabiri offered me a reasonable salary, nothing close to what I was earning before but a respectable amount nonetheless. I certainly needed a paying job after losing my St. Regis salary so I could pay the rent on an apartment for Denyse and I to live in, buy groceries so we could eat, not to mention continue to pay the expensive legal team I had hired. What else could I say but yes?

No sooner had I agreed to take the job than Dabiri got to work trying to sell me one of his hair treatments. My "no" was firm, stated without a trace of hesitation. I would rather have turned down the job than been forced to wear one of his toupees. Anyway, I had absolutely nothing on my head to which he could attach his hair extensions. I was essentially bald by this point.

Obviously, my answer was not what Dabiri had expected because he made it clear that he did not want customers noticing that one of his very own employees was hairless. My decision left him with no choice, he explained. He was obliged to require me to hide in the back office every time a customer walked in.

If he felt so strongly about hiring employees with hair, it struck me as absurd that he would choose me of all people to manage his business, a man with no hair and no experience whatsoever with the product. Even more preposterous was that part of my job involved hiring employees for his new business and acquiescing to his preference for interviewees with lots of hair, preferably thick, flowing locks tumbling over their shoulders.

Hiding in the office every time the door opened was humiliating enough, but the job itself hardly felt dignified either. My days consisted mainly of trying to fend off legal cases from customers who tried to sue Dabiri for a variety of reasons, mostly related to dissatisfaction with their astronomically expensive treatment. I also spent hours each week organizing Dabiri's entire office, doing all his administrative paperwork, and getting him the permits he needed to operate legally.

Dabiri had never owned a credit card, always opting to pay in cash instead. But he finally decided he needed one, and I found myself having to educate him about how important it is in the US to earn a good credit rating and that the only way to do so was to get a card and use it properly. Through my contacts with American Express, I managed to get him approved for a credit card, but he complained when they issued him the basic green credit card. True to form, he only wanted platinum, and he did not seem to understand when I tried to explain to him that he couldn't just go out and get one. He would need to earn a platinum card by first proving he could pay his monthly bills on the green card in a timely fashion. If he did so, it wouldn't be long before American Express would offer him an upgrade. This subject was difficult to understand for a self-made entrepreneur who wore custom-made suits, lived in Trump Tower, and flew the Concorde on his monthly trips to Paris.

If I learned anything at all of value from Dabiri, it was his definition of what it means to be an entrepreneur. He asked me if I knew the answer to this question once when we were sitting together in his office. Then he replied to his own question. "An entrepreneur," he said, "is someone who is prepared to give up everything he possesses for an idea he believes in and who will spare no effort to make this idea successful." Looking at Dabiri, I could not but agree because the best example was sitting right in front of me.

Meanwhile, Dabiri continuously boasted about the wonderful growth opportunities available in his company, how much he planned to expand, how illustrious his clients were. But it soon became evident that this was all mostly talk. Selling the illusion of having a full head of hair was not enough to put a business on solid ground because what his customers didn't realize was that once the expensive initial treatment was done, an equally expensive monthly maintenance of the system was required in order to keep up the effect.

Soon the daily realities and humiliations of working for him began to reach an intolerable level. Functioning in such a degrading environment made the job unsustainable beyond the short-term benefit of an immediate paycheck.

After working with him for a little less than a year, I felt I couldn't take it anymore. I was ready to leave, but I hesitated to turn in my resignation. I needed to do something with my time, and I needed to earn money. Where would I find another job?

This time, at long last, luck was on my side. Another opportunity presented itself just in time. This one sounded far better suited for my skills and promised to involve absolutely no ducking behind a door to hide from customers and no $50,000 hair treatments.

The Bristol Hotel Beirut

A stranger's voice echoed through my phone one morning as I prepared to go to Trump Tower for another day of shuffling papers for Dabiri. "Peter?" The man on the phone introduced himself as Pierre Doumit and wasted no time in revealing what his call was about. His family owned Le Bristol, a renowned hotel in Beirut. Unhappy with their property's current standing, they wanted to hire an experienced consultant to bring the hotel back to its potential.

I knew of the Bristol, one of Beirut's most elegant hotels and a social center before the Lebanese civil war of 1975–90. Situated on the edge of the lively retail and restaurant districts of Hamra and Verdun, the hotel, built in the 1950s and distinguished by its curved ship-like facade, had hosted celebrities ranging from Charles Lindbergh to Dizzy Gillespie, Prince Albert of Monaco, and Princess Souraya of Iran. But I had heard that after surviving the war, the hotel had fallen into neglect and disrepair over the years and never quite managed to reclaim its former status.

This was what Pierre wanted to speak with me about, the idea of my taking on the job of restoring the hotel to its former grandeur. I agreed to meet with him that week. On the morning of our appointment, as I headed to Dabiri's office, my soul felt a little bit brighter at the prospect of finally escaping the world of hair replacement. The possibility made me look into the future with hope for the first time in quite a while.

While Pierre's phone call had come as a surprise at first, it was not completely out of the blue. Denyse and I knew Pierre Doumit's aunt, Mary Kettaneh, who lived in Manhattan and belonged to the prominent Kettaneh family of Lebanon. Since Pierre, also based in New York, had taken on the task of helping his father look for a hotelier to straighten out the Bristol, he must have spoken to Mary, who in return might have told him: "I have somebody for you: Peter Tischmann, the former general manager of the St. Regis."

The position at Le Bristol sounded intriguing, but during my first meeting with Pierre, I quickly learned that it would involve more than the usual hotel consultant's job description. Pierre spoke with me in great detail about the hotel, how it was not properly run, and how it needed a significant amount of work to recapture its former splendor. I had guessed at that part, but Pierre also hinted to me about a messier problem, a long-standing family conflict concerning the future of the hotel. The argument involved his own father, mother, sister, and a former Canadian-based cousin, who had been in charge of the family's interests in Canada and who had almost driven the entire company into bankruptcy through his mismanagement. Then there was the issue of the hotel's general manager, Mrs. Arakelian, who had been running the hotel for decades and managed to keep it open during the civil war. The family had no intention of replacing her.

As we continued our meeting, Pierre made it clearer what the expectation would be for my role: to function as a consultant based on-site at the hotel, tasked with the job of modernizing the Bristol so it could compete in the current environment. I would work alongside Mrs. Arakelian, and our roles would be distinct but overlapping. He was not yet formally offering me the job, however, and I have to admit that I was slightly wary by this point, after hearing him detail the various family conflicts and complications. But I was intrigued.

The war had ended several years ago by this point, and the Bristol was still the only hotel of reputation operating in Beirut. The city's famous Phoenicia, the centrally located downtown hotel that had long served as the headquarters for VIPs and government officials visiting Beirut, had been destroyed and not yet rebuilt. Other upscale competitors were also either wrecked or still closed, and luxury hotels such as the Four Seasons, the Ritz Carlton, and other leading luxury brands had yet to enter the Beirut market.

Therefore, the Doumits needed to seize the opportunity to bring the Bristol back up to an international standard, and they needed to do it fast.

"Ho ho," I thought, "with pleasure." Yes, the job did sound appealing despite the ongoing family conflicts, which I felt comfortable I could handle with a professional approach. But what I did not realize at this point was that this family squabble ran much deeper than Pierre described. But the work of modernizing the hotel sounded perfectly aligned with my skills, and it would scratch the itch I'd been feeling to return to the hospitality world. The Doumits arranged to fly me to Beirut with Denyse to meet with Pierre's father.

After we arrived in Lebanon and went directly to his beautifully appointed villa, surrounded by lavish gardens and situated only a few steps away from the Lebanese president's residence outside Beirut, Pierre's father got right down to business. As we talked, it became even more evident to me how deep the family conflict really was. Pierre and his father were committed to renovating the hotel to bring it up to international standards. Meanwhile Elias, Pierre's cousin, the one who had almost drowned the Doumit empire because of his mismanagement in Canada, used every opportunity to contradict Pierre. Elisabeth, Pierre's sister, thought she was a born hotelier, and although she had little or no hotel experience, she continuously tried to impose her own ideas of how to run the Bristol. Pierre's aunt Laura, a very sweet lady, tried to smooth the conflict when things got out of control. And last but not least, Mrs. Arakelian got involved whenever she suspected she could carve out some kind of benefit for herself.

A perfect background for a soap opera, and I was confident it would have been a successful one.

I got the sense that Pierre's father supported him in the decision to begin major renovations at the hotel, but he did not want to personally take a strong position on the issue so as not to upset the rest of the family.

Pierre's earlier description of the family mess now came to life in far more vivid detail than I would have ever wanted to hear.

Still, I felt confident that if I accepted this consulting job, I would somehow find a way through this mess. I was willing to take on the challenge. When I received a formal offer to take the position, I said yes with no hesitation.

Returning to Beirut a few weeks later, after bidding farewell to Dabiri and packing up my luggage in New York, I moved into a room at the Bristol to begin work. Denyse remained in New York for the first few months to stay close to Carine and Peter, both attending university on the East Coast.

Things immediately got off to a rough start with Mrs. Arakelian. My working relationship with her, as much as I tried to begin on a positive and congenial note, took on a tense and negative tone from the first day. It was obvious that she was afraid I would take her job, and although I tried repeatedly to explain to her my role at the hotel, her hostile attitude toward me would not budge. I had no intention of moving to Beirut long-term and becoming the GM at the Bristol, nor was that job even offered to me. I had only a short-term consulting contract to oversee the renovations and reestablish the status of the Bristol. Nonetheless, Mrs. Arakelian remained suspicious of me and treated me as such.

To her credit, she had worked extremely hard to keep the hotel open throughout the war, brokering a series of business arrangements and meeting the demands of the militias and the occupying Syrian forces that ran rampant in Beirut in those years. It was what she had to do to keep the hotel in one piece, and she rose to the occasion with courage and savvy. At one point, her daughter was kidnapped to put pressure on the wealthy Doumit family, and she had to use her personal contacts to negotiate her release. Mrs. Arakelian navigated conditions far more difficult than I would ever know in her efforts to keep the hotel open, and everyone connected to it got through the civil war unscathed. If I could have talked her out of her fear that I wanted to take her job, we would've enjoyed a supportive working relationship. But she considered me a necessary evil and was unrelentingly negative toward me at first, until she eventually agreed to work with me, but only grudgingly.

I spent my days at the Bristol studying every aspect of the hotel and the local hospitality landscape. Over the ensuing weeks and months, I created a detailed master plan for restoring the Bristol to match its illustrious reputation and restore its position at the top of the hotel market in the city. As I worked on the proposal, I did my best to navigate the competing motives of the various family members. Nonetheless, one group of relatives seemed intent on blocking any changes whatsoever, while Pierre and his immediate family were eager to go ahead. I was caught in the middle.

A Family Conflict, a Roadblock to Success

Even though most family members claimed to want to restore the Bristol to its former glory, and they paid me handsomely for my consulting work, they ultimately did not agree to implement the master plan. The only exception was my suggestion that they change the windows because everyone agreed the rooms were too noisy.

I hid my frustration and tried to keep it in perspective. I reminded myself that a consulting job for the Doumit family was better than working for Dabiri and that the internal family conflict was really beyond my control. But contrary to most consultants, who present their recommendations for improvement then collect their fees and say bye-bye, I felt more of a personal connection to the Bristol. I took responsibility for my recommendations and wanted to be a part of the solution, having grown to care about the hotel and its staff.

I could not understand how the owners could be so blind to the enormous opportunities they were missing.

The lack of action at the Bristol started to impact me personally, as my efforts to persuade the family went nowhere. Money was not an issue, as they had plenty of it. They simply could not come to terms about anything whatsoever.

Exasperating as the situation was, I had to force myself to let it go. It was incredibly difficult to give up, since I knew that if the family allowed me to implement my ideas, we could guide the hotel through the renovation process and reposition it at the top of the luxury market within one year. Without a doubt, the Bristol would soar beyond any other hotel in Beirut. Business was returning to the city in those days, the early 1990s, but visitors still had no suitable place to stay. The timing would have been perfect.

Sure enough, the Bristol lost a huge opportunity in those years. The family stubbornly allowed its internal conflicts to destroy any hope of renewal and any chance of a quick return on its investment.

The hotel did retain one saving grace, however: its restaurant, a popular lunch destination since the years before the war.

From its earliest days, the Bristol had established a reputation for its cuisine and the quality of its banquets. Starting in the 1960s and up until the eighties, the Bristol employed a famous chef named George Rayess, author of an influential cookbook called *The Art of Lebanese Cooking*. George Rayess essentially did for Lebanese cuisine what Auguste Escoffier did for French cooking, refining the regional dishes and documenting the recipes for posterity.

Although George Rayess was long gone, and the other chefs at the hotel were not nearly as talented, the hotel was still benefiting from his reputation, and the banquet business remained an important source of income. The restaurant, especially, was still doing very well, thanks in large part to the fish kibbe, a much-anticipated special every Friday.

Fish kibbe is a classic Lebanese dish made with the fleshy meat of the fresh local catch, roasted with pine nuts and onions, and served in a dramatic presentation on a large platter. It's not easy to find the dish in Beirut, and the Bristol served the best one in town. The restaurant would get packed every Friday when they served it, and the dish remained popular all the way up until the Bristol closed down permanently in 2020.

In my final weeks of working there, I saw the opportunity to implement any of the ideas in my Bristol proposal disappear completely. I sensed no progress toward the goal of getting the owners to break their impasse for the good of the hotel and to agree to make the desperately needed changes. I knew my days of eating fish kibbe would soon come to an end. My one-year contract was winding down. I had nothing more to contribute at the Bristol under these circumstances and no other opportunity on the horizon.

But good fortune struck again, out of the blue. Around the end of my Bristol year, I received a surprise phone call from an old colleague.

An Unexpected Call from a Former Colleague

Years ago, when I was still at the St. Regis, I did a favor for the Kempinski hotel company by conducting a market survey and feasibility study on the Plaza Hotel for them since they had an opportunity to take over a lease for the Plaza. Fortunately for Kempinski, the deal to take over the hotel never materialized, as the very seasonal business in New York, combined with major operational problems, would have drained Kempinski's financial reserves in no time.

When my telephone rang one day after I had concluded my year of consulting in Beirut, it was Kempinski calling again. But this time, the person on the phone was a former Hannover colleague of mine, someone with whom I had not spoken in years. I recognized his voice immediately: It was Michael Maas, the same Michael Maas from whom I took over the job as chief steward at the InterContinental Hotel in Hannover many years ago. Since that time, Michael had made fantastic strides in his career and was now one of the top corporate executives at Kempinski.

Michael got right to the point. "Peter," he asked me, "how would you like to join us at the Ciragan Palace in Istanbul as general manager?"

I didn't need to do much thinking. I gave Michael an immediate yes. As I hung up the phone with him, I realized that my stalled career was about to get a badly needed kick in the backside. I would have a real job again. A big job. I was not exactly sure what lay in store, but I braced myself and Denyse for a dramatic transformation in our lives.

In my excitement about the move to Istanbul, I had neglected to consider an important detail. I did not yet have a job offer. Michael Maas wanted me to go to Istanbul first to understand what the job at the Ciragan would actually involve. I told him this would not be necessary, as I knew Istanbul already from my previous corporate position with Sheraton, and anyway, a visit to the hotel would not sway my decision one way or the other.

Positioning the Ciragan as the best hotel in Istanbul was going to require an enormous amount of work. I knew this since I had been in these situations before and had a profound understanding of what they involved. I assured Michael that I really didn't have to waste the company's money by traveling to Istanbul before the decision was finalized. Of course, I also knew that every hotel is different, and the Ciragan would surely have specific circumstances I could not yet predict. But I knew one thing. I wanted the job.

It soon became clear that the decision, at this point, was not up to me, and it turned out that it was not up to Michael either. The job offer was subject to the approval of the Ciragan's owners ADIA, the Abu Dhabi Investment Authority, who wanted to meet with me in person in Abu Dhabi. Naturally, I agreed to take the trip to Abu Dhabi. But scheduling the meeting turned out to be trickier than I expected, as Kempinski's director of operations, who was supposed to accompany me to the owners, had his own ideas about the travel schedule.

The problem with him was that he never worked on Saturdays or Sundays. And the problem with planning the interview in Abu Dhabi was that the owners wanted to meet me on a Sunday, as Friday and Saturday is the official weekend in much of the Arab world. So to satisfy the owners' request, we had to fly on Saturday to be available on Sunday, which did not coincide with the private schedule of Kempinski's director of operations.

A few days after I told Michael Maas I would be happy to fly to Abu Dhabi, he called me, sounding very frustrated that the meeting still hadn't happened. Apparently, the owners in Abu Dhabi had called Michael to ask, "Where is this person you have proposed that we meet?"

I explained the situation, and before I knew it, I had an airline ticket in my hand. I suspect Michael had sent his operations director a carefully worded memo. The following Sunday morning, we sat at a huge table in one of the meeting rooms at the owners' office in Abu Dhabi. The entire board of directors sat facing us, each of them dressed in a perfectly ironed white dishdasha and the traditional head scarf worn by men in the Gulf region.

The owners began the meeting by giving Kempinski's executive a piece of their mind. After congratulating him for finally making it to Abu Dhabi to meet with them for the very first time—obviously they had learned about his travel preferences—they unleashed a tirade of complaints about how Kempinski was managing their Istanbul hotel, complaining bitterly that the operation was well below their expectations.

While Kempinski's representative was still wading through the cascade of owners' complaints, Ahmed al Mohamed , the chairman of the board, continued with a statement I'll never forget, further adding to the discomfort of the Kempinski executive.

"We gave you a Rolls Royce in Istanbul," Ahmed al Mohamed continued, "and you drive it like an ordinary car."

He could not have chosen a more vivid image to illustrate the owners' extreme dissatisfaction with Kempinski's performance. For me, his comment made it crystal clear what was expected of me in Istanbul should I get the job.

Nothing further happened at that meeting, and soon we walked out of the room to head back to the airport. The Abu Dhabi meeting had gone badly, through no fault of my own. I was feeling discouraged, wondering if an opportunity like this would ever come up again.

Two days later, back in our temporary home in New Hope, Pennsylvania, I received a phone call from Michael. "Congratulations," he said, "the owners liked you and want to extend you an offer. When can you start?"

Visiting Harvard University

Before packing our suitcases again and preparing for our move to Turkey, Denyse and I had to take a long scheduled trip to Harvard, where Carine was studying for her MBA. On this visit, I had been looking forward to the opportunity to sit in one of Carine's business classes. But first I needed to get her okay, to make sure that she would be comfortable having me in the classroom.

"Daddy," she said, "you can sit in, but please do me one favor: shut up."

The lecture in her class that day happened to be about digitization in the hospitality industry. A representative from Marriott Hotels and Resorts was visiting the class and discussing a new system by which customers would be able to check themselves in and minimize the service required from hotel personnel. As the discussion about the advantages and disadvantages went on, the professor suddenly turned around to me and said, "Well, we have Carine's dad sitting with us, and he has managed international luxury hotels worldwide. Why don't we ask him if something like this could be applicable in luxury hotels?"

My face turned so red, a tomato would have looked pale by comparison. I absolutely did not want the spotlight on me, especially after my well-publicized career fiasco of a few years ago. Most of all, I did not want to humiliate Carine. I looked up at my daughter, sitting all the way at the top of the classroom amphitheater, and watched as she put her head in her hands, almost diving under the bench to seek shelter from what was about to happen.

Embarrassed as I felt, it would have been impolite to ignore the professor's question. I said simply, "I don't think this is applicable in luxury hotels because luxury hotel customers expect personalized service and attention to details." Then I added, "Why don't you ask your visitor if he is planning to implement this system in Marriott's hotels?"

The guest speaker and the professor turned to discuss this among themselves, as I felt a wave of relief. I had managed to answer the question without getting embroiled in any further discussion about myself or my career. I remained quiet from then on. Carine looked relieved too.

Even though this Harvard visit had come at an awkward moment, while the St. Regis disaster still loomed, I found myself enjoying the classroom atmosphere. I was also happy to have received a close-up view of a Harvard MBA lecture, and I felt glad once again that Carine had chosen this program over others to which she had been accepted.

Denyse and I had been proud of our daughter for her acceptance into multiple prestigious MBA programs, including not only Harvard but also INSEAD, or Institut European d'Administration des Affaires, which had its main campus in Fontainebleau, France. Founded in 1957, INSEAD had quickly earned an excellent reputation, and by the time Carine was sending out her applications, it was ranked by the *Financial Times* as one of the best business schools in the world.

Carine had faced a tough decision between the two schools, and at one point, she was leaning toward INSEAD since it could be completed in only three semesters instead of the four required by Harvard. I was hoping she would choose Harvard, in large part because of its name recognition. It so happened that during the decision-making process, Carine was having dinner with Denyse and me along with our invited guest for the evening, a highly placed executive at Bear Stearns. When he professed not to have heard of INSEAD, Carine took notice, and then our guest asked, "Carine, if you asked ten students accepted at Harvard how many of them would prefer to switch to INSEAD, what do you think the answer would be?" She paused. "And then if you posed the reverse question to ten students at INSEAD, what do you think their reaction would be?"

I believe it was those questions that changed Carine's mind, since from then on, it was Harvard and nothing else. And while I am sure Carine would have received a fantastic education at INSEAD, her decision did turn out to be perfect for her. When she graduated from Harvard, Denyse and I were overflowing with pride, just as we were when our son Peter graduated with an undergraduate diploma from Cornell two years before. Of course, true to form, Peter Jr. decided to add his own personal flair to Cornell's graduation ceremony by walking in sneakers and shorts under his robe.

In 1997, when Carine received her diploma from Harvard, we felt confident that Carine and Peter's decisions about where to attend school, along with their distinct personalities and their commitments to the paths they had chosen, would pave the way for wonderfully successful careers.

As for me, the experience of sitting in for one of my daughter's Harvard lectures made me wonder whether I should consider teaching at a business or hospitality school one day. But another big adventure awaited me first.

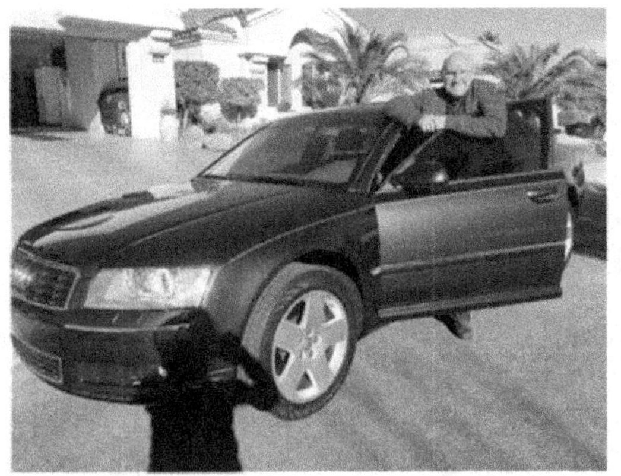

HAPPY OWNER OF AN AUDI 8L

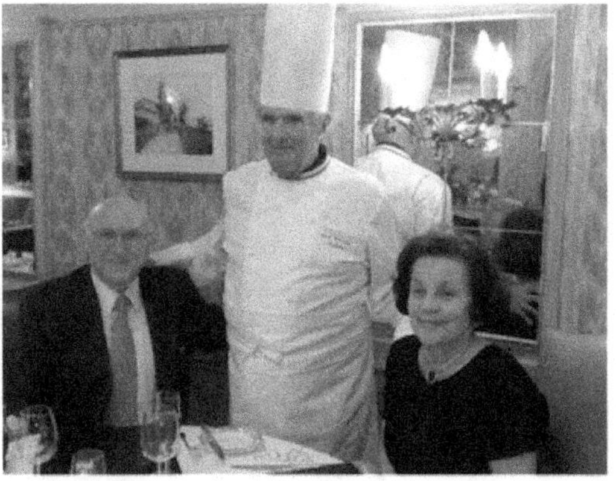

DINNER AT MY FRIEND PAUL BOCUSE

SELF EXPLANATORY

DANCING WITH FABIENNE

ENJOYING A CRUISE

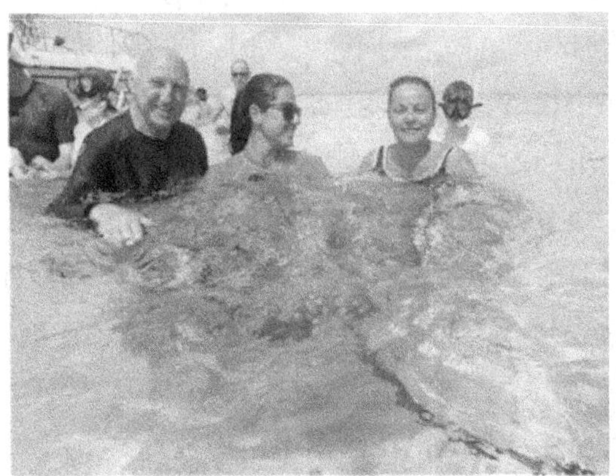

SWIMMING WITH STING RAYS AT THE CAYMANS

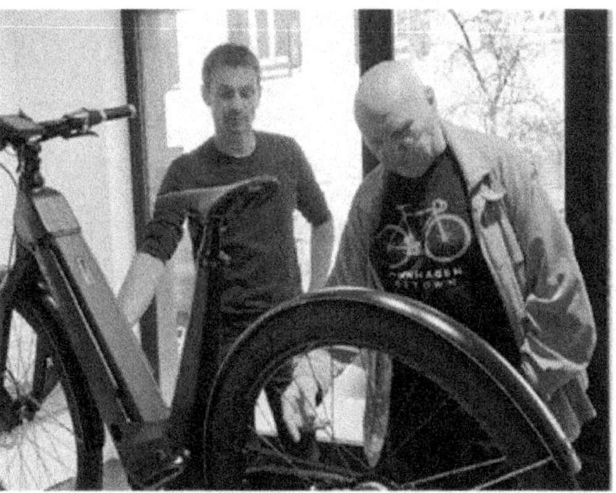

MY NEW ELECTRIC BIKE

The Pearl on the Bosporus 29

A Spectacular Location

I had barely caught my breath in New Hope when it was time to pack my bags again and get ready to embark on my new role at the Ciragan Palace in Istanbul.

On past visits to Istanbul, the city had enchanted me with its beauty and its history. The ancient metropolis spanned three empires, from the Roman to the Byzantine to the Ottoman, and its position along the Bosporus Strait straddled two continents, Europe and Asia. The Ciragan, originally built as a home for Ottoman sultans, holds a prime location on the shoreline, near the nineteenth-century imperial Dolmabahce Palace and the Ottoman splendors of the Yildiz Palace and Park. A visitor heading southwest from the Ciragan along the Yeni Galata Bridge will soon find himself standing in front of Istanbul's famous fifteenth-century Topkapi Palace, a prime residence of the Ottoman sultans, and gazing at the Hagia Sophia and Blue Mosque nearby. For anyone fascinated by magnificent old buildings, jaw-dropping seaside landscapes, and bustling skylines, Istanbul is a city not to miss.

Pulling up in front of the hotel as I arrived from the airport, I felt a sense of excitement and suspense that I had not experienced in a long time. This felt like a rebirth, a chance to start again in a vibrant cosmopolitan city, to revitalize the energy and passion I had always felt about my career, feelings that had grown dormant in recent years. Istanbul was a city of imagination, of change and renewal. Perhaps this job would do the same for my own life.

Arriving at the Ciragan

Ciragan's general manager stood waiting for me when I walked into the soaring lobby of the hotel building, a modern structure built alongside the original Ottoman-era Ciragan Palace and similar in style, with its waterfront-facing white stone facade and blue-green roof. While the company prepared to move the GM elsewhere, his last job was to guide me through all the systems and departments until I was ready to take over.

In our first few moments together, I could tell that our hotel management work styles were as different as day from night. His schedule was strictly 9:00 a.m. to 4:00 p.m., at which point he would leave—very punctually—for his residence outside the hotel. Once he was gone, the staff did not see him again until the next morning, as he would spend the late afternoons and evenings out and about, zooming around Istanbul on his Harley Davidson.

It came as no surprise that my soon-to-be predecessor had prepared no handover notes of any kind for me, leaving me dependent on the information I received from the various department heads. Not that this bothered me, but the presence of proper handover notes would have made my first day a little easier.

My first order of business was to immediately acquaint myself with everyone on the management staff, figure out the procedures and rhythms of the Ciragan, and identify what the place was doing right and wrong—mostly wrong, as I quickly discovered.

From my experiences overhauling the St. Regis and working in many other hotels around the world, I knew how to gain a rapid understanding of what's going on behind the scenes. Within a few days, I felt I had enough grounding to fully take over the job from my predecessor, giving him some additional days to cruise on his Harley Davidson. Much to the staff's surprise, I immediately introduced them to my twenty-four-hour management style.

Unlike my predecessor, I insisted on living on the premises. Denyse and I moved into a suite in the palace, the grander and more historic half of the Ciragan property. I had no plans to live like a sultan while stationed in this job, and I had not specifically requested a palace suite for Denyse and myself. But for business reasons, the company decided that it made sense to put us in the palace because those suites were the most difficult to book. Guests preferred to stay in the hotel building, close to where the activity was and conveniently situated near the reception desk.

Originally, the suites of the Ottoman-era Ciragan Palace had ceilings seven meters high, but during the restoration phase before the property opened as a hotel in 1991, most of these spaces had been converted into duplexes. This required cutting the spaces in half horizontally, leaving the bedroom on the top level and the living room downstairs. The accommodations Denyse and I moved into looked like nearly every other palace duplex—rather cramped for a suite but felt comfortable enough as an on-site residence for Denyse and myself, especially as we had a guest room where Carine or Peter could stay with us when they visited. But unlike the spacious apartment we had access to at the St. Regis, this suite was not conducive to entertaining guests, so Denyse and I resolved to invite our friends to the main restaurant whenever we wanted to host a dinner party.

I could only imagine what Ciragan guests who booked palace suites and paid handsomely for the privilege might think of their accommodations. Clearly, there was much work to be done to bring the Ciragan up to the expected standards of a luxury property.

One evening not long after we arrived in Istanbul, I suggested to Denyse that we take a stroll through the entire Ciragan complex. The property spans an area of about four hundred or five hundred meters in length, quite a distance for a guest wanting to get from one end of the grounds to the other. Beginning at the palace, we walked through the connecting wing, down the long corridor, passing the Ciragan Bar and the All-Day Dining restaurant to arrive in the hotel lobby. The moment we arrived, the staff looked up at us, startled, their eyes peering at me as if I had just landed there from Mars. I could sense what was going through their minds: "What is wrong with the new general manager, and what is he doing here?" They had never seen the old GM after four o'clock in the afternoon.

"Well, they had better get used to it now," I whispered to Denyse.

History of the Palace

I challenge any traveler to name a more spectacular location for a hotel than what the Ciragan has to offer. The sumptuous nineteenth-century palace, with its lush gardens of tulips and palm trees overlooking the waterfront, is among the most romantic sights in the world. In the daytime, the Ciragan's white marble columns stand starkly against the sparkling waters of the Bosporus, and in the evening, its lights twinkle against the breathtaking skyline of domed mosques, palaces, and imperial monuments, mingling with the electric street life of a modern metropolis.

The history of the Ciragan dates back to the sixteenth century, when the palace was home to the last sultans of the Ottoman Empire. In the 1550s, High Admiral Kilic Ali Pasha built a house on this formerly forested stretch of land along the shoreline and used it for hunting wild game. The land then passed down through the families of the Ottoman sultans, who replaced the original house with their own series of mansions in the seventeenth and eighteenth centuries. When Ibrahim Pasha tore down an existing wooden mansion on the property and built his own gilded, marbled palace in the early eighteenth century, he began hosting "ciragan" (torchlight) parties in the gardens, giving the place a name that has lasted through the ages.

Ottoman rulers demolished and rebuilt the palace several times in the 1800s, until Sultan Abdulaziz oversaw its restoration by the Armenian palace architect Nigoğayos Balyan and his sons, in a style influenced by the ornate Arab palaces of Spain and North Africa.

The palace entered its last era under the Ottomans, when the deposed Murad V moved into the Ciragan in 1876 and continued to live there even after an attempted coup failed to restore him to power. In the early twentieth century, Parliament began holding its meetings in the palace, until a devastating fire ravaged the Ciragan in 1910 and burned it almost to the ground in only five hours. The palace's gutted shell stood empty for decades, a grim sight along the city's picturesque waterfront, and a poignant reminder of the rise and fall of one of the world's great empires.

Various plans hatched in the early and mid-twentieth century to restore the Ciragan once again and turn it into a hotel or a museum, but none of them materialized. In the meantime, the remains of the ruined palace served as a public swimming pool and even a football stadium.

It was not until the late 1980s that the restoration idea finally gained momentum. The Turkish government sold the palace to a Japanese company, launching its transformation into a hotel intended to capture a share of the country's growing tourism market. The government insisted that the restorations resemble as closely as possible what the palace looked like before the fire, approving only plans that used mostly original materials in the reconstruction.

By 1991, the Ciragan stood prepared to accommodate the needs of modern travelers. The rebuilt palace building offered a dozen guest suites, while the newly built hotel structure nearby boasted 310 balconied rooms, the majority overlooking the Bosporus. An ornately carved staircase rising in front of the columned white marble facade of the palace led into a majestic atrium hung with an enormous crystal chandelier, the largest on the European continent. Elegant function rooms, luxury shops, fine dining restaurants, nightclubs, and an original Turkish hammam would ensure guests had plenty to explore and do during their stay. Walking through the grounds, visitors could stroll past a glittering infinity pool overlooking the Bosporus and into the white six-level hotel building that resembled a more contemporary version of the palace. Both buildings stood facing the shore along a waterfront walkway, their facades greeting travelers from near and far, ushering in a new era for Istanbul and its stunning legacy of imperial architecture.

With the renovations almost complete, the Abu Dhabi investment authority bought the hotel from the Japanese, who were running out of funds to complete the renovation. Once the hotel was finished, Kempinski was awarded the management contract.

The Ciragan was ready to open its doors to the world. But things didn't go exactly as planned.

A Dream of a Hotel

Dr. Mehmet Tekbas, a friend of mine and professor at Istanbul University, once said to me when we talked about the beauty of the Bosporus: "The river is the same, but the water changes all the time."

His description is one I always remembered when I looked out onto the Bosporus. It made me think about the changing waters this famous strait had seen over the centuries, as one civilization after another passed through this land and as the Ottoman Empire grew to conquer much of Europe, North Africa, Asia, and the Middle East over six centuries, only to collapse after World War I and give way to the modern era.

The Ciragan grounds too had seen so many changes, from one sultan to another, and one palace to another, and now here we were, welcoming in a new wave of travelers and explorers who would stand in this very same spot and look out onto the ever-changing waters.

The Ciragan's breathtaking location resonated with history and magic. But despite the majesty of its position along the Bosporus, despite its historic architecture, despite its newly restored buildings, the Ciragan did not quite manage to bewitch visitors in the days, weeks, and months after it flung open its doors to a new era of hospitality. Disappointingly for its owners and management company, the Ciragan failed to secure a position at the top of Istanbul's hotel market and soon slid into an unremarkable existence as just another moderately upscale Istanbul hotel. Whether this was a result of poor management or of a dysfunctional working relationship between the owners and the on-site team tasked with running the hotel, one thing was clear to visitors: The Ciragan did not offer anywhere near the experience a guest should expect from a luxurious property of such distinction.

By the time I joined the Ciragan three years after its grand opening, in 1994, the newer portion of the complex had long been functioning like an ordinary hotel, as far as the guest experience was concerned. Nothing about the hospitality, the service, or the operational concepts bespoke luxury or the attention to detail that the most exclusive hotels can promise. Guests might as well have booked at a business hotel in any big city. Meanwhile, the palace building, owing to its combination of disappointingly undersized suites, high nightly rates, and distance from the entertainment options available in the main hotel, failed to create the sense of magic that guests who pay astronomical rates might hope for.

In virtually every respect, the Ciragan was significantly underperforming. Even the coffee was terrible.

The Importance of Turkish Coffee

One evening, not long after we arrived at the Ciragan, Denyse and I were having dinner in the main restaurant of the hotel when I said to her, "Here we are in Turkey, so why don't we order a real Turkish coffee?" If there was one place where we should be able to taste the original Turkish coffee, it would be right here.

Along came a little cup filled with a liquid of dark brown color, no foam, no nothing, and totally different to the Turkish coffees I knew from my trips through the Middle East. Somehow confused, I looked in my cup and asked the waitress still standing at our table.

"What is this?"

"That's Turkish coffee," she said.

"When you serve Turkish coffee at home, is this how you prepare it?" I asked again.

"No, sir," she answered.

"So why is it like this?"

"Because it comes from a machine," she replied.

I could not believe what I had just heard, so I went into the kitchen to see this famous machine with my own eyes. A Turkish coffee from a machine? Sure enough, there was a machine sitting on the counter, tasked with the important job of brewing the signature Turkish coffee served to Ciragan guests.

One brief telephone call later, two hotel engineers rushed into the kitchen, and I stood there watching the machine getting dismantled part by part. Starting that very same evening, Turkish coffee at the Ciragan was prepared the old-fashioned way again.

For hotel guests in Istanbul, encountering a cup of mechanically brewed Turkish coffee should be cause for alarm, because in Turkey, coffee is more than simply a caffeinated beverage. It's deeply embedded in the culture, as it is in certain other parts of the world.

I'd once heard that in the past, when Turkish parents arranged a marriage for their daughter, the woman was expected to impress her intended fiancé by demonstrating that she could make a proper cup of Turkish coffee. At times, however, the woman intentionally served terrible coffee to avoid marrying the man her parents had chosen. Whether this was true or just a rumor, I don't know. There must be some truth to it, though, because a film I recently saw about Turkish families in Germany had a scene in which a woman goes to the kitchen to prepare coffee for a suitor her family had arranged. But the woman was in love with another man, so she threw salt into the cup.

At the Ciragan, if we wanted our guests to fall in love with us, we had to at least get the Turkish coffee right.

Bit by bit, I attempted to learn as much as I could about Turkey, the Turks, and the Turkish culture, and it didn't take long to feel love and a close connection to the country and its people.

Most Germans remain largely ignorant about Turkish culture, and my sister Jenny was no exception. When I told her that my next job would be in Turkey, her reaction was very much opposed. She questioned me about my decision, sounding almost upset.

"Turkey? What are you going to do with the Turks?"

"Jenny," I said, "you don't know anything about the Turks."

"Of course, I do," was her answer. "I see them every day hanging around the railway station."

My sister's impression of Turkish people was based only on glimpses she experienced in Hannover. But now, I realized, I had the opportunity to change her mind about Turkey and the Turkish people, if she would simply agree to visit us in Istanbul.

Luckily, Jenny and her husband accepted our invitation not long after we moved to Istanbul. Denyse and I devised an enjoyable itinerary for their trip based on what we had learned about the city so far. We took them to wonderful restaurants and shops around Istanbul and on a lovely tour on the Bosporus. They met warm, friendly locals, toured beautiful gardens around the city, and experienced the spectacular architecture of the palaces and mosques all over Istanbul.

By all accounts, the trip was a huge success. Even if Jenny did not admit it right away, I could tell the visit had opened her eyes about Turkey. Since then, she has returned five or six times, even traveling beyond Istanbul to Anatolia and other cities with her husband, sometimes without even telling me. That first visit resulted in a 180-degree turnaround in her perception of who the Turks are and what Turkey is all about.

Without realizing it, my sister reminded me of why I love working in the hospitality industry. Travel has the power to transform people's understanding of their fellow humans and the world around them. Beyond merely running hotels, my job was about welcoming guests to a life-changing cultural experience, both inside the hotel and beyond its walls.

One stereotype that I cannot dispute when it comes to my own people, however, is that the Germans are maniacal about punctuality. I believe it's fair to say that we Germans are far more obsessive than the Turks about time. I discovered this when I held my first department head meeting, supposed to start at nine o'clock in the morning.

With the clock turning nine o'clock, I found myself sitting alone in the room, with the first department head walking into the room at five minutes past nine o'clock, another arriving ten minutes past nine, and the rest of them arriving one by one even later. As they arrived, they appeared completely unperturbed by their lateness, almost as if time didn't exist. I realized I would need to change this attitude immediately if I wanted to avoid losing my mind.

"If the meeting is scheduled to be at nine o'clock," I announced to the staff, "it means that I expect everybody to be in the room at nine o'clock, so I can start the meeting rather than waiting for everybody to get here. That takes valuable time away from our schedule, time which could be better used to serve our guests."

The Ciragan needed rescuing, and it was up to me and our entire staff to succeed at this monumental task. Not only did the owners need to recoup their investment, but my team and I would have to see to it that the Ciragan achieved the number-one ranking in Istanbul and a position near the top of the lists of best hotels worldwide.

How would we accomplish this, when the Ciragan, apart from its location on the shore of the Bosporus, had nothing else to offer to make it stand out among its competitors? I knew there was nothing I could physically do with the property, at least not for now. I could not go to the owners or to Kempinski and say, "We have to start spending money at once." That approach would never work, certainly not so soon after I arrived. The only thing it would succeed in doing was ruining my credit as a world-class hotelier and might even get me fired.

But what I could do without spending any money, starting immediately, was to dramatically improve our commitment to hospitality and service, our attention to details, our food and beverage program, the impeccable spotlessness of our premises, and every other element that was within my power to change. Those improvements, taken together, would help create an impression befitting a world-class luxury hotel. I could redefine the operational concepts to make them worthy of a five-star property. I could introduce expert training to make sure the staff fully understands what luxury service and hospitality are all about. I could structure the entire operation to function properly, so the Ciragan could begin to live up to its potential. Yes, a round of renovations would absolutely help us achieve the high rankings we aimed to get, but for the time being, we could go a long way with all the big and small improvements that I intended to implement. After all, there are plenty of hotels worldwide that haven't physically changed for many years and that still play in the upper league of the world's leading hotels.

Another big goal of mine, beyond reshaping our operation, was to defeat the Swissotel and other competitors that had started attracting the business that should belong to the Ciragan and had risen in the meantime to the rank of best hotel in the city.

So there were plenty of challenges ahead of us, no doubt about that. But I felt encouraged while I was attending ITB—the annual international tourism fair in Berlin—when the GM of the Swissotel introduced me to his corporate staff with the following words: "This is Mr. Tischmann, the new general manager of the Ciragan in Istanbul," he said to his team. "And by the way, since Peter is at the Ciragan now, our honeymoon is over."

I knew that his statement was meant seriously, and that what sounded like a nervous joke might have been a first attempt to get his corporate staff used to the idea that the Swissotel's reign would soon come to an end.

The Swissotel had nothing special about it, aesthetically speaking. Its location on a hillside offered a nice panoramic view of the Bosporus but could not even begin to compare with the Ciragan's prime spot along the waterfront. But it was a very active hotel, hosting many events throughout the year that attracted not only tourists but Istanbul locals too. And from an operational point of view, the Swissotel at that time was indeed the best hotel in Istanbul, definitely better than the Ciragan.

A Company Without Culture Is Not a Company

"The fish always stinks at the head first," as the saying goes. The attitude of the general manager impacts the employees because they assume that if a certain detail or behavior is not important to their boss, why should they bother with it? It is difficult to blame the line employees for not caring about the details if the management clearly cannot be bothered. And if the general manager is not interested in promoting his hotel, or if the hotel is not active in its community, it will never be anything more than just a hotel. I had to make it clear to the entire Ciragan staff that this was a new era, and we would be doing things very differently from my predecessor.

The problem reached higher than the Ciragan's previous GM, as I soon discovered. During my first months at the Ciragan, I attended a meeting of Kempinski's general managers in Hamburg. I found myself sitting around a table with about a dozen other general managers, most of whom were engaged in pointless chatter. I got the impression that we were all there to just talk and talk, simply to hear ourselves talking. Someone would mention a problem at his hotel, but nobody in the room would seem particularly concerned with offering a solution. I decided to take matters into my own hands. "If this is what you consider to be your problem," I would say to a GM who raised an issue, "then here is a solution to try. Why don't you give it a shot?" I would offer up a course of action based on my own experience because nobody else seemed interested in doing so. But the problems didn't stop there.

At the time, Kempinski was managed by a trio of executives: Mr. Michael Maas in Berlin, Mr. Theodor Walterspiel in Hamburg, and Mr. Rehfeld in Koeln. As Kempinski's office was in Frankfurt am Main, the trio arrived every Monday morning from their respective home destinations to manage the company during the week, then disappeared again on Friday mornings to return to their cities. Lufthansa was a major shareholder of Kempinski at that time, which made travel for the trio very convenient.

All three executives had their own areas of responsibility, but their real preoccupation was to team up with a second person to blame the third one if something went wrong in the company. And there were a great many things that needed management's attention, starting with the need to introduce a management culture in the first place.

The management culture of the company, as far as I could tell, was to meet occasionally, complain about problems, assign blame, and show no interest in trying new approaches that might actually fix the issues.

Everything changed shortly after the Hamburg meeting, when Reto Wittwer, formerly the head of Swissotels, took over as president and CEO of Kempinski. Lufthansa had recently sold its participation in Kempinski to a Thai company, Dusit Thani, owned by the royal crown. The chairman of Dusit Thani had attended hotel school with Reto Wittwer in Switzerland, so when he took over Kempinski, he brought Wittwer over. The trio was out. I felt bad for Michael Maas since he had brought me in, but I suppose that's life.

Under Reto Wittwer, the structure and management of Kempinski began to improve. The strength of Kempinski had been in its mostly excellent general managers, who were typically very talented at their jobs, but the company culture did not foster the slightest sense of collaboration or improvement.

Ciragan's previous GM appeared to have run the hotel on autopilot, allowing it to stagnate and operate far below its potential. Somehow the Ciragan had managed to make money anyway, most likely due to its location, although not as much as its potential should have allowed.

Managing a hotel like the Ciragan as if it were just a hotel seemed to me like buying a Lamborghini, then only driving it to the corner shop to buy your groceries. The owner's comments that they had offered us a Rolls Royce, only to see it driven like a regular car, suddenly made a lot of sense.

With Reto Wittwer taking over, I felt optimistic that change was on the way, especially under the leadership of Dusit Thani, known for operating luxury hotels of high standing.

Founded in 1948, Dusit Thani had grown to become the premier player in the hospitality business in Thailand, developing a strong reputation for offering the quality and service that made hotels in the Far East justifiably famous. With the Thailand royal crown investing in the company, Dusit Thani now found itself in the position to expand internationally, and the Kempinski purchase signaled its intent to establish a strong foothold in Europe.

The President's First Corporate Meeting

To introduce himself and his new ideas for repositioning Kempinski within the highly competitive international hotel world, Reto Wittwer called a general manager meeting in Istanbul. I had met Reto Wittwer once before at the St. Regis years ago, and we had occasionally stayed in touch over the years. Maybe it was because of this professional relationship, and because he knew what we had achieved at the St. Regis, that he decided to hold his first meeting as new president and CEO of Kempinski at the Ciragan Palace Hotel.

I was honored that Reto entrusted me to organize his event from the beginning to the end, and I felt this gave me the chance to stand out from the pack of GMs at the company. I was eager to prove myself worthy of his trust.

Reto was already under a great deal of pressure from his Dusit Thani bosses when they learned that Kempinski had cancelled the membership of all of its hotels with the Leading Hotels of the World, a valuable marketing organization for luxury hotels.

Highly frustrated, the chairman was seriously thinking of pulling Dusit Thani out of the purchase deal he had recently signed with Kempinski.

The only hotel to resist the move to leave Leading Hotels of the World was the Ciragan, as my predecessor had the wisdom to insist on retaining this membership. The reputation of the Leading Hotels brand was simply too important for the Ciragan to follow blindly in the money-saving efforts of Kempinski's marketing department. I had to applaud his foresight.

The company-wide meeting in Istanbul would give me a chance to position the Ciragan as a star hotel in the new Kempinski firmament. I had a hunch about this, and I knew I needed to do everything in my power to ensure that Reto's first meeting as CEO went smoothly.

We created a theme for the meeting, "Moving forward to become the best." I believe this message worked subliminally in helping me motivate my staff to create a first-rate event. As the leadership teams of every Kempinski hotel converged at the Ciragan to meet Reto Wittwer and listen to his remarks about the company's new path forward, my staff displayed seamless service and impeccable coordination throughout the entire day. The meeting went off without a hitch and was a unanimous success. Reto commended my staff and myself for our efforts, and I am convinced the meeting also helped me, as the new kid on the block, to earn some respect from my peers in the company.

Considering my not-so-long-ago crisis at the St. Regis, and my less than stellar experiences with Dabiri and the Bristol, I was hungry for this level of acclaim and for the chance to prove I could still do my job extremely well indeed.

I was not prepared for the surprise that came my way soon after Reto's meeting.

Traveling with the President

One morning at the Ciragan, I received a phone call from Reto. He was about to fly to Dubai for a business meeting and wanted to know if I would join him.

The purpose of the sudden trip, Reto explained, was to meet a potential investor for a first Kempinski Hotel in the Middle East. I had a few guesses as to why Reto wanted me to participate. My extensive experience with Sheraton in the Middle East was likely one reason, but I suspected, or hoped, that my performance at the St. Regis was the main motivation. By taking me along to Dubai, Reto would be able to point to the St. Regis relaunch as an example of the level of experience and quality Kempinski's general managers could offer.

Saying yes to the Dubai trip was one decision I did not regret. When we arrived, Sheikh Ahmed Bin Ahmed, a wealthy investor, invited us for a meeting in his sumptuous home. Recently built by a European architect, the house represented a mixture of various European styles, French interior design, and gilded surfaces as far as the eye could see. We walked into an enormous oval reception area furnished with sizable leather armchairs designed for large, heavy individuals. Sitting down in one of the chairs, I almost disappeared into the upholstery.

After the customary "Ahlan wa sahlan" ("welcome" in Arabic) and a round of small talk, the sheikh's household staff offered us the traditional welcome coffee. But this time, after my experience years ago in Kuwait, I knew how to politely avoid receiving unwanted refills over and over again. I simply shook my cup when the server came by with the coffee pot. I felt proud of myself, having remembered this lesson from a former life.

Moments later, the sheikh invited us to join him for lunch in his dining room. If one would have expected a richly dressed table with chandeliers and golden cutlery, one would have been disappointed, because there was no table. Instead, a huge embroidered tablecloth covered the floor, and the Middle Eastern specialties our host's chefs had prepared for lunch rested on large silver platters directly on the cloth.

The sheikh sat down and invited Reto and me to sit to the right and to the left of him, a very special honor. The seating followed a strict protocol, with the sheikh and his guests at the top of the floor arrangement, followed by members of the family, and at the end, opposite to the sheikh, the guests of lesser importance.

Sitting on the floor with legs crossed was not, for me, a comfortable way to eat lunch. I found myself wishing the architect had designed a lower level below the seating area where we could dangle our legs, a style one finds in many Japanese restaurants and dining rooms in which guests sit on the floor. But what could I do? One had to adapt oneself to the customs of the host, and certainly every other aspect of this lunch was extraordinarily luxurious.

"Sahtein," the sheikh said, offering the Arabic version of "Bon appetit." He took a few large pieces of meat with his hand from the leg of roasted lamb in front of him and handed them to Reto and to me before helping himself. The trays on the floor displayed generous portions of not just roasted lamb but also grilled fish and a wide variety of Lebanese mezze, all looking extremely inviting.

"I have the best Lebanese chef in the Middle East," the sheikh announced. I had no doubt that he did, because when I was at Sheraton, one reason why we'd had a serious problem finding Lebanese chefs for our Middle East hotels was because the sheikhs had hired them all, at astronomical salaries we were not able to offer at our hotels.

As we ate, the other guests sat silently watching us, until the sheikh decided to send the food platter further down to reach them, and then further down again until everyone all the way on the other side had something to eat. Obviously, the best pieces of meat were gone by then, and the fish platter had nothing but bones left. The mezze bowls were almost empty. For those unlucky guests, I hoped that the experience of sitting at the same table as the sheikh was enough to counteract the disappointment of eating last, but who knows.

In the United States, a long business lunch like this one, during which absolutely no business is discussed, would be considered a waste of time. But in this part of the world, socializing and business are often strictly separated, at least on the surface. The sheikhs can make up their mind about whether they want to do business with you by simply watching and listening to you during lunch and observing how you handle the casual moments.

Different cultures, different habits.

The next morning Reto received notice from the sheikh that Kempinski had won the offer to manage the investors' first hotel in the Middle East, in Ajman, a small emirate close to Dubai. Today, Kempinski operates fifteen hotels in the Middle East, including the Emirate Palace in Abu Dhabi and the Emerald Palace in Dubai, both among the most spectacular hotels in the Middle East.

Reshaping the Ciragan

At last, I was back in the game. After the stellar success of the meeting, I had organized for my boss at the Ciragan, and the lucrative effects of our lunch with the sheikh in Dubai, I had finally returned to the position I enjoyed most: creating transformative changes and getting strong results for a luxury hotel in an exciting cosmopolitan location. My professional life appeared to be rising from the ashes and not a moment too soon.

Until then, as much as I hate to admit it, the St. Regis fiasco was still preoccupying my mind. Denyse kept telling me to forget about it, to put it all behind me. But this was impossible. I could not forget about what had happened in New York not so long ago.

From the start, the assignment at the Ciragan allowed me to concentrate on a project that required my complete focus, and the challenges did shift my attention away from my personal troubles, at least in part. But it was not until I started to see those early signs of success, until I won accolades from my boss and my peers, that I could truly begin to put the St. Regis disaster behind me.

Did what happened at the St. Regis impact the way I did my job and how I interacted with staff at the Ciragan? I have asked myself this, but I don't have an easy answer to the question. The change in environment made it difficult for me to compare the two situations. What I mean by this is that in Turkey, if you put your hand on someone's shoulder, they are likely to see it in a positive rather than a negative light. A certain warmth and style of joking is perceived in different terms than it might be in certain American contexts. After what had happened to me at the St. Regis, I was well-aware of the need to avoid any misunderstandings, but in the Istanbul environment, or in Europe where I worked years ago, I do not believe my conduct would have disturbed anyone in the least. If I had continued to work in the US, I would have changed my way of dealing with my staff and would have been more formal and exceedingly conscious of how certain words and gestures might be misconstrued or used against me.

My goal at the Ciragan was, as it always had been everywhere else, to build a sense of teamwork and a staff dedicated to impeccable service and professionalism. Our shared ambition was to bring the hotel operation to a world-class level that reached or exceeded its potential.

I relished this challenge, and as the weeks went by, my work at the Ciragan allowed me to put the darkness of the recent past behind me. But I admit that I did follow the ongoing developments at the St. Regis with some interest. Many of my former staff members at the St. Regis kept in contact with me, colleagues such as the director of banquet operations Joe Prezioso, the deputy housekeeping head Monika Krebs, the marketing associate Jude Rozenveld, the former butler and now banqueting staff member Arndt Oesterle, along with twenty or thirty people from the opening team, including line employees, chefs, bellmen, and all levels of staff.

If I heard an overarching theme in the comments of my former colleagues, it was that things were not the same at the St. Regis anymore. I could interpret this in many different ways: Perhaps my old staff was referring to my twenty-four-hour style of management, always walking around to check in on each department, talking to employees at all levels, trying to inspire them to do their best. No one did that anymore, apparently. Obviously, it's pleasing to hear that your former team misses you, and misses your management style too, after you leave.

But in the end, what does it all mean? It didn't mean much, since I was no longer part of the St. Regis, and whatever happened at that hotel was no longer my business. I did have a sparkle of satisfaction that maybe I did something right while I was there. But the most important thing is that many of my former St. Regis employees remained loyal friends, and still do to this day.

Together, what we had created at the St. Regis was a sense of belonging, a feeling of camaraderie, a common commitment to serving the customer with the utmost hospitality and professionalism. Those values had bonded our team together. I knew I wanted to achieve that same feeling, that same commitment to excellence at the Ciragan too.

If I had taken a job in the New York City area, I would have rehired some of the St. Regis staff to come work for me. But now that I was in Istanbul, the option to do so was more limited. However, I did poach a few people, including one of the St. Regis department heads. It may sound surprising to hear that this person was Christel Schmitt, the former executive housekeeper at the St. Regis. Christel had avoided me in the days after I was fired, even though her deputy, Monika Krebs, had helped organize a petition that hundreds of my staff members signed to protest ITT Sheraton's action against me. But I understood why Christel felt she needed to be cautious and keep her distance. I did not hold this against her, and the reason why I chose to bring her to the Ciragan was because she is a topnotch housekeeping professional. I knew she could help me establish the standards of impeccable cleanliness and polish that we had at the St. Regis, standards that were lacking at the Ciragan when I started.

No doubt Christel felt uncomfortable hearing from me and receiving my offer to join our staff in Istanbul, considering her behavior toward me after my St. Regis dismissal. But I knew that when I was fired from the St. Regis, everyone who showed sympathy for Peter Tischmann in the days afterward ran the risk of not keeping their job. Staff members sensed an unwritten threat not to show too much appreciation for the good old days. I think Christel was afraid to lose her job, and she was probably right to worry.

When Christel started at the Ciragan, I never mentioned anything about what had happened at the St. Regis and neither did she. It was as if we had silently agreed to put it behind us. She arrived in Istanbul ready to do what she does best, which is to ensure a spotless hotel. With Christel leading the housekeeping staff at the Ciragan, I knew I didn't have to supervise her all the time to get the hotel looking exactly the way I wanted it to.

A few specific positions at a hotel are absolutely vital to its image: One is the head housekeeper, one is the executive chef, and one is the front office manager. These are the roles which you need to fill with exactly the right person in order to make a fast and visible impact on your operation.

When I took over at the Ciragan, I cannot say that it was not clean, or was not spotless, but there is an important distinction between basic cleanliness and the "wow" factor. A hotel might look perfectly clean, but its brass surfaces are not quite polished to a brilliant shine, for example. A discerning guest will notice, even if most will not. Christel knew how to get every one of those details perfectly right. She had the rare skill of achieving a "wow" effect across the entire hotel.

Hiring Christel and the other key positions mean dismissing some existing staff members, which I did not relish doing but needed to do in order to create noticeable improvements.

The chief engineer had to go, as he simply did not grasp how to handle guest complaints at a luxury hotel. If a guest has a problem with a room, you don't just take that order and put it at the end of the list of maintenance problems. You have to prioritize it and make that customer happy as quickly as possible, even if you have twenty other maintenance orders waiting. I gave him a rough time about his slow approach to fixing problems, so he left. In his place, I hired a chief engineer who was exceptional at his job and who understood that the number-one person to please in a hotel is the customer, always. My new hire changed the entire attitude of the engineering department, turning them into a guest-focused rather than a hammer-and-nail-focused crew.

The culinary program needed a dramatic change too. The existing chef had a habit of using convenience foods in the kitchen, rarely serving a freshly cooked dish. He and his team prepared nearly everything in advance. This would not do at the Ciragan. In his place, I hired an excellent culinary talent named Michael Norman from South Africa, and for the main restaurant, I brought in a chef from the Four Seasons in New York, a colleague of my son Peter Jr. The chef I dismissed later joined SwissAir to run its airline food program, which made sense since that is the type of food he was cooking at the Ciragan. A wonderful pastry chef from Australia joined us too, and I hired Heinz Grub, formerly of the Frankfurt Sheraton, as the F&B director. Heinz was a workaholic, a tough cookie, someone for whom a twenty-hour workday was a half-day. He had an innate understanding of quality and service, and he could manage a crisis, both of which are extremely important when you're running the food department at a hotel.

I didn't fire anyone else from the existing culinary team. Most of them were locals and needed the work. Under new leadership, I saw no reason why they could not perform their jobs at a higher level.

Each day, I tried to instill in my staff a sense that every single detail matters and makes an impression on guests. Every detail contributes to the ultimate success or failure of a hotel. One cannot exaggerate the importance of even the littlest things. For example, I've always had a tendency to glance down at the floor in search of any scraps of paper or tiny bits of trash that would ruin the overall look of spotlessness.

If details like this don't matter to the boss, why should they matter to other employees? It is easy to underestimate the ripple effect that even the tiniest evidence of sloppiness can have on a hotel aiming to win over the most discerning guests in the world.

Leading the Way

"A leader is somebody who knows the way, goes the way, and shows the way." The author John Maxwell's quote rang through my mind as I walked around the Ciragan, trying to model the behavior I wanted my staff to adopt.

As general manager of the Ciragan, and before that of the St. Regis, I saw it as an important part of my job to get staff into the habit of noticing and fixing the little imperfections they saw. Soon enough, after a few weeks of bending over to pick up every piece of paper I spotted on the carpet, I had only to glance at a wayward scrap, or cast my eyes in the direction of a dirty ashtray, and an employee who saw me noticing it would immediately rush over to clean it up.

In Istanbul, I knew I was working in a different cultural environment from the St. Regis, but I wanted to keep the operational approach as similar as possible. Now that I had the right people in place in the key positions, it was time to make sure everyone obtained the skills and attitude required of a world-class luxury hotel. The entire staff needed to get to the point where they took ownership of their jobs and felt personal responsibility and pride in upholding the image of our hotel.

We had no choice but to think this way, which required a major shift from the management culture the Ciragan's previous leadership had established. As a result of the failure to implement an operational philosophy worthy of a luxury hotel, and a lack of care in overseeing a hotel of this scale, the Ciragan's physical quality had declined, along with its reputation, at an alarmingly fast rate in the first few years before I arrived.

Imagine you have this beautiful location on the Bosporus and you promote your hotel as the Ciragan Palace, a property that once housed the sultans of a legendary empire. Guests arrive with monumental expectations, but soon enough, they find themselves checking into an ordinary hotel where the rooms have nothing special to offer.

During the restoration of the late 1980s, the spaces in the hotel as well as in the palace building had been designed with practicality in mind. The quality of the furnishings looked simply mediocre, and nearly all the furniture was attached to the wall. A housekeeper would come into the room with a vacuum cleaner and would be able to move around without even touching or displacing any furniture, with the exception of the desk chair.

In addition to the poor design of the rooms, in which practical considerations about how to clean the spaces apparently took priority over the guests' comfort, all the materials and fabrics were cheap. This had the effect of making the rooms look extremely worn after a short time, leading to more than a few embarrassing moments.

I learned later that the owners had spent much more than anticipated to finish the hotel, but I believe that the selection of cheap materials had happened much earlier, as a result of poor design and a lack of understanding of the needs of a luxury hotel.

I will never forget the first time I wanted to show some guest rooms to a potential customer. Walking into what was supposed to be one of our premium rooms, I immediately noticed a hole in the carpet in the middle of the room. I quickly dashed over to the area, stood on the piece of the damaged carpet, and let the guest walk alone to the balcony so he could enjoy the magnificent vista of the Bosporus and of Asia across the strait. While the guest looked around the room, I remained standing in the same spot the entire time with my foot covering the hole.

After that nearly disastrous tour with the guest—luckily, he didn't seem to notice the damaged carpet—we prepared one room exclusively as a showroom, to spare ourselves the humiliation.

Conrad Hilton, when asked what he considered the three most important elements for a good hotel, answered: "Location, location, location." But without contradicting Mr. Hilton, the location alone doesn't guarantee a good hotel, if the rest of the hotel doesn't live up to the expectation generated by the location.

For sure the Ciragan, alongside the waters of the Bosporus, did have one of the most spectacular sites in Istanbul, but to become the best hotel in town takes much more than just location. Much more. Any customer who came to us expecting something extraordinary, beyond just the view, faced a terrible disappointment.

A luxury hotel has to be something you see, feel, and experience, in every element from the high quality of the towels in the bathroom, to the unobtrusive sound of the air-conditioning, to every little detail that signifies quality and refinement. At the Ciragan, the walls were bare and the carpets were falling apart. The hotel was only a few years old at this point, but if you put in cheap materials to begin with, they will require renovation much sooner than if you had invested in higher quality materials in the first place.

I knew the owners had no intention of spending money to make the necessary changes, at least not until we started bringing in more revenue. I couldn't go to them and say, "I need six million dollars for a renovation."

They would say, "We didn't bring you over so you could ask for money."

They brought me over because they expected miracles from me. The miracle of driving an ordinary car like a Rolls Royce. I wanted to say to them, "If you want to drive a Rolls Royce, you have to have a Rolls Royce in the first place."

Yes, I was already sprucing up the lesser car they gave me and doing everything imaginable to make it drive like a Rolls. Still, I found myself caught in a Catch-22. How do we make as much money as we need to bring in, with the hotel looking the way it does, so the owners will agree to give us the money to keep it from looking this way?

First, the owners needed to see that I was doing everything possible to take care of their interests. The management company expected me to defend its interests as well. As a GM, you're caught in the middle, because not everything that helps the management company is also good for the owners. This is a situation I had faced before, most recently at the Heliopolis. The St. Regis had a slightly different arrangement: ITT owned the hotel and Sheraton was the management company, but since they were the same entity, no such conflict existed.

The situation at Ciragan was much more sensitive than at the Heliopolis. This was because the owners, the Abu Dhabi Investment Authority, also owned the Lanesborough Hotel in London, which was clearly the number one hotel in London. The Lanesborough's occupancy was very high and was only outperformed by its average room rate, producing a healthy return for the owners.

Comparing the Lanesborough with the Ciragan would be like comparing apples with pears, but still the owners took every opportunity to compare operational results among the two properties. They would come to me and ask why the room rate at the Ciragan was lower than the room rate at the Lanesborough, without realizing that Istanbul could not be compared with a financial center such as London.

I had no doubt the owners were well-aware of this, as they were highly educated and intelligent and understood the hotel industry very well. Nonetheless, they stuck to their strategy, coming back every month with the same questions about the rates, to keep up the maximum amount of pressure on me, and to make me sweat.

Training for Success

Losing my job was not an option. Not now, not after I had worked so hard to restore my name. To stay employed at the Ciragan and to continue rescuing my reputation from the ashes of the St. Regis, I had no choice. I had to find new ways of improving the Ciragan Palace quickly and dramatically, not by spending money but simply by continuing to find ways to do everything better each and every day.

The key department heads I installed had already made a difference in our overall quality. But I knew what I needed to do next: implement an extensive training program to ensure that every employee in every department, from my new hires to the longtime staff, knew what it would take to perform at the highest level.

Training people who've worked in a certain hotel for years and developed specific habits and routines is quite a bit more difficult than training employees from scratch. It takes approximately double the time, in my experience. At the St. Regis, we hired an almost entirely new team for the opening, a team who had no previous habits associated with that particular hotel. We essentially started with a blank slate, which allowed us to create the culture we wanted to implement. At the Ciragan, we had to undertake two processes: unlearning old work habits first, then learning new ones.

I managed to allocate a small budget so I could invite expert consultants from outside the hotel to run training activities. This turned out to be well worth the expense. I sat in on the training sessions myself, to signal to my staff that I valued this process and expected them to do the same.

Unlearning old ways of thinking about your job can be even harder than it sounds. Some people aren't just unprepared to take on this responsibility; they're afraid to do so. A waiter who is used to having the head waiter tell him, "You have to do this and this and this," now suddenly has to make his own instant decisions about what is best for the customer in a certain situation. That waiter will likely feel terrified of making a mistake. So a big part of the training is to help staff members understand that everybody makes mistakes, and it's not the end of the world as long as you learn from it and don't make the same error again and again.

Giving our employees the authority to make their own decisions when serving customers was not enough. We also had to instill them with the sense of confidence to do so. We had to remind employees of their important role at the center of the service experience. All members of the staff, no matter what their position, needed to feel an ownership stake, a sense that "This is my restaurant, and you are my guest."

To train our restaurant waiters, we had them act out scenes in which a guest is seated at a table and ready to order. How would the waiter approach the guest? How would he take the order and answer the guest's questions? Waiters needed to learn that when they greet and serve the guest, they're the main point of contact. They're ultimately responsible for that customer's sense of satisfaction and happiness with the overall experience.

At the front desk, staff members play-acted the role of customers who complained about their invoice at checkout. A customer might say, "You are charging me for a beer from the mini bar, but I didn't have anything to drink, and I don't even like beer," to which a typical hotel receptionist would reply, "Please wait one moment while I check with housekeeping." But that's the worst situation you can create because the guest is probably waiting to go outside, and his taxi has already arrived. The receptionist at a luxury hotel must instead say, "Sir, we will take the charge off your bill, no problem at all." We had to authorize each staff member to make decisions like this, which is a challenging goal in a workplace culture that operated very differently before.

Sometimes, watching a negative situation unfold during the training can be more effective than simply talking about the right way to do things. For example, you can tell stewards not to stack more than twenty plates at a time when they're carrying them across the room. But instead of just giving verbal instructions, we decided to show our staff a training film in which a steward stacks up thirty plates and starts to walk through the dining room. The plates begin to sway, and as he tries to catch them, they crash loudly to the floor. Everyone in the restaurant turns around and gawks.

In an even more instructive hands-on exercise, we sent our staff to other hotels in the city to see how they do things differently. We gave staff members a budget to spend on lunch or dinner at other hotel restaurants in Istanbul, for instance at the Swissotel, and take note of service behaviors that impressed them in a positive or negative way. Then they had to report back about what they'd learned.

Cash incentives and public recognition never hurt either, so we created awards like Employee of the Month, which came with a check for $100. Every month, we gave the recognition to one staff member in the front of the house and another in the back of the house, so a pot washer or an engineer had an equal chance at the prize. We hung a plaque in the lobby with the winner's name on it. We also threw a monthly party in the dining room for all the employees celebrating a birthday. We used every single trick in the book to motivate our staff and get them to think differently about what their job means for the hotel.

A majority of the staff, around 75 or 80 percent, took well to the training. It is nearly impossible to achieve 100 percent compliance with an entirely new system when you're dealing with so many staff members who are used to the old ways. But we created enough changes in employee behavior to make a significant difference.

The moment when staff members begin to feel they're part of something special and can experience the positive impact of their work, it's like a breakthrough. Their attitude shifts immediately. They can see the results when a customer thanks them personally, and especially when higher tips start to roll in. In many cases, changes like these can be enough to inspire resistant staff members to alter their habits entirely.

Guests who had stayed at the Ciragan before started to notice that something new was happening. The owners certainly noticed too, but they said nothing. Any positive transformations that I delivered to them during this era were, in their eyes, merely a given. Even if I yearned for a reaction, I understood why they remained silent.

To earn the owners' praise, and especially if I hoped to get them to spend money on major renovations, I needed to do something even more visible than simply revolutionize the service. Luckily, I had some big ideas in mind.

Luring Istanbul's High Society Back to the Ciragan

An iconic hotel offers much more than just a place to stay. To reach top-of-mind status, a hotel must position itself at the center of a city's social and cultural life. Ciragan's main competitor, the Swissotel, only a year older than our hotel, had already gained the center-stage position with events like the annual Swiss National Day, a de rigueur event on Istanbul's social calendar. But I felt confident that by making a few of the right moves, the Ciragan could easily compete and with even more flair than our competitors. It was a matter of coming up with the perfect promotions and marketing them properly. I had done this before at the Heliopolis, with wildly successful results.

At the Ciragan, I knew we needed to start smaller. We had a new chef, along with the other key staff members I had recently hired, and they would need time to get organized. The big splashy productions would have to come later, but first we could run a series of promotions to introduce our new menus or to highlight new specialties at the Turkish restaurant. We got off to a strong start with a seasonal promotion around asparagus season, which drew visitors from around the city eager to taste menu items made with the popular ingredient. Then we announced a number of equally small-scale, crowd-pleasing culinary events to follow, to get the chef and the rest of the staff into the habit of developing new ideas, implementing special menus, and running promotions.

I quickly discovered that Istanbul likes a special event just as much as Cairo does, and it certainly appreciates a great party. Once we got a few successful small-scale promotions off the ground at the Ciragan, it was time to plan something a little bigger.

As it happened, the fifth anniversary of the Ciragan's 1991 launch was coming up, a perfect excuse for a party. I wanted to organize an unforgettable event to celebrate this milestone in the life of the Ciragan Palace Hotel, and I was determined to outdo the Swissotel's own Swiss-themed anniversary party the year before, with its live cows grazing on grass and its elegant buffet of Swiss cuisine.

How much would our party cost? I budgeted roughly $10,000, which was more in 1996 dollars of course than it is now, but still not a staggeringly large sum for an anniversary party at a hotel like the Ciragan. It was probably not even a tenth of what the Swissotel had spent on its own anniversary bash, but I knew we could make that relatively small amount go a long way.

I decided to throw a black-tie anniversary gala, a rare event back then for hotels in Istanbul. With a few judicious decoration ideas, we could use our modest budget to create a dramatic impact, and our invited guests' elegant dress code would add to the sense of occasion.

On the day of the party, we enrobed the palace gate with a large red ribbon and a red carpet leading up to the terrace. We lined the terrace with red and white balloons and lit lanterns all along the edge overlooking the Bosporus, creating a spectacular lighting effect once evening settled in. Five giant candles glowed on the roof, visible all the way to the Asia side of the Bosporus.

At the top of the central staircase, we placed a fifteen-foot-tall replica of our birthday cake with a number-five candle on top. The dummy cake stood ready to be lit up later in the evening by two candle-lighters, who would climb up to reach it via hidden staircases on each side of the cake.

As guests began to arrive on the terrace, waiters greeted them with champagne glasses on silver trays decorated with orchids. Instead of displaying buffet tables loaded with food, we decided to assign waiters wearing coattails and white gloves to move among the guests and offer finger foods on silver platters, each decorated with small butter sculptures. Like waves at the beach, the waiters rolled through the crowd, presenting one item after another, serving a total of twenty-five different specialty finger foods, followed by ten assorted desserts at the end.

The advantage was that nobody had to queue up for food, and guests could keep a hand free to hold a glass of champagne. Invitees could move around, mingle, and try as many of the foods as they liked without interruption.

Guests told us they had never seen a culinary parade extravaganza of this kind before. In those years, this was still something of a novelty.

People claimed this was one of the best galas they had ever been to. Everyone seemed pleased that our concept allowed them to socialize rather than standing in line at the buffet, and they assured us they'd had more than enough to eat and drink throughout the evening. We later adopted this food concept for most of our future receptions, setting a new standard for parties at the Ciragan.

Even our musical selection for the evening set a new trend. We decided we would not offer the type of live music generally played at these events, and instead, we hired the sixty-piece Istanbul Symphony Orchestra to entertain our guests with classical music.

Listening to the string instruments as they complemented the soft whispers of the Bosporus waters was an experience in itself, a sensory reverie interrupted only by the horn sounds of the few big ships that passed in front of the hotel.

This was the first time that the symphony orchestra had played for such an event, and our guests said they enjoyed it tremendously. Ever since that evening, the orchestra, albeit in a reduced version, became a frequent guest at the Ciragan's many special events.

What would such an evening be without a speech? Guests waited for the "Genel Müdür" to take the podium, and he did. Much to the amusement of our invitees, I presented my speech in Turkish, mostly by relying on the help of a piece of paper. But nobody seemed to care. The crowd applauded the speech, showing enthusiastic support for my attempt to speak Turkish. I was happy to have survived.

The highlight of the evening was the lighting of the big number-five candle on top of the dummy birthday cake. Two beautiful women in white dresses floated up the central staircase, and then up the hidden stairs behind the cake, arriving at the top with great fanfare to light the candle with torches. This involved a delicate coordination of the timing because once the candle-lighters held the torch up to the candle, we had to open the gas supply to make sure that the 5 would light up properly and shine out into the dark night. Fortunately, everything worked out smoothly.

All in all, it was a very successful evening, the talk of the town for many days afterward. The media raved about the spectacular evening and showered us with compliments. What more could we have hoped for?

The evening showed Istanbul society what the Ciragan Palace is all about. The entire event and its aftermath would have been perfect, had I not received a telephone call from Abu Dhabi the next morning, questioning the amount of money we had spent and asking if this event was really necessary.

As I listened to the owners' personal advisor interrogate me about the party expenses, I heard the voice of the hotel's comptroller in my mind. She had asked me the same questions about the budget a few weeks before, and I had no doubt now where the owners' information was coming from.

It took me some time to convince the owners that the return on the money we had spent would be tenfold if not more, and that the hotel would benefit to a great extent from this event for months or even years to come.

"You should have informed us before," was the answer from the owners' side. I could tell that they realized the party was in fact in the best interests of the hotel but still felt compelled to tell me that it was my job to keep them informed of such events. I had never before notified or asked the owners about any promotions we did at the hotel, nor did they seem to want to get involved in details of this nature. Why should I have sought permission this time? I had a strong hunch the comptroller had decided to step in and elevate herself in the owners' eyes by questioning my decisions. I decided it was best if I appeared to go along with his advice.

"Yes," I said to the owners' advisor on the phone that day. "You are right. I should have thought about informing the owners. We'll do it for the tenth anniversary party."

Although the conversation ended on a friendly note, it left a bitter taste. My trust and confidence in the comptroller was now hurt beyond repair. A few months later, I would learn how right I was in my assumptions when the comptroller decided to lobby for a 10 percent raise for her staff only because, apparently, they were working so much harder than the rest of us. The owners approved the raise as soon as she asked for it. I was worried that by giving a raise to only one department, after the entire staff had put so much effort into getting retrained and developing new work habits, we would hurt morale. When I complained to Kempinski about the comptroller's move, they said they agreed with me and vowed to fire her. But they never did. I think they were too scared to hurt their relationship with the owners.

In any case, our anniversary party had accomplished its goal of launching the Ciragan onto the city's social scene, despite the owners' complaints. We still had a long way to go before we could knock the Swissotel out of the top position, but we had started to rattle their foundation.

Our momentum was building now, stronger and stronger every day. I was convinced that soon enough, the Ciragan would be unstoppable.

VIEW FROM THE GARDEN & POOL

THE FAMOUS HALAS OF MRS. SIMAVI

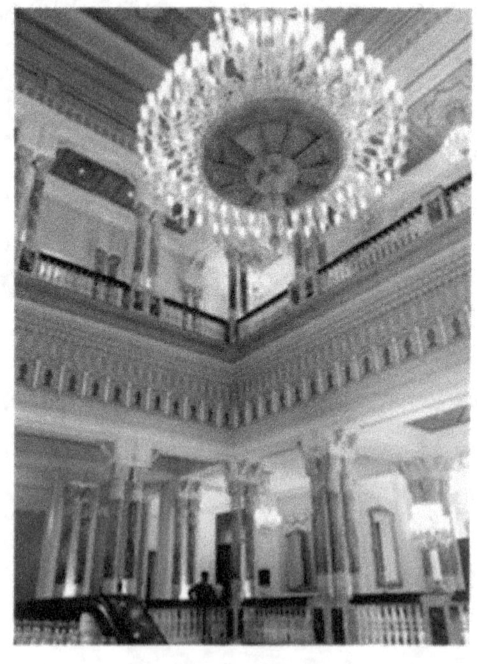

5 TONS OF CRISTAL IN
THE PALACE LOBBY

The Who's Who of Istanbul 30

Meeting the First Lady of Istanbul

Not long before our anniversary bash, I had been fortunate to make the acquaintance of a society lady named Cigdem Simavi. Her husband was the former owner of a prominent newspaper in Istanbul, and Cigdem was as powerful a presence in Istanbul society as Brooke Astor in New York. Cigdem and her husband owned a private yacht called *Hallas*, one of those classic Bosporus ferry boats, which they had bought and converted into a magnificent vessel of twenty cabins. They were always inviting top international personalities to spend time on the yacht as it docked in the south of Turkey during the summer months or along the Bosporus in Istanbul in winter. Princess Margaret was an annual guest of the Simavis and would join them on cruises on the *Hallas* yacht.

Like Brooke Astor, Cigdem had a great deal of personal charm, and her parties attracted the crème de la crème of Istanbul. But Cigdem had run into an obstacle with the Ciragan's former general manager. Due to the hotel's unique location on the Bosporus, Cigdem had approached the former GM to ask if she could dock her boat in front of the Ciragan, but he had refused. Instead, he suggested that she ask her international guests to stay at the Ciragan. He felt the yacht would compete with his hotel business.

Shortly after I joined the Ciragan, Cigdem approached me and asked for an appointment. As she introduced herself in my office, she told me about the company she runs to help promote Turkish culture and art in international exhibitions. I liked her as a person immediately. I did not yet know how prominent she was in Istanbul. Later, when I asked around, people said, "Oh, Cigdem Simavi! Of course, we know who she is."

Cigdem told me about her efforts to dock her yacht in front of the Ciragan, explaining that when she hosts VIP friends like Princess Margaret, it would be awkward to ask them to stay in a hotel since she has private cabins on her yacht. I said of course I would permit her to dock her boat in front of our hotel and that it would be a pleasure for me to have the *Hallas* parked there. An old-fashioned, elegant-looking boat owned by one of society's grande dames could only serve as an asset for the hotel.

On the day when I met with Cigdem for the first time, it never occurred to me that Denyse and I would soon develop a warm friendship with the Simavis. But as the months went by, we got to know them well. They invited us for dinner, and we invited them. Cigdem introduced me to people in Istanbul society, allowing me to forge relationships that helped establish the Ciragan at the center of the city's cultural life. Cigdem began to host Turkish art exhibitions in our hotel. Over time, the friendship between our two families blossomed, and we remain in touch to this day, many years after we left Turkey.

The local society people to whom Cigdem introduced me began to throw their functions at the hotel, and slowly but surely—as we continued to improve the quality of our service and our attention to detail—the Ciragan began to move closer into the social center of Istanbul.

As society moved in, the political class didn't wait too long to adopt our hotel as their preferred event space too. Once word got around, we built up momentum, and soon we began hosting VIPs and their events on a regular basis.

At the time, Recep Tayyip Erdogan was the mayor of Istanbul, and he visited the hotel once or twice a week for lunches or events. As a general manager, you have to greet these people with a sense of occasion. "Mr. Mayor, welcome to the Ciragan," would be a typical greeting, followed by the traditional kiss on the right cheek and on the left cheek. His aftershave smelled terribly sweet, but what could I do?

In Turkey, as part of the welcome greeting, men often kiss each other on the cheek, which wasn't my favorite habit. But as a hotelier, you adapt to the local culture everywhere you go.

The official delegations from the Turkish capital of Ankara began to stay in our hotel when they came to Istanbul. At this point, we were leaving the Swissotel and Conrad, another somewhat new competitor, in the dust, and this was exactly where we wanted to be. Our hotel was still badly in need of a physical upgrade, but we were managing to compensate for this with a high quality of service and a considerable amount of flair.

Luckily, not every accommodation at the Ciragan was substandard. The majority of rooms did fall below the quality that one would expect from a luxury hotel, but we still had some suites and rooms which were acceptable. We also had suites in the palace, although those were difficult to book since they were very expensive, and we could not exactly market them as state-of-the-art accommodations. But at least they were higher in quality than the hotel rooms, and their location in the palace gave them heightened appeal.

The VIPs, by now arriving in ever greater numbers, included the most prominent government officials and celebrities from around the world.

US president Bill Clinton visited in 1995, and Denyse and I still have a photo of ourselves welcoming him to the Ciragan. The former Soviet Union president Mikhail Gorbachev also visited in 1995, five years after winning the Nobel Peace Prize.

First Lady Hillary Clinton arrived at the Ciragan during her Istanbul visit on her way back from Bosnia in 1996. She was invited to speak at our hotel by the Turkish American Chamber of Commerce, an organization to which I belonged, since as a hotelier, you have to join all kinds of civic associations.

Mrs. Clinton gave a speech to around eight hundred businessmen in our ballroom. She talked about the importance of Turkey, and how Ataturk, the founder and first president of the Turkish state, had liberated the country's women and introduced the right to vote. She mentioned the history of development in Turkey and the role of women in the country's business sector, and she talked for at least half an hour without ever looking at her notes. When she finished, she received a standing ovation from the entire room. Considering that business in Turkey was still a man's world, the applause Mrs. Clinton received was quite impressive. She was a brilliant speaker.

Because of the position the Ciragan had achieved by this point, virtually every big corporation in Turkey was hosting its galas and activities at our hotel. One summer evening in 1995, Liza Minelli held a concert at the Ciragan when a Turkish company invited her to Istanbul to perform for its guests. We had Whitney Houston at our hotel for another event. One weekend at a huge wedding we hosted, one of the guests was Vanessa Mae, a famous young violinist whose signature white violin added a lovely visual flourish to the celebration.

We were clearly the number one hotel in Istanbul at this point, by a sizable distance. No competitor could come close to the Ciragan now, even with rooms and suites more elegant than ours. I felt an immense sense of pride that we had reached this status, after all our hard work. But I was not sure how long this situation could last.

The Nights of Culinary Stars

Despite the Ciragan's increasingly dire need of a renovation, we still had a few spectacular amenities to offer that no other hotel could claim. For instance, the palace with its impressive open spaces, majestic staircases, huge crystal chandeliers, and Ottoman decoration, which made the palace unique.

Not exposed to the public was the old Turkish bath and hammam with beautifully carved Carrara marble and unique Ottoman design elements.

When in 1910 the fire totally destroyed the mostly wooden structure of the palace, keeping only the outside walls standing, the marble hammam survived as well, with little damage to the Carrara marble, but traces of the fire remained all over.

Although during the renovation the marble had been cleaned to restore its original splendor, the hammam had not been used as a bath since, as it was too costly to renovate. But it served as a showpiece and a symbol of the sultan's lifestyle.

The hammam was a fantastic space, and one day, it occurred to me that we should use it as a private dining room. We put out the word that we would allow guests to book the hammam space for dinner parties and cocktail events of up to fifty people. From the moment we made the announcement, the hammam became an instant smash hit as a party room. Since the space didn't have a kitchen, however, we had to get creative when we hosted dinners there. But we pulled it off, making use of our main restaurant kitchen and shuttling dishes back and forth.

Now that we had Istanbul's attention, it was time to expand the scope and ambition of our hotel promotions. At the Heliopolis, we had enjoyed great success with our celebrity chef events, so I decided to see how those would do at the Ciragan. We came up with an event series called the Night of Culinary Stars, in which every month we would bring a three-star French chef to Istanbul to cook exclusively at the Ciragan.

We announced every dinner as a one-night-only gala and brought in famous Michelin-starred French chefs like Georges Blanc, Michel Troisgros, Alain Ducasse, and Paul Bocuse to headline each event.

Each chef brought his own sous chefs and special ingredients with him so he could produce an unforgettable dinner, in the same style as what guests might experience in the chef's own restaurants in France. One chef even arrived with his own potatoes, and another lugged in twenty kilos of his favorite butter for a sauce.

As the Ciragan had become known for hosting the city's best banquets, I wanted to maintain the same level of service and exclusivity for these chef promotions. We set the price at $120 a person for the Culinary Stars dinners, which was a lot of money at the time. To maintain our quality of service, we could only accommodate a hundred guests, since the restaurant space we were using only had a hundred seats. We also had only a hundred silver domes to cover the plates to ensure that the food arrived at the table as hot as possible.

Nobody had ever tried to sell a gala dinner for $120 per person, and we were very concerned we might end up with a flop on our hands. But within two days, the first gala dinner was sold out, with many more people begging us for a seat or at least a place on the waiting list.

The first gala evening was a smashing success, and most of the customers who had a reservation for the first night immediately reserved for the second, third, and all the other dinners in the series.

The reservation list of our guests for the gala events looked like a page from the who's who of Istanbul, with many of them adjusting their personal schedules to be present the day of their reservation.

With the word out, and people all over Istanbul hearing reports of the magnificent dinner, hopeful attendees called for reservations for the other nights in the series, only to learn that we were totally booked.

One customer pleaded with me, "Mr. Tischmann, you have to give me a table."

I told him I was sorry, but we had none left.

"I am not leaving town," he insisted. "If someone doesn't show up, call me immediately. I will be there."

In Istanbul, people wear Ataturk pins to show their appreciation of what the former Turkish president did for his country. Out of respect, I was wearing an Ataturk pin too, which was greatly appreciated by the majority of our guests and helped me get accepted as one of them. I enjoyed hobnobbing with our guests and building connections that would solidify the status of the Ciragan. Once you impress the members of society, this creates a domino effect, as they keep bringing each other into the fold.

For the last dinner in the series, I invited my old acquaintance Paul Bocuse to be the featured chef. Who hadn't heard of Paul Bocuse? His event was anticipated with great enthusiasm. The first question Paul asked me when he arrived was: "Peter, how many guests will we have?"

I said, "One hundred, as usual."

He said, "What? Only a hundred? You made me come here for only a hundred covers?"

I explained to Chef Bocuse that we didn't have enough seats or silver cloches to serve more than a hundred guests at a time. But I asked him how many covers he would like to do if he could.

"Two hundred," he replied.

I digested this for a moment. Then I said okay. We divided the night into two seatings, allowing us to give Paul Bocuse the two hundred covers he wanted. I got on the phone with our sales and marketing department, and in less than an hour, we had filled the second seating of one hundred.

The man who told me he would remain in Istanbul, practically waiting by the phone for us to call, finally got his chance to attend one of the dinners. At the Ciragan, we were in the business of making people happy, and I was delighted when we could please an eager customer as well as an internationally famous chef at the same time.

We certainly needed to spread all the cheer we could and to build as much loyalty as possible with people in the position to raise the Ciragan's status in Istanbul and the world.

His Holy Highness—the First among Equals

A former New York colleague of mine surprised me with an unexpected connection in Istanbul. Years ago, my former St. Regis coworker John Stavros had introduced me to his friend Father Alexander, a highly placed member of the Greek Orthodox Church in the US who lived in New York City at the time. Coincidentally, Father Alexander was visiting Istanbul around the same time Denyse and I arrived. When we reconnected at the Ciragan, he offered to introduce me to his good friend in Istanbul, the Holy Highness Patriarch Bartolomeos. I had not heard of the Patriarch, but I was intrigued.

As I quickly learned, the Patriarch is head of the Greek Orthodox Church worldwide, a position that makes him one of the two highest-ranking leaders in Christianity according to the church's canons. The Pope of the Catholic Church in Rome is one of the leaders, and the Patriarch of the Eastern Orthodox Church in Constantinople, otherwise known as Istanbul, is the other. I'm a Lutheran myself, and I had never met the Pope, but I considered it a great honor to meet the Patriarch.

I soon discovered that not everyone felt this way about the Patriarch, at least not in Istanbul. As the leader of a minority religion in Turkey, especially one that has been subject to suppression by the government, Patriarch Bartolomeos did not typically receive a formal welcome around Istanbul. Nor was he a habitual guest of the Ciragan, as he generally held his meetings in other locations. Father Alexander would often send Greek Orthodox visitors from the US to meet with the Patriarch during their travels in Turkey, a tremendous privilege for members of the sect, and after the visit, they would usually leave a large fundraising check for the Orthodox church.

From the day when Father Alexander introduced us to the Patriarch, I welcomed him with fanfare at the hotel, and since that moment, he became a frequent guest at the Ciragan. I believe he was quite surprised the first time this happened, as he had never experienced such treatment before at our hotel. But as far as I was concerned, a highly ranked religious figure deserves this kind of welcome.

Later, I learned how grateful the Patriarch had been for the dignified treatment we gave him at the Ciragan, especially in the presence of world leaders and VIPs. We received the Patriarch as an honored guest during events featuring people such as Henry Kissinger and Ahmet Ertegun, the Turkish-born head of Atlantic Records. Ertegun already held the Patriarch in high esteem, but Kissinger had apparently never heard of him before, and he seemed to take note of the ceremonious way we treated him at the Ciragan. Similarly, with other diplomatic and political figures we hosted at our hotel, when we honored the Patriarch's presence, the effect was to elevate him in the esteem of Istanbul society and the international community.

When Denyse's mother visited us in Istanbul, the Patriarch gave us a private audience, just Denyse and her mother sitting with him in his office at the heart and center of the Greek Orthodox religion. A devout Greek Orthodox, my mother-in-law was beside herself with gratitude.

I developed a deep respect for the Patriarch myself, even though, despite the humorous efforts of Father Alexander and John Stavros to convince the Patriarch to convert me to the Greek Orthodox faith, "Leave him in peace," the Patriarch said to Father Alexander. "Lutherans are good people too."

Denyse and I grew fond of the Patriarch as a person as well, beyond his esteemed role in the church, and we enjoyed hosting him once in our suite at the Ciragan. That time, he and three other Greek Orthodox patriarchs joined us for a social visit before a wedding that he was officiating that day at the palace.

As the bride and groom had not quite organized themselves yet, the beginning of the wedding was delayed, but the four patriarchs had arrived at the hotel well ahead of time.

What to do with four patriarchs who are supposed to enter the wedding party last, after everyone has been seated? Keep them waiting in the public hallway of the palace? Impossible!

Without any hesitation, I invited all four of them to our apartment to pass the time comfortably as they waited. As we sat in our living room, chatting to kill time, Denyse asked the patriarchs, "What can I offer you to drink?" They charmed us by replying, "Do you have whiskey?"

When they left after half an hour to finally join the wedding party, I turned to Denyse and said with a big smile, "When was the last time you were surrounded by so much holiness?"

"Never," she answered. "This should last for a very long time."

Finally the Renovation

Celebrities and VIPs swarmed around the Ciragan nearly every day now, and the hotel was a busy hive of activity from morning to night. The weeks flew by, one after the other. I looked up to realize that it was now two and a half years since I had joined the hotel. In that time, we had raised the quality of the Ciragan tremendously and improved operational results, despite the physical shortcomings of our buildings and guest accommodations. There was no longer any question about the Ciragan's standing in Istanbul. Now it was only a matter of bringing the rooms and suites to the level expected by the distinguished guests who had started coming to us before booking at any other hotel. We could not risk losing the status we had worked so hard to build.

I now felt it was the right moment to talk to the owners about investing money in renovations. What we needed amounted to relatively minor fixes in the grand scheme of things, but any changes we could make would have a visible impact on the quality of the hotel and the experience of our guests, especially those who stayed overnight.

The owners were well-aware that the hotel had grown into a success story, as they showed up to visit us once every two months. So when I prepared a presentation for them about the need for renovations, they sounded immediately receptive in a way I had not anticipated despite our strong results. This willingness to say yes may have been due in part to the recent opening of a Four Seasons Hotel near the Topkapi Palace.

The Four Seasons took over a building that had previously housed a prison for journalists and writers who were deemed dangerous to the regime, and the hotel offered fewer rooms than the Ciragan. But even though it lacked the jaw-dropping views of the Bosporus that we had, its newer and more luxurious interiors, combined with its closer proximity to the center of town, presented us with serious competition. We needed to enhance our offerings and upgrade our product quickly to maintain our position.

We immediately got to work finding the right interior designer for the project. I recommended the designer who had done the Adlon, a uniquely elegant Kempinski Hotel in Berlin. But the owners wanted to make a competition out of it, so we invited three designers to submit their designs. One eventually dropped out, leaving us with two options, and of those, the owners selected the designer I had initially suggested, Julian Reed.

His concept would bring the most exceptional aspects of Ottoman design into the hotel, focusing on luxurious fabrics and furnishings that evoke the beauty and culture of Turkey, along with subtly symbolic accents such as bouquets of tulips, a flower that originated in the country. We all agreed that the design of the common spaces and the guest accommodations should create a seamless flow and visually tie the palace to the hotel. This way, visitors can experience the same level of quality no matter what part of the Ciragan they were in.

The owners approved the design concept but insisted that the Ciragan needed to pay for the renovations, budgeted at roughly $16 million, and declined to finance the project out of their own significant resources. Hotels typically have what is called a replacement reserve, created by taking a small portion of the revenue and putting it in reserve to cover repairs or replacement parts needed throughout the year. We had a replacement reserve of 4 percent, which the owners agreed to increase to 8 percent in order to help fund the renovation. But there was a catch:

The owners offered to double the percentage only if the management bonus would be calculated after applying the replacement reserve, which would reduce Kempinski's benefits for some time.

A conflict arose when Kempinski's corporate comptroller refused to accept the owners' proposal and, by remaining stubborn, almost jeopardized the entire project. The owners took offense at this and informed me that they were committed to doing the renovation under the condition they had proposed, and if Kempinski would not accept this, maybe another management company would. Suddenly I was caught in the middle of a vital decision, as general managers often are, wanting to alienate neither the owners nor the management company.

I was left with only one choice in order to save Kempinski's contract with the Ciragan. I called Reto Wittwer to ask for help in reversing the orders of his corporate comptroller. I convinced Reto that even though the renovations would come at a stratospherically high cost for the Ciragan, we would be able to make up for it in no time, since once we completed the renovation, we would be able to charge a much higher room rate.

I never heard from the comptroller again, but the renovation project did get off the ground, starting in 1997. We rolled it out in phases, without needing to close down the hotel as we had done at the St. Regis. Over the course of the two years it took to renovate the Ciragan, we redesigned the hotel lobby, the corridors, and most of the rooms and suites in the hotel and palace buildings, as well as all of the restaurants. Usually, I am not in favor of undertaking renovations while customers are staying in the building. But with the Ciragan, I could physically separate the hotel in two parts, allowing us to renovate one half at a time without inconveniencing our customers.

Near the beginning of our renovation process, a journalist from the *New York Times* stayed at the Ciragan for an assignment in which he compared us to the Four Seasons. In his article, he pointed out the rather ordinary, somewhat tacky furniture in our rooms, but he did mention that the renovation had just begun and would result in an upgrade of every room and suite. He also decided not to pick a winner between the Ciragan and the Four Seasons, choosing instead to point out each hotel's strengths and weaknesses. I felt relieved, but I knew that after the renovation, the Ciragan would emerge as the clear victor, a hotel with no equal in Istanbul.

Attempting the renovation without closing the hotel had an impact on our revenues, as I predicted it would, since we only had half of the rooms available at any given time. Our hotel had been running at close to 80 percent occupancy, very high in the industry, so the reduced inventory hurt us. On the plus side, we remained nearly full for the entire two years of the renovation. We could have certainly used more space, but we had to make do.

A Financial Windfall

Illustrious guests continued to stay at the Ciragan during the renovation period. One memorable set of visitors was the family of the emir of Qatar at the time, Hamad bin Khalifa al Thani. His wife and daughters came to stay at the Ciragan in 1997, during a turbulent time in Qatar after an attempted coup by the education minister who wanted to depose Hamad. Two years before, Hamad had deposed his own father in a coup and had been engaged in trying to freeze his father's overseas bank accounts to prevent him from attempting to seize control again.

Hamad's wife, Sheikha Mozah Bint Nasser Al-Missned, and their two daughters arrived in Istanbul by private plane. She rented the Sultan suite, our largest, for herself along with two smaller suites for her daughters, for a stay that was scheduled for four weeks but ended up lasting six months. This turned into a tremendous windfall for our budget. The

Sultan suite had an official nightly published rate of $20,000, although the sheikha was paying a much-reduced amount in view of her long stay. In one room, adjacent to the sheikha's suite, sat six metal suitcases, guarded day and night by her own security staff. There was speculation as to whether the suitcases were stuffed top to bottom with money taken out of the country by her husband.

Every day, the sheikha went shopping, and on Fridays, she went by car to the mosque nearest the hotel. When people would come up to the car, she would ask, "Are you poor?" If they said yes, she would hand out money through the window, thinking she was doing good. I don't know how many people who took her handouts actually needed them, but her actions created a commotion around the hotel. Our chief security guard was on high alert.

After her daily shopping expeditions, the sheikha brought back silverware, carpets, clothes, or furniture, sometimes all of the above. We had one suite packed with just her purchases. One of the family's assistants said to me, "Mr. Tischmann, this is nothing. In their house outside London, we have containers full of their purchases and no one knows what to do with them all." The sheikha would periodically ship her stuff to their England residence as she continued shopping every single day.

From time to time, the sheikha received a visit from her son Tamim, who stayed in another hotel and would come to the Ciragan only to see his mother. Tamim eventually became the emir of Qatar in 2013 when his father stepped down.

When the sheikha and her daughters first arrived at the Ciragan, a few people warned me that renting accommodations to wealthy Arabs of her status would result in major damage to our suites, since members of that class are known for throwing lavish parties with lots of drinking and no regard for property.

The entire time the sheikha stayed in our hotel, I had no idea what went on in the suites she and her daughters had booked, since the sheikha had brought her own maids and did not want our housekeeping staff coming in to clean. I only entered the main suite once, briefly, to escort Tamim on one of his visits, and I saw all the sofas protected with white sheets. When the family moved out six months later, everything looked impeccable. There was absolutely no damage. In fact, the rooms were cleaner and in better condition than before.

A few years later, I learned that the sheikha had passed away in Mecca during the Hajj. For many Muslims, dying while doing the sacred pilgrimage in Mecca is considered a blessing, but I had lost contact with the family by then, and I did not know the circumstances of her passing. Still, I felt sadness at the loss of someone who, along with her children, had become practically a member of our own hotel family for several months and who had contributed her own dramatic chapter to the Ciragan storybook.

Becoming Number 14 of the World's Best Hotels

Breathing new life into the Ciragan meant not only spending millions of dollars to update the interior design, as we had finally begun to do. Along with the renovations, we also needed to transform the entire experience of staying at the hotel and palace. This meant ensuring that our staff received an elevated level of training so they could deliver the service worthy of the five-star rankings we would now be in a position to achieve. The training sessions I'd provided before the renovation had raised the overall performance of our staff, but now we needed to set the bar even higher, improving on and polishing every aspect of our operation.

Creating the Ciragan's new training manuals was the easy part. I found copies of the volumes I had created at the St. Regis, including the thick, detailed manual intended for the butlers. I adapted these manuals to suit the cultural environment of Istanbul, but mostly, I kept the same operational principles I had implemented in New York. Why invent something completely new when I had already created a tool that achieved such successful results before?

With the renovations still underway, we established a butler staff for the first time at the Ciragan, to service the palace suites and turn them into truly extraordinary accommodations. Just as I had done at the St. Regis, I wanted to ensure that the butlers followed a philosophy of service modeled on the Asian luxury hotels that had inspired me many years ago.

In our training sessions for the entire staff, we emphasized that everyone in the hotel needed to behave like a personal butler, even if this was not their official job description. I took this idea from the Four Seasons Hotel that had debuted in New York City shortly after the St. Regis reopened. The Four Seasons had no butlers; instead, everyone operated like a butler. The Four Seasons ingeniously imparted this philosophy to its staff without designating a million-dollar payroll for butlers. Staff members who serviced the rooms would ask guests if any clothes needed to go out for dry cleaning, for instance, and would offer personalized assistance in much the same way that a butler would.

While I did designate a budget for certain staff members to serve specifically as palace butlers at the Ciragan, I set up the butler service in a different way from what I had done at the St. Regis. Instead of assigning each suite its own butler, I hired a pool of butlers to work at the palace and take responsibility for all twelve suites.

Each newly hired butler had to undergo our extensive training program to learn how to provide the highest quality service to our guests and deliver beyond expectations. The manual I gave our butler staff weighed as much as a doorstop and left no detail out. The book described, for instance, exactly how to pack a guest's suitcase and handle each item correctly, including draping trouser legs over the side of the luggage while layering the other clothes, to prevent wrinkles.

We play-acted scenarios to teach butlers how to handle guest complaints and what to say or not to say when someone has a gripe. We showed butlers how to do everything from searching the furniture for scuff marks to identifying any tiny details of the room that need repair. We even trained them in how to politely ask dignitaries to sign our guest book. Even though we never revealed the identities of any of our customers while they stayed with us, we liked to keep a record of VIP guests at the Ciragan, a list that included everyone from supermodel Claudia Schiffer to actor Peter Ustinov, opera singer Luciano Pavarotti, actors Goldie Hawn and Kurt Russell, royal figures from Prince Rainier of Monaco to King Juan Carlos of Spain, and countless heads of state from French president Francois Mitterand to American president and first lady Bill and Hillary Clinton.

Two years of renovations followed by rigorous training sessions are a tiring process for the entire staff, and by 1999, when we finally reached the end of the project, we all breathed more easily. The results were well worth the wait and all the trouble. The Ciragan now looked more magnificent than ever, its rooms, suites, and common areas finally worthy of the breathtaking surroundings.

The millions of dollars spent on the redesign, along with our meticulous training program and elevated overall product, earned us rankings that outdid even the high marks we had aimed for. *Institutional Investor* magazine, which lists annual rankings of the best hotels based on input from frequent business travelers, gave us the number 14 slot worldwide. The same magazine had ranked the St. Regis at number 11 or 12 after the extensive renovations that closed down the hotel for a few years, but the Ciragan had nearly matched that ranking with a shorter and far less costly renovation process. *Gourmet* magazine and *Conde Nast Traveler* raved about the Ciragan too, and the media accolades continued to roll in.

In my St. Regis years, I used to visit comparable hotels in other cities and notice that many of them had something in common that the St. Regis did not have, for instance they were situated in a beautiful garden, or along a waterfront, or in another spectacular setting. Most hotels of that caliber had an element that the St. Regis could never match, a feature that was produced and presented by mother nature. Yes, guests of the St. Regis do enjoy its location in the middle of the hustle and bustle of Manhattan's Fifth Avenue. But I always used to say that one day, I would like to paint Fifth Avenue blue and plant palm trees along the street.

At the Ciragan, we had everything that the St. Regis could not offer. We had the mystique of an ancient city, the lavish gardens and grounds that surrounded us, the magical Bosporus with the ships passing by, and the sparkling evening lights of the Asian side of the city, visible across the strait. All those elements, combined with a multimillion-dollar renovation and the upgraded level of service of a world-class luxury hotel, helped to earn us the prestigious international rankings we coveted.

Now the Ciragan was truly ready for prime time. And just in the nick of time. By the fall of 1999, our hotel would find itself at the epicenter of the world's attention, so we needed to look our very best.

But first, we needed to survive the momentous events in store for us.

PRINCE FILIPE OF SPAIN
FUTURE KING OF SPAIN

ROBERT KENNEDY AT HIS VISIT
TO THE CIRAGAN

EROL SABANCI LEADING
TURKISH BUSINESSMAN

MRS. HILLARY RODHAM - CLINTON VISITING

THE "HALAS" MRS. SIMAVI'S PRIVATE YACHT

ON A BUSINESS TRIP TROUGH THE MIDDLE
EAST WITH THE PRESIDENT OF KEMPINSKI
HOTELS ENJOYING ARABIAN HOSPITALITY.

HIS HOLY HIGHNESS PATRIARCH
BARTHOLOMEUS AND HEAD OF THE GREEK
ORTHODOX CHURCH, A FREQUENT VISITOR
TO THE CIRAGAN PALACE

Learning Never Ends 31

Joining the MBA Program

Four years can fly by in the blink of an eye, but for a general manager, that's a long time to stay at a hotel. Suddenly, it was 1998. I had been at the Ciragan nearly four years, one of the longest time spans I had spent in any one city during my career of constant travel. But as it turned out, my full-time life in Istanbul was about to undergo a dramatic change.

Reto Wittwer, the president of Kempinski, called one morning to inform me that Kempinski was underwriting a new MBA study program for general managers, and that I was among the first group selected. Earning the degree would enhance the prestige of my position at Kempinski, and the coursework would involve some travel, while no doubt offering stimulating intellectual and managerial challenges. As a bonus, it would be almost free.

I was ready for a change of scenery, especially one that would not immediately overturn the life Denyse and I had built in Istanbul. My answer was a quick and easy yes.

Reto told me he was convinced of two things. First of all, he did not want to expand Kempinski into North America, which to him would be a fool's errand. He was sure that unless the company intended to run a hotel in every major business center in the United States and build a referral system, it would merely hemorrhage money. Reto's main ambition at the time was to expand Kempinski into China, a goal he did achieve, as today the company has about twenty hotels there.

His second conviction was that all his general managers should have MBAs in order to give Kempinski a competitive edge when competing for hotel management contracts against formidable peers from Hilton, Sheraton, Hyatt, InterContinental, Radisson, and all the big names. Those companies all dwarfed Kempinski in terms of size and brand recognition, so Wittwer needed to figure out how to differentiate his offering and gain an upper hand in the negotiations. As a result, he had decided to launch a two-year program overseen by the Reims Management School in France to give his general managers the added distinction of a business degree from a renowned institution.

The concept had a downside, as those of us who pursued the program would be required to give up two weeks out of our month of vacation every year in order to participate in four different four-week courses, three at Kempinski's training center outside Berlin and one during the last semester in Beijing, China.

At the end of each of the first three courses, we had to return to our hotels and do homework and exercises for the rest of the year, before spending the last four weeks in China to finish the curriculum. It would be a demanding program, over and above the pressures of our hotel jobs, and we would get little to no rest. But the end result for each of us, as well as for the company, seemed well worth the investment.

In preparation for my months at Kempinski's Training Academy in Bad Saarow, near Berlin, I decided to entrust the day-to-day operations of the Ciragan to my second-in-command. I had complete confidence that he and the rest of the team could do their jobs extremely well and leave me to focus on my studies.

Bad Saarow, a small spa resort in the Brandenburg district, is famous for its hot springs and mineral-rich mud. It sounded like an appealing location to spend time in during the MBA course, although my colleagues and I in the program would likely have very little time to do anything else but attend class and study. Still, this was a chance to spend time in a beautiful lakeside region, a place whose close distance to Berlin and location along the shore of the Scharmutzelsee made it a preferred weekend destination for the rich and famous of pre-war Berlin.

Before World War II, members of the upper class maintained stately houses around the lake and transferred their social life from Berlin to Bad Saarow on the weekends. At the end of the war, most of the villas were confiscated by the Soviet Army or were taken over for private use by the cultural and political elite of the German Democratic Republic, who made sure nobody had the opportunity to peek inside to watch the elite members of the Communist party enjoying life. Erich Honecker, the Communist party official, general secretary of the Socialist Unity Party in Eastern Germany, and head of state of East Germany in the 1970s and 1980s, was among the many elite politicians living in Bad Saarow.

With the fall of the Berlin Wall and the reunification of Germany, the villas returned to their original owners or their legal inheritors, making Bad Saarow and the shores of the Scharmutzelsee accessible to ordinary citizens once again. Business started to boom in the area, and within a short time, Bad Saarow had established itself again as the spa resort of preference for the Berliner and even for the western part of Germany.

It was therefore no wonder that Kempinski seized the opportunity to take over the management of a resort hotel on the shores of the lake in Bad Saarow, offering along with its traditional hotel services a tennis academy, a riding school, a sailing school, two golf courses, and a business training center, which later was renamed the Kempinski Training Academy.

Using the hotel to host Kempinski's first MBA training program was a decision that made sense for the company, especially as it helped improve the occupancy rates during the off-season. Giving up half of my vacation time certainly felt like a sacrifice, but the facilities would at least provide a very comfortable place to stay, with views of the lake and surrounding region.

I arrived at the Training Academy as part of the first group of students, which consisted of twenty general managers selected by the Reims Management School—now known as the NEOMA Business School—and by our company's president, Reto Wittwer. Our group knew each other already from the GM meetings, but spending such an extensive time together would be a challenge we'd all need to get used to and likely an intentional part of the exercise.

Inevitably, some of the general managers packed tennis rackets and golf clubs in their luggage, knowing they would be living at a resort but having no idea what actually awaited them. From the very first day and continuing through the end of the program, our studies began at eight o'clock in the morning and, except for a one-hour lunch break, went straight through until 5:00 p.m., leaving us just enough time to drop our books in our rooms, refresh briefly, and show up for dinner. The evening meal was a two-hour mandatory social event designed to allow us to exchange thoughts about the various subjects covered during the day.

Dinner rarely signaled the end of the day's activities, as we often went back to work immediately after eating. Laurent Choain, the director of the Reims Management School and supervisor of our program, kept us busy with case studies that extended our days far beyond our normal hotel working hours. We worked on the case studies in small groups and could usually meet only after dinner, since our days were taken up by classroom lectures. The late meetings often went well past midnight, interrupted only by quick trips to the soft drink and cookie buffet. For those of us who had arrived in Bad Saarow thinking this would be an easy path to an instant MBA, the grueling schedule was a rude awakening.

Still, I enjoyed the program and even more so starting in the second week, when guest lecturers from distinguished universities joined us from the US. Spending time with the professors from the States was enlightening, as their teaching style was quite different. While the European professors spent more time lecturing on the various subjects, the American professors got the class involved in discussions and encouraged a more collaborative approach to learning.

The many years I had spent in the US helped me to understand their philosophy of teaching, and I became friends with most of the guest professors. Some of them later gave me the opportunity to guest lecture at the University of Nevada in Las Vegas, New York University, Cornell University, and the Humboldt University in Berlin.

The days went by quickly, and although there were no classes on Sundays, not too many of us could be found on the golf course or tennis courts, as we needed to rest and prepare ourselves for another challenging week. Of course, some still thought the program was mainly a chance to have fun and spent more time on the golf course than in their study groups. I was lucky that the working groups I joined always consisted of younger, ambitious general managers, and we all learned from and benefited from our collective hard work and dedication.

Meanwhile, throughout the training in Bad Saarow, I noticed how some general managers in the MBA program received updates from their deputies almost hourly: reports on the occupancy rates, on who was staying in the hotel, and so forth. This struck me as ridiculous. You should trust the people you hired. I may be the top manager at the hotel, but I'm only as good as the people I work with. Since we had a great rooms division manager, an excellent F&B director, a wonderful head of housekeeping, and first-rate department heads in all the key positions at the Ciragan, I was able to give my full attention to my studies during the entire training and didn't have to worry about the hotel. The staff left in charge of the Ciragan during my absence knew that they could call me in case of an emergency, but they never did.

China, an Experience Not to Miss

For the last and shortest part of the program, in China, our accommodations at the Kempinski Hotel in Beijing were perhaps not as scenic as the lakeside resort in Bad Saarow, but they were certainly comfortable and well-appointed. The program itself continued to be challenging and stimulating. In addition to our studies, which built on the concepts we had learned at the Kempinski Training Academy, each of us had the chance to work with local entrepreneurs to coach and consult with them on their businesses. My assignment was a man who owned several restaurants in Beijing and wanted to grow bigger than McDonald's. I helped him develop business plans for how to expand in China first.

Even though the MBA program added to my workload and eliminated my vacation time, and meant I was away from Denyse during most of my time in Berlin and Beijing, it was a positive experience overall. I was pleased to achieve the highest honors at graduation. Denyse and Carine flew to Beijing for the graduation ceremony at the Hall of the People, applauding enthusiastically as they watched me receive one certificate in Chinese and one in English.

Living in Beijing for six weeks, I barely had any time to see the city in between my intensive coursework. But during the graduation week, the school organized special events for graduates and our families so we could enjoy a bit of tourism. Some of the events were better than others.

The most memorable adventure, perhaps not for the right reasons, was our visit to the Great Wall. As this was January, it must have been minus twenty degrees, and while I toured the wall with my wife and daughter, the wind blew like ice sheets around us. I still had my old movie camera, the Bolex-Paillard, which I had bought years before in Switzerland. But it was so cold at the Great Wall that the oil in the camera's motor froze. I would start the film rolling, only to hear it go *ZZZZzzzzzzz*, then stop. The tour bus driver had given our group an hour and a half to visit the wall, but within half an hour, everyone had climbed back into the bus to escape the freezing wind.

More successful was our visit to the Chinese National Circus, an impressive acrobatic event that predated the Cirque du Soleil. The performers bent their bodies every which way, as if they had no bones at all. Others balanced towering stacks of fragile plates without breaking them, a feat that any hotelier can appreciate.

The highlight of my family's week together in China was a dinner one night with old friends of mine who lived in Beijing, Rene and Catherine Schmitt. Rene, my former assistant at Sheraton, had been promoted to general manager of a hotel in Beijing. His wife, Catherine, was Chinese, and the two of them took Denyse and me to a wonderful restaurant in an old quarter in the city, a tiny house of three or four rooms. Every room had its own private table for eight, and our group feasted on a twenty-course tasting menu inspired by the Ming Dynasty. The evening gave me a renewed appreciation for the magnificence of Chinese cuisine, far beyond anything I had tasted before.

Our Chinese adventure over, Carine returned to München, and Denyse and I flew back to Istanbul, not at all ready for what awaited us.

CELEBRATING AT THE GRADUATION
IN BEJING/CHINA

MY DIPLOMA IN CHINESE

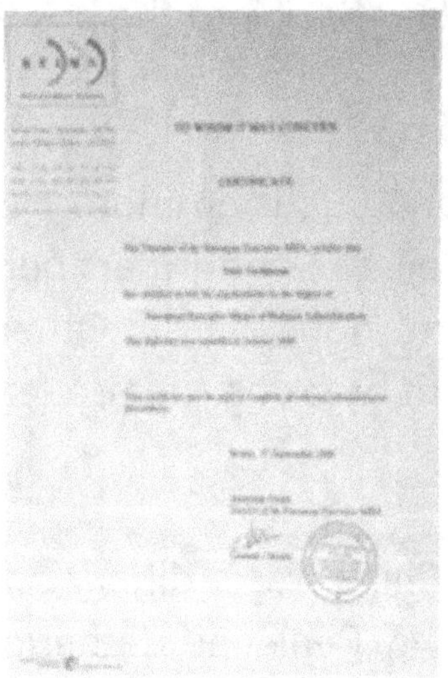

CERTIFICATE OF ACHIEVEMENT

CELEBRATING WITH ME IN CHINA
DENYSE AND CARINE

FREEZING ON THE GREAT WALL
AT MINUS 20 CELSIUS

CONGRATULATIONS
FROM THE PRESIDENT

Our Thirtieth Wedding Anniversary 32

Thanks to My Staff

Thanks to my staff's considerable skills in managing the daily challenges of hotel life, I returned from Beijing to find the Ciragan running smoothly, a cheerful summertime atmosphere in the air. As usual in the summer, we hosted a series of grand weddings at the Ciragan. Now that I was back in Istanbul, I looked forward to resuming my duties overseeing the events that filled up our social calendar.

We had a big wedding planned for the sixteenth of August 1999. As the banqueting team got to work putting all the final details in order, that morning began like any other busy summer Friday at the Ciragan. The hotel was almost full, and tables in our restaurants were in high demand as usual. In the early evening, once the staff had arranged the terrace with elegant tables and lit it up with lanterns, the wedding guests began to arrive, a guest list of Istanbul's rich and famous. Business couldn't be better, and I relished the feeling of being back in Istanbul, especially now that the renovations were all but complete.

I was very pleased that everything went smoothly at the hotel because I did have one special trip coming up, for vacation, not business this time. A few weeks before for our wedding anniversary, I had surprised Denyse with airline tickets for a trip to Botswana to go on a photo safari. We were scheduled to leave on that Saturday evening, flying on Lufthansa to Johannesburg via Frankfurt. Denyse had no idea that both of our children planned to meet us in Johannesburg and join us on the safari.

But first, the wedding party on that Friday night had to go smoothly. Fortunately, the dinner and dancing and ceremony all went beautifully, with no problems at all, and the festivities continued merrily until the last guests left around 11:00 p.m. It was a relatively early night by Turkish standards, which proved convenient since Denyse and I had to wake up early and prepare for our trip. By midnight, the banquet team had cleaned and arranged the terrace as if nothing had happened.

Istanbul Is Shaking—7.6 on the Richter Scale

A last round through the hotel to check that everything was fine, a little chat with the night manager, and soon I was climbing into bed at 1:00 a.m., ready to get a full night of sleep before our flight the next day. Another busy day in Istanbul had finally drawn to a close, and tired from my long day, I fell asleep immediately.

The next thing I knew, it was the middle of the night and Denyse was pushing me to wake me up. "Can't you stop moving in bed? I'm trying to sleep," she pleaded. But I wasn't moving at all. To the contrary, I had been in a deep sleep when Denyse woke me up.

As I turned around and tried to sink back into unconsciousness, I felt the whole palace begin to shake. The drawers on the night tables and sideboards flew open, their doors swinging loudly on their hinges. The chandelier in our suite swayed like the pendulum of a grandfather clock.

"Let's get out of here!" I screamed. "This is an earthquake! We must get downstairs immediately." Denyse and I have never dressed so fast in our lives. Moments later, we stepped on to the small staircase from our bedroom to the ground floor of our suite, getting thrown from one side of the stairs to the other as we made our way down. We grasped the handrail on the wall and desperately tried not to lose our balance.

While we were running out of our apartment and down to the ground floor of the palace, the shaking grew stronger and stronger, making it impossible to run in a straight line. The tremors were flinging us right to left and back again.

As the shaking intensified, we heard a terrible noise that grew louder and louder. It sounded as if a series of construction trucks loaded with heavy stones were rumbling along an unpaved road, crushing the rocks as they thundered on.

We looked up to see the giant five thousand–pound crystal chandelier over the palace stairs start to swing from one side to the other. Terrified, we braced ourselves for a catastrophic crash on the palace floor. But just before that disaster could happen, the shaking and the noise of rumbling stones suddenly calmed down. It was 3:03 a.m., and finally, after a seemingly endless forty-five-second earthquake, everything around us fell into an eerie silence.

Denyse and I, our hearts pounding, started to cautiously walk the four hundred–yard path from the palace to the hotel. We found a few guests already in the lobby, having woken up abruptly from their sleep with no idea what had just happened.

As we soon learned, we had just witnessed a 7.6 earthquake on the Richter scale, the strongest Istanbul had experienced for many years.

That night, 17,000 people lost their lives and 250,000 were left homeless. The city suffered tremendous damage to its structures, much of it irreparable.

Our emergency protocols at the Ciragan prepared us for a variety of disasters and eventualities, but such a massive earthquake was not in our plans. Still, this was no time to panic. We needed cool heads and common sense to get through this crisis. Since aftershocks typically follow nearly every big quake, we alerted guests and staff to be on guard for more shakes to happen. And happen they did, in intervals, with some aftershocks shaking us up again much more powerfully than we had expected.

Evacuating all guests and employees out of the hotel building and into a safe area was our top priority. Along with the small crew of staff on overnight duty, we checked floor by floor to ensure that our guests had left their rooms and herded everyone outside on to the pool deck. Whatever might happen next, the outdoors would surely be the safest place to wait. Following the procedure of our fire drill, we cleared the hotel from top to bottom and double-locked all the rooms and suites to prevent unauthorized access.

As I walked around, I noticed that the water level in the pool had dropped substantially. Did the earthquake damage the foundation of the pool and cause it to leak out? After a thorough check, we realized that cracks were not the issue. The shaking must have produced huge waves in the pool, pushing the water over the edge into the Bosporus.

As the guests could not yet go back to their rooms, at least not until everything was safe again, we did our best to keep them comfortable. Heinz Grub, my assistant, and Christel Schmitt, the executive housekeeper, arrived at the hotel shortly after from their respective homes to help take care of the stranded customers as they sat through one aftershock followed by another. Housekeeping passed out blankets to all the guests, and Heinz produced trays of freshly baked croissants and pots of coffee, seemingly out of nowhere, earning him big smiles and cheers from our guests.

When would the aftershocks finally end? It was impossible to know. But as we waited for the tremors to wind down, I learned that animals act as nature's first alarm system. They sense aftershocks well before they actually happen, and their panicked reaction gives us less-sensitive humans advance notice of what is coming our way.

It appeared that the giant birdcage in our gazebo lounge, home to many colorful lovebirds, was giving us an important warning. I noticed all the birds start to fly up and down at the same time, chirping as they flew nervously around the cage. This became our clear sign that the next aftershock was coming, and sure enough, a few minutes after the birds went into a frenzy, the earth started shaking beneath our feet again.

Some People Are Deep Asleep

The scene on our pool terrace grew communal, as we all looked out for each other and helped our fellow human beings cope with the anxiety and disruption. After what must have been no fewer than five hours from the moment the first shaking and rumbling began, John Roberts, our food and beverage director, appeared in the hotel, looking confused. He walked around, questioning why all our guests were sitting around the pool drinking coffee and eating croissants.

"What's going on here?" John asked, puzzled.

The crowd looked at him, even more puzzled at his question. Then I realized what had happened. John had slept through one of the biggest earthquakes to ever hit Turkey. He only learned about what had happened when he arrived at the hotel.

When the aftershocks finally calmed down, we did a thorough inspection of the hotel and palace, checking all the technical installations and emergency systems for damage. We discovered that, to our surprise, the Ciragan had sustained no major damages, with the exception of a few cracks here and there. The hotel building had an exceptionally solid structure and was designed to be earthquake resistant. As for the palace, the Ottomans certainly knew how to construct a sturdy imperial building in an earthquake-prone area. Besides the chandelier that had swung in the central court of the palace and now needed repairs to make it safe again, the Ciragan had escaped mostly unscathed.

The same could not be said for the rest of the country. The tremor, known as the Izmit earthquake, had a rupture length of 150 kilometers and extended all the way into the Marmara Sea. One of the major naval bases on the sea had suffered tremendous damage when the earth opened up under it, swallowing up the officers' housing and taking hundreds of young sailors into the depths of the earth.

Any part of the naval base not destroyed by the earthquake fell victim to a three-meter-high tsunami shortly after. In just a few hours, a natural disaster had decimated the Turkish Navy.

In view of this tremendous tragedy and the loss of so many lives, I sent a letter of sympathy to Admiral Ilhami Erdil, commander-in-chief of the Turkish Navy, who was a frequent guest of the Ciragan Palace Hotel and had become a personal friend of mine.

It was a relief that he had survived this catastrophe, and shortly afterward, I received a letter from Admiral Erdil, saying:

> *My dear friend, thank you very much for your kind and sincere letter of condolences. This tragic earthquake gave our Navy family irreparable pains and sufferings. We have lost dear friends and comrades. Your offer of help and friendship in these difficult days is very appreciated.*

It was a deeply sad time for the entire country. Under the circumstances, going on vacation felt very strange. But the day after the earthquake, Denyse and I had yet to know the full scope of Turkey's losses. As a result of its sturdy construction and no small amount of luck, the Ciragan was able to bounce back almost immediately. With the hotel in the capable hands of my staff, I left with my wife on our African safari.

Fortunately, the Istanbul airport was still standing. Meanwhile, before the earthquake, I had been secretly planning for months to engineer all the details so I could pull off the biggest surprise gift my wife had ever received.

A Surprise Trip to Botswana

Denyse did not look terribly excited when she first opened her anniversary present. For weeks before our anniversary earlier in the summer, I had brainstormed ideas for a completely unexpected gift. The concept of the Botswana safari came from Carine. Our daughter had already done two photo safaris in Botswana and raved about the experience, and I decided this would make the perfect gift for Denyse. It would be a trip my wife would never plan for herself, a chance to view and photograph the most incredible wild animals in the world in a beautiful country we had never seen before.

For the gift presentation on our anniversary night, I had bought binoculars and made an album featuring the map of Botswana along with the airline ticket. Over our celebratory dinner, I presented Denyse with the wrapped gift. When she opened the box, at first, she didn't know what to do with binoculars. Then she glanced at the airline ticket. Her first response? "I'm not going to fly alone to Botswana."

"No, no," I said. "I'm flying with you."

She appeared happy when I told her this, or at least she did a good job of acting the part. But she still had no idea about the full extent of the plans I had in store.

Carine and Peter would be flying in from Germany and the US, respectively, then meeting in London and arriving together in Johannesburg two hours after we did. We would spend a few days there before heading to Botswana. I had arranged for a separate driver to meet our son and daughter at the Johannesburg airport and transfer them to the hotel, so that we would not run into each other at the airport. I did not want Denyse to know they were joining us until later that day, when they would surprise her at the hotel.

When our flight to Johannesburg was delayed, I worried that our plans would get thrown off and we would accidentally run into Peter and Carine at the airport. Luckily, we did not, and once at the hotel, as Denyse settled into our room, I told her that I was going outside to take pictures. In fact, I walked directly to Peter and Carine's room to make sure they had arrived. They were sitting there waiting for further instructions, and I briefed them on the plan. A few minutes later, I coaxed Denyse to join me at the rooftop restaurant for lunch.

As my wife and I sat on the terrace soaking up the sunshine, I suddenly saw her eyes open as wide as saucers. She shrieked, "What are you doing here?"

Sure enough, Peter and Carine were approaching our table, shouting, "Happy anniversary, Mom!" and giving her hugs.

"Are you going with us on the safari?" she asked them, her eyes still blinking.

"No," Peter said in his joking fashion, "we are just joining you for lunch and will have to return in the afternoon."

"Of course we're going with you!" they yelled at the same time, just as Denyse's smile started to fall.

As tears of happiness streamed down Denyse's face, I stood behind the table, filming the scene. The surprise vacation was off to a promising start.

Spending the Night with Crocodiles

To get the most out of our short stay in Johannesburg, the concierge of our hotel had recommended that we visit the crocodile sanctuary, which was only a few miles outside of the city. As this sounded very intriguing, we all decided to head there to see the crocodiles.

When we arrived at the sanctuary, we entered through the souvenir shop, bought our tickets, then walked outside to the elevated bridges and walkways from which guests can observe the huge crocodiles moving slowly underneath. They were enormous.

Denyse and I had never seen crocodiles up close like this before, so we were happy to kick off our animal-themed vacation with this encounter. But after an hour or so of admiring the fearful animals, we were ready to leave. The four of us walked back to the entrance that led to the souvenir shop, only to find all the doors closed. The booth where we had bought the tickets was empty. Everyone was gone. Perhaps, we assumed, they had closed the sanctuary because it was late afternoon and we were the last visitors. But how could they have forgotten about us?

Clearly, no one had remembered we were still out here, and now it was only us stranded outside with all the crocodiles. I tried again to open all the doors, but there was no way of getting out of the sanctuary. As we all silently tried to calm ourselves down, I noticed that the sanctuary buildings were essentially all made of light wood structures. That gave me an idea. I swung my leg back and flung it hard against the door. I heard a creak. I swung again, and this time I felt the door give way to my foot, then fly wide open into the souvenir shop. We then opened the shop door and ran outside, to find our chauffeured car waiting for us where we had left it, the driver in a deep sleep at the wheel.

Having avoided a massacre by crocodiles, we were ready to leave Johannesburg and embark on our safari adventure the next day. We boarded our short flight to Botswana, then transferred to the Okavango Delta area to begin our small safari camp tour. Contrary to other African safari destinations, Botswana does not allow mass tourism, so instead of big tour buses, the trips tend to involve private jeeps. The safari camps of Botswana are small and often temporary, creating a sense that you are living out in the wild among the animals. And the varieties found there do not disappoint. The Okavango area's forested wetlands attract a tremendous variety of wild animals, from giraffes and lions to wildebeest, antelopes, and many more.

The Safari Adventure

A photo safari in Botswana is all about moving from one place to another to follow the animals, traveling by small Cessna planes from camp to camp. The up-close animal sightings can take some getting used to, as

I quickly learned. In our first camp, I woke up in the tent I shared with our son Peter and heard a loud sound of ripping branches. Opening the zipper of the tent and looking outside, I saw, not more than ten feet from our tent, a huge elephant tearing branches off the trees. I was shocked, as I had never been that close to an elephant before, not even in a zoo.

Monkeys like to steal towels, so at one of our camps the guides warned us not to leave our towels unattended in the outside shower. We saw monkeys everywhere at that camp, climbing the trees above our huts, jumping on the roofs, sliding down, and hopping to the next tree, enjoying what looked like a tremendously fun time.

I realized later that I had experienced most of the photo safari through my movie camera lens. I never actually looked at anything with my own eyes, obsessed as I was with filming all the animals and all the action. Carine took pictures the entire time too. Peter, in typical fashion, decided to simply enjoy himself without any additional goals, so he walked around carrying nothing in his hands. It did not occur to me at the time that I could learn a valuable lesson about living in the moment simply by watching my son.

We had a terrifying scare one day after we had to take a helicopter to one camp since the area around it had not yet built a landing strip for a Cessna. Arriving at our destination after a low and exciting flight over the Delta, which allowed us to watch herds of antelopes from the air, the pilot dropped us off and left us waiting on the ground, promising us that our driver should be arriving to pick us up shortly. Then he flew off. There we stood, alone in the middle of the savannah, waiting with our luggage for someone to pick us up. After what seemed like hours of watching elephants go by, much too close to us as far as I was concerned, Denyse turned to me and said, "I'm scared. The kids are scared." What would we do if nobody shows up?

Defenseless in the middle of nowhere, we heard noises from all kinds of animals, but thankfully, all we saw were elephants. I prayed a lion or a leopard would not show up before the driver and devour us all. I had to make an effort not to look scared, and I had to admit to myself that I was feeling very uncomfortable as well. After what felt like an eternity, we heard a vehicle rumble along, and we all breathed sighs of relief when the driver stepped out with a smile on his face and loaded us into the jeep to take us to our next camp.

Hippos are extremely dangerous, as we learned on this trip. In one part of the river delta, our guide took us out in tiny boats. The canoe captain promised he would only take us where the water is shallow because where it's deeper, there are hippos. Hippos are the most dangerous animals to see on a safari, apparently, far more dangerous than lions and many other wild animals. They live in the water a large part of the time, but to find food, they wander around on the land. Hippos are very territorial animals, and if they detect a human or another animal entering the area between the water and where the herd is grazing, they feel threatened and attack. I was told there are more deadly incidents with hippos during safaris than with lions or any other animals.

We encountered many deadly incidents on our trip—involving only animals, not people—but luckily, we only witnessed the aftermath. On a night safari we took one evening, we passed by a dead antelope and saw two lions eating its flesh. We never witnessed the actual kill, but we were sure the bloody incident must have happened shortly before we arrived. The next morning, passing by the same spot again, we noticed that the only thing left over was the skeleton with a few pieces of meat left on it. The vultures must have stood waiting in the trees for their chance to pounce. We again passed by the same spot later that day, and found only the skeleton, cleaned down to the last shred of meat. The day after that, we observed that even the skeleton was gone, and only the head and the horns remained. Perhaps the hyenas had played a role too. Nature takes care of everything.

Not long after our first dead antelope sighting, we saw another one, this time courtesy of a leopard that had just nabbed its prey. To protect their catch, leopards pull the antelope up into a tree and leave it there, then come back to eat it later. We could not take our eyes off the poor dead antelope in the branches.

Cheetahs and lions were among the most exciting animal sightings of our trip. On one drive, we saw lion cubs playing together while a group of female lions rested nearby. It's the female lions that are the most dangerous, since they do all the hunting. We did not see any male lions on our entire safari, until a surprise encounter on our last day. On our way back to the airport, the tracker—the person who sits at the front of the jeep to look out for signs of animals—noticed the traces of lions around us. We followed those traces to a spot under a tree and found two male lions resting there. We all sat in the jeep, gawking.

The guides and trackers always told us that when we approach an animal by car, we should never stand up. If the animals see the car and the people in it as one big and scary object, bigger than they are, they will not be in the mood to attack. But if someone gets up, they might identify that person as an individual, and if they're hungry they might have ideas for what to do with that human. We remained seated and observed the lions from a few feet away, Carine snapping photos the entire time while I watched the lions through the lens of my movie camera. A minute later, I heard Denyse's voice saying, "That's enough! Let's go." She'd been scared the entire time and was holding her breath. It was time to listen to her and get ourselves out of there.

Happily, we all survived the safari, and we had a marvelous time admiring the way the wild animals lived and hunted, up close to us but at a safe distance. We had excellent guides at every camp. The safari was a huge success, even for someone like Denyse who hates surprises and hates not knowing everything in advance.

This trip had caught her totally off-guard, and even if she had faked excitement when I first handed her the airline ticket, I could tell she had enjoyed the trip tremendously. I had too, and I promised myself I would do it again, but next time without bringing a camera. I would enjoy it empty-handed like our son.

As for Denyse? "I've seen enough safari camps," she said. I could hardly blame her. We had gotten through a safari without getting devoured by wild animals. Why tempt fate?

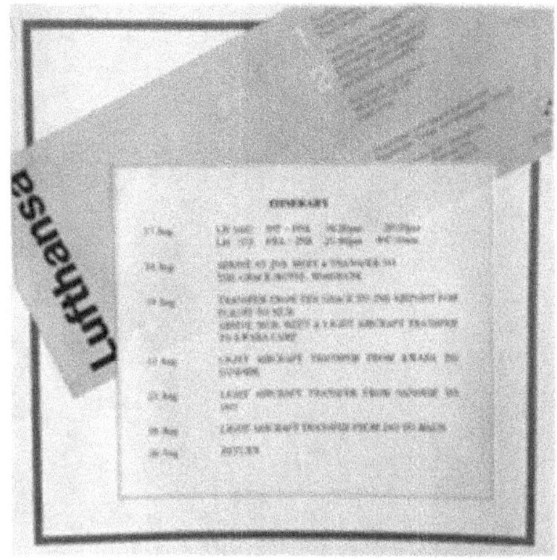

THE SURPRISE TRIP TO BOTSWANA

AND THE CHILDREN ARE HERE TOO

NOT ALLOWED TO TAKE

LOCKED IN WITH CROCODILES

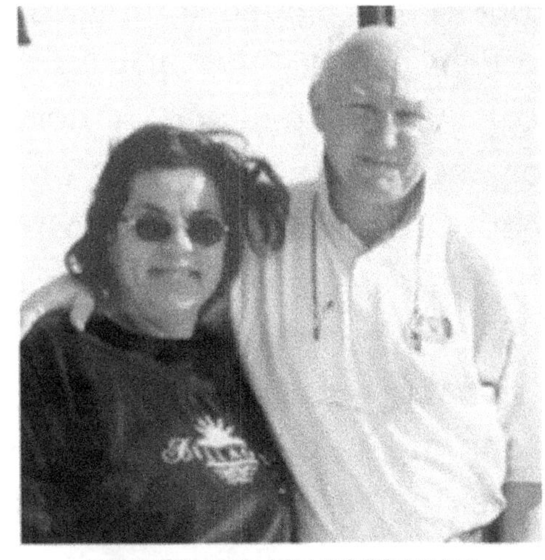

DENYSE AND I IN BOTSWANA

THE SAFARI TEAM

Hosting the World 33

The OSCE Conference

The Ciragan looked refreshed and ready to make a splash on the international scene by the fall of 1999, when the global spotlight was about to shine on our hotel. We were soon to receive a level of attention from international VIPs that would exceed any experience I had ever witnessed at the Ciragan, the St. Regis, or anywhere else.

That year, an organization whose membership included the heads of state of more than fifty nations in North America, Central Asia, and Europe chose the Ciragan as the site of its annual meeting. Although the group, called the Organization for Security and Cooperation in Europe (OSCE), formed in the 1970s, it had only recently started hosting annual events, and I was honored they had selected the Ciragan for their November 1999 summit. We had faced steep competition in our bid to host the conference, and the decision went in our favor as a result of our success in establishing the Ciragan at the center of Istanbul's social and political activities. We were by far the best hotel in the city by now, and here was our chance to prove it.

The fact that we were the Turkish government's hotel of choice and maintained friendly relations with Suleyman Demirel, the president of Turkey at the time, might have helped as well.

Despite our newly completed renovations, we faced a monumental amount of work before we could host such an illustrious group at the Ciragan. For the summit, the highest-ranking government officials among the member countries would be staying in our palace, in addition to attending daytime meetings in our conference rooms. Other heads of state would stay in other hotels because we simply did not have enough suites available at the Ciragan. The presence of just one head of state required an enormous security presence, and now we were about to host dozens.

Working with the conference organizers to arrange the heavy security that such an event required turned out to be a giant logistical challenge. We planted security guards all over the property, from the roof of the hotel down to every part of the grounds. All the heads of state would be arriving for the conference within a certain time frame on the same day, which meant a finely choreographed routine of welcome greetings. At the appointed time, I parked myself at the entrance to the palace, and soon I began welcoming the heads of state one by one as they arrived, then escorting them to the Sultan suite to be welcomed by the president of Turkey. I then had to rush back down and welcome the next head of state, repeating the same walk again and again until all the dignitaries had finally arrived.

This summit had all the marks of a once-in-a-lifetime event, and I had hired a photographer for the sole task of taking pictures every time I welcomed a head of state into the palace. But after the day was over, I discovered that this photographer had somehow not managed to take a single proper picture. Maybe he had tried to change the film in his camera and accidentally exposed it to the light. Whatever happened, he never offered any explanation for why he had virtually no pictures to show for all his work. I was furious.

Except for the reports in the press and the few pictures we secured at the hotel, the event nearly vanished into thin air after it ended. The only photos I have of the event are from other people who attended and shared their images with me. These include a few shots of me with Bill Clinton and Jacques Chirac, and one with Boris Yeltsin, and that's about it. But I suppose that is not too bad at all, now that I think about it.

With so many heads of state staying at the Ciragan, Denyse and I had to wear special badges to get into the palace and up to our suite. Yeltsin was staying right next to us. President Demirel of Turkey occupied the Sultan suite, the largest, since he was hosting and welcoming all the individual heads of state to the conference.

Because of my special badge, I could move around the palace and even had access to the conference hall. I could even peek into the room and at the O-shaped table with all the luminaries sitting around it. One of the most amusing moments I remember is when Yeltsin sat in a press conference and a journalist asked him, "Mr. President, are you an alcoholic?" Yeltsin replied that no, he is not an alcoholic. He is Russian.

Bill Clinton, a man of tall stature, is a person who commands respect by his appearance alone. I remember noticing that when he entered a room, the whole crowd went silent. Clinton would greet and salute everybody as he entered, exchanging at least one or two words with each person. You had the feeling the room was not only quiet, but that it had also gotten brighter and shinier when he walked in. He has an extraordinary presence. Before sitting down at a table, he would look around and make eye contact with each person seated around it. I could understand how this man had risen to win the presidency of the United States, twice over.

The summit was a huge success, at least from the standpoint of the Ciragan experience. We offered world-class service, luxurious accommodations, and impeccable security to our guests, and I felt proud—not to mention relieved—when it was all over. As a diplomatic event, it appeared to succeed quite well too, resulting in historic agreements on arms reduction and the prevention and resolution of conflicts. But as far as I was concerned, the hotel had delivered on its reputation and exceeded expectations, and for me, this was the only true measure of our success.

What I did not expect was that soon after the conference ended, Denyse and I would have the opportunity to attend a cruise with our friends, in which the guests of honor were none other than Bill and Hillary Clinton and their daughter Chelsea.

Yachting with the Clintons

The yacht owned by our friend Cigdem Simavi, the wonderfully old-fashioned Bosporus ferry boat that we allowed her to dock in front of the Ciragan, continued to pay social dividends not just for the hotel but for my personal life as well. The friendship Denyse and I had developed with Cigdem led to an invitation to join her and a few of her family members and friends, including the Clintons, for a boat trip around the Bosporus after the conference. Of course, we said yes.

Hosting the cruise on the Bosporus was Mustafa Koc, the eldest of the three sons of Cigdem Simavi, who was destined to take over the family's business, which had an interest in all the major industrial and business branches in the country.

They were manufacturing everything from automobiles to refrigerators, and they owned supermarkets and even private universities. Cigdem had once been married to Rahmi Koc, though she had since divorced and remarried. She and Rahmi had three sons together: Mustafa, Omer, and Ali, the youngest one. Coincidentally, Ali was studying at Harvard at the same time as our daughter Carine and was even enrolled in the same class.

As friends of the family, we had a cordial relationship with the three sons too, and from time to time, I even played golf with Mustafa.

For security reasons, Bill Clinton and his family had to remain inside the yacht, until it reached a certain distance from the shore.

After we had arrived at a safe position in the middle of the Bosporus, Bill Clinton was finally cleared to walk out onto the deck and socialize, which he did with his characteristic flair. Soon I found myself standing with President Clinton and Mustafa Koch talking about golf. This time I had a chance to observe him at a closer range than I did during the conference. When Mr. Clinton talked, you had a feeling that he was talking only to you. He had a way of attracting attention and drawing people into his conversation. It was incredible. I have never personally witnessed anyone quite like that. In the context of our conversation, I had the chance to talk briefly with him one-on-one. We discussed hotels, and when the St. Regis came up, he commented on what a great hotel it was. I have no idea if he had ever even been there, but it was gratifying to hear his compliments and an honor to have the opportunity to talk with him. The cruise remains a fantastic memory from our Istanbul years.

A Secret Honeymoon Not So Secret

Certain other memories from the Ciragan did not fill me with quite as much pride. One day, I received a telephone call from Christiane Amanpour of CNN, informing me that she had a couple she would like to send to our hotel for their honeymoon. But their identity, she cautioned me, had to remain top secret. I promised her the confidentiality we always grant to our guests, along with an extra effort to ensure the staff knows they must reveal nothing about the visit.

The couple in question turned out to be John Kennedy Jr. and his wife, Carolyn Bessette. I informed the front office manager about the visit, reiterating the extreme confidentiality we owed these guests. The front office manager had been a former member of the St. Regis opening team, and I had hired him to join me at the Ciragan because of his wonderful customer service skills and personal charm.

Although scheduled to leave on a business trip to the USA, I still had the opportunity to welcome John-John (as he was known) and Carolyn to the Ciragan and escorted them to their suite.

Leaving on my trip the following day, I made a point to instruct my key department heads, one by one, about our special guests and the confidentiality promise I had given to Christiane Amanpour.

Barely two days into my trip, I received a phone call from the front office manager telling me, "Mr. Tischmann, please don't be surprised when you read *People* magazine."

I asked, "Why? What's in the magazine?"

He said, "Well, there is a story about John-John Kennedy and his wife at the Ciragan. I just wanted to inform you."

Sure enough, there it was, an article in *People* magazine, with pictures and everything. I have no proof of my suspicion, but I am fairly convinced that it was our front office manager who could not keep his mouth shut and had informed the media. I suspected this because (1) he was American, and none of the Turkish employees would likely have heard of *People* magazine, and (2) he called me to warn me, which to me seemed like a sign he had gotten cold feet. I knew that he was very talkative, the kind of person who liked to talk, so maybe he didn't spill the secret intentionally.

Journalists are smart, as I had discovered over the years, particularly during my fateful interview at the St. Regis years ago, when I had made a joke about the Peninsula. Reporters ask you sly questions which you think don't mean anything, and before you even realize it, you've just revealed a secret or made an embarrassing comment you will soon regret.

As a lawyer would put it, our front office manager had a bad case of verbal diarrhea.

The Kennedys checked out several days early since their cover had been blown. This was a low point for me at the Ciragan, but fortunately, I enjoyed many positive experiences during my time in Istanbul.

After the renovation, I stayed at the Ciragan for another two years, adding up to a total of eight years on the job. I would have happily stayed longer, but around this time, the Kempinski executives began to talk about bringing in a new general manager to implement new ideas.

Eight years at a hotel is a long time for a GM, as traditionally the position tends to revolve every three years to make room for a new person and, at least theoretically, some new ideas too.

Now, this might be true for general managers who are not in a position to renew themselves and do not have a lot of fresh, innovative ideas. But if a company has a GM who is always innovating, who shows himself to be a strong performer and is well-established and respected within the local community, changing merely for the sake of changing makes no sense. Unfortunately, corporate offices have their own ideas for how to do things, and their decisions can be difficult to understand.

So I was disappointed, not to say upset, when I learned that my time in Istanbul was about to come to an end. But another exciting city awaited me, one I had ranked high on my list. It was a city of intrigue, of fascinating history, and novelistic drama. I prepared Denyse to make another giant leap into the unknown.

KURT MASUR, CONDUCTOR OF THE NEW YORK PHILHARMONIC

BOUTROS BOUTROS GHALI, EX UN SECRETARY GENERAL

OSCAR DE LA RENTA, AMERICAN FASHION DESIGNER

PRINCE PHILIP, DUKE OF EDINBURGH

MIKHAIL GORBACHEV, EX PRESIDENT OF RUSSIA

KENZO, A FREQUENT GUEST AT THE CIRAGAN

LIZA MINELLI IN CONCERT AT THE CLRAGAN PALACE HOTEL

HANS-DIETRICH GENSCHER, GERMAN MINISTER OF FOREIGN AFFAIRS

Leaving the Ciragan Palace Hotel 34

"Hi Peter, this is Reto. We need to talk about your next assignment."

The end of my time at the Ciragan did not come as a complete surprise. I knew I had outlasted most of the palace's previous general managers. Rumors that I might be on my way out had been flying around the Ciragan for months. So after the endless speculation and uncertainty, it was a relief to finally hear from Reto—even though our conversation got off to an awkward start.

"After so many years in Istanbul, the owners wish to make a change in management," he said to me on the phone.

I had a hunch the decision was coming more from Kempinski than from the owners. Every GM in the company was angling for my job, and Kempinski could not keep me in the prime spot forever. Still, I decided to press Reto on the reasons behind the decision, since now that we had finally completed the renovation, I felt I should at least have the chance to bring the hotel up to its true potential.

"Are the owners not happy with my performance and the results of the renovation?" I asked Reto.

"To the contrary," Reto answered, "they have been extremely happy with what you have done. Nevertheless, they feel that a change would be for the benefit of the hotel."

Nonsense talk, I thought to myself. I knew that if Reto insisted on keeping me on for a while longer, the owners would most likely accept. But Reto had obviously made his decision. I needed to accept this and move on.

"What do you have in mind for my next assignment?" I asked him.

"The Baltschug Kempinski in Moscow. You know that Hans Sebasta wants to take a one-year sabbatical, and we need somebody like you to give the hotel a new push and an international flair, just as you did at the St. Regis and the Ciragan Palace."

"And when do you expect me to start?"

"As soon as possible, but if you wish to take some vacation before, that's fine with me."

"Yes, I wouldn't mind taking my overdue vacation before I go to Moscow, but when do you want me to leave the Ciragan?"

"At the end of August at the latest, because I don't want you to start too late in Moscow."

I paused to let Reto's timeline sink in. Leaving that summer would mean I would no longer be in Istanbul for Carine's scheduled wedding at the Ciragan.

Not that I believed mentioning that personal timing conflict to Reto would change anything, but I decided to bring up the issue anyway. "Reto," I said, "our daughter was planning to get married at the Ciragan next summer, and I would appreciate a few favors from Kempinski to make her wedding a nice one."

"Whatever you need, it's granted," Reto answered. "After all, the Ciragan Palace owes you something." He vowed to tell the owners himself about the wedding and promised it would be no problem.

"August 11 of next year," I announced. "Take note that you are invited, and we would be pleased if you could make it."

Little did I know how important this last part of our conversation would prove to be.

Leaving Istanbul would feel bittersweet for both Denyse and me, but at least we had four weeks to savor the city and say goodbye to dear friends. I could take the time to ensure a smooth handover to my successor.

The idea of moving to Moscow excited me. I was aware of the opportunity to turn the Kempinski Hotel there into an extraordinary property. Money was no object, from what I understood, as the company's top priority was bringing a surge of creativity and vision to the hotel. I was gratified that they had chosen me for this assignment.

Denyse was not quite as eager as I was, especially since our son-in-law had sent her an article describing how a general manager of another Moscow hotel had been found murdered in his office. Rumor had it the Russian Mafia was responsible. Nonetheless, Denyse bought an English-Russian dictionary and began learning her first words in the language.

Even though nearly all general managers at Kempinski had the Ciragan Palace at the top of their wish lists, the honor could only go to one. Ostensibly, this should be the person most qualified to run this magnificent hotel. But as often happens in corporate life, it's not the most qualified employee but the one with the best connections who gets the lucky assignments. Kempinski was no exception.

So when the company announced my successor, many general managers were struck by disappointment and even disbelief that they had picked this particular person. But it pays to be a personal friend of the president. I wished this man well, as I looked ahead to the new adventure in Russia.

Before Denyse and I left Istanbul, we had a grand farewell party in the true style of the Ciragan. A huge replica of the Kremlin and its Basilica set the stage, and Russian and Turkish music regaled the crowd throughout the evening.

It was heartbreaking to bid goodbye to the colleagues and personal friends we had come to cherish over the years. I knew this moment would eventually happen, but I had hoped for a few more years in Istanbul. That fascinating city had become home, and I knew I would always miss Turkey and its wonderful people.

During our last week there, Denyse and I went to our friend Garo's boutique, so we could each buy a reverse lamb-fur coat to prepare for the freezing winters in Moscow.

If I had only guessed what games the general manager of the Moscow hotel would play, I would have skipped the vacation and flown to Russia immediately without wasting any time.

Employed but No Job

Our vacation went smoothly for the first two weeks, as Denyse and I took time to unwind, reflect on our time in Istanbul, and mentally prepare for the move to Russia. Then at the end of the second week, I got an unexpected telephone call.

It was Reto, my boss, informing me that the company was having a problem with my transfer to Moscow since the general manager had decided not to take his sabbatical. As the owners were supporting his decision, my Moscow assignment was canceled.

Of course, anyone could choose to cancel a planned sabbatical. But something sounded fishy about this decision. The general manager's job at the Baltschug Kempinski was, at the time, a job like none other I had heard of in the hotel industry. Besides the respectable salary, the GM had access to an unlimited expense account, with no questions asked.

This particular GM also happened to sit on the board of directors and took its members with him on pleasure trips twice a year. I remembered the time they had all visited the Ciragan together a few years before.

Did he have second thoughts about leaving for a sabbatical, since during my tenure there I might happen to find out what else was secretly going on in the hotel?

It doesn't take a Harvard degree to figure out that the close connection of the general manager to the board of directors, and the freewheeling expense account they all enjoyed together, would be ample reason for them to decide to keep their heads down and maintain the status quo.

Unfortunately, the general manager passed away one year later. But in the meantime, my transfer to Moscow fell through permanently. And although I was still technically employed by Kempinski, I was without a job.

"Don't worry," Reto said, "we will keep you on the corporate payroll until a new opportunity comes along. For now, you can help us to develop our new operational and quality standards."

This didn't sound like a promising future, but at least it gave me something to do. Disappointingly, I learned that I could not do the work out of the company's head office in Geneva since they would have had to pay for a place for me to stay there. I had to do it from our house in New Hope, or the home office as such arrangements are called today.

The work itself was stimulating, and I enjoyed drawing on my longtime experience, but it was still not as satisfying as a full-time job. I kept waiting for the phone to ring with a new employment offer from the company.

When the phone finally did ring one day, I did not hear the news I was waiting for. Instead, I learned Kempinski could no longer afford to carry an expensive general manager on their payroll, as they had no opportunities coming up in the near future.

So here I was again, without a job. The company did buy me out of my contract, so I didn't have to worry financially. But the fact that they would pay me for another three months was hardly comforting when I had no prospects ahead. I could see my future crumbling in front of my eyes.

The situation was especially difficult to face considering all the years I had spent rebuilding my life after the St. Regis crisis. You go down into a ditch, then you finally pull yourself out of it, and the future looks bright. Then there you are, back in the ditch again. It didn't help that I was now sixty-one.

There I sat in New Hope, Pennsylvania, with the chances of getting a new job looking very slim, because who is going to hire somebody at this advanced age when even younger general managers were having trouble finding jobs?

What else could I do but go back to calling old colleagues, making new contacts, seeing what might happen? Maybe all the networking would turn up a consultancy offer somewhere. But weeks went by, and day after day, nothing happened.

Well, one thing did happen.

My First Heart Problem

One night after I had been lying in bed, wondering what to do with my life, I finally fell asleep, only to wake up in the middle of the night with a terrifying burn in my chest.

This was not the usual heartburn. I was gasping for air. I could barely breathe as I sputtered to Denyse to please wake up.

"Let's go to the hospital," I wheezed. I didn't have to do much convincing. I looked like I was on my deathbed.

It was a rainy, foggy autumn night as Denyse drove me to the hospital in Doylestown, about fifteen miles away from our home.

"Drive faster, I can't breathe anymore!" I pressured Denyse, as she did her best to ferry us safely through the rainy night, with barely any visibility on our windshield. "Just drive through the red light," I urged when I saw no other cars at an intersection. Finally, we pulled up in front of the emergency entrance, and I hobbled inside to the reception desk.

By the time Denyse had parked and come running into the hospital, I was already in the emergency room, connected to all types of machines. The Nitro pills had already taken care of my terrible pain.

Twenty-four hours and two stents later, I felt fine again, having just survived my first cardiac problem. It was a mild heart attack, but a heart attack no less.

The ups and downs of the last years, the politics, the intrigues, the worrying, and the concerns had finally taken their toll on my health.

A first warning, and a lot of food for thought.

FAREWELL TO ISTANBUL WITH FRIENDS AND FREQUENT HOTEL GUESTS

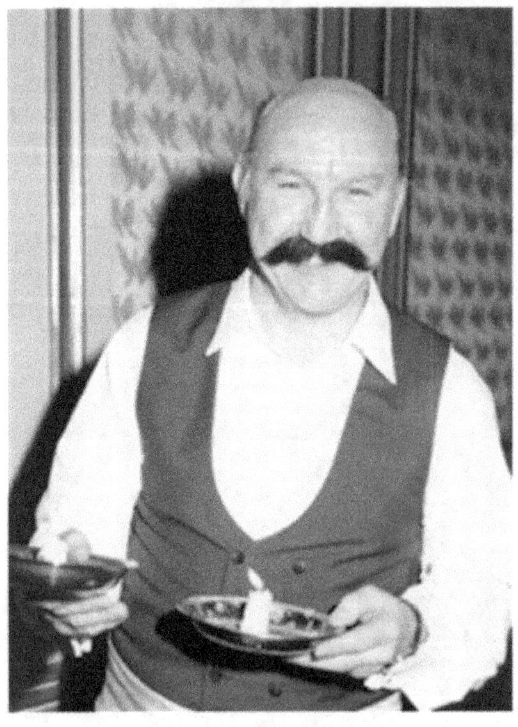

FAREWELL PARTY WITH THE ASSOCIATES OF THE CIRAGAN PALACE HOTEL

Discovering America the Beautiful 35

The fact that my first heart attack had not succeeded in killing me was reason to feel grateful about my life. But I had a difficult time summoning any optimism about my future. A sense of pride kept me from admitting to my friends how low I felt about my shrinking career prospects.

At least the time off from working had a few benefits. The break gave Denyse and myself a chance to spend time unwinding for the first time in years. We decided to tour the US, driving from New Hope to Las Vegas to surprise our son Peter for his birthday. This way, we could also take our time contemplating where we might like to live after we returned. The small town of New Hope was a pleasant place to spend weekends and vacations, but we both knew it was not meant to be our full-time home.

Our road trip across the United States would be the first big outing for the new Mercedes Benz 560 SL that Denyse and the children had given to me as a gift a few years before, to celebrate my career successes and symbolize the adventures ahead. It had languished in the garage while we were in Istanbul, and upon our return, we only used it for short trips around New Hope.

The car proved a trustworthy partner for our drive out west, except for the electrical failure halfway through the trip that almost caused us to miss our son's birthday. But for the week or so that we were on the road, we took our time and enjoyed the long, mostly smooth ride from Pennsylvania to Nevada. We took our mind off day-to-day concerns, reminisced about years past, planned the future, and delighted in the highlights of our trip, large and small: from the relaxing dip we took in the hot springs bubbling up in an Indiana river to the day we spent touring the stunning Grand Canyon in Arizona.

One unexpected highlight of the trip was the Buffalo Bill Museum in Iowa. A legend of the Old Wild West, Buffalo Bill's real name was Bill Cody. He became famous for his Wild West Shows, which traveled around the United States and even Europe in my grandfather's day. I remembered Opa talking about Buffalo Bill, probably after seeing one of his shows in person.

Visiting the museum reminded me of the fascinating stories my Opa told me about the Gold Rush, the Indians, the cowboys, and the Wild West. Although he had never lived in the West himself, he was a great storyteller. I especially enjoyed the story he told me about his travels from the East coast to the West coast, and about how he slept on the train for a week during that trip, a concept I found unimaginable at the time. As if this did not sound exciting enough, Opa added the story of the pageboy in his white uniform and pillbox hat, who would walk down the aisles and shake a bell to draw everybody's attention whenever he announced yet another of the four time-zone changes during the trip.

One long week, days and nights spent on a train, and passing through four time zones along the way, all while staying in the same country, was an idea I could not imagine, having grown up in a country with the same time zone from the North to the South. As a young boy, I would hang on his every word, eager to learn about this new world called America.

I later learned that it was the railroad industry in America that first established the system of using time zones. The industry created the four time zones in 1883 in order to standardize the local methods of time-telling, which had relied on the sun, and to make way for a new railroad era that depended on strict schedules and that, for the first time, made it possible to travel quickly from one end of the country to the other.

One small moment of the trip made an everlasting impression on me, when I met an old chief of the proud tribe of Sioux Indians. Sitting in front of a store, he was allowing passersby to take pictures with him for five dollars a photo. It must have been humiliating for the one-time proud chief of the Sioux tribe to have to make money off tourists. I suppose everybody needs to make a living, but this was a poignant symbol of the fate of the Native Americans in the United States.

The owner of a nearby store told me that in the chief's younger years, he was famous for his skill at dressing wild horses. Nobody could beat him at taming those animals that no one else would dare to go near. Taking a picture with him had just fulfilled another of my youth dreams.

For anyone passing near South Dakota, crossing into the state for a visit to Mount Rushmore is a must. Located near the little town of Keystone, Mount Rushmore receives more than two million tourists every year, making it the US's most visited national monument. After leaving Iowa, on South Dakota's southeast border, we knew we could not miss the chance to see the famous sculpture for ourselves.

Created between 1927 and 1941, the sixty-foot high sculpture displays the heads of four presidents: George Washington, Thomas Jefferson, Theodore Roosevelt, and Abraham Lincoln. The four were chosen to be immortalized in granite on the Black Hills of South Dakota because they witnessed the nation's birth (in the case of Washington), growth (Jefferson), development (Roosevelt), and preservation (Lincoln). The magnificent site did not disappoint, and we took our time in walking around and enjoying the views of the monument and the stunning mountains. But after a day, it was time to get on our way.

Our next stop was Murdo, a small, sleepy South Dakota town stretching along Interstate 90. As we settled into the Sioux Motel for the night, the receptionist told us that few people knew the Murdo area had provided the location for Kevin Costner's film *Dancing with Wolves*. Many of the Native Americans who performed in the film actually live nearby on an Indian reservation, she explained, and some of them even work in the hotel.

Curious to see Murdo's local American Indian community and visit the area where they live, we were looking forward to the next morning, having no idea that a major technical problem with our car would soon make us forget our plans altogether.

First, we planned to eat dinner at a local restaurant and enjoy a relaxing evening after our many hours of driving. Murdo, a small midwestern town, consisted of only a few houses, the Sioux Motel, and a gasoline station with an attached drugstore. Nothing else, as far as we could tell. The only place to get something to eat was a family-owned restaurant in one of the houses, which had its living room converted into a small dining room for guests. The family's daughter, a teenager named Susan, was doing the table service, and as I learned during a conversation with her when she came to take our order, she had never left Murdo, not even to go to Sioux City a handful of miles away.

Our dinner that night was pleasant enough, if not quite memorable from a culinary standpoint, but my one regret from our Murdo visit is that I did not buy a memento I had noticed at the restaurant that evening.

Displayed for sale on a shelf in the living room where we had dinner was a mug with the following inscription: "When you visit your grandmother in the evening and the following day it becomes the headline on the front page of the local newspaper, then you know you are in Murdo." Nothing could have described this small, sleepy, but charming town better than this statement.

A long trip awaited us the following day, so we decided to get ourselves completely packed the night before so we could be ready to leave early in the morning. Comfortably installed in the driver's seat of our car after breakfast that morning, I turned the key and waited to hear the familiar humming of the engine, but nothing happened. Another turn of the key and again nothing.

The car had worked fine when we came back to the motel from the restaurant the night before, but now, only a few hours later, total silence. Fortunately, AAA had a service number in Murdo, and we felt relieved that help would soon be on the way.

About fifteen minutes later, an antique F150 Ford pick-up truck drove up and came to a halt right next to our car. As the door opened, a skinny six-foot-tall man with cowboy boots, jeans, a checkered shirt, and a huge cowboy hat squeezed himself out of the car and came walking toward our Mercedes.

He reminded me of the Lucky Strike cowboy, a familiar character from the advertisements for this popular cigarette brand.

"Are you from AAA?" I asked him.

"Yeah," he answered, "what can I do for you, man?"

I explained that the engine would not start and proceeded to open the hood to show it to him.

"Wow," he said, pushing his hat back toward his neck. "What an engine! I have never seen an engine like this! Let me call my friend. He has to see this engine. I'm sure he has never seen an engine like it either." Ten minutes later I had two cowboys standing around the Mercedes, admiring the eight-cylinder engine but unable to help us.

I'm sure they continued to talk about our engine for a long time, while in the meantime, we tried to figure out what to do. We ended up putting the car on a flatbed and riding in the noisy cabin of a Diesel tow truck to the nearest competent Mercedes repair shop, which was in Denver, Colorado, about four hundred miles away. We crossed Nebraska and Kansas, watching endless cornfields and farms with thousands of livestock go by from the cabin of the truck as we rode all the way to Denver, arriving four hundred miles and $500 later.

At 7:00 a.m. the next morning, we stood waiting in front of the repair shop. After a while, the chief mechanic showed up and took the car to the diagnostic center, leaving us pacing nervously outside the workshop. Not long afterward he finally returned. "It's what I thought," he said. "The electronic master switch needs replacing." Fine with me, I told him. Let's get it done, please.

"It won't be cheap," he continued. "It will cost you at least $1,200 to replace."

"That's fine," I said, "do it so we can continue our trip."

"The problem," he went on, "is that I don't store such expensive parts. I have to order it from Mercedes in Los Angeles. It may take a few days."

Hearing "a few days," Denyse couldn't stop tears from running down her face. Our plan to visit our son Peter in Las Vegas for his birthday on September 6 suddenly seemed in jeopardy. It was going to be impossible to make it there in time.

"I will do my best," the mechanic continued, "but you have to allow me a few days."

Realizing that letting the mechanic do his best was too big a gamble to take, we decided to abandon the car while it got repaired and hop a flight to Las Vegas so we could make it for Peter's birthday. Missing the big day was not an option, especially since we'd been planning the surprise visit for weeks.

When we rang his doorbell on the afternoon of his birthday, he was genuinely stunned to see us. It was a joyful reunion, and we spent a memorable few days touring the city and catching up with our son.

After flying back to Denver to retrieve our car, we drove to Las Vegas again to continue our visit. This time we got to see the famous "Welcome to Las Vegas" sign sparkling in the sunset as we approached.

We spent a few more days with Peter before driving briefly into California to visit the giant redwood trees and watch the sea lions sunbathe on the Pacific beaches. Crossing back east into Arizona, we made sure not to miss the famous cactus forest, where we saw cactus plants almost thirty feet high, their trunks so big that it would take four people to surround them. The needles were so long and thick, they could be used for knitting.

Arizona's White Sands National Monument was on our way as we drove to New Orleans, and it gave us an excellent photo opportunity for our red Mercedes convertible as we parked it amid white sand dunes that looked like snow.

In New Orleans, a visit to the legendary Preservation Hall, birthplace of New Orleans jazz, was at the top of our list. The hall is a tiny, cramped room where jazz enthusiasts must usually stand in the back since there are so few seats. Visitors can eventually advance to the benches by staying long enough for seats to becomes available and can finish by sitting in the front on the floor, if they're lucky.

Guests sitting on the floor can't get any closer to the musicians, unless they wanted to be hit in the face when Jim Robinson extended his trombone to create some of jazz music's most artful tones and improvisations. Every minute in Preservation Hall was an unforgettable experience.

Before leaving New Orleans, we made sure not to miss getting a coffee and a beignet at the legendary Cafe du Monde before we crossed the mighty Mississippi River. It reminded me of my boyhood days reading Tom Sawyer and Huckleberry Finn.

After a stop in Florida to visit our friends and former New Hope neighbors George and Anneliese Plosa, we enjoyed a scenic drive across Georgia, the Carolinas, Virginia, and Maryland on our way home to Pennsylvania.

The trip had renewed our spirits, just as we had hoped. We met incredible people, drove through impressive landscapes, visited sites and monuments not too many locals have ever seen, and got to spend time with our son. Yes, we had our challenges, but even in moments of trouble we had fun.

After five weeks of traveling 15,000 miles and crossing over twenty-five states, we finally arrived back in New Hope, realizing again what a great country America is and that there is still so much to see.

But the decision about where to live loomed over us. It was by now the beginning of 2001, and we needed to figure out where to settle as the new century unfolded.

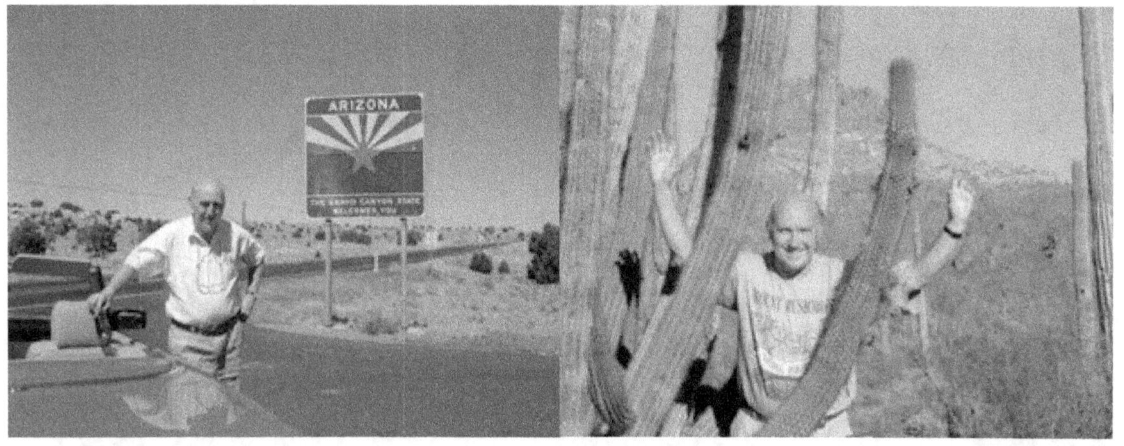

CROSSING ANOTHER STATE LINE

THE CACTUS FOREST IN NEW MEXICO

SAND AS WHITE AS SNOW

WHITE SANDS NATIONAL PARK

DENYSE AT FOUR CORNERS

CRUISING THE MISSISSIPPI RIVER

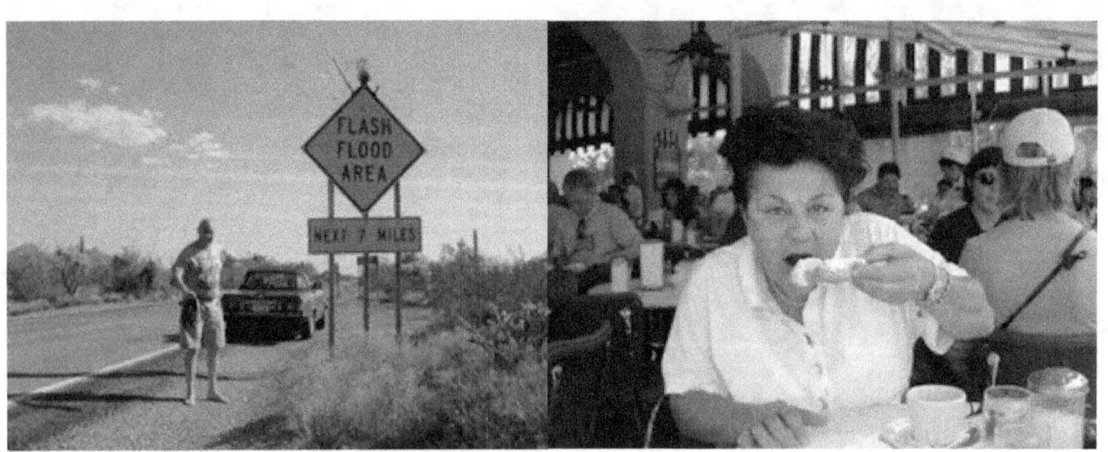

FLASH FLOOD IN NEVADA'S DESERT

CAFE DU MONDE'S FAMOUS DONUTS

Shopping for a City to Call Home 36

The rainy, middle-of-the-night drive from our house in New Hope to the nearest hospital on the night of my heart attack had made one thing clear: Neither Denyse nor I wanted to live in the countryside. We both missed the cosmopolitan energy and the convenience of city life. The question was, which city should we choose?

New York or Paris, That's the Question

We liked the idea of returning to New York City, since we both loved it and still had many friends there, and of course, it would have to be in Manhattan. But the real estate situation was too prohibitive. For a tiny Manhattan apartment with a "space shuttle design" kitchen, the price would be about a million-plus. We would be falling over each other every second. If we wanted to buy a bigger, more comfortable place, we would need a loan—but with no job and no payroll slip to show, no bank would even talk to you. With the starting price for a two-bedroom apartment at two million, not to mention the annual charges amounting to another twenty thousand dollars, New York was simply out of reach, and time was running out to make our decision.

Our New Hope home had sold much faster than we thought it would. When we first told our real estate agent that we wanted to sell the house, she'd said our asking price was too high, and would make the house the most expensive one of its kind for sale in the area. But before we knew it, she had sold the house at the price we wanted. Now the new owner wanted to move in within four weeks.

Competing with New York was Paris, not just because Denyse and I had met in the city of lights, but also because her mother and sister still lived there. But as much as we adored Paris, I could not help thinking of all the dog poop garnishing the city's walkways, making it difficult to walk a straight line, unless one could afford to live on the Champs-Élysées, Avenue Kleber or any of the other prestigious avenues, home to the rich and famous, and the largest amounts of capital in the world. So it was bye-bye to Paris too.

"How about Hannover?" Denyse asked. "You own a building there, and we could take one of the apartments and fix it."

I could tell my wife was proposing my hometown as a favor to me. Even though my sister Jenny and her family were still living there, which was a plus, I had no illusion that Denyse would be happy in what was essentially a big village.

I said, "Hannover? Forget about Hannover, it's a big village which only comes alive once a year for the world's biggest industrial fair, then falls back to sleep once the fair is over. No way! Even the local soccer team, Hannover 96, doesn't play in the first league. Forget it."

We soon realized that the answer to our dilemma lay not too far away, in München, one of Germany's greatest cities. It was where everyone wanted to live and where our daughter's job at McKinsey had happily settled her for the time being.

Home of the famous Oktoberfest and Bavarian "Gemütlichkeit," München is only a short drive from the surrounding lakes and mountains. The Alps weren't far, and we still had our small pied a terre in a nearby mountain resort there. Our whole family loved to ski in the winter. What better place could we choose?

München, get ready, we are coming!

Finding an Apartment in München

Apartment-hunting typically starts with high hopes and turns into a headache. Our experience in München was no exception. We had narrowed our options by deciding to look at apartments only, no houses, since we still planned to travel frequently. Denyse wanted to be able to lock the door, turn the key, and leave.

But München had a housing shortage at the time, and our dream apartment failed to materialize even after my two trips there from the US. Both times I spent endless days looking at place after place. I even had a look at a beautiful house at the Starnberger See, weekend destination of München's rich and famous, just in case it might be our dream home. It wasn't.

I soon grew discouraged after looking at all the spaces our friends Alice and Sigi Steber had so tirelessly found for us. I'm giving up, I told them. "Not so fast," Alice said. "Peter, I think I found a beautiful place. At least the location is outstanding. Let's go have a last look, please?"

"No way," I responded. "If Denyse wants to have an apartment here, let her come and look for one herself."

If Alice gave up so easily, she would not have been Swiss. I finally agreed to this last visit before I took the next flight back to the States.

The apartment was on the twelfth floor of a beautiful building surrounded by a big garden with mature trees. The large balcony offered an unrestricted view over the Alps, the München skyline, and the Englischer Garten. It had underground parking too, making the daily stress of searching for a parking space a thing of the past.

After the apartment tour, I decided my job was done. Denyse would have to make a trip to München after all, but there was no need for her to conduct a search. All she had to do was look at this one place, the apartment I had almost refused to see. It fit our needs perfectly. It was absolutely ideal, and I hoped she would agree.

Moments after Denyse's visit, we had our pens in hand. Knowing that this apartment was one of the last ones available on a high floor of this wonderful building, we signed a letter of understanding immediately. We vowed to be back in early September to sign the final contract, so we could start the renovations before we moved in. This was now July, so we had plenty of time to sketch out a few changes we wanted to make.

In the meantime, we would spend a little time in Las Vegas and visit friends in New York, where we would also meet with our banker to discuss the details of the money transfer necessary to purchase our new home in München. We also had another project to attend to: Carine's August wedding in Istanbul, at the Ciragan, a place I had left with mixed feelings not so long ago.

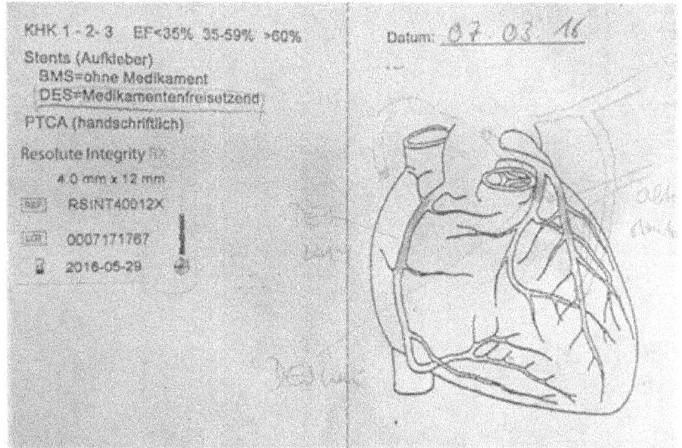

THE DOCTORS EXPLANATION ABOUT MY HEART

ONE OF MY PAINTINGS

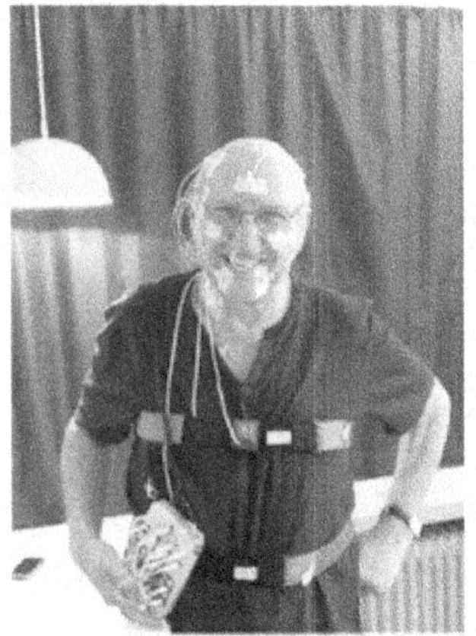

CHECK UP FROM TOP TO BOTTOM

THE REHABILITATION CENTER "LAUTERBACHER MÜHLE"

CARINE AND HER FAMILY VISITING

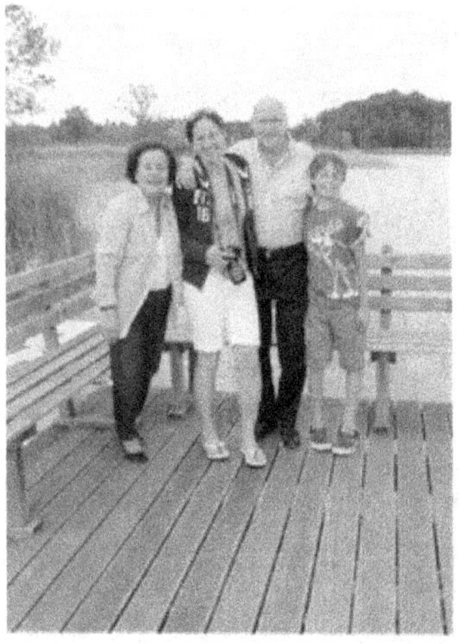

DENYSE, CARINE & TOMMY

Carine and Martin's Wedding 37

Thousand and One Nights on the Bosporus

The day when Carine and her fiancé Martin first announced they wanted to get married in Istanbul, I felt immense joy and pride. Not just because my daughter was marrying a wonderful person, but also because I knew I could help make their wedding an unforgettable experience.

What better place in the world to have a wedding than Istanbul, a city with ancient history, a rich cultural heritage, and spectacular views? With the Ciragan Palace's majestic location at the shore of the Bosporus, and with the father of the bride as the general manager, everything would be in place for a dream wedding straight from the "Thousand and One Nights."

Once the date was fixed, Carine and Martin had visited us for a few days to discuss every single detail of the special day. Our daughter, organized and determined about what she wants, rarely changes her ideas, although she allows room for discussion and listens carefully. But in the end, once she has set her mind on something, that's it.

I forced myself to hold back on my own ideas as I listened carefully to make sure the hotel could deliver every little detail the couple wanted for their special day. But I still planned a few surprises of my own. Because if Carine had an ability to get things done her way, I did too. After all, I was her father.

What I did not know back then was that by the time the wedding happened the following summer, on August 11, 2001, I would no longer be the general manager of the Ciragan.

Yes, it's true that when Reto dismissed me from my job, not long after Carine and Martin's weekend of wedding-planning in Istanbul, he had promised that the wedding would continue just as we had envisioned it, even without me as GM.

But promises are only that: promises.

The Arrangements Not Quite as Planned

In the early summer of 2001, with Carine's wedding rapidly approaching, I gave the new general manager of the Ciragan a courtesy call. I knew my former boss Reto had every intention of honoring his word that the Ciragan would throw a very special event for my daughter, even if I was no longer running the hotel. I only wanted to reassure myself that the wedding arrangements were proceeding as planned.

Contacting the various department heads would have been more efficient than phoning Richard, the new GM, but I didn't want to insult him by going over his head. I would not appreciate it if someone did that to me.

I also suspected Richard would not take kindly to such a slight. He had gotten off to a rough start at the Ciragan, with employees secretly revolting against his management style. The local newspapers published a string of negative stories about him, and the Ciragan's owners would no doubt have replaced him immediately had Reto not stepped in. But as Reto would find out later, his protege would let him down when he needed him the most. In any event, the hotel's problems were no longer my concern. I simply wanted my daughter's big day to go smoothly.

It was a good thing I called the GM because no one at the Ciragan seemed to have gotten the memo about Carine's upcoming wedding. On the phone with me, Richard questioned every single arrangement we had made for the wedding. He refused to give me the special rate for the hundred-plus rooms, insisting he could sell them for more. The food and beverage discount I'd been promised was unacceptable to him because it would mean losing money. And he wasn't sure if he could give me the Palace terrace for the two hundred–person event, as he knew he could book it for a bigger party at a higher rate.

Detail by detail, he went back on every promise I had counted on. I could feel my blood pressure rising as he put my daughter's entire wedding day in jeopardy.

My upbringing and education forbid me to write down the words that passed through my head as I listened to him. He was obviously out to play the big shot, to put on a show, and make clear exactly who is now the boss at the hotel.

It took me a while to calm down before I picked up the phone again to call Reto. I tried to play it cool, but my former boss must have sensed my frustration and concern. Relax, he said. Everything we agreed upon stands, and if I need anything else I should not hesitate to call him.

It was a lucky thing I had called that day. If I'd learned one thing in my decades in the hotel world, it's that you should never, ever take anything for granted. Especially the plans for an event as detailed and momentous as a wedding, when so much can go wrong.

My Surprise

Carine and Martin had intricately arranged every aspect of their wedding, but they had no idea that secret plans were underway behind their back.

With my training as a chef and the years I'd spent organizing elaborate banquets, I could not miss the opportunity to put my own little culinary stamp on my daughter's ceremony. I wanted to make sure she had the perfect cake.

The only person to call was Sylvia Weinstock, the undisputed queen of wedding cakes in New York, who had become a very close personal friend of ours. I had brought Sylvia to Istanbul on two occasions when a couple wanted an extraordinary wedding cake for their celebration.

"Sylvia," I said, "our daughter is getting married, and I want to surprise her with a six-foot wedding cake. Can you send me some flowers, a lot of white and pink flowers?"

She agreed to ship her exquisite decorations directly to me but said she could not go to Istanbul in August. I would have to apply the flowers to the cake myself. I'm no Sylvia Weinstock, but I had a feeling I could handle the job. It would take me back to my days working in the cold kitchen in Hannover and at Fauchon in Paris.

One month before the wedding date, three huge boxes filled with white and pink flowers arrived for me at the hotel. I had a delicate task to accomplish, and I had to keep it a secret from Carine and Martin until it was time to unveil the cake.

Other big surprises awaited. Carine had accepted my offer to handle the invitations we would send out. But I didn't tell her I had arranged for Sami Alouf, who had designed spectacular menus for me in my Sheraton days, to also create the program for the wedding weekend and the menu for the reception.

Sami created a stunning set of invitations, with a design inspired by Istanbul, the Ottoman Empire, and the Ciragan Palace. I let Carine preview only the invitations before the wedding and kept the menu and program as a surprise. She was very happy to see what Sami had come up with. The elegant invitations soon found their way to mailboxes around the world, as Carine had always stayed in touch with her many friends from high school, Dartmouth College, and Harvard University. Martin's contacts ranged all over the globe too, and the couple's invitations went out to Hong Kong, Singapore, Australia, and points all over the United States, Europe, and beyond. Denyse and I were delighted that Sami and his wife, Sophie, could join us for the wedding too.

The biggest surprise was the most difficult one to keep from Carine and Martin. For the evening before the wedding, our dear friend Cigdem Simavi offered a tour around the Bosporus on her *Hallas* boat, followed by a dinner at Zeyrekhane, a most extraordinary place overlooking the Golden Horn, the Blue Mosque, and the Bosporus. Cigdem had mentioned the idea to Denyse and me during Carine and Martin's planning trip to Istanbul the year before, and I managed to hold on to the secret until the last minute. I hoped the soon-to-be newlyweds would be as excited about the idea as we were.

A Religious Challenge

The first surprise we encountered when we arrived in Istanbul the week before the wedding was not the kind of news we hoped to hear.

Our plans were already set for the wedding ceremony to take place on the Ciragan Palace terrace. The couple had asked a Catholic priest to preside over the ceremony, in keeping with the groom's denomination. Although the priest had already agreed in preliminary talks, he changed his mind mere days before the ceremony. He decided he would only hold the wedding in his own church, refusing to come to the Ciragan instead.

I have no idea what caused his change of heart, but transporting two hundred guests from the hotel to the church and back again through the Istanbul traffic would have been a logistical nightmare. We had no intention of inconveniencing our guests or disrupting the carefully planned festivities.

Luckily, an easy solution presented itself. Carine called the Lutheran pastor, and within moments, he agreed to officiate at the ceremony on the Ciragan's terrace. Another crisis averted.

One More Surprise

The trip on Cigdem's yacht with Bill Clinton several years before had been one of our most unforgettable Istanbul memories, but the cruise she arranged for our daughter's wedding easily rivaled it. Carine and Martin were delighted at the chance to experience a boat ride on the *Hallas*, and the entire evening Cigdem organized for us was a tremendous success. Starting a wedding weekend with a cruise on the Bosporus is an experience one cannot easily beat.

Leaving the Unkapani Bridge and making your way along the strait to the Aqueduct of Valens, you will see up on the ridge to your right a large, old stone building with a number of domes and impressive walls. That building is the former Monastery of Christ Pantokrator, once a triple church that housed a chapel and two Eastern Orthodox churches. It is known today as the Zeyrek Mosque, since during the fifteenth-century Ottoman conquest, Istanbul's churches, including famous monuments such as the St. Sophia, were converted into mosques.

We enjoyed a wonderful dinner at the nearby Zeyrekhane restaurant, which we entered by walking through old stone houses that lead into the dining room. Truly, there couldn't have been a more magnificent place to begin a weekend of festivities, especially as Carine and Martin had no idea about what we had planned. Our private cruise, followed by a Turkish feast overlooking the Bosporus and the glorious city of Istanbul, added up to a magical evening we would not soon forget. Denyse and I felt immense gratitude for our dear friend Cigdem and great excitement about the weekend to come. All eyes were now on the wedding day.

Here Comes the Bride

True to his commitment, the Lutheran priest arrived on time on the wedding day. He opened the small black suitcase he carried with him and placed a golden cross on top of the prepared altar table that looked out onto the Bosporus. He was ready to go.

It was a lovely summer evening as the invitees filtered in and took their seats facing the altar. When it was time to start the religious ceremony, Carine and Martin arrived on the terrace, looked out onto the view, and smiled at the gathered guests. As the priest gave his blessing, large ships sailed along the Bosporus in front of the Ciragan. They blew their horns across the water, making a joyful sound that traveled miles beyond the hotel. Music from a church organ could not have sounded better.

Besides the many international friends joining Carine and Martin on their big day, the wedding created an occasion for a true family reunion we had not experienced in many years. Our son, Peter, joined from Las Vegas, Denyse's brother from England, her sister from France, and even Denyse's mother, Meme, despite her advanced age, did not spare the long travel from Paris to be present at her grandchild's wedding.

That evening, guests took their seats in the palace garden, waiting for the bride to come down the majestic staircase decorated in a sea of white roses. Meanwhile, my daughter and I waited in the palace for the music to start. Carine looked beautiful in her elegant yet simple white wedding dress.

I had prepared myself to feel sad at the moment the music started, knowing I was about to give away my only daughter. But Carine and I had a lot of fun as we waited, joking around while we listened for the familiar notes telling us to step outside.

Minutes later, the organ sounds boomed over our laughter. "Here comes the bride." It was time for us to walk outside and down the white Carrara marble stairs.

"Why don't we keep them waiting a little bit?" I said to Carine as we continued to joke around.

"Good idea," Carine said, "let's give them a small version of the runaway bride." But then the palace butler swung open the door to the top of the stairs, and we had no choice but to step out, accompanied by the music and the chorus of "wows" from the crowd of guests waiting at the bottom of the steps.

The Wedding Cake Surprise

The Ciragan had hosted many unforgettable gala dinners in my time, and the one we enjoyed at the wedding was no exception. The chef and his outstanding brigade produced an exquisite culinary experience that delighted us and our guests. But the highlight was still to come, when the waiters and waitresses in traditional Ottoman costumes arrived on the terrace rolling a cart topped with a six-foot-tall wedding cake, covered with white and pink flowers from top to bottom. Sylvia Weinstock would have been proud of the work I did on the cake. I made sure to send her pictures of myself decorating it with her flowers, tucked away in a hiding spot so my daughter wouldn't find me.

It was a joy to surprise Carine and Martin with the enormous cake and to watch them cut it with an antique silver Ottoman épée. The waiters served small individual replicas of the wedding cake to every guest, and it tasted as fabulous as it looked. The pastry chef had outperformed himself.

Compliments about the wedding poured in as I stood on the side, watching Carine and Martin bask in their special day. I felt satisfied, not to mention relieved, at the way the evening had gone so far. For this one night, I was once again the head of the Ciragan Palace Hotel.

Moments later, the palace's wedding event staff released white pigeons to fly out above the crowd, as canons shot golden confetti from the top of the palace roof. Magic all the way.

The newlyweds' first dance ushered in a long festive night ahead. The dance floor on the terrace quickly filled up with the younger generation as they gathered to celebrate and keep the disc jockey busy until the early morning.

As our own "Thousand and One Nights" drew to a close, Denyse and I, feeling tired but very happy, retired to our room to fall into a restful sleep in our treasured old home, the magnificent Ciragan Palace Hotel.

THOUSAND AND ONE NIGHT AT THE BOSPHORUS

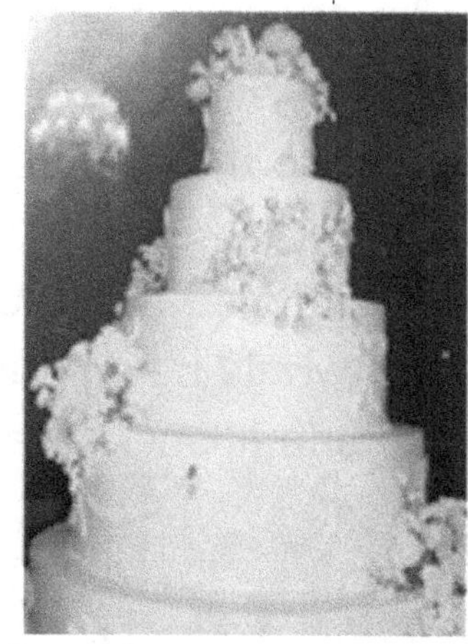

Stuck in the Big Apple **38**

When Everything Came to a Standstill

Fall in New York is the city's most glorious season. Crisp air, clear skies, and a promenade in a horse carriage through Central Park to watch the changing leaves is an experience like no other.

A friend of ours had offered the use of his empty apartment on Lexington Avenue until he returned in mid-September, and the timing could not have been more perfect for our planned trip to New York to see friends and take care of paperwork for the München apartment purchase. While not quite fall yet, those early September weeks in New York are like a long, sweet goodbye to summer, as the mood in the city shifted to settle into the quieter joys of autumn.

We still loved New York, and deep down, we regretted that our new home would be in München and not the Big Apple, but a dream is one thing and financial reality another.

September 11, 2001, our travel day back to Germany, we woke up to bright blue skies and a cool, fresh breeze, making our farewell to

New York even more difficult. But there was no chance of delaying our departure because the lawyers were waiting for us to sign the purchasing agreement for our new apartment in München. Our suitcases stood by the door ready to go as we prepared to call a taxi to take us to the airport. The only thing left to do was to call our friend May Fernaine to say bye-bye.

"You are on your way to where?" she asked.

"To the airport," I said. "We are just calling to say bye-bye and hope to see you in München soon."

"Haven't you watched TV this morning?" she asked. "Haven't you seen what has happened in the city and to the World Trade Center? You're not going anywhere. You'll be staying in New York for a while."

Denyse and I don't like to turn on the TV when we wake up, and we're not in the habit of keeping it on morning to night in our home. Had we missed something important? I went over to the TV to switch it on, and Denyse and I stood frozen in place as we absorbed the horrific news and watched what happened to the twin towers.

A call to the airline confirmed that all flights that day were canceled. The airport was now closed indefinitely. New York was in a panic, the entire nation was stunned, and we were stuck in Manhattan with nowhere to go.

Thankfully, we have friends like May, who would not hear of us trying to find a hotel and told us to come stay with her. Finding a cab to her place on 87th Street was another story. Taxis rushed by us, occupied or not, and we stood there until our arms ached from holding up our hands in vain. Finally, one cab driver took pity and stopped. He was off-duty and heading to fetch his kid from school, but he agreed to take us to May's since it was on his way.

Ten minutes and a healthy tip later, we got out in front of May's building and took an elevator up to the thirtieth floor. We greeted each other somberly this time, as we walked to her living room windows overlooking downtown, all the way south to where the World Trade Center towers had stood tall only yesterday.

Dark smoke filled the horizon over the southern tip of Manhattan, and even up on Eighty-Sixth Street, we would soon start smelling it. In the days after, all we could do was watch the terrible news, hour after hour, and call our families, and try again to get a flight out of New York. But repeated calls to the airlines only confirmed that no flights were going in or out of New York anytime soon. For how long? Nobody knew. The city we loved dearly, the city that was always on the move, had come to a complete standstill.

"Rien ne va plus," as they say in the casinos. "Nothing is going anymore," as the spinning wheel slows to a halt.

The entire world knew about the event, of course, so our broker in München, Mr. Huelsebusch, was not surprised when I called to tell him we were stuck in New York. I gave him an optimistic guess that it would be only a few days before we could return to München to sign the purchase documents.

But as day after day went by, with no available flights on the horizon, I had to keep calling Mr. Huelsebusch to reassure him that we still had every intention of buying the apartment.

Finally, a week later, the New York airports reopened. Now it was only a matter of finding a flight, as hundreds of thousands of stranded passengers scrambled to rebook their travel. Two days later, we managed to get a return flight to Germany, but as all flights to München were fully booked, we had to fly to Frankfurt instead. We rented a car and drove the four hours to München as soon as we landed and finally signed all the documents for the apartment purchase in the lawyer's office the next day.

"Thank you for waiting for us," I said to Mr. Huelsebusch as I stood pen in hand.

He smiled and answered, "Do you realize I could have sold your apartment ten times while you were stuck in New York?"

I had no doubt he was telling the truth. After what we had just witnessed in New York, I knew more than ever just how fortunate we were. I hoped our luck would not soon run out.

First Return to Cairo

Sitting in a lovely new München apartment doing absolutely nothing was not the plan I had in mind for the next phase of my life. It was also not an option. For my sanity, not to mention our finances, I needed to start working again, the sooner, the better.

Fortunately, a job prospect had come up out of nowhere while we were still in New Hope. One day, I had received a telephone call out of the blue from a man named Ednan Galali, who introduced himself as an Egyptian hotelier. He said he wanted to meet me while he was in New York, so when Denyse and I passed through Manhattan after Carine's wedding, I scheduled a time to talk to him in person. I had no idea how he had learned about me, but his call had piqued my curiosity.

During our meeting, he wasted no time in making his intentions clear. He needed my help in Cairo, where he was managing the Helnan International Hotels for the Egyptian government, a portfolio that included the Shepheard Hotel in Cairo, the Palestine Hotel in Alexandria, and one hotel at the Red Sea in Sharm El Sheikh. All three were renowned and had long been considered among the leading hotels of Egypt, but they had been neglected for many years after being nationalized during the reign of Abdel Nasser.

Ednan sounded like a typical self-made man, full of confidence and proud of his achievements. He had made his fortune in Denmark, where he also owned two hotels. But he admitted that the Cairo hotels were not performing as he had hoped, and he was under pressure from the Egyptian government to make them succeed. He was convinced he could make more money on the hotels if they were properly managed. Perhaps the Midas touch I had brought to the St. Regis, as well as to the Heliopolis Sheraton Hotel just outside Cairo, could transform the failing properties?

Our discussion resulted in a job proposal on the spot. Ednan offered me the position as chief operating officer of Helnan International Hotels, based in Cairo. This was an intriguing proposal, to say the least. Job offers were not exactly falling out of the sky. The position would include full board at the Shepheard Hotel plus the use of the company car whenever we needed it. Returning to Cairo was an appealing prospect too since we had felt at home in Egypt during our time at the Heliopolis. Denyse agreed this would be a good move for us, and I accepted immediately.

With my reputation from my time at the Heliopolis preceding me, Ednan was expecting a small miracle from me, as I found out the moment I arrived once again in the land of the Nile.

But as soon as Denyse and I moved into the Shepheard, I discovered just how right Ednan was about the mismanagement. The Shepheard was nearly falling apart, and the other hotels in the group were in poor condition too. Ednan's company, Helnan Hotels, was obliged by the management contract to maintain the hotels properly for the Egyptian government, but the properties did not make enough money to allow for high-quality upkeep. This was a situation in which money needed to be spent in order to make money, but neither Helnan Hotels nor the government were willing to open their wallets. It was a vicious circle with no solution in sight.

Making the best of a situation like this was a familiar predicament for me. Figuring out how to make money without spending any money was a huge challenge, but I was convinced that with the goodwill of all parties involved, it would be a task not so impossible to surmount.

How wrong I would turn out to be!

Arriving in Cairo, I got to work immediately, cleaning up the hotels, introducing new operational concepts, and conducting countless training sessions for the staff. We were able to make progress with those moves, but considering just how badly the hotels had been maintained for years, we had no choice but to allocate funds for renovations if we wanted any chance of increasing revenues.

But after a month, we still saw no light at the end of the tunnel. Despite our constant meetings and tireless attempts to search for a solution, the Egyptian government refused to change its position. Helnan Hotels was also not prepared to advance the funds to make even the most minor of improvements. I would sit up in bed at night, attempting to find a way out of this impasse.

The situation was looking hopeless, until the phone rang one morning. It was a telephone call from my lawyer Steven Eckhaus, who had handled the ITT lawsuit. This time he was calling with a job prospect of all things. The position was in New York City, and he wondered if I would be willing to consider moving back. Before Steven had a chance to give me all the details, I agreed to say yes to the new challenge, having only the vaguest idea of what it would involve. Steven's call, I decided, was a fateful sign that it was time to move on.

Visiting the Burned Out Shell of My Old Hotel

In the meantime, Denyse and I decided to stop by Heliopolis again before we left Egypt, to visit our old stomping grounds and see what had become of the hotel we once called home. Five years after we left, the hotel had experienced a huge fire that burned two-thirds of the building to the ground, resulting in a battle between the owners and the insurance company. When Denyse and I passed through before departing to New York, we found a burned-out shell in the spot where the once-grand Heliopolis had stood. The damaged portions still lay in ruins.

As we walked through the burned-out spaces, only the colors of the floors, as familiar as the ones in our own home, allowed us to guess where the once-busy restaurants had stood. White marble for the Vienna Café, green marble for the Italian restaurant Alfredo, and a checkered marble floor for the German Bierstube.

It was a surreal experience to see the deserted, ghostly restaurant spaces, which not so long ago rang out with the sounds of lively guests and rushed waiters dashing around serving exquisite food and drinks. The Heliopolis visit broke our hearts. The last thing we wanted was to leave Egypt with this image in our heads.

But New York City was calling again, and it was time to say goodbye to Cairo. What did the Big Apple have in store for us this time? Never in my wildest dreams could I have imagined what awaited me there.

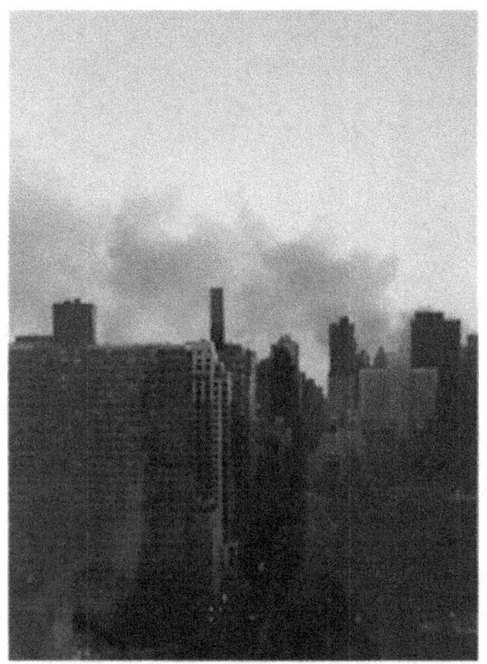

NEW YORK 11. SEPTEMBER 2001

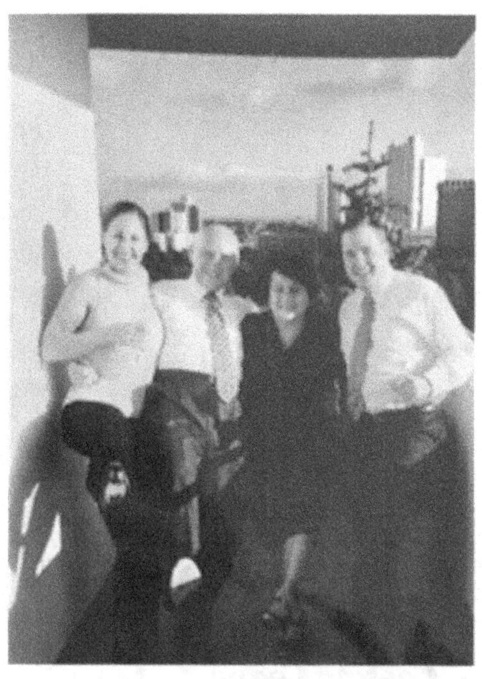

FAMILY REUNION AT OUR NEW APARTMENT

SEPTEMBER 11TH, 2001 VIEW FROM THE BALCONY OF OUR FRIENDS ON 86TH STREET TO DOWNTOWN

The Queen of Mean 39

Meeting Leona

"The palace does not serve wet lettuce!"

In the last decades of the twentieth century, Leona Helmsley and her opulent hotels achieved an international celebrity status that eludes most hospitality brands. But the nature of her fame was not exactly the envy of her peers in the hotel industry. Stories about her crude, abusive managerial style filled the headlines back when I was at the St. Regis. Everyone in New York City had heard of Leona Helmsley. The hotelier and wife of real estate billionaire Harry Helmsley, whose vast holdings included the Empire State Building and the Flatiron Building, was well-known for verbally and publicly berating her staff at the nearly thirty hotels she ran with her husband, among them the Park Lane and the Helmsley Palace in Manhattan. The Helmsley Hotels advertisements appeared all over the newspapers, with a big picture of Leona's face alongside a series of grandiose slogans. "The only palace in the world where the queen stands guard," said one ubiquitous ad.

In 1990, a made-for-TV movie called *The Queen of Mean*—Leona's real-life nickname—dramatized her horrible behavior, in scenes where she screamed at her staff for serving a room service salad with lettuce that had not been sufficiently dried. I did not see the movie when it first aired, and I was at the time too busy with the St. Regis renovations to care much about Leona Helmsley one way or another. But in the late 1980s, I did hear the news of her tax evasion conviction, for which she served eighteen months in jail.

By the time Steven Eckhaus called me in Las Fuentes, Spain, in 2003, Leona Helmsley and her legal troubles were the furthest thing from my mind. As it happened, Steven had been Leona's lawyer too, and the job he was calling about involved working directly for Mrs. Helmsley.

Everyone takes advantage of Leona, Steven said to me on the phone that day, and she needs someone like you to help manage her hotel business. As my mind attempted to conjure a picture of myself working for a person like Leona Helmsley, Steven interrupted my silence to explain that even though she has a terrible reputation, in person she is not so bad.

Despite my doubts about this, I had to admit Steven's timing was impeccable. I could give Ednan my one-month notice, then fly to New York to meet with Leona. Even if I could never imagine working for her after meeting her in person, and even if she decided not to hire me after all, I would eventually find a job somewhere else. I knew this was a gamble, but I suspected there was no future for me anyway at the Cairo hotels.

Arriving in New York four weeks later, I contacted Steven to arrange a meeting with Mrs. Helmsley. I learned she was on an extended visit to her hotel in Sarasota, Florida, and she expected me to meet her there. There was one catch: If I'm interested in the job, she let me know through Steven, I would have to buy my own plane ticket.

Unbeknownst to me, I was getting my first taste of how Leona Helmsley operates. I agreed to purchase the ticket and fly to Florida, hoping that she wouldn't charge me for the hotel accommodations too.

Paying for my own flight was only the first surprise. The second surprise was that I quite liked her during our meeting. Our interaction was cordial, and she took charge of the conversation by asking a lot of questions, but through it all, she was very charming and even revealed a healthy sense of humor.

She started by asking if I knew she had been in prison for tax evasion. Of course, I knew. Not only was her conviction big news in New York at the time, but a comment she made to one of her housekeepers had hit the headlines too: "We don't pay taxes. Only the little people pay taxes," Leona had allegedly said to her employee. The phrase quickly became a Helmsley trademark.

Leona seemed almost proud of her time in jail, as if it made her a martyr. But she was defensive about her behavior and insisted to me that the whole thing was ridiculous.

"I don't understand!" she said. She claimed she always paid hundreds of thousands of dollars in taxes, and the government reimbursed her for hundreds of thousands of dollars that she overpaid. "And then they punish me for a piece of jewelry that I didn't pay taxes on?" From what I had read in the news, that "piece of jewelry" was actually a collection of hundreds of thousands of dollars' worth of items from Van Cleef and Arpels. But I was not about to argue with her.

During our first meeting in Sarasota, Leona told me she was obsessed with an idea for a new advertising campaign featuring her little white Maltese dog Trouble as the spokesperson for the hotel. The ads would show Trouble, "the Helmsley's favorite four-legged guest," posing on a velvet chair. In one ad, he would direct prospective guests to call for reservations. In another, he would pout, saying, "It's a sad day when you leave a Helmsley Hotel." The idea struck me as innovative, especially compared to the many boring hotel ads out there. Leona seemed pleased that I genuinely liked her idea and was even receptive to some changes I recommended.

I had to admit I had difficulty imagining that this was truly the Queen of Mean, known for making the lives of her employees miserable and firing them on a whim.

In every conversation during our extended Florida interview, Leona seemed concerned about making me feel at ease with her. She took an interest in my life, asking me about myself and my family. Her quick wit and her lesser-known social graces came through during my entire three days in Sarasota, as she presented herself from her best side and oversaw all the details of making my stay comfortable. She even avoided talking about hotels or business for most of my visit.

After three days of socializing in the sun, sipping drinks on the hotel restaurant terrace, and chatting casually, I returned to New York not knowing if I had a new job or if the whole exercise had just been a leisurely poolside weekend in Florida.

A phone call from Steven Eckhaus the next day shed some light on the situation.

"She likes you," Steven said. "When can you start?"

I told him I had to fly back to our München apartment to pick up some belongings, and I could start in ten days.

This was impossible, Steven told me. If I don't start immediately, she'll see that I'm not in the hotel when she returns from Florida and will assume I've changed my mind.

"No problem," I said. "If she is prepared to buy me a couple of suits, shirts, ties, underwear, and shoes, I'll be ready to start tomorrow."

"I'll call you back," Steven answered, and hung up.

One week later, I flew back from München with my luggage, and on December 1, 2003, I started as the new general manager of the Helmsley Park Lane Hotel, the latest in a long list of Leona Helmsley veterans.

My New Job at the Park Lane

My first day at work began in grand style, as I ascended to the top of the Park Lane Hotel to meet with Leona in the duplex where she lived and worked. She greeted me cheerfully, and we began to talk business as I stole glances at the amazing view overlooking Central Park. It was a perfect postcard of Manhattan in all its gleaming, early twenty-first-century glory.

Little did I realize then that I would have the opportunity to enjoy this view many more times, unfortunately far more than I ever wanted.

But on my first day of work, I had to admit it felt wonderful to be back in the Big Apple. After all, nothing beats New York City. It's still the most exciting city in the world, and Denyse and I had plenty of close friends there whom we could not wait to see.

Of course, the Park Lane Hotel was not the St. Regis, but it had tremendous potential. Its location directly across from Central Park was its biggest asset, and the property itself had the makings of a luxury hotel—although it needed a great deal of work. I looked forward to giving the Park Lane the Tischmann touch.

The hotel was uniquely situated to take advantage of the changes happening in the uptown hotel landscape. Many hotels on Central Park South had begun the process of converting into condominiums, even the Plaza. The Park Lane stood to capitalize on the increased demand for rooms, as long as we could build and cement its reputation as the best hotel in the area. I knew this would be a challenge, but the circumstances seemed ripe for doing exactly the type of work I felt born to do.

On a bright December morning, after meeting with Leona and preparing myself for my first day at my job, I walked eagerly to my new office. Opening the door and stepping inside, I got the shock of my life. The office looked like a neglected storage room, with papers strewn all over, boxes piled up in the corners, and a desk and sideboard cluttered with dirty glasses and half-empty water bottles.

Colleagues in the industry had warned me that the general manager position at the Park Lane had a high turnover rate, but I wondered just how miserable my immediate predecessor could have been to leave the office in this condition. And could it be that nobody had set foot in here since then to clean up the space? If this was how the general manager's office looked, I shuddered to think what the rest of the spaces might look like. I took a deep breath, tried to find a place to sit down amid the mess, and prepared myself to roll up my sleeves and dig in.

Getting the hotel into shape, retraining the staff to the level of a luxury hotel, and managing the entire operation would be a big enough job in itself. I was certainly not new at this, though I had yet to encounter a hotel that had been falling apart to quite this degree. But after a few days in the hotel, I realized that my new responsibilities involved much more than just managing the hotel.

My most urgent priority was to protect the department heads from Mrs. Helmsley. She had a habit of calling them all day long to complain about things of no importance, leaving them with little time to do their jobs. As a result, each department in the hotel remained stalled and directionless.

Another discovery I made in my first week is that my ability to zero in on the tiniest speck of dust was outmatched by Leona's. I have always had an eye for detail, and my employees as well as my friends and family have resented me for this because nothing escapes my eyes, not a drop of water on an otherwise impeccable sink and not a single finger smudge on a tabletop.

I would be escorting Leona into the hotel restaurant for a lunch meeting, and she would say, "Mr. Tischmann, why are there fingerprints on the mirror?" I would look and sure enough, I would see a fingerprint on the surface. In the moment between when I checked every detail in the room and then brought Leona in, the head waiter must have put his hand on the mirror. She never, ever missed a thing.

Outmatched, I began to direct my attention to every detail of every room each time I walked into a space, and I would notify department heads and staff members so they could stay one step ahead of Leona. This drastically reduced the time left each day to do the real work of analyzing the hotel operation, identifying areas to improve, and implementing the changes I wanted to make. To catch up, I worked long hours that began in the early morning and did not end until late in the evening, seven days a week.

One day at 4:30 a.m. when I was still asleep, a rare morning when I was not already sitting at my desk or walking around to inspect the hotel as I sometimes did in the predawn hours, the phone rang. It was Leona on the line.

"Mr. Tischmann, are you trying to kill me?" she asked.

My heart stopped. I was still half-asleep, and hearing Leona's imperious voice accuse me like this sounded like a nightmare.

"I'm freezing to death in my apartment," she went on. "Do you want me to jump out of the window?"

"You can't jump out of the window," I told her, blinking my eyes and snapping awake. The windows of the hotel were always locked. "But I'll be up in a minute."

There I was, in the middle of the night, hitting the elevator button to go to the forty-sixth floor and investigate my boss's latest bizarre complaint.

"Thank you, darling," she said as she opened the door. She liked to call everybody darling when she was in a cheerful mood.

A quick look at the thermostat explained what was happening. Leona must have played with the thermostat in her room, reducing the temperature to freezing. Although her complaint that the room was too cold was legitimate, she had inflicted the problem on herself, or was she just desperate for attention?

I fixed the thermostat, wished her good night, and left.

"Thank you for coming, darling" she said, as I exited her apartment, under the watchful eyes of one of the security guards she had sitting in front of her door twenty-four hours a day.

The situation had gone smoothly, perhaps too smoothly. As for me, I had no intention of receiving any more absurd middle-of-the-night wakeups like this one. I instructed the chief engineer to bypass her thermostats and set her room temperature himself from the control room. This would still allow her to play with the temperature controls, but without any consequences. Nobody besides the chief engineer, the engineer on guard, and myself were supposed to know about this arrangement. It wasn't the only scheme we came up with to save Leona from herself and to keep us all from losing our minds.

Straightening Out the Hotel

A poorly run hotel cannot hide behind elegant curtains. I've always believed that if the back of the house did not operate smoothly, the failures would soon reveal themselves in the front of the house. My old philosophy turned out to be true once again.

As I walked the Park Lane from top to bottom, inspecting every space of the hotel and casting my eye into every storeroom and every corner, it became immediately obvious to me that the entire place was a mess, not just my office. No wonder the hotel occupancy and revenues were not living up to the potential of a luxury property located across from Central Park. The operation was rotting from the inside out. I had to undertake a major clean-up of the back of the house before I could even begin to address the public areas.

Over the following days, I met with each department head to assess the problems in his or her respective area and to create timetables and deadlines for bringing each part of the hotel up to the highest standards. I instructed the chief engineer to clean his department from top to bottom, remove the clutter piled up everywhere, and restore the machinery to tip-top condition. Meeting with the executive chef and chief steward, I reminded them that the kitchen is the heart of the food and beverage operation and needs to adhere to the highest standards of hygiene, from the cooking equipment to the work tables to the refrigerators, which I expected their staff to clean and sanitize twice a day. I told the executive housekeeper to get all the carpets in the guest corridors and rooms professionally cleaned so the original colors would reappear. That task proved so difficult, the contractor had to charge us a premium to achieve the expected results.

When I asked someone on the housekeeping staff when was the last time the carpets had been deep-cleaned, he said it had never happened during his tenure.

"How long have you been in the hotel?" I asked him.

"Eight years, Mr. Tischmann." I couldn't believe my ears.

Even the comptroller had to join in the clean-up. After all, if the office of the person in charge of the hotel's finances looked like a dump, what would that say about the health of the entire operation? I instructed him to reorganize his offices and store all the important papers and documents in the archive.

"Mr. Tischmann," he said, "we have no space, but we can put all the papers in our outside storage."

"Outside storage?" I asked. Why did we need outside storage? The hotel had plenty of storage facilities on the premises, at least in theory. But because of the amount of clutter and rubbish to be found everywhere, the in-house spaces were already full to capacity, and I learned that the hotel was paying exorbitant fees to rent storage in external facilities. The waste and mismanagement were truly epic.

After spending four weeks overseeing the clean-up of every inch of the hotel, a project that involved our entire staff, it was time to start anew. Painters arrived to refresh the entire back of the house. To rebuild the staff's morale and prepare them for a new era, I had the employees' dining room redecorated with new furniture and attractive wall hangings. The chef did his part and began offering a daily choice of dishes to entice staff. I closed the separate department heads' commissary and turned it into a much-needed storage space for supplies, which had until now piled up in every corner of the hotel, without anyone paying attention to which department was consuming which supplies, or how often.

To revive an esprit de corps among the demoralized staff, I explained to all employees and department heads that they were expected to have lunch in the same room. They would eat the same food, as the days of serving a lesser quality meal to rank and file employees were now over. All staff members, regardless of their title, would clean up their tables when they were done. I hoped the employees would notice this change, and that it would reinforce the sense of respect and camaraderie I wanted to bring to the hotel.

With the back of the house now running more efficiently, I could finally turn my attention to the significant management challenges. I needed to examine all the expenses, contracts, and operating structures to find out why the hotel, despite the fact that Leona owned it free and clear, always lost money—big money.

Solving the financial mysteries would keep my boss from wasting away her fortune and bleeding the hotel dry and would help bring the Park Lane up to its full potential. But Mrs. Helmsley had a way of always diverting attention to trivial matters and wasting time that should go to far more pressing issues. No matter how much I arranged my time so I could tackle the important challenges, she kept me busy with her constant requests that I visit her on the forty-sixth floor to act as a go-between for her disputes. She was always accusing her two personal maids of this or that oversight. Before I even made it to the forty-sixth-floor apartment, I would often find one of the maids standing in the hallway crying, having just been fired by Mrs. Helmsley.

The turnover on the forty-sixth floor was mind-boggling. Of course, we could never appoint one of the existing hotel maids to replace a personal attendant whom Leona had just dismissed, since no staff member who had spent any time at the hotel was willing to work on the forty-sixth floor. This meant we had to constantly hire new maids for Mrs. Helmsley and spend time training them, only to see them fired again in no time.

The staff even had a method for protecting each other from their boss's wrath. They had developed a warning system by which someone at the Park Lane would notify employees at another hotel the moment when Leona got into her car to go check on that property. But no matter how much warning her staff had received that the Queen was arriving, she would find ways to catch them off-guard and yell at them in front of their colleagues and guests. It was her signature management technique. And it was failing miserably.

Where Is the Money?

The Park Lane hemorrhaged so much money every day, it was hard to believe the hotel was still standing. Considering its long history of poor management, even a single penny in profits would count as a miracle. My close examination of the finances revealed an unimaginable amount of waste. Looking at the service and maintenance contracts, I found over twenty agreements amounting to more than $200,000 monthly.

Never before in my life had I seen so many service contracts for a single hotel. Why did we need so much staff, I wondered, when nearly all the work was done by outside contractors? Each individual contractor had seemingly figured out they could charge an arm and a leg without anyone noticing. For years, contractors had been taking advantage of Mrs. Helmsley and her famous riches, and they'd no doubt spread the word that this hotel had no one at the controls.

Now the game was over. After analyzing and renegotiating every contract, from the elevator service to the brass polishing contract, I canceled more than half. I reassigned those jobs to the hotel's existing employees, spreading out the additional responsibilities equally from the engineering staff to the housekeepers. All staffers got their fair share of new tasks, each of which should have been their responsibility to begin with.

The moves paid off, yielding considerable savings and cutting the hotel's losses to a great extent.

One day soon after completing the financial makeover, I ran into Mrs. Helmsley having lunch in the restaurant with Albert Cohen, the corporate CFO. Leona's little Maltese dog Trouble sat comfortably on Albert's lap as I approached the table to say hello and see if everything was to their satisfaction.

"Sit down," Mrs. Helmsley ordered, her way of inviting me to join them at the table. She asked how everything was going with my new job, and I proudly informed her about the enormous savings we had recently achieved, substantially reducing the hotel's losses.

I glanced in her direction, expecting to see a smile and, with any luck, to hear a compliment about my work. Instead, she turned to me and said, "Mr. Tischmann, I don't know what you are doing, but when I was managing the hotel, we were not losing any money!"

Perhaps she was joking? Or had she lost all touch with reality? I paused to contemplate what she had just said, when she continued: "Since you've saved so much money, Peter, where is that money?" She made the classic "give me the cash" signal with her fingers, as if expecting me to actually lay the money down on the table.

Cautiously, I glanced over at Albert Cohen, thinking he might give her a quick lesson in financial principles, or at the very least explain to her that reducing losses doesn't mean cash in the bank. But he simply sat in his chair quietly, petting Trouble and saying to Mrs. Helmsley, "Isn't she a cute little dog!"

This behavior from a CFO would be shocking in any other context, and Albert's behavior took me by surprise at first. But as I soon learned, this was completely typical conduct from her top executives, who went along with anything she said in order to protect their own comfortable jobs.

Well, their jobs may have seemed plush from a salary standpoint, but they came at a very high price: saying goodbye to any glimmer of self-respect. Would I let this happen to me too? Never, I promised myself.

Dealing with Leona

Working for Mrs. Helmsley was, by normal standards, an absolute nightmare. Her staff suffered daily as she scolded them, threatened to fire them, and subjected them to humiliation in front of their colleagues. She made my job very difficult too, and a big part of the challenge was retaining my dignity in the face of her constant attempts to diminish me and everyone else who worked for her. But in my daily dealings with Leona, I have to admit there were a few moments here and there when she made me laugh with her wit, her insanity, or both.

One morning, she called me to her apartment. She was sitting at a gueridon room service table in front of her TV, having breakfast. In order not to talk down to her while standing next to her, I knelt down so I could be at eye level with her as she talked to me. She looked directly at me and said, "What are you doing, Peter? Are you proposing? The answer is no."

I took my laughs where I could get them. In general, working for Leona made every day unpredictable, and not pleasantly so. Even though she was still quite sharp and maintained her unusual attention to detail, she was starting to show early signs of Alzheimer's as the months went by. Every week, she had her good days, but I noticed an increasing number of not-so-good days. In case any of her employees had ever underestimated her volatile personality before, they certainly were not doing so anymore.

My own job evolved to include a role as Mrs. Helmsley's personal medical assistant, to help administer the pills her doctor prescribed to help with her memory loss. The same physician had treated her late husband Harry Helmsley, and he insisted on involving me to ensure that Mrs. Helmsley took her medications on time every day. It was a responsibility I could have done without, but what could I say?

If only the medications had helped. Perhaps they had some effect, but despite all the pills she took, Leona constantly forgot things we had discussed, questioned agreements we had made together, and worst of all, denied any awareness of decisions she had approved only the day before. I had to change the way I worked with her in order to keep her from destroying the business and everyone around her.

In the new system I devised, Mrs. Helmsley would need to sign off on every agreement and decision she made, so we could have it in writing. Not that adding this extra step ended up making any difference at all. She simply refused to recognize her own signature. But at least her approval was documented.

"Imagine a Swiss cheese," her personal adviser John, a supporter of mine, once explained to me. Every hole represents dead brain cells and affects her capacity to remember and to react even to the most typical everyday situations.

Visualizing her internal condition in this way helped me understand her illness, which now seemed to be worsening rapidly. But her behavior would still sometimes take me by surprise. So one day, when I saw a Swiss cheese replica in a shop selling decorative items, I could not help buying it. I put it on my desk, as a daily reminder of the reality I was facing. Of course, Leona had no idea what the Swiss cheese represented and probably assumed it was merely symbolic of my love of food and my background as a chef.

As her mental state continued to deteriorate, a situation that was even leaking out to the gossip columns of New York City's local newspapers, dealing with Leona turned into even more of a slippery, deceptive experience. We could have a pleasant conversation about the hotel one minute, followed by a frustrating encounter the next moment, when her mind started to wander. But she did still manage to show concern for how her reactions were impacting me, as I sensed during certain conversations. Once in the restaurant, after she had called me to complain about something or other, she said this to me:

"I hope I do not frustrate you, Peter."

"No, not yet, Mrs. Helmsley," I lied. "And if that should happen, I'll tell you about it, and then I'll go take a walk in the park."

"Are you being truthful?" she asked. "I don't want to frustrate you."

"Absolutely, Mrs. Helmsley," I insisted.

"I like you, and I don't want you to be frustrated."

"I don't either, Mrs. Helmsley. I like you too, and I do appreciate your support," I replied, hoping this useless conversation would come to a rapid end.

Sure enough, she nodded at me, smiled, grabbed Trouble, and walked off to the elevator.

As little confidence I had that this brief show of lucidity would have any impact on my daily reality, at least it was reassuring to experience hours or even an entire day when she seemed perfectly normal. In those moments, she sounded fully aware of what was happening around her—until her mind took a turn for the worse in the next hour or the next day.

Leona and I had a number of subjects around which we went in circles, day after day. One of these was the question of which coffee to serve at the hotel. We had chosen Jamaica Blue Mountain, the most expensive kind money could buy at the time, its tiny coffee beans selected for their exquisite aroma. We ground the beans a la minute for each order and brewed them in a special machine just moments before serving the coffee in a preheated coffee pot. We served Jamaica Blue Mountain coffee for weeks without any issues, which seemed too good to be true, when suddenly Leona found a reason to complain about the coffee.

"I don't like the coffee you serve me and my guests," she told me one day. She handed me a paper cup of coffee one of her maids had picked up from a pizzeria around the corner.

"This is the coffee I like, and we should offer this to our guests," she said, "not the poison you are serving."

Well, she was the boss. From that day on, when she ordered her breakfast every morning, a waiter would run around the corner to the pizzeria to get the coffee, then pour it into a silver coffee pot and serve it to her. Problem solved. At least for now.

Smoked salmon was another of her obsessions. We served the best smoked salmon in the city, but she still found a way to make our lives difficult. This was partly because the chef did not follow the instructions I gave him.

Smoked salmon, traditionally a very fatty fish, has the tendency to bleed some of its fat onto the plate when sliced too early. This gave Leona a reason to complain, and there was no talking sense into her. To circumvent the issue, I instructed the chef that every salmon order for Mrs. Helmsley needed to be sliced a la minute immediately before serving, so not a single drop of oil would have a chance to appear.

One morning, Mrs. Helmsley phoned me: "Good morning, Mr. Tischmann, this is your favorite complainer calling." She informed me that her plate of salmon did not meet with her approval. I immediately knew what had happened. In anticipation of her order and contrary to my instructions, the chef had prepared her plate in advance. There I was, on the elevator again heading up to the forty-sixth floor.

"Do you know why I understand so much about salmon?" Mrs. Helmsley asked me as soon as I arrived.

"Absolutely, Mrs. Helmsley," I said, trying to charm her. "You are a world-class hotelier. Of course, you know a lot about food and specifically about smoked salmon."

"No," she replied. "It's because I'm a good Jewish girl."

Leona always liked to stay one step ahead of the conversation, at least whenever her mind would allow her to.

But with every passing day, her memory was playing more and more tricks on her, and often cruel ones. Although Harry Helmsley had passed away eight years before, I would frequently find her sitting in the lobby staring at his portrait. Sometimes her profound sense of loss would leave her completely disoriented.

"Can you please call Harry for me?" she asked me one day.

"Of course," Mrs. Helmsley, I said. I went into my office to do some work and returned after half an hour.

"I'm sorry, Mrs. Helmsley, but I couldn't find your husband anywhere in the hotel."

"Never mind," she said, "he probably went to town to buy a gift for me."

Another morning, what was supposed to be a short visit to respond to one of her complaints turned into a two-hour conversation about her life and how she met Harry Helmsley. She wanted to make a few things clear: She had been married twice before she met Harry. It was not the money but the dancing that made her relationship with Harry click. And even though everyone is after her money, it doesn't belong to her. It belongs to Harry. Nobody will get a penny when she dies, as she can't make decisions about his fortune. Even still, every man who meets her wants to marry her, which is fine with her, but they have to put the same amount of money on the table.

I nodded and smiled as she explained these points to me and reassured her that I understood and would make sure others did too.

Working for Mrs. Helmsley was exhausting on every level, but I never spent one boring day in my life as general manager of the Park Lane Hotel. Despite my boss's unpredictable behavior and her meanness to her staff, I did mostly enjoy what I was doing. And I even liked Leona Helmsley, at least at times. The personal charm I had witnessed during our first meeting in Sarasota still emerged on a regular basis. In the moments when she expressed concern for the frustration she was causing myself and others, she accidentally revealed a gentle and sensitive side too, even if she tried hard to hide it.

She would hate to know that I felt pity for her too. After all, she was a deeply lonely person, with no friends, and nobody ever coming by to visit her. Her only child had died of a heart attack two decades before, in his forties, and she was not on close terms with her four grandchildren.

As luck would have it, her birthday was on July 4, which helped hide just how disastrous the event turned out to be. We had prepared a wonderful party for Leona in the garden court of the hotel and invited everyone on the small list of friends she had given us. But nobody showed up, no birthday cards arrived, and even her doctor, with whom she thought she had a close friendship, did not appear. Steven, her lawyer, was the only one who showed up, so he and I quickly assembled staff to surround her as she cut her perfectly decorated birthday cake, acting like the life of the party.

Did she realize what a pathetic situation this was? We could not quite tell. The fact that this was a national holiday created confusion, which was convenient for her and for us.

"The whole country is celebrating my birthday, and tonight they'll organize beautiful fireworks for me," she said to the assembled guests with a big smile on her face. Her only real friend at the party, Trouble, barked as she spoke, as if confirming what she just said.

I was personally surprised that more guests had not appeared, for the simple reason that some of the people she considered friends were using her in every conceivable way. These so-called friends circled around her like sharks, hoping she would give them a job on the board of her multimillion-dollar trust or include them in her will.

Perhaps everyone knew that her memory was fading and it would not matter whether or not they showed up for her birthday party. If so, they were probably right. Her failing mental health was increasingly impossible to ignore.

One afternoon, during a rare moment of quiet as I sat in my office working, I received an urgent call from the front desk. Three police officers had just arrived at the hotel, responding to a 911 call from Mrs. Helmsley.

My heart jumped. Apparently, she had heard noises from the floor above her and was afraid that somebody was in her apartment.

I rushed down to the lobby and met the officers as they waited for the elevator. They did not seem terribly concerned.

"This isn't the first time she's called us," one of the officers said to me. "It's probably nothing, but we have to respond to every call."

As we arrived at her forty-sixth-floor apartment, Mrs. Helmsley flung open the door and greeted us, with Trouble sitting on her arm. She looked at each of the police officers, one by one. Then her face twisted into a slow smile.

"Oh, you're cute," she said to one of the officers. "Are you married?" They asked about the noise she had heard, and she brushed it off, trying to flirt a bit more while she had their attention. Leona apparently felt entitled to make a nonsense call to 911, wasting the officers' time and taxpayers' money. Or perhaps, once again, she was just confused.

In the elevators, the officers laughed about the incident, much to my relief. Clearly, they already knew about her eccentric ways and had no intention of charging us with a violation. I returned to my office to try to restore some normalcy to the day. At least I was one story richer.

Incredibly, we did manage to get some actual work done at the hotel. The financial clean-up I had initiated, along with the more rigorous staff training and the systemic changes throughout the hotel, had led to a higher average room rate, increasing operational results, and improving the bottom line. I felt pleased about these accomplishments, and despite Mrs. Helmsley's many ongoing complaints, I and the other hotel executives saw no need to alter the path we were taking to improve the Park Lane.

Nearly every area of the hotel looked much better at this point, a result of a heightened attention to detail, a more intensive cleaning regimen, and the elimination of any clutter that interfered with the elegance of the common spaces. The Park Lane was finally beginning to live up to its potential, even without a major investment in renovations. But while the guest rooms were quite large and well-furnished and offered a spectacular view of Central Park, the bathrooms needed upgrading. We could no longer postpone the necessity of investing in the bathrooms if we wanted to compete with newer hotels like the Four Seasons and the Ritz Carlton.

The entire team of corporate executives agreed with me about the need to update the bathrooms, but they recommended that I get Mrs. Helmsley's approval first. Of course, I knew we would have to do so, but I dreaded the process since it would no doubt end in frustration.

Her answer came as a total surprise to me.

"Mr. Tischmann," she said, "I have spent so much money on this hotel." I had a feeling she would begin this way. Then she went on: "If you want to do the bathrooms, please go ahead, but spend your own money."

This was a shocking new tactic, even for Leona. But then my mind flashed back to the Sarasota trip, when she made me pay for my own travel for the job interview.

Then as now, there was no changing her mind. I knew that was the end of our discussion and the end of our plan to renovate the bathrooms. Not only did she hate to spend money, but she was haunted by the idea that everybody was stealing from her. She probably thought this was yet another scheme to separate her from her fortune.

Her paranoia about getting cheated was not far off the mark, as I had discovered in my earliest weeks at the hotel, as I analyzed every angle of the operation and found an enormous amount of waste. I suspected that a significant portion of the waste did in fact have to do with stealing and embezzlement, rather than merely inefficiency.

In any case, on the day when I lost the argument about the badly needed bathroom renovation project, I lost my chief engineer as well.

Unfortunately for him, he couldn't answer some question or other for which Mrs. Helmsley wanted an immediate response.

"If you don't know the answer to my question, I don't need you anymore," she barked at him. Out he went. She had not earned her Queen of Mean nickname for nothing, and she kept reminding us of her ability to fire anyone on the spot, for even the most trivial reason.

It was no surprise that staff members often took any excuse they could get away with to miss a workday. One morning in late January of 2004, the weather was bitterly cold, and eight inches of snow fell on the ground. We were heavily short-staffed that day, and I'm sure a lot of our employees didn't even make an effort to get to work, deciding to take a free mental health day at home.

But by noon that day, I still hadn't heard anything from the forty-sixth floor, which was highly unusual. I called my boss, and the following conversation took place:

"Good afternoon, Mrs. Helmsley, this is Peter Tischmann. How are you?"

"It's cold!"

"Cold outside or inside?"

"Outside. Inside my room it's fine."

"Yes, we had a lot of staff not reporting to work because of the snow."

"I don't blame them."

"Mrs. Helmsley, can I interest you in some lunch? We have some interesting specials on the menu today."

"I don't think so because I'm not getting out of bed."

"Are you sure you are not hungry?"

"I'm fine, don't worry."

"Well, have a nice afternoon and please call me if I can do anything for you."

"Thank you, you too."

One hour later, when I passed through the kitchen, I learned that she had just ordered her lunch: fried courgette, the special of glazed scallops, and a cappuccino.

Was this a mind game she was playing? Or dementia rearing its head again? Or perhaps both?

Whatever she was up to, I could hardly blame her for her lunch choices. I wish I could have stayed in bed eating scallops, but she would have asked for my head on a platter.

Suddenly Allergic to Garlic

Friday the thirteenth is a famously unlucky day. While I do not place much stock in superstitions, I could not help noticing the date when I woke up one cold, sunny Friday morning in mid-February. That night, I was going to dinner at our friends Toni and May Fernaine's apartment on the Upper East Side. Denyse was out of town that week so I would be going alone to spend the evening with a couple who felt like family. Toni, a prominent cardiologist, was also my own heart doctor, about which I felt quite lucky.

From Toni and May's beautiful apartment on the thirtieth floor of a high-rise on Second Avenue, I always enjoyed looking over at the wonderful views over the Manhattan skyline, the Empire State Building, and the Chrysler Building. They were both from Lebanon, so being invited for dinner meant feasting on one of my favorite cuisines, and this time was no exception.

After a delicious dinner that included some of my beloved Lebanese dishes and a leisurely conversation with our dear friends, I took a pleasant stroll back to the hotel. Toni liked to eat early and go to bed at a decent hour, so our dinner did not go late. It was February but not an especially freezing night, and walking all the way to Fifty-Ninth Street gave me a chance for exercise and fresh air. Back at the hotel, I planned to read for a while and prepare myself for the next day.

After a lovely evening like this, I was in the best possible frame of mind to go through a pile of correspondence that needed my attention. As I settled into my desk chair, I felt an unusual pressure and heat wave in my head. So unusual that I decided to take my blood pressure. I couldn't believe what I saw on the screen: 150/90, very high indeed for someone whose blood pressure never exceeds 120/80. I opened the window, hoping a bit of fresh air would do the trick, only to feel the pressure in my head getting stronger and stronger. When the second reading of my blood pressure showed an astronomical 190/120, I got worried—not to say terrified, but quite concerned.

It was not long ago that Denyse had driven me through a rainy night to a hospital in New Hope. I decided to call Toni.

"Take a taxi and proceed immediately to the emergency room of the Lenox Hill Hospital," he told me. "I'll call them, and they'll be waiting for you."

Minutes later, I found myself in a packed emergency room. I mentioned my problem to the desk clerk and said Dr. Toni Fernaine had sent me. I received a blank look in response, along with a stack of papers to fill out and a request for my credit card. Did they not give priority to patients with heart problems?

My head felt worse and worse, as if it would explode any second, as I sat there waiting. I watched patients with what appeared to be bruises, cuts, and other minor injuries get taken in one after the other as I continued to sit. The pressure kept increasing in my head, and I decided to call Toni again to let him know I was still waiting in the ER, where nobody was paying any attention to me.

Not one minute later, a team of doctors came running into the waiting room to find me, and the next thing I knew, I was in an intensive care room. They gave me Nitro spray, connected me to an EKG machine, took a blood sample, and hooked me up to an IV. Suddenly I felt like the most important person in the emergency department.

Soon the pressure in my head began to dissipate, and a doctor appeared at my bed to speak with me.

"Mr. Tischmann, everything seems to be fine," he said, "but we would prefer to keep you overnight for observation. Tomorrow morning, we want to take an angiogram to be on the safe side."

It was comforting to see May walk into my room the next morning, to keep me company and wait with me until I was released in the afternoon. But I left the hospital knowing as little as I did when I arrived. The doctors could not explain what had happened to me and why my blood pressure had suddenly shot up the night before, causing that exploding sensation in my head.

The situation remained puzzling until a few days later when I met with Joe Prezioso, my former colleague and friend from the St. Regis.

"Did you eat garlic?" he asked me.

"Well, I had some Lebanese food and salad with friends that night. It's possible there was some garlic involved."

"That's it," he said, "the garlic!"

Garlic? What was he talking about? But shortly afterward, I learned about other friends who had experienced the same symptoms after eating raw garlic.

How strange. Don't doctors prescribe garlic pills to keep the heart healthy and blood pressure down? So why did mine go through the roof? Since that night, I've avoided raw garlic, one of my favorite ingredients. A shame, but there are worse problems in life.

Enough Is Enough

"Don't do this to me! Never ever do this to me!" Mrs. Helmsley screamed when I told her about my hospital emergency.

True to form, she found a way to turn my medical scare into her own personal inconvenience.

But in the next moment, she did a 180-degree turn. "Are you okay, darling?" she asked, expressing what seemed like genuine concern.

This erratic behavior on her part was nothing new, but like her memory, it was getting worse by the week.

She exploded at me one day soon afterward, when I was overseeing the badly needed cleaning project for our lobby. This involved shining the marble walls, polishing the brass entrance doors, and cleaning the two large, beautiful handwoven carpets. I had discussed all these elements with Mrs. Helmsley weeks before and had begun negotiating with contractors to decide which one to hire.

Finding and procuring the right contractor for the job took some time. Obviously, it was too much time for Leona Helmsley to remember having ever authorized the project in the first place because she flew into a furious rage one day as the clean-up was starting. The front office manager called me to the lobby.

"What can I do for you, Mrs. Helmsley?" I addressed her with my usual big smile.

"Don't smile like this at me!" she yelled. "Who has given you authorization to remove the carpet and move the furniture? Are you an interior decorator?"

I looked at her silently, shaking my head no.

"I'm the interior decorator in this hotel! How dare you change my decoration?"

She went on like this while I stood there silently. As she grew more and more abusive, I realized that any response on my part would be useless. So I decided to take the heat until she finally ran out of steam and walked away.

While I had seen her loudly berate other members of her staff time and time again, I had not yet received such a public shaming from her. This must have been what she was like twenty years ago, at the height of her reign as the Queen of Helmsley Hotels, I thought to myself.

She greeted me with a cheerful smile the next day, as if nothing had happened. I too pretended everything was normal and took comfort in looking at the Swiss cheese replica on my desk.

As her mental condition worsened, she had a difficult time walking steadily, one of the symptoms of Alzheimer's. One day, her legs started buckling in the middle of the lobby, and the director of security and I rushed over to support her and escort her on her way.

"I'm getting pretty good at falling," she said with a smile as we walked her to the limousine that waited for her outside.

But it was impossible to monitor her every move, and a few days later, her maid called to tell me Leona had fallen in her apartment. Rushing up to the forty-sixth floor, I found her sitting on one of her sofas, her face bloody and scratched up, a scene from a horror movie.

"Get away from me!" she screamed.

"Mrs. Helmsley, your wounds do need some attention or they will get worse."

"Who the hell are you? Are you a doctor?" she yelled, glaring at me.

I finally talked her into letting me disinfect her face and put some Neosporin on her open wounds. She looked frightening, so much so that she refused to leave her apartment for three weeks.

Now every time I spoke with her, she found a reason to hurl insults at me. I understood she was struggling with a medical condition, but she was growing more and more irrational and developed a new habit of screaming at me in front of employees. So far, I had managed to brush off all the bad behavior I had seen and endured from her, but now, for the first time since I took the job, I started seriously thinking about leaving.

I no longer needed the job, and I certainly didn't need to be treated this way. I told Steven Eckhaus and Albert Cohen that I wanted to resign, but both of them chimed in to convince me to hang in there. She didn't mean what she was saying, they assured me, and by tomorrow, she will have forgotten it already. Together they managed to persuade me to stay on. For now.

It did feel gratifying to see the hotel continue to improve, and I hoped Leona acknowledged the positive changes to herself even if she rarely complimented me or any of our staff anymore. Perhaps she was too confused at this point to notice.

To take advantage of the pedestrian traffic on Central Park South, we had recently opened a garden café at the Park Lane. Accessible from the street, it was the only café of its kind on Central Park South, and it quickly became very popular for a quick, light lunch and for coffee and tea in the afternoon after office hours. One afternoon, Denyse had arranged to invite a group of ladies, all married to ambassadors at the UN, to introduce them to the Park Lane and in particular to our new garden café.

As Denyse sat enjoying the afternoon tea with her guests, I walked by and noticed Mrs. Helmsley sitting in the lobby in front of Harry's portrait, with a full view of my wife's table. I decided to leave her alone. Later I learned Leona had asked the waitress in the café to identify the lady who was entertaining that big group of women and wanted to know who was paying for the event.

"Mrs. Tischmann," the waitress told Leona. I discovered afterward that Mrs. Helmsley had even asked the financial comptroller of the hotel to check that Denyse had indeed paid for the afternoon.

Was her trust in me eroding? I again talked myself out of letting this bother me and blamed her worsening condition instead.

On her bad days, she had grown increasingly aggressive, as if she was fighting her deteriorating health condition by turning meaner than ever.

As a blessing, moments of accidental humor started happening with greater frequency, enough to keep me and other staff members sane.

One evening, about half an hour after she allowed her driver, Nicholas, to go home for the night, she called me to ask where he was.

I reminded her that he had left for the day with her permission.

"Tell him I need him," she replied.

Calling Nicholas on his cell phone, I reached him as he was exiting a subway station. He took the next train back, got the limousine out of the garage, and pulled up in front of the Fifty-Ninth Street entrance of the hotel to wait for Mrs. Helmsley.

She arrived a few minutes later with Trouble on her arm.

"Good evening, Mrs. Helmsley," Nicholas asked her politely, "where do you wish to go?"

"I want to go home," she answered, getting into the car with her dog. Nicholas acted as unruffled as ever, and I guessed he must have been used to this. He drove her around the block twice and then dropped her exactly where he had picked her up only ten minutes before.

She smiled, bid him good evening, and disappeared into the elevator to go up to her apartment on the forty-sixth floor.

Mercifully, her Connecticut mansion still tempted her away from time to time for brief getaways from the hotel. Those trips were a badly needed vacation for myself and the entire staff, but unfortunately, they happened less and less often. She went to her Sarasota hotel much less frequently too, much to the joy of the general manager there.

One day in early October, she announced she would be traveling to Connecticut in the company of John Huntington , her personal advisor and trusted friend. I felt sorry for John, but suspected he wasn't spending time with Leona out of a sense of charity. I knew there must be more to it, especially as I saw him endure the same kind of abuse that I did, without saying a word.

Eventually, unable to contain my curiosity anymore, I asked him why he tolerated the mistreatment. He confided in me that he was hoping she would name him the director of her trust, a prize that would be well worth all the abuse.

Poor Mrs. Hemsley. She obviously had a crush on John and was simply devising ways to spend time with him. Dinners that involved consuming more than three dozen oysters and emptying a bottle of vintage Chateau d'Yquem were a frequent event, during which she even bickered with him constantly, as a romantic partner might, and became miserable when he was not around. She would ask everyone about his whereabouts all day long until he reappeared.

John came up with creative ways to get her off his back without arousing her suspicions. The position at her trust surely remained at the top of his mind, but even he needed breaks from the Queen. I remember the time he received his annual invitation to the Kentucky Derby. He claimed he had to go to his grandmother's funeral so Leona wouldn't act like a jilted lover if he traveled there without her.

John started using the grandmother's funeral story every time he needed to get away for a few days, and considering Leona's mental condition, it seemed to work every single time.

Her trips to Connecticut became less and less frequent. She was in such bad shape at this point that she would return to the hotel a few hours after she left "for the weekend," having no idea she had missed out on her vacation. We would watch her limousine pull up in front of the hotel on the same day she had left. Again and again, we said goodbye to our dreams of having even the smallest break from our exasperating boss.

By November of that year, I had all but lost the will to continue working for Mrs. Helmsley. Drop by drop, the jug reached capacity. All it needed was one last drop, and it would finally overflow.

That drop came a few days later, when Leona was having dinner with Steven Eckhaus and Albert Cohen in the restaurant. I received a message that Mrs. Helmsley was looking for me. As usual, I heeded the call immediately and showed up at her table moments later, only to realize she couldn't remember why she had called me. But that didn't stop her from using my arrival as an opportunity to start complaining—about everything in the restaurant, from the terrible menu to the high prices. No wonder the restaurant is empty, she yelled.

Turning away to pet her dog, Trouble, she left me standing there looking at Steven and Albert, wondering what to say. The three of us began discussing the changes she might like to see implemented at the restaurant, when she suddenly turned her face back to me:

"How dare you do this to me!"

I looked at her quietly, unsure what she meant.

"When I talk to you, you look at me," she hollered. "I'll never put my feet back into this place. I don't like what you are doing to my hotel. The restaurant was never so empty when I was running this hotel."

I continued to look at her without saying a word.

"You better get your act together and straighten this place out," she yelled, "or I will look for somebody else. How dare you treat me like this."

Silence fell over the restaurant when she finished her tirade. Steven and Albert sat there silently, and I stood frozen in place, having just received the most humiliating shower of unjustified accusations I had ever heard in my life. Even though I knew her mind wasn't working properly, I had no intention of taking this kind of treatment anymore. I turned around and walked away from the table. Enough was enough.

Don't take her seriously, Albert and Steven said to me a little while later in the bar. Tomorrow she won't remember any of this.

But that was that. My decision was made. I resigned that day, politely refusing any attempts to talk me out of it.

The relief of saying goodbye to the Helmsley chapter of my life faded a month later, when Leona moved to Connecticut permanently. What had I done? The chance to manage the Park Lane Hotel without Leona around would have been a perfect job, one I would have held happily for as long as I decided to work. But it was too late now.

Leona Helmsley passed away a few years later at the age of eighty-seven. Upon her death, the world learned that she had left a $12 million fortune to her dog, Trouble, and had directed that when the dog died, its remains would be buried next to hers in the Helmsley mausoleum. Even from her grave, she planned to remain in charge, insisting that the mausoleum should get steam-cleaned annually according to her specifications.

Unfortunately for Leona and for her last will, to have Trouble put to rest next to her, her order ran into an obstacle as a result of Connecticut law, which did not allow animals and humans to be buried together.

The dog still did very well for himself in his last years, even after a judge ruled that he would only receive $2 million of the inheritance Leona had willed him. Trouble died in 2011, at the respectable age of twelve, or eighty-four in human years, almost the same age as his owner.

Although part of Trouble's inheritance would be contested by various parties—including a former housekeeper who filed multiple lawsuits alleging that Trouble had caused her nerve damage with his constant bites—the dog did far better than two of her four grandchildren, who received nothing in her will.

The end of the Helmsley era of my life would signal the beginning of a new phase, one filled with challenges and achievements of its own. But there was no question that my time on the hotel roller coaster was winding down.

I did have one big surprise in store for my family, however—one that nobody saw coming.

THE HELMSLEY PARK LANE HOTEL

MRS. LEONA HELMSLEY

A BUSINESS CONVERSATION WITH LEONA HELMSLEY
WITH TROUBLE ON HER ARM

Studying for PhD 40

Working for Leona Helmsley required a strong constitution and the ability to come up with creative ways of coping. During my year at the Park Lane, I had a secret pursuit that kept my mind off the constant abuse. In my room sat stacks of books and papers that I consulted in the late hours of the evening, and often at my private office at our friends Toni and May Fernaine's apartment, as I studied for my PhD.

Yes, a PhD.

Since 2002, when I was between jobs and deciding what to do next, I had the idea of undertaking a difficult academic program that would satisfy my need to be constantly challenged. I already had my MBA, so why not add a PhD to my CV?

In truth, I had another, more compelling reason for pursuing a doctorate: to compete with my son-in-law, Martin, who enjoyed being the only person in our family with a PhD.

Although Martin had not studied at an internationally renowned institution like Harvard, as Carine had, he had still crowned his studies with a doctoral achievement.

When Carine and Martin sometimes jokingly argued about the value of their education, Carine would congratulate Martin on his PhD but could not resist adding that it could never match the prestige of a Harvard degree.

Nevertheless, Martin was very proud of his doctor title, and he had every reason to be. The Germans are crazy about titles. In Germany, a title ensures respect and can bring advantages in every aspect of life. When Germans have a doctorate, they get upset if you don't address them with that title. The rest of the world does not operate this way, but Germany is indeed an exception—surpassed only by Austria, where married women often use their spouse's doctor title without having completed any studies.

Martin enjoyed flaunting his doctorate title in our family, and when the competitive urge finally overtook me, I conveniently had a bit of time on my hands.

I began to search for doctoral programs I could pursue online. One advantage about studying in the USA is that nearly every university offers distance learning courses in business, starting long before the days of the COVID-19 pandemic. This is true primarily for online MBA programs, which are always very much in demand, as the participants are typically already working and don't want to give up their income to study on campus.

But distance learning programs for a PhD are not offered by many institutions, as the lower demand does not make them profitable enough.

After searching for weeks and checking references, I finally decided to apply to Madison University, an institution that specialized in distance learning for the PhD. Its course in philosophy and management seemed a perfect match, and when I spoke with advisers at the university, they encouraged me to send in my application with a detailed CV and references from my past career.

Four weeks later, I received a big envelope with a letter offering acceptance into the program. Besides Denyse and our friends the Fernaines, nobody was aware of what I was about to do and definitely not Martin, who had inspired this entire adventure.

At the start of 2003, I received the next heavy envelope, containing my syllabus and a long list of books I needed to buy, read, and study.

Little did I realize that this was only the beginning of buying and reading books, and that by the end of my studies, I would have enough books to fill a library.

Even though I was studying for a PhD, I had not quite counted on the enormous amount of work that lay ahead. As I already had an MBA and had spent decades in business, I had perhaps underestimated the coursework necessary to complete a doctorate. Studying for the PhD turned out to be no promenade on a sunny Sunday afternoon. It was hard work indeed, and to receive the title at the end, one had to earn it.

The next months passed with homework, plenty of homework, and endless hours of writing essays and solving case studies. Harvard had pioneered the use of case studies in business classes as a way of adapting the academic curriculum to the realities of business life. Many universities have since built upon this idea, but even today, most of the serious case studies in business school are based on the Harvard model.

The PhD program at Madison University was divided into four semesters, and it was up to students to decide how much time they wanted to take to complete the studies.

Most of my peers planned to complete their degree in two years, allowing for some time off between each semester, just as in every other university.

As for myself, impatient as I was, I decided to take semesters one to three without a break. I wanted to finish my studies as quickly as possible, so I could present my family with a surprise and free up my time to accept work that came my way.

As I read through one book after the other, I realized very quickly that business books could easily be divided into two categories. The first category is books written by professors for professors, because that's what you have to be in order to make any sense out of the jargon. If you are not an academic, you only have one choice: to read the book one more time, sometimes three times, to understand what the author is trying to say.

Those books reminded me a little bit of instruction manuals for electronic equipment, which are written by the engineers who developed the equipment and are nearly incomprehensible to most consumers. Why can't they write the manuals in a language a normal persons can decipher?

The second category were the books by famous authors who had already written successful business books and made a name for themselves. I imagined a publisher approaching a best-selling author about writing another book, even specifying the title and the number of pages, because bigger books sell for a higher price. And here our famous author starts to write, with the word count on his computer telling him when the required number of pages has been achieved. The problem for the reader is that he has to read 550 pages of a stretched-out subject, when the same topic could be covered more succinctly in a maximum of 250 pages.

I vowed that if I ever wrote a business book, it would be very different, designed to meet the needs of business professionals who have no time to read but still want to absorb the main points. As I worked through my first two semesters, I had no idea how close I was to actually writing my first business book.

When I learned that at the end of the studies we had to write a dissertation of two hundred pages minimum, I decided to schedule some time off before the last semester to concentrate on this project. Now, in addition to my studies, I had to find a subject for my dissertation that was promising enough for the university to accept.

As the wildest ideas crossed my mind, I remembered the essay I had written for my final MBA exam. Although it was only a short summary of twenty pages, and no comparison with the scope of the dissertation that awaited me, the subject was still very much up-to-date. It was about the courage it takes to implement changes in a business context when nobody else believes in the need for transformation.

Talking to my adviser, I explained to him my basic ideas and the changes I had implemented at the Ciragan. After listening carefully, and a long period of reflection, he said: "Peter, that's it. It obviously needs more depth, but that's it."

I could not have found a better subject, as it allowed me to draw from my many years of experience as a hotelier, but particularly from the reopening of the St. Regis and the repositioning of the Ciragan. I felt motivated by the opportunity to deepen the work I had already done, and so I plunged into writing what I titled "The Challenges of Change." Based on my own experience and in-depth research, I examined how to deal with the impact of change on the attitudes and human behaviors of those who are most affected by it.

As the year came to an end, I bid farewell to the coursework and written exams, now happily behind me, and finished up my final project. With a sense of satisfaction and great relief, I prepared a dozen copies of my 238-page bound dissertation to be sent to the university.

With Christmas approaching, the whole family planned to spend the holidays together in Germany, something that did not happen often. This would be a wonderful opportunity to surprise them with my PhD achievement and to watch the look on my son-in-law's face. Unfortunately, beyond simply telling them what I had been doing during the past two years, I still had nothing concrete to show for my accomplishment.

An idea sprang to mind at the last minute. I called the university and explained my intention of surprising the family with my doctorate and inquired as to when we would receive our diplomas.

"Not before March," they told me, "but if it helps you, we could send you the official student transcript." Obviously, I would have preferred to surprise the family with the actual diploma, but in the meantime, the transcript had to do.

One week later, I received my copy listing the most important achievements:

Student name:	Peter W. Tischmann
Degree conferred:	Doctor of Philosophy and Management
Special Honor:	Summa Cum Laude
Graduation:	12/22/04

On Christmas day, I walked into the festively decorated living room at our daughter's home holding four rolls of paper wrapped with a red ribbon. The entire family looked at me curiously and, more specifically, at the rolls I was clutching in my hand.

I waited until everyone had opened all their Christmas gifts, then I began to hand one roll each to our son, Peter, our daughter, Carine, our son-in-law, Martin, and of course my wife, Denyse, who was the only one who knew what the rolls contained.

As everyone slowly removed the red ribbons to unroll the manuscripts, their faces showed a wide variety of reactions.

Peter nodded his head gravely, perhaps feeling pressured now that I had not only an MBA but a PhD too and he had neither.

Martin, after reading the transcript, sank into a deep silence. I guess it took some time to realize that he was not the only doctor in the family anymore.

Carine, screaming with joy, took me in her arms and congratulated me for this achievement.

My Christmas surprise had succeeded as planned. As the evening went on, everyone asked me to talk more about my doctoral project and to explain how I had managed to sneak in two years of PhD study without them ever suspecting anything.

So besides shocking my family, what did I do when I earned my own doctorate? Nothing, and today, many years later, my passport, my ID card, and my driver's license still show the same name, Peter W. Tischmann, because as I had learned from my international travels, a title like "Dr." may add value to your CV, but it is not important in daily business life, unless you are a medical doctor.

I am, however, proud that I was able to add my name and my doctoral credentials to the management book that I finally did publish a few years later, in 2007, under the same title, *The Challenges of Change*. It was based 90 percent on my dissertation, and as I prepared to write it, I took into consideration the lessons I learned from all the business books I read for my degree. I kept it short and included easy to read graphics and summaries.

By making the book easy to understand, I hoped that all the CEOs to whom I sent a copy could actually find the time to read it and to decipher what it said without having to earn a doctorate first.

Based on the reactions I received from the executives who received my book, at least the ones who took the time to open it, my attempt to break down challenging ideas about change management into an approachable format was well appreciated. I sent copies to the CEOs of all the Fortune 500 companies, including one to Jack Welch, for example. I received two or three letters thanking me. Most probably it was the secretary who had written the letter, and I had no way of knowing if the executives had ever laid eyes on the book. But still, I could now say to people, "This book is on the shelf of every Fortune 500 CEO."

So all those hours of reading books for my PhD proved useful in the end, if not for my passport, then at least for my ability to write a business book without scaring away my audience. And of course, the best gift of all was the chance to shock my family with the biggest Christmas surprise of the year.

Madison University

The Board of Trustees of Madison University upon the recommendation of the President and Faculty have conferred upon

Peter W. Tischmann

the degree of

Doctor of Philosophy

Management

Summa Cum Laude

with all the rights, privileges and honors pertaining thereto.

In testimony thereof we have affixed our signatures and the seal of the University on this twenty-second day of December, in the year of our Lord two thousand and four.

Chief Executive Officer

President

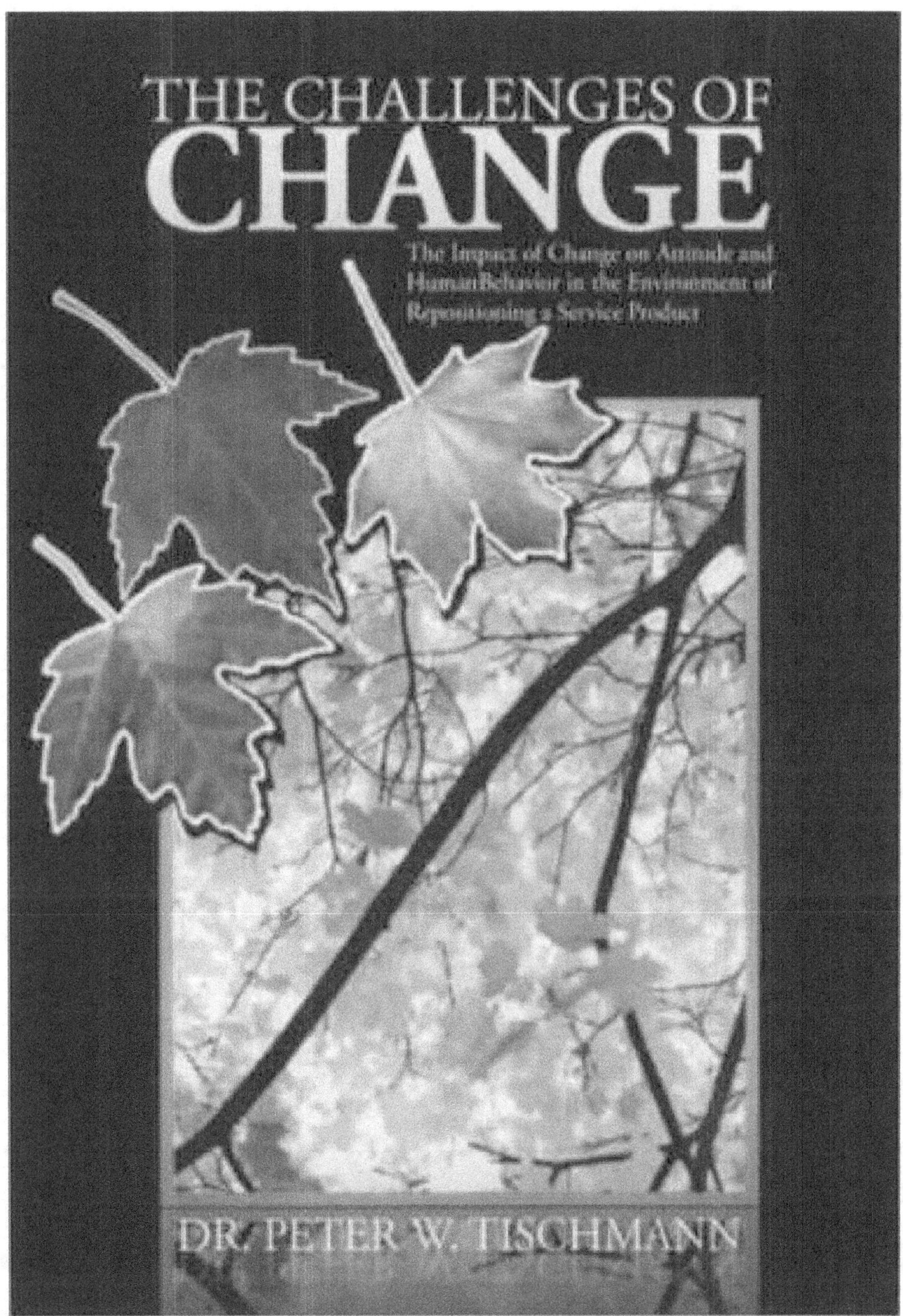

MY PUBLISHED MANAGEMENT BOOK

MADISON UNIVERSITY

OFFICIAL STUDENT TRANSCRIPT

Student Name: Peter Tischmann
Student Number: 148282
SSN: 067-70-5249
DOB: 12/26/1939

Degree Conferred:
Doctor of Philosophy
Management
Summa Cum Laude
Graduation: 12/22/04

REIMS Management School, MBA

COURSE ID	COURSE TITLE	GRADE	HOURS	QUALITY PTS
BADM 701	ADVANCED BUSINESS COMMUNICATION	A	6	24.0
BADM 751	ADVANCED ORGANIZATIONS	A	6	24.0
BMGT 701	ADVANCED MANAGEMENT I	A	6	24.0
BMGT 711	ADVANCED LEADERSHIP	A	6	24.0
BMGT 721	ADVANCED MANAGEMENT II	A	6	24.0
DISS	DISSERTATION	A	24	96.0

	AHRS	EHRS	GPA
Current	54.00	54.00	4.00
Cumulative	54.00	54.00	4.00

ISSUED TO STUDENT

MADISON UNIVERSITY
PURSUIT ERUDITIO EXCELLENTIA

A BLACK AND WHITE TRANSCRIPT IS NOT OFFICIAL

PURSUANT TO THE FAMILY RIGHTS ACT AND PRIVACY ACT OF 1974, INFORMATION CONTAINED HEREIN SHALL NOT BE RELEASED TO A THIRD PARTY WITHOUT THE WRITTEN AUTHORIZATION OF THE STUDENT.

This official document is printed on SCRIP-SAFE security paper with the name of the college printed in white type across the face of the document. When photocopied the word COPY should appear. A BLACK ON WHITE OR A COLOR COPY SHOULD NOT BE ACCEPTED!

AN OFFICIAL SIGNATURE IS WHITE WITH A BLUE BACKGROUND

Office of the Registrar

OFFICIAL ACADEMIC DOCUMENT

THE REPORT CARD AS A CHRISTMAS GIFT

Las Vegas Here We Come 41

"You must be from New York."

I heard a strange voice call out those words to me one day, as I walked through a parking lot in Las Vegas. I turned around and saw a woman looking right at me. "The way you walk, you must be from New York," she said, smiling.

This amused me, and I took it as a compliment. I had spent a pleasant day in our new city and felt in no particular hurry, but I suppose all my years in New York had given a certain urgency to my step.

That year, 2004, we had spontaneously decided to buy a house in Las Vegas. Now that I had resigned from my job with Leona Helmsley and completed my PhD, we felt a newfound freedom to enjoy life and spend time anywhere we wanted to go.

We did have our apartment in Munich, but we'd been visiting Las Vegas frequently to stay with Peter Jr., who was managing the food and beverage department at the Wynn Hotel there. Apart from our joy at spending more time with our son, we also grew charmed by Las Vegas itself, with its combination of sparkling city lights, high-quality restaurants, and live musical entertainment, not to mention the unique scenery of desert landscapes and red-rock mountains in the background.

Our regular visits gave us time to catch up with Peter Jr. during the hours when he wasn't working, and we'd spend the rest of our time exploring the city and its surroundings. Denyse would make our son his favorite Lebanese dishes, filling up his refrigerator with kibbe and baba ghanoush and tabbouleh, so he would have home-cooked food throughout our visit and for weeks after. This arrangement, mutually convenient for a year or two, ended when Peter got himself a girlfriend. She moved into his house, making it difficult for us to stay for five or six weeks at a time whenever we wanted.

But we were not yet ready to say goodbye to a city that had become a second home for us. Denyse enjoyed the warm and dry climate of Nevada, so different from the weather in Munich, and felt its positive effects on her arthritis. I enjoyed the ongoing adventure of exploring Las Vegas and its surroundings.

We decided to look around for a home to buy, and it did not take long before we found a beautiful house by a golf course with a spectacular view overlooking the mountains. Despite the neglected interior, which would require a lot of work, we bought the house without any hesitation. This turned into a time-consuming project and a costly one too, as we invested quite a bit of money to bring everything up to our standards. By the end, the house looked like a custom-designed European home. It was a wonderful place to spend time, and we were very happy with our decision.

As luck would have it, the year after we completed the renovations on the house, Peter's job transferred him to Hawaii. I saw no point in keeping our home base in Las Vegas, and I had a feeling time would be on our side since real estate prices in Vegas were going through the roof that year. Peter had bought his house for $320,000 and was able to sell it quickly for twice that amount. The money he made on his house proved to be well-timed, as he and his girlfriend had been making secret plans which would soon surprise Denyse, myself, and the rest of our family.

As the days went by, Denyse and I debated whether we should sell our house immediately or wait. "What is the point in going to Las Vegas now?" I said to Denyse. "Peter is gone." We had spent a total of $400,000 on the house after the renovations, and we could have sold it within a week for $800,000 or more. But Denyse didn't agree with my reasoning. Since we've just completed work on a house we love, and since we enjoy the climate in Vegas, she thought, why don't we keep it for some time and see how it goes?

The following year, the city's real estate market took a nosedive. After all the speculation from investors, including all the Californians who kept buying and selling Las Vegas houses within a short time to make money, it was suddenly a terrible time for us to sell. We had no choice but to keep enjoying Las Vegas as much as we could until the real estate market picked up again.

It was not difficult to find reasons to fly off to Las Vegas, even after our son moved away. The city became our hub for visiting with friends around the US, and it also turned into our landing spot for trips to see Peter Jr. wherever his company decided to relocate him for his work.

And relocate him they did often.

After leaving Las Vegas for Hawaii in 2006, Peter was soon transferred to Miami, followed by Chicago, the Cayman Islands, and then back again to Miami, with every transfer advancing him in his career as a hotelier.

He was truly following in the footsteps of his father.

We visited Peter and Christina in each one of these locations, sometimes more than once.

We especially enjoyed the Cayman Islands, a dream of a destination. Known as a tax-free haven and a home to over six hundred international banks, the Cayman Islands are also famous as the location of the novel *The Firm*, a legal thriller by American writer John Grisham.

There is much more to see in the Cayman Islands besides banks, and Denyse and I enjoyed exploring local sites, such as the turtle sanctuary. The islands are home to giant water turtles, which usually swim slowly in the water very close to the beaches and disappear quickly if they sense someone approaching. We also visited Sting Ray City, a spot fifteen minutes off the coast where we went swimming with stingrays in the middle of the ocean. One time, we went whale-watching and had the chance to observe huge buckle whales and their families cruising slowly through the water, sometimes even jumping out of the ocean and landing again with a big splash.

The eleven-mile beach is an alluring place to take long promenades, and we would pass one hotel after the other, as well as spectacular condominium buildings housing the rich and famous. It's a paradise on earth for those who can afford to live there, unless they're there for work reasons. We were lucky to experience this part of the world as a result of Peter's time working at the best hotel on the islands.

It was five years after Peter Jr. and Christina left Las Vegas that on St. Patrick's Day 2011, in Chicago, their daughter Lily Eloise, our grandchild number four, was born. Lily couldn't have picked a better date to remember.

With Lily's birth, Denyse decided to extend the vacation from Munich by one month, so she could assist Christina and Peter as much as possible as they got used to their new responsibility and change of lifestyle.

For the time being, it was still convenient to us in many ways to keep the house in Las Vegas while still basing ourselves mostly in Munich. From there Las Vegas was not exactly the most convenient vacation destination, since it's a twenty-hour trip door to door, but we discovered that the journey remained worthwhile to us, at least for the first few years after Lily's birth.

We liked being able to place ourselves a few hours' flight from Peter Jr. and from our friends around the US. We also continued to enjoy spending time in our new house and relaxing in Las Vegas whenever we had the chance. In addition to its comfortable weather, Las Vegas offers plenty of things to do in and around town. Living there is like living in any big city in the US, with the exception of a big buzzing metropolis like New York or Los Angeles or Chicago.

Our house was not quite in the middle of all the action, but we could get anywhere we wanted to go within a short drive. The Strip and all its noise was a full twelve miles away, and even though we didn't like to go there much, if we wanted to see a show or take a guest to see the lights, we could drive there in minutes. We also had plenty to keep us busy near our house, since it was located in a retirement community full of cultural amenities. You had to be a minimum age of fifty-five to buy a property in the community, and residents could enjoy activities on the grounds throughout the year, from movies to concerts to all kinds of arts and performance events.

We occasionally made the three-hour drive to LA or drove an extra hour to visit San Diego, but one of our favorite destinations was the Valley of Fire with its beautiful red rock formations, less than an hour outside Las Vegas. This otherworldly landscape is where parts of the Elvis Presley movie *Viva Las Vegas* were filmed, and it has also featured in *Star Trek* episodes and other movies. In the valley, we experienced one of the most incredible Easter mass ceremonies at 5:30 one morning just as the sun came up, lighting the rocks and making the entire valley look as if it were engulfed in flames.

Denyse and I continued to feel a deep love for Nevada as the years went by. It also didn't hurt that the state had no income taxes, but we eventually realized that the financial commitment we were making no longer made as much sense as it once did, and that this was finally the right time to sell. Even though we only spent six or seven months in Las Vegas, our sunny escape during the winter months in Germany, we still had to pay the maintenance, taxes, landscaping fees, and assorted expenses for the other half of each year when the house sat empty. I figured out that those fees were costing us around $20,000 per year. If we sold the house, we could spend six months in a hotel at that cost and get rid of the other worries that come with owning a home.

Mathematics aside, it was eventually a medical reason that drove us out of Las Vegas. I had been seeing an internist there for my heart condition, and one day, when I had high blood pressure, he gave me pills to treat it and sent me on my way. We had spent that entire year in the States instead of going back in the summer to Munich, as we usually did. The following year, when I went in for a checkup with my cardiologist in Munich, he ran some tests, looked at me with a frown, and said, "I don't like what I see." The angiogram he prescribed found that I had 90 percent blockage in one of my arteries. I had to get two stents inserted and spend a few days in the hospital.

What did my Las Vegas doctor think he was doing? He knew my health history but decided to only give me pills when my blood pressure went up, when here I was, sitting on a time bomb with my arteries. Denyse and I decided we couldn't stay in Las Vegas anymore. All the factors were pointing in the same direction: It was time to go.

Munich beckoned to us more than ever, and we reinvested our time and energy into making it our year-round home. But even though we began to travel less and less to Las Vegas, we did not actually get around to selling the house right away. In the months before we finally said goodbye to the city, we enjoyed memorable vacations there with our growing family. One time, Carine's kids flew from their camp in Maine to Las Vegas to spend a few weeks with us, and we spent fantastic days watching them play in the swimming pool, taking them hiking around the nearby Red Rock Canyon, cycling along the Grand Canyon, rafting on the Colorado River, and taking a roller coaster ride that was particularly thrilling for Carolina.

In 2016, five years after Lily's birth, our era of traveling back and forth across the Atlantic finally ended, and we sold our house in Las Vegas.

Denyse and I both loved our time in Las Vegas, and we still miss the city. Sometimes I hear Denyse raving about Vegas the way you rave about an old boyfriend. That chapter of our lives is over now, but it has been the source of many happy memories ever since.

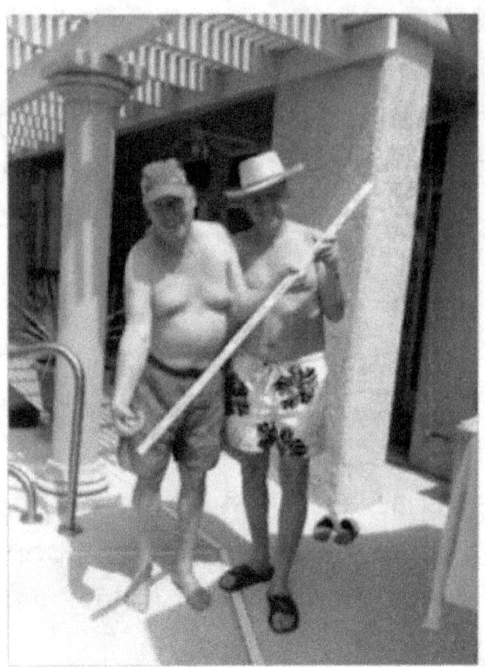

MY BEST FRIEND SIGI STEBER CHECKING IF THE GRASS IS CUT AT PERFECT LENGTH.

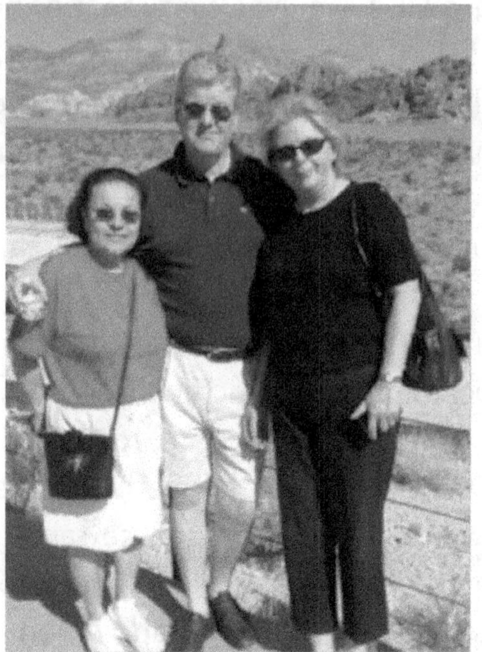

MY SISTER JENNY WITH HER HUSBAND DIRK AND DENYSE VISITING RED ROCK CANYON

DENYSE'S COUSIN FADI AND I ON THE STRIP GETTING A TASTE OF LAS VEGAS

Peter and Christina's Wedding in Paris 42

Our son had his own way of saying goodbye to Las Vegas. In the weeks before he moved to Hawaii, as his transfer to the Four Seasons Hotel in Maui approached, Peter and his girlfriend Christina had apparently decided to get married without telling anyone in our family.

A hush-hush wedding was, perhaps, the ultimate way to bid farewell to Las Vegas, the world capital of secrets and instant marriage ceremonies. At least Peter and Christina had the wedding in their own style. Not in a hotel chapel, not with an Elvis Presley impersonator officiating the wedding in his sparkling outfit, and not in a white stretch limousine cruising up and down the Strip.

Peter had instead taken my red Mercedes Benz 560SL convertible, and with his bride, Christina, in the passenger seat, had gotten married in a drive-through ceremony to complete the civil formalities. Evil tongues say that there are two signs after leaving the Las Vegas wedding drive-through: Exit to the left and divorce to the right. I never checked on this personally, and I never asked Peter, but I would not be surprised if this is the truth, because in Las Vegas, everything is possible.

Denyse and I needed a little time to adjust to the news, as we did not realize Peter and Christina had intended to get married so soon. Then again, they had been living together in Las Vegas for some time now, so it should not have come as a surprise.

Fortunately, they were not simply planning to elope without allowing any family or friends to celebrate their marriage. They had another secret plan, one that would follow the Las Vegas drive-through ceremony by a few months: a big, beautiful wedding in Paris.

Since Denyse and I had met in Paris and have great fondness for the city, we were delighted by this announcement. I did regret that I was not working at that time, so I could not offer them a venue as I had done for Carine and Martin at the Ciragan. But I had every intention of ensuring that Peter and Christina's day would be a truly special one.

I quickly discovered I would have very little work to do. By the time they revealed their plan to get married in Paris, Peter and Christina had already arranged most of the details. For the ceremony, they had booked the Press Club, a prestigious address off the Champs-Élysées with lovely facilities furnished in Louis XIV style, sure to impress the many foreign invitees. For the evening before the wedding, they had hired one of the Bateaux Mouches as a venue for a cocktail party on the Seine.

Everything seemed to be under control, at least as far as the planning was concerned. But all my years in the hospitality industry had taught me one thing: An event like this always, always requires that someone show up in advance, in person, to check on all the details.

With Maui located more than 12,000 miles away from Paris, the couple could not simply take quick weekend trips to oversee such matters. So how convenient it was that Mom and Dad had, in the meantime, established their main residence in München—not exactly around the corner from Paris, but not so far for anyone willing to zoom along the German Autobahn and the French highways.

Denyse and I did not want to impose, but when Peter asked us if we could drop by to make sure that the planning was on track, we accepted without hesitation. Since planning elaborate events to perfection was a big part of my life's work, I was honored my son had asked, and Denyse was thrilled to get involved.

Our first trip to Paris made it all too clear someone needed to be on the ground to oversee the details.

"Ne vous en faites pas," the director of banqueting of the Press Club told us during our first meeting with her. "Don't worry."

We felt quite worried, however, for the simple reason that she couldn't find any answers to any of our questions about the details Peter had discussed with her only a few months ago. She nervously turned one page after the other, the expression on her face growing more and more hopeless with every passing moment. Denyse and I looked at each other. We had a challenge on our hands.

The food tasting turned out to be another catastrophe, as the presentation of the individual menu courses fell way below our expectations for a gala dinner in a stunning facility like the Press Club. While I was busy with the chef de cuisine and the director of banqueting, Denyse had her arguments with the photographer, the florist, and the Bateau Mouche to ensure that Peter and Christina received what they were expecting.

As we realized again and again on that trip, the French staff of the Press Club wanted to do everything their own way and had little or no flexibility to accommodate special wishes. If they had been displaying a professional attention to detail and a high quality of planning and execution, we might have been willing to listen. But so far, everything they had shown us was a disappointment.

Unfortunately for them, they didn't know me yet. I was determined not to let them get away with the mediocrity they were offering. After all, we were the customers, and we owed Peter and Christina the wedding they wanted, the one the Press Club had led them to believe they could have.

As the big day approached, Peter and Christina arrived in Paris a few days ahead of time. Denyse and I brought them up-to-date on the latest developments, which by now looked far more buttoned-up than they had a few weeks before. Peter took over to arrange the final details, and Denyse continued to oversee the florist and the photographer. We were ready at last for the special moment to come.

But first, we had arranged a surprise for Peter and Christina, a late breakfast at Ladurée on the Champs-Élysées the morning after the ceremony. Ladurée is a famous rendezvous spot for Parisians and visitors alike and an ideal venue to wrap up the wedding event.

Louis Ernest Ladurée had opened his first bakery in 1862 at 16 Rue Royal, when the area was already home to a collection of deluxe boutiques. A few years later, he converted the bakery into a pastry shop, and in order to compete with the elegant boutiques and chic restaurants of the district, Mr. Ladurée built a small room next to the patisserie to serve coffee, tea, and his exquisite pastries. He contracted Jules Chéret, a well-known artist of that time, to decorate the walls and ceilings.

It did not take long for the Patisserie Ladurée to become the preferred destination for Parisian high society and for the city's poets and artists, who would meet for coffee, pastries, and conversation. The first salon de thé in Paris was born, and it has kept up its formidable reputation until today. Now Ladurée's macarons are internationally renowned, and the pastry shop and tea salon has opened several branches in cities around the world.

By the time Denyse and I helped Peter and Christina finalize the last few details for the wedding ceremony, most of the invitees had arrived in Paris. Our friends George and Anneliese Plosa flew in from Florida, Denyse's cousin Makram and his wife, Elisabeth, from Riyadh in Saudi Arabia, Christina's family from Brooklyn, and my sister and her family from Hannover in Germany. Denyse's mother and relatives who lived close by in Paris had the good fortune of traveling a very short distance to join us.

Now that all the guests were in Paris, the party could finally begin. As everyone boarded the Bateau Mouche, Peter and Christina welcomed each of their guests with a wreath of fresh Hawaii flowers. A touch of the islands in the middle of Paris.

The stunning flowers signaled the beginning of a magical evening, as we all floated together on the Seine River along the Quai de Paris and watched the famous Paris monuments passing by. The Eiffel Tower sparkled with a thousand lights, the Louvre lit up to show every detail of its magnificent architecture, and the Grand and Petit Palais, with their crystal roof shining like a diamond in the night, demonstrated why Paris had earned its nickname. It was indeed the city of lights.

A selection of delicious cocktails and exquisite canapés completed our trip along the Seine, a successful preview of an even more wonderful day to follow.

With the details finally organized and ready to go at the Press Club, the wedding ceremony the next day turned out to be the spectacular event that the bride and groom had anticipated. Christina, escorted by her father, walked elegantly down the aisle, to the spot where a handsomely dressed Peter stood waiting for his future wife.

After the drive-through wedding in Las Vegas, I had braced myself for Peter and Christina to attempt a similar gesture in Paris, maybe driving into the room in a Citroen 2CV. But to our great joy and relief, they decided to do things the traditional way.

The gala reception afterward capped off the day magnificently, as the menu selected by Peter proved exceptional indeed. Between our son's discussions with the Executive Chef and my own conversations with the kitchen staff in the weeks before the wedding, the chef had finally understood what a high quality of food and presentation truly meant.

As guests prepared to hit the dance floor, a spectacular French wedding cake made of macarons emerged into a room now lit with sparkling candles, while projections on a screen showed photos of Peter and Christina from their youth. Guests danced the rest of the evening away as the entire room gleamed with the glow of candlelight and newlywed bliss.

Midnight approached, and the evening slowly drew to an end. Peter and Christina slipped out and guests began to say their goodbyes as the moonlight twinkled over Paris.

Brunch at Ladurée is an event not to miss, and most of the wedding guests accepted our invitation for the farewell feast the next morning. As everyone talked about the festivities of the night before, we relaxed over an eight-course brunch menu filled with exquisite pastries and delicious surprises.

After a shaky beginning to the arrangements at the Press Club a few months before, the wedding weekend in Paris had turned into a huge success. Denyse and I were relieved, but most of all very happy for the newlyweds, as we rested to recover from all the champagne and rich Parisian food that signals a French weekend well spent.

PETER'S WEDDING IN PARIS

IMPRESSIONS FROM A WONDERFUL EVENING

And Cairo Again 43

A Call From a Former Associate

"Hello, Peter, where are you?"

We had just returned to Munich from a summer trip to the US in 2006 when I received an urgent telephone call from the office of a former associate named Ali Abdel Aziz.

During my time as general manager at the Heliopolis Sheraton, Ali was my right-hand and resident manager, a loyal and extremely supportive colleague. Working with him had been a pleasure indeed. Why was he calling now?

His assistant informed me that Ali needed to speak to me immediately, and I could reach him at his current location, a spa at the Bodensee in Germany. This piqued my curiosity.

I always knew Ali was destined for big things. An alumni of the Victoria College in Alexandria, Egypt, he had studied at the Glion Hotel School in Switzerland, giving him an extraordinary foundation for a successful career, and he came from a well-respected family in Egypt, where descent is held in great esteem. His excellent relations with highly ranked members of government circles made him a valuable assistant to me in the Heliopolis days. The success I was able to achieve at that hotel was due to a great extent to Ali's support and help.

Unfortunately for me, our time working together ended too soon. During my tenure in Heliopolis, Ali was promoted to general manager at the Sheraton Hotel in Medina, the second holiest city in Saudi Arabia. He returned to Cairo a few years later to take over the Giza Sheraton and later ran the Le Meridien Hotels in Egypt.

I was convinced that one day I would see him appointed minister of tourism. So it came as no big surprise when I learned on that summer day in 2006 that Ali was now CEO of HOTAC, a subsidiary of the ministry of development, managing all government-owned hotels in Egypt as well as real estate and other tourism-related properties.

When I called him, Ali wasted no time in asking me to go see him immediately. "We have very important matters to discuss," he said, sounding rushed as always. "Alatoul," as he liked to say in Arabic.

Ali was apparently under the impression that since we were both in Germany that week, I could simply materialize in front of his eyes. But the drive from München to the Bodensee would take several hours, so we agreed that I'd visit him with Denyse that weekend.

I have no idea who recommended this specific spa to Ali, as he was clearly paying a lot of money to be served cabbage soup every day as part of a dubious weight loss regimen.

We were all very happy to see each other again, and Ali got right to the subject. His job was to privatize as many of the government hotels as possible, with the exception of Egypt's landmark hotels, which needed to be consolidated into a new group of government-owned hotels. To renovate the old landmark hotels, Ali continued, the government had agreed that he could use the money from the hotels sold. Ali was excited about the prospects of this program and wanted me to help him make it a reality.

As all the hotels were under the authority of EGOTH, the Egyptian General Organization for Tourism and Hotels, I would have to work closely with Nabil Selim, its chairman and managing director, but I would report to Ali on issues related to the landmark program.

Not too many years ago, Ali was my employee at the Heliopolis Sheraton, and now he was about to become my new boss. I remembered the saying, "You'd better be nice to everybody, because they could be your boss one day."

I guess I must have been nice enough to Ali that he thought to call me now. His job offer did appeal to me, there was no doubt about it. Still, my gut feeling told me things would turn out to be even more complicated than they sounded. But how would I ever know if I didn't jump in with both feet?

The Waters of the Nile

An Egyptian proverb says, "He who once drank from the waters of the Nile will always return."

Of course, I never literally drank from the waters of the Nile—nobody in their right mind would—but here I was again, back in Cairo, as a hotel consultant to the government.

Arriving in the midst of the disorganized jumble at the Cairo airport, Denyse and I felt relieved to have someone waiting to whisk us through passport control and customs, all the way into the limousine that took us to the Shepheard Hotel, our home away from home for the foreseeable future.

The night before my first meeting with Ali Abdel Aziz and Nabil Selim, I had difficulty falling asleep. My head was full of ideas about how to address this new challenge.

It was a quarter to ten the next morning when I left the hotel for the five-minute walk to my new office. The official working hours of government offices in Cairo were 9:00 a.m. to 1:00 p.m., but nobody showed up before 10:00 a.m., and certainly I had no intention of changing this habit.

As it happened, the meeting did not reveal anything beyond what I had already heard from Ali during our first talk at the Bodensee. But I noted that during the one hour in which Nabil and I sat in Ali's office, as he simultaneously juggled incoming telephone calls, talked to us, and gave orders to his secretary, the total time that we enjoyed his full attention was less than fifteen minutes. Typical Ali, trying to do ten things at the same time.

Even though I learned nothing new in the meeting, it became clear to me that, in my role, I would be much more than just a simple consultant. Ali's busy schedule allowed him no time to handle the transformation of EGOTH himself, and Nabil Selim, a former general of the Egyptian Army, had no hotel or tourism experience and could not take on that role himself. My job, it quickly dawned on me, was to be the professional brain behind the scenes, making the magic happen while allowing Nabil and Ali to shine.

This was no problem, as far as I was concerned. The job sounded stimulating enough, and I respected both Ali and Nabil.

Despite Nabil's limited English, my relationship with him was off to a strong start from the minute we met. He understood English much better than he led everyone to believe, and when we talked on our own, we understood each other perfectly well. I would have loved my Arabic to be as good as his English.

I met daily with Nabil to exchange thoughts and ideas and, most important of all, to allow him to feel in charge of the project. And what a project it was. The program was riddled with grave problems from the beginning, as I soon discovered.

Of the ninety-plus hotels controlled by EGOTH, the majority were in such poor condition that only a few could make plausible candidates for the new hotel group Ali had in mind. But even those hotels, although managed by foreign companies, would need major renovations if we wanted our project to succeed.

The problem for Nabil was that EGOTH not only had an inventory of dilapidated old hotels, but it also employed five thousand people, many of whom never showed up in their office but still cashed their salary at the end of the month.

I once asked Nabil how many employees he would need to run EGOTH successfully. About four hundred, he answered, but the rest are all government employees and cannot be dismissed. Not only that, but this number keeps growing as every day a minister or an official high up in the government had to do someone a favor and give the son of a friend a job at EGOTH.

Meanwhile, Ali kept busy using his sales talent to find investors so that most of the hotels could be privatized. I decided my time would be well-spent in examining each of the hotels on our shortlist to assess whether we should include it in the program. The hotels under consideration spanned Egypt, from Alexandria in the north all the way to Luxor and Aswan in the south, and we had three potential candidates in Cairo.

We would rate each hotel based on several criteria: the importance of the city in which the hotel was situated, the location of the property within the city, the standing and history of the hotel within its community, and last but not least, the potential for the hotel to be successful in the future.

My first trip took me to Alexandria, Egypt's second most important city after Cairo and a preferred summer destination for many Cairotes. Every year, its population ballooned from about 350,000 in winter to more than one million in summer.

Founded by Alexander the Great in 331 bc, Alexandria was one of the greatest cities in Hellenistic civilization. Only Rome, which gained control of Egypt in 30 bc, surpassed Alexandria in size and wealth. Alexandria spent nearly a millennium as the capital of Egypt, before losing its central status after the Arab conquest in ad 641. But Alexandria's famous ancient sites, including the Great Library and the Alexandria Lighthouse, one of the Seven Wonders of the World, continued to bring fame and tourism through the centuries. Today, the lighthouse doesn't exist anymore, but the library remains a magnificent site, along with the city's unparalleled waterfront, miles-long white beaches, and historic buildings such as the Montaza Palace.

The Alexandria property under consideration for our new landmark program was the Palestine Hotel, located near the Montaza Palace complex and its gardens overlooking the blue Mediterranean Sea. Although the hotel itself was a modern building with no particularly noteworthy features, its location next to a beautiful park and with such close proximity to the Montaza Palace and beaches made it a suitable candidate for the prestigious group.

In Cairo, we had several options. The city has no shortage of international hotels, but while most of the new ones were constructed with foreign investment, EGOTH still owned three major landmarks: the Omar

Khayyam Palace, managed by Marriott; the Mena House at the Pyramids, managed by the Indian hotel group Oberoi; and the Shepheard Hotel, which fell back under EGOTH's control after Helnan Hotels lost the management contract.

All three of those properties, along with the city's oldest hotel, the Nile Hilton, met our initial criteria for the new landmarks group, although they would need millions of dollars in renovations to hit the mark.

The only other two hotels in Egypt to qualify were the Winter Palace in Luxor and the Cataract Hotel in Aswan, both under management contracts with the French Accor group. Those two cities were popular destinations for Nile cruises and had other attractions that brought tourists in significant numbers.

Dating back more than three millennia, the Luxor Temple is where Egypt's pharaohs were crowned, according to legend, and the site typically draws thousands of visitors annually, especially in years when the temple stages a performance of Verdi's *Aida* opera. Watching the opera in this majestic location is a once-in-a-lifetime experience, and the Winter Palace Hotel, only steps away, could not be more perfectly situated.

What the temple was for Luxor, Lake Nasr and the spice bazaar were for Aswan. In Aswan, the Cataract Hotel, set in a beautifully manicured garden overlooking the Nile, allowed guests to enjoy the sites of the city and to watch the feluccas, the classic Egyptian sailing boats, passing by along the legendary waters. It was another Egyptian sight not to miss.

Historic Hotels of Egypt

The hotels we chose for our landmark collection represented the most breathtaking locations in Egypt, and now we were ready to implement our ambitious concept. The next step was to develop an identity, one that would stand out and unify the hotel group, without offending the management companies that operated the properties.

I was excited to tackle this challenge. I knew it would be a complex puzzle to solve. The brand identity would need to communicate the sense of history that each hotel embodied, along with the unrivaled locations. Most important of all, our chief goal was to promote Egypt as the destination.

For several days, I carried the themes around in my head and played with various word combinations, until the answer popped up: Historic Hotels of Egypt. I instantly knew that was it. The identity of our new hotel group was born.

Nabil and Ali would still need to approve the idea, and I decided to develop a logo and a complete design package to present to them so they could visualize what I was talking about.

My designer friend Sami Alouf in Brussels was only a telephone call away and ready to assist me with the artwork. I gave him a few ideas I had sketched out to help steer the design in the direction I thought would win their approval, since the brand identity needed to not only sound Egyptian but to visually highlight Egyptian pride.

I also knew the final approval of the brand concept would need to come from higher up than Ali and Nabil, much higher as a matter of fact.

Sami Alouf did an extraordinary job and hit the idea right on target. He created two classically designed capital H letters, one for "Historic" and one for "Hotels," framing a lotus flower, and he placed the words "Historic Hotels of Egypt" underneath in elegant script. This identity represented everything I was looking for.

When I presented the graphic design to Nabil, his facial expression transformed from nervous curiosity into a big smile. I knew we had a winner on our hands. It was time to visit Ali in his office.

While I let Nabil do the talking, I watched Ali's reaction.

"Fantastic!" Ali said instantly. "Let's go ahead."

Nabil and I looked at each other, relieved, knowing we had just cleared one of the most important hurdles.

From then on, it was full steam ahead. It was now time to expand the design into other pieces of collateral, and within a few weeks, I had developed a set of quality standards and operational concepts for the hotels, in preparation for a presentation to the board of directors of HOTAC.

As I handled all the details related to staff training and guest experience at the Historic Hotels of Egypt, Ali was making other important decisions, ones which would likely spark controversy but would improve the hotels' quality, reputation, and standing.

One of those decisions was to not renew the management contract with Hilton for the Nile Hilton and to instead sign a contract with Ritz Carlton, which was owned by the Marriott Hotel Group. As Marriott was already managing our Omar Khayyam Palace, we expected some synergies, along with added profitability, if we entrusted the former Hilton to the Ritz Carlton instead. The contracts with Accor for the Winter Palace and the Old Cataract Hotel were allowed to run out, and Ali had started discussions with Four Seasons as a potential operator.

As far as we could tell, the only remaining ingredient was the money to restore each of these hotels to its original glory, as the minister of development had promised, and as the future hotel operators expected us to do. But a big obstacle stood in our way first.

An Unscheduled Presentation

The door to my office swung open one morning and in walked Ali. I don't remember Ali ever visiting me in my office before, as he was the type of person who preferred to order people to drop everything and come to his office.

He seemed agitated, and I quickly learned why.

"Peter," he said, "I have to make a presentation to Prime Minister Ahmed Nazif about the Historic Hotels of Egypt tomorrow. I want you to join me and do the presentation."

"How much time do we have?" I asked.

"No idea, but we have to be in his cabinet at 11:00 a.m. I would suggest making it short and sweet, because I don't think they have too much time to listen." Then out the door he went.

It was 11:00 a.m. sharp the next morning when we walked into the prime minister's office and took seats around the large conference table. The prime minister sat at the head of the table, with our group on one side and the minister of development, the minister of tourism, and several other ministers sitting on the other side.

A huge portrait of President Mubarak decorated the wall behind the prime minister. While I sat patiently waiting for my turn to speak, a lively discussion erupted in Arabic between Ali, the prime minister, and a few other ministers. It sounded as though they were fighting, if their cheerful faces and body language had not suggested otherwise.

When I was summoned to speak, I stood up and gave my presentation. It took less than ten minutes, as I flipped through the various charts I had prepared and explained the operational philosophy and the opportunity for Egypt to establish itself within the international market of luxury hotels.

A thank you from the prime minister ended the session, and out we went.

Ali later told me that the minister of development had initiated the presentation and that everything had gone well. Apparently, the prime minister was impressed by the presentation, and most important of all, he did like the idea.

A crucial step, successfully completed.

But a surprise awaited us. In the preceding weeks, Ali had sold the only remaining piece of land on Tahrir Square to the French hotel company Accor for the construction of a new hotel, but he had not foreseen what was about to happen. Ali suddenly received a telephone call from the minister of development informing him that President Mubarak requested the cancellation of the purchase, as he did not want another hotel on Tahrir Square.

Ali was in shock. How could he cancel the agreement now, with the down payment received and his and the minister's signatures on the contract?

On the other hand, the president had just given an order, and who dared to contradict Mubarak? Ali was panicked, running in circles, not knowing what to do. All he knew was that he was in trouble, deep trouble.

Contacting Accor did not produce the desired result. Accor flatly refused to even talk about a cancellation, and to make things worse, the next day they posted a huge sign saying "Site of the new Accor Hotel" on the piece of land under dispute. This provoked a new call from the president to the minister of development.

Soon enough, even Accor realized it would not make any sense to go against President Mubarak. They grudgingly agreed to a cancellation of the agreement, but not before securing a twenty-year extension of their management agreement for the Winter Palace in Luxor and the Cataract Hotel in Aswan.

Here we were, watching our high-flying plans for the Historic Hotels of Egypt come crumbling down.

In the Newspapers Again

The media always craves a juicy story. In Egypt, the press can write just about whatever it wants as long as it doesn't criticize the president.

But an investigation into a government plan gone awry is often fair game, and the story about the sale of the Tahrir Square property to Accor—and the president's decision to cancel the contract—attracted a lot of interest in the press. The activities of Ali Abdel Aziz, HOTAC, and EGOTH came under close scrutiny in the newspapers.

The situation reminded me of my time at the Heliopolis Sheraton when a certain newspaper columnist enjoyed attacking me over and over again. The only difference this time was that I was not mentioned by name but referred to simply as a foreign consultant.

Considering how the media was now spinning our program in a negative light, it was bad timing to try to introduce the idea of the Historic Hotels of Egypt to the various old and new operators. Ali had also lost interest in the plan as he devoted his energy to keeping his name out of the newspapers.

The media would not let up, increasing its pressure against HOTAC and focusing on Ali's compensation too. The press also trumpeted the money the program was spending on foreign consultants, when there were supposedly plenty of Egyptians in the country who could do the job.

Ali needed to react to all the bad press, because to him, in this moment, there was nothing more important than Ali. Forgotten were the ambitious plans for the Historic Hotels of Egypt and forgotten too was his urgent plea to me several months ago to lend my professionalism to his program.

My days of working for the Egyptian government were clearly about to end. The countdown had begun.

To reach a mutually acceptable understanding, Nabil and I agreed to change my contract from one of permanent employment to an as-needed agreement. We both saw this as a fair solution under the circumstances, one that would allow the government to save some money while retaining my services for the continuation of the project. We agreed that I would return to Cairo once things had cooled down.

The agreement would also achieve the most important goal: keeping Ali out of the press.

On August 15, 2007, Denyse and I returned to München and never again heard from either Ali or Nabil.

Adel Wally, a former colleague and director of technical services for EGOTH, called me in München a few weeks later to inform me that several days after I left, Ali had emptied my office to convert it into a meeting room. All my documents had been packed into boxes and put into storage.

So much for the ambitious plan for the Historic Hotels of Egypt and my triumphant return to the land of the Nile.

Until today, the Historic Hotels program has yet to be implemented, and my operational guidelines, concepts, policies, and procedures are sitting somewhere collecting dust in one of the government storerooms. A missed opportunity to introduce Egypt's beautiful, gracious accommodations to new generations of travelers.

PRESENTATION TO THE PRIME MINISTER AND HIS CABINET

MY OFFICE AND HQ OF HISTORIC HOTELS

سياحة وسفر

الفنادق التاريخية.. من دائرة الاهمال، إلى دائرة الاهتمام!

"Europe from EGP 1999."

THE MEETING WITH THE PM IN THE MEDIA

Contemplating Retirement 44

In *The Godfather* film, there is a moment when Michael Corleone, the character played by Al Pacino, says, "Just when I thought I was out, they pulled me back in." Corleone had been trying to avoid his family's attempts to lure him into the Mafia, and at the point when he thought he had finally escaped, he realized he would never be free.

That line is one of the most famous ones from the movie and seemed to resonate with people facing all kinds of situations from which they have a difficult time breaking free. To some extent, my situation was very similar. Once a hotelier, always a hotelier, but I had reached a point when I was ready to slow down so I could have more freedom in my life and more family time.

A part of me wanted to retire, or at least to create a far less demanding schedule for myself. Still, every time I thought my career was winding down, I would find myself pulled into a new assignment.

I would usually accept these projects for the simple reason that I enjoyed them and found them energizing. But the fact remained that after four decades of hard work, I needed more peace and quiet in my life.

The idea of retirement appealed to me more and more with every passing month, although I kept delaying any decisions about when I would officially end my career. As time went by, and as Denyse and I began to feel an increasing urge to travel freely, not to mention a need to address the health problems we now faced on a regular basis, the leisure time we had became a lifesaver.

One of these health issues was my recurring heart problem, which, unbeknownst to me, was on the brink of erupting again. Denyse had also developed a mysterious shoulder pain, which crept up on her slowly and eventually demanded an urgent resolution.

We Don't Walk On Our Hands

Her shoulder aches, more crippling by the day, led us to seek an appointment with a highly recommended doctor at the New York University Hospital in Manhattan, a decision we would soon regret.

The doctor's office looked quite impressive at first, decorated with pictures of all the famous athletes he had treated. Between checking Denyse's shoulder condition and explaining that in order to make her pain-free he would need to clean the arthritis from her shoulder, he spent no more than twenty-five minutes with us during our first appointment. In that short time, he succeeded in convincing us that the treatment he was proposing would be the right solution to end Denyse's suffering.

We agreed to the procedure, and he made sure we understood that Denyse would also have to spend one day in the hospital to recover. The procedure went by smoothly, and we were pleased at first.

The first surprise came once the intervention was done, and I received a bill for $25,000 to be paid within one week. I thought the zero button on his computer must be stuck. But we paid the absurdly high fee, enough for a down payment on a home anywhere but in New York City. At least we had solved her shoulder problem, or so we thought.

After her brief hospital stay, Denyse came home, hopeful that her shoulder was cured. No such luck. The pain returned only a few months later, while we were visiting Paris.

Taking advantage of being in a city renowned for its excellent medical care, we wasted no time in searching for a shoulder specialist who could finally help Denyse. Dr. Jaques Dutront seemed to be the person we were looking for, and we were lucky to get an appointment the following day.

Yes, he could help us, Dr. Dutront said, after thoroughly checking Denyse's shoulder and examining her x-rays. But she would have to plan to spend a few days in the hospital after the operation.

That would be difficult, I responded, because we do not live in Paris. As soon as I began to explain that our home is in Germany, Dr. Dutront jumped in. "You have Europe's best shoulder specialist in Germany. Why are you coming to me? His name is Professor Habermeyer, and he practices in Heidelberg, which I think is not too far from where you live."

Once we returned home to Munich, we immediately went to Heidelberg to see Prof. Dr. Peter Habermeyer, who by his international peers was called respectfully the Shoulder Pope.

Examining the reports we had brought from the New York City hospital where Denyse had her $25,000 treatment, Dr. Habermeyer said, "Mrs. Tischmann, what they did for you in New York, we have not done for at least fifteen years because it does not cure the problem. It only delays the pain, but the pain will return."

He paused. "Thank God we don't walk on our hands," he said, looking at Denyse. "Or else you wouldn't be able to walk."

As we continued our conversation, Prof. Habermeyer explained that only a shoulder replacement would free Denyse from the suffering caused by this particular kind of arthritis, which eats up every bit of cartilage between the bones. Inquiring how long it would take before she was rid of the pain, Prof. Habermeyer responded to Denyse, "From the moment you leave my operating room, you will have no pain anymore."

After a four-week rehabilitation, Denyse had to rest her shoulder on a special cushion for six more weeks, day and night, but Prof. Habermeyer was right. The pain never returned.

Unfortunately, one year later, Denyse's second shoulder started having the same problem. That time we decided to visit Prof. Habermeyer right away and asked him to do the same operation. Now she has two artificial shoulders, but she can move her arms like a professional athlete. The operation and hospital stay cost $7,500 Euros altogether, about a third of what we paid in New York for one failed, outdated procedure that did nothing but make the doctor even richer.

Denyse's shoulder issue was finally behind us, but another health crisis emerged in the summer of 2002, when a return of my heart symptoms sent me right back to the hospital.

This time I found out I would need to undergo a triple bypass.

Stress Is Taking Its Toll

Luckily, a friend of ours knew a well-known heart surgeon in Munich and recommended him without reservation, so off we went to meet with him. My first impression of Prof. Dr. R. Lange at the German Heart Center in Munich was not what I would call either encouraging or positive. The Professor seemed entirely too busy to be bothered, keeping his remarks brief and taking no time to answer any of my questions. Still, as he was considered the number 1 heart doctor in the region, I reminded myself that it's not important for me to like the guy. The important thing is that he knows what he is doing.

In the days before the surgery, I felt at peace with the operation and confident about our choice of doctor, to the point where I was joking about the operation with Denyse, until she couldn't hear my story anymore. I think during the days leading to the operation, she felt nervous about it, especially when I described to her what would happen. "You know how it goes," I said. "They cut you open and spread your chest open with a wrench. Then the surgeon removes the heart and throws it to the nurse and says, 'Put it in the heart-lung machine while I fix this guy here!'" I don't think Denyse found this funny at all.

Despite my efforts to lighten the mood, I became anxious myself on the night before the surgery, when the nurses arrived in my hospital room to shave my chest. Now I could no longer deny that things were getting serious.

I woke up nervous on the morning of my operation and could not hide that I was very concerned during the brief moments while I was still conscious, before they put me under. But the bypass surgery went very well, evidently. It was all over before I knew it, and now all I had to do was to rest and recover in the hospital, then undergo a rehabilitation program for four weeks afterward.

Rehab proved to be a rejuvenating experience in ways I did not foresee. My program emphasized art activities alongside all the breathing exercises, fitness regimens, and stress tests. I learned pottery, and I started to paint again under the guidance of a professional painter, who coached a group of us and hung the best paintings in the dining room every week. I felt proud that my paintings started to line the walls.

Not long after my bypass surgery, I went back to visit the doctor who did the operation, thinking he would have an interest in knowing how I was doing. A visit which took less than three minutes total. When I was called into his office, rather than asking me how I felt, he surprised me with his rude manner. "What are you doing here? What do you want?"

This was not the welcome I had expected. "I thought you might be interested to learn how your patient is doing?" I replied.

"No, I have nothing to do with it anymore. You have to see your cardiologist from now on."

The last thing I wanted to do now was spend one additional moment with this man, but since I had no cardiologist in Munich, I asked him if he could recommend anyone. He referred me to Dr. Edward Wildfeuer, who is still my cardiologist today. My farewell visit to the heart surgeon, as unpleasant and brief as it was, taught me an important lesson: Surgeons are no longer interested in their patients after the operation is done. The only thing they're interested in is that their patients leave the operating theater alive. Once you're stable and sent to intensive care to begin the recovery, they're finished with you.

I still follow the news about Prof. Dr. R. Lange and his accomplishments in the newspaper on a regular basis, and he remains at the top of his field. But I am glad not to have had to go back and see him again.

One positive side effect of my heart surgery is that after the rehab program and the art sessions, I have been more inspired to paint than ever before. I continue to paint nearly every week, to the point that Denyse and I have no more space left to hang any paintings in our Munich apartment.

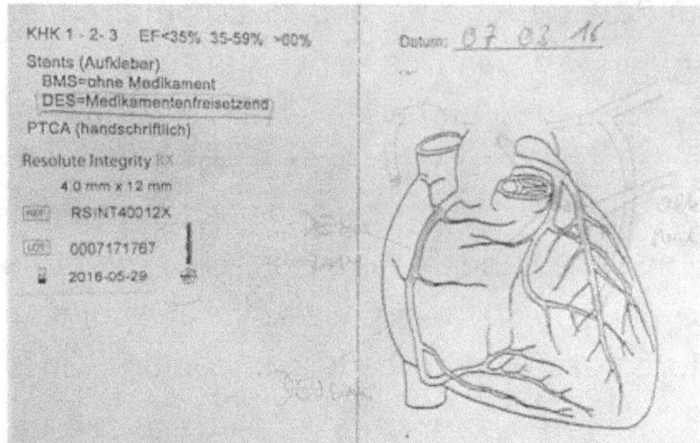

THE PROFESSOR EXPLAINING THE STATUS OF MY HEART

ONE OF MY PAINTINGS

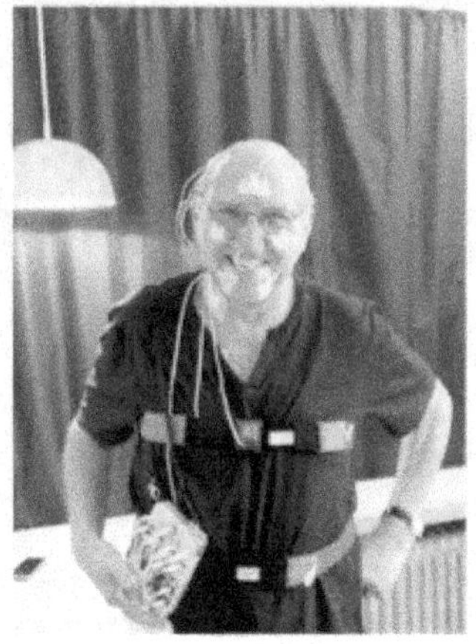

AND MORE TESTS

THE LAUTERBACHER MÜHLE, MY REHAB

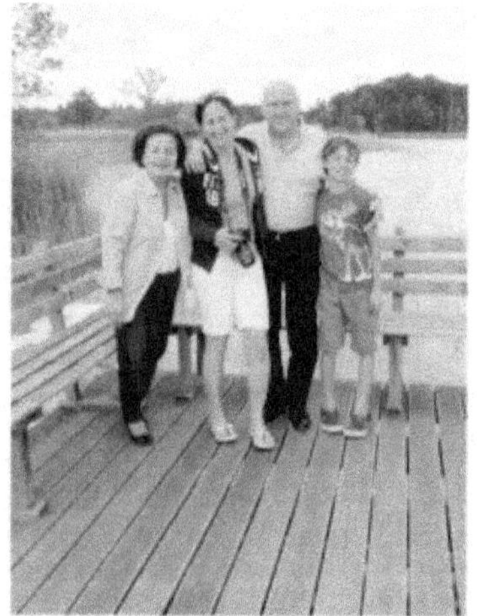

THE FAMILY VISITING AT THE REHAB CENTER

Becoming Grandparents 45

A career in hotels is one of the most thrilling experiences anyone can have in a lifetime, at least in my opinion. But there is another job which provides ongoing change and excitement, and with which I also soon fell in love. This is a job to which no one needs to either apply or appear for an interview, or even dress up in business clothes. All that is required is love and time. I am speaking of the role of grandparent, a position to which Denyse and I found ourselves recruited by our children. We were, of course, overjoyed to be tapped for this new position.

So as I continued to wrestle with the decision about whether or not to officially retire, Denyse and I felt increasingly tempted by one of the biggest reasons to create more leisure time in our lives: our grandchildren. Our important new job as grandparents was a role that immediately brought with it a completely new level of fulfillment and pride, and we wanted to create more time for it. One of the fringe benefits of this role, needless to say, is that grandmothers and grandfathers are not the ones doing all the hard work. We simply get to enjoy the children.

On the day in 2003 when our first grandchild arrived, Denyse and I had been spending the weekend at a resort hotel managed by a former colleague of mine. A phone call from Carine made us jump. "Mama, can you come?" she said. "I think it's time." We rushed to pack and drive the few hours back to Munich and straight to the hospital where Carine was delivering, but little Tommy had already arrived.

A Different Challenge

Suddenly, we were grandparents. Meeting Tommy, the tiniest member of our family, was one of the most profoundly joyful moments in our lives, an experience that would repeat itself with the same level of excitement each time another of our grandchildren was born, three more over a decade. Carine and Martin had Carolina two years later, and Fabienne two years after that. Then Peter Jr. and his wife, Christina, had Lily in Chicago in 2011.

Somehow, we were always outside Munich when our German grandkids were born, and too far from Chicago when Lily was born. But we felt extremely fortunate to become grandparents four times, and it was especially lucky that Lily was born on St. Patrick's Day, which symbolizes good fortune.

As much pleasure and fun as we have watching our grandchildren grow up, it's also a rude reminder of how fast time is running. As they grow, we are getting older.

This year, Tommy has passed his baccalaureate and is getting ready to join Europe's leading business school in St. Gallen, Switzerland. This reminded me of when our children left home to go to Dartmouth College and Cornell University.

Becoming grandparents also made me remember that when Carine and Peter Jr. were young, I traveled frequently, no fewer than 250 days a year. Consequently, I missed a great many events in their childhood. I was not around to watch them grow up from week to week, or to experience all the challenges and milestones of childhood and adolescence. Now that I have the time to spend with our grandchildren as they grow up, I have a closeup view of what I missed before. I can read books to the kids and sit in the audience at their school plays and sports competitions, and I could not be happier about this.

Denyse and I are fortunate to have a strong relationship with all our grandchildren, although sometimes we might question a decision that one of their parents makes. On this matter, the less said, the better. Age brings with it the wisdom to keep our mouths shut. We are simply here to have fun with our grandchildren and to keep them safe and happy when we babysit. Their parents are doing a wonderful job anyway, and it is no longer our business to be the boss.

Definitely Not Opa

When Tommy was an infant and started to say his first words, Carine asked us, "What do you want your grandchildren to call you?"

I said, "Definitely not Opa. Opa makes me feel old. Maybe they should call me Mr. Tischmann." I was joking of course, and little Tommy had a better idea anyway. The first time Tommy said my name, it came out as "Pupa." I don't know what he was trying to say, maybe "Papa," but the nickname stuck.

Soon enough, even Carine's au pair was calling me Pupa. Ever since then, I have been Pupa to all of Carine's children, and to Lily, Peter's daughter. They call Denyse Mamie (Carine is Mama). I do think Pupa is cute, but in any case, it's better than Mr. Tischmann, and certainly preferable to Opa.

Even though we live on the other side of Munich from Carine's family, and on the other side of the Atlantic from Peter's, we've done our best to spend as much time as possible with our grandchildren over the years. We see them on a regular basis, although we didn't have to do any babysitting when Carine and Martin went out for the evening, as they had an au pair girl living with them. But we were available when needed.

Watching our four grandchildren develop unique personalities and cultivate distinct talents and hobbies has been a delightful adventure, year after year. Tommy began taking climbing lessons when he was a child, and he is quite athletic now and a good student too. Carolina is grownup for her age, and during one year that she spent in boarding school in Colorado, she became even more independent, mastering winter sports such as snowboarding. Fabienne is an A student and even receives an A+ from teachers who are hesitant to give such a high grade. We have a deal that if she earns an A+ throughout, and in particular in German, her most difficult subject, I would smash my piggy bank and fulfill her wish to fly first-class somewhere. And, as no surprise to me, at the end of the year, I received a FaceTime video call from Fabienne presenting me with her all A+ report card. Her big smile said it all.

Unfortunately, the coronavirus pandemic has limited the choice of destinations we could fly to, but during Fabienne's Easter holiday, we took advantage of the first possible opportunity and booked a flight to Dubai.

Emirates Airlines, the local carrier, was named for three consecutive years as having the best first-class service in the air, so this seemed to be the right choice. Indeed, they exceeded our expectations and delivered an unforgettable experience. Fabienne was thrilled, and flying on board an

Airbus 380, the world's biggest airplane, was another bonus, although the invitation by the hostess to take a shower at 35,000 feet above the ground was a little bit too much for her.

Promise delivered!

Video calling has also given us the chance to maintain regular contact with our son's family and to watch our granddaughter Lily grow up, even though living across the Atlantic means we cannot see her as much as we would like. Over the years, we have enjoyed taking Lily out and about in Miami during our visits there, surprising her with a gingerbread house for Christmas, and watching her grow into a wonderful young girl.

Lily is almost ten years old now, and Carine's kids are teenagers. But we're still Pupa and Mamie to them all. Every year, we take pleasure in making new memories with each of them and reminiscing about the times we had together when they were smaller.

NO MONEY FOR THE 50TH
ANNIVERSARY PARTY

COMPETING WITH THE KIDS,
THE WINNING JUMP

NOTHING BEATS A REAL HAVANNA CIGAR

THE AUDI 8 L ON IT'S WAY
TO FLORIDA

THE BEER KIDS ARE
VISITING US IN LAS VEGAS

A New Toy 46

Giving gifts to grandchildren and watching their faces light up is a joy that grandparents cannot resist. But sometimes grandparents are in the mood to acquire their own new toys too.

I have always reserved a place in my heart for automobiles, and as Denyse and I began to embark on the retirement lifestyle, we needed a vehicle that would suit us. In 2008, we realized it had been some years since we had purchased a new car. The one we chose this time was a Volkswagen Tiguan, a small SUV that drives like a VW Golf. Since we had more free time these days, we decided to take advantage of a ritual available to those who purchase a VW in Germany: a tour of the company's enormous, state-of-the-art factory in Wolfsburg, in north Germany, not far from Hannover. Included in the tour is an overnight stay with dinner at the luxurious Ritz Carlton Hotel.

As it turned out, we would have an unexpected adventure even before we arrived. When the day of our appointment came, we went to the München station early in the morning to board the Intercity, the fast train to Wolfsburg, to pick up our new Tiguan. The journey required one stop and change of train in Goettingen, which was no problem, as the train to Wolfsburg was supposed to arrive immediately after us on the same platform.

Watching the train speed into the station, we started to make our way to the wagon number indicated on our ticket and found our reserved seats, only to discover that there were people already sitting in them.

"I'm very sorry, but you are sitting in our seats," I said, as two confused faces looked up at me.

The passengers who had taken over our seats said no, that is not possible, and showed me their tickets. We argued for a while, then finally they got up, allowing us to take our seats just in time for the train to leave the station.

Moments later, we heard the conductor announce, "Welcome to the Intercity 945, on our way to Hamburg with our next stop in Hannover."

I looked at Denyse. Oops. Hannover was definitely not our destination. Are we on the wrong train? How had this happened? While our new car was waiting for us in Wolfsburg, we were moving at over two hundred kilometers per hour to Hannover.

"Isn't this train supposed to go to Wolfsburg?" I asked the conductor. He glanced at me with a pitying expression.

"No," he said, "the train to Wolfsburg is behind us. Since we had a delay, they gave us priority and allowed us to depart ahead of the Wolfsburg train at our stop in Kassel. So your train that will be stopping in Wolfsburg is actually the train behind us, not this one."

This last-minute change had left us stuck on the wrong train and, much to our regret, had forced an elderly couple from their rightful reserved seats.

At our next stop, Hannover, we were told we would have five minutes to catch a regional train to Wolfsburg. As soon as the train came to a stop, we picked up our luggage, got off the train in a hurry, and ran through the railway station to board the train to Wolfsburg that was waiting on another platform. This time, I asked other passengers on the train to confirm that we were going to Wolfsburg, and Denyse and I were relieved to find two unoccupied seats in one of the wagons. Thinking of the couple we forced out of their seats, I felt embarrassed to have been so pushy. I don't know why they even agreed to give their seats up to us.

Despite the bumpy start, the rest of our trip went much more smoothly. The VW rep picked us up from the station and drove us to the hotel before we were picked up again to drive to the factory to claim our car. We toured the factory grounds, visited the VW Museum, and finished the day with a wonderful gourmet dinner at the hotel before we retired into the comfortable beds of the Ritz Carlton. Not a bad deal at all.

The factory tour itself was impressive indeed. The entire facility takes up five square kilometers, making it one of the largest automobile factories in the world. The area where they assemble the cars is impeccable, with lacquered floors and shiny machinery, and it is tempting to set up a picnic blanket and eat right there. I said to Denyse, "This car factory is cleaner than most restaurant kitchens."

After the two-hour tour, you get to relax in a comfortable lounge and wait for your turn to pick up your car as you stare at a big board, just like the type you watch at an airport. We waited until we saw "Mr. and Mrs. Tischmann, position 12" pop up on the screen. Then we walked into the hall, admiring all the freshly made cars lined up like pieces of candy in tidy rows. We made our way to position 12, and there we spotted our shiny new Tiguan. A friendly representative introduced the car, took a picture with us in front of it, and familiarized us with all its features before wishing us well and sending us on our way. We received the photos of ourselves posing with the car, proud new parents showing off their baby, and drove out triumphantly into the sunset. Of course, by the time we were out of the gate, our car had already lost 20 percent of its value.

A New Car, Empty Tank Included

As soon as Denyse and I drove out of the VW parking lot, we discovered that our brand-new car had only five liters in the tank—and there was no gas station for miles. I later learned that manufacturers only partly fill the tanks up on purpose. This is because they put so many new cars into the waiting lot at the same time, and if the tanks are all full of gas, it could cause an inferno. Nonetheless, driving into the countryside with hardly any gas in the tank is a terrifying proposition, but luckily, we found a gas station just in time, as I suppose every driver who leaves the VW factory in Wolfsburg does. Soon we hit the gas pedal and drove back to München, ready for the adventures that awaited us.

PICKING UP OUR NEW VW TIGUAN AT THE FACTORY IN WOLFSBURG

Our Fortieth Anniversary River Cruise 47

Time always seems to move faster and faster as the years go by. With the memories of our surprise safari for our thirtieth anniversary still fresh in our minds, here we were in 2009, ten years later, with our fortieth anniversary date rapidly approaching.

A lot had happened during the past decade. Our family now numbered nine people—as our granddaughter Lily had not been born yet at the time—making our group more than double the crew of four that had traveled to Botswana for our thirtieth anniversary.

With three small children among us, any complicated adventure would be out of question, so we limited our search to what Germany and Europe had to offer. After juggling a few thoughts, Denyse and I came up with the idea of a river cruise, just in time to send our invitations out early enough so everybody had time to plan.

Invitation

For our upcoming fortieth wedding anniversary, we take great pleasure in inviting you to join us for a cruise on the Danube River.
The Danube, Europe's second longest river, winds through ever-changing, beautiful landscapes, offering the chance to visit famous cities such as Vienna and Budapest.
We are looking very much forward to this time together, especially as it will unite the entire family for the first time.

See you soon, yours,

Mom & Dad

The river trip turned out to be a wonderful idea, and the children especially enjoyed every minute. As we discovered Vienna in a fiacre and strolled through the charming streets of Budapest, we made a point of not missing any ice cream parlors on our way, ensuring the kids had a lot of fun every day.

In comparison to the Caribbean cruise ships, the boats that go along the Danube are quite small, as they have to pass through narrow locks while they make their way down the river. One hundred cabins are the most these boats can offer, so our trip felt almost like our family's own private cruise.

As we went through the many locks on the Danube, we were surprised by how tightly the boat fit through each one, often leaving less than ten inches on either side. Even more startling was the sensation of dropping down. With the sinking water levels in each lock, the boat slowly went from street level to a much lower point as we continued our voyage along the Danube.

By the day of our anniversary, we had arrived in Vienna, and after visiting the elegant and historic city, we invited the entire family to a surprise dinner back on the boat so we could toast forty happy years and many more to come.

As the champagne flowed, even the children joined for the toast, their glasses filled with ginger ale. The sparkling soda couldn't look any closer to the real stuff in the bottles of Laurent Perrier Grand Siècle we kept popping as we celebrated.

If the dinner was an unexpected treat, my thank-you speech was a different kind of surprise. I informed the family jokingly that my pockets were empty after this cruise, so it would be their turn to open their wallets for our fiftieth anniversary. Everybody laughed, but little did I realize at this moment that ten years later, they would remember my joke.

2009 OUR 40TH ANNIVERSARY FAMILY CRUISE ON THE DONAU

Another Heart Problem 48

With the first decade of the twenty-first century coming to an end, and the many harrowing experiences of recent years behind me, I now welcomed the days with a newfound peace. The lifestyle Denyse and I had envisioned had finally turned from fantasy to reality, as we filled our time with travel, relaxation, and memorable moments with our grandchildren, which soon numbered four after Lily's birth in 2011.

But professional opportunities continued to find me, even when I thought of myself as more or less retired and was not looking for a job. I had a difficult time saying no to the work that came my way, since I remained passionate about the hospitality industry and enjoyed its challenges. The paychecks were a bonus.

Staying involved in the hotel industry in one way or another allowed me to maintain my contacts with old colleagues and to stay current on developments in hospitality, a constantly evolving industry whose trends and evolutions always captivated me. But as much as keeping my hands in the profession was energizing for me, I soon discovered it was perhaps too energizing.

In May 2014, I decided to register for a conference of the European Hotel Managers Association (EHMA) in Leipzig, Germany, not realizing that it would turn into a frightening reminder that it was time to put the brakes on my career once and for all.

The trouble began after the EHMA meeting ended, while Denyse was still spending time in the United States. I had returned to München via Hannover to pay a short visit to my sister Jenny, a visit that was long overdue.

It was wonderful to see my sister, and after a few days, I left for München on the ICE, one of Germany's high-speed trains, arriving four hours, twenty minutes, and almost four hundred miles later. The trip was restful, and I returned home in good spirits.

Friday, May 2, was a wonderfully warm and sunny day, inspiring me to do some work on the balcony to prepare the planting for the summer. But as I walked outside, I suddenly felt cramps in my stomach. I could not remember having eaten anything which could have provoked this apparent malaise, but I opened a can of Coke, as it normally soothes me in situations of poor digestion and stomach pain.

The soda helped for a few minutes, but the cramps came back much stronger than before, this time climbing into my chest and reaching all the way to my neck.

Since I had experienced heart problems before, I grew concerned and called my cardiologist, Dr. Wildfeuer. It was one o'clock in the afternoon on a Friday, and I knew Dr. Wildfeuer was closing for the weekend in less than an hour.

"Are you short of breath?" was his first question.

"No," I answered.

"Do you have pain in your left arm?"

"No, I do not have any pain, only this strange pressure in my upper chest and esophagus."

"How fast can you be here?" was his next question.

"If all goes well, in about ten minutes," I said, dropping everything I was doing and proceeding into the garage to take our car downtown.

Racing to See My Cardiologist

A trip which should not take more than ten minutes took much longer this time. Every traffic light turned red when I approached it, and a garbage truck in front of me stopped at every house to empty the garbage cans.

When I finally stepped into the clinic, Dr. Wildfeuer and his nurses were already waiting for me, and immediately connected me to an EKG and drew a blood sample to rush over to his laboratory on-site.

"It doesn't look too good," Dr. Wildfeuer's expression seemed to say, as he measured my blood pressure. He called out to his staff to summon an ambulance. Meanwhile, my pain increased, and I felt that my chest would explode, so he gave me injections and a fast-acting Nutriat spray, allowing me to breathe a little easier.

Moments later, the ambulance and emergency doctors arrived, immediately loading me into the vehicle and speeding off, the sirens echoing off the surrounding buildings. I was on my way to the hospital in Schwabing, whose staff had already been alerted by Dr. Wildfeuer.

By the time we arrived at the hospital, my pain had become intolerable, and the doctor decided to inject me with morphine to reduce the pressure in my chest. I started to realize that I might be in trouble, deep trouble.

Denyse was still in the United States, our daughter was at work, and nobody knew what had happened to me.

As per Dr. Wildfeuer's instructions, the hospital staff took me from the ambulance directly into the operating theater, where a whole emergency team of doctors and nurses were waiting for me to arrive. No registration, no check-in, no paperwork. Time was of the essence.

While I was taken care of in the hospital, Dr. Wildfeuer tried to reach Carine, who was on assignment in Düsseldorf. Normally, Carine never answers calls from unknown numbers, but this time she did and informed the doctor that she would be back in München in the late afternoon.

Meanwhile, the intervention went smoothly, and I now had two more stents in my arteries. As I recovered in the intensive care unit, I felt deep gratitude to Dr. Wildfeuer. His early intervention and immediate call for an ambulance had saved me from the worst. From the first moment of discomfort on our balcony to the emergency room to the hospital, hardly forty minutes had elapsed, and this speed combined with the right treatment at the right time made all the difference, preventing serious damage to my heart.

I learned that what I had experienced that day was in fact another heart attack, but this time, it had happened in the back heart chamber. Typically, the symptoms are very different and therefore difficult to identify as a heart attack, and for this reason, it can be quite dangerous.

When Carine arrived at the hospital, I was already feeling much better and had regained my smile. We took a picture and sent it to Denyse to keep her from worrying, but she did not believe us and rushed to München the following day.

Before finally going home to her family, Carine removed our car from the parking garage, where it had already accumulated a substantial amount in parking fees and drove it back to our home.

Rehabilitation Again

After one week in the hospital, I was transferred directly to a specialized rehabilitation center about one hour south of München in the Bavarian countryside. I had started to know this specialized center quite well, as this was the second time I was spending time here. Even though I almost never drank alcohol, never smoked, and did a reasonable amount of exercise, I seemed to be constantly prone to heart problems, from the triple bypass back in 2002 to the placement of various stents over the years.

Could this heart attack have been a last warning? The future will tell. In the meantime, I am paying extra attention to my lifestyle and my nutrition, and I report for regular checkups and stress tests with my cardiologist. I feel very good, but then again, before May 2, 2014, I had no clue that anything was amiss.

Life is full of unforeseen situations. The least I could do was to take the hints my body was giving me and try my best to prepare for any surprises that might come my way.

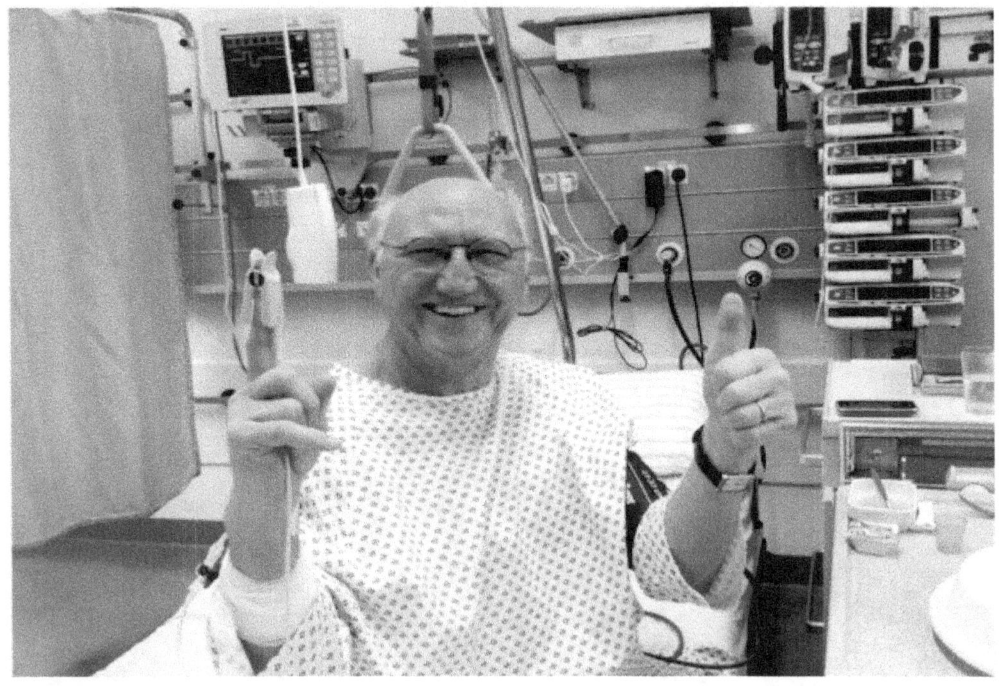

MAY 2ND, 2014 IN THE INTENSIVE CARE UNIT, BUT SMILING AGAIN

THE FAMILY VISITING AT THE REHAB CENTER "LAUTERBACHER MÜHLE"

Welcome to the Past **49**

*F*acts, Impressions, and Stories

Human beings live in a complex universe we will never fully understand, and so we cope by believing certain truths about ourselves and others around us, from facts we learn and impressions we form, from stories we are told, and stories we tell ourselves.

Especially when they have been told over and over again, those stories become our own and turn into the truths we believe in. Until we are confronted with the past, and with truths we did not know before, creating total confusion and a new reality.

But how important is this new reality? Could it wipe out years of imaginary truth, built like a protective wall and tailored to the special needs of a particular moment or time? Wipe out stories we have been told, and which we made our own, and which have guided us through our lives, year after year?

What I have been confronted with is indeed a heartbreaking story, one that placed me, within a fraction of a second, into the center of a brand-new script of my life. The story has also led to more questions than answers.

The reality is, I'm Peter W. Tischmann, born into a world at war in Hannover, Germany, in 1939.

Reality is, I'm married to a wonderful wife named Denyse, with whom I have a daughter, Carine, and a son, Peter Jr. We have four grandchildren.

Reality is that my mother was a classical dance teacher who owned her own dance school, and that my father died at the Eastern front during the early days of World War II.

Reality is that I had two sisters.

All the above facts have accompanied me throughout my life, or at least part of it, until I learned differently.

Despite all that has happened, I consider myself as one of the lucky ones. I have had many difficulties in my life, but they have been among the kinds that human beings typically face merely by living on earth. Yes, I have experienced times of war and political instability, and I have suffered my share of interpersonal conflicts, career reversals, and health problems. But my family and I have always managed to spare ourselves from the ravages of poverty, violence, or lifelong struggle.

Nothing describes this part of my life better than the following statement from Charles Schulz, creator of the Peanuts, Snoopy, and Charlie Brown comic strip figures, whose continuing popular appeal stems, to a great extent, from Schulz's ability to connect to his audience.

We all face difficulties and discouragement from time to time.
But we also have a choice in how to handle it.
If we are persistent and if we hold fast to our faith,
and discover and develop the unique talents that each of us have,
then there is no limit to our potential.

Farewell to My Mother

When my mother passed away in 1983, she took with her much of our family history. Her experiences of being bombed out of a comfortable life, my father missing in action in an ever-expanding war, bringing up three children on her own, and struggling every day to make a living are ones she never shared with any of us. Even as I grew older and asked more questions, I never received an answer.

I guess my mother was just doing what she thought was best to give us a childhood free of worries, even covering up how hard she was working, at times desperately, to run the household as a single mother of three in the most difficult of times.

Looking back, she did a remarkable job, but I'm sure it must have drained her energy, physically and mentally.

Maybe forgetting the past and concentrating on the present was the recipe for survival at that time. We'll never know what was going on in her mind because it was not out of character for my mother to say as little as possible. If confronted with uncomfortable questions, her answer was a vague "ja ja", or she simply walked away whistling one of her favorite melodies.

A visible symbol of this attitude was a big closet in our living room, which she kept locked at all times, with the keys firmly secured in her pocket.

From time to time when she opened the cupboard, we had a chance to peek inside, but besides the cookies and chocolate she rationed for us, there was nothing we could see which would justify keeping the closet locked at all times.

How wrong we were, as I found out many years later.

Leaving Home

In the meantime, I had completed my apprenticeship, and as I was aspiring to become a chef, I had started to travel, first in Germany and then abroad, to widen my knowledge and experience so I could eventually become a grand chef.

In between assignments, I visited home whenever possible to spend some time with my mother and my sisters. By that point, I had decided not to ask any questions anymore, and as for the closet, it was still locked. Nothing had changed.

At times, I would ask myself if I would find a skeleton in that closet if I ever got the keys to it.

By the time my mother passed away in 1983, I had advanced in my career and was working as a general manager of the Heliopolis Sheraton Hotel. My responsibilities made it difficult to find the time to go back to Hannover to sort through all her belongings, which I left to my two sisters to do. I let them decide what to toss and what to keep.

My mother had informed us that she wanted to be cremated, and when she died, my sister Jenny took care of the preparations until I was finally able to return to Hannover for the funeral a few weeks later. In the meantime, Jenny had been cleaning out the closet, which besides the cookies and chocolates contained the little jewelry my mother possessed, along with paper files, a lot of them.

"I have put all the papers for you to sort out in Mutti's travel bag," my sister Jenny said. She handed me my mother's brown leather bag, which I knew well from the various times she visited us wherever we were.

The bag felt very heavy, filled as it was to the brim with papers and photo albums. At the top, I glimpsed some letters and photographs we had sent her from the places where we lived during my assignments and from the trips we took as a family. It appeared that Mutti had saved every single piece of paper she felt was important.

"Keep it for me until I come the next time," I said to Jenny. I saw no need to carry the bag with me to Cairo because I did not have the time nor the interest to look through it. It had been in Mutti's closet for so long, and a few more months wouldn't make a difference.

It would take almost twenty years before Jenny reminded me that she still had Mutti's travel bag in the basement, and maybe it was time now for me to take it with me. By then, I was semi-retired, and my substantially reduced work schedule involved only some consultancy work from time to time, so I agreed.

I took the bag with me to Munich, only to put it into our basement again. I still had no interest in sorting out all the papers since I felt I had better and more important things to do. Maybe I was still scared of the potential surprises I could find.

"Was ich nicht weiß, macht mich nicht heiß," a German saying goes, meaning "what I don't know can't excite me."

That brown bag, filled with potentially boring and potentially scary documents, had by now spent a total of thirty years in different basements. Should I simply dispose of them all, I wondered, instead of allowing them to take up space and remain a bother? In the absence of any decision, that bag spent another few years in our basement.

It was only in 2016 while I was sorting out our basement that I came across the bag again. This time I finally decided to have a look at its contents, my curiosity having finally beat all the other emotions and procrastination strategies I could come up with.

As I started to empty the bag, piles of pictures, so many pictures, came tumbling out. Then came papers, lots and lots of papers, followed by more old pictures. Soon a few intriguing documents, such as diplomas from William Hähnel, my grandfather, began to appear in the jumble.

Going through the documents, some of them over a hundred years old, I was happy that I had kept the bag, because years of family history were now unfolding in front of my eyes. My grandfather's entire life was coming into view: awards from the Hoboken high school he attended, employment references, Honorary Citizenship from our family's hometown of Hannover in Germany, pictures of the first transatlantic flight that arrived in New Jersey, and other photos of historical interest. I found several pictures that were more than a century old and were printed on cardboard.

It became clear that I was looking at a historical treasure of our family's history and the history of an entire era. It was at this moment that I decided to rescue the photos and documents from their long imprisonment in that brown leather bag and arrange them in a special album.

Unfortunately, many of the pictures did not have an inscription on the back to identify the persons on the photo. As it made no sense to keep pictures of people I didn't know, I decided to discard those.

Little did I realize at this moment what other surprises the bag was holding for me.

What Does Truth Mean?

As I was sitting on the floor, surrounded by old pictures and piles of paper, one folder filled with letters caught my attention. The cover said "Fritz Tischmann," written in my grandfather's characteristic handwriting. As I began to peruse its contents, one letter, written in French and dated July 30, 1942, stood out for the anxious tone of its introduction and what appeared to be hastily penned blue handwriting.

I held the letter in my hand and began to read.

> *It's been a long time since I've heard from you or from Benno. During this time, I've been in several camps, from which it has been impossible to write. I hope with all my heart that your health has been good, and that of little Peter. How I long for him! As for me, my morale has been low, and I've been quite unhappy. In my last camp at Compiegne, everyone experienced the same situation as Aunt Lilly and Hanz Schweitzer of Hannover. To avoid the same thing here and as proof for the authorities, I need immediately the proof of your Aryan origin and your maiden name, as well as our wedding certificate from October 29, 1934. Also, if possible, the birth certificate of Peter . . . This is of the gravest importance to me. It could result in my liberation . . . Do not waste one minute in sending what I am asking for. Send me recent photos of yourself and of Peter and details of your life. I hope I can be free for Christmas and bring presents for our dear son. Give my father Benno my address so he can write to me. Kisses to you and Peter, your sad Fritz. PS Please reply in French so the intermediary can translate.*

I picked up another piece of correspondence, this one a postcard in the same handwriting, its message tightly crowded onto the small space.

> *My dear Wilma, your kind letter to Drancey I received shortly before my departure. Unfortunately, too late. I am writing on the train and hope that this card will reach you. Maybe the train will go via Hannover . . . I'll try to keep in touch with you, but it will be easier for you to find my location with the Red Cross in Hannover, as you know that I have left the Drancey camp . . . If possible, send me some clothes, something to eat, a big backpack, and a woolen blanket. Try to find me as soon as possible . . . Maybe I can improve my situation through the papers you send me. I'll always think of you and Peter. My sentiments and my heart will always be with you. Please take care of me, and don't leave me.*

Obviously, this was a letter from my father, who had been felled at the Eastern front at the beginning of the war. But the letter was dated 1942, and the war had started in 1939. My curiosity started to mount.

As I continued to sort through the file, my fingers moving more quickly now, I came across another letter addressed to my mother from the World Jewish Congress, Search Department. Dated May 18, 1947, it said, "With response to your inquiry, we have now been informed by our office in Belgium: Fritz Tischmann, born May 28, 1900, Hannover, was deported on August 21, 1942, through the concentration camp of Drancey (France) and has not returned. Should any further information reach us, we will get in touch with you. Meanwhile, we would convey to you our deepest sympathy in your anxiety. We remain yours sincerely, Search Department."

I put the letter down and sat still, trying to make sense of what I was reading. For the first time in my life, as I held one letter after another in my hand, I began to understand that the reason for my father's absence from my life was not because he was away fighting in the war. Yes, he had disappeared, but for a different reason than I was led to believe by my mother for all these years.

I learned from the papers that my mother had first contacted the German Red Cross and the offices that dealt with war victims as she attempted to search for her husband, before she finally turned for help to the World Jewish Congress. By that point, she must have had an idea of what might have become of him after he fled from Germany to Belgium.

During that time, he had been moved from one concentration camp to another, before he finally shared the fate of more than a million others and ended up in Auschwitz, where he was sent to the gas chamber in October of 1942. He was forty-two years old.

Having seen what was happening around Germany in the late 1930s, including to relatives such as his aunt Lilly, my father must have known it was only a matter of time before he faced the same fate. His decision to flee Germany in 1939 to go to Antwerp in Belgium and to hide there for a time with friends was his desperate bid to save his life and wait for the carnage to end so he could return to his family.

During an attempted business trip to Paris, he was arrested by the French police and sent to a concentration camp in Perpignan, from where his unfortunate journey to Auschwitz began.

At some point before he was sent to Auschwitz, my father must have been informed by family friends that my mother was now with another partner and had become pregnant, soon to give birth to my sister Bärbel. The situation resulted in my parents' divorce in February of 1942. By then, my father had been absent for years, never having been able to return to Hannover to see his newborn son.

A Last Sign of Life

The last sign of life from Fritz Tischmann was the postcard he had written to my mother and thrown out of the train transporting him from Paris, via Metz and Kassel, to Auschwitz, possibly passing through Hannover.

What an unimaginably terrible feeling this must have been as he wrote the letter and tossed it out the window, hoping for one last chance to escape what he knew awaited him.

The card was later found by a railroad worker who was kind enough to forward it to Wilma Tischmann.

My father died in a gas chamber, one of Germany's six million Holocaust victims, having never met his only child, having never met me. A few months later, his seventy-two-year-old father, Benno, was deported to Auschwitz too to meet the same fate.

As I continued reading through the many documents, I wondered why my mother had chosen to keep all this information from us for the remainder of her life. And if she had no intention of telling us about these papers, why did she retain them for so many years? To break with the past, it would have made more sense to simply destroy any remnants of what had happened. My guess is that she did want us to find out, eventually, but did not want to be confronted with questions she had avoided for so long.

Since those dark times reflected in the papers my mother kept, Germany has changed. It has dealt with its past and has developed into a committed democracy that subordinates its own national interest to the goals of a united Europe. It has grown into a society that remembers the past and is, on the whole, determined never to allow the kinds of devastating events that took place in my childhood to happen again.

As I was reading those letters, those papers that contained so much and yet had been hidden so well as to have nearly disappeared, unseen, I could almost hear a voice behind every word, every page. Almost, as the voices slowly faded, disappearing into a vast silence.

Confronting a New Reality

When I opened the bag and reality escaped into my life like the ghost from Aladdin's lamp, I was suddenly confronted with a part of German history which had not played a large role in my life, as our mother had done a great job in protecting us from her experience of this terrible time.

Unexpectedly, I was not only confronted once again with Germany's dark past, but suddenly, I had become an integral part of it.

Sorting out my late mother's papers, I did not expect to discover the secret my mother had kept hidden from us. I did not expect to come face-to-face with a family catastrophe, one that I still do not know how to fully comprehend, all these years after my father and everyone is gone.

Madame
Vilma Tischmann
Grosse Wallstr. 13. I
Hannover
Allemagne

Camp de Drancy
Seine
France

POSTCARD FROM MY FATHER FRITZ TISCHMANN THROWN OUT OF THE TRAIN TRANSPORTING HIM TO HIS FINAL DESTINATION IN AUSCHWITZ.

UNITED KINGDOM SEARCH BUREAU FOR GERMAN AUSTRIAN AND STATELESS PERSONS FROM CENTRAL EUROPE.

Telephone: MUSeum 6811

CF 1o8.7o8

BLOOMSBURY HOUSE
BLOOMSBURY STREET
LONDON, W.C.1

AWW/CH

6th March,1947

Sehr geehrte Frau Tischmann,

Wir beziehen uns auf Ihre Suchanfrage fuer Ihren Gatten Herrn Fritz Tischmann,and wir bedauern ausserordentlich,Ihnen eine sehr traurige Nachricht uebermitteln zu muessen. Wir haben Nachforschungen in Belgien gemacht und haben erfahren,dass Herr Tischmann am 21.8.42. from Camp de Drancy nach Auschwitz deportiert worden ist. Wir werden uns wieder an Sie wenden,sobald irgend eine andere Information bei uns einlaeuft. Wir verstehen,wie sehr Sie um das Schicksal Ihres Gatten besorgt sein muessen und versichern Sie unserer aufrichtigen Anteilnahme.

Mit freundlichem Gruss

W. Guthmann

Secretary

Mrs.Wilma Tischmann
Maasen ueber Sulingen Nr 59
Kr.Grafschaft Diephols
British Zone of Germany.

St. Regis Twenty-Fifth Anniversary Reunion 50

The late summer of 2016 brought with it an occasion for a happier rendezvous with the past. September of that year would be the twenty-fifth anniversary of the St. Regis reopening. Much had happened since then, enough for a few lifetimes perhaps, but September of 1991 still stood out as one of the most vivid, memorable times of my life.

I still felt pride when I thought about the tireless dedication and spirit our opening team had shown in the months leading up to the reopening of the legendary hotel. For the past year, I had been in contact with my colleagues and friends from that era to plan a celebration that would reunite our team, so we could toast everything we had accomplished together and catch up on the paths our lives had taken since then. We agreed to invite only the opening team to the party so we could keep the celebration to a close-knit group.

The Planning

Our initial idea was to throw the party in its natural venue, at the St. Regis, and Jude Woodstock and Joe Prezioso volunteered to contact the current general manager to book a private event space there. After several weeks, however, it became clear their efforts were going nowhere. Perhaps this GM did not want to get involved with a reunion party, considering the drama that had taken place around my firing. I decided to try calling the regional president of Sheraton in Europe, Africa, and the Middle East, since I had known him from my own days at the company. He said he would be pleased to get in touch with the St. Regis GM on my behalf. This should seal the deal, I thought, feeling relieved.

The next thing I knew, my friend was calling me on the telephone to tell me the GM was unwilling to host the celebration at the St. Regis because he was afraid it would create problems at the hotel. Even a quarter-century later, the bad blood of that era had apparently not yet washed away. It was time to move on to plan B.

My next try was the Peninsula Hotel across the street. When the St. Regis reopened, I liked to joke that the best thing about the Peninsula was its view of the St. Regis. But in truth, the Peninsula was and is a wonderful hotel. In any case, I had no luck there either. The GM told me they would love to host us, but their private rooms were fully booked.

During my initial excitement about planning the party, I had set up an organizing committee consisting of a few former colleagues. Jude had warned me from the beginning that it would be difficult to plan this party by committee, but I had insisted on trying. She was right, of course. When we were about two months away from the anniversary and the plans were still up in the air, I said to Jude, "You are my wonder girl. You make it happen."

She got on the phone immediately and looked into a number of options, eventually deciding on Le Pain Quotidien on Park Avenue, part of the international collection of casual French restaurants started by Belgian chef Alain Coumont. The Park Avenue location gave her a good price for our group, allowing us to keep the costs to $75 per guest for a party that would include a table of appetizers, a main course, and a dessert buffet. It would not be fancy, but it would feature the type of well-prepared French food and warm ambience for which the restaurants had built a following.

I had wanted to make a special lapel pin and a certificate to commemorate the anniversary, but we realized this would involve a large price tag, and we did not want to have to pass the cost on to our guests. So in the end, we scrapped all those crazy ideas. A joyous, festive party would be enough.

As the date of the event approached, I began to wonder: Would people show up? Would it feel strange to see some of the team again after so many years? Would the party live up to expectations?

The Mystery Guest

To create suspense and intrigue, Jude had printed on the invitation that a mystery guest would arrive at some point during the party. That person was me. Between the two of us, we managed to keep my attendance a secret until the night of the celebration.

That evening, I decided not to walk in until half an hour after the party had started. I was feeling a little bit nervous, I have to admit. I had not seen many of these people in twenty-five years, and my time at the St. Regis had not ended on a particularly pleasant note.

Much to my surprise, the crowd erupted in shouts of "Hello, Peter!" when I walked in at 7:30 p.m., followed by Denyse and Peter Jr. right behind me. I was proud to have my son fly in from Miami to join us for the special event.

As soon as I arrived, I could tell that the ambience in the room was wonderfully loud, boisterous, and warm. Everyone seemed delighted to see each other and appeared to be having a fantastic time.

In total, sixty-five guests showed up that night, even more than Jude and I had expected. Some arrived without making a reservation, presumably to avoid paying the fee, but we made sure they paid. The event was worth every penny.

Most of the former colleagues who came to the party were people I had not seen in twenty-five years. I had seen Joe and Jude over the years, as well as John Stavros, Maria Peralta, and a few other team members on occasion, but I had lost touch with many. The desire to reunite was apparently strong, as guests traveled to New York City from all over to be together that night. It was fantastic to see everyone and realize the efforts they had made to reunite. People showed up from the front office department, engineering, housekeeping, and all the various roles that made up our opening team.

Throughout the evening, guests would come up to me and say, "Do you remember me?" And I would say, "Of course I remember you," even though sometimes I did not, to tell the truth. Among the crowd, an impressive number had made tremendously successful careers and were GMs by now, while others had left the hotel business and gone in another direction.

We spent hours mingling, catching up with each other, and gathering departmental teams to pose for group photos. There were many pictures taken, hugs given and received, and the feeling of a big, happy reunion of the dozens of us who had spent so much time together back in those days, working hard and achieving great things.

I got to see pictures of my former colleagues' children and felt delighted about how their families and lives had progressed since we last saw each other. I enjoyed introducing old friends to my now-grown son Peter, a highly accomplished hotelier, whom some had known when he was a little boy. Carine could not make it over from Germany, but she sent a wonderful message of congratulations by video, which we played for guests. I felt proud of our entire St. Regis opening team and thrilled to be surrounded by my family on this special night.

Another Speech

At one point, guests began to ask me to make a speech. So of course, I had to say a few words. I started by thanking everybody for their strong support of me during the roller coaster ride of the St. Regis reopening, and for helping our team to make it the best hotel in New York City and one of the very top hotels in the world. I congratulated some former colleagues on the successful careers they had built as a result of the hard work they had done at the St. Regis. We had a moment of silence for several employees who had passed away in the meantime, including Christel Schmitt and Anne Power. Guests cheered each other and expressed joy and pride in our shared history at the St. Regis and our ability to stay connected all these years later.

The occasion turned out even better than I had hoped. For the entire night, I felt as if I were floating on clouds. The party also made it clear to me that, considering the level of affection and respect everyone showed each other at the reunion, we must have been doing something right when we assembled our team. After we had put in so many nights and days of hard work together, and committed ourselves to opening the best hotel we could possibly imagine, none of us had ever forgotten the experience.

I was half-expecting the issue of my firing, and the dark days that surrounded it, to come up in conversation at some point that evening. But no one brought it up. I have to admit I was grateful for this.

Since I still had an old VIP book from the St. Regis opening back in 1991, I had decided to bring it with me to the anniversary party. Many people signed it to commemorate this extraordinary night, twenty-five years later.

Eileen McGill, a former associate, wrote: "The St. Regis was and is one of the most important places in my life. Not just because of the hotel, but because of the incredible people that worked there and will forever be my family."

Joe Prezioso, former director of banquet operations, remembered a statement I have repeated many times in my training sessions: "Perfection not only consists in doing extraordinary things, but also doing ordinary things extraordinary well."

Tatako Suzuki, a member of the guest relations team, wrote: "I'm so proud to be part of this amazing team."

And Marie Wittorp-Dejonje, still at the St. Regis and today the hotel's head concierge, wrote: "To be part of the opening butler team and to continue the beautiful legacy of the St. Regis is such an honor."

And finally, Maria Peralta, my executive secretary and personal assistant, said: "The St. Regis, Mr. Tischmann, and all the 'young' go-getters taught me all about teamwork, selflessness, and true caring for each other.

There is no better opening team ever. Thank you for all your love and caring."

The laughter and smiles throughout the night more than repaid the efforts Jude and I had made to pull the event together. The party ended very late, as stories, gossip, memories, and experiences were exchanged long into the evening.

Before leaving, we agreed not to wait another twenty-five years for the next reunion. When will it happen? We will see. The pandemic made it difficult to plan an in-person event for the thirtieth anniversary in 2021, but we are all determined to have another get-together again as soon as we can.

Hopefully the management at the St. Regis will be a little more open-minded next time and allow us to do it at the hotel we opened together in 1991, a place which has changed the lives of so many former employees for the better.

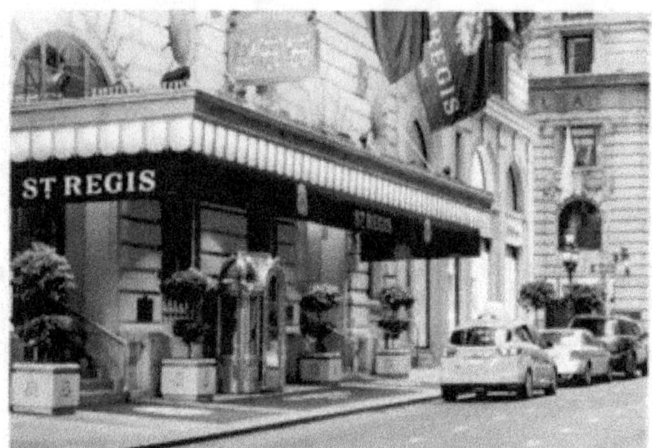

THE ST. REGIS 25 YEARS
AFTER THE OPENING

25TH ANNIVERSARY OF THE ST. REGIS OPENING
CELEBRATING WITH FORMER ASSOCIATES

JAN ROZENVELD A FORMER BUTLER TO MY RIGHT
AND OUR SON PETER TO MY LEFT

Reuniting with My Old Boss 51

Since my departure from the St. Regis Hotel in 1992, and the years of legal disputes that followed, I have had no contact with John Kapioltas or any of the Sheraton executives. They had destroyed my career, and although the court had cleared me of any wrongdoing, my name had been tainted and my future opportunities had been in question as a result of the company's actions.

Fortunately, I was able to rebuild my career and go on to many exciting adventures, and the twenty-fifth anniversary party in New York was a reminder of the wonderful time I had working with the talented team we had built together at the St. Regis.

But not long after the party, I found myself one day reflecting back on the terrible time that led up to my departure. I had been deeply disappointed by the little support I had received from John and, in particular, by his lack of courage to stand up and stop this nonsense right from the beginning as soon as he became aware of the accusations made against me. I had been working for him for almost twenty years, and he should have known me better.

My thoughts also wandered to Bud James, the previous president of Sheraton Hotels. Bud was a man of character and would have stood up for his people, the same way he had stood up for Sheraton as a company against the attempts by ITT to try to dictate its day-to-day operations. A situation like this would have never happened with Bud at the helm.

One of the disappointing memories I have of that era is that after I was dismissed from Sheraton, John had stated in a conversation with Denyse that he only learned about the accusations the same morning that I was confronted by Jim Smith. Could this really be possible, that the president and CEO of the company were not in the picture? The fact that John had cancelled his room reservation at the St. Regis to stay at the Sheraton Center Hotel instead speaks volumes about what he may have known. Was he afraid of what might happen to his own job if he had opposed whatever games the company was up to?

Observing John on the witness stand being cross-examined by Steven Eckhaus, my lawyer, I could see how uncomfortable he was, looking desperately for help to the bench where the ITT lawyer was sitting. And help he certainly could have used, as he was contradicting himself time and time again, making different statements than in his deposition.

But despite the excellent job Steven did, success was not on our side. The power of a company such as ITT was simply too strong.

It would be twenty-eight years later before I met John again.

Jumping Over a Shadow

While visiting our son, Peter, and his family in Bay Harbor Islands, Florida, in January of 2018, I learned that John and his wife, Katherine, were spending the winter months not far away from where our son was living.

Under normal circumstances, it would be up to the senior-most person to make the first move, but I decided that enough years had passed, and it was time to renew an old friendship. I decided to give John a call.

His wife, Katherine, picked up the phone, and much to my surprise, she expressed how pleased she and John were to hear from me. We agreed to meet the next day for lunch at Timos's in Sunny Isles Beach, their favorite restaurant.

When we arrived, John and Katherine were already waiting for us at the bar. The welcome was very cordial, and despite his ninety-one years of age, John looked very good. He hadn't really changed.

Our conversation was pleasant, as we talked about the good old times in Sheraton's Europe, Africa, and Middle East office, carefully avoiding any mention of the St. Regis and what had happened to me. Certainly, I would not be the one to open the subject.

As we talked about our years in Brussels, John suddenly admitted that the time in Brussels was the most rewarding of his career and that he had hated being in Boston.

Yes, Mr. President, I couldn't agree more.

I was very pleased with myself that I had taken the initiative to meet with John again after so many years.

When a few weeks later I told some former associates about my meeting with John, they congratulated me for taking the first step after so many years. "Only great people have the courage to do what you did," was their comment. I don't know about that, but I felt humbled by their compliment and grateful once again to have such a loyal group of former colleagues and lifelong friends.

MEETING MY FORMER BOSS AND HIS WIFE IN FLORIDA AGAIN

1976 AT THE CULINARY OLYMPICS

2018 IN FLORIDA

Looking Back

52

Two Questions

Whenever Denyse and I get together with friends and the subject turns to my life and career, two questions always come up.

"Peter, of all the places you have lived in, which one did you enjoy the most?" and "If you could turn the clock back and start all over again, what would you have done differently in your life?"

For anyone who knew us well, those questions were legitimate ones to ask, and they might appear easy to answer. But I always struggled for the right answer, especially when the first question presented a big challenge.

The truth is that I enjoyed every single one of the many different assignments and countries in which I had the opportunity to spend time over the years, with one exception, which I'll come to later.

While Denyse and I have always loved to travel, our frequent moves were always due to my getting transferred somewhere to manage a hotel. Moving the entire family was never an easy process, and making a city our new home always took time. This was largely because anytime we arrived somewhere, I had to get to work immediately, sparing no effort in making the hotel successful. Still, even though I typically found myself working extremely long hours, I made it a priority to explore the country at every opportunity. It was important for our family to get to know our surroundings, to connect with the people and the culture around us. This was particularly important for me in creating a sense of fulfillment in my work and crucial for our family in our attempt to have meaningful experiences everywhere we went.

Even though the quality and reputation of the hotels I managed did have an influence on the lifestyle that Denyse and I were fortunate to enjoy in our overseas postings, the associates I worked with every day, and the friends we made, were the most significant factors in making each place memorable.

Our First Foreign Assignment

As I let my mind parade through the cities where we lived, I have tried to remember the key factors that could make any particular location special enough to call it our preferred place, among all of the contenders.

Was it Brussels? This was where Denyse and I spent our first years after leaving Germany, where the international phase of my career began, and where our children went to kindergarten and started their first years in school.

Indeed, Brussels was a city of many firsts for our family. But even on its own, Brussels would have ranked high on the list. Situated in the center of Europe, with many European destinations within a few hours' drive, Brussels is in many ways a perfect place to live. There is only the matter of the weather.

Those who know Brussels have often described it as the only place on earth where one can experience all four seasons in a single day. But Brussels has more than enough charm to overcome its weather. The city is a truly international metropolis, with English, French, German, and Dutch spoken everywhere, and people from around the world living and working there.

The city's old district, with its small streets lined with restaurants like pearls on a string, was a true pleasure to stroll through. There were no bad restaurants in Brussels. One can walk into any place and would almost never end up with a disappointing experience, contrary to Paris, where one had to know where to go.

My favorite street in Brussels, Rue de Boucher, is where the best restaurants in town could be found. We particularly enjoyed going to Vincent, where before entering the dining room, one had to walk through the kitchen. I always noticed that no matter how busy the chefs were, they always found the time to wish every passing customer "bon appetit." Dining at Vincent was a unique experience, one of those memories that made our time in Brussels stand out.

Brussels would certainly be a candidate for the city we enjoyed living in the most, but it was the first stop along our international expatriate journey, and many more exciting destinations awaited. So I will set Brussels aside for the time being as I sift through all the places that shaped our lives.

Certainly Not This One

I have to admit that the country I enjoyed living in the least was England. When Sheraton moved our area office from Brussels to Denham in the UK, I already knew that I would do anything possible to make our stay on the island as short as possible.

This was the result of impressions I had formed during the many trips I took to London for the opening of my first Sheraton Hotel. Observing a general sense of superiority in the conduct of the people with whom I came into contact in London and noticing certain hypocritical attitudes among those I interacted with day to day, I determined that the UK was not for me, or maybe I was not made for the UK. Even Harrods and its extraordinary food market could not change my mind.

The idea of living in the UK permanently filled me with discomfort, and the behavior of our neighbors when we moved into a house there did not help matters either. I was grateful for every day when I had to travel outside of England on business.

Even the beautiful countrysides of the region, from Cornwall to the Lake District and Scotland, and all those charming mountain landscapes, lovely lakes, and picturesque shores with inviting beaches, could not change my mind. Still, if there was anything positive about our short stay in England, it was that our children managed to learn the English language extremely well, Oxford accent included.

However, the many British people I worked with throughout my career, typically those who had left the UK long ago to live abroad, seemed to me to have a different attitude. Maybe the foreign experience and the exposure to various cultures and environments had changed their perspective and made them more open-minded and welcoming.

The Land of the Pyramids

What a difference we felt as soon as we moved from England to Cairo. On arrival, we were met by people who managed to turn their entire face into one big smile, greeting us with a hearty "ahlan wa sahlan." This Arabic expression of welcome was one that sounded sincere to our ears, accompanied as it was by an exceptionally warm, hospitable manner.

In my experience, Egyptian people were especially generous in their attitude and behavior. One got the sense that, once you have earned their friendship, they would go through fire for you. The feeling was mutual. Denyse and I valued the many friends we made in Egypt within a short time, as well as the relationships we developed with people all the way to the government level. We are still in touch with many of our Egyptian friends today.

As a family, we were quite happy during our time in Egypt, and we would not have objected to staying a few years longer. But as my company had other plans for my career, those priorities had to take precedence over my own. So when the big boss called me, it was time to move.

The Big Apple

Our next stop would be the Hudson River, in New York, the city that never sleeps, the city whose heartbeat would make even the slowest-moving person run fast.

I fell in love with New York from our very first minute there. This is my type of town, I used to say, because New Yorkers, no matter whether they were born there or were just drawn to it, instinctively related to my way of working: No talking nonsense, no wasting time, just do it, and do it now.

"New York, New York, if you can make it there, you can make it anywhere," as Frank Sinatra used to sing. That song, famous around the world, was very true then and remains true today.

Moving to New York was also a way of going back to my roots. Just across the river in New Jersey, the city of Hoboken—Sinatra's birthplace—was the place where my grandfather had been born, spent his childhood, and gone to school.

Unfortunately, despite all my years in Manhattan, I never made it to Hoboken to visit Opa's birthplace. The closest I came was buying a sweatshirt with HOBOKEN written in big letters all over the front, a celebration of my grandfather's hometown.

Little did I know during our time in New York that my other grandfather, from my father's side, originally came from Boston, a city I had to visit many times for meetings at Sheraton's home office.

Unlike my time in England, when I was always glad to have an excuse to travel, in New York City, I was generally happy to just stay put. The cultural life New York has to offer is on par with anywhere else in the world, offering anything one could wish for, from the musical performances at Lincoln Center and Carnegie Hall, to the entertainment and sports events at Madison Square Garden, and of course, the many theatrical venues offering unbelievable shows, from the Rockettes at Radio City Music Hall to the smaller spaces all over the city.

There is virtually nothing New York City doesn't offer, but having the time to take advantage of all of it is another story. If you ask a New Yorker if he has been to the top of the Empire State Building, don't be surprised to hear "nope." If you ask why, most of them will not have an answer. At best, they will say they haven't gotten around to it yet, it's not a priority, it's there anytime they decide to go.

From what I have seen, this phenomenon is the same in every big capital of the world. Ask a Parisian if she has been to the top of the Eiffel Tower, and you'll get a similar answer. It's as if the most extraordinary sites in the world are reserved for tourists only.

Despite my around-the-clock work schedule during the years when we lived in Manhattan, and despite the lack of time to explore my surroundings to my heart's content—and most of all, despite the conflict at the St. Regis that led to my dismissal and damaged my reputation as a hotelier—I still love New York.

Looking back on my years there, I take enormous pride in what my team was able to do at the St. Regis. The hotel still ranks at the very top in New York City, and nobody can take anything away from what our hardworking group accomplished. We set a new standard in hospitality in New York City, and we returned the historic St. Regis hotel to its rightful position as one of the finest in the world.

The fact that our original St. Regis team remains close after all these years, and that our anniversary party felt like a joyful celebration with old friends, is another gift I cherish from the years Denyse and I spent in New York City.

As we contemplated where we would like to settle down after retirement, New York remained high on our list for a long time, but the dream soon succumbed to a reality check. Buying an apartment in Manhattan, where we most wanted to be, was simply out of reach, not to mention the fact that the cost of living kept rising and rising. Unless one is part of the rich and famous 1 percent, survival in Manhattan seems incomprehensible.

Luckily, the world is full of other exciting cities in which to retire, and we had the good fortune of already having experienced life in more than a few. The truth is that within several weeks after we moved to Istanbul, New York City began to rapidly fade from our minds.

Back to the Bosporus?

It's no surprise why this happened. The magnificent city of Istanbul, formerly Constantinople, is tremendously rich in culture and natural beauty, and everywhere you look are spectacular sites remaining from the city's Byzantine, Roman, and Ottoman eras. Walking along the Bosporus waterfront, it is impossible not to fall madly in love with the place. We felt welcome and at home in this cosmopolitan, historic metropolis.

If asked about the difference between living in New York City and in Istanbul, the answer would be easy. In New York, the mind is set on business and nothing but business most of the time, while in Istanbul personal relationships are at least as important if not more so than business. Making a friend in Istanbul means having that friend for as long as you wish. Friendship in New York, with a few exceptions of course, is often transactional. Your friendship exists for as long as your mutual business interests require. If the business interest fades, the friendship goes along with it. But as I said, there are exceptions to this. The long-time friendships from the St. Regis, which have lasted for decades after the relatively brief time we worked together, are among the relationships I value most.

Anyone who asks us which city is our favorite among them all would certainly hear Istanbul on our shortlist, not just because of the mythology of the city or because of my job as a general manager of one of the finest hotels in the world. Our lasting impressions of Istanbul revolve mainly around the friendships we were able to establish there, which existed and still exist independently of my job as general manager of the Ciragan.

As exciting as our frequent international moves might have appeared to outsiders, the constant packing and unpacking, and all the school changes, and the efforts to settle in a new environment again and again did take their toll. For one thing, they limited the possibility of establishing roots and making lifelong friends from a young age, especially for our children.

On the other hand, the chance to live in a variety of cultural environments and gain exposure to a range of lifestyles has enlarged their view of the world they live in. It has given them a deeper understanding and allowed them to live alongside and respect people of different backgrounds, cultures, and upbringings, an experience neither of our two children would have wanted to miss.

So, Peter, what would you do differently if you could start again?

Answering the second most-asked question did not require a lot of thinking on my part.

If you are passionate about the work you are doing, if your job becomes your hobby, and if you look forward to the next day with excitement, then there is only one answer to this question. You are doing what is right for you.

Yes, I would choose the same path all over again because I am still as passionate about hospitality as I was from the moment I started in this very demanding business, and the idea of doing something different with my life never crossed my mind.

I believe I was destined to excel in the world of hospitality, to be a dedicated ambassador of high-quality service and attention to detail, and to be a role model for young hoteliers who want to follow this dream.

But if I would have known in advance what professional pitfalls might lie ahead, I would have spared myself a few of the not-so-pleasant moments in my life. I am speaking mainly of the St. Regis chapter, when my different cultural assumptions about workplace dynamics led to a situation that seemed to spin rapidly out of control, for reasons that were puzzling to me.

Nonetheless, if my actions in the workplace unintentionally hurt anyone, I am deeply sorry for this. I did not have reason to believe that this was truly the case. But I do believe that anyone whose behavior has caused discomfort to anyone else owes an apology and is required to spend significant time on self-reflection.

After many months, and subsequent years, spent thinking about what had unfolded, and working hard to rebuild my career, I was fortunately able to return to doing the work I loved. I was able to once again recruit and train talented employees, build effective teams, and contribute to the success of some of the most illustrious hotels in the world.

As I reflect on my life, I am happy that my first attempt to start a career as a graphic designer came to an end before it even started. I am equally glad that I did not capitulate when people tried to talk me into being a salesman, because today I know that this line of work would not have allowed me to develop the love and passion I found in my career in the hospitality industry.

My initial attraction to design never disappeared but, instead, turned into a hobby I still enjoy. Over the years, I developed my skills in sketching and bringing ideas to life on paper, and these proved useful in my work too. The techniques were helpful when I needed to express what words could not achieve, even if this meant that hotel architects had to give orders to hide the tracing paper whenever I entered their office.

Can't Deny My Roots

I do not regret my early career as a chef, either, despite all the butt kicking, the sawdust kissing, the kitchen mishaps, and the funny and not-so-funny pranks of my bosses and coworkers.

"Yes, sir" was the response expected anytime they gave an order in the kitchen. There was to be no arguing, no debating, and certainly no complaining. Working in a busy kitchen, forced to perform under intense pressure from morning to night, and hitting all mental and physical limits is the closest one can get to serving in the military.

As I remember the many long hours I spent in kitchen after kitchen, I realize I am proud to have done my chef training at a time when the climate in the profession was quite rough, sometimes even amounting to physical abuse. But I survived it all, and I have to credit that time in my life for laying the foundation for a successful career.

My decade of working as a chef is a part of my life I would never want to go back and change because it gave me the experience and the tools that allowed me to communicate with all the hotel chefs I would later interact with, in a language they could understand. Most important of all, the experience allowed me to earn their respect, and the confidence to make friends with many of the finest three-star chefs to ever grace the pages of the Michelin guide.

I will never forget the day when I went to visit Georges Blanc and found him and his chefs in the middle of a tasting of new signature dishes for his menu.

Georges was a dear friend of mine and one of the top three-star chefs in France. We knew each other for almost forty years and organized many successful food promotions together during the unforgettable Nights of Culinary Stars, which excited gourmets and gourmands alike in New York and Istanbul.

But Georges is more than just a three-star chef. I considered him to be a culinary perfectionist because he did not simply create a new menu item. He planned every detail of it extensively, testing and tasting every ingredient and every step of the preparation, until he was satisfied that he had perfected the dish and it could not be done better any other way.

He left no room for error and kept going until he felt the process was done and the impeccable new dish was finally ready to be introduced to his demanding clientele.

"Sit down, Peter," Georges said as soon as I walked into his restaurant that day. Before I realized what was happening, I was part of the group of chefs tasked with tasting, evaluating, and suggesting improvements to his new creation.

It filled me with tremendous pride to see how Georges and his chefs listened carefully to my feedback, and I'm sure that they noticed in each of my comments how much passion and commitment I felt for this wonderful profession.

But destiny had other plans for me, as it turned out. It took a nasty bout with hepatitis to end my career as a chef and force me once again into a desperate search for what to do next. But without this difficult episode in my life, I would have never found the road I eventually took in my career.

Any move from the tough kitchen environment to the front office is not an easy one to make because the language used in the kitchen is rough and abrasive and certainly not appropriate when dealing with hotel customers at the front desk.

As much as I felt offended at the time to hear someone suggest that I might not be fit for a front-office job, in retrospect, I came to understand very well the concern of the person interviewing me. From day one in my first front-office job at a hotel, I made sure to break any lingering kitchen habits and rely on my politest manners. I still felt at home in kitchens and among chefs, but learning the ways of the front office and rapidly adapting to that environment, served me well as I launched my new career.

None of these changes could have gone nearly as smoothly had it not been for the willing participation and open-minded spirit of Denyse and our children. Constantly moving from one country to another put a significant burden on us all, and I'm grateful that they supported me without complaining, or at least not to me.

Wherever my career took me, from the Atomium in Brussels, built for the World's Fair in 1958, to the five-thousand-year-old pyramids in Egypt, and all the way to the Statue of Liberty in the Big Apple, the moves were exciting but also demanding on our family.

Still, every change we made added a new piece to the puzzle, adding a challenging dimension to our lives but resulting in a perfect picture at the end, especially when it comes to our children.

Starting in Brussels, Carine and Peter Jr. learned French. Our short stay in England was enough to prepare them for the American school in Cairo, followed by their high school time in New York, and last but not least, by Ivy League universities including Harvard and Cornell.

We were worried at first that our children would not cope well with the constant moves, and with the need to keep making new friends, but our fears turned out to be unfounded. They adjusted everywhere we went, and even if they enjoyed certain experiences more than others, they gained something and enlarged their horizons in each new place we moved to.

In America, children leave home much too early for college, and this is something Denyse took some time to get used to. I wonder if she ever did. But we could not be more proud of the people our children grew to become. What more could parents hope for but to give their children the best education possible and to set them up to succeed in the world, no matter where they choose to go.

As for myself, the opportunity to take the helm of the St. Regis and to bring the hotel back up to the standard it deserved was a challenge which allowed me to put into place everything I had learned up until then. It was the culmination of all my experiences as a hotelier for so many years.

Following in John Jacob Astor's footsteps and reopening this grande dame ninety-five years later, turning it once again into one of the best hotels in the world, was a hotelier's dream. I feel grateful to have had this once-in-a-lifetime opportunity to play a role in New York City hotel history and to have worked with my outstanding opening team in helping the St. Regis to realize its destiny.

For dedicated professionals in the hotel industry, working on the St. Regis relaunch was a feather in our caps. It has led to a long-lasting sense of pride and accomplishment, not to mention all the cherished memories and the friendships that I will treasure forever.

But as my secretary in Brussels once said, the higher you climb, the deeper you fall. And right she was because the St. Regis was not just the place of my greatest professional success but also the place that led to the darkest period of my career.

I had hoped that by successfully reopening the St. Regis to enormous international acclaim and earning it recognition as one of the best hotels in the world, this would naturally lead to the next step in my career, the opportunity to lead the new luxury hotel segment the company planned to create.

"If you can dream it, you can do it." I have heard this saying many times. Not only did I dream about this exciting next step in my career, but I had dedicated decades of hard work and many months of around-the-clock planning, strategy, and innovation at the St. Regis to help the hotel achieve the highest caliber of success. Who else within the Sheraton Corporation had the experience, understanding, and commitment necessary to take charge of the company's luxury segment in the making? I knew a great many talented people at Sheraton, but the specific combination of skills necessary to take on the challenges of this new position were ones I felt particularly suited to bring.

But in this case, the dream did not come to pass. I had to learn the hard way that it takes two to tango, as I watched my dreams, together with my career at Sheraton, come crashing down.

The loss of this dream devastated me for a time, but after grieving it, I managed to rise again, bruised but not destroyed. A former colleague helped me to get back on my professional feet again, by entrusting me with one of Europe's most beautiful landmarks, the Ciragan Palace Hotel in Istanbul. This role gave me the chance to set the hotel on the same path as the St. Regis, renewing it after a long period of decline and pushing it, in a short time, into the top fifteen hotels worldwide.

I am thankful to have had the opportunity to catapult two great hotels on two different continents and in two different cultural environments on to the list of the best hotels in the world. How could I not love what I was doing?

Twenty-Five Years Later

As more than five dozen associates from the opening team of the St. Regis reunited to celebrate the twenty-fifth anniversary of the relaunch in 2019, it was a joy to see how many of them are general managers today or are occupying other leading positions in the hotel industry.

It also brought me tremendous gratitude and pride that more than fifty years after stepping for the first time into the rough environment of a professional kitchen, I was awarded the prestigious Six Star Diamond and Lifetime Achievement Award from the American Academy of Hospitality Science. The words engraved on the plaque read:

Recognized for your leadership, vision,
and commitment to excellence,
during your exemplary career over the course of 45 years,
reaching the status as one of the finest renowned hoteliers
who has ever reigned in the luxury hospitality industry worldwide.
Thank you for setting the highest of standards
for quality and service
and paving the way for all outstanding future hoteliers to follow.

So for the question of what I would have done differently with my life, there is only one answer. I would have chosen the exact same path all over again, every single minute and every single day. Well, perhaps with the exception of a few moments that I wish had never existed.

Epilogue

When I decided to write my autobiography, it was a challenge not to get carried away by the temptation to include every memorable anecdote that stood out in my mind. I tried to restrict my story to those experiences that seemed important and interesting enough not just to myself or my family but to readers who might not know anything about me.

It was also important to me that I not only tell my story through my own eyes but that I give voice to the associates and friends who supported me, allowed me to have a successful career, and enriched my life in so many ways. For this reason, I have invited former employees to let me know how it felt to work for Peter W. Tischmann, and their own recollections and comments have found their way into my life story as it is told on these pages.

Still, writing an autobiography also requires one to make decisions about what to share and what not to share, because every life has its private moments, confidences, and dreams.

"Are there no personal secrets you want to write about?" a curious friend asked me recently.

"Well," I replied, "if I did, they would not be secrets anymore, would they?"

"But shouldn't your innermost thoughts and dreams have a place in your life story too?" he continued.

As he kept drilling for answers, I felt as if I were being pursued by a paparazzi chasing a red-hot story or a tantalizing bit of gossip. But I was not willing to dig down and reveal any other private impressions or thoughts that I had decided a long time ago to keep to myself.

When I was talking to a dear friend of mine about this question, she surprised me by sharing the following philosophy, which struck me as profoundly true, not just of myself but probably of everyone I know:

Every human being has a secret garden
where nobody is allowed to enter.
A place to dream, to step into a different world,
sometimes simply to cheer up.
A place where a person can share in the beauty and mystery of life,
where nobody is standing in opposition,
and where there is always a smile and complicity.

A truth not to deny, and to which philosophy one can only respond with a "Declaration d'Amour" to a secret garden, which against my will I had to say farewell, and which beauty of roses I'll never forget. A place of smile and love I was privileged to share, and which secret nobody will ever enter.

What to many readers might sound like an exciting and impressive career felt quite normal to me as it unfolded, following along the path set out by my dreams and my vision. One step seemed to naturally follow another. At least this is how I experienced it from the inside.

In part, I was too busy and distracted with work most of the time to step back and see how my career might look to others. To be a successful hotelier requires the ability to overcome the constant challenges that pile up every day and the willingness to reinvent oneself and one's vision on a regular basis in order to master it all.

Certainly, I had my share of challenges in my career, but looking back, I am grateful that none of them were as demanding as the recent coronavirus pandemic.

To stand up to this challenge, one whose impact on the hospitality industry will not be fully clear for some time, hoteliers of today will have to do some serious thinking with nowhere to look for answers. They'll have to reinvent themselves, because the hospitality industry as we have known it will likely never be the same again.

The experiences of the pandemic will shape our lives for a long time to come, and the more quickly hoteliers can implement new concepts and new styles of service, the greater success they will see for themselves and the hotel industry as a whole.

Hotels will need to introduce innovative ways of operating in order to survive and to gain an edge over their competitors. Hoteliers who are up to the challenge will not only save their industry, but they will also determine the success of their own careers and lives.

A Wish for My Readers

I do wish to thank all my readers who have joined me on my journey through this episode of my life, and I hope that what lies ahead of me will be as exciting and rewarding as the past.

I'm certainly ready for it.

In closing, I wish to share with you an American Indian saying I learned from an old Sioux chief many years ago, while we were traveling through the Black Hills in South Dakota on our way to the Mount Rushmore National Memorial.

The wisdom of the beautiful proverb he shared with me has touched me profoundly through the years.

May the sun bring you new energy by day

May the moon softly restore you by night

May the rain wash away your worries

May the breeze blow new strength into your being

May you walk gently through the world

and appreciate its beauty all the days of your life.

I wish to thank you again for joining me on my travels throughout my life, and I wish you good luck and Godspeed wherever you might be.

Dr. Peter W. Tischmann, PhD

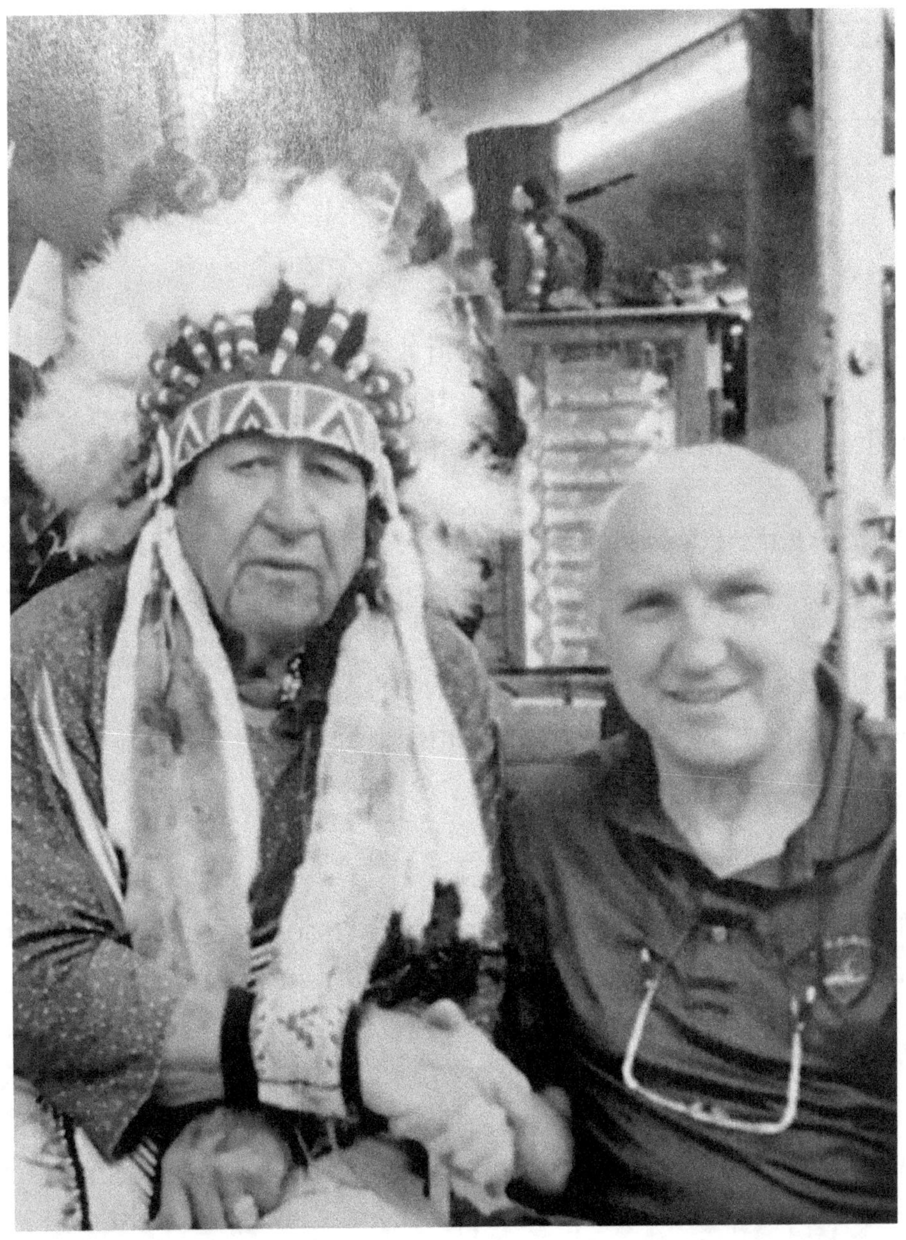

Credits

A great thank you to my co-writer Mrs. Salma Abdelnour, which literary professionalism and writing talent have contributed to turn a simple life story into something striking to read.

As in a four star cuisine, she has added the missing salt, pepper and spices, necessary to turn basic cuisine into a signature dish.

Salma Abdelnour is a writer and editor based in New York, and has been a travel editor of "Food and Wine" and the restaurant editor of

"Time Out New York".

Her writing has appeared in the New York Times, Travel and Leisure and in Forbes Life. She has been anthologized in two volumes of Best Food Writing.

In her free time she has taught writing courses at the new York University continuing education department and has appeared in television segments about travel and food for CNN, CNBC, and the Fine Living Network.

The combination of her experience as a travel journalist and her love for food and wine, together with the life story of an international hotelier, known for his passion for quality, attention to smallest details and a commitment to exemplarily service culture, resulted in an ideal mix to create this extraordinary life story, I could not have achieved alone.

Thank you Salma !

Index of Chapters with subtitles

www.ingramcontent.com/pod-product-compliance
Lightning Source LLC
Chambersburg PA
CBHW080749120626
46557CB00005B/1203

* 9 7 8 1 9 6 0 5 4 8 3 6 8 *